LEED-EB

FOR EXISTING BUILDINGS

REFERENCE GUIDE

Version 2.0

First Edition
June 2005

Disclaimer

Copyright

Trademark

LEED-EB Reference Guide

Version 2.0

ISBN # 1-932444-02-5

Acknowledgements

The LEED-EB Reference Guide has only been made possible through the efforts of many dedicated volunteers, staff members and others in the USGBC community. The Reference Guide drafting was managed and implemented by USGBC staff and included review and suggestions by many TAG members and the EB Core Committee. We especially extend our deepest gratitude to all of our LEED committee members who participated in the development of this guide, for their tireless volunteer efforts and constant support of USGBC's mission. They are–

LEED-EB Core Committee

Michael Arny (Chair), Leonardo Academy
Stu Carron (Vice-Chair), JohnsonDiversey
Steve Ashkin, The Ashkin Group
Bob Cline, National Geographic
Barry Giles, Moss Landing Marine Laboratories
Don Horn, U.S. General Services Administration
Mike Italiano, Sustainable Products Corporation
Bob Lawler, Kansas City, MO Government
Dirk Meyer, U.S. Department of Interior
Teresa Pohlman, Pentagon Renovation Office
Sheila Sheridan
Mike Spishock, Johnson and Johnson
Paul Walitsky, Phillips Lighting
Craig Williamson, Abacus

Special thanks to: Gay Bindocci, U.S. Department of Interior, Lance Davis, U.S. General Services Administration, and the Leonardo Academy staff, Jenny Carney, Dan Ackerstein, Steve Olson, Erica Eisch, and Michael Arny for their significant contributions to the creation of the LEED-EB Reference Guide.

Energy & Atmosphere TAG

Greg Kats (Chair), Capital-E
Marcus Sheffer (Vice-Chair), 7group
Saad Dimachkieh, HOK
Chad Dorgan, Farnsworth Group, Inc.
Jay Enck, Commissioning & Green Building Services
Donald Fournier, Building Research Council
Jonathan Heller, Ecotope Inc.
Tia Heneghan, Sebesta Blomberg
John Hogan, City of Seattle Department of Design, Construction, and Land Use
Bion Howard, Building Environmental Science
Michael Lorenz, Kling
Cheryl Massie, Flack + Kurtz
Brenda Morawa, BVM Engineering, Inc.
Erik Ring, CTG Energetics, Inc.
Mick Schwedler, Trane Company

Indoor Environmental Quality TAG

Bob Thompson (Chair), EPA Indoor Environments Management Branch
Steve Taylor (Vice-Chair), Taylor Engineering
Jude Anders, Johnson Controls, Inc.
Terry Brennan, Camroden Associates
Brian Cloward, Mithun
Larry Dykhuis, Herman Miller, Inc.
Greg Franta, Ensar Group, Inc.
Francis Offerman, Indoor Environmental Engineering
Christopher Schaffner, The Green Engineer
Dennis Stanke, Trane Company

Materials & Resources TAG

Nadav Malin (Chair), BuildingGreen, Inc.
Kirsten Ritchie (Vice-Chair), Scientific Certification Systems
Paul Bertram, PRB Design
Chris Dixon, Mithun
Ann Edminster, Design AVEnues
Lee Gros, Austin Energy Green Building Program
Debra Lombard, RETEC
Nancy Malone, Siegel & Strain Architects
Dana Papke, California Integrated Waste Mgmt. Board
Wayne Trusty, Athena Institute
Denise Van Valkenburg, Steelcase
Melissa Vernon, Interface Flooring Systems
Mark Webster, Simpson Gumpertz & Heger
Gabe Wing, Herman Miller, Inc.

Sustainable Sites TAG

Bryna Dunn (Chair), Moseley Architects
Susan Kaplan (Vice-Chair), Battery Park City Authority
Ann Abel Christensen
Gina Baker, Burt Hill Kosar Rittelmann
Ted Bardacke, Global Green USA
Stephen Benz, Judith Nitsch Engineering, Inc.
Mark Brumbaugh, Brumbaugh & Associates
Meg Calkins, University of Illinois at Urbana-Champaign (and ASLA representative)
Stewart Comstock, Maryland Department of the Environment
Jay Enck, Commissioning & Green Building Services
Jim Frierson, Advanced Transportation Technology Institute
Ron Hand, G&E Environmental
Richard Heinisch, Acuity Lighting Group
Michael Lane, Lighting Design Lab
Mark Loeffler, The RETEC Group, Inc.
Marita Roos, Andropogon Associates
Zolna Russell, Hord Coplan Macht, Inc.
Eva Wong, U.S. EPA Heat Island Reduction Initiative (HIRI)

Water Efficiency TAG

Gunnar Baldwin, TOTO USA, INC
Neal Billetdeaux, JJR
David Carlson, Columbia University
Bill Hoffman, City of Austin - Water Conservation
Heather Kinkade-Levario, ARCADIS
John Koeller (Vice-Chair), Koeller and Company
Geoff Nara, Civil & Environmental Consultants
Shabbir Rawalpindiwala, Kohler Company
David Sheridan (Chair), Aqua Cura
Stephanie Tanner, National Renewable Energy Laboratory
Bill Wall, Clivus New England, Inc.
Bill Wilson, Environmental Planning & Design, LLC

USGBC Staff for their invaluable efforts in developing the LEED-EB Reference Guide.

NEW LEAF PAPER

ENVIRONMENTAL BENEFITS STATEMENT

This project is printed on New Leaf Opaque and New Leaf Everest, both made with 100% post-consumer waste, processed chlorine free. By using this environmental paper, the US Green Building Council saved the following resources:

trees	water	energy	solid waste	greenhouse gases
93 fully grown	39,764 gallons	67 million BTUs	4,446 pounds	8,673 pounds

Calculated based on research done by Environmental Defense and other members of the Paper Task Force.

© New Leaf Paper www.newleafpaper.com 888.989.5323

Printed on 100% post-consumer recycled paper that is processed chlorine free and using 100% soy-based inks that are virtually free of environmentally toxic metals.

Table of Contents

Foreword from the USGBC

The built environment has a profound impact on our natural environment, communities, economy, health and productivity. Breakthroughs in building science, technology and operations are now available to designers, builders, operators, and owners who want to build green and maximize economic and environmental performance, as well as occupant well-being.

The U. S. Green Building Council (USGBC) is leading a national consensus to produce new and existing buildings that deliver high performance inside and out. Council members work together to develop industry standards, design practices and guidelines, operating practices and guidelines, policy positions, and educational tools that support the adoption of environmentally sustainable design and building practices. Members also forge strategic alliances with key industry and research organizations, federal government agencies, and state and local governments to transform the built environment. As the leading organization that represents the entire building industry on environmental building matters, our unique perspective and collective power provides our members with enormous opportunity to affect change in the way buildings are designed, built, operated and maintained.

USGBC Membership

The Council's greatest strength is the diversity of our membership. The USGBC is a balanced nonprofit association representing the entire building industry, consisting of companies and organizations in the following member categories:

Architects
A/E
Attorneys
Builders/Contractors
Commissioning Providers
Consultants
Corporate & Retail
Engineers
Federal
Finance
Interior Designers
Landscape Architects
Nonprofit Organizations
Planners
Press
Product Manufacturers
Professional Societies
Real Estate
State and Local Governments
Universities
Utilities

Since its inception in 1993, the USGBC has played a vital role in providing a leadership forum and a unique, integrating force for the building industry. Council programs are:

Committee-Based

The heart of this effective coalition is our committees in which members design strategies that are implemented by staff and expert consultants. Our committees provide a forum for members to resolve differences, build alliances, and forge cooperative solutions for influencing change in all sectors of the building industry.

Member-Driven

The Council's membership is open and balanced and provides a comprehensive platform for carrying out important programs and activities. We target the issues identified by our members as the highest priority. We conduct an annual review of achievements that allows us to set policy, revise strategies and devise work plans based on members' needs.

Consensus-Focused

We work together to promote green buildings and in doing so, we help foster greater economic vitality and environmental health. The various industry segments bridge ideological gaps to develop balanced policies that benefit the entire industry.

Contact the US Green Building Council

1015 18th Street NW, Suite 508

Washington, DC 20036

(202) 828-7422 Office

(202) 828-5110 Fax

www.usgbc.org

Introduction

What Does "Green" Mean?

"Green" has become the shorthand term for the concept of sustainable development as applied to the building industry. Also known as high-performance buildings, green buildings are intended to be environmentally responsible, economically profitable, and healthy places to live and work.

Why Make Your Building Green?

The building sector has a tremendous impact on the environment. Buildings in the U.S. consume more than 30% of our total energy and 60% of our electricity annually. They consume 5 billion gallons of potable water per day to flush toilets. A typical North American commercial construction project generates up to 2.5 pounds of solid waste per square foot of floor space. The industry appropriates land from other uses such as natural habitats and agriculture. These are just a few examples of the environmental impacts associated with the construction and operation of buildings.

Green building practices can substantially reduce these negative environmental impacts and reverse the trend of unsustainable building activities. As an added benefit, green performance reduces operating costs, enhances building marketability, increases worker productivity, and reduces potential liability resulting from indoor air quality problems. For example, energy efficiency measures have reduced operating expenses of the Denver Dry Goods building by approximately $75,000 per year. Students in day-lit schools in North Carolina consistently score higher on tests than students in schools using conventional lighting fixtures. Studies of workers in green buildings reported productivity gains of up to 16%, including reductions in absenteeism and improved work quality, based on "people-friendly" green design. At a grocery store in Spokane, Washington, waste management costs were reduced by 56% and 48 tons of waste was recycled during construction. In other words, green performance has environmental, economic, and social elements that benefit all building stakeholders, including owners, occupants, and the general public.

I. The LEED® Green Building Rating System

History of LEED

Following the formation of the U.S. Green Building Council (USGBC) in 1993, the membership quickly realized that a priority for the sustainable building industry was to have a system to define and measure "green buildings." The USGBC began to research existing green building metrics and rating systems. Less than a year after formation, the membership followed up on the initial findings with the establishment of a committee to focus solely on this topic. The diverse initial composition of the committee included architects, realtors, a building owner, a lawyer, an environmentalist, and industry representatives. This cross section of people and professions added a richness and depth both to the process and to the ultimate product.

The LEED Pilot Project Program, also referred to as LEED Version 1.0, was launched at the USGBC Membership Summit in August 1998. After extensive modifications, the LEED Green Building Rating System Version 2.0 was released in

March 2000. This rating system is now called LEED for New Construction and Major Renovations, or LEED-NC.

As LEED has evolved and matured, the LEED program has undertaken new initiatives to address the many different stages and sectors of the U.S. building market aside from new construction. Owners, tenants, property managers, designers and building teams who wish to certify their buildings should choose the appropriate LEED Rating System for the scope of their project.. Currently, the LEED product portfolio is being expanded to the following areas:

LEED-NC
LEED for New Construction

LEED-EB
LEED for Existing Buildings

LEED-CI
LEED for Commercial Interiors

LEED-CS
LEED for Core & Shell*

LEED-H
LEED for Homes*

LEED-ND
LEED for Neighborhood Development*

** under development as of June 2005*

Features of LEED

The LEED Green Building Rating System is a voluntary, consensus-based, market-driven building rating system based on existing proven technology. It evaluates environmental performance from a whole building perspective over a building's life cycle, providing a definitive standard for what constitutes a "green building." LEED is a measurement system designed for rating new and existing commercial, institutional, and high-rise residential buildings. It is based on accepted energy and environmental principles and strikes a balance between established practices and emerging concepts.

LEED is organized into the five environmental categories of Sustainable Sites, Water Efficiency, Energy & Atmosphere, Indoor Environmental Quality and Materials & Resources. An additional category, Innovation in Upgrades, Operations, and Maintenance addresses building measures not covered under the five environmental categories, as well as sustainable building expertise. It is a performance-oriented system where points are earned for satisfying criteria. Different levels of green building certification are awarded based on the total points earned. The system is designed to be comprehensive in scope, yet simple in operation.

II. LEED for Existing Buildings (LEED-EB)

LEED-EB provides the existing building stock an entry point into the LEED certification process, and is applicable to:

- ❑ building operations, processes, systems upgrades, and minor space use changes.
- ❑ buildings new to LEED certification as well as buildings previously certified under LEED-NC.

LEED-EB is a method for building owners and operators of existing buildings to implement sustainable operations and maintenance practices and reduce the environmental impact of a building over its functional life cycle. Specifically, it addresses exterior building site maintenance programs; water and energy use; environmentally preferred products for cleaning and alterations; waste stream management; and ongoing indoor environmental quality.

LEED-EB Registration

Project teams interested in obtaining LEED-EB Certification for their project must first register with the USGBC. Registration is an important step that establishes the primary contact between the project and the USGBC. This connection allows the project to receive periodic errata, other updates, and access to the LEED-EB Version 2.0 project resource page on the USGBC website. The project administrator should also send the project access code to other members of the project team to give them access to the online projects resources. The project resources include access to the LEED-EB Letter Templates, an electronic document which contains pre-formatted submittal sheets for each prerequisite and credit, and includes integrated calculation tables when necessary. The Letter Templates and Reference Guide are to be used as companion documents.

LEED-EB Submittals

Once a project is registered, the project team begins to collect information and perform calculations to satisfy the prerequisite and credit submittal requirements. It is helpful to identify an individual who will champion LEED goals, facilitate communication, track progress and compile the components of the final LEED submittal for certification.

Submittal documentation should be gathered throughout the process. The project team should compile documentation in one three-ring binder with a CD, or entirely in electronic format (note: online submission may be required once the online project workspace is operational; please check the related LEED-EB Web page for the most up to date instructions). Submittals should include the following:

- ❑ The completed LEED-EB Version 2.0 Letter Templates
- ❑ Overall project narrative including at least three project highlights
- ❑ LEED-EB Project Scorecard indicating projected prerequisites and credits and the total score for the project
- ❑ Drawings and photos illustrative of the project:
  - Site plan
  - Typical floor plan
  - Typical building section
  - Typical or primary elevation
  - Photo or rendering of project

Performance Period for LEED-EB Applications

Documentation required for LEED-EB Certification Applications include performance data for the building and site over the performance period.

Performance Period for first time LEED-EB Applications:

- ❑ The performance period can be as short as 3 months. This allows first time LEED-EB participants to get all their policies, programs and tracking systems in place and reviewed quickly, to assure that these are set up to meet the requirements for ongoing LEED-EB recertification. First time LEED-EB Applications include both applications for buildings never LEED certified and buildings previously certified under LEED-NC.

Performance Period for Recertification under LEED-EB for buildings previously certified under LEED-EB:

- ❑ These buildings can apply for recertification as frequently as annually and must file for recertification at least once every 5 years to maintain their LEED status.
- ❑ The performance period for recertification applications runs from the time of the last certification under LEED-EB to the date of the time of the filing of the recertification application.
- ❑ As a result the performance period for these recertification applications can be as short as 1 year and as long as 5 years.
- ❑ Performance data for the entire performance period needs to be provided with LEED-EB Applications. Performance data needs to be provided for each year of the performance period so that ongoing annual performance is demonstrated. If data cannot be provided for a building for the entire performance period, then an application for first time certification needs to be submitted instead of a recertification application under LEED-EB and there will be a gap in the buildings certification history.

Credit Interpretation Rulings

In some cases, the project team may encounter difficulties in applying a LEED-EB prerequisite or credit to their particular project. These problems arise from specific instances where the Reference Guide does not sufficiently address a specific issue or there is a special conflict that requires resolution. To address such problems, the USGBC offers technical support through Credit Interpretation Requests and Rulings (CIRs). See the LEED-EB Web page for more information.

The Credit Interpretation process is summarized as follows:

1. Project teams should review the Ruling Page to read previously posted Credit Interpretation Requests and USGBC responses. Many problems can be resolved by reviewing existing Credit Interpretation Rulings.
2. If no existing Credit Interpretation Rulings exist, the project team should follow instructions for submitting a CIR posted on the CIR resources page on the USGBC website. The problem encountered by the project team should be brief but explicit and should be based on prerequisite or credit information found in the Rating System and Reference Guide, with a special emphasis on the intent of the prerequisite or credit. If possible, the project team should offer potential solutions to the problem, and solicit approval or rejection of their proposed interpretation.
3. For each CIR, the USGBC applies a committee and staff review process and posts decisions on the Ruling Page per the posted schedule. All Credit Interpretation Rulings are available on the Ruling Page for the benefit of all registered LEED projects and Ruling Page subscribers.

Certification

To earn LEED-EB certification, the applicant project must satisfy all of the prerequisites and a minimum number of points to attain the established LEED-EB project ratings as listed below. LEED-EB projects will need to comply with the version that is current at the time of project registration.

LEED-EB Certification Levels:

- ❑ Certified 32-39 points
- ❑ Silver 40-47 points
- ❑ Gold 48-63 points
- ❑ Platinum 64-85 points

To begin the certification process, the project team submits a complete application to the USGBC for review. The review process cannot begin until the application is complete and the project has paid the certification fees. Certification review fees and procedures are detailed on the LEED-EB Web page

Updates & Addenda

As LEED-EB continues to improve and evolve, errata and addenda may be developed to correct, substitute and augment the current material. Errata and addenda will be accumulated between revisions and will be formally incorporated into the next version. In the interim between major revisions, the USGBC may use its consensus process to clarify criteria.

The prerequisites, credits and credit rulings current at the time of project registration will continue to apply to the project throughout its documentation and certification processes. Credit rulings posted after that time may be applied if desired. A newer version of a referenced standard may be used if considered at least as stringent as the version cited herein.

III. LEED-EB Reference Guide

The LEED-EB Reference Guide is a supporting document to the LEED-EB Green Building Rating System. The Guide is intended to assist project teams understand LEED-EB criteria and the benefits of the requirements. The Guide includes examples of strategies that can be used in each category, case studies of buildings that have implemented these strategies successfully, and additional resources that will provide more information. The guide does not provide an exhaustive list of strategies for meeting the criteria. Nor does it provide all of the information that building teams need to determine the applicability of a credit to their project.

Prerequisite and Credit Format

Each prerequisite and credit is organized in a standardized format for simplicity and quick reference. The first section summarizes the key points regarding the measure and includes the intent, requirements, required submittals for certification, and a summary of the referenced standard. The subsequent sections provide supportive information to help interpret the measure and offer links to various resources and examples. The sections for each credit are described in the following paragraphs.

Intent identifies the main goal of the prerequisite or credit.

Requirements & Submittals specify the criteria to satisfy the prerequisite or credit, the number of points available, and the documentation required for the LEED application. The prerequisites must be achieved. While each credit is optional, it contributes to the overall project score. Some credits are divided into two or more measures with cumulative points. For example, Materials & Resources Credit 4: Recycled Content is divided into Credit 4.1 for achieving 25% (worth one point), and Credit 4.2 for achieving 50% (for an additional point). In contrast, Energy Credit 1: Optimize Energy Performance is divided into five measures and a project can only apply for one of the measures, depending on the degree of energy savings realized. Checkboxes are used to identify required documents for submittal.

Summary of Referenced Standards, where applicable, briefly introduces the required standards used to measure achievement of the credit intent. Users are strongly encouraged to review the standard and not rely solely on the summary.

Green Building Concerns related to the prerequisite or credit are explained in this section and divided into environmental and economic issues.

Environmental Issues address the environmental impacts of the prerequisite or credit and attempt to relate specific goals or concerns with the influence on our natural environment.

Economic Issues address considerations related to first costs, life-cycle costs and estimated savings.

Strategies are specific methods or assemblies that facilitate achievement of the requirements.

Technologies are specific products or systems that can be employed to achieve the measure.

Synergies & Trade-Offs identify areas of significant interaction with other building operations, upgrades, and maintenance issues as well as other LEED-EB credits. Users are advised to carefully evaluate the benefits and disadvantages of pursing these related credits.

Calculations are sample formulas or computations to assist with the determination of achievement of a particular prerequisite or credit. Some calculations are facilitated by the LEED-EB Letter Templates, which are available to registered projects via the USGBC Web site in order to facilitate the application process.

The **Documentation** section contains additional information for documenting prerequisite and credit achievements and successfully developing the submittals required for the LEED-EB application.

Other Resources are are suggested for further research and may include web sites or print media that provide examples or illustrations, detailed technical information, or other information relevant to the prerequisite or credit..

Web sites list resources available on the Internet.

Print Media are books and articles related to the prerequisite or credit and may be obtained directly from the organizations listed.

Definitions clarify the meaning of certain terms relevant to the prerequisite or credit. Listed definitions may be general descriptions of terms or have meanings that are specific to LEED-EB..

Case Studies are provided to present an example of the successful implementation of the goals stated for the prerequisite or credit. As an illustration, the selected project exemplifies one method to achieve the intent of the measure, although there may be other methods.

Sustainable Sites

Maintenance of a building's site infrastructure is a fundamental component of comprehensive, sustainable building operation. Implementing sustainable, long-term site maintenance practices is especially important when considering that the successful preservation or restoration of site ecology may only be realized after several years of careful planning and execution.

Site design and management issues affect local ecology. Planting and landscaping maintenance practices dictate the use of irrigation water and fertilizer. Impervious surfaces on the site may contribute to urban heat island effect and cause stormwater runoff that harms water quality, aquatic life, and recreation opportunities in receiving waters. Exterior building lighting may exacerbate nighttime light pollution, which interferes with nocturnal ecology. Development of building sites can encroach on agricultural lands and/or adversely impact wildlife habitat.

Broader scale environmental concerns related to building sites include the environmental impacts of travel to and from the site. The travel impacts of building occupants include vehicle emissions and heightened need for vehicle infrastructure. Emissions contribute to climate change, smog, acid rain and other air quality issues. Parking, roadway and building surfaces alter runoff flow and contribute to urban heat island effect by absorbing heat energy.

Responsible, innovative and practical site management techniques that are sensitive to plants, wildlife, and water and air quality can mitigate some of the negative effects buildings have on the local and regional environment. Proactive management of the exterior site may also improve indoor environmental quality and safety by reducing the amount of dirt and allergens tracked into the building and reducing the potential for slips and falls.

Environmentally sensitive site maintenance practices have been proven to reduce site operation and maintenance costs while creating and maintaining an outdoor space that is healthy for building occupants and local plant and wildlife. The LEED-EB Sustainable Sites prerequisites and credits encourage these practices.

Overview of LEED® Prerequisites and Credits

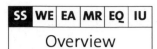

Overview of LEED® Prerequisites and Credits (continued)

SS Credit 6.2
Heat Island Reduction – Roof

SS Credit 7
Light Pollution Reduction

SS	WE	EA	MR	EQ	IU

Prerequisite 1

Required

Erosion & Sedimentation Control

Intent

Control erosion to reduce negative impacts on water and air quality.

Requirements

Develop and implement a site erosion and sedimentation control policy that incorporates best management practices. The policy shall address ongoing maintenance of the facility's site to prevent soil erosion and sediment transfer under ongoing operation, as well as addressing erosion and sedimentation control for any future infrastructure repairs or other construction activities. The policy provisions shall address restoring eroded soil areas and eliminating conditions that result in erosion or sedimentation. The provisions addressing erosion and sedimentation control for additions and repairs shall require a sediment and erosion control plan, specific to the site, that conforms to U.S. Environmental Protection Agency (EPA) Document No. EPA 832/R-92-005 (1992), Storm Water Management for Construction Activities, Chapter 3: Sedimentation and Erosion Control, OR local erosion and sedimentation control standards and codes, whichever is more stringent. The person responsible for its ongoing implementation will sign off the facility sedimentation and control policy.

The plan shall meet the following objectives:

- ❑ Prevent loss of soil during construction by stormwater runoff and/or wind erosion, including protecting topsoil by stockpiling for reuse,
- ❑ Prevent sedimentation of storm sewer or receiving streams,
- ❑ Prevent polluting the air with dust and particulate matter, and

Log building operations and maintenance activity to ensure that plan has been followed.

Submittals – Initial Certification

- ❑ Provide a narrative summary of the site construction and erosion control policy that conforms to the referenced EPA standard. If local standards are followed, describe how they meet or exceed the EPA best management practices. The narrative summary should provide detailed information on all erosion and sedimentation control measures that may be implemented on the site.
- ❑ Provide the organization's erosion and sediment control policy that mandates implementation of erosion and sediment control techniques into all site construction plans and requires the techniques' inclusion into contract documents for any construction projects carried out on site.
- ❑ Provide copy of document committing organization to implement its erosion and sediment control policy.
- ❑ Provide a log showing that the plan has been followed.
- ❑ Provide photos documenting site problems identified and solutions implemented.
- ❑ For any construction projects begun or completed at the building over the performance period:

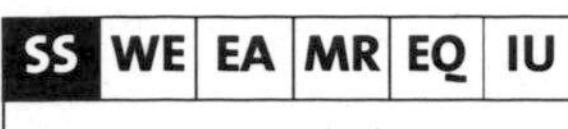

- Declare that the project followed the erosion control policy.
- Submit relevant sections of the erosion control plan (or drawings and specifications) highlighting the sediment and erosion control measures implemented during the performance period.

Submittals – Recertification

Provide an update of previous filings:

- ❑ Provide a statement that there have been no changes to the policy or plan since the initial LEED-EB filing.

OR

- ❑ If there have been changes to the policy or plan since the initial LEED-EB filing, provide the same information that is required for initial LEED-EB filings.

Provide performance documentation:

- ❑ For any construction projects begun or completed at the building site over the performance period, submit relevant sections of the erosion control plan (or drawings and specifications) highlighting the sediment and erosion control measures implemented.
- ❑ Provide a log showing plan has been followed.
- ❑ Provide photos documenting site problems identified and solutions implemented.

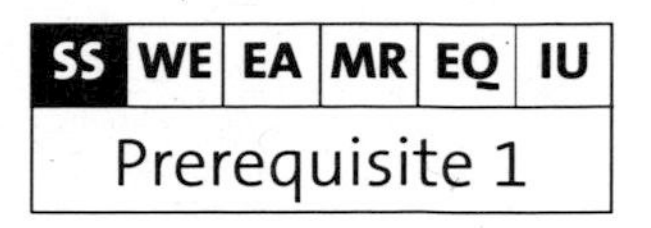

Summary of Referenced Standard

Storm Water Management for Construction Activities: Developing Pollution Prevention Plans and Best Management Practices – Chapter 3: Sediment and Erosion Control

U.S. EPA Publication No. 832-R-92-005

(202) 564-9545

http://cfpub.epa.gov/npdes/stormwater/swppp.cfm

This standard describes two types of measures to control sedimentation and erosion. Stabilization measures include temporary seeding, permanent seeding and mulching. Each of these measures is intended to stabilize the soil to prevent erosion. Conversely, structural control measures are implemented to retain sediment after erosion has occurred. Structural control measures include earth dikes, silt fencing, sediment traps and sediment basins. These measures depend on the conditions at a specific site. If local provisions are substantially similar, they can be substituted for this standard. However, applicants must demonstrate that local provisions meet or exceed the EPA best management practices.

Green Building Concerns

Erosion results from precipitation and wind processes, leading to degradation of property as well as sedimentation of local water bodies. Erosion negatively affects water quality, navigability, fishing and recreation activities. Building sites can be a major source of sediment delivered to water bodies. Although developed sites make up a relatively small percentage of land within a watershed, erosion on highly disturbed land (such as building sites) is often 100 times greater than on agricultural land.[1] Fortunately, measures can be implemented to minimize site erosion during construction and avoid erosion once buildings are occupied.

First, ongoing prevention of erosion and control of sedimentation can be integrated into an existing building's O&M procedures. This involves establishing and maintaining control features on the site and identifying and resolving problems that develop. Second, erosion must be controlled during periodic construction activities. Clearing and earth moving during construction can result in significant erosion without adequate environmental protection strategies. Erosion and sedimentation threats can be prevented by implementing a policy that specifies which control measures to undertake during construction. These strategies help mitigate the on-site and off-site environmental degradation associated with erosion and sedimentation.

Environmental Issues

The loss of topsoil is the most significant on-site consequence of erosion. Topsoil is the soil layer that contains organic matter, plant nutrients and biological activity. Loss of topsoil greatly reduces the soil's ability to support plant life, regulate water flow, and maintain the biodiversity of soil microbes and insects that controls disease and pest outbreaks.[2] Loss of nutrients, soil compaction, and decreased biodiversity of soil inhabitants can severely limit the vitality of landscaping. This can lead to additional site management and environmental concerns, such as increased use of fertilizers, irrigation and pesticides; and increased storm water runoff that heightens the pollution of nearby lakes and streams.

The off-site consequences of erosion from developed sites include a variety of water quality issues. Runoff from developed sites carries pollutants, sediment and excess nutrients that disrupt aquatic habitats in the receiving waters. Eutrophication, the process by which lakes and ponds age and lose the ability to support aquatic life, is accelerated by excess nutrient contribution from erosion and runoff. Nitrogen and phosphorous from runoff hastens eutrophication by causing unwanted plant growth in aquatic systems, including algal blooms that alter water quality and habitat conditions. Algal blooms can also result in decreased recreation potential and diminished diversity of indigenous fish, plant and animal populations.[3] Sedimentation also contributes to the degradation of water bodies. The build-up of sedimentation in stream channels can lessen flow capacity, potentially leading to increased flooding. Sedimentation also affects aquatic habitat by increasing turbidity levels. Turbidity reduces sunlight penetration into the water and leads to reduced photosynthesis in aquatic vegetation, causing lower oxygen levels that cannot support diverse communities of aquatic life.[4]

Economic Issues

Erosion and sedimentation control measures do not necessarily add cost to ongoing building operation or construction. Reduction of sedimentation and erosion through landscaping and other measures can reduce the size, complexity and cost of stormwater management measures. While costs may be associated with monitoring soil conditions, the information gathered can help avoid problems over the building lifetime. For example, inspection may identify unstable soil formations that could potentially lead to structural instability in the building's foundation. Identification and correction of this type of situation will likely save significant amounts of money and prevent unsafe conditions. Early knowledge and reporting of these conditions can also lead to better planning for future development.

Landscaping strategies for preventing soil erosion include augmentation of soil prone to erosion and inclusion of additional plantings in the landscape design to retain soil in place. Additional landscaping may require initial expenditures and maintenance over time, resulting in additional operation costs. Using native plants reduces both watering and maintenance needs.

Strategies & Technologies

Develop an erosion and sedimentation control policy for ongoing site maintenance and future construction. Consider strategies such as temporary and permanent seeding, mulching, earth dikes, silt fencing, sediment traps and sediment basins. Erosion on existing sites typically results from foot traffic killing the vegetation, steep slopes where stormwater sheet flow exceeds vegetation holding power, or point stormwater outflow that exceeds vegetation holding power. Identifying and eliminating these and other causes of erosion can control erosion and sedimentation.

The general approach for earning this prerequisite involves conducting a building site survey to classify the different types and composition of soil, identifying potential site problems, and planning and implementing control measures as needed. The ongoing erosion and sedimentation control policy should outlines strategies for stabilizing areas prone to erosion and protecting them during construction activities. The policy should mandate stringent erosion and sedimentation control requirements in construction drawings and specifications. In addition to construction controls, the policy should specify ongoing site maintenance practices such as landscaping and site design strategies to minimize erosion and sedimentation processes. It may be beneficial to consult with an expert on sustainable landscape architecture and land planning as the policy is developed and implemented. Finally, consider also addressing stormwater management in the policy as it is closely connected to erosion control.

Consider including the following information in the policy:

1. An introduction section that includes a general overview of site flow conditions
2. A statement of erosion control and stormwater control objectives
3. An analysis of current stormwater runoff conditions to establish a baseline with which to compare runoff conditions following construction projects or site alterations
4. A description of all temporary and permanent erosion control and stormwater control measures implemented on the site
5. A description of the type and frequency of maintenance activities required for erosion control facilities utilized on the site.

The referenced standard, *Storm Water Management for Construction Activities*, Chapter 3, lists numerous control measures such as silt fencing, sediment traps, construction phasing, stabilization of steep slopes, and establishment and maintenance of vegetated ground that will meet this credit. **Table 1** describes technologies for controlling erosion and sedimentation as recommended by the referenced standard.

Synergies & Tradeoffs

Measures for erosion and sedimentation control depend on site location and conditions. These measures are often integrated with stormwater management plans because uncontrolled stormwater flows can contribute to erosion. For this reason, consider addressing stormwater management in the erosion and sedimentation control policy. Also, landscaping strategies and other site uses have a significant effect on controlling erosion and providing sedimentation control.

LEED-EB prerequisites and credits related to these issues include:

- ❑ SS Credit 1: Plan for Green Site and Building Exterior Management
- ❑ SS Credit 4: Reduced Site Disturbance
- ❑ SS Credit 5: Stormwater Management
- ❑ SS Credit 6.1: Heat Island Reduction – Non-Roof, Options C and D

Table 1: Technologies for Controlling Erosion and Sedimentation

Control Technology	Description
Stabilization	
Temporary Seeding	Plant fast-growing grasses to temporarily stabilize soils.
Permanent Seeding	Plant grass, trees and shrubs to permanently stabilize soils.
Mulching	Place hay, grass, woodchips, straw or gravel on the soil surface to cover and hold soils.
Structural Control	
Earth Dike	Construct a mound of stabilized soil to divert surface runoff volumes from disturbed areas or into sediment basins or sediment traps.
Silt Fence	Construct posts with a filter fabric media to remove sediment from stormwater volumes flowing through the fence.
Sediment Trap	Excavate a pond area or construct earthen embankments to allow for settling of sediment from stormwater volumes.
Sediment Basin	Construct a pond with a controlled water release structure to allow for settling of sediment from stormwater volumes.

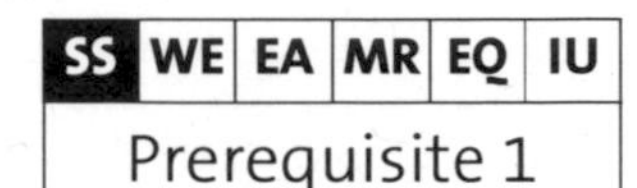

Calculations & Documentation

Calculations

None.

Documentation

- ❑ Erosion and sediment control policy
  - Provide a copy of the policy that details specifications and instructions for erosion and sedimentation control on the project site.
- ❑ Document committing organization to implement policy
  - This document should be a signed statement from an officer of the organization on organization letterhead.
- ❑ Log showing that the plan has been followed
  - The log should note any projects requiring erosion and sedimentation control and track specific measures enacted to prevent or control erosion and sedimentation.

Other Resources

In addition to the resources below, check with state and local organizations for information on erosion and sedimentation control specific to your region.

CPESC Inc.

(828) 655-1600

www.cpesc.net

Search the directory on this web site to find certified erosion and sedimentation control professionals in your state.

Environment Canada's Freshwater Web – Sediment Page

(819) 953-6161

www.ec.gc.ca/water/en/nature/sedim/e_sedim.htm

This site includes information on the environmental effects of sedimentation.

EPA Erosion and Sediment Control Model Ordinances

(202) 566-1155

www.epa.gov/owow/nps/ordinance/erosion.htm

This resource, developed by the EPA, is geared towards helping municipalities draft ordinances for erosion and sedimentation control and might serve as a helpful tool in developing company policies for meeting this LEED-EB Prerequisite.

Erosion Control Technology Council

(651) 554-1895

www.ectc.org

This nonprofit organization develops performance standards, testing procedures, and guidance on the application and installation of rolled erosion control products.

International Erosion Control Association (IECA)

(970) 879-3010

www.ieca.org

This organization's mission is to connect, educate and develop the worldwide erosion and sediment control community.

Soil Erosion and Sedimentation in the Great Lakes Region

(734) 971-9135

www.great-lakes.net/envt/pollution/erosion.html

This resource from the Great Lakes Information Network provides links to general resources, education and training opportunities, materials, manuals, maps and other resources related to soil erosion, sedimentation and watershed management.

Definitions

Erosion is a combination of processes by which materials of the Earth's surface are loosened, dissolved, or worn away, and transported from one place to another by natural agents.

Eutrophication is the process by which lakes and ponds age. Water, through natural or human sources, becomes rich in nutrients and promotes the proliferation of plant life (especially algae) that reduces the dissolved oxygen content of the water and often causes the extinction of other organisms within the water body.

Sedimentation is the addition of soil particles to water bodies by natural and human-related activities. Sedimentation often decreases water quality and can accelerate the aging process of lakes, rivers and streams.

Turbidity is the state of having sediment stirred up or suspended. Turbidity in lakes or estuaries affects water clarity, light penetration, and their suitability as habitat for aquatic plants and animals.

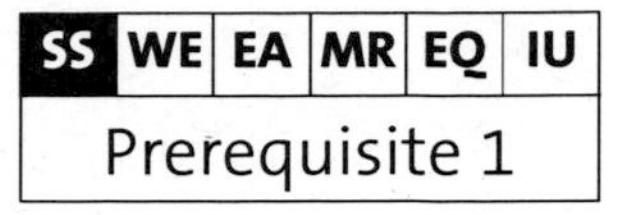

SS	WE	EA	MR	EQ	IU

Prerequisite 2

Required

Age of Building

Intent

Provide a distinction between buildings that are eligible to apply for LEED-NC certification and buildings that are eligible to apply for LEED-EB certification.

Requirements

Buildings that have not been certified under LEED-NC must be at least two years old before they can achieve certification under LEED-EB.

- ❑ Buildings that are more than two years old can register to participate in LEED-EB and apply for LEED-EB certification as soon as they are prepared to do so.
- ❑ LEED-NC Certified buildings that are less than two years old can also register to participate in LEED-EB and apply for LEED-EB certification or re-certification as soon as they are prepared to do so.
- ❑ Buildings that are less than two years old that have not been certified under LEED-NC can register to participate in LEED-EB but must reach two years of age before LEED-EB certification will be awarded by USGBC.

Submittals – Initial Certification

- ❑ Provide a statement that the building covered by the certification application will be at least two years old before certification is received.

OR

- ❑ If the building will be less than two years old when certification is received, provide a statement that the building covered by the certification application has been previously certified under LEED-NC.

Submittals – Recertification

- ❑ Provide all dates of previous LEED-NC or LEED-EB certifications.

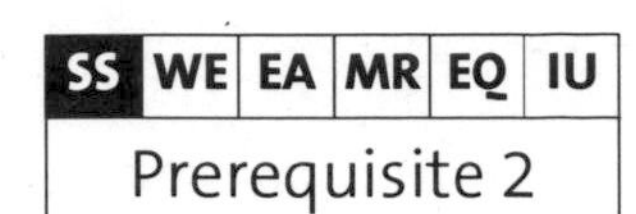

Summary of Referenced Standard

There is no standard referenced for this credit.

Green Building Concerns

This prerequisite is included in LEED-EB to encourage new buildings that are being designed and built to seek LEED Certification under LEED-NC.

Environmental Issues

This prerequisite is included in LEED-EB to encourage new buildings to seek certification under LEED-NC in order to minimize the environmental impacts of new building design and construction. Using LEED-NC to incorporate green building principles into the design and construction phase of a building's life expands opportunities for operating the building sustainably throughout its lifetime.

Economic Issues

LEED-EB and LEED-NC certification standards are equally challenging so there are no economic benefits to using one or the other rating system.

Strategies & Technologies

Project teams with control over the design and construction of new buildings are encouraged to register and earn certification under LEED-NC and then apply for ongoing recertification under LEED-EB. If the opportunity for LEED-NC certification has been missed for buildings younger than two years old, project teams may register the building for LEED-EB and utilize the reporting and documentation tools available to registered LEED-EB projects. Early implementation of sustainable operations and maintenance strategies, coupled with data collection and documentation of performance, will enable buildings to develop the building performance data needed to achieve LEED-EB certification once the building is two years old.

Synergies & Tradeoffs

LEED-NC focuses on the event of sustainable building design and construction, while LEED-EB focuses on the journey of sustainable building operation and upgrades over the long term. Given the different but complementary purposes of LEED-NC and LEED-EB, the ideal approach for new building design and construction is to apply for LEED-NC certification and then immediately register and begin preparing for recertification under LEED-EB. Applying for LEED-NC certification reduces environmental impacts during construction and encourages the design of a building with a high potential for sustainable operation. Registering and applying for recertification under LEED-EB guides the development and implementation of a sustainable building operating plan. Recertification under LEED-EB will ensure that the potential for sustainable performance designed into the building is achieved over the long term.

Calculations & Documentation

Calculations

None.

Documentation

All information needed to successfully document this credit can be found in the Submittals section of the LEED-EB Rating System and the LEED-EB Letter Templates.

Other Resources

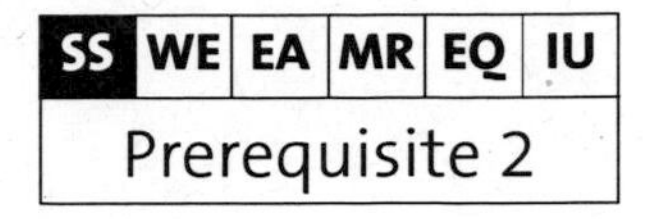

If you are designing and building a new building, review the LEED-NC rating system and consider registering your building for certification under LEED-NC. The LEED-NC rating system can be downloaded at no cost and the LEED-NC Reference Guide can be purchased on the USGBC web site (www.usgbc.org).

SS	WE	EA	MR	EQ	IU

Credits 1.1 & 1.2

1–2 Points

Green Site and Building Exterior Management

Intent

Encourage grounds/site/building exterior management practices that have the lowest environmental impact possible and preserve ecological integrity, enhance diversity and protect wildlife while supporting building performance and integration into surrounding landscapes.

Requirements

Have in place over the performance period a low-impact site and green building exterior management plan that addresses the topics listed below. One point is earned for each four items addressed.

1. Maintenance equipment
2. Plantings
3. Animal and vegetation pest control
4. Landscape waste
5. Irrigation management
6. Fertilizer use
7. Snow removal (where applicable)
8. Cleaning of building exterior
9. Paints and sealants used on building exterior
10. Other maintenance of the building exterior

Submittals – Initial Certification

- ❑ Provide a narrative overview of an organizational management plan for establishing/maintaining a low-impact site and building exterior plan that addresses and specifically highlights the actions from the list in the requirements that are being implemented.
- ❑ Provide quarterly reports over performance period documenting that this management plan is being implemented on an ongoing basis.

Submittals – Recertification

Provide an update of previous filings:

- ❑ If there has been no change to the organizational management plan for establishing/maintaining a low-impact site and building exterior plan, clearly state this in update.

OR

- ❑ If there have been changes to the organizational management plan for establishing/maintaining a low-impact site and building exterior plan, provide an updated narrative overview of this plan that addresses and specifically highlights the actions from the list in the requirements that are being implemented.

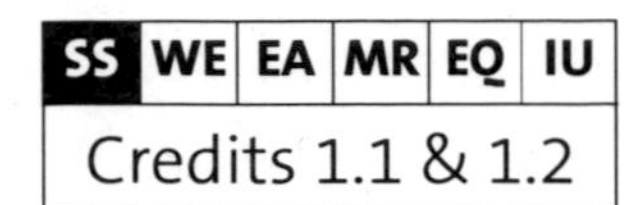

Provide performance documentation:

- ❑ Provide quarterly reports over the performance period documenting that the organizational management plan is being implemented on an ongoing basis.

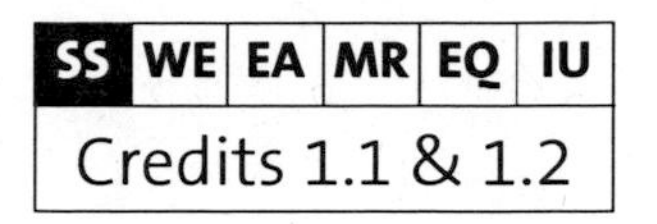

Summary of Referenced Standard

There is no standard referenced for this credit.

Green Building Concerns

Grounds management affects the sustainability of the site itself, the quality of the building's indoor environment, and the environment beyond the building grounds. Adopting a green site and building exterior management plan provides a framework to address exterior maintenance in a manner that preserves the health of building occupants and the environment. The development and implementation of this plan may require altering or expanding current building exterior and ground management activities.

Environmental Issues

A variety of environmental issues are associated with the manner in which building sites are used and maintained. See **Table 1** below for the potential negative environmental effects of various areas of building exterior management.

Economic Issues

Sustainable site management requires attention to the details of site management, but does not necessarily require significant investments in equipment or supplies. Generally, the cost of sustainable site management should be equivalent to other approaches.

Strategies & Technologies

Develop a low-impact site and green building exterior management plan that addresses as many items listed in the credit requirements as possible. One point, up to a total of 2 points, is awarded for every four items addressed. Some site management practices may address multiple items from the list.

Consider including the following elements in the plan:

- ❑ Overall site management practices, chemical/fertilizer/pest management/ snow removal practices, building exterior cleaning and maintenance practices.
- ❑ Green cleaning and maintenance practices and materials.
- ❑ Green landscape management actions such as: using a greater variety

Table 1: Environmental Impacts of Site and Building Exterior Management Practices

Building Exterior Management Practice	Potential Negative Environmental Impacts
Maintenance Equipment	Noise, emissions, soil compaction
Plants	Use of non-native or invasive plants can interfere with local ecology
Animal and Vegetation Pest Control	Use of toxic chemicals poses a risk to other plants, animals and humans
Landscape Waste	Added volume to landfills
Irrigation Management	Excessive water use for irrigation burdens the water supply, as well as treatment and delivery systems
Fertilizer Use	Contamination of groundwater; degradation of lake, river, and stream ecology
Snow Removal (where applicable)	Snow-melting chemicals can be harmful to vegetation, pollute water bodies, and irritate the paws of pets
Cleaning of Building Exterior	Cleaning compounds can harm vegetation and pollute groundwater
Paints and Sealants	Many of these products contain VOCs

of plants, using more native plants, reducing size of lawns, changing maintenance practices, reducing the use of power equipment, controlling stormwater, using fertilizer on an as-needed basis, composting waste, applying integrated pest management, creating wildlife habitat, avoiding/removing invasive plants, protecting natural areas, and using plants to reduce heating and cooling needs.

- Integrated Pest Management (IPM). IPM is a safer and usually less costly option for effective pest management. An IPM program employs common-sense strategies to reduce sources of food, water and shelter for pests in your buildings and on the grounds. IPM programs take advantage of effective pest management strategies and minimize the use of pesticides.
- Mulching mowers that leave grass clippings on the lawn to significantly reduce yard waste generation, fertilizer needs, and water consumption through retention of organic matter. Further reduce the amount of yard waste delivered to landfills by composting other types of yard waste or using them for mulch. Shredding devices can be used on leaves and woody debris to hasten the composting process or to generate mulch. Composting of yard waste can be done onsite, and requires maintaining the appropriate mix of organic materials and moisture/temperature conditions to facilitate decomposition. Compost generated onsite can then be used to add organic matter to the grounds, which reduces the need for fertilizer and water input. Alternatively, some municipalities may operate composting sites where yard waste can be delivered.

Synergies & Tradeoffs

Many aspects of sustainable site maintenance are aligned with other areas of sustainability. Native plantings can reduce irrigation requirements and prevent soil erosion and sedimentation. Animals and vegetation pest management practices implemented near the building can reduce pest problems inside the building. Using low-VOC paints and sealants on exterior projects can meet green materials requirements. Cleaning equipment, practices and supplies can meet purchasing and green cleaning credit requirements.

Related LEED-EB prerequisites and credits include:

- SS Prerequisite 1: Erosion and Sedimentation Control
- SS Credit 4: Reduced Site Disturbance
- SS Credit 5: Stormwater Management
- WE Credit 1: Water Efficient Landscaping
- MR Credit 3: Optimize Use of IAQ Compliant Products
- MR Credit 4: Sustainable Cleaning Products and Materials
- IEQ Credit 10: Green Cleaning

Calculations & Documentation

Calculations

None.

Documentation

- Narrative overview of an organizational management plan
  - The narrative should describe the management plan and note each of the site management items it addresses. A copy of the plan, with applicable sections clearly identified, will aid application reviewers in assessing compliance with credit requirements.

SS	WE	EA	MR	EQ	IU
Credits 1.1 & 1.2					

Other Resources

Green Landscaping with Native Plants

(312) 353-2117

www.epa.gov/greenacres

This U.S. EPA web site details benefits and practices related to landscaping with native plants.

Green Seal

(202) 872-6400

http://greenseal.org

Green Seal is a nonprofit organization that identifies and promotes sustainable products and services. The web site lists certified products, including paints/coatings and various cleaning related products.

Integrated Pest Management In Schools

www.epa.gov/pesticides/ipm/

This U.S. EPA resource contains information about the risks associated with conventional pest control, IPM strategies, and case studies of successful implementation of IPM in schools.

Mid-Atlantic Region Green Landscaping

(215) 814-2744

www.epa.gov/reg3esd1/garden/what.htm

The U.S. EPA Mid-Atlantic Region's web site provides comprehensive information regarding multiple aspects of green landscaping.

National Pesticide Information Center (NPIC)

(800) 858-7378

http://npic.orst.edu/

NPIC is a cooperative effort of Oregon State University and the U.S. EPA. Its web site and hotline services provide information about pesticide handling, toxicity, regulations, and pesticide alternatives.

Pennsylvania Green Building Operations and Maintenance Manual

www.dgs.state.pa.us/dgs/lib/dgs/greenbldg/greenbuildingbook.pdf

This manual includes chapters on green landscaping, snow removal and de-icing, and other green site management practices.

Definitions

Integrated Pest Management (IPM) is the coordinated use of pest and environmental information and pest control methods to prevent unacceptable levels of pest damage by the most economical means, and with the least possible hazard to people, property and the environment.

SS | WE | EA | MR | EQ | IU

Credit 2

1 Point

High Development Density Building and Area

Intent

Channel development to urban areas with existing infrastructure, protect greenfields and preserve habitat and natural resources.

Requirements

Occupy a building that has a density of at least 60,000 square feet of building floor space per acre located within an area with a density of at least 60,000 square feet of building floor space per acre (two-story downtown development). The goal is to encourage the occupancy of high development density buildings in high development density areas. Once earned and for subsequent re-certifications, the only requirement is that the building itself have the required density.

Submittals – Initial Certification

The following must be provided for the first time this point is earned:

- ❑ A signed statement that the building meets the required development density.
- ❑ A signed statement that the buildings in the surrounding area meet the required development density.
- ❑ Calculations showing that the building has a density of at least 60,000 square feet of building floor space per acre area.
- ❑ An area map and calculations showing that on average the buildings in the surrounding downtown area are at least two stories tall.

Submittals – Recertification

In re-certifications after this point has been earned once, only the following must be provided:

- ❑ A signed statement that the building meets the required development density.
- ❑ Calculations showing that the building has a density of at least 60,000 square feet of building floor space per acre area.

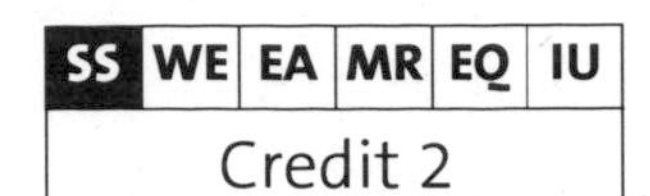

Summary of Referenced Standard

There is no standard referenced for this credit.

Green Building Concerns

The development of open space away from urban cores and other existing developments often reduce property costs, but have negative consequences on the environment and the community. Building occupants become increasingly dependent on private automobiles for commuting and, as travel distances increase, this results in more air and water pollution. Prime agricultural land is lost and inner city neighborhoods fall into disuse and decay. In addition, infrastructure must be installed to support new development areas.

In contrast, occupying an existing building in a more densely developed area helps avoid urban sprawl and reduces the loss of greenfields. Continuing to occupy an existing building and upgrading it to achieve LEED-EB certification helps revitalize and enhance existing communities while preserving non-urban spaces.

Environmental Issues

By maintaining high density in cities, agricultural land and greenfield areas are preserved for future generations. Mass transportation in urban areas can be an attractive alternative mode of transportation, reducing impacts associated with automobiles. Continuing to occupy an existing building in an urban area reduces the number of vehicle miles traveled and, thus, reduces pollution caused by automobiles. The use of existing utility lines, roadways, parking, landscaping components and other services eliminates the environmental impacts of constructing these features for expanding non-urban developments.

Economic Issues

A significant economic benefit of continuing to occupy an existing building is the reduction or elimination of the need for new infrastructure, including roads, utility services and other amenities. If mass transit serves the urban site, significant cost reductions are possible by downsizing the project parking capacity.

Strategies & Technologies

For most projects seeking LEED-EB certification, the building site is already determined. Owners of existing buildings can become involved in the zoning and development decisions about areas around their buildings to encourage high-development density. Also, an organization that plans to eventually seek certification for all the buildings it owns or occupies can give preference to high density locations during the acquisition of additional properties, construction of new properties, or leasing of additional building space.

Synergies & Tradeoffs

Building siting can affect the feasibility of implementing some green building operations. For example, existing buildings in urban areas may have limited space available for construction waste management and occupant recycling programs. Urban sites may have negative IEQ aspects such as contaminated soils, undesirable air quality or limited daylighting applications. Conversely, access to alternative transportation and other sustainable actions may be more feasible in dense urban areas. Green building and other organizational priorities should be considered when siting decisions arise for organizations seeking LEED certification.

SS	WE	EA	MR	EQ	IU
Credit 2					

Calculations & Documentation

Calculations

To determine the development density of a property, calculate both the project density and the densities of surrounding developments. The extent of neighboring areas to include in density calculations depends on the size of the building. Larger buildings are required to consider a greater number of neighboring properties than smaller buildings. To calculate density:

1. Determine the total area of the building property and the total square footage of the building.
2. Calculate the development density for the building by dividing the total square footage of the building by the total property area in acres. This development density must be equal to or greater than 60,000 square feet per acre (See **Equation 1**).
3. Convert the total property area from acres to square feet and calculate the square root of this number. Then multiply the square root by three to determine the appropriate radius for calculating the density of the surrounding buildings (See **Equation 2**).
4. Overlay a circle (with the radius calculated above) on a map that includes the building property and surrounding areas. The center of the circle should be located at the center of the building applying for certification. Include a scale on the map.
5. For each property within the circle defined in step 4, as well as for properties that intersect the circle boundary, create a table with the building square footage and property area of each property. Include all properties in the density calculations except for undeveloped public areas. Undeveloped public areas are defined as public parks, gardens and water bodies. Do not include public roads and right-of-way areas. Information on neighboring properties can be obtained from your city or county zoning department.
6. Sum all of the building square footage values and property areas in a table. Divide the total square footage by the total property area to obtain the average property density within the circle. The average property density of the properties within the circle must be equal to or greater than 60,000 square feet per acre.

The following example illustrates the property density calculations: A 95,126-square-foot building is located on a 0.70-acre urban property, and the calculations are used to determine the building density. The building density is above the minimum density of 60,000 square feet per acre required by the credit (95,126 [SF] / 0.70 [Acres] = 135,894 [SF / Acre]).

Next, the density radius is calculated (3 × √ 0.70 [Acres] × 43,560 [SF/Acre] = 524 [LF]).

The density area circle is applied to a map of the building property and surrounding area (**Figure 1**). The map identifies all properties that are within or are intersected by the density area circle, and includes a scale and a north indicator.

Table 1 below summarizes the information about the properties identified on

Equation 1

Development Density [SF / Acre] = Building Square Footage [SF] / Property Area [Acres]

Equation 2

$$\text{Density Radius [LF]} = 3 \times \sqrt{\text{Property Area [Acres]} \times 43{,}560\ \text{[SF/Acre]}}$$

Figure 1: Example of Density Circle Applied to Map of Building and Surrounding Area

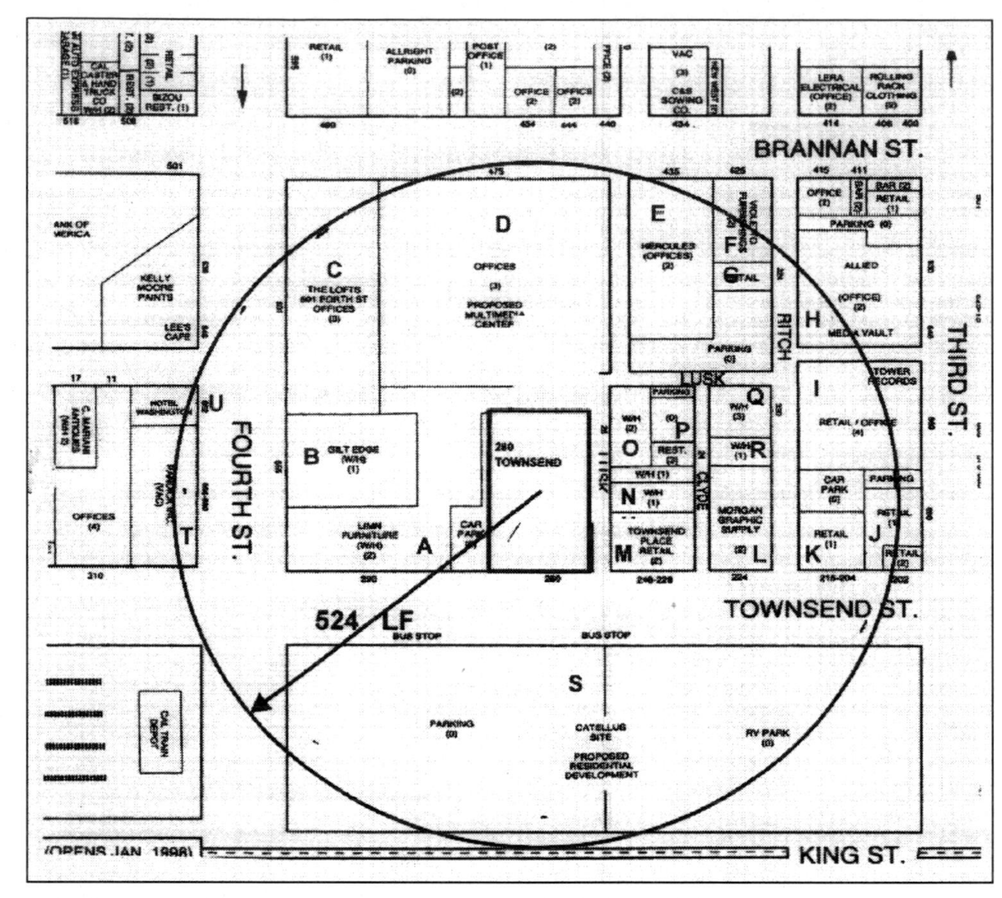

Swinerton Inc. Headquarters, 260 Townsend Street, Certified LEED-EB Gold.

Table 1: Sample Area Properties

Buildings w/in Density Circle	Building Space [SF]	Property Area [Acres]	Buildings w/in Density Circle	Building Space [SF]	Property Area [Acres]
A	43,000	0.90	L	12,500	0.14
B	15,000	0.40	M	5,000	0.06
C	116,513	0.87	N	9,032	0.21
D	255,000	2.41	O	15,196	0.17
E	40,000	0.46	P	7,686	0.06
F	19,600	0.22	Q	22,743	0.17
G	3,766	0.09	R	4,016	0.09
H	41,750	0.48	S	1,100,000	6.50
I	85,000	0.50	T	89,664	0.51
J	43,304	0.25	U	19,650	0.15
K	43,304	0.25			

Total Building Space [SF]	1,991,724
Total Property Acres [Acres]	14.90
Average Density [SF/Acres]	**133,673**

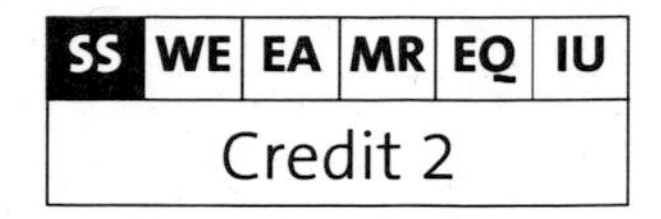

the map. The building space and property area are listed for each property. These values are summed and the average density is calculated by dividing the total building space by the total property area.

For this example, the average building density of the surrounding area is greater than 60,000 square feet per acre and thus, the example qualifies for one point under this credit.

Documentation

All information needed to successfully document this credit can be found in the Submittals section of the LEED-EB Rating System and the LEED-EB Letter Templates.

Other Resources

Changing Places: Rebuilding Community in the Age of Sprawl by Richard Moe and Carter Wilkie, Henry Holt & Company, 1999.

Density by Design: New Directions in Residential Development by Steven Fader, Urban Land Institute, 2000.

Green Development: Integrating Ecology and Real Estate by Alex Wilson et al., John Wiley & Sons, 1998.

International Union for the Scientific Study of Population

33 1 56 06 21 73

www.iussp.org

The IUSSP promotes scientific studies of demography and population-related issues.

Once There Were Greenfields: How Urban Sprawl Is Undermining America's Environment, Economy, and Social Fabric by F. Kaid Benfield et al., Natural Resources Defense Council, 1999.

Suburban Nation: The Rise of Sprawl and the Decline of the American Dream by Andres Duany et al., North Point Press, 2000.

Urban Land Institute

(703) 390-9217

www.washington.uli.org

The Urban Land Institute is a nonprofit organization based in Washington, D.C. that promotes the responsible use of land in order to enhance the total environment.

Definitions

Building density is the floor area of the building divided by the total area of the property (square feet per acre).

A **Greenfield** is undeveloped land or land that has not been impacted by human activity.

Property Area is the total area within the legal property boundaries of a building and includes all areas of the site including constructed areas and non-constructed areas.

The **Square Footage** of a building is the total floor area in square feet of all rooms, including corridors, elevators, stairwells and shaft spaces.

Case Study

260 Townsend St.

San Francisco, California

LEED-EB Gold
Owner: Swinerton Inc.

Photo courtesy of: Swinerton Inc.

260 Townsend St., the corporate headquarters for the Swinerton Companies, is a 90,000 square foot office building located in an urban renewal zone in San Francisco. The building's immediate surroundings include a wide variety of offices, retail, and warehouses, and extensive redevelopment for mixed-use and residential projects is currently underway. Nearby neighbors include Pacific Bell Park and Caltrain. To determine the density of development in the surrounding area, Swinerton surveyed the square footage of 21 buildings within its density radius, calculating an average density of over 133,000 square feet per acre.

SS	WE	EA	MR	EQ	IU
Credit 3.1					

1 Point

Alternative Transportation

Public Transportation Access

Intent

Reduce pollution and land development impacts from automobile use.

Requirements

Meet the criteria of at least one of the following three options:

Option A

- ❑ The building is located within 1/2 mile of a commuter rail, light rail or subway station.

Option B

- ❑ The building is located within 1/4 mile of two or more public or campus bus lines usable by building occupants.

Option C

- ❑ Building occupants are provided with a conveyance (shuttle link) that supplies transportation between the building and public transportation meeting the criteria in Option A or Option B above.

Submittals – Initial Certification

- ❑ Provide an area drawing or transit map highlighting the building location, the fixed rail stations and bus lines. Include a scale bar for distance measurement and indicate the distance between the building and each service.
- ❑ Provide records and results of quarterly contacts over the performance period with transit services to verify that service continues to be provided within specified distances from the building.

Submittals – Recertification

Provide an update of previous filings:

- ❑ Provide a signed statement declaring that there have been no changes to the distance between the building and the fixed rail stations and bus lines.

OR

- ❑ If there have been changes since the previous filing, provide updated information that meets initial LEED-EB filings requirements for Option A, B or C above.

Provide performance documentation:

- ❑ Provide records and results of quarterly contacts over the performance period with transit services to verify that service continues to be provided within specified distances from the building.

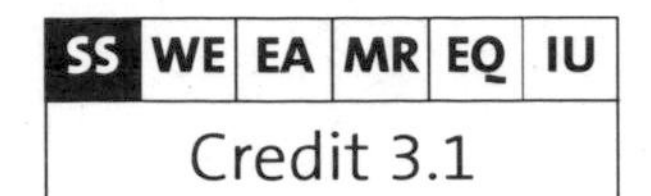

Summary of Referenced Standard

There is no standard referenced for this credit.

Green Building Concerns

Transportation accounts for 27.4 percent of energy use in the United States, the vast majority (96.4 percent) of which is powered by petroleum-based fuels.[5] Light vehicles, including automobiles, motorcycles, and light trucks, consume more energy than any other transportation mode.[6] In 2001, Americans were estimated to own more than 200 million private vehicles.[7] Along with steady increases in vehicle ownership, the number of miles traveled by Americans has also steadily increased over the past few decades. In 2001, on average each American (excluding persons ages 0 to 4) traveled 40.25 miles per day, with 88.2 percent of all daily travel attributed to private vehicles.[8] Travel to and from work makes up a significant portion (nearly 30 percent) of the vehicles miles traveled in personal vehicles, and the average length and duration of these commuting trips has steadily increased over the past few decades.[9]

The extensive use of private automobiles and their heavy reliance on petroleum contributes to a number of environmental problems. Fortunately, alternatives to conventional transportation methods exist. A surprisingly large number of people are willing to use alternative means of transportation such as mass transit if it is convenient. Encouraging the use of mass transit reduces the energy demand for transportation needs and affects building sites by reducing the space needed for parking lots, which encroach on green space. Minimizing parking lots reduces the building footprint and sets aside more space for natural areas or greater development densities.

Environmental Issues

The environmental effects of automobile use include vehicle emissions that contribute to smog and other air pollutants, as well as environmental impacts from oil extraction and petroleum refining. Increased use of public transportation can improve air quality. For every passenger mile traveled, public transportation emits 95 percent less carbon monoxide, 92 percent fewer volatile organic compounds (VOCs), and almost 50 percent less carbon dioxide and nitrogen oxides than private vehicles.[10]

Fewer private vehicles also reduces fuel consumption. On the basis of passenger miles traveled, public transportation is twice as fuel efficient as private vehicles, and annually saves 45 million barrels of oil.[11] Another benefit of public transportation is the associated reduction in the need for infrastructure used by vehicles. Parking facilities and roadways for automobiles have negative impacts on the environment because impervious surfaces like asphalt increase stormwater runoff while contributing to urban heat island effects.

Economic Issues

Many building occupants view proximity to mass transit as a benefit, and this can influence the value and marketability of the building. For building occupants, access to public transportation can reduce commuting costs. For this reason, providing access to public transportation may provide an economic benefit in attracting and retaining employees. Existing building project teams have little to no control over their building's proximity to mass transit. If a building is not near mass transit, a shuttle can earn this credit, but this would add an operating cost for the building.

Reducing the size of parking areas based on anticipated use of public transit may

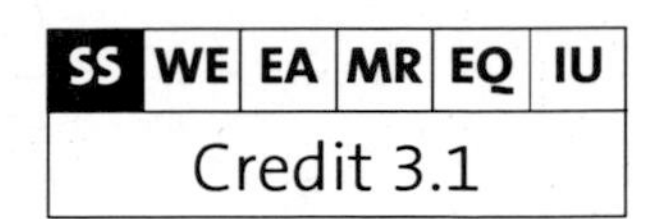

alter operating costs associated with parking lot maintenance. If local utilities charge for stormwater runoff based on impervious surface area, minimization of these areas can also result in lower stormwater runoff charges.

Strategies & Technologies

- ❑ Survey potential building occupants and determine if the available mass transportation options meet their needs.
- ❑ Use existing transportation networks to minimize the need for new transportation lines.
- ❑ Provide sidewalks, paths and walkways to existing mass transit stops.
- ❑ Provide incentives such as free or discounted transit passes to encourage occupants to use mass transit.
- ❑ Provide a shuttle to public transportation to meet the requirements for this credit. The schedule and frequency of shuttle services must be adequate to serve employees during standard commuting times for all shifts, as well as periodic service at other times.
- ❑ Explore the possibility of sharing facilities with other groups for a transportation link service.

Synergies & Tradeoffs

Increased use of public transportation by building occupants reduces the need for parking spaces on site, thus reducing the need for impervious surfaces and potential water runoff problems. A reduction in hard surface parking areas could also increase the amount of open space on the site while reducing heat island effects and stormwater runoff volumes. Consider how reduced parking needs could facilitate earning the following LEED-EB credits:

- ❑ SS Credit 4: Reduced Site Disturbance
- ❑ SS Credit 5: Stormwater Management
- ❑ SS Credit 6: Heat Island Reduction

Calculations & Documentation

Calculations

None.

Documentation

- ❑ Area drawing or transit map
  - The map should clearly demarcate locations of public transit options, the routes/lines available and the distance to each stop or station that services the building within the required radius.
  - If a shuttle between the building and transit points is used to meet the requirements of this credit, provide information on the distances between transit points and the building, schedule and frequency of shuttle operation, and shuttle capacity.

Other Resources

Best Workplaces for Commuters

(888) 856-3131

www.bestworkplacesforcommuters.gov/index.htm

This program, established by the U.S. EPA and U.S. DOT, publicly recognizes employers for their exemplary commuter benefits programs. It provides tools, guidance and promotion to help employers incorporate commuter benefits into their employee benefits plan, reap financial benefits, and gain national recognition.

Transportation and Air Quality

www.epa.gov/otaq/

This U.S. EPA web site provides information on the types and effects of air pollution associated with automobile use,

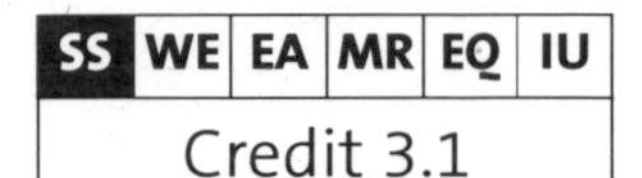

information for consumers, and links to resources for organizations interested in promoting commuter choice programs.

Definitions

Mass Transit consists of transportation facilities designed to transport large groups of persons in a single vehicle such as buses or trains

Case Study

Oregon Convention Center

Portland, Oregon

LEED-EB Certified

Owner: Oregon Convention Center/Metro

Photo courtesy of: Nancy Erz

The Oregon Convention Center (OCC) is highly accessible by major bus lines and light rail, making public transportation convenient to both visitors and employees. The facility is served by three light-rail stops operated by the Tri-Met transit system within a ¼-mile radius of the building, as well as over a dozen bus lines at the nearby Rose Quarter Transit Center. To encourage use of public transit by employees, the OCC is a member of the Lloyd District Transport Management Association. Through this association, OCC is able to purchase discounted annual Tri-Met transport passes and provide them to qualified employees who use public transportation.

SS	WE	EA	MR	EQ	IU
Credit 3.2					

1 Point

Alternative Transportation

Bicycle Storage & Changing Rooms

Intent

Reduce pollution and land development impacts from automobile use.

Requirements

For commercial or institutional buildings, provide secure bicycle storage with convenient changing/shower facilities (within 200 yards of the building) for regular building occupants. Maintain bike storage and shower capacity that is sufficient for the greater of 1% of the building occupants or 125% of peak demand for these facilities.

For residential buildings, provide covered storage facilities for securing bicycles for 15% or more of building occupants in lieu of changing/shower facilities. These facilities may be provided incrementally as long as the capacity of the facilities supplied exceeds the demand for these facilities.

In campus settings, if secure bicycle storage and showers are provided for all buildings occupants on a campus-wide basis, the maximum distance from individual buildings to showers requirement can be replaced with a requirement that two lines be drawn at 90 degrees to each other through the center of the campus on a campus map and that it be documented that the bicycle storage and showers requirements are met for all buildings occupants within each quadrant.

Submittals – Initial Certification

- ❑ Provide site drawings (drawings showing where the showers and bike storage are located do not need to be the original building architectural drawings of the building), product cut sheets and/or photographs highlighting:
  - Bicycle securing apparatus.
  - Changing/shower facilities.
- ❑ Provide records and results of quarterly inspections over the performance period to verify that the initially identified number of bicycle securing apparatus and shower/changing facilities continue to be available and that bicycle storage peak usage is being tracked on a quarterly basis.
- ❑ Provide record of quarterly assessments of the number to building occupants and associated calculations to verify that these facilities continue to meet the credit requirements.
- ❑ If a LEED-NC certified building is less than two years old:
  - Document that secure bicycle storage with convenient changing/shower facilities (within 200 yards of the building) are provided for at least 5% of all building users.
- ❑ If building is more than two years old, document that:

  (1) The initially installed bike storage capacity is equal to the greater of the following:

  a) 125% of the peak demand for bicycle parking.

b) 1% of the full-time equivalent building users.

(2) The initially provided shower capacity is adequate based on required bike storage capacity calculated in (1) above.

(3) The bike storage capacity has been increased within six months for each time there is an increase in peak usage so that the bike storage capacity is maintained at 125% of the peak demand for bicycle parking until a maximum bike storage capacity of 5% of the building users is reached.

(4) The number of showers has been increased to provide the required shower capacity for any increase in the required number of bike storage identified in (3) above.

Submittals – Recertification

Provide an update of previous filings:

- ❑ Provide a signed statement declaring that there have been no changes to either number of building users, bike storage capacity or shower/changing facilities and that these facilities continue to meet the needs of the building occupants.
- ❑ Provide quarterly checks on the number to building occupants to verify that the bike storage capacity or shower/changing facilities continue to meet the needs of the building users and that bicycle storage peak usage is being tracked on a quarterly basis.

OR

If there have been changes in the number of building users and/or storage/shower/changing facilities, provide:

- ❑ Current site drawings, product cut sheets and/or photographs highlighting:
  - Bicycle securing apparatus.
  - Changing/shower facilities.

Provide performance documentation:

- ❑ Provide records and results of quarterly inspections to verify that the initially identified number of bicycle securing apparatus and shower/changing facilities continue to be available and that bicycle storage peak usage is being tracked on a quarterly basis.
- ❑ Provide a record of quarterly assessments of the number of building users and associated calculations to verify that these facilities continue to meet the credit requirements.
- ❑ Document that:

(1) The installed bike storage capacity continues to be the greater than the larger of the following:

a) 125% of the peak demand for bicycle parking.

b) 1% of the full-time equivalent building users.

(2) The bike storage capacity has been increased as necessary (within six months of identification of need), each time there has been an increase in peak usage so that the bike storage capacity is maintained at 125% of the peak demand for bicycle

parking until a maximum bike storage capacity of 5% of the building users is reached.

(3) That the provided shower capacity continues to be adequate based on required bike storage capacity calculated in (1) above.

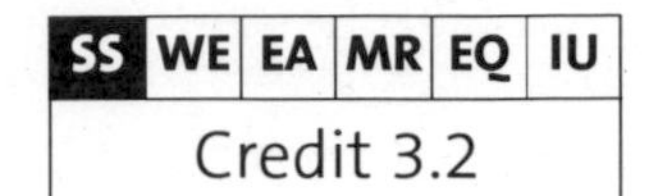

Summary of Referenced Standard

There is no standard referenced for this credit.

Green Building Concerns

Transportation accounts for 27.4 percent of energy use in the United States, the vast majority (96.4 percent) of which uses petroleum-based fuels.[12] Light vehicles, including automobiles, motorcycles, and light trucks, consume more energy than any other transportation mode.[13] In 2001, Americans were estimated to own more than 200 million private vehicles.[14] Along with steady increases in vehicle ownership, the number of miles traveled by Americans has also steadily increased over the past few decades. In 2001, on average each American (excluding persons ages 0 to 4) traveled 40.25 miles per day, with 88.2 percent of all daily travel attributed to private vehicles.[15] Travel to and from work makes up a significant portion (nearly 30 percent) of the vehicles miles traveled in personal vehicles, and the average length and duration of these commuting trips has steadily increased over the past few decades.[16]

The extensive use of private automobiles and their heavy reliance on petroleum contributes many environmental problems. Since the early 1990s, the U.S. Department of Transportation (DOT) has increasingly focused on bicycling as an environmentally friendly, cost-effective, healthy option. This has increased knowledge about bicycling rates and barriers to participation, funding for bicycling facilities, and programs promoting bicycle use and safety.[17] Building owners can help promote bicycling for commuters by ensuring that building grounds offer the appropriate facilities.

Environmental Issues

The environmental effects of automobiles include vehicle emissions that contribute to smog and other air pollutants, as well as environmental impacts from oil extraction and petroleum refining. Bicycling offers environmental benefits. It produces no emissions or demand for petroleum-based fuels. Bicycle commuting also relieves traffic congestion, reduces noise pollution and requires far less infrastructure for roadways and parking lots. Roadways and parking lots produce stormwater runoff, contribute to the urban heat island effect and encroach on green space.

Bicycles are more likely to be used for relatively short commuting trips. Displacing vehicle miles with bicycling even for short trips carries a large environmental benefit, since a large portion of vehicle emissions occur in the first few minutes of driving following a cold start, as emissions control equipment is less effective at cool operating temperatures.[18]

Economic Issues

If local utilities charge for stormwater runoff based on impervious surface area, minimization of these areas (like vehicle parking lots) can result in lower stormwater runoff charges. The cost increase for bike storage areas is typically relatively small. Adding changing facilities and showers in existing buildings can cost more. Local and state governments may assist employees in meeting the cost of bicycle facilities through commuter choice incentive programs. Encouraging bicycle commuting can improve employee health and reduce sick leave.

Strategies & Technologies

Design and construct safe bike pathways and secure bicycle storage areas. Provide shower and changing areas that are easily accessible from bicycle storage areas. Explore the possibility of sharing facilities

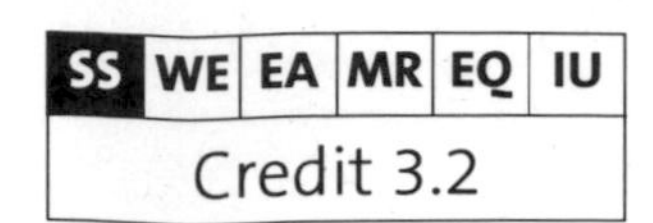

and bike paths with other groups. A variety of bicycle storage and locker products are currently available. Choose the type, location and quantity of bike racks that will maximize their usefulness. Seek user input, investigate local municipal recommendations or criteria, and consider the following guidelines when adding bicycle racks to building grounds[19]:

Type

- ❑ Rack design – Racks should be designed to support a bicycle by its frame, allow for the frame and one or both of the wheels to be secured, and support the use of U-shaped bicycle locks. Inverted "U" shaped, "A" shaped, and "Post and Loop" shaped racks are recommended. Designs that do not support the bike frame can easily lead to bicycle damage, and should be avoided. "Wave" shaped racks should also be avoided as they are often used in a manner that limits capacity below the manufacturer specified capacity and, when used as intended, do not supply as much support to the bicycle frame as other designs.
- ❑ Rack material – Racks should be constructed out of durable, sturdy materials that cannot be easily damaged or tampered with by thieves or vandals. Racks should be resistant to cutting or disassembling with bolt cutters, pipe cutters, pry bars, wrenches, handsaws or other tools.
- ❑ Spacing – Spacing between individual parking spots within a rack, spacing between aisles of racks, and spacing between racks and building walls or other obstructions are important considerations. Poor spacing can inhibit use of the racks, decrease capacity or result in accidental damage to parked bicycles. Generally, plan to allow an area 2 feet by 6 feet for each individual bike parking space. Aisles should be at least 4 to 5 feet wide.
- ❑ Anchoring – Choose a rack style that can be securely anchored with tamper-proof bolts.

Location

- ❑ Visibility – Racks should be located in a convenient area. Locating bike racks in visible areas also prevents theft and vandalism.
- ❑ Security – In addition to placing racks within view of passersby, windows, or security cameras, select an area that is well lit at night.
- ❑ Accessibility – Racks should be located in an area convenient to corridors used by bicyclists, such as street or bike path access, and near building entrances.
- ❑ Protection from weather – If possible, locate bike racks in an area protected from the elements. Building overhangs, protected walkways, covered lots, or spaces within the building interior can prevent damage to bicycles from rain, snow, and sunlight.
- ❑ Proximity to other types of traffic – Locate bike racks in an area that avoids conflict with pedestrian or motor vehicle traffic. Bike racks in pedestrian areas can impede pedestrian traffic or lead to bicycle/pedestrian collisions. Keeping bike racks separate from vehicular traffic protects the safety of bicyclists and prevents damage to bicycles from vehicle parking mishaps.

Quantity

The appropriate number of bicycle facilities depends on the number of bicyclists and building type:

- ❑ Buildings previously certified under LEED-NC that are less than two years old must have in place or add enough bike racks for 5 percent of building occupants and showers equal to 0.625 percent of building occupants.
- ❑ For all other buildings, bike racks must accommodate 1 percent of full-time

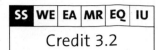

equivalent building users or meet 125 percent of the peak demand for bicycle parking, whichever is greater. Shower facilities must be provided at a rate of one shower per eight bicycle parking spaces. To aid compliance with this credit, regularly inspect the number of bikes parked at bike racks to determine demand. Routine assessment of bicycle parking demand should be integrated into the job description of appropriate building personnel. When the peak usage multiplied by 125 percent exceeds the number of bike racks, additional facilities must be added within 6 months.

- ❑ Assessment of bicycle parking demand might be coordinated with security measures that involve routinely patrolling bike parking areas.
- ❑ See the Calculations section for more information about determining the appropriate quantity of bicycle racks.

Synergies & Tradeoffs

Provisions for bicycles as a viable transportation mode reduces the need for parking spaces, thus reducing impervious surfaces and potential water runoff problems. A reduction in hard surface parking areas could also increase the amount of open space on the site while reducing heat island effects.

Shower and changing facilities take up space, and in some existing buildings finding space for these facilities can be difficult. These facilities also increase water and material usage. However, commuter choices can be attractive to prospective employers, and incorporated into employee benefit packages.

Calculations & Documentation

Calculations

To determine the number of secure bicycle spaces and changing/showering facilities required for the building, follow this calculation methodology:

1. Identify the total number of full-time and part-time building occupants.
2. Calculate the Full-Time Equivalent (FTE) building occupants based on a standard 8-hour workday. A full-time occupant has a FTE value of 1.0 while a half-time occupant has a FTE value of 0.5 (see **Equation 1**).
3. Calculate the FTE building occupant values for each 8-hour shift. For buildings used for multiple shifts each day, use data from the shift with the greatest number of FTE building occupants to set the overall FTE building occupants for the building.
4. Determine the peak demand for bicycle facilities by conducting a survey of building occupants and/or counting the number of bicycles parked at the racks. Conduct rack counts on different days of the week and times of day to account for variation in bicycle commuting. Reassess peak demand every quarter.
5. Determine the minimum number of bicycle racks required. This is equal to the greater of (a) 1 percent of the FTE building occupants during the maximum shift or (b) 125 percent of the peak demand for bike racks. (See **Equation 2**.) Bicycle rack requirements can be met with outdoor bicycle racks, bicycle lockers or indoor bicycle storage rooms.
6. Determine the number of changing and showering facilities required. This

Equation 1

FTE Building Occupants = Hours spent by all occupants in building per day [hours] / 8 [hours]

SS | WE | EA | MR | EQ | IU

Credit 3.2

Equation 2

Bicycle Racks = Greater of:

(a) FTE Building Occupants x 0.01

OR

(b) Peak usage of bike racks x 1.25

is based on the required number of bike racks. A minimum of 1 shower for every 8 bicycle racks from Equation 2 is required. Showering facilities can be unit showers or group showering facilities (see **Equation 3**).

Example: A building is occupied by a company with two shifts. The first shift includes 240 full-time workers and 90 half-time workers. The second shift includes 110 full-time workers and 60 half-time workers. Calculations to determine the total FTE building occupants for each shift are shown in **Table 1**.

The first shift is used to determine the number of occupants because it has the greater FTE building occupant total. Based on a total of 285 FTE building occupants, 15 bicycle racks are required. Based on 125 percent of the peak usage in that quarter, 13 bike racks are required. Since 15 is greater than 13, the required number of bike racks is 15. The number of required bike racks (15) divided by 8 indicates that the changing room for bicycle users needs to have at least two showers to earn this credit.

Documentation

All information needed to successfully document this credit can be found in the Submittals section of the LEED-EB Rating System and the LEED-EB Letter Templates.

Other Resources

Bicyclinginfo.org

www.bicyclinginfo.org

This resource from the Pedestrian and Bicycle Information Center provides information and resources for a number of issues related to bicycle commuting, including health and safety, engineering, advocacy, education, facilities and more.

Table 1: Sample FTE Calculation

Shift	Full-Time Occupants		Part-Time Occupants		Total FTE Occupants
	Occupants	[hr]	Occupants	[hr]	
First Shift	240	8	90	4	285
Second Shift	110	8	60	4	140

Table 2: Quartery Survey of Peak Bike Rack Usage

Survey Days in Last Quarter	Dates	Bike Rack Positions in Use
Monday	October 18, 2004	8
Tuesday	October 26, 2004	10
Wednesday	November 17, 2004	7
Thursday	November 11, 2004	8
Friday	October 22, 2004	10
Saturday	November 20, 2004	5
Sunday	December 5, 2004	2
125% of peak demand		13

Equation 3

Showering Facilities = Bicycling Racks Required / 8

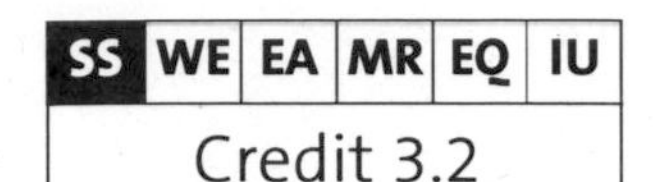

Information and links for bicycle parking issues can be found at http://www.bicyclinginfo.org/de/park.htm.

Bicycle & Pedestrian Program

www.fhwa.dot.gov/environment/bikeped/

(202) 366-5007

This program of the Federal Highway Administration's Office of Human and Natural Environment promotes bicycle and pedestrian transportation accessibility, use and safety.

Bike To Work

www.biketowork.com

This online resource for bicycle commuters provides a variety of links and information.

Commuting Guide for Employers

www.self-propelled-city.com/employ-comm.html

This web site outlines strategies employers can use as they try to encourage employees to bicycle commute.

Employer's Guide to Encouraging Bicycle Commuting

(207) 623-4511

www.bikemaine.org/btwemployer.htm

This web site from the Bicycle Coalition of Maine suggests ways to encourage and facilitate bike commuting.

Definitions

Bicycle Racks include outdoor bicycle racks, bicycle lockers or indoor bicycle storage rooms.

Full-Time Equivalent Building Occupants refers to the total number of hours all building occupants spend in the building during the peak 8-hour occupancy period divided by 8 hours. For buildings used for multiple shifts each day, the shift with the greatest number of FTE building occupants sets the overall FTE building occupants for the building.

Case Study

Microsoft Buildings 30, 31 & 32

Redmond, Washington

Photo courtesy of: Microsoft Corporation

LEED-EB Certified

Owner: Microsoft Corporation

Buildings 30, 31 and 32 on the Redmond campus of Microsoft provide parking spaces for 160 bicycles, serving roughly 10% of the building occupants. Bicycle parking is provided in parking garages and at the base of stair wells where feasible, allowing bicyclist to park their bikes in areas protected from inclement weather. The buildings also have eight showers for commuters.

Microsoft uses data from commuter surveys and inspections of the facilities to verify that bike facilities are meeting the needs of building occupants.

SS	WE	EA	MR	EQ	IU
Credit 3.3					

1 Point

Alternative Transportation

Alternative Fuel Vehicles

Intent

Reduce pollution and land development impacts from automobile use.

Requirements

Have a communication program in place over the performance period that promotes the use of alternative fuel vehicles for building occupants. In addition, meet the criteria of at least one of the following three options:

Option A

- ❑ Alternative fuel refueling station(s) for 3% of the total vehicle parking capacity of the site. NOTE: liquid or gaseous fueling facilities must be separately ventilated or located outdoors.

Option B

- ❑ Provide (or achieve result in some other way) alternative fuel vehicles or hybrid vehicles for 3% of building occupants.
- ❑ Provide preferred parking for these vehicles.

Option C

- ❑ Provide preferred parking programs for hybrid or alternative fuel vehicles for at least 3% of the total vehicle parking capacity and increase as necessary the amount of preferred parking to meet the demand for preferred parking up to 10% or more of the total vehicle parking capacity.

Submittals – Initial Certification

Option A

- ❑ Provide specifications and site drawings documenting that the installed alternative fuel refueling stations have the capacity to accommodate 3% or more of the total vehicle parking capacity.
- ❑ Provide records and results of quarterly inspections to verify that the initial alternative fueling capacity continues to be available.
- ❑ Provide evidence that the program to promote use of alternative fuel vehicles is communicated to building occupants.
- ❑ Perform quarterly checks of the total vehicle parking capacity to verify that these refueling facilities continue to have the capacity to accommodate 3% or more of the total vehicle parking requirements.

Option B

- ❑ Provide proof of ownership or leaseagreement of at least two years to prove that alternative fuel vehicles are being provided for 3% of building occupants.
- ❑ Provide specifications and site drawings documenting that preferred parking is being provided for these vehicles.

- ❑ Provide evidence that the program to promote use of alternative fuel vehicles is communicated to building occupants.
- ❑ Perform quarterly checks of the total vehicle parking capacity to verify that alternative fuel vehicles continue to be provided to accommodate 3% or more of the total vehicle parking requirements.

Option C

- ❑ Provide specifications and site drawings and calculations documenting that:
  - Preferred parking for hybrid or alternative fuel vehicles is being provided for at least 3% of the total vehicle parking capacity
  - The amount of preferred parking has been increased as necessary so that the amount of preferred parking meets the demand for this preferred parking up to 10% or more of the total vehicle parking capacity.
- ❑ Perform quarterly checks of the total vehicle parking capacity to verify that preferred parking for alternative fuel vehicles continues to be provided and that it continues to meets the demand for this preferred parking up to 10% or more of the total vehicle parking capacity.
- ❑ Provide evidence that the program to promote use of hybrid vehicles is communicated to building occupants.

Submittals – Recertification

- ❑ If no changes in parking or building occupancy have occurred, provide a signed letter stating that there have been no changes, and reaffirm that the alternative fuel vehicle strategy certified in the initial LEED-EB Certification remains valid.

OR

- ❑ If there have been any changes to how option (A), (B) or (C) above is being met, provide documentation of the nature of any such changes. Provide specifications, drawings, calculations and the results from quarterly inspections over the performance period to demonstrate that the requirements certified under the initial LEED-EB Certification continue to be met and that the annual capacity of the alternative refueling stations meets demand.

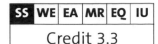

Summary of Referenced Standard

There is no standard referenced for this credit.

Green Building Concerns

Transportation accounts for 27.4 percent of energy use in the United States, the vast majority (96.4 percent) of which is powered by petroleum-based fuels.[20] Light vehicles, including automobiles, motorcycles, and light trucks, consume more energy than any other transportation mode.[21] In 2001, Americans were estimated to own more than 200 million private vehicles.[22] Along with steady increases in vehicle ownership, the number of miles traveled by Americans has also steadily increased over the past few decades. In 2001, on average each American (excluding persons ages 0 to 4) traveled 40.25 miles per day, with 88.2 percent of all daily travel attributed to private vehicles.[23] Travel to and from work makes up a significant portion (nearly 30 percent) of the vehicles miles traveled in personal vehicles, and the average length and duration of these commuting trips has steadily increased over the past few decades.[24]

The extensive use of private automobiles and their heavy reliance on petroleum contributes to a number of environmental problems. Fortunately, alternatives to conventional transportation methods exist. Alternative fuel vehicles (AFVs) can reduce the environmental impacts associated with automobiles. Although alternative fuel made up only 0.3 percent of fuel consumption in the United States in 2003, alternative fuel use increased 59 percent from 1993 to 2003.[25] The four most commonly owned AFVs in the United States are powered by liquefied petroleum gas (LPG), mixes of 85 percent ethanol and 15 percent gasoline (E85), compressed natural gas (CNG), and electricity.[26] These AFVs require special refueling facilities to be viable alternatives to conventional vehicles.

Advanced technology vehicles (ATVs) provide another alternative to conventional vehicles. Hybrid technology uses petroleum fuels and electricity, and vehicles of this type are becoming increasingly popular. Hybrid sales in 2003 increased 31 percent over 2002,[27] and several additional light-duty models are expected in the coming years. Fuel cell technology is also continually developing, and may become a more widely available option in the future.

Providing refueling stations and preferred parking for building occupants using alternative vehicles encourages their use and helps minimize the environmental impact associated with people traveling to and from the building.

Environmental Issues

Operation of vehicles significantly contributes to global change and air quality problems through the emission of greenhouse gases (GHG) and other pollutants generated from combustion engines and fuel evaporation. Motor gasoline is estimated to account for 60 percent of all carbon dioxide (a major GHG) emitted in the United States in the last 20 years.[28] Personal vehicles also generate large portions of the air pollutants responsible for smog and ground-level ozone, both of which have negative affects on human health. **Table 1** below shows the contribution (percentage) of gasoline-powered light vehicles to total U.S. emissions of various pollutants.

AFVs and ATVs offer the possibility of reducing air pollutants from vehicular travel as well as the environmental effects of producing gasoline. However, the extent to which alternative vehicles produce an environmental benefit depends on the complete lifecycle of their fuels and the

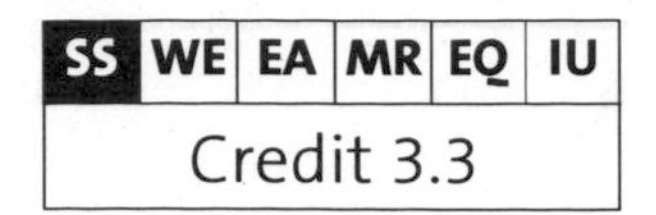

Table 1: Percent of Total U.S. Emissions Attributed to Light Vehicles.

Pollutant	Light Vehicles Share of U.S. Emissions in 2001
Carbon Monoxide	58.4%
Nitrogen Oxides	17.4%
Volatile Organic Compounds	24.6%

U.S. Environmental Protection Agency, National Emission Inventory. Air Pollutant Emission Trends January 2005. 2 March 2005 <www.epa.gov/ttn/chief/trends>.

vehicle technology. For example, electric vehicles generate zero GHGs during operation, but the amount of GHGs emitted during the production of the electricity that these vehicles run on varies greatly depending on the electricity source. Furthermore, alternative fuels may be superior to conventional gasoline on the basis of one pollutant, but carry a higher pollution load for another pollutant. **Table 2** shows the changes in per-mile fuel-cycle energy use and emissions for different fuel types relative to conventional gasoline passenger cars. Energy use and emissions for complete fuel-cycles include energy-use and pollutants generated during the extraction and production of fuels, as well as those generated during vehicle operation.

Because the environmental benefit of AFVs and ATVs depends on complete fuel-cycle energy-use and emissions, carefully consider available vehicle technologies and fuel sources before purchasing vehicles or installing fuel stations.

Economic Issues

Initial costs for alternative vehicles are higher than for conventional vehicles, and this may delay their purchase, decreasing the necessity for refueling stations.

Table 2: Comparison of Fuel-cycle Energy Use and Emissions for Different Alternative Fuel Technologies Relative to Gasoline-Powered Passenger Cars

Alt Fuel		CNG	E85			LPG		Electric		
Vehicle Technology	Bi-fuel spark ignition engine	Dedicated spark ignition engine	Flexible-fuel vehicle spark ignition engine			Dedicated spark ignition engine		-		
Fuel Source			Corn	Woody Biomass	Herbaceous Biomass	Crude	Natural Gas	US mix	North Eastern US mix	California mix
Total Energy	6.7%	3.3%	17.9%	90.4%	79.1%	-8.6%	-9.6%	-14.7%	-14.0%	-16.9%
Fossil Fuels	5.7%	2.3%	-41.8%	-81.8%	-72.7%	-8.6%	-9.3%	-34.7%	-46.0%	-65.6%
Petroleum	-99.4%	-99.4%	-73.8%	-71.2%	-73.2%	-99.4%	-3.4%	-98.4%	-96.9%	-99.5%-
VOC	-48.7%	-71.2%	54.0%	4.5%	0.4%	-58.2%	-64.1%	-88.0%	-90.6%	-95.2%
CO	-34.8%	-42.7%	-37.4%	-30.3%	-31.7%	-39.3%	-39.7%	-98.0%	-98.0%	-98.7%
NOx	26.6%	18.6%	101.9%	125.7%	139.8%	-17.7%	-22.4%	64.5%	11.5%	-51.3%
PM10	-35.9%	-37.8%	615.2%	139.9%	124.4%	-34.1%	-43.0%	48.5%	10.5%	-31.7%
SOx	-37.5%	-39.5%	168.8%	-151.8%	-95.8%	-57.3%	-77.4%	462.8%	217.2%	-13.9%
CH_4	211.0%	205.1%	-14.3%	-62.9%	-48.9%	-5.7%	2.8%	-15.5%	-23.5%	-49.2%
N2O	-38.4%	-19.4%	500.3%	187.1%	607.8%	-1.8%	-1.8%	-89.9%	-90.2%	-92.9%
CO_2	-13.9%	-16.7%	-36.4%	-113.1%	-85.5%	-12.6%	-14.3%	-24.3%	-42.8%	-70.7%
GHGs	-8.2%	-10.7%	-26.3%	-106.4%	-72.2%	-12.2%	-13.6%	-25.3%	-43.1%	-71.5%

Wang, M.Q. *GREET 1.5 – Transportation Fuel-Cycle Model, Volume 2: Appendices of Data and Result*. Center for Transportation Research, Energy Systems Division, Argonne National Laboratory. Argonne, IL, 1999.

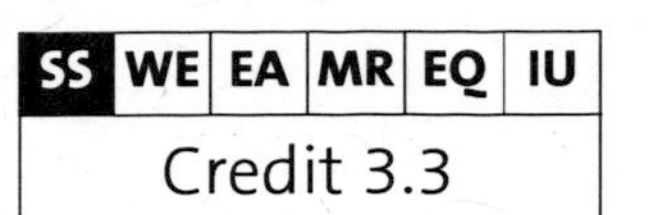

Federal, state and local government may offer tax incentives for purchasing alternative vehicles, which can help offset their higher initial costs. Different AFVs need different refueling stations, and the costs vary. Hybrid vehicles are gaining traction in the marketplace, which should start to drive down their cost. For fuel-efficient vehicles, reduced operating costs on a per-mile basis can offset higher initial purchase prices or higher fuel costs.

Strategies & Technologies

Option A

Establishing alternative fuel refueling stations requires the consideration of a number of legal, technical and safety issues, which vary by fuel type. Consider the following while developing alternative fuel station infrastructure:

- ❑ Poll building occupants to determine which alternative fuel type is in highest demand.
- ❑ Compare the environmental and economic cost/benefits of different alternative fuel types to determine which alternative fuel type would provide the highest benefit.
- ❑ Investigate local codes and standards for refueling stations in the area.
- ❑ Compare different fuel station equipment options and fuel availability. Depending on the type of alternative fuel provided, equipment requirements will differ in terms of expense and complexity of installation. Lack of availability may limit the feasibility of providing refueling stations for some types of fuels.
- ❑ Learn about the safety issues associated with alternative fuel types. Ensure that appropriate building personnel are trained to operate and maintain refueling stations.

Option B

Encourage use of AFVs or ATVs by 3 percent of building occupants, and designate preferred parking. Increasing the use of alternative vehicles can be done by encouraging private ownership through incentive programs, or by providing company-owned alternative vehicles.

Incentive programs for encouraging alternative vehicle ownership might include monetary grants to assist in purchasing alternative vehicles, preferred parking for alternative vehicles (required by this credit) or other benefits specific to alternative vehicle owners. A communication program should be developed to convey to building occupants the rewards of the incentive program, as well as the environmental benefits of alternative vehicles.

Option C

Provide preferred parking spaces for AFVs or ATVs equal to or greater than 3 percent of the total vehicle parking capacity on the site. Use employee newsletters, postings, signs or other forms of communication to inform occupants about the preferred parking. Perform quarterly checks of the total vehicle parking capacity to verify that preferred parking for alternative fuel vehicles continues to be provided and that it continues to meet the demand. Following quarterly inspections, if necessary add preferred parking spaces so that the number of preferred parking spaces is at least 125 percent of peak usage.

Synergies & Tradeoffs

This credit primarily affects parking facilities on the building site. Adding preferred parking or refueling stations may be difficult at building sites with limited parking space. Building sites with no available parking spaces are not eligible to achieve this LEED-EB credit unless parking spaces are added to the site that provide preferred parking for the necessary percentage of alternative fuel

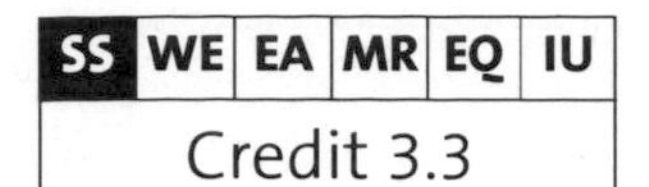

vehicles. Expanding lot size to accommodate these facilities may affect other LEED-EB credits, including SS Credit 4: Reduced Site Disturbance; SS Credit 5: Stormwater Management; and SS Credit 6: Heat Island Reduction.

Prior to installing or designating additional space for alternative vehicle parking and refueling, project teams should assess how these activities will affect current parking facilities and capacity. Space allocation and installation of refueling stations may not be cost-effective if there is not enough actual or potential demand for these facilities.

Alternative fuel refueling stations require staff time for operations and maintenance. Procedures for maintaining the safety and proper operation of refueling stations should be included in the Plan for Green Site and Building Exterior Management if your project is seeking SS Credit 1.

Calculations & Documentation

Calculations

Option A

To calculate the number of required alternative fuel refueling stations, multiply the total number of vehicle parking spaces by 3 percent (see **Equation 1**).

Example: In the example under SS Credit 3.2, the building has a parking area with 250 parking spaces. For this building, the number of alternative fuel refueling stations required is 3 percent of the 250 parking spaces or 8 vehicles.

Option B

To calculate the number of alternative fuel or hybrid vehicles and parking places, multiply the total number of building occupants by 3 percent (see **Equation 2**).

Option C

The number of preferred parking spaces for hybrid or alternative fuel vehicles is equal to the greater of: (a) the total number of vehicle parking spaces multiplied by 0.03 or (b) the peak demand for preferred parking spaces for hybrid or alternative fuel vehicles and parking places multiplied by 1.25 (see **Equation 3**).

Documentation

Option A

❑ Specifications and site drawings

- Submission should include calculations showing total parking capacity and number of vehicles that can be served by refueling stations. Drawings should clearly identify parking associated with the building.

Equation 1

Number of alternative fuel refueling stations = Total number of vehicle parking spaces x 0.03

Equation 2

Number of alternative fuel/hybrid vehicles and parking places =
Total number of building occupants x 0.03

Equation 3

Required number of preferred parking spaces is the greater of:

Total number of vehicle parking spaces x 0.03

OR

Peak demand for preferred parking spaces x 1.25

- ❑ Evidence of communication to building occupants.
  - Evidence of communications may include signage, flyers, emails or other methods of formal communication with building occupants, employees and staff.

Option B

- ❑ Proof of ownership or lease agreement for alternative vehicles
  - Proof of ownership/lease should specifically identify the type and number of vehicles.
- ❑ Specifications and site drawings documenting preferred parking
  - Drawings should illustrate location and number of spaces for alternative fuel vehicles.
- ❑ Evidence of communication to building occupants.
  - Evidence of communications may include signage, flyers, emails or other methods of formal communication with building occupants, employees and staff.

Option C

- ❑ Specifications and site drawings and calculations
  - Drawings should illustrate location and number of spaces for alternative fuel vehicles.
  - Calculations must identify the total number of parking spaces and number of preferred parking spaces.
  - As-necessary increases should be documented by submitting summaries of quarterly monitoring and findings by a responsible officer of the organization about the need for additional parking.
- ❑ Provide evidence that the program to promote use of hybrid vehicles is communicated to building occupants.
  - Evidence of communications may include signage, flyers, emails or other methods of formal communication with building occupants, employees and staff.

Other Resources

Alternative Fuels Data Center

www.afdc.doe.gov

A section of the DOE Office of Transportation Technologies that has information on alternative fuels and alternative fueled vehicles, a locator for alternative refueling stations and other related information.

American Council for an Energy-Efficient Economy (ACEEE)

www.greenercars.com

Online searchable green car guide based on a combination of fuel efficiency and tailpipe emission levels. Also offers hardcopy Green Guide to Cars and Trucks, an annual publication of the American Council for an Energy-Efficient Economy,

CARB Cleaner Car Guide

(916) 323-6169

www.driveclean.ca.gov/en/gv/home/index.asp

The California Air Resources Board (CARB) has developed a comprehensive searchable buyer's guide to find the cleanest cars on the market, which lists advantages clean vehicles offer.

California Certified Vehicles List

www.arb.ca.gov/msprog/ccvl/ccvl.htm

This site provides a list of all vehicles certified by the California Air Resources Board.

Clean Cities Vehicle Buyer's Guide For Consumers

www.eere.energy.gov/cleancities/vbg/

The Vehicle Buyer's Guide for Consumers explains the alternative fuel and advanced technology vehicles—including hybrid

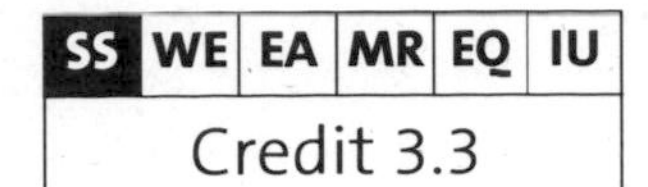

and neighborhood electric vehicles—available. You can use this site to learn more about the vehicle technologies, obtain pricing and technical specifications, locate the nearest alternative fuel station, contact a dealer, industry expert, or manufacturer, research financial incentives and laws in your state, and more.

Clean Cities Vehicle Buyer's Guide For Fleets

www.eere.energy.gov/cleancities/vbg/fleets

The Vehicle Buyer's Guide for Fleets is designed to educate fleet managers and policy makers about alternative fuels and vehicles to help them determine whether the Energy Policy Act of 1992 (EPAct) affects them. Use the site to figure if your fleet is covered under EPAct, obtain pricing and technical specifications for light- and heavy-duty AFVs, find an alternative fueling station in your area, or research information about state AFV purchasing incentives and laws.

CREST

www.crest.org/hydrogen/index.html

The Center for Renewable Energy and Sustainable Technology's fuel cell and hydrogen page.

Electric Auto Association

www.eaaev.org

This nonprofit education organization promotes the advancement and widespread adoption of electric vehicles.

Electric Vehicle Association of the Americas

www.evaa.org

This industry association promotes electric vehicles through policy, information, and market development initiatives.

Fuel Economy Web Site

www.fueleconomy.gov/feg

This U.S. Department of Energy site allows comparisons of cars based on gas mileage (mpg), greenhouse gas emissions, air pollution ratings, and safety information for new and used cars and trucks.

Natural Gas Vehicle Association

www.ngvc.org

The Natural Gas Vehicle Association consists of natural gas companies, vehicle and equipment manufacturers, service providers, environmental groups and government organizations.

Rocky Mountain Institute Transportation Page

www.rmi.org/sitepages/pid18.php

This web site offers information on the environmental impact of transportation, and extensive information about Hypercar® vehicles.

Union of Concerned Scientists Clean Vehicle Program

www.ucsusa.org/clean vehicles/index.cfm

This site provides information about the latest developments in alternative vehicles, the environmental impact of convention vehicles, and information for consumers such as the guide Buying a Greener Vehicle: Electric, Hybrids, and Fuel Cells.

Definitions

Advanced Technology Vehicles (ATVs) are a type of alternative vehicles that use advanced technologies for powertrains, emissions controls, and other vehicle features that allow for improved environmental performance. Electric hybrid vehicles and fuel cell vehicles are examples of ATVs.

Alternative Fuel Vehicles (AFVs) are a type of alternative vehicles that use low-polluting fuels such as electricity, propane or compressed natural gas, liquid natural gas, methanol and ethanol.

Hybrid Vehicles are vehicles that use a gasoline engine to drive an electric generator and use the electric generator and/or storage batteries to power electric motors that drive the vehicle's wheels.

Preferred Parking is parking that is preferentially available to particular users.

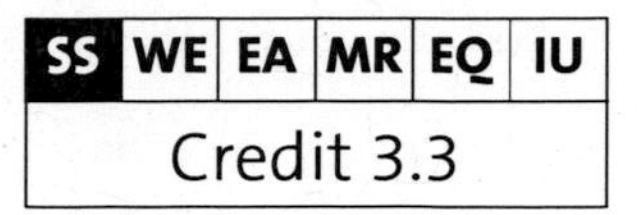

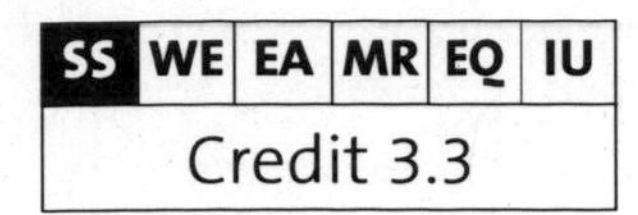

SS | WE | EA | MR | EQ | IU

Credit 3.4

1 Point

Alternative Transportation

Car Pooling and Telecommuting

Intent

Reduce pollution and land development impacts from single-occupancy vehicle use.

Requirements

Option A

- ❑ Provide preferred parking and implement/document programs and policies for car pools or van pools capable of serving 5% of the building occupants and add no new parking.

Option B

- ❑ Operate an occupant telecommuting program over the performance period that reduces commuting frequency by 20% for 20% or more of the building occupants and provides the necessary communications infrastructure in the building to accommodate telecommuting.

Submittals – Initial Certification

Option A

- ❑ Provide a description, calculations, parking plan and company literature describing carpool and vanpool programs designed to serve 5% of the building occupants.
- ❑ Submit a summary for the performance period and an excerpt from underlying daily or weekly reports on car pool and van pool usage.
- ❑ Submit a letter verifying that the project has added no new parking over the performance period.

Option B

- ❑ Provide a detailed description of telecommuting program (including specific information on baselines, assumptions and calculation methodology) designed to reduce the commuting frequency by 20% for 20% or more of the building occupants.
- ❑ Submit a summary for the performance period and an excerpt from underlying daily or weekly reports on telecommuting participation documenting that this program is reducing the commuting frequency by 20% for 20% or more of the building occupants on an average basis over the performance period.

Submittals – Recertification

- ❑ Provide a letter of verification that there have been no changes that affect the building's achievement of the requirements of the credit.

OR

Option A

- ❑ If there have been changes in any of the credit achievement requirements:
  - Submit a summary for the performance period and an excerpt from underlying daily or weekly reports on car pool and van pool usage.

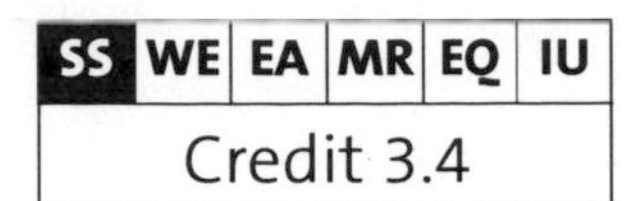

- Submit a letter verifying that the project has added no new parking over the performance period.

Option B

- ❑ Provide a detailed description of telecommuting program (including specific information on baselines, assumptions and calculation methodology) designed to reduce the commuting frequency by 20% for 20% or more of the building occupants.
- ❑ Submit a summary for the performance period and excerpts from underlying daily or weekly reports on telecommuting participation documenting that this program is reducing the commuting frequency by 20% for 20% or more of the building occupants on an average basis over the performance period.

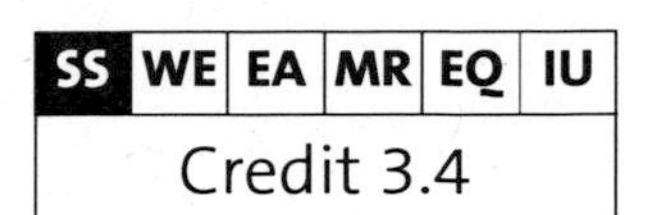

Summary of Referenced Standard

There is no standard referenced for this credit.

Green Building Concerns

Transportation accounts for 27.4 percent of energy use in the United States, the vast majority (96.4 percent) of which is powered by petroleum-based fuels.[29] Light vehicles, including automobiles, motorcycles, and light trucks, consume more energy than any other transportation mode.[30] In 2001, Americans were estimated to own more than 200 million private vehicles.[31] Along with steady increases in vehicle ownership, the number of miles traveled by Americans has also steadily increased over the past few decades. In 2001, on average each American (excluding persons ages 0 to 4) traveled 40.25 miles per day, with 88.2 percent of all daily travel attributed to private vehicles.[32] Travel to and from work makes up a significant portion (nearly 30 percent) of the vehicles miles traveled in personal vehicles, and the average length and duration of these commuting trips has steadily increased over the past few decades.[33]

The extensive use of private automobiles and their heavy reliance on petroleum contributes to a number of environmental problems. A surprisingly large number of people are willing to use alternative means of transportation such as carpools if they are convenient and facilities are provided to encourage their use. For example, a survey at North Dakota State University discovered that 69 percent of students and 31 percent of faculty and staff would be willing to carpool if they were guaranteed better parking.[34]

Environmental Issues

Reducing the use of private automobiles saves energy and avoids environmental problems associated with automobile use, such as vehicle emissions that contribute to smog and other air pollutants and the environmental impacts associated with oil extraction and petroleum refining. The environmental benefits of carpooling are significant. For example, 100 people who carpooled (2 people per car) 10 miles to work and 10 miles home instead of driving separately would prevent emission of 7.7 pounds of hydrocarbons, 55 pounds of carbon monoxide, 3.3 pounds of nitrogen oxides, 990 pounds of carbon dioxide and 50 gallons of gasoline per day.[35] Telecommuting also reduces the number of vehicle miles traveled by reducing the frequency of travel to the office.

Parking facilities for automobiles also have negative impacts on the environment, since asphalt surfaces increase stormwater runoff and contribute to urban heat island effects. By restricting the size of parking lots and promoting carpooling, buildings can reduce these effects while benefiting from reduced parking requirements and more and healthier green space.

Economic Issues

Carpooling and telecommuting reduce the size of the parking areas needed to support building occupants, allowing the building to accept more occupants without enlarging the parking area. Reduced stormwater charges can also save money, as some local utilities charge for stormwater based on impervious surface area. Also, many municipalities and state governments offer tax incentives to carpooling programs, since fewer cars on the road reduces pollution, traffic congestion and damage to roadways.

The minimum costs of implementing an organizational carpool program include signs marking parking spaces, program promotion and employee incentives. Comparatively, the costs associated with implementing a telecommuting program can be more expensive depending on the technology needed. However, benefits for

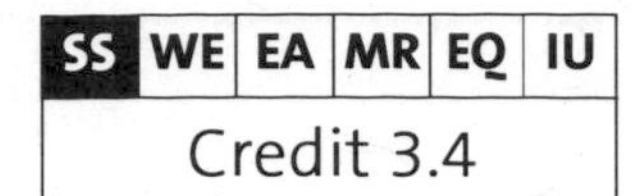

these programs include increased employee productivity, improved morale, expanded hiring opportunities, improved recruitment and retention of employees, reduced absenteeism and expanded office space.[36]

Strategies & Technologies

Option A

Provide preferred parking while implementing and documenting programs and policies for car/vanpools capable of serving 5 percent of the building occupants, and do not add any new parking over the performance period. Have in place a communications program encouraging building occupants to carpool. Produce posters, fliers, company emails or other forms of information promoting car/vanpool programs.

Provide incentives for occupants to carpool. For example, eliminate parking subsidies for non-carpool vehicles, reward building occupants who give up their parking passes, or offer added personal time for employees who carpool regularly. A valuable incentive that encourages many people to carpool is a guaranteed ride home program, which provides transportation fares to carpooling employees who must leave work early or late for unexpected situations.

Option B

Operate over the performance period a telecommuting program that reduces commuting frequency by 20 percent for at least 20 percent of occupants: equivalent to 20 percent of employees working from home one day each week. Telecommuting is usually a flexible program that works around the needs of the organization and of individual employees. For example, telecommuting programs can include flexible scheduling to reduce or eliminate the hours that need to be worked outside the office, as this method reduces commuting frequency as well. Provide the necessary communications infrastructure in the building and homes of telecommuters, and develop communication and incentives programs encouraging building occupants to telecommute.

Synergies & Tradeoffs

Car/vanpooling and telecommuting reduce the number of parking spaces required, therefore reducing the need for additional paving and associated problems. A reduction in impermeable parking areas could also increase the amount of open space on the site while reducing heat island effects and stormwater runoff volumes. Telecommuting also reduces the number of building occupants, saving water and energy in the building without the loss of productivity. Carpooling programs can also be integrated with other alternative transportation programs, such as a public transportation program.

Other LEED-EB credits related to these issues include:

- ❑ SS Credit 3.1: Alternative Transportation: Public Transportation Access
- ❑ SS Credit 4: Reduced Site Disturbance
- ❑ SS Credit 5: Stormwater Management
- ❑ SS Credit 6.1: Heat Island Reduction – Non-roof

Calculations & Documentation

Calculations

Option A

To calculate the required number of carpool spaces required, multiply the number of building occupants by 5 percent and divide by the number of occupants per vehicle. Assume that the Average Number of Occupants per Carpool Vehicle is equal to 2 unless documentation can be provided showing a carpool vehicle occupancy rate greater than 2. In the example in SS Credit 3.2, 285 building occupants requires a minimum of 8 carpool spaces. (See **Equation 1**)

Option B: Telecommuting

To calculate the reduction in commuting frequency, divide the reduction in commuting frequency for an individual building occupant and multiply the product by 100 (See **Equation 2**).

Documentation

Option A

- ❑ Description, calculations, parking plan and literature describing carpool/vanpool programs
  - Submittal should describe the operation of the program and program capacity to serve the required portion of the occupants. Identify preferred parking, and illustrate methods of communicating with building occupants about the program.
- ❑ Summary and excerpts from daily or weekly reports on carpool and vanpool usage
  - An excerpt from regular reports is requested as an illustration of monitoring methods to determine participation levels.

Option B

- ❑ Description of telecommuting program
  - Submittal should describe the operation of the program and program capacity to serve the required portion of the occupants. Identify any incentives or employee benefits, and illustrate methods of communicating with building occupants about the program.

Other Resources

Association for Commuter Transportation

http://tmi.cob.fsu.edu/act/

The ACT is an association of professionals who specialize in commute options and solutions and organizations interested in creating a more workable transportation system. ACT serves as an information resource, provides advocacy on transportation issues involving commute alternatives, and offers networking and professional development opportunities to its members.

Benefits of Using Alternative Transportation Costs Calculator

www.metrocommuterservice.org/costcal.asp

This online calculator helps commuters estimate the costs associated with driving a single occupancy vehicle and the savings associated with carpooling.

Online TDM Encyclopedia

www.vtpi.org/ted

Transportation Demand Management (TDM) is a general term for strategies that result in more efficient use of transportation resources. This online encyclopedia from the Victoria Transport Policy Institute is a comprehensive source of information about innovative management solutions to transportation problems.

Smart Commute

www.smartcommute.org/

Smart Commute is a program of Research Triangle Park that has valuable information about telecommuting and carpool programs useful for any organization.

Equation 1

Required number of carpool spaces =
(Number of building occupants x 0.05 / Average number of occupants per carpool vehicle)

Equation 2

Reduction in Commuting Frequency [Percent] = (Reduction in Commuting Frequency / Initial Commuting Frequency) x 100

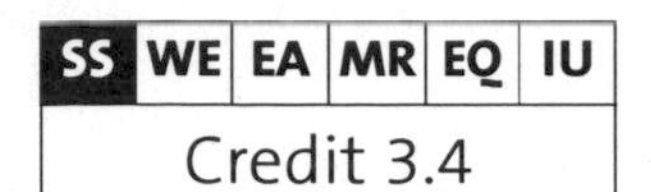

State of Arizona Telecommuting Program

www.teleworkarizona.com

This web site provides background information on the significance of telecommuting and an example of the development, implementation and results of a telecommuting program.

Teletrips

www.teletrips.com

Teletrips helps create, implement and manage public-private partnership programs to reduce commuter congestion, improve air quality and reduce energy consumption.

Telework Collaborative

www.teleworkcollaborative.com

The Telework Collaborative combines the expertise and resources of five western states (Texas, Arizona, California, Oregon and Washington) to deliver some of the most respected telework program implementation materials in the field.

Definitions

A **Carpool** is an arrangement in which two or more people share a vehicle together for transportation.

High Occupancy Vehicles are vehicles with more that one occupant.

Parking Subsidies are the costs of providing occupant parking that are not recovered in parking fees.

Preferred Parking is parking that is preferentially available to particular users, usually located closer to the building.

Telecommuting refers to work done through the use of telecommunications and computer technology from a location other than the usual or traditional place of business — for example, home, a satellite office or a telework center.

Case Study

King Street Center
Seattle, Washington

LEED-EB Gold

Owner: King County, State of Washington

Photo courtesy of: Ned Ahrens

Located in Seattle, WA, the King Street Center is home to 1,450 King County employees. As an urban building, parking and transportation issues are significant. King County has adopted a Transportation Management Plan (TMP) to encourage responsible transportation practices. A minimum of 50 carpool spaces and two 100% subsidized van pool spaces are available at the facility. Additional vanpoolers have access to the 150-space valet parking, located on the top two levels of the parking garage. This amounts to 16% of all available onsite parking. In addition to these parking space allowances, King County provides financial incentives to vanpool and carpool users. These include vanpool stipends of $45, discounted membership in a car sharing program, cash vouchers of $20 per month for carpool riders, and guaranteed taxi rides home for staff members who are unexpectedly required to work late. The TMP 2002 Annual Report shows that 11% of building occupants use car/vanpooling.

SS	WE	EA	MR	EQ	IU

Credits 4.1–4.2

1–2 Points

Reduced Site Disturbance

Protect or Restore Open Space

Intent

Conserve existing natural areas and restore damaged areas to provide habitat and promote biodiversity.

Requirements

Have in place over the performance period, native or adapted vegetation or other ecologically appropriate features:

- ❑ SS Credit 4.1: Covering a minimum of 50% of the site area excluding the building footprint. (1 point)
- ❑ SS Credit 4.2: Covering a minimum of 75% of the site area excluding the building footprint. (1 point)

Improving/maintaining off-site areas with native or adapted plants or other ecologically appropriate features can count toward earning both SS Credit 4.1 and 4.2. Every 2 square feet off-site will be counted as 1 square foot on-site. Off-site areas must be documented with a contract with the owner of the off site area that specifies the required improvement and maintenance of the off-site area.

Native/Adapted Plants are those that are indigenous to a locality or cultivars of native plant materials that have adapted to the local climate and are not considered invasive species or noxious weeds. Such plants require only limited irrigation water for sustenance once established, and do not require active maintenance such as mowing. Native/Adapted Plants should provide habitat value and promote biodiversity through avoidance of monoculture plantings.

Other ecologically appropriate features are natural site elements beyond vegetation that maintain or restore the ecological integrity of the site, and may include water bodies, exposed rock, un-vegetated ground, or other features that are part of the historic natural landscape within the region and provide habitat value.

Submittals – Initial Certification

- ❑ Provide highlighted site drawings with area calculations demonstrating that the declared percentage of the site area excluding the building footprint has been covered with native or adapted vegetation or other ecologically appropriate features over the performance period.
- ❑ Provide a list of the native or adapted plants used in earning this credit.
- ❑ Provide records and results of quarterly inspections for performance period to show that the declared percentage of the site area excluding the build footprint remains covered with native or adapted vegetation or other ecologically appropriate features.

Submittals – Recertification

Provide an update of previous filings:

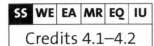

- ❑ Provide a letter stating that no change has occurred if there has been no change in the site area.
- ❑ Provide summary results of quarterly inspections over the performance period to document that the declared percentage of the site area excluding the build footprint remains covered with native or adapted vegetation or other ecologically appropriate features.

OR

- ❑ If there have been changes since the previous filing, provide the same information as is required for initial LEED-EB filings.

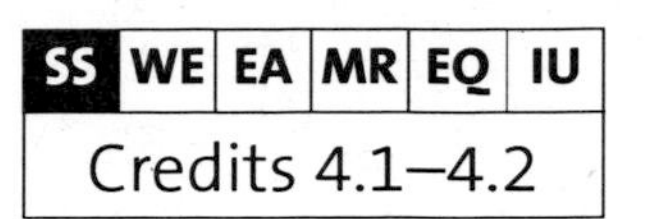

Summary of Referenced Standard

There is no standard reference for this credit.

Green Building Concerns

Development on building sites often damages site ecology, indigenous plants and regional animal populations. Ecological site damage can be reduced by restoring native and adapted vegetation and other ecologically appropriate features on the site, which in turn provides habitat for fauna. Other ecologically appropriate features are natural site elements beyond vegetation that maintain or restore the ecological integrity of the site. They may include water bodies, exposed rock, unvegetated ground, or other features that are part of the historic natural landscape within the region and provide habitat value. When construction occurs on the site, protection of open space and sensitive areas through the use of strict boundaries reduces damage to the site ecology, resulting in preservation of wildlife corridors and habitat.

Environmental Issues

Developed building sites disturb or destroy wildlife and plant habitat, as well as eliminate wildlife corridors that allow animal migration. As animals are pushed out of existing habitat, they become increasingly crowded into smaller spaces. Eventually, their population exceeds the carrying capacity of these spaces and they begin to invade surrounding developments or perish due to overpopulation. Overall biodiversity, as well as individual plant and animal species, may be threatened by reduction in habitat areas. Restoring native and adapted vegetation and other ecologically appropriate features on the site reduces habitat destruction.

Economic Issues

Indigenous plantings require less maintenance than non-native plantings and reduce maintenance costs over the building lifetime by minimizing inputs of fertilizers, pesticides and water. In many cases, trees and vegetation raised off site are costly to purchase and may not survive transplanting. Additional trees and other landscaping, as well as soil remediation and water elements, can incur first costs. It may be advantageous to implement site restoration in phases to spread costs out over time. Strategic plantings can shade the building and site impervious areas, which can decrease cooling loads during warm months and reduce energy expenditures.

Strategies & Technologies

Protect or restore open space either on or off the building site (Options A and B below).

Option A

Preserve and enhance natural site elements including existing water bodies, soil conditions, ecosystems, trees and other vegetation. Perform a site survey to identify site elements, and adopt a master plan preserving and enhancing natural site elements including existing water bodies, soil conditions, ecosystems, trees and other vegetation. Identify opportunities for site improvements that increase the area of native/adapted vegetation or other ecologically appropriate features. Activities may include removing excessive paved areas and replacing them with landscaped areas, or replacing excessive turf-grass areas with natural landscape features. Work with local horticultural extension services or native plant societies to select and maintain indigenous plant species for site restoration and landscaping. The growing number of ecological consultants and sources of native/adapted plant stock may be helpful. If applicable, coordinate

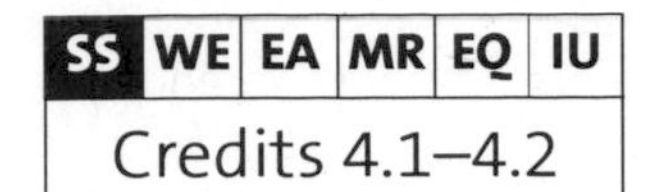

site restoration with the elements of the Building Exterior Management Plan developed for SS Credit 1.

Option B

Identify an off-site area that would benefit from improving/maintaining areas with native or adapted plants or other ecologically appropriate features. The building owner can own these off-site areas, or building owners can contract with the owners of an off-site area. If different from the building owner, the owner of the off-site area must be committed to the required improvement or maintenance of natural areas. Every 2 square feet of off-site area devoted to native or adapted plants counts as 1 square foot on site.

Preserve and enhance natural site elements on the off-site area through the same strategies for Option A. Receive approval from the owner of the off-site area before maintaining or restoring the site.

Synergies & Tradeoffs

The existing building site will largely dictate what is possible for increasing/maintaining open space with native or adapted vegetation or other ecologically appropriate features. Trees and other vegetation can reduce heat island effect through shading of buildings and paved surfaces. Site vegetation is also related to irrigation practices and stormwater management.

Calculations & Documentation

Calculations

Calculate Site Open Area

1. Determine the area of the building footprint. This is the area of the site that is occupied by the building structure. Parking lots, landscapes and other non-building facilities are not included in the building footprint.
2. Determine the total area of the entire site.
3. Calculate the open area of the site (see **Equation 1**).

Option A: Calculate Percent Onsite Natural Area

1. Determine the area of the site covered by native or adapted vegetation or other ecologically appropriate features.
2. Calculate the percentage of the site area covered by native and adapted vegetation or other ecologically appropriate features (see **Equation 2**).

Option B: Calculate Percent Offsite Natural Area

1. Determine the off-site natural area [SF] that includes native or adapted vegetation or other ecologically appropriate features.
2. Calculate the percentage of the building's open site area that one-half of the off-site natural area would cover if it were located on site (See **Equation 3**).

Equation 1

Open Site Area [SF] = Total Site Area [SF] - Building Footprint [SF]

Equation 2

Onsite Natural Area [%] = Onsite Natural Area [SF] / Open Site Area [SF])

Equation 3

Offsite Natural Area [%] = Offsite Natural Area [SF] / (Open Site Area [SF] * 2)

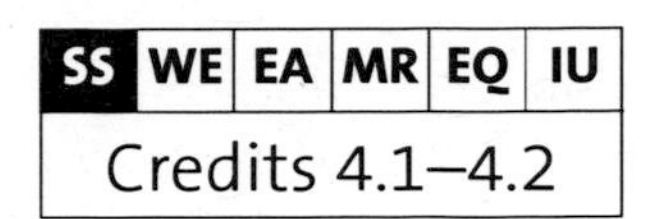

Documentation

- ❑ Highlighted site drawings with area calculations
  - Site drawings should demarcate all areas of vegetation, clearly identifying areas of native or adapted vegetation. Area calculations should include notation of site area, total vegetated area, and native or adapted vegetated area.

Other Resources

American Society of Landscape Architects

www.asla.org

ASLA is the national professional association representing landscape architects. The web site provides information about products, services, publications and events.

Design for Human Ecosystems: Landscape, Land Use, and Natural Resources, by John Tillman Lyle, Island Press, 1999.

This text explores methods of landscape design that function like natural ecosystems.

Ecological Restoration

http://ecologicalrestoration.info

This quarterly print and online publication from the University of Wisconsin-Madison Arboretum provides a forum for people interested in all aspects of ecological restoration.

Lady Bird Johnson Wildlife Center

www.wildflower.org

The center, located in Austin, Texas, has the mission of educating people about the environmental necessity, economic value and natural beauty of native plants. The web site offers a number of resources, including a nationwide Native Plant Information Network and a National Suppliers Directory.

Landscape Restoration Handbook, by Donald Harker, Marc Evans, Gary Libby, Kay Harker, and Sherrie Evans, Lewis Publishers, 1999.

This resource is a comprehensive guide to natural landscaping and ecological restoration, and provides information on 21 different ecological restoration types.

North American Native Plant Society

www.nanps.org

A nonprofit association dedicated to the study, conservation, cultivation and restoration of native plants. Its web site contains links to state and provincial associations.

Plant Native

www.plantnative.org

This organization is dedicated to moving native plants and nature-scaping into mainstream landscaping practices.

Society for Ecological Restoration International

www.ser.org

Nonprofit consortium of scientist, planners, administrators, ecological consultants, landscape architects, engineers, and others has the mission of promoting ecological restoration as a means of sustaining the diversity of life and reestablishing an ecologically healthy relationship between nature and culture.

Soil and Water Conservation Society

www.swcs.org

An organization focused on fostering the science and art of sustainable soil, water, and related natural resource management.

Definitions

The **Building Footprint** is the area of the site that is occupied by the building structure, not including parking lots, landscapes and other non-building facilities.

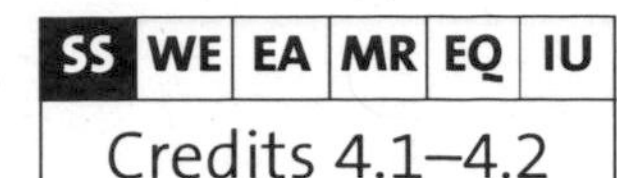

Ecological Restoration is the process of assisting in the recovery and management of ecological integrity, which includes a critical range of variability in biodiversity, ecological processes and structures, regional and historical context, and sustainable cultural practices.

Ecologically Appropriate Site Features are natural site elements that maintain or restore the ecological integrity of the site, and may include native/adapted vegetation, water bodies, exposed rock, un-vegetated ground, or other features that are part of the historic natural landscape within the region and provide habitat value.

A **Greenfield** is undeveloped land or land that has not been impacted by human activity.

Landscape Architecture is the analysis, planning, design, management and stewardship of the natural and built environments.

Local Zoning Requirements are local government regulations imposed to promote orderly development of private lands and to prevent land use conflicts.

On-site and off-site Natural Areas are areas covered with native or adapted vegetation or other ecologically appropriate features.

Native/Adapted Vegetation are plants indigenous to a locality or cultivars of native plants that are adapted to the local climate and are not considered invasive species or noxious weeds, and which require only limited irrigation following establishment, do not require active maintenance such as mowing, and provide habitat value and promote biodiversity through avoidance of monoculture plantings.

Open Site Area is the total site area less the footprint of the building.

Case Study

Moss Landing Marine Laboratory
Moss Landing, California

LEED-EB Gold
Owner: California State University

Photo courtesy of: Barry Giles

The Moss Landing Marine Laboratory is located in an ecologically unique environment, on the edge of the Monterey Submarine Canyon, and surrounded by natural features including sand dunes, beaches, wetland, and rocky shoreline. Protecting the ecological integrity of the building site is essential to MLML's educational mission. An extensive rehabilitation project was undertaken to restore the landscape so it more closely models its native state. This involved soil rehabilitation, the removal of non-native, invasive vegetation, and the reintroduction of appropriate native vegetation. No non-native plants or animals are currently present in the restored areas, and disturbed soils are reforming natural structure and now support a more diverse flora and fauna.

A portion of the site's east slope and cypress forest still contain some non-native vegetation. This area comprises less than 10% of the total site, and gradually will be rehabilitated by eliminating weeds and replacing them with native plants. Though the native vegetation is largely self-sustaining, MLML continuously monitors the health and status of the site's vegetation to ensure its success.

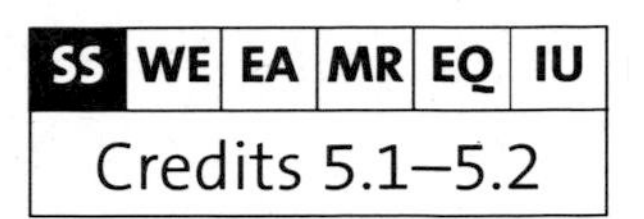

1–2 Points

Stormwater Management

Rate and Quantity Reduction

Intent

Limit disruption and pollution of natural water flows by managing stormwater runoff.

Requirements

Have a stormwater management plan in place over the performance period that is designed to mitigate runoff from the site. Mitigated stormwater is the volume of precipitation falling on the site that does not become runoff by leaving the site via means of uncontrolled surface streams, rivers, drains, or sewers. This mitigation can be accomplished through a variety of measures including perviousness of site, stormwater management practices (structural and non structural), capture of rainwater for reuse or other measures.

- ❑ SS Credit 5.1: Have measures in place on the site that mitigate at least 25% of the annual stormwater falling on the site. (1 point)
- ❑ SS Credit 5.2: Have measures in place on the site that mitigate at least 50% of the annual stormwater falling on the site. (1 point)

Submittals – Initial Certification

- ❑ Document Stormwater Runoff Mitigation.
  - Provide a narrative description and calculations showing the impact of the implemented stormwater management plan and the annual stormwater falling on the site mitigation percentage provided.
  - Provide records and results of quarterly inspections over the performance period to determine if the stormwater management plan on the site is being maintained and functions properly.

Submittals – Recertification

Provide an update of previous filings:

- ❑ If there has been no change to the stormwater management plan since previous LEED-EB filing, provide statement that there has been no change.
- ❑ If there has been a change to the stormwater management plan since previous LEED-EB filing, provide updated information.
  - Provide a narrative description and calculations showing the impact of the stormwater management plan that has been implemented and how much mitigation of the annual stormwater load on the site it provides.
  - Provide records and results of quarterly inspections over the performance period to determine if the stormwater management plan has been implemented on the site is being maintained and functions properly.

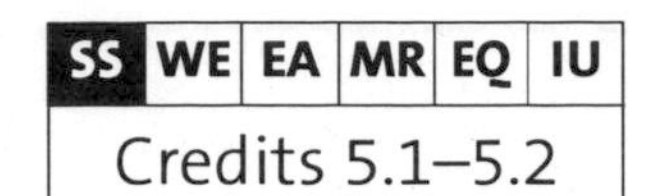

Summary of Referenced Standard

There is no standard reference for this credit.

Green Building Concerns

The volume of runoff generated on a site depends on perviousness of the surfaces covering the site and any systems for capturing stormwater. In natural areas, the majority of precipitation infiltrates into the ground while a small portion runs off on the surface and into receiving waters. As areas are constructed and urbanized, surface permeability is reduced, resulting in increased runoff volumes that are transported via urban infrastructure (e.g., gutters, pipes and sewers) to receiving waters. These runoff volumes contain sediment and other contaminants that have a negative impact on water quality, navigation and recreation. Furthermore, if sewer systems capture the stormwater runoff, these systems need the capacity to convey and treat runoff volumes, which may require significant infrastructure and maintenance.

Environmental Issues

Reduction and treatment of runoff volumes reduces or eliminates contaminants that pollute receiving water bodies. For instance, parking areas contribute to stormwater runoff that is contaminated with oil, fuel, lubricants, combustion by-products, material from tire wear and deicing salts. On a larger scale, runoff volumes delivered directly to waterways via gutters, pipes and sewers increase the volume and accelerate the flow rate of waterways, which causes erosion, habitat alteration and downstream flooding issues. Minimized stormwater infrastructure also reduces construction impacts and the overall footprint of the building. Finally, infiltration of stormwater on site can recharge local aquifers, mimicking the natural water cycle.

Economic Issues

If natural drainage systems are designed and implemented at the beginning of site planning, they can be integrated economically into the overall development. Water detention and retention features require cost for design, installation and maintenance. However, these features can also add significant value as site amenities. Water features may pose safety and liability problems, especially in locations where young children are playing outdoors. The use of infiltration devices, such as pervious paving, may reduce the need for expensive and space-consuming detainment options such as water runoff collection systems. However, the initial cost for pervious pavers may be up to three times higher than solid asphalt or concrete.

Strategies & Technologies

The most effective method for coping with runoff volumes is to reduce the amount generated. Reducing volumes can minimize stormwater runoff infrastructure. Methods to minimize runoff volumes include reducing impervious surfaces or capturing and reusing rainwater. Using pervious materials on site or installing garden roofs on the building encourages the natural process of evaporation and infiltration. Rainwater capture systems direct water falling on impervious systems into a collection and treatment system. The captured rainwater is then used inside the building and on the site for applications that would otherwise require the unnecessary use of potable water.

If runoff volumes cannot be completely prevented through minimization of impervious surfaces and rainwater capture and reuse, detention systems and other strategies can control runoff flow and remove pollutants. These include constructed wetlands, filtering systems, bioswales, bioretention basins and veg-

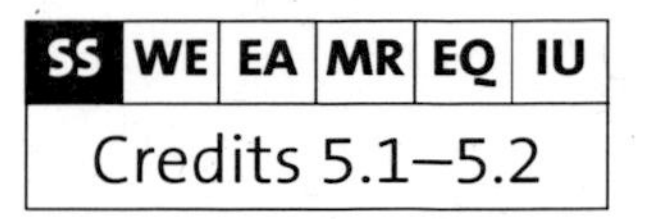

etated filterstrips. In many cases, detention structures can be designed to allow runoff water to slowly infiltrate on site, rather than being discharged off site.

When developing stormwater management strategies, consider the replacement costs and maintenance requirements of different options, as well as natural site features that affect rainwater infiltration rates and dictate management opportunities. On-site soil characteristics can greatly influence which strategies can be effectively implemented. For example, infiltration strategies will not be effective in soil with high clay content.

Minimizing the Use of Impervious Surfaces

Pervious paving systems reduce stormwater runoff by allowing precipitation to infiltrate the undersurface through voids in the paving material. These systems can be applied to pedestrian traffic surfaces as well as low vehicle traffic areas such as parking spaces, fire lanes, and maintenance roads. Use pervious paving materials such as poured asphalt or concrete with incorporated air spaces, or use concrete unit paving systems with large voids that allow grass or other vegetation to grow between the voids.

Pervious paving has several options, including systems that use grass and a plastic grid system (typically 90 percent pervious), concrete grids with grass (typically 40 percent pervious), and concrete grids with gravel (typically 10 percent pervious). Pervious paving requires different maintenance procedures than impervious pavement. Some systems require vacuum sweeping to prevent the voids from clogging with sediment, dirt and mud. Systems that use vegetation, such as grass planted in a plastic matrix over gravel, may require mowing. Snow removal from pervious paving requires more care than from conventional paving. Check existing codes on the use of pervious surfaces for roadways.

Minimize impervious surfaces by clustering or concentrating developments to reduce the amount roads, parking lots, sidewalks and other paved surfaces. Widths and lengths of roads, parking lots and sidewalks can also be minimized. For instance, turning lanes in roads can be removed to minimize the width of the paved surface. This requires the sharing of traveling and turning lanes.

Rainwater Capture and Reuse

Stormwater from impervious areas can also be captured for reuse within the building. Stormwater harvesting from roofs and hardscapes go for non-potable uses such as sewage conveyance, fire suppression and industrial applications.

Garden roofs or green roofs are vegetated surfaces that capture rainwater and return a portion of it back to the atmosphere via evapotranspiration. They consist of a layer of plants and soil, a cup layer for collection and temporary storage of stormwater, and a synthetic liner to protect the top of the building from stormwater infiltration. Garden roofs also provide insulating benefits and aesthetic appeal. Some garden roofs require plant maintenance and are considered active gardens, while others have grasses and plants that require no maintenance or watering. All types of garden roofs require semiannual inspection but are estimated to have a longer lifetime and require less maintenance than conventional roofs.

Structural Management and Detention Facilities

Install structural detention facilities that retain stormwater and allow it to infiltrate into the ground over time. Design detention ponds to remove contaminants, increase on-site infiltration, and release remaining water volumes to local water bodies in a controlled manner. Utilize biologically based and innovative stormwater management features for pollutant load reduction such as constructed wetlands, stormwater filtering systems, bioswales, bio-retention basins and vegetated filter strips. Use vegetated filter strips around impervious areas, such as parking lots, to remove oil, grit and other runoff pollutants. Specify and install water quality ponds or oil/grit separators for pretreatment of runoff from surface parking areas. Oil/grit separators use gravity to separate oil, grit and "pretreated" water into separate chambers.

Do not disturb existing wetlands or riparian buffers when constructing ponds at the lowest elevations of a site, and consider constructing additional on-site wetlands. Constructed wetlands incorporate plants in a shallow pool. As runoff volumes flow through the wetland, pollutants and sediment are filtered out of the water through settling and biological uptake. Wetlands are among the most effective stormwater management practices for pollutant removal, and also add to the aesthetic value of the site.

Design stormwater runoff to travel into vegetated swales rather than into structured pipes for conveyance to detention ponds or wetlands. Bioswales provide filtration for stormwater volumes and require less maintenance than constructed stormwater features. Install sequences of ponds whenever possible for more complete water treatment.

In some cases, such as heavily wooded sites where larger ponds are not feasible, smaller bio-retention areas that use subsurface compost and plantings to accelerate the filtering of contaminants can be distributed around the site. To moderate water runoff along drainage paths, construct water ponds to temporarily store stormwater flows and improve water quality through settling and biodegradation of pollutants. Bio-retention areas are also commonly located in parking lot islands, where surface runoff is directed into shallow, landscaped depressions.

Synergies & Tradeoffs

Runoff volumes are in part determined by site design. Improving stormwater management on an existing building site may require altering existing impervious surfaces, investing in rainwater capture systems or altering the site landscape. Adding any of these features could result in additional site maintenance issues. Pervious paving systems usually have a limit on transportation loads and may pose problems for wheelchair accessibility and stroller mobility. If stormwater volumes are treated on site, additional site area may need to be disturbed to construct treatment ponds or underground facilities.

Strategies for earning this credit could present other green building benefits. It may be possible to reuse stormwater for non-potable water purposes such as flushing urinals and toilets, custodial applications, and building equipment uses. Underground parking and green roofs, strategies that reduce stormwater runoff volumes, can also reduce heat island effects. However, installation of garden roofs reduces stormwater volumes that may be intended for collection and reuse.

When choosing stormwater management strategies, consider how they interact with the other LEED-EB prerequisites and credits listed below:

- ❑ SS Prerequisite 1: Erosion and Sedimentation Control
- ❑ SS Credit 1: Plan for Green Site and Building Exterior Management
- ❑ SS Credit 4: Reduced Site Disturbance
- ❑ SS Credit 6: Heat Island Reduction
- ❑ WE Prerequisite 1 and Credit 3: Minimum Water Efficiency and Water Use Reduction
- ❑ WE Credit 1: Water Efficient Landscaping
- ❑ WE Credit 2 Innovative Wastewater Technologies

Calculations & Documentation

Achievement of this credit requires mitigating 25 percent (1 point) or 50 percent (2 points) of the annual volume of precipitation falling on the site from becoming runoff. Mitigated stormwater is equal to the volume of precipitation falling on the site that does not become runoff. Runoff is defined as stormwater leaving the site via means of uncontrolled surface streams, rivers, drains or sewers. Factors affecting stormwater mitigation include site permeability, site management practices (structural and non-structural), and on-site capture and reuse of rainwater.

Three components of mitigation can contribute to earning this credit.

1) **Infiltration Based on Permeability of Site Surfaces**

   Follow the calculation protocol below to determine how much of the average annual precipitation falling on the site is prevented from becoming runoff through infiltration into the ground. This is determined based on the permeability of site surfaces.

2) **Rainwater Capture and Reuse**

   Follow the calculation protocol below to determine how much of the average annual precipitation falling on the site is prevented from becoming runoff through the capture and reuse of rainwater. This is determined based the area served by the capture system and system storage capacity, the rate at which capture water is used, and the typical distribution of rainfall throughout the year.

3) **Structural Detention Facilities**

   Follow the calculation protocol below to determine how much of the average annual precipitation falling on the site is prevented from becoming runoff by detention facilities that retain water and allow it to infiltrate over time. This is determined based on detention facilities size (volume) and type, detention time, annual distribution of rainfall, and infiltration rate from the detention facility into the ground. Note that a system that delays runoff peak flows but does not result in increased infiltration into the ground does not achieve the credit requirements.

Calculations

First calculate the average amount of rainwater falling on the site that does not become stormwater runoff using **Equation 1**.

Next, calculate the average amount of rainwater that can be mitigated on the site so that it does not become runoff. The three mitigation strategies can be used individually or in combination to meet the credit requirements.

Infiltration Based on Permeability of Site Surfaces

To calculate the annual stormwater infiltrated into the ground based on site permeability, use the values in **Table 1** to determine the area-weighted site runoff coefficient, as described below.

Step 1: Identify the different surface types on the site: roof areas, paved areas (e.g., roads and sidewalks), landscaped areas, natural areas, roof garden areas, and other areas.

Step 2: For each different types of surface on the site, calculate the area it covers and the runoff coefficient for this surface type. Use the values in **Table 1**, from the U.S. EPA publication Guidance

Equation 1

On-site Annual Precipitation = Average Annual Precipitation per unit area x Area of Site

Table 1: Typical Runoff Coefficients

Surface Type	Runoff Coefficient	Surface Type	Runoff Coefficient
Pavement, Asphalt	0.95	Turf, Flat (0–1% slope)	0.25
Pavement, Concrete	0.95	Turf, Average (1–3% slope)	0.35
Pavement, Brick	0.85	Turf, Hilly (3–10% slope)	0.40
Pavement, Gravel	0.75	Turf, Steep (> 10% slope)	0.45
Roofs, Conventional	0.95	Vegetation, Flat (0–1% slope)	0.10
Roof, Garden Roof (<4 in)	0.50	Vegetation, Average (1–3% slope)	0.20
Roof, Garden Roof (4-8 in)	0.30	Vegetation, Hilly (3–10% slope)	0.25
Roof, Garden Roof (9-20 in)	0.20	Vegetation, Steep (> 10% slope)	0.30
Roof, Garden Roof (>20 in)	0.10		

Specifying Management Measures for Sources of Non-point Pollution in Coastal Waters, to assign a runoff coefficient to each surface type.

Step 3: Use a spreadsheet similar to the one in the LEED-EB Letter Templates to list each surface type, the area of the surface type, and the runoff coefficient for each surface type.

Step 4: Calculate the area-weighted average runoff coefficient for the site (**Equation 2**).

Step 5: Determine the amount of precipitation infiltrated into the ground based on the area-weighted average runoff coefficient (**Equation 3**).

Rainwater Capture and Reuse

The effectiveness of rainwater capture systems is controlled by the interaction of rainfall patterns (frequency, duration, seasonal variation and intensity), storage tank capacity and seasonal use rate of the captured water.

The preferred method of determining the amount of rainwater captured is to install a meter that measures all water used from the holding tank.

If metering data is not available, estimate the volume of rainfall captured by the rainwater collection system using **Equation 4**. Note that the quantity of rainwater collected may be limited by cistern capacity, and this should be accounted for when calculating the amount of stormwater mitigated by the system.

Equation 2

Weighted Average Runoff Coefficient = [(Area of Surface Type A x Runoff Coefficient Surface Type A) + (Area of Surface Type B x Runoff Coefficient Surface Type B) + (...)] / (Area of Surface Type A + Area of Surface Type B + ...)

Equation 3

Annual Precipitation Mitigated by Infiltration =
Onsite Annual Precipitation – (Onsite Annual Precipitation x Area-Weighted Average Site Runoff Coefficient)

Equation 4

Annual Precipitation Mitigated by Rainwater Collection System =
(Area of Impervious Surfaces the Feed into Collection System x Average Annual Precipitation per unit area) – Annual Storage Tank Overflow

Structural Detention Facilities

Structural stormwater management facilities implemented at the site can also be used to mitigate stormwater runoff. The characteristics of the system must be fully documented, and calculations must be used to demonstrate the amount of water that falls onsite that is channeled into detention facilities.

Use **Equation 5** to estimate the amount of stormwater mitigated through detention facilities. Note that any overflow volumes should be reflected in the calculations.

Total Annual Stormwater Mitigation Rate

Finally, calculate the percentage of the annual precipitation that falls on the site that is mitigated through the three strategies. Use **Equation 6** to calculate the percent of annual rainfall mitigated.

If the percent of stormwater mitigated is greater than 25 percent, 1 point is earned. If it is greater than 50 percent, 2 points are earned.

Documentation

All information needed to successfully document this credit can be found in the Submittals section of the LEED-EB Rating System and the LEED-EB Letter Templates.

Other Resources

Center for Watershed Protection

www.cwp.org

Nonprofit dedicated to the dissemination of watershed protection information to community leaders and watershed managers via online resources, training seminars and the publication of Watershed Protection Techniques.

EPA Office of Wetlands, Oceans & Watersheds

www.epa.gov/owow

This web site offers general information about watersheds, and information about protecting water resources, water conservation, landscaping practices, water pollution reduction and more.

Post-Construction Storm Water Management in New Development & Redevelopment

http://cfpub.epa.gov/npdes/stormwater/menuofbmps/post_7.cfm

Information from the U.S. EPA about catch basins as a tool for sediment control.

Stormwater Manager's Resource Center

www.stormwatercenter.net

Site for stormwater practitioners, local government officials and others in need of technical assistance on stormwater management issues.

Definitions

Constructed Wetlands are wastewater treatment systems designed to simulate natural wetland functions for water purification by removing contaminants from wastewaters.

Detention Ponds are ponds that capture stormwater runoff and allow pollutants to drop out before release to a stormwater or water body. A variety of detention pond

Equation 5

Annual Precipitation Mitigated by Structural Detention Facilities = [(Collection Area of Site that Feeds into Detention System x Area Weighted Average Runoff Coefficient for Collection Area) x Average Annual Precipitation per unit area] – Annual Detention Facility Overflow

Equation 6

Stormwater Mitigated [%] = (Sum of Annual Precipitation Mitigated by Infiltration, Rainwater Collection System, and Structural Detention Facilities / Total Annual Precipitation) x 100

designs are available, with some utilizing only gravity while others use mechanical equipment such as pipes and pumps to facilitate transport. Some ponds are dry except during storm events and other ponds permanently store water volumes.

Filtration Basins are basins that remove sediment and pollutants from stormwater runoff using a filter media such as sand or gravel. A sediment trap is usually included to remove sediment from stormwater before filtering to avoid clogging.

Grassed Swales consist of trenches or ditches covered with vegetation and encourage subsurface infiltration, similar to infiltration basins and trenches. They utilize vegetation to filter sediment and pollutants from stormwater.

Impervious Surfaces are surfaces that promote runoff of precipitation volumes instead of infiltration into the subsurface. The imperviousness or degree of runoff potential can be estimated for different surface materials.

Infiltration Basins & Trenches are used to encourage subsurface infiltration of runoff volumes through temporary surface storage. Basins are ponds that can store large volumes of stormwater. They need to drain within 72 hours to maintain aerobic conditions and to be available for the next storm event. Trenches are similar to infiltration basins except that they are shallower and function as a subsurface reservoir for stormwater volumes. Pretreatment to remove sediment and oil may be necessary to avoid clogging of infiltration devices. Infiltration trenches are more common in areas where infiltration basins are not possible.

Mitigated Stormwater is equal to the volume of precipitation falling on the site that does not become runoff. Runoff is defined as stormwater leaving the site via means of uncontrolled surface streams, rivers, drains, or sewers. Factors affecting stormwater mitigation include site perviousness, stormwater management practices (structural and non-structural), and onsite capture and reuse of rainwater.

Permeable Surfaces are used as a substitute for impermeable surfaces to allow runoff to infiltrate into the subsurface. These surfaces are typically maintained with a vacuuming regime to avoid potential clogging and failure problems. Porous pavement is one type of permeable surface.

Stormwater Runoff consists of water volumes that are created during precipitation events and flow over surfaces into sewer systems or receiving waters. All precipitation waters that leave project site boundaries on the surface are considered to be stormwater runoff volumes.

Case Study

JohnsonDiversey Global Headquarters

Sturtevant, Wisconsin

LEED-EB Gold

Owner: JohnsonDiversey, Inc.

Photo courtesy of: JohnsonDiversey

Detention ponds and restored wetlands at JohnsonDiversey's Global Headquarters site in Sturtevant, Wisconsin collect 100% of the site's stormwater runoff. Additional runoff from neighboring sites and roadways is also collected by the 12 acres of restored wetlands and ponds. An estimated 34% of the 57-acre site consists of impervious surface, making the role of the detention ponds in providing sediment, pollution and flood control essential.

JohnsonDiversey monitors and maintains the site actively to ensure the effective management of stormwater and reduced impacts on the site environment. Native prairie plants covering 30 acres of the site also aid in stormwater management while providing habitat and protecting open space.

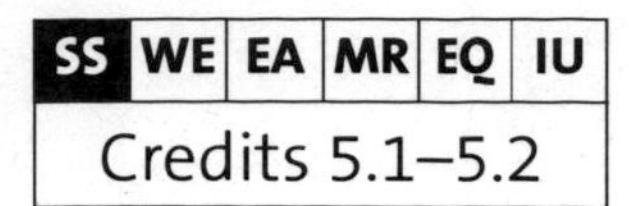
SS WE EA MR EQ IU
Credits 5.1–5.2

SS	WE	EA	MR	EQ	IU
Credit 6.1					

1 Point

Heat Island Reduction

Non-Roof

Intent

Reduce heat islands (thermal gradient differences between developed and undeveloped areas) to minimize impact on microclimate and human and wildlife habitat.

Requirements

Choose one of the following options:

Option A

- ❑ Provide (from existing canopy or within five years of landscape installation) shade on at least 30% of non-roof impervious surfaces on the site, including parking lots, walkways, plazas, etc.

Option B

- ❑ Use/maintain light-colored/high-albedo materials (reflectance of at least 0.3) for 30% of the site's non-roof impervious surfaces on the site, including parking lots, walkways, plazas, etc.

Option C

- ❑ Place/maintain a minimum of 50% of parking space underground.

Option D

- ❑ Use/maintain an open-grid pavement system (net impervious area of LESS than 50%) for a minimum of 50% of the parking lot area.

Submittals – Initial Certification

In addition to the documentation required for each specific compliance path, provide records and results of quarterly inspections over the performance period to determine that one of the following features are being maintained:

Option A

- ❑ Provide site plan highlighting all non-roof impervious surfaces and portions of these surfaces that will be shaded within five years. Include calculations demonstrating that a minimum of 30% of non-roof impervious surface areas will be shaded within five years.

Option B

- ❑ Provide third-party reflectance documentation, site plan, calculations and photographs documenting use of high-albedo materials on 30% of non-roof impervious surfaces.

Option C

- ❑ Provide a parking plan demonstrating that a minimum of 50% of site parking spaces are located underground.

Option D

- ❑ Provide third-party documentation on paving system perviousness, site plan, calculations and photographs for a pervious paving system with a minimum perviousness of 50%. Include calculations demonstrating that this paving system covers a minimum of 50% of the total parking area.

Submittals – Recertification

Provide an update of previous filings:

- ❑ If no change in the policies or techniques used to earn this credit has occurred, provide records and results of quarterly inspections over the performance period to determine that the specific feature used to earn this credit is being maintained.

OR

- ❑ If the policy or technique used to earn this credit in previous LEED-EB Certifications has changed, in addition to the documentation required for each specific compliance path, provide records and results of quarterly inspections over the performance period to demonstrate that the requirements continue to be met and maintained to reduce heat islands in non-roof areas.

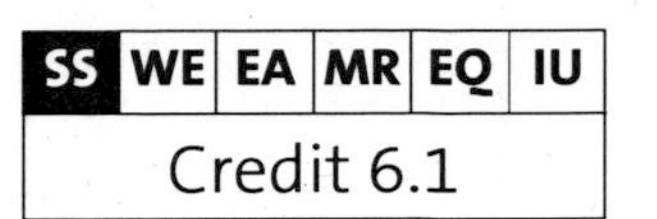

Summary of Referenced Standard

There is no standard referenced for this credit.

Green Building Concerns

The use of dark, non-reflective surfaces for parking, roofs, walkways and other surfaces contributes to heat island effect. Dark, non-reflective surfaces absorb incoming solar radiation. Heat is then re-radiated from the material surface back to the surrounding areas. As a result of heat island effect, ambient temperatures in urban areas are artificially elevated by 2–10°F compared to surrounding suburban and undeveloped areas.[37] This results in increased cooling loads in the summer, requiring larger HVAC equipment and greater energy use for building operations. Heat island effects can be mitigated through shading and the use of light colors that reflect solar radiation rather than absorbing it.

Environmental Issues

Heat island effect raises the localized temperature. Plants and animals sensitive to large fluctuations in daytime and nighttime temperatures will not thrive in areas affected by heat islands. Heat islands also exacerbate air pollution for two reasons. First, smog is produced faster at higher temperatures. For example, for every degree the temperature in Los Angeles rises above 70°F, 3 percent more smog is created.[38] Secondly, rising temperatures lead to increased cooling requirements, requiring energy and causing associated emissions. Electricity use in Los Angeles increases by 2 percent for every degree the temperature rises over 70°F.[39]

Economic Issues

The Lawrence Berkeley National Laboratory estimates that one-sixth of electricity consumed in the nation is to cool buildings. If full-scale implementation of reflective surfaces and vegetation were performed, the nation could save $4 billion a year in reduced cooling energy demand by 2015.[40] Site-specific heat island reduction can reduce the cost of cooling buildings and servicing HVAC equipment.

Conversely, higher initial costs result from installation of additional trees and reflective surfaces. However, these items can have a high aesthetic value and a rapid payback when integrated into a whole systems approach that maximizes energy savings. Proper planning can increase the value of the site and reduce energy costs at minimal implementation costs. If the initial costs associated with the installation of shade and reflective devices are not financially feasible, long-term benefits can be realized as opportunities present themselves during ongoing site improvements and construction activities.

Strategies & Technologies

Employ strategies, materials, and landscaping techniques that reduce heat absorption of exterior materials.

Option A – Vegetative Shading

Vegetative shading can increase a site's surface albedo. Employ design strategies and landscaping schemes to reduce solar radiance on exterior materials. Provide shade with native or climate-tolerant trees and large shrubs, vegetated trellises, or other exterior structures supporting vegetation on parking lots, walkways and plazas. Where tree planting is not possible, consider architectural shading devices to block direct sunlight radiance. Shading from architectural devices can be included in this credit only if you can demonstrate that the architectural devices do not themselves contribute to heat island effect.

Option B – High Solar Reflectance Materials

LEED-EB requires emissivity performance in addition to reflectivity, which is more stringent than ENERGY STAR®. Therefore, look for materials that exhibit a high reflectivity and a high emissivity over the life of the product. These materials will also maximize energy savings and minimize heat island effects. Read the manufacturer's data carefully when selecting a product based on a material's reflective properties. Not all manufacturers conduct solar reflectivity and emissivity testing as a matter of course, although research on urban heat islands has helped to expose the problem and encourage such testing. Far more often, manufacturers measure visible reflectance. Visible reflectance correlates to solar reflectance, but the two quantities are not equal because solar reflectance covers a wider range of wavelengths than visible light. A material that exhibits a high visible reflectance usually has a somewhat lower solar reflectance. For example, a good white coating with a visible reflectance of 0.9 typically has a solar reflectance of 0.8. Therefore, it is necessary to measure the solar reflectance of the material even if the visible reflectance is known. Measurements of the solar reflectance must be conducted according to ASTM Standard E408–71 (1996)e1 - "Standard Test Methods for Total Normal Emittance of Surfaces Using Inspection-Meter Techniques" (Reapproved 2002)

Explore elimination of blacktop and the use of new coatings and integral colorants for asphalt to achieve light-colored surfaces with higher albedo. Paving materials with high values of solar reflectivity can be difficult to find in the marketplace. Most traditional paving materials are mineral-based and have low solar reflectivity. Therefore, concentrate efforts on materials with high reflectivity values for non-parking impervious surfaces such as sidewalks and plazas in order to keep costs down. There are new coatings and integral colorants for parking surfaces that improve solar reflectance.

Option C – Underground Parking

Minimize the size of parking surfaces by placing parking areas below the building or constructing multi-tier parking ramps. For existing buildings, restructuring parking areas may be difficult or impossible without major renovations.

Option D – Open-grid Pavement Systems

Consider an open paving system that increases perviousness by at least 50 percent, reducing the amount of low reflective material present and increasing water infiltration. Pervious paving systems can be applied to pedestrian traffic surfaces and low-vehicle traffic areas such as parking spaces, fire lanes and maintenance roads. Pervious paving systems usually have a limit on transportation loads and may pose problems for wheelchair accessibility and stroller mobility, so these systems should only be used in certain areas.

Use pervious paving materials such as poured asphalt or concrete with incorporated air spaces, or use concrete unit paving systems with large voids that allow grass or other vegetation to grow between the voids. Pervious paving has several options, including systems that use grass and a plastic grid system (typically 90 percent pervious), concrete grids with grass (typically 40 percent pervious), and concrete grids with gravel (typically 10 percent pervious). Pervious paving requires different maintenance procedures than impervious pavement. Some systems require vacuum sweeping to prevent the voids from clogging with sediment, dirt, and mud. Systems that use vegetation, such as grass planted in a plastic matrix over gravel may require mowing like conventional lawns. Snow removal from pervious paving requires more care than conventional paving. Check existing codes on the use of pervious surfaces for roadways.

Additional Heat Island Reduction Opportunities

If the site utilizes photovoltaic cells to offset electricity consumption, position them to shade applicable areas. Also consider water features to mitigate heating, which will increase the beauty of the site while preventing the formation of heat islands.

Synergies & Tradeoffs

Site planning has a significant effect on urban heat islands, especially transportation planning. There may be a tradeoff between material durability and material reflectance. Some coatings with high emissivity require periodic maintenance, and these costs should be considered before installation. Highly reflective surfaces may also create glare, posing a hazard to vehicle traffic and annoyance for building occupants.

Planting indigenous trees that are low-water users or fruit producers adds environmental benefit to the site by conserving water and supporting native wildlife. Conversely, trees that require extensive watering, fertilizing or pesticide application could pose greater negative environmental impacts than the effects of heat islands. Vegetative shading strategies should be coordinated with site landscaping and management plans. All shading strategies should also be integrated with solar strategies such as daylighting, solar heating and photovoltaic cells.

Calculations & Documentation

Calculations

The following calculation methodology is used to support the credit submittals listed on the first page of this credit.

Option A: Shading of Non-Roof Impervious Surfaces

1. Identify all non-roof impervious surfaces on the project site and sum the total area. Non-roof impervious surfaces include all surfaces on the site with perviousness of less than 50 percent, except the roof of the building. Examples of typically impervious surfaces include parking lots, roads, sidewalks and plazas.
2. Identify all trees and vegetation that contribute shade to non-roof impervious surfaces. Shading from architectural devices can be included only if it is demonstrated that the architectural devices themselves do not contribute to heat island effect. If the shading trees and vegetation are already mature, use the current shading in the calculations. If the shading trees and vegetation are fewer than five years old, estimate the shading they will provide when they are five years old.
3. Calculate the shading on all non-roof impervious surfaces on June 21 at noon solar time to determine the shading provided. Sum the total area of shade provided for non-roof impervious surfaces.
4. Shade must be provided for at least 30 percent of non-roof impervious surfaces to earn this point (see **Equation 1**).

Option B: Light-Colored/High-Albedo Surface

1. Identify all non-roof impervious surfaces on the project site and sum the total area.
2. Identify all of these surfaces with surface reflectance greater than 0.3 and sum the area. The measurements for high reflectance need to be carried

Equation 1

Shade [%] = Shaded Impervious Area [SF]/Total Impervious Area [SF]

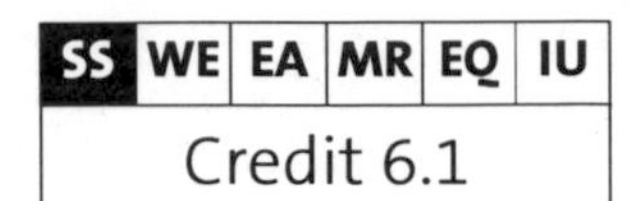

out according to ASTM Standard E408–71 "Standard Test Methods for Total Normal Emittance of Surfaces Using Inspection-Meter Techniques" (Reapproved 2002).

3. Calculate the percentage of non-roof impervious surfaces that have a solar reflectance of greater than 0.3 (see **Equation 2**). At least 30 percent of non-roof impervious surfaces must have a surface reflectance greater than 0.3 to earn this point.

Option C: Parking Spaces Underground

1. Calculate the percentage of parking spaces that are underground.
2. A minimum of 50 percent of the total parking spaces must be underground (see **Equation 3**).

Option D: Pervious Parking Area

1. Calculate the total parking lot area onsite. Parking lots include parking spaces and driving lanes in the parking lot. Exclude areas that are not exposed to direct sunlight (e.g. underground parking, parking on floors below exposed top floor), as well as sidewalks and other surfaces that cannot support vehicle loads.
2. Calculate the perviousness of any pervious paving materials used in the parking lot (see **Equation 4**). Perviousness of a given type of paving surface must be equal to or greater than 50 percent in order to count towards satisfaction of this credit.
3. Calculate the parking area that is paved with material that is at least 50 percent pervious. A minimum of 50 percent of the total parking area must be comprised of pervious paving materials (see **Equation 5**).

Documentation

Option A

❑ Site plan highlighting all non-roof impervious surfaces and portions shaded

- Site drawings should demarcate all areas of impervious surface, clearly designating both areas that are currently shaded as well as areas that will be shaded within 5 years. Area calculations should include notation of site area, total impervious area, and area anticipated to be shaded within 5 years.

Option B

❑ Third-party reflectance documentation, site plan, calculations and photographs

- Manufacturer or roofing contractor documentation is appropriate for third-party documentation.

Equation 2

High Albedo [%] = Area of high reflectance [SF]/Total Impervious Area [SF]

Equation 3

Parking Spaces Underground [%] = Parking Spaces Underground / Total Parking Spaces

Equation 4

Perviousness [%] =
Area of paving system permeable to moisture [SF] / Total Area of Paving System [SF]

Equation 5

Pervious Portion [%] = Pervious Parking Area [SF] / Total Exposed Parking Area [SF]

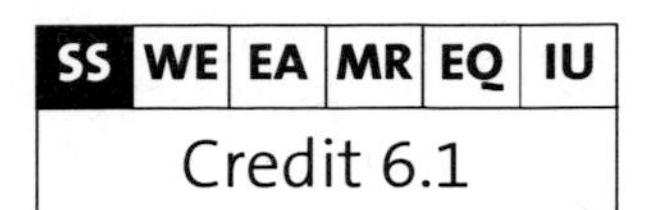

Option C

All information needed to successfully document Option C can be found in the Submittals section of the LEED-EB Rating System and the LEED-EB Letter Templates.

Option D

- ❑ Provide third-party documentation of paving system perviousness, site plan, calculations and photographs for a pervious paving system
  - Site plan should demarcate all areas of impervious and pervious paving surface. Area calculations should include notation of site area, total impervious area and pervious area.

Other Resources

American Concrete Pavement Association

www.pavement.com

National association representing concrete pavement contractors, cement companies, equipment and material manufacturers, and suppliers. See the R&T Update #3.05, June 2002, "Albedo: A measure of Pavement Surface Reflectance" (http://www.pavement.com/techserv/RT3.05.pdf).

EPA Heat Island Effect Web Site

www.epa.gov/heatisland

Basic information about heat island effect, its social and environmental costs, and strategies to minimize its prevalence.

Lawrence Berkeley National Laboratory Heat Island Group

http://eetd.lbl.gov/HeatIsland/

LBL conducts heat island research to find, analyze, and implement solutions to minimizing heat island effect, with current research efforts focusing on the study and development of more reflective surfaces for roadways and buildings.

Definitions

Albedo is synonymous with solar reflectance (see below).

Emissivity is the ratio of the radiation emitted by a surface to the radiation emitted by a blackbody at the same temperature.

Heat Island Effect refers to urban air and surface temperatures that are higher than nearby rural areas. Principal contributing factors include additions of dark, non-reflective surfaces, elimination of trees and vegetation, waste heat from vehicles, factories, and air conditioners and reduced airflow from tall buildings and narrow streets.

Imperviousness is resistance to penetration by a liquid and is calculated as the percent of area covered by a paving system that does not allow moisture to soak into the earth below the paving system.

Infrared Emittance is a parameter between 0 and 1 that indicates the ability of a material to shed infrared radiation. The wavelength of this radiant energy is roughly 5 to 40 micrometers. Most building materials (including glass) are opaque in this part of the spectrum, and have an emittance of roughly 0.9. Materials such as clean, bare metals are the most important exceptions to the 0.9 rule. Thus clean, untarnished galvanized steel has low emittance, and aluminum roof coatings have intermediate emittance levels.

Non-roof Impervious Surfaces include all surfaces on the site with a perviousness of less than 50 percent, not including the roof of the building. Examples of typically impervious surfaces include parking lots, roads, sidewalks and plazas.

Perviousness is the percent of area covered by a paving system that is open and allows moisture to soak into the earth below the paving system.

Solar Reflectance is a measure of the ability of a surface material to reflect

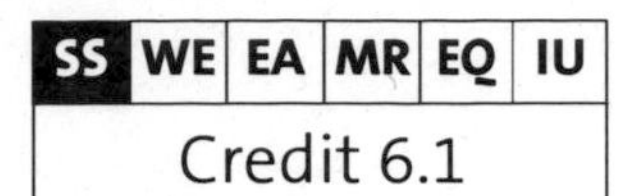

sunlight – including the visible, infrared, and ultraviolet wavelengths – on a scale of 0 to 1. Solar reflectance is also called albedo. White paint (titanium dioxide) is defined to a have a solar reflectance of 1 while black paint has a solar reflectance of 0.

Underground Parking is a "tuck-under" or stacked parking structure that reduces the exposed parking surface area.

SS	WE	EA	MR	EQ	IU
Credit 6.2					

1 Point

Heat Island Reduction

Roof

Intent

Reduce heat islands (thermal gradient differences between developed and undeveloped areas) to minimize impact on microclimate and human and wildlife habitat.

Requirements

Option A

- ❑ Have in place over the performance period ENERGY STAR®–compliant, high-reflectance and high emissivity roofing material that has a minimum emissivity of 0.9 when tested in accordance with ASTM 408 for a minimum of 75% of the roof surface.
- ❑ Provide records and results of quarterly inspections over the performance period to determine that these features are being maintained

Option B

- ❑ Install/maintain a "green" (vegetated) roof for at least 50% of the roof area.
- ❑ Provide records and results of quarterly inspections over the performance period to determine that these features are being maintained

Combinations of roofing materials that meet the requirements of Option A and Option B can be used providing they collectively cover the designated area. See the LEED-EB Reference Guide for guidance on calculating achievement of credit requirements based on using a combination of Option A and B roofing materials.

Submittals – Initial Certification

Option A

- ❑ Provide documentation demonstrating that roofing meets roofing material requirements of Option A. Documentation must include a roof plan, photographs and measurements of reflectance and emissivity. Manufacturer measurements are acceptable if the materials have been in place less than five years. If the materials have been in place more that five years, current measurements must be provided.
- ❑ Include area calculations demonstrating that the roofing material covers a minimum of 75% of the total roof area.
- ❑ Provide records and results of quarterly inspections over the performance period to determine that these features are being maintained.

Option B

- ❑ Provide documentation demonstrating that the requirements of Option B are met.
- ❑ Provide photographs and a roof plan documenting the installation/maintenance of a green vegetated roof system. Include a description of the green roof system being used and the types of vegetation being grown in the green roof. Include area calculations demonstrating that the roof system covering a minimum or 50% of the total roof area.

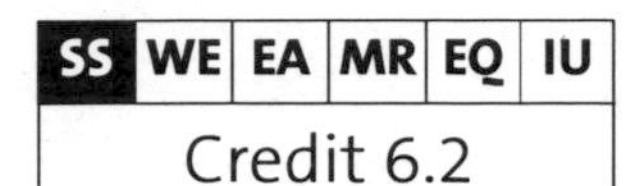

- ❑ Provide records and results of quarterly inspections over the performance period to determine that these features are being maintained.

Submittals – Recertification

Provide an update of previous filings:

- ❑ If no change in the policies or techniques used to earn this credit has occurred, provide records and results of quarterly inspections over the performance period to determine that the specific features used to earn this credit are being maintained.

OR

- ❑ If the policy or technique used to earn this credit in previous LEED-EB Certifications has changed, in addition to the documentation required for each specific compliance path, provide records and results of quarterly inspections over the performance period to determine that the roofing area continues to meet the requirements of Options A or B.

Summary of Referenced Standards

ENERGY STAR® Roof Compliant, High-Reflectance, and High Emissivity Roofing

U.S. EPA

(888) 782-7937

www.energystar.gov

This standard is used for determining reflectivity. The EPA's ENERGY STAR program allows for voluntary partnerships between the U.S. Department of Energy, the U.S. Environmental Protection Agency, product manufacturers, local utilities and retailers. ENERGY STAR is dedicated to promoting energy efficiency, reducing air pollution, and saving money for businesses and residences through decreased energy use. In addition to other building products, the ENERGY STAR program addresses roofing products. By choosing roofing products wisely, air conditioning needs can be reduced or eliminated. Roofing products with the ENERGY STAR logo meet the EPA criteria for reflectivity and reliability. Roof solar reflectance requirements for ENERGY STAR roofing products are summarized in **Table 1**. More information on roof products is available at these two web sites: www.energystar.gov/index.cfm?c=roof_prods.pr_roof_products or www.energystar.gov/ia/partners/product_specs/eligibility/roofs_elig.pdf.

ASTM Standard E408 – 71 (1996; Reapproved 2002): Standard Test Methods for Total Normal Emittance of Surfaces Using Inspection-Meter Techniques

ASTM

(610) 832-9585

www.astm.org.

This standard describes how to measure total normal emittance of surfaces using a portable inspection-meter instrument. The test methods are intended for large surfaces where non-destructive testing is required. See the standard for testing steps and a discussion of thermal emittance theory.

Green Building Concerns

Dark, non-reflective surfaces for roofs contribute to the heat island effect when heat from the sun is absorbed and re-radiated back to surrounding areas. As a result, ambient temperatures in urban areas are artificially elevated by 2–10°F when compared with surrounding suburban and undeveloped areas.[41] This results in increased cooling loads in the summer, requiring larger HVAC equipment and more energy for building operations. Heat island effects can be mitigated through shading and light colors that reflect heat instead of absorbing it.

Environmental Issues

The heat island effect raises the localized temperature. Plants and animals sensitive to large fluctuations in daytime and night-time temperatures will not thrive in areas affected by heat islands. Heat islands also

Table 1: EPA ENERGY STAR Roof Criteria

Roof Type	Slope	Initial Solar Reflectance	3-Year Solar Reflectance
Low-Slope Roof	< 2:12	0.65	0.50
Steep Slope Roof	> 2:12	0.25	0.15

Source: ENERGY STAR Program Requirements for Roof Products: Eligibility Criteria

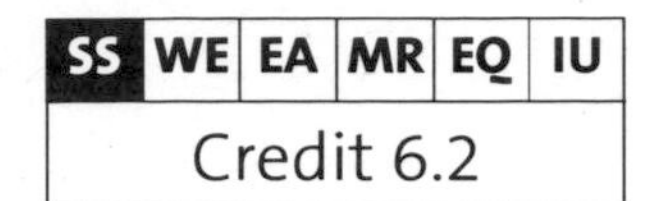

exacerbate air pollution for two reasons. First, smog is produced faster at higher temperatures. For example, for every degree the temperature in Los Angeles rises above 70°F, 3 percent more smog is created.[42] Secondly, rising temperatures lead to increased cooling requirements, requiring energy and causing associated emissions. Electricity use in Los Angeles increases by 2 percent for every degree the temperature rises over 70°F.[43]

Economic Issues

It is unlikely that an otherwise sound roof would be replaced just to earn this credit. However, there is little or no additional cost associated with earning this credit over time by carrying out each needed roof repair and replacement in a manner that contributes to the eventual achievement of the credit. Green roofs or roofs with high reflectance reduce costs associated with cooling and HVAC equipment. Energy costs for cooling buildings are a substantial expense over the building lifetime. The Lawrence Berkeley National Laboratory estimates that one-sixth of electricity consumed in the nation is used to cool buildings. If full-scale implementation of reflective surfaces and vegetation were performed, the nation could save $4 billion a year in reduced cooling energy demand by 2015.[44]

Strategies & Technologies

Gradually implement this credit as opportunities present themselves for ongoing roof repair and replacement. Visit the ENERGY STAR® web site (www.energystar.gov) to research compliant products. Install high-albedo and/or vegetated roofs to reduce heat absorption.

To maximize energy savings and minimize heat island effects, materials must exhibit a high reflectivity and a high emissivity over the life of the product. Read the manufacturer's data carefully when selecting a product based on a material's reflective properties. Not all manufacturers conduct solar reflectivity and emissivity testing as a matter of course, although research on urban heat islands has helped to expose the problem and encourage such testing. Far more often, manufacturers measure visible reflectance. Visible reflectance correlates to solar reflectance but the two quantities are not equal because solar gain covers a wider range of wavelengths than visible light. A material that exhibits a high visible reflectance usually has a lower solar reflectance. For example, a good white coating with a visible reflectance of 0.9 typically has a solar reflectance of 0.8. Therefore, it is necessary to measure the solar reflectance of the material even if the visible reflectance is known.

Table 2 provides example values of initial solar reflectance and infrared emittance for common roofing materials. Typically, white roof products exhibit higher performance characteristics than nonwhite products. Performance varies by roofing materials as well as brand. Check with roofing manufacturers and the Lawrence Berkeley National Laboratory's Cool Roofing Materials Database (http://eetd.lbl.gov/CoolRoofs) for specific information.

Membrane roofing is fabricated from strong, flexible waterproof materials. It

Table 2: Type of Roofing

Roofing Material	Initial Solar Reflectance	Infrared Emittance
Roof Coating, White	0.60–0.85	0.90–0.91
Roof Coating, Tinted	0.16–0.79	0.90–0.91
Roofing Membranes	0.06–0.83	0.86–0.92
Concrete Tile, Off-White	0.74	0.90

Source: LBNL Cool Roofing Materials Database. http://eetd.lbl.gov/CoolRoofs.

may be applied in multiple layers or as a continuous single-ply membrane. Membranes usually contain a fabric made from felt, fiberglass or polyester for strength that is laminated to or impregnated with a flexible polymeric material. The polymeric material may be a bituminous hydrocarbon material such as asphalt, synthetic rubber known as EPDM, or a synthetic polymer such as polyvinyl chloride (PVC). The color of the polymer itself ranges from black to white, depending on the amount of carbon black present. The upper surface of the membrane may be coated with a colored material that determines the solar reflectance, or it may simply be ballasted with roofing gravel. When a dark membrane is surfaced with roofing granules, the membrane has the appearance and low solar reflectance of asphalt shingles.

Metal roofing is typically steel or aluminum based, although a small amount of copper and tin roofing is used today. Steel roofing is usually produced with a galvanic corrosion protection coating of zinc or zinc/aluminum. This corrosion coating may be covered by a colored paint-like polymeric coating, which influences the overall emissivity of the roofing product. Bare aluminum and steel typically have a solar reflectance of 60 percent and low infrared emittance. The reflectance and emittance of bare metals are very sensitive to the smoothness of the surface and the presence or absence of surface oxides, oil film, etc. Usually, bare metals are not very cool in the sun. For example, in one outdoor experiment, a bare clean sheet of galvanized steel with a solar reflectance of about 0.38 reached temperatures nearly as high as a reference black surface.

Garden roofs, or green roofs, are vegetated surfaces that minimize heat island effect by reflecting solar radiation and cooling through evapotranspiration. Garden roofs provide insulating benefits, aesthetic appeal, and lower maintenance than standard roofs. Some garden roofs require plant maintenance and are considered active gardens, while other gardens have grasses and plants that require no maintenance or watering. All types of garden roofs require semiannual inspection but have longer lifetimes than conventional roofs.

Synergies & Tradeoffs

Buildings in very cold climates may not experience year-round energy benefits from reflective roofing due to high emittance and low absorption, which may increase heating costs. However, increasing the reflectance of a roof reduces annual cooling energy use in almost all climates.

Garden roofs reduce stormwater volumes that may be collected and used for non-potable purposes. Stormwater runoff volumes from garden roofs depend on the local climate, depth of soil, plant types, and other variables. However, all garden roofs decrease runoff volumes substantially.

Calculations & Documentation

Calculations

High Reflectivity/Emissivity Roofing Materials Calculations

1. Calculate the total roof area of the project. Deduct areas with equipment and appurtenances.
2. Determine the area of the roof that is covered by Energy Star-compliant roofing materials that meet the emissivity requirements.

Equation 1

Compliant Roof [%] = Compliant Roof Area [SF] / (Total Roof Area [SF] – Equipment & Appurtenance Area [SF]) x 100

3. Calculate the percentage of the total roof area that is surfaced with ENERGY STAR-compliant roofing materials that meet emissivity requirements (see **Equation 1**). This value must be at least 75 percent in order to earn this point.

Vegetated Roof Calculations

1. Calculate the total roof area of the project. Deduct areas with equipment and appurtenances.
2. Determine the area of roof that is surfaced with a vegetated roof system.
3. Calculate the percentage of the total roof area that is covered with a green vegetated roof system (see **Equation 2**). This value must be equal to or greater than 50 percent in order to earn this point.

Combination of Vegetated Roof and Reflective/Emissive Roofing Calculations

1. Calculate the total roof area of the project. Deduct areas with equipment and appurtenances.
2. Determine the area of the roof that is covered by ENERGY STAR-compliant roofing materials that meet the emissivity requirements.
3. Determine the area of roof that is surfaced with a vegetated roof system.
4. Use Equation 3 to weight the square footage of each type of roof covering that is either surfaced with ENERGY STAR-compliant roofing materials that meet emissivity requirements or covered with a green vegetated roof system
5. If the value determined in **Equation 3** is greater than or equal to the actual roof area (Total Roof Area [SF] – Equipment & Appurtenance Area [SF]), this credit is earned.

Documentation

All information needed to successfully document this credit can be found in the Submittals section of the LEED-EB Rating System and the LEED-EB Letter Templates.

Other Resources

Cool Roof Rating Council

www.coolroofs.org

A nonprofit organization dedicated to implementing and communicating fair, accurate, and credible radiative energy performance rating systems for roof surfaces, supporting research into energy-related radiative properties of roofing surfaces, including durability of those properties, and providing education and objective support to parties interested in understanding and comparing various roofing options.

EPA ENERGY STAR Roofing Products

www.energystar.gov/index.cfm?c=roof prods.pr roof products

This site provides solar reflectance levels required to meet ENERGY STAR labeling requirements.

Extensive Green Roofs

www.wbdg.org/design/resource.php?cn=0&rp=41

This Whole Building Design Guide article by Charlie Miller, PE details the

Equation 2

Vegetated Roof [%] = Vegetated Roof Area [SF]/ (Total Roof Area [SF] – Equipment & Appurtenance Area [SF]) x 100

Equation 3

Weighted Square Footage of Compliant Roofing Material Types = (ENERGY STAR-Compliant Roof Area [SF]/0.75) + (Vegetated Roof Area [SF]/0.5)

features and benefits of constructing green roofs.

Greenroofs.com

www.greenroofs.com

The green roof industry resource portal offers basic information, product and service directory, and research links.

Lawrence Berkeley National Laboratory Heat Island Group – Cool Roofs

http://eetd.lbl.gov/HeatIsland/CoolRoofs/

This site offers a wealth of information about cool roof research and technology, including links to the Cool Roofing Materials Database.

Penn State Center for Green Roof Research

http://hortweb.cas.psu.edu/research/greenroofcenter/

The Center has the mission of demonstrating and promoting green roof research, education and technology transfer in the Northeastern United States.

Definitions

Solar Reflectance is a measure of the ability of a surface material to reflect sunlight – including the visible, infrared, and ultraviolet wavelengths – on a scale of 0 to 1. Solar reflectance is also called albedo. White paint (titanium dioxide) is defined to a have a solar reflectance of 1 while black paint has a solar reflectance of 0.

Thermal Emittance is the ratio of the radiant heat flux emitted by a sample to that emitted by a blackbody radiator at the same temperature.

Weathered Radiative Properties refer to the solar reflectance and thermal emittance of a roofing product after three years of exposure to the weather.

Case Study

National Geographic Society Headquarters Complex

Washington, D.C.

LEED-EB Silver

Owner: National Geographic Society

Photo courtesy of: NGS Staff

Due to the urban setting of its four-building Headquarters Complex, the National Geographic Society (NGS) made reducing its contribution to urban heat island effect a priority for this facility. The entire roof area of two of the complex buildings have light colored roof ballast, and the recently completed roofing renovation on a third building included the use of EPA Energy Star-compliant roofing materials. Because measured albedo characteristics of existing roofing materials can be difficult to ascertain, NGS engaged a third party to demonstrate the light-colored roofing material performance and contribution to reducing the heat island effect. This was done by using a direct measured performance based method, where actual roof surface temperature readings were compared between standard, dark-colored roofing materials and the NGS roofs. The Energy Star-compliant roofing was nearly 18 degrees F cooler than standard roofing, and the light colored roof ballast was 4.45 degrees F cooler.

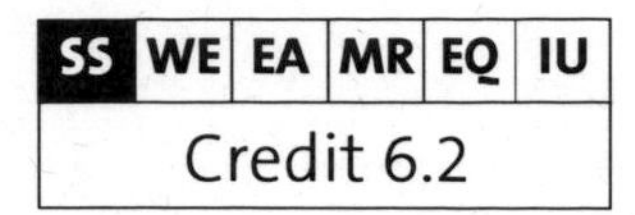
SS WE EA MR EQ IU
Credit 6.2

SS	WE	EA	MR	EQ	IU
Credit 7					

1 Point

Light Pollution Reduction

Intent

Eliminate light trespass from the building and site, improve night sky access and reduce development impact on nocturnal environments.

Requirements

Option A

❑ Light to the Night Sky

- Shield all outdoor luminaries 50 watts and over so that they do not directly emit light to the night sky.

OR

- Provide calculations showing that less then 5% of light emitted by all outdoor lighting reach the night sky on an annual basis.

❑ Light Trespass

- With the building interior, exterior and site lights on and off, measure the illumination levels at the same locations at regular intervals around the perimeter of the property. At least eight measurements are required with documentation that the measurements made are sufficient in quantity to be representative of the illumination levels on the perimeter of the property. The property perimeter illumination levels measured with the lights on must not be more than 10% above the levels measured with the lights off.

❑ Performance

- Provide records and results of quarterly inspections to determine if required features are being maintained.

Option B

❑ Light to the Night Sky

- Shield all outdoor luminaries 50 watts and over so that they do not directly emit light to the night sky.

OR

- Provide calculations showing that less then 5% of light emitted by all outdoor lighting reach the night sky on an annual basis.

❑ Light Trespass

- Provide calculations showing that the maximum candela value of all interior lighting falls within the building (not out through windows) and the maximum candela value of all exterior lighting falls within the property. Provide documentation that all luminaires within a distance of 2.5 times their mounting height from the property line have shielding that allows less that 5% of the light from these fixtures to cross the property boundary.

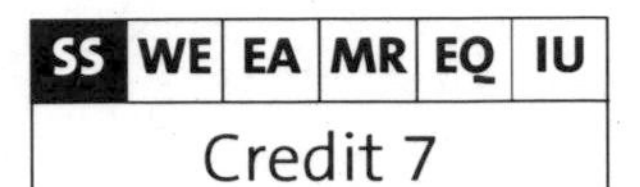

- ❑ Performance
  - Provide records and results of quarterly inspections to determine if required features are being maintained.

Submittals – Initial Certification

Option A

- ❑ Provide documentation showing that the requirements for Option A have been met.

Option B

- ❑ Provide documentation showing that the requirements for Option B have been met.

Submittals – Recertification

Provide an update of previous filings:

- ❑ If changes have occurred that affect the site or building lighting, provide updated documentation that the site or building lighting continues to meet the certification submittal requirements for Option A or B.

Provide performance documentation:

- ❑ Provide records and results of quarterly inspections over the performance period to show that the requirements for Option A or B continue to be maintained.

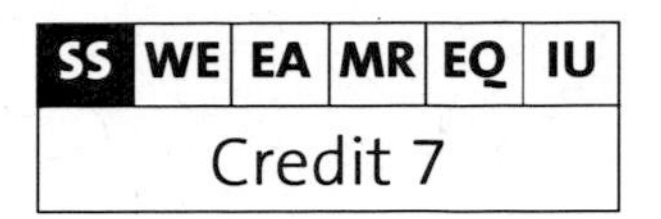

Summary of Referenced Standard

There is no standard referenced for this credit.

Green Building Concerns

Outdoor lighting is necessary for illuminating connections between buildings and support facilities such as sidewalks, parking lots, roads and community gathering places. Through thoughtful planning, outdoor lighting can meet these needs while creating a low lighting profile that does not contribute to light pollution of the night sky.

Environmental Issues

Light pollution from poorly designed outdoor lighting schemes affects the nocturnal ecosystem on the site and hinders enjoyment of the night sky by building occupants and neighbors. Reduction of light pollution encourages nocturnal life to thrive on the building site. Thoughtful exterior lighting strategies reduce infrastructure costs and energy use over the lifetime of the building.

Economic Issues

By avoiding unnecessary outdoor lighting, infrastructure costs are reduced. Also, energy savings over the lifetime of the building can be substantial.

Strategies & Technologies

Adopt site lighting criteria to maintain safe lighting levels while avoiding off-site lighting and night sky pollution. Minimize site lighting where possible by avoiding unnecessary lighting of architectural and landscape features.

Where lighting is necessary, utilize downlighting techniques rather than uplighting. Technologies to reduce light pollution include full cutoff luminaries, low-reflectance surfaces, and low-angle spotlights. Controls should be used wherever possible to turn off lighting after normal operating hours or in post-curfew periods. Select lighting equipment carefully, as any type of luminaire can produce excessive brightness in the form of glare.

Use computer models, lighting professionals, and other resources for determining strategies and technologies appropriate to the site. Also review local or regional lighting ordinances that might effect site lighting options.

Synergies & Tradeoffs

Exterior lighting strategies are affected by the transportation features of the site as well as the total area of developed space on the project site. Exterior lighting choices will affect energy consumption, and the exterior lighting system should be included in EA Prerequisite 1: Existing Building Commissioning.

Care should be taken when designing exterior lighting to provide enough illumination for safety, accessibility, and public perception while at the same time avoiding unnecessary light pollution.

Calculations & Documentation

Calculation of Light to the Night Sky from Exterior Lighting

Shield all outdoor luminaries 50 watts and over so they do not directly emit light to the night sky, or carry out calculations that document that less than 5 percent of light emitted by all outdoor lighting reach the night sky on an annual basis.

1. Prepare a spreadsheet listing (1) all the exterior light on the site, (2) the lumen output of each exterior light, (3) annual hours of night time operation, and (4) the percent of light output lost directly to the sky. The percent of light output lost directly to the sky

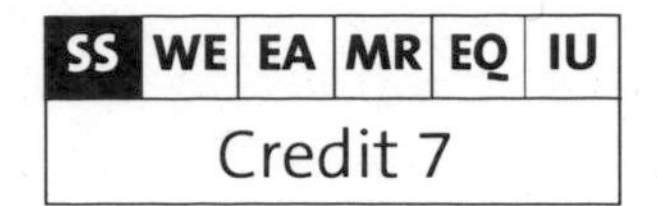

for each exterior light is dependent on the extent to which the light is shielded. Lights that are completely shielded from the night sky will lose zero percent of light output directly to the sky. Those that are partially shielded will lose varying percentages of total light output to the night sky, based on the design of the shield. The percent of light output lost directly to the sky should be estimated based on the characteristics of the light and any shielding devices in place.

2. Calculate for each exterior light (1) the annual lumen-hour output of each exterior light, (2) the annual lumen-hours of light lost directly to the sky from each exterior light.
3. Calculate site totals of (1) the annual lumen-hour output of all exterior lights, (2) the annual lumen-hours of light lost directly to the sky from all exterior lights.
4. Calculate average percentage of light lost to the night sky from exterior lights using **Equation 1**.

Calculation of Light Trespass from the Building and Site

Calculate light trespass in the following manner:

Option A

1. With the building interior, exterior, and site lights on and off, measure the illumination levels at the same locations at regular intervals around the perimeter of the property.
2. Prepare a table showing the lighting levels around the site perimeter (1) measured with interior and exterior lights on, and (2) measured with interior and exterior lights off.
3. Make at least 8 measurements, and more as necessary, to document that the measurements accurately represent the illumination levels on the perimeter of the property.
4. Calculate for each site perimeter measurement location using **Equation 2**.

The requirement is met if the property perimeter illumination levels measured with the lights on is not more than 10 percent above the levels measured with the lights off.

Documentation

Option A

- ❑ Light to the Night Sky
  - If choosing the luminary shielding option, submit a brief list of 50+ watt outdoor luminaries, their location and purpose, and a description of the shielding approach employed to eliminate light emission to the night sky.
  - If choosing the calculation method, provide calculations.
- ❑ Light Trespass
  - Submit a table comparing on/off measurements at each of the eight (or more) measurement points, and average the percentage increase in illumination to determine achievement of the 10 percent standard.

Equation 1

Light lost to the night sky from exterior lights [Average %] =
(Annual site total of light lost directly to the sky from all exterior lights [lumen-hours] / Annual site total output of all exterior lights [lumen-hours]) x 100.

Equation 2

Light trespass at each site perimeter location [%] =
((Site perimeter lighting levels measured with interior, exterior and site lights on [fc] – Site perimeter lighting levels with interior, exterior and site lights off [fc]) / Site perimeter lighting levels with interior, exterior and site lights off [fc]) x 100

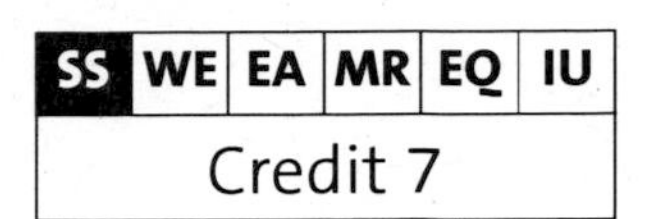

❑ Performance

- Provide records and results of quarterly inspections to determine if required features are being maintained.

Option B

❑ Light to the Night Sky

- If choosing the luminary shielding option, submit a brief list of 50+ watt outdoor luminaries, their location and purpose, and describe the shielding approach employed to eliminate light emission to the night sky.
- If choosing the calculation method, provide calculations.

❑ Light to the Night Sky

- Submit a footcandle contour map that shows that the maximum candela value of all interior lighting falls within the building (not out through windows).
- Submit a footcandle contour map that shows that the maximum candela value of all exterior lighting falls within the property.
- Provide documentation that all luminaires within a distance of 2.5 times their mounting height from the property line have shielding that allows less that 5% of the light from these fixtures to cross the property boundary.

Other Resources

Illuminating Engineering Society of North America

www.iesna.org

This organization provides general exterior lighting design guidance and acts as a link to other IESNA outdoor lighting Recommended Practices

International Dark-Sky Association

www.darksky.org/ida/ida_2/index.html

A nonprofit agency dedicated to educating and providing solutions to light pollution.

New England Light Pollution Advisory Group

http://cfa-www.harvard.edu/cfa/ps/nelpag.html

A volunteer group to educate the public on the virtues of efficient, glare-free outdoor night lighting as well as the benefits of no lighting for many outdoor applications.

Sky & Telescope

http://skyandtelescope.com/resources/darksky/default.asp

Includes facts on light pollution and its impact on astronomy, and information about purchasing light fixtures that minimize light pollution.

The Design of Lighting by Peter Tregenza and David Loe, E & F N Spon, 1998.

Definitions

Curfew Hours are locally determined times when greater lighting restrictions are imposed.

Footcandle (fc) is a unit of light intensity and is equal to the quantity of light falling on a one-square foot area from a one candela light source at a distance of one foot.

Light Pollution is waste light from building sites that produces glare, compromises astronomical research, and adversely affects the environment. Waste light does not increase nighttime safety, utility, or security and needlessly consumes energy and natural resources.

Case Study

Ada County Courthouse and Administration Building

Boise, Idaho

LEED-EB Silver

Owner: Ada County, Idaho

Photo courtesy of: Maria Bracci

Ada County's Energy Specialist worked in cooperation with staff from the Energy Division of the Idaho Department of Water Resources to create a measurement and analysis plan that would accurately ascertain light pollution generated by this 350,000 square foot public building. Exterior light readings were taken at eight different locations along the perimeter of the property. Measurement locations were selected to take into account off-site light sources like city street lights and lamp posts. Using a handheld light meter, illumination levels were recorded to determine levels of light trespass.

Results were reviewed with the Idaho Lighting Design Lab in order to gain a better understanding of the nuances of light readings and measurements, and then retaken to better account for variables like sensor placement, environmental conditions, and meter error. The final readings showed that property perimeter illumination levels, when measured with the site lights on, were less than 10 percent greater as compared to illumination levels when the lights are off.

Endnotes

[1] Brady, Nyle C., and Ray R. Weil. The Nature and Properties of Soils. 12th ed. Upper Saddle River, NJ: Prentice Hall, 1999.

[2] United States. Department of Agriculture, Natural Resources Conservation Service, Soil Quality Institute. Erosion and Sedimentation on Construction Sites. Soil Quality – Urban Technical Note No. 1, March 2000. 21 February 2005 <http://soils.usda.gov/sqi/files/u01d.pdf>.

[3] United States. Environmental Protection Agency, Mid-Atlantic Integrated Assessment, Office of Research & Development. Eutrophication September 2003. 21 February 2005 <http://www.epa.gov/maia/html/eutroph.html>.

[4] United States. Department of Agriculture, Natural Resources Conservation Service, Soil Quality Institute. Erosion and Sedimentation on Construction Sites. Soil Quality – Urban Technical Note No. 1, March 2000. 21 February 2005 <http://soils.usda.gov/sqi/files/u01d.pdf>.

[5] United States. Department of Energy, Energy Information Administration. Annual Energy Review 2003. Report No. DOE/EIA-0384(2003). 1 March 2005 <http://www.eia.doe.gov/emeu/aer/contents.html>.

[6] Davis, Stacy C. and Susan W. Diegel. Transportation Energy Data Book: Edition 24. Center for Transportation Analysis, Engineering Science & Technology Division, Oak Ridge National Laboratory. U.S. Department of Energy, 2004.

[7] Hu, Patricia S., and Timothy R Reuscher. Prepared for the U.S Department of Transportation, Federal Highway Administration. Summary of Travel Trends: 2001 National Household Travel Survey December 2004. 25 February 2005 <http://nhts.ornl.gov/2001/pub/STT.pdf>.

[8] Ibid.

[9] Ibid.

[10] Shapiro, Robert J., Kevin A. Hassett, and Frank S. Arnold. Prepared for the American Public Transportation Association. Conserving Energy and preserving the Environment: The Role of Public Transportation July 2002. 25 February 2005 <http://www.apta.com/research/info/online/documents/shapiro.pdf>.

[11] Ibid.

[12] United Sates. Department of Energy, Energy Information Administration. Annual Energy Review 2003. Report No. DOE/EIA-0384(2003). 1 March 2005 <http://www.eia.doe.gov/emeu/aer/contents.html>.

[13] Davis, Stacy C. and Susan W. Diegel. Transportation Energy Data Book: Edition 24. Center for Transportation Analysis, Engineering Science & Technology Division, Oak Ridge National Laboratory. U.S. Department of Energy, 2004.

[14] Hu, Patricia S., and Timothy R Reuscher. Prepared for the U.S Department of Transportation, Federal Highway Administration. Summary of Travel Trends: 2001 National Household Travel Survey December 2004. 25 February 2005 <http://nhts.ornl.gov/2001/pub/STT.pdf>.

[15] Ibid.

[16] Ibid.

[17] United States. Department of Transportation, Federal Highway Administration. National Bicycling and Walking Study: Ten Year Status Report October 2004. 28 February 2005 <http://www.fhwa.dot.gov/environment/bikeped/study/>.

[18] United States. Department of Transportation, Federal Highway Administration. Transportation Air Quality – Selected Facts and Figures: Vehicle Emissions 2004. 28 February 2005 <http://www.fhwa.dot.gov/environment/aqfactbk/factbk13.htm>.

[19] Information compiled from multiple sources: Association of Pedestrian and Bicycle Professional. Bicycle Parking Guidelines 2002. 28 February 2005 <http://www.bicyclinginfo.org/pdf/bikepark.pdf>; Bicycle Parking Criteria, Bike Rack, Bicycle Locker, Cycle Stands & Bike Storage Systems. International Bicycle Fund. 28 February 2005 <http://www.ibike.org/engineering/parking.htm>; Bicycling Parking: The Basics. Pedestrian and Bicycle Information Center. 28 February 2005 <http://www.bicyclinginfo.org/de/park_basics.htm>; Bicycle Parking Facilities Guidelines. City of Portland, Office of Transportation. 28 February 2005 <http://www.trans.ci.portland.or.us/bicycles/parkguide.htm#Rack>.

[20]United States. Department of Energy, Energy Information Administration. Annual Energy Review 2003. Report No. DOE/EIA-0384(2003). 1 March 2005 <http://www.eia.doe.gov/emeu/aer/contents.html>.

[21]Davis, Stacy C. and Susan W. Diegel. Transportation Energy Data Book: Edition 24. Center for Transportation Analysis, Engineering Science & Technology Division, Oak Ridge National Laboratory. U.S. Department of Energy, 2004.

[22]Hu, Patricia S., and Timothy R Reuscher. Prepared for the U.S Department of Transportation, Federal Highway Administration. Summary of Travel Trends: 2001 National Household Travel Survey December 2004. 25 February 2005 <http://nhts.ornl.gov/2001/pub/STT.pdf>.

[23]Ibid.

[24]Ibid.

[25]Eudy, Leslie and Jarett Zuboy. Overview of Advance Technology Transportation, 2004 Update. Technical Report, National Renewable Energy Laboratory, Energy Efficiency and Renewable Energy, U.S. Department of Energy, 2004.

[26]United States. Department of Energy, Energy Information Administration. Alternatives to Traditional Transportation Fuels. Washington, DC, 2003.

[27]Eudy, Leslie and Jarett Zuboy. Overview of Advance Technology Transportation, 2004 Update. Technical Report, National Renewable Energy Laboratory, Energy Efficiency and Renewable Energy, U.S. Department of Energy, 2004.

[28]Davis, Stacy C. and Susan W. Diegel. Transportation Energy Data Book: Edition 24. Center for Transportation Analysis, Engineering Science & Technology Division, Oak Ridge National Laboratory. U.S. Department of Energy, 2004.

[29] United States. Department of Energy, Energy Information Administration. Annual Energy Review 2003. Report No. DOE/EIA-0384(2003). 1 March 2005 <http://www.eia.doe.gov/emeu/aer/contents.html>.

[30] Davis, Stacy C. and Susan W. Diegel. Transportation Energy Data Book: Edition

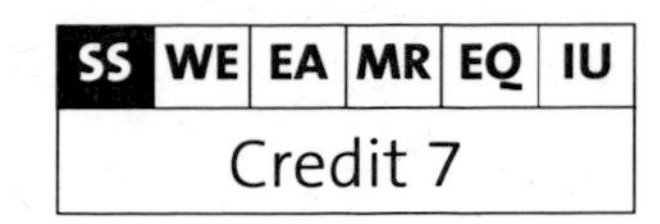

24. Center for Transportation Analysis, Engineering Science & Technology Division, Oak Ridge National Laboratory. U.S. Department of Energy, 2004.

[31] Hu, Patricia S., and Timothy R Reuscher. Prepared for the U.S Department of Transportation, Federal Highway Administration. Summary of Travel Trends: 2001 National Household Travel Survey December 2004. 25 February 2005 <http://nhts.ornl.gov/2001/pub/STT.pdf>.

[32] Ibid.

[33] Ibid.

[34] Peterson, Del and Jill Hough. Carpooling to NDSU. Upper Great Plains Transportation Institute. October 2003. 3 March 2005 <http://www.surtc.org/research/university/SP-156/index.html>.

[35]United States. Environmental Protection Agency, Research Triangle Park. Carpool Emissions and Gas Savings February 2005. 3 March 2005 <http://www.epa.gov/rtp/transportation/carpooling/emissions.htm>.

[36]Commute Solution: Telecommute. Mar 2005. SmartCommute. 3 March 2005. <http://www.smartcommute.org/Telecommute.htm>.

[37] United States. Environmental Protection Agency. Heat Island Effect February 2005. 1 March 2005 <http://www.epa.gov/heatisland/>.

[38] Lawrence Berkeley National Laboratory. Environmental Energy Technologies Division, Heat Island Group. Air Quality Apr 2000. 2 March 2005 <http://eetd.lbl.gov/HeatIsland/AirQuality/.>

[39] Lawrence Berkeley National Laboratory. Environmental Energy Technologies Division, Heat Island Group. Energy Use June 2000. 2 March 2005 <http://eetd.lbl.gov/heatisland/EnergyUse/>.

[40] United States. Environmental Protection Agency. Heat Island Reduction Initiative July 2001. 2 March 2005 <http://www.epa.gov/globalwarming/greenhouse/greenhouse14/reduction.html>.

[41]United States. Environmental Protection Agency. Heat Island Effect February 2005. 1 March 2005 <http://www.epa.gov/heatisland/>.

[42]Lawrence Berkeley National Laboratory. Environmental Energy Technologies Division, Heat Island Group. Air Quality Apr 2000. 2 March 2005. <http://eetd.lbl.gov/HeatIsland/AirQuality/.>

[43]Lawrence Berkeley National Laboratory. Environmental Energy Technologies Division, Heat Island Group. Energy Use June 2000. 2 March 2005. <http://eetd.lbl.gov/heatisland/EnergyUse/>.

[44]United States. Environmental Protection Agency. Heat Island Reduction Initiative July 2001. 2 March 2005 <http://www.epa.gov/globalwarming/greenhouse/greenhouse14/reduction.html>.

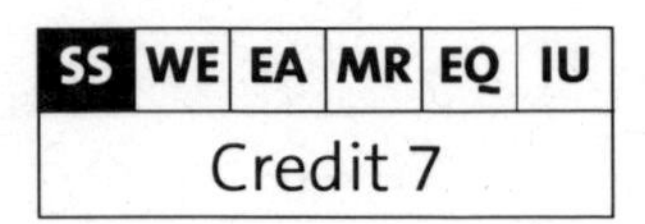
SS WE EA MR EQ IU
Credit 7

Water Efficiency

Americans' use of public supply water is increasing. The U.S. Geological Survey estimated that between 1990 and 2000, public supply water use increased 12 percent, to 43.3 billion gallons per day.[1] Public supply water is delivered to users for domestic, commercial, industrial and other purposes, and is the source of water for most water consumption in buildings. In 2000, these uses represented about 11 percent of total withdrawals and slightly less than 40 percent of groundwater withdrawals, comprising the third largest category of water use in the U.S., behind thermoelectric power (48 percent of total withdrawals) and irrigation (34 percent of total withdrawals). This high demand for water is straining supply stocks, and in some parts of the United States, water levels in underground aquifers have dropped more than 150 feet since the 1940s.[2]

Only about 14 percent of withdrawn water is consumed through evaporation, transpiration, or incorporation into products or crops; the rest is used, treated and discharged to the nation's water bodies.[3] Returned water contaminates rivers, lakes and drinking water with bacteria, nitrogen, toxic metals and other contaminants.[4] The U.S. Environmental Protection Agency (EPA) estimates that one-third of the nation's lakes, streams and rivers are now unsafe for swimming and fishing.[5]

On a positive note, water bodies in the United States are 50 percent cleaner[6] than in the mid- 1970s. And although public water supply consumption is rising, total U.S. water withdrawals declined by nearly 9 percent between 1980 and 1985, and have varied by less than 3 percent for each 5-year interval since then.[7] These achievements can be largely attributed to the Clean Water Act and reductions in industrial, irrigation and thermoelectric-power withdrawals since 1980. Although these statistics show improvement, we are still far from harvesting, using and discharging water sustainably.

Using large volumes of water increases maintenance and life cycle costs for building operations, and also increases consumer costs for additional municipal supply and treatment facilities. Conversely, facilities that use water efficiently can reduce costs through lower fees, less sewage volumes to treat, reductions in energy and chemical use, and lower capacity charges and limits. The LEED-EB Water Efficiency (WE) prerequisites and credits encourage the use of strategies and technologies that reduce the amount of potable water consumed in buildings. Many water conservation strategies are either no-cost or provide a rapid payback from more expensive water-conserving fixtures. Other water conservation strategies, such as biological wastewater treatment systems and graywater plumbing systems, often require more substantial investment and are only profitable under certain building and site conditions.

Efficiency measures can easily reduce water use in average commercial buildings by 30 percent or more.[8] In a typical 100,000-square-foot office building, low-flow fixtures coupled with sensors and automatic controls will save a minimum of 1 million gallons of water per year.[9] In addition, non-potable water volumes can be used for landscape irrigation, toilet and urinal flushing, custodial purposes and building systems. Depending on local water costs, utility savings can represent thousands of dollars per year, resulting in rapid payback on water conservation infrastructure. For example, the City of Seattle estimates that a 30 percent reduction in water use in a 100,000-square-foot office building saves $4,393 annually.[10]

Overview of LEED® Prerequisites and Credits

WE Prerequisite 1
Minimum Water Efficiency

WE Prerequisite 2
Discharge Water Compliance

WE Credit 1.1
Water Efficient Landscaping – Reduce Water Use by 50%

WE Credit 1.2
Water Efficient Landscaping – Reduce Water Use by 95%

WE Credit 2
Innovative Wastewater Technologies

WE Credit 3.1
Water Use Reduction – 10% Reduction

WE Credit 3.2
Water Use Reduction – 20% Reduction

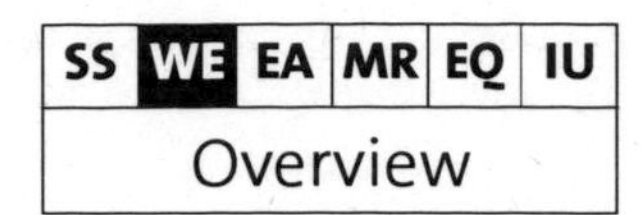
SS WE EA MR EQ IU
Overview

SS	WE	EA	MR	EQ	IU

Prerequisite 1

Required

Minimum Water Efficiency

Intent

Maximize fixture water efficiency within buildings to reduce the burden on potable water supply and wastewater systems.

Requirements

Reduce fixture potable water usage to a level equal to or below water use baseline, calculated as 120% of the water usage that would result if 100% of the total building fixture count were outfitted with plumbing fixtures that meet the Energy Policy Act of 1992 fixture performance requirements. If the building does not have separate metering for each water use (fixture use, process use, irrigation and other uses), the water use reduction achievements can be demonstrated with calculations. At least one meter for the overall building water use is required and metering for cooling towers and other process water uses are encouraged but not required.

Submittals – Initial Certification

- ❑ Provide documentation showing the baseline calculations. The baseline is calculated as 120% of the water usage that would result if 100% of the total building fixture count were outfitted with plumbing fixtures that meet the Energy Policy Act of 1992 fixture performance requirements.
- ❑ Demonstrate that the existing building fixture potable water use over the performance period is equal to or less than the baseline. Do this by providing annual water meter data for the performance period for potable water use inside the building OR by providing calculations, fixture cut sheets, and photographs.
- ❑ Provide calculations showing fixture potable water use per occupant and per square foot.

Submittals – Recertification

- ❑ If there has been no change to building potable water consumption relative to the 120% baseline since the previous LEED-EB filing:
  - Provide a statement that there has been no change.
  - Provide quarterly and annual fixture potable water meter data for water use inside the building showing that the annual potable water use is equal to or less than the calculated baseline over the performance period OR provide a statement confirming that the calculations, fixture cut sheets, and photographs initially submitted to demonstrate fixture potable water use are still valid.
- ❑ If there has been a change to building fixture potable water consumption relative to the 120% baseline, provide the same information as is required for initial LEED-EB filings.

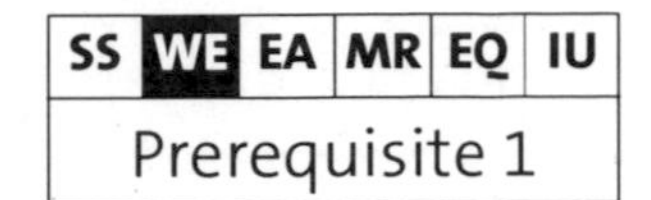

Summary of Referenced Standard

Energy Policy Act of 1992, Section 123 of Public Law 102–486

Publication 10CFR430.32 pages 266–273

U.S. Department of Energy (DOE)

www.doe.gov

(800) 363-3732

The Energy Policy Act of 1992 (EPAct) establishes minimum energy and water efficiency levels for many products. The EPAct standards relevant to LEED-EB set efficiency levels for plumbing fixture water usage performance. The types of plumbing fixtures that must be considered for establishing a LEED-EB water use baseline are listed in Subpart C – Energy and Water Conservation Standards of the act, and include: (o) Faucets, (p) Showerheads, (q) Water Closets, and (r) Urinals. **Table 1** below summarizes the standards for fixture water use.

To obtain a copy of EPAct, go to the U.S. Government Print Office (GPO) document retrieval web site (www.gpoaccess.gov/cfr/retrieve.html) or the following web link:

http://a257.g.akamaitech.net/7/257/2422/12feb20041500/edocket.access.gpo.gov/cfr_2004/janqtr/pdf/10cfr430.32.pdf

Green Building Concerns

The increasing demand on U.S. freshwater supplies creates the need for existing buildings to install plumbing fixtures that reduce potable water use. Less water consumption decreases the building's operating costs (i.e., water and sewer costs) and environmental impact. Reducing potable water consumption may require building upgrades such as installing more water-efficient fixtures, installing flow restrictors on existing fixtures, using electronic controls, installing dry fixtures such as composting toilet systems and non-water using urinals, and using graywater or collected rain water for non-potable applications.

Environmental Issues

Lower potable water use for toilets, showerheads, faucets and other fixtures reduces the total amount withdrawn from rivers, streams, underground aquifers and other water bodies. This conserves potable water and protects aquatic ecosystems. Reduced water consumption also minimizes the amount of water discharged to municipal water treatment facilities. Reduced volumes of discharge water require lower chemical inputs at treatment facilities and lessen the need for water supply and treatment infrastructure.

Water conservation also lowers energy use. Water heating in commercial buildings accounts for nearly 15 percent of

Table 1: Energy Policy Act of 1992 Standards for Plumbing Fixture Water Usage

Fixture	Energy Policy Act of 1992 Standards for Plumbing Fixture Water Use
Water Closets [gpf]	1.60
Urinals [gpf]	1.00
Shower Heads [gpm]*	2.50
Faucets [gpm]**	2.20
Faucet Replacement Aerators**	2.20
Metering Faucets [gal/cycle]	0.25

** When measured at a flowing water pressure of 80 pounds per square inch (psi).*
*** When measured at a flowing water pressure of 60 pounds per square inch (psi).*

building energy use.[11] For this reason, water conservation that reduces the use of hot water also conserves energy and reduces energy-related pollution.

Economic Issues

The cost of potable water use reduction measures in existing buildings varies widely. For example, installing tamper-proof faucet aerators is a small expense compared to rainwater harvest or gray-water systems. Different strategies are economical for different buildings, depending on location and building design. Water-conserving fixtures that meet the requirements of the EPAct are readily available. Most jurisdictions' building codes require new plumbing fixtures to comply with EPAct minimum requirements. Fixtures that exceed EPAct standards, including high-efficiency toilets and dry fixtures like composting toilet systems, often have higher initial costs than standard models. Finding a balance between reducing potable water use immediately and continually implementing additional water use reductions as practical opportunities become available is a good way to manage upgrade costs in existing buildings.

In the United States, potable water generally comes from large municipal water systems that rely on surface water (such as rivers, lakes and reservoirs) or wells that draw water out of underground aquifers. With increased demand on finite water resources, the price of water is expected to continually rise. Global climate change could also contribute to rising water costs, as altered precipitation patterns and an increased need for irrigation could further strain the water supply. Water conservation reduces building operating costs and insulates building owners from price increases, and also can lead to more stable municipal taxes and water rates. Reducing water demand at treatment facilities can delay the need for costly infrastructure expansion projects and help maintain stable prices.

In many buildings, the most significant savings associated with water reduction efforts stem from reduced energy and maintenance costs. Water efficiency saves energy by reducing the volumes of water heated or chilled. Building maintenance costs also decrease as water volumes are reduced.

Some municipalities have incentive programs to encourage water use reduction. These programs have become a cost-effective way for municipalities to defer, reduce or avoid capital costs of additional water supply and wastewater facilities. For example, New York City invested $393 million in a 1.6 GPF toilet replacement rebate program that has reduced water demand and wastewater flow by 90.6 million gallons per day (MGD), equal to 7 percent of the city's total water consumption. The rebate program accomplished net-present-value savings of $605 million from a 20-year deferral of water supply and wastewater treatment expansion projects.[12]

Strategies & Technologies

Follow the methodology outlined in the Calculations & Documentation section for this prerequisite to calculate a water use baseline that includes all plumbing fixtures required for building occupancy. Develop a water use inventory to identify significant potable water demands and determine methods to minimize or eliminate these demands to achieve water use below the calculated baseline. Strategies for reducing potable water consumption are described below and in WE Credit 3.1–3.2: Water Use Reduction. Examples of potential water use reduction actions include:

- ❑ Installing flow reduction aerators in faucets
- ❑ Installing automatic controls on lavatory faucets

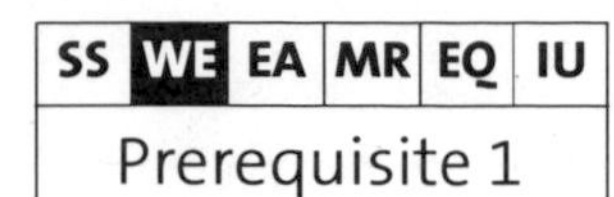

- Using graywater volumes captured from showers, sinks and lavatories for use in water closets
- Replacing conventional urinals used in male restrooms with high-efficiency urinals (HEUs)
- Replacing fixtures on lavatories and kitchen sinks with fixtures that use 1.8 gpm or less
- Replacing showerheads with high-efficiency showerheads that use 1.8 gpm or less
- Installing high-efficiency toilets (HETs) that reduce per-flush water consumption by 20 percent or more.

High-Efficiency Plumbing Fixtures

Install water-conserving plumbing fixtures that exceed the fixture requirements stated in the EPAct. Consider high-efficiency toilets (HETs) and urinals (HEUs), faucets, showers, and other fixtures. A variety of high-efficiency plumbing fixtures are currently available. Most can be installed and used the same way as conventional low-flow fixtures. **Tables 2 and 3** below show the ranges of efficiency in available plumbing fixtures.

Water closets use a significant amount of potable water. A number of water closets are available that use considerably less than 1.6 gpf, including pressure-assisted water closets at 1.0 gpf and dual-flush water closets that provide for "short flushes" (liquid only) of between 0.8 and 1.1 gpf and "long flushes" (liquid and solids) at 1.6 gpf. Actual water consumption, which includes water used by extra flushes needed because of inadequate

Table 2: Sample Flush Fixture Types

Flush Fixture Type	Water Use [gpf]
Conventional Low-Flow Toilet (Water Closet)	1.6
High-Efficiency Toilet (Water Closet)	Below 1.3*
Dual-Flush Toilet	0.8 to 1.1/1.6**
Composting Toilet	0.0
Conventional Low-Flow Urinal	1.0
High-Efficiency Urinal	0.5 or below***
Non-Water Consuming Urinal	0.0***

**High-efficiency toilets (HETs) include dual-flush toilets, 1.0-gpf pressure-assist toilets and 1.28-gpf gravity-fed single-flush toilets.*
*** Dual-flush toilets have an option of full flush (1.6 gal) or liquid-only flush (ranging between 0.8 gpf and 1.1 gpf, depending upon design). When calculating water use reductions from installation of these fixtures, use a composite (average) flush volume of 1.2 gpf.*
****High-efficiency urinals are currently available at 0.5 gpf and 0.0 gpf. Urinals at 0.25 gpf will be available in 2005.*

Table 3: Sample Flow Fixture Types

Flow Fixture Type	Water Use [gpm]
Conventional Low-Flow Lavatory Faucet	2.2
High-Efficiency Lavatory Faucet	1.8
Conventional Low-Flow Kitchen Sink Faucet	2.2
High-Efficiency Kitchen Sink Faucet	1.8
Conventional Low-Flow Showerhead	2.5
High-Efficiency Showerhead	2.0 and below
Low-Flow Janitor Sink Faucet	2.5
Low-Flow Hand Wash Fountain	0.5
Conventional Low Flow Self Closing Faucet	0.25 gals./cycle
High Efficiency Self Closing Faucet	0.2 gals./cycle and below

performance, can only be determined by sub-metering.

Water-efficient showerheads are also available that require less than 2.5 gpm. Bathroom faucets and fixtures typically used only for wetting purposes can be effective with as little as 1.0 gpm. Some water-saving faucet aerators do not change the feel of the water flow and can be installed for a fraction of the cost of new fixtures.

Communication with Building Occupants

Water-efficient fixtures must be used correctly to capitalize on their water-saving potential. Communicating with building occupants about water conservation goals, water-saving features, and the overall function of building water systems will maximize the benefits of the upgrades. Consider posting signs that educate users on the proper way to operate fixtures. This is especially important for technologies that function differently than conventional models, such as low-flow fixtures, dual-flush toilets, composting toilet systems or fixtures that deliver non-potable water

Other Options

Automatic sensors, non-water using urinals, composting toilet systems and use of graywater or harvest rainwater can also contribute to achieving this prerequisite. More information on these technologies can be found under WE Credit 2 and WE Credit 3.1–3.2.

Synergies & Tradeoffs

Water and energy efficiency are related, so consider the energy implications of water-efficiency improvements. For example, installing low-flow faucets or showers will not only save water, but also will reduce the amount of water to heat.

Water use reduction strategies for existing buildings depend on the existing fixtures and systems, as well as the physical constraints of the building and site. Reduction strategies also depend on financial constraints that limit how quickly investments can be made to conserve water. Some technologies, such as graywater or rainwater collection, may not be economically feasible in an existing building unless extensive remodeling is taking place.

WE Credit 2: Innovative Wastewater Technologies and WE Credits 3.1–3.2: Water Use Reduction provide opportunities for earning points and additional information on potable water reduction measures in buildings.

Calculations & Documentation

Calculations

Calculate the Fixture Water Use Baseline

The LEED-EB Calculated Water Use Baseline is developed as follows, and is used for WE Prerequisite 1, WE Credit 2 and WE Credit 3.

1. Create a spreadsheet (see LEED-EB Letter Templates) listing each type of water-using plumbing fixture and data concerning frequency of use. Frequency data must assume that:
   - The ratio of males to females is 50:50 unless specifically documented otherwise.
   - Female building occupants use water closets three times daily.
   - Male occupants use water closets once and urinals twice daily.
   - All occupants use faucets for 15 seconds three times daily.
   - If there are showers in the building, 10 percent of building occupants use shower facilities for 5 minutes per day.

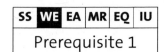

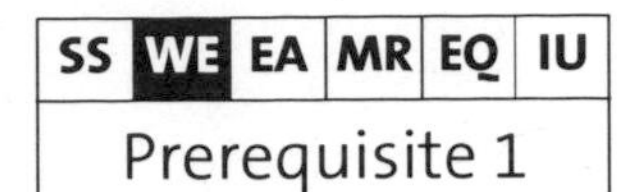

Use EPAct fixture flow rates or fixture water usage for each fixture type in the baseline case (see **Table 1**). With these values, calculate the total potable water used for each fixture type and gender (see **Equation 1**).

2. Sum all of the water volumes used for each fixture type to obtain male and female total daily potable water use.
3. Multiply male and female potable water volumes by the number of male and female building occupants and sum these volumes to obtain the daily total potable water use volume (see **Equation 2**).
4. Multiply total daily potable water volume by the number of workdays in a typical year to obtain the total annual potable water volume use for the building (see **Equation 3**).
5. Multiply the total annual potable water use volume for the building (calculated in Equation 3 above) by 120 percent to get the Calculated Water Use Baseline for fixture water use in the building.

Table 4: Calculated Water Use Baseline Example

Flush Fixture	Daily Uses	Flowrate [gpf]	Duration [flush]	Auto Controls	Occupants	Water Use [gal]
EPAct Equivalent Water Closet (Male)	1	1.6	1	N/A	150	240
EPAct Equivalent Water Closet (Female)	3	1.6	1	N/A	150	720
EPAct Equivalent Urinal (Male)	2	1.0	1	N/A	150	300
EPAct Equivalent Urinal (Female)	0	1.0	1	N/A	150	0
Flow Fixture	**Daily Uses**	**Flowrate [gpm]**	**Duration [sec]**	**Auto Controls**	**Occupants**	**Water Use [gal]**
Conventional Lavatory	3	2.2	15	N/A	300	495
Kitchen Sink	1	2.2	15	N/A	300	165
Shower	0.1	2.5	300	N/A	300	375
					Total Daily Volume [gal]	2,295
					Annual Work Days	260
					Total Annual Volume [gal]	**596,700**
					Multiply by 120%	**1.2**
					Calculated Water Use Baseline	**716,040**

Equation 1

Potable Water Use per Fixture per Gender [gal] = Daily Uses x Duration [minutes or flushes] x (Water Volume [gal] / Use [min or flush])

Equation 2

Daily Potable Water Volume [gal] = (Male Occupants x Male Water Use [gal]) + (Female Occupants x Water Use [gal])

Equation 3

Total Potable Water Use [gal] = (Water Use [gal]/Occupant Day [day] x Occupants) x Workdays/Year

Table 4 illustrates a potable water use baseline calculation for a two-story office building with 300 occupants. Fixtures using potable water include water closets, urinals, lavatories, kitchen sinks and showers. Calculations are based on a typical 8-hour workday and 260 workdays per year. In the calculation of the baseline, all fixtures are assumed to be standard fixtures that comply with the Energy Policy Act of 1992 (EPAct). Also, the baseline assumes no use of automatic sensors or reuse of graywater. This example uses the required assumptions listed at the beginning of this section and estimates an Annual Baseline Potable Water Use of 716,040 gallons. An example of further reductions in potable water use is included in WE Credits 3.1–3.2.

Determine Fixture Water Use

Determine fixture water use through metering data (preferred for WE Prerequisite 1 and WE Credit 3.1, mandatory for WE Credit 3.2) or through calculations similar to those used in establishing the baseline. This second method can be used to earn WE Prerequisite 1 and WE Credit 3.1, but not WE Credit 3.2.

Method A: Determine Fixture Water Use with Metering Data

If the building has separate metering for fixture use, use these data to compare fixture water use to the calculated baseline.

If the building does not have separate metering for fixture water use, but does have metering for all non-fixture water uses (for example, process, HVAC and irrigation loads) and total water use, calculate the building's actual annual fixture water use with **Equation 4**. Water used in cooling towers is considered process water.

Method B: Calculate Fixture Water Use Based on Fixture Flow Rates

If there is insufficient metering in the building to use Method A, calculate fixture water use with a table similar to the baseline calculation example (Table 4). This alternate methodology can be used to earn this prerequisite and WE Credit 3.1, but not the additional point from WE Credit 3.2. Calculate fixture water use based on fixture flow rates with these guidelines in mind:

- ❑ Instead of using flow rates consistent with the Energy Policy Act of 1992, use actual building fixture flow rates or water usage based on the manufacturer's flow rate listed on the fixture.
- ❑ Assumptions about fixture use frequency should remain consistent with those used in calculating the baseline.
- ❑ Unlike the baseline calculation, the fixture water use figure calculated should not be multiplied by 120 percent.
- ❑ For buildings with multiple fixture models with different flow rates, the flow rate entered into the table should be the weighted average flow rate for that fixture type. To calculate the weighted average flow rate, use **Equation 5**.
- ❑ Subtract any graywater volumes delivered to fixtures from the total fixture water use to determine the potable water used by fixtures.

Equation 4

Total Annual Fixture Volume [gal] =
Total Measured Water Use for Building and Site [gal] – (Measured Process Water Use [gal] + Measured Irrigation Water Use [gal] + Other Measured Non-fixture Water Use [gal])

Equation 5

Weighted Average Flow Rate =
[(Quantity Model A x Flow Rate Model A) + (Quantity Model B x Flow Rate Model B)] / (Quantity Fixture Model A + Quantity Fixture Model B)

Table 5: Calculated Weighted Average Flow Rates Example

Flush Fixture	Model A		Model B		Weighted Average Flow Rate [gpf]
	Quantity	Flow Rate [gpf]	Quantity	Flow Rate [gpf]	
Water Closet (Male)	4	1.6	2	4.5	2.57
Water Closet (Female)	12	1.6	2	4.5	2.01
	Model A		Model B		
Flow Fixture	Quantity	Flow Rate [gpm]	Quantity	Flow Rate [gpm]	Weighted Average Flow Rate [gpm]
Lavatory	6	2.2	8	1.8	1.97

Table 6: Calculated Fixture Water Use Example

Flush Fixture	Daily Uses	Flowrate [gpf]	Duration [flush]	Auto Controls	Occupants	Water Use [gal]
Weighted Average Water Closet (Male)	1	2.57	1	N/A	150	385.50
Weighted Average Water Closet (Female)	3	2.01	1	N/A	150	904.50
Conventional Urinal (Male)	2	1.00	1	N/A	150	300.00
Conventional Urinal (Female)	0	1.00	1	N/A	150	0.00
Flow Fixture	**Daily Uses**	**Flowrate [gpm]**	**Duration [sec]**	**Auto Controls**	**Occupants**	**Water Use [gal]**
Weighted Average Lavatory	3	1.97	15	N/A	300	443.25
Kitchen Sink	1	2.2	15	N/A	300	165
Shower	0.1	2.5	300	N/A	300	375
					Total Daily Volume [gal]	2,573.25
					Annual Work Days	260
(A) Total Annual Fixture Volume [gal]						**669,045**
(B) Total Annual Graywater Fixture Volume [gal]						**0**
(C) Total Annual Potable Fixture Volume [gal] (Line A – Line B)						**669,045**
(D) Calculated Water Use Baseline						**716,040**

Table 5 and **Table 6** below provide a summary for calculating weighted average flow rates and calculating fixture water use based on fixture flow rates.

Compare Fixture Water Use to Calculated Water Use Baseline

If the building's total annual fixture volume is less than the calculated water use baseline, the building meets WE Prerequisite 1.

Calculate Fixture Potable Water Use per Occupant and per Square Foot

Calculate the total fixture water use per building occupant and per square foot, using the fixture use figures calculated above and **Equations 6 and 7**. This information is used for comparing LEED-certified buildings and guiding future metrics for the LEED-EB program.

Equation 6

Fixture Water Use per Occupant [gal] = Total Fixture Water Use [gal] / # of Building Occupants

Equation 7

Fixture Water Use per Square Foot = Total Fixture Water Use [gal] / Building Area [SF]

Documentation

All information needed to successfully document this credit can be found in the Submittals section of the LEED-EB Rating System and the LEED-EB Letter Templates.

Other Resources

Smart Communities Network

www.sustainable.doe.gov/efficiency/weinfo.shtml

This U.S. Department of Energy project provides information about water efficiency and national and regional water efficiency assistance programs, and links to additional resources.

Water Closet Performance Testing

www.ebmud.com/conserving_&_recycling/toilet_test_report/NAHBRC%20Toilet%20Report.pdf

This report summarizes findings of the NAHB Research Center on the performance, reliability and water efficiency of a variety of different toilets. Report No.: P01-1660902. September 2002.

Water Efficiency Manual for Commercial, Industrial and Institutional Facilities

www.p2pays.org/ref/01/00692.pdf

Several North Carolina government departments collaborated on this straightforward manual on water efficiency.

Water Measurement Manual: A Water Resources Technical Publication

www.usbr.gov/pmts/hydraulics_lab/pubs/wmm/

This U.S. Department of the Interior publication is a guide to effective water measurement practices for better water management.

Water Wiser: The Water Efficiency Clearinghouse

www.awwa.org/waterwiser

(800) 926-7337

This web clearinghouse provides articles, reference materials and papers on all forms of water efficiency.

Water Use Efficiency Program

www.epa.gov/owm/water-efficiency

This web site provides an overview of the U.S. EPA's Water Use Efficiency Program and information about using water more efficiently.

Definitions

Blackwater does not have a single definition that is accepted nationwide. Wastewater from toilets and urinals is always considered blackwater. Wastewater from kitchen sinks (perhaps differentiated by the use of a garbage disposal), showers, or bathtubs may be considered blackwater by state or local codes. Project teams should comply with blackwater definition as established by the authority having jurisdiction in their areas.

Composting toilet systems are dry plumbing fixtures that contain and treat human waste via microbiological processes.

Fixture sensors are motion sensors that automatically turn on/off lavatories, sinks, water closets and urinals.

Graywater is defined by the Uniform Plumbing Code (UPC) in its Appendix G, titled "Gray Water Systems for Single-

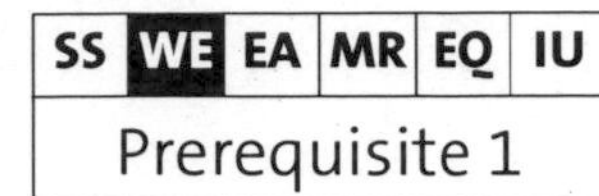

Family Dwellings" as "untreated household waste water which has not come into contact with toilet waste. Grey water includes used water from bathtubs, showers, bathroom wash basins, and water from clothes-washer and laundry tubs. It shall not include waste water from kitchen sinks or dishwashers." The International Plumbing Code (IPC) defines graywater in its Appendix C, titled "Gray Water Recycling Systems" as "waste water discharged from lavatories, bathtubs, showers, clothes washers, and laundry sinks." Some states and local authorities allow kitchen sink wastewater to be included in graywater. Other differences with the UPC and IPC definitions can probably be found in state and local codes. Project teams should comply with graywater definitions as established by the authority having jurisdiction in their areas.

Potable water is water that is suitable for drinking and is supplied from wells or municipal water systems.

Process water is water used for industrial processes and building systems such as cooling towers, boilers and chillers.

A **non-water using urinal** is a urinal that uses no water, but instead replaces the water flush with a specially designed trap that contains a layer of buoyant liquid that floats above the urine layer, blocking sewer gas and urine odors from the room.

SS **WE** EA MR EQ IU

Prerequisite 2

Required

Discharge Water Compliance

Intent

Protect natural habitat, waterways and water supply from pollutants carried by building discharge water.

Requirements

Option A

If regulated by EPA National Pollution Discharge Elimination System (NPDES) Clean Water Act requirements, demonstrate NPDES permit compliance including use of any required oil separators, grease interceptors and other filtration for in-building generated discharges and proper disposal of any wastes collected.

Option B

If the facility is not regulated by a NPDES Permit, this prerequisite is achieved.

Submittals – Initial Certification

Option A

- ❑ If regulated by the EPA NPDES Clean Water Act requirements, provide documentation demonstrating ongoing NPDES permit compliance and ongoing discharge monitoring reporting (DMR) over the performance period being reported.

Option B

- ❑ Provide a letter of confirmation that the facility is not regulated by the EPA NPDES Clean Water Act requirements.

Submittals – Recertification

Option A

- ❑ If regulated by the EPA NPDES Clean Water Act requirements, provide documentation demonstrating ongoing NPDES permit compliance and ongoing discharge monitoring reporting (DMR) over the year being reported.

Option B

- ❑ Provide a letter of reconfirmation that the facility is not regulated by the EPA NPDES Clean Water Act requirements.

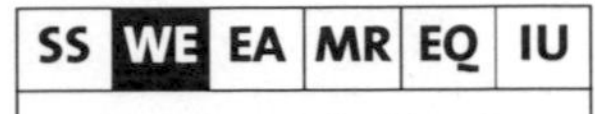

Summary of Referenced Standard

National Pollution Discharge Elimination System (NPDES)

U.S. Environmental Protection Agency

www.epa.gov

(202) 564-2051

The National Pollutant Discharge Elimination System (NPDES) permit program is part of the Clean Water Act. It controls water pollution by regulating point sources that discharge pollutants into U.S. waters. Industrial, municipal and other facilities must obtain permits if their discharges go directly into surface waters. In most cases, authorized states administer the NPDES permit program, but the EPA still retains oversight responsibilities. Since its introduction, the NPDES permit program has significantly improved U.S. water quality. Information about the NPDES Program can be found at: http://cfpub.epa.gov/npdes.

Green Building Concerns

The discharge of water from buildings into ground or surface water can cause pollution. Because of the importance of controlling discharge water, the Clean Water Act prohibits discharging "pollutants" through a "point source" into "water of the United States." NPDES permits allow exemptions from the Clean Water Act in certain circumstances. An NPDES permit defines limits on what can be discharged, requirements for monitoring and reporting compliance with the permit, and other provisions for controlling discharge.[13]

Depending on the facility, one or more NPDES programs may apply. The number of facilities required to have a permit is expected to grow as the scope of the NPDES program expands.[14] For example, requirements implemented in 2003 mean that stormwater runoff from roofs, parking lots and construction sites may require a permit under the NPDES stormwater program, particularly if the runoff discharges directly to a water body. In general, standard commercial buildings that comply with local stormwater treatment requirements will not require significant effort to comply with NPDES rules and, in many cases, will not be regulated by NPDES. Industrial facilities may more likely fall under NPDES jurisdiction.

LEED-EB applicants should check with their state or municipality to confirm stormwater and other NPDES permit requirements.

Environmental Issues

Contaminant discharge and runoff from parking lots, construction sites and industrial facilities can contain pollutants such as sediment, debris and chemicals. Polluted stormwater runoff can cause stream bank erosion and harm or kill fish and other wildlife, and sedimentation can destroy aquatic habitat.[15] Pollutants regulated in the NPDES program include conventional pollutants (such as BOD5, total suspended solids, pH, fecal coliform, and oil and grease), toxic pollutants, and non-conventional pollutants (additional substances that require such regulation, such as ammonia, nitrogen, and phosphorus).

When the NPDES permit program was implemented in 1972, only one-third of all U.S. rivers, lakes and coastal waters were safe for fishing and swimming. Today, two-thirds of them, or approximately twice as many as in 1972, are considered healthy. More than 50 categories of industry (including several hundred thousand businesses) and the nation's network of more than 16,000 municipal sewage treatment systems comply with the NPDES permit standards. These permits have resulted in the removal of billions of pounds of conventional pollutants and millions of pounds of toxic pollutants annually.[16]

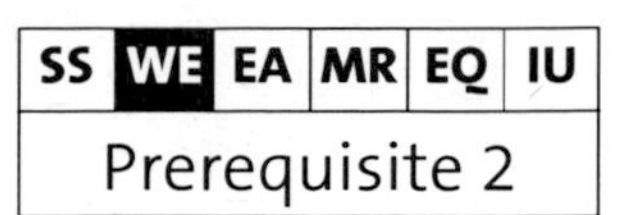

Economic Issues

Minimizing the amount of pollutants discharged into public waters ensures that clean water remains accessible, reducing and stabilizing the probable cost of potable water in the future. Clean water is also important for recreation and other industries, and keeps property values from falling due to polluted water. Observance of NPDES regulations prevents criminal and civil fines and other liabilities resulting from noncompliance.

Strategies & Technologies

NPDES Permit Acquisition or Renewal

If the building is not currently regulated by an NPDES permit, determine if discharge activities on the building site require a permit. If the building currently holds an NPDES permit, verify that the permit covers all pollutants discharged from the site, no additional permits are necessary, and the permit is valid. If necessary, apply for or renew the appropriate NPDES permits. If the building site does not require a permit, provide documentation to that effect and take no further action. The following guidelines on NPDES permits are from the *NPDES Permit Program Basics: Frequently Asked Questions*:[17]

Do I need an NPDES permit?

It depends on where you discharge pollutants.

- ❑ If you discharge from a point source into the waters of the United States, you need an NPDES permit.
- ❑ If you discharge pollutants into a municipal sanitary sewer system, you do not need an NPDES permit, but you should ask the municipality about their permit requirements.
- ❑ If you discharge pollutants into a municipal storm sewer system, you may need a permit depending on what you discharge. You should ask the NPDES permitting authority.

What is a pollutant?

The term pollutant is defined very broadly in the Clean Water Act because it has been through 25 years of litigation. It includes any type of industrial, municipal, and agricultural waste discharged into water. Some examples are dredged soil, solid waste, incinerator residue, sewage, garbage, sewage sludge, munitions, chemical wastes, biological materials, radioactive materials, heat, wrecked or discarded equipment, rock, sand, cellar dirt and industrial, municipal, and agricultural waste. By law, a pollutant is not sewage or discharges incidental to the normal operation of an Armed Forces vessel, or water, gas, or other materials injected into an oil and gas production well.

Where do I apply for a NPDES permit?

NPDES permits are issued by states that have obtained EPA approval to issue permits or by the EPA Regions in states without such approval.

Typically, how long are NPDES permits effective?

The Clean Water Act limits the length of NPDES permits to five years. NPDES permits can be renewed (reissued) at any time after the permit holder applies. In addition, NPDES permits can be administratively extended if the facility reapplies more than 180 days before the permit expires, and EPA or the state regulatory agency, which ever issued the original permit, agrees to extend the permit.

Permit Compliance

For facilities regulated by the NPDES requirements, control and monitor pollutant discharge levels as mandated by the permit. The permit held by a facility specifies an acceptable level of a pollutant or pollutant parameter and the sampling procedures necessary to demonstrate com-

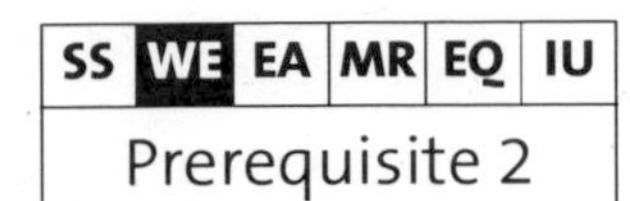

pliance. Ensure pollutants are maintained below the level stated in the permit and that discharge is monitored in a manner that conforms to the regulations. Strategies for maintaining pollutant discharge at the permitted level depend on the nature and source of the pollutant(s) being discharged. Some permits may contain generic "best management practices," such as installing a screen over discharge pipes to keep debris out of the waterway.

Below is a summary of permit compliance enforcement as described in *NPDES Permit Program Basics: Frequently Asked Questions*:[18]

How are the conditions in NPDES permits enforced by EPA and the states?

There are various methods used to monitor NPDES permit conditions. The permit will require the facility to sample its discharges and notify EPA and the state regulatory agency of these results. In addition, the permit will require the facility to notify EPA and the state regulatory agency when the facility determines it is not in compliance with the requirements of a permit. EPA and state regulatory agencies also will send inspectors to companies in order to determine if they are in compliance with the conditions imposed under their permits.

Federal laws provide EPA and authorized state regulatory agencies with various methods of taking enforcement actions against violators of permit requirements. For example, EPA and state regulatory agencies may issue administrative orders which require facilities to correct violations and that assess monetary penalties. The laws also allow EPA and state agencies to pursue civil and criminal actions that may include mandatory injunctions or penalties, as well as jail sentences for persons found willfully violating requirements and endangering the health and welfare of the public or environment. Equally important is how the general public can enforce permit conditions. The facility monitoring reports are public documents, and the general public can review them. If any member of the general public finds that a facility is violating its NPDES permit, that member can independently start a legal action, unless EPA or the state regulatory agency has taken an enforcement action.

Additional Information

Many different types of NPDES permits regulate pollutant discharge, and requirements vary by location. For information on whom to contact for more information about NPDES permits in your state, visit http://cfpub.epa.gov/npdes/stateinfo.cfm.

Additional NPDES program information can be found on the NPDES Permit Program Basics – Regulations web site (http://cfpub.epa.gov/npdes/regs.cfm?program_id=45) and in the EPA document *Protecting the Nation's Waters Through Effective NPDES Permits* (http://www.epa.gov/npdes/pubs/strategicplan.pdf).

Synergies & Tradeoffs

Compliance with NPDES regulations may have some associated costs; however, it prevents environmental degradation and fines that may result from failing to receive a permit.

Facilities regulated by the NPDES Stormwater Program should consider the synergies between compliance activities and SS Prerequisite 1: Erosion and Sedimentation Control and SS Credit 5: Stormwater Management.

Calculations & Documentation

Calculations

None.

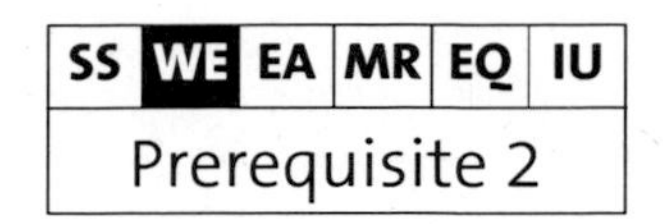

Documentation

- ❑ Option A: Demonstrate ongoing NPDES compliance and discharge monitoring reporting
  - Provide a copy of the NPDES permit(s) for the facility
  - Provide copies of all documents submitted over the performance period to the EPA NPDES program demonstrating compliance with the permit requirements. If no such documentation has been submitted to the EPA during the LEED-EB performance period, provide a copy of the most recent submittal to the EPA.
  - Provide narrative descriptions and/or schematic drawings of the pollution discharge control techniques and monitoring procedures employed on the site.
- ❑ Option B: Provide a letter confirming that an NPDES permit is not required for the facility
  - This letter should be signed by the responsible officer of the organization and appear on organization letterhead.

Other Resources

Low Impact Development (LID) Center

www.lowimpactdevelopment.org

(301) 982-5559

The LID Center is a nonprofit organization dedicated to protecting water resources by promoting site development techniques that replicate pre-existing hydrologic site conditions. The Resources section of the LID Center web site provides information about techniques for meeting regulatory requirements and water protection goals for site retrofits, redevelopment projects and new development sites.

Water Permits Division Strategic Plan

www.epa.gov/npdes/pubs/strategicplan.pdf

This plan provides an analysis of the past, present and future of the NPDES permit program.

Definitions

A **point source** is a discrete conveyance of a pollutant, such as a pipe or man-made ditch. As stated in the NPDSES Permit Program Basics: Frequently Asked Questions[19], a point source is "any discernible, confined and discrete conveyance, such as a pipe, ditch, channel, tunnel, conduit, discrete fissure, or container."

Pollutants include "any type of industrial, municipal, and agricultural waste discharged into water.[20]" Those regulated in the NPDES program include conventional pollutants (such as BOD5, total suspended solids, pH, fecal coliform, and oil and grease), toxic pollutants (such as metals and manmade compounds), and non-conventional pollutants (such as ammonia, nitrogen, phosphorus). The definition of "pollutant" as it pertains to the Clean Water Act and NDPES permitting is subject to change based on ongoing litigation and increased understanding about the environmental affects of discharged substances. An agent of the NPDES should be consulted regarding the pollutant status of discharge from specific buildings.

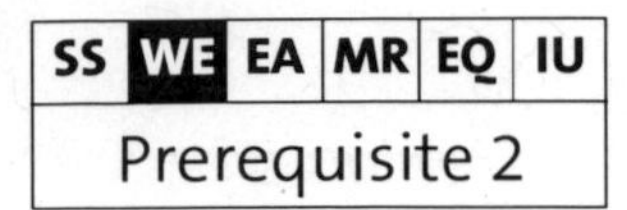
SS
WE
EA
MR
EQ
IU
Prerequisite 2

SS WE EA MR EQ IU

Credits 1.1 & 1.2

1–2 Points

Water Efficient Landscaping

Reduce Water Use

Intent

Limit or eliminate the use of potable water for landscape irrigation.

Requirements

Use high-efficiency irrigation technology, captured rain/recycled site water, or landscaping and other techniques to reduce potable water consumption for irrigation in comparison to conventional means of irrigation. If the building does not have separate metering for each water use (fixture use, process use, irrigation and other uses), the water use reduction achievements can be demonstrated with calculations. At least one meter for the overall building water use is required and metering for cooling towers and other process water use is encouraged but not required. In urban settings, where there is no lawn, credits can be earned by reducing the use of potable water for watering any roof/courtyard garden space or outdoor planters.

- ❑ WE Credit 1.1: 50% reduction in potable water use for irrigation over conventional means of irrigation. (1 point)
- ❑ WE Credit 1.2: 95% reduction in potable water use for irrigation over conventional means of irrigation. (1 point)

Submittals – Initial Certification

- ❑ Provide a brief narrative description, system schematics, photographs and calculations or meter readings demonstrating how much potable water use for irrigation is reduced in comparison to conventional means of irrigation. The head of facility management for the facility is required to sign off on the calculation of reduction in the amount of potable water used for irrigation.
- ❑ Provide a description of the type of irrigation system that is "conventional" in the area and the extent that the conventional type of irrigation system is used in the area.
- ❑ Provide quarterly reports over the performance period that document the maintenance activities implemented to ensure proper operation of the irrigation system.

Submittals – Recertification

- ❑ If there has been no change to the irrigation system or organizational policy regarding landscape irrigation:
  - Provide a letter stating that there has been no change.
  - Provide quarterly water meter readings for the performance period demonstrating how much the potable water use for irrigation is reduced in comparison to conventional means of irrigation OR provide a statement confirming that the calculations initially submitted to demonstrate irrigation water use are still valid OR update these calculations if conditions have changed.
  - Provide quarterly reports for the performance period that document the maintenance activities implemented to ensure proper operation of the irrigation system.

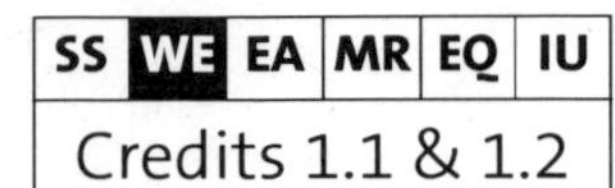

OR

- ❑ If there has been a change to the irrigation system or organizational policy regarding landscape irrigation, provide a brief narrative description, system schematics, photographs and calculations demonstrating how much potable water use for irrigation is reduced in comparison to conventional means of irrigation.

  The head of facility management for the facility is required to sign off on the calculation of reduction in the amount of potable water used for irrigation.

- ❑ Provide quarterly reports over the performance period, that document the maintenance activities implemented to ensure proper operation of the irrigation system.

Summary of Referenced Standard

There is no standard referenced for this credit.

Green Building Concerns

Landscape irrigation practices in the United States consume large quantities of potable water. Outdoor uses, primarily landscaping, account for 30 percent of the 26 billion gallons of water consumed daily in the United States.[21] Improved landscaping practices can dramatically reduce and even eliminate irrigation needs. Maintaining or reestablishing native plants on building sites fosters a self-sustaining landscape that requires minimal supplemental water and provides other environmental benefits.

Improved irrigation systems can also reduce water consumption. Irrigation typically uses potable water, although non-potable water (e.g., rainwater, graywater or reclaimed water) is equally effective. Irrigation system efficiency varies widely, and high-efficiency irrigation systems can also reduce potable water consumption. For example, high-efficiency drip irrigation systems can be 95 percent efficient, while sprinkler or spray irrigation systems are only 60 to 70 percent efficient.[22]

Environmental Issues

Reduction in the amount of potable water used for irrigation lessens demand on limited supplies. Since landscape irrigation uses large amounts of potable water, it is an important opportunity to reduce overall consumption.

Native landscaping can reduce the amount of water needed for irrigation while also attracting native wildlife and creating a building site integrated with its natural surroundings. In addition, native plants tend to require less fertilizer and pesticides, and thus reduce water quality degradation and other environmental impacts.

Economic Issues

Currently, the most effective strategy to avoid escalating water costs for irrigation is to design landscaping adapted to the local climate and the site's microclimate. The cost can be reduced or eliminated through thoughtful planning and careful plant selection and layout. Native plants further reduce operating costs because they require less fertilizer and maintenance than turf grass.

Although the additional design cost for a drip irrigation system may make it more expensive than a conventional system, a drip system usually costs less to install and has lower water use and maintenance requirements. This usually leads to a very short payback period. Many municipalities offer rebates or incentives for water-efficient irrigation systems, dedicated water meters and rain or moisture sensors.

Strategies & Technologies

Landscaping Choices

Design landscaping with climate-tolerant plants that can survive on natural rainfall quantities after initial establishment. Contour the land to direct stormwater runoff through the site to give vegetation an additional water supply. Minimize the amount of site area covered with turf, and use techniques such as mulching, alternative mowing and composting to maintain plant health. These practices conserve water and help foster optimal soil conditions.

Perform a soil and climate analysis to determine which plants will adapt best to the site's soil and climate, and specify plants most suitable to site conditions. Use evapotranspiration data and crop coefficients to determine which plants to use or to budget irrigation water demand for existing plants. A landscape with a variety of indigenous plants may not require watering while contributing to the aesthetic beauty of the site.

Research the lifetime water requirements of landscaping plants, as they may change as the plant matures or the seasons change. The water needs of plants usually decrease significantly once their root systems are established, and it is important that irrigation techniques are adjusted to reflect these changes. Over-watering plants not only wastes water, but can also damage the plants.

Efficient Irrigation Policies and Practices

Efficient irrigation practices and policies can significantly reduce the amount of water needed for irrigation without replacing current systems. For example, installing and monitoring dedicated meters for irrigation can allow better water budgeting and help landscaping staff detect leaks or other problems. Checking ground moisture levels and the weather report and adjusting irrigation activities can also save a significant amount of water.

Compile and follow a seasonal maintenance schedule to optimize a healthy landscape. The schedule should address specific times for pruning, watering and inspecting for pests. Address seasonal changes in irrigation requirements, since most plants do not need as much water in winter. A simple way to increase the efficiency of a conventional system is to schedule watering early or late in the day, when evaporation is minimal. This allows more water to soak into the ground and reach the roots of the plants. Irrigation systems and controllers should be commissioned to ensure they are working optimally. This includes inspecting, maintaining and adjusting the systems on a regular basis.

Advanced and High-Efficiency Irrigation Systems

High-efficiency irrigation systems include micro or drip irrigation systems, moisture sensors, clock timers and weather-data based controllers. These systems are widely available and more water-efficient than conventional systems. Drip systems apply water slowly and directly to the roots of plants, using 30 to 50 percent less water than sprinkler irrigation.[23] Moisture and rain sensors save water by ensuring that plants only receive water when necessary.

Non-Potable Water Use

A rainwater collection system can significantly reduce or completely eliminate the amount of potable water used for irrigation. Rainwater can be collected from roofs, plazas and paved areas and then filtered by combination of graded screens and paper filters to prepare it for use in irrigation. Filtration needs should be determined based on collector surface, potential pollutants and jurisdictional requirements. Metal, clay or concrete-based roofing materials are ideal for rainwater harvest, as asphalt or lead-containing materials will contaminate the water. Rainwater with high mineral content or acidity may damage systems or plantings, but pollutants can be filtered out by soil or mechanical systems prior to being used by plantings. It is important to check local rainfall quantity and quality, as collection systems may be inappropriate in areas with rainfall of poor quality or low quantity.

Graywater can also be used for irrigation purposes to reduce potable water consumption. Graywater consists of wastewater from sinks, showers and washing machines; cooling tower bleed down water; condensation from air conditioning systems; and other building activities that do not involve human waste or food processing. These graywater volumes can be filtered and stored in a tank on the site prior to use for irrigation.

Synergies & Tradeoffs

Successful water-efficient landscaping depends on site location and design. It is advantageous to couple landscape improvements with water use reduction strategies. The use of native plants can reduce site maintenance needs. Landscape plantings can mitigate climate conditions and reduce building energy consumption, for example by shading south-facing windows. Vegetation can aid passive solar design, serve as a windbreak, provide pleasant views for building occupants and muffle off-site noise. Indigenous plantings can restore habitat for native wildlife.

In addition to reducing potable water consumption, rainwater capture systems can be used to manage stormwater runoff. Using graywater for irrigation reduces the amount of wastewater delivered to water treatment facilities.

LEED-EB prerequisites and credits related to these issues include:

- ❑ SS Prerequisite 1: Erosion and Sedimentation Control
- ❑ SS Credit 1: Plan for Green Site and Building Exterior Management
- ❑ SS Credit 4: Reduced Site Disturbance
- ❑ SS Credit 5: Stormwater Management
- ❑ EA Prerequisite 2 and Credit 1: Energy Performance
- ❑ IEQ Credit 8.1–8.4: Daylighting and Views

Calculations & Documentation

Calculations

The calculations for WE Credit 1 consist of establishing a baseline of average irrigation volumes in your area and then comparing irrigation volumes on the project site to that baseline.

Calculating Baseline Irrigation Water Use

Calculate Baseline Irrigation Water Use by determining the water use that would result from using an irrigation system typical of your region. Use the following steps to develop the baseline for your site.

1. Identify Conventional Irrigation Systems

   Determine which irrigation systems are commonly used in the area for sites with standard landscaping, such as turf grass and other common landscaping features. To find this information, survey facility managers of nearby building sites or contact an irrigation specialist that services and operates irrigation systems in the area. If your building site used conventional practices prior to improvements made for LEED-EB certification, baseline calculations can include data from pre-improvement site irrigation practices.

2. Determine Irrigation Water Use of Conventional Systems

   Collect information about the annual volume of potable water delivered by conventional irrigation systems. Metered data from your site prior to landscaping and irrigation improvements or from nearby sites using conventional irrigation practices is the preferred method to establish conventional irrigation volumes. If metered data are not available, consult an irrigation contractor to determine annual irrigation water use typical for your region. Use a table similar to **Table 1** to summarize the average annual irrigation water use for vegetated sites in your region.

3. Calculate Average Annual Conventional Systems Irrigation Rate

   Based on the information collected from nearby sites using conventional

Table 1: Sample Average Annual Conventional Systems Irrigation Rate Calculations

Building Site	Description of Irrigation System	Annual Irrigation Volume [gallons]	Irrigated Site Area [acres]	Annual Irrigation Rate [gallons/acre]
Building Site A	Permanent sprinkler system	23,500,000	6.2	3,790,323
Building Site B	Hose-base sprinkler system	3,000,000	0.7	4,285,714
Building Site C	Permanent sprinkler system for turf, drip irrigation in landscaped beds	10,400,000	3.2	3,250,000
Building Site D	Permanent sprinkler system	12,600,000	3.6	3,500,000
Average Annual Irrigation Rate for Convention Systems				**3,706,509**

Notes:Annual Irrigation Rate = Annual Irrigation Volume / Irrigated Site Area
Average Annual Irrigation Rate = Sum of Annual Irrigation Water Use for all Sites / Number of Sites

irrigation practices, determine the average annual irrigation water use per unit area for your region. Use metered irrigation data from a number of sites if possible. If metered data are not available, determine the average annual irrigation rate by contacting an irrigation specialist who can provide information about annual irrigation volumes typical of the region based on typical systems and practices. The final row in Table 1 shows the average annual irrigation water use rate calculated for the example.

4. Calculate the Annual Irrigation Baseline

   To determine the irrigation baseline for your site, first determine its landscape area. This is equal to the total site area less the building footprint, paved surfaces, water bodies, and patios. Once the landscape area of the site is determined, use the information from Step 3 and **Equation 1** to calculate the irrigation baseline for your site.

Example: For a landscape area of 4 acres, based on the example shown in **Table 1**, the Annual Irrigation Baseline for the site is 14,826,037 gallons of water (3,706,509 gallons/acre x 4 acres).

Actual Irrigation Potable Water Use

Next, determine the actual amount of potable water used for irrigation on an annual basis on the building site. Do not include graywater and captured rainwater in this figure. Use either of the two options below to determine actual irrigation use of potable water.

Option A: Meter Data

The preferred method for determining actual irrigation water use is through submetering. To determine the amount of potable water used annually for irrigation, sum the irrigation data recorded by meters over the performance period. If the performance period is longer than one year, determine the average irrigation water use by month or quarter, and then sum the averages from each month/quarter to get an annual value.

Equation 1

Annual Irrigation Baseline = Landscape Area [acres] x Average Annual Conventional System Irrigation Rate [gallons/acre/year]

Option B: Estimated Data

If the building does not have submetering, estimate the amount with calculations based on information from an irrigation specialist, manufacturer's data on the irrigation system in place, the area of the site being irrigated, and information about the irrigation practices used on the site. **Equation 2** below illustrates a method to calculate irrigation water.

Percent Reduction

After determining the baseline value and the actual irrigation water use, calculate the percent reduction. Use **Equation 3** below.

If the Percent Reduction is greater than 50 percent, WE Credit 1.1 is earned. If the Percent Reduction is greater than 95 percent, both WE Credit 1.1 and 1.2 are earned.

Additional Considerations

If the building site uses no potable water for irrigation, you do not need to calculate a baseline, as the percent reduction would automatically be 100 percent from any baseline. In this case, document that no potable water is used for irrigation instead of performing calculations.

For LEED-EB projects with a performance period under 1 year, you can extrapolate data for a shorter period as long as you account for seasonal variations in irrigation loads.

Documentation

- ❑ System schematics and photographs demonstrating potable water use reduction strategies
  - Schematics and photographs should clearly illustrate the irrigation system in place, its design and layout, and the technologies employed.
- ❑ Description of the type of irrigation system that is "conventional" in the area
  - Documentation should include a narrative description of conventional irrigation techniques, as well as methods employed to determine conventional approaches. This description should include a discussion of climate and rainfall factors, sources of irrigation water, and the general landscaping designs and approaches employed in the area.

Other Resources

America Rainwater Catchment Systems Association (ARCSA)

www.arcsa-usa.org

ARCSA was founded to promote rainwater catchment systems in the United States. Its web site provides regional resources, publications, suppliers and membership information.

Graywater Systems, Compost Toilets, & Rain Collection

www.rmi.org/sitepages/pid287.php

This web resource from the Rocky Mountain Institute provides general information and links to resources on rain collection and graywater systems.

The Irrigation Association

www.irrigation.org

Equation 2

Total Annual Potable Irrigation Water Use [gallons/year] =
Irrigated Area [acres] x Best Estimate of Actual Irrigation Water Use [gallons/acre/year]

Equation 3

Percent Reduction = ((Baseline Irrigation Water Use – Actual Potable Water Use for Irrigation) / Baseline Irrigation Water Use) x 100

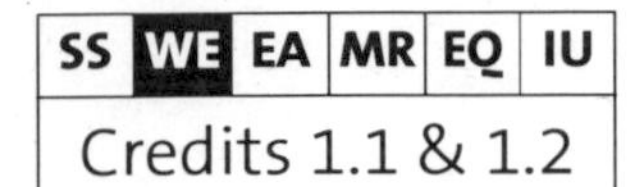

This nonprofit organization focuses on promoting products that efficiently use water in irrigation applications.

Landscape Irrigation: Design and Management by Stephen W. Smith, John Wiley and Sons, 1996.

This text is comprehensive guide to landscape irrigation strategies, techniques, and hardware.

Texas Evapotranspiration Website

http://texaset.tamu.edu

This web site provides evapotranspiration data from the State of Texas with a discussion of crop water use and sprinkler efficiencies.

Turf Irrigation Manual, Fifth Edition by Richard B. Choate and Jim Watkins, Telsco Industries, 1994.

This manual covers all aspects of turf and landscape irrigation.

Water-Efficient Landscaping

http://muextension.missouri.edu/xplor/agguides/hort/g06912.htm

This web site has general descriptions and strategies for water efficiency in gardens and landscapes.

Water-Efficient Landscaping: Preventing Pollution and Using Resources Wisely

www.epa.gov/owm/water-efficiency/final_final.pdf

This manual from the Environmental Protection Agency provides information about reducing water consumption through creative landscaping techniques.

Water Wiser: The Water Efficiency Clearinghouse

www.awwa.org/waterwiser/

This clearinghouse provides articles, reference materials and papers on all forms of water efficiency.

Definitions

Blackwater does not have a single definition that is accepted nationwide. Wastewater from toilets and urinals is always considered blackwater. Wastewater from kitchen sinks (perhaps differentiated by the use of a garbage disposal), showers, or bathtubs may be considered blackwater by state or local codes. Project teams should comply with blackwater definition as established by the authority having jurisdiction in their areas.

Conventional irrigation refers to the most common irrigation system used in the region where the building is located. A common conventional irrigation system uses pressure to deliver water and distributes it through sprinkler heads above the ground.

Drip irrigation is a high-efficiency irrigation method in which water is delivered at low pressure through buried mains and sub-mains. From the sub-mains, water is distributed to the soil from a network of perforated tubes or emitters. Drip irrigation is a type of micro-irrigation.

Graywater is defined by the Uniform Plumbing Code (UPC) in its Appendix G, titled "Gray Water Systems for Single-Family Dwellings" as "untreated household waste water which has not come into contact with toilet waste. Grey water includes used water from bathtubs, showers, bathroom wash basins, and water from clothes-washer and laundry tubs. It shall not include waste water from kitchen sinks or dishwashers." The International Plumbing Code (IPC) defines graywater in its Appendix C, titled "Gray Water Recycling Systems" as "waste water discharged from lavatories, bathtubs, showers, clothes washers, and laundry sinks." Some states and local authorities allow kitchen sink wastewater to be included in graywater. Other differences with the UPC and IPC definitions can probably be found in state and local codes. Project teams should comply with graywater definitions as established by the authority having jurisdiction in their areas.

The **Landscape area** of the site is equal to the total site area less the building footprint, paved surfaces, water bodies, patios, etc.

Micro-Irrigation involves irrigation systems with small sprinklers and microjets or drippers designed to apply small volumes of water. The sprinklers and microjets are installed within a few centimeters of the ground, while drippers are laid on or below grade.

Potable water is water suitable for drinking and supplied from wells or municipal water systems.

Case Study

Roosevelt Facility

Scottsdale, Arizona

LEED-EB Certified

Owner: General Dynamics, Inc.

Photo courtesy of: General Dynamics

General Dynamics achieved a 59% reduction in potable water use for irrigation on the Roosevelt Campus when compared to conventional standards, and a 35% reduction compared to historical use on the site. This reduction was accomplished through two significant steps to reduce irrigation. First, General Dynamics eliminated winter irrigation on roughly six acres of the site, saving over 12 million gallons of potable water each year. In addition, General Dynamics began converting the turf grass on site back to desert landscaping. Drought-tolerant native species and crushed granite have been installed on 1.6 acres, and General Dynamics plans to convert the remaining site acreage in the coming years.

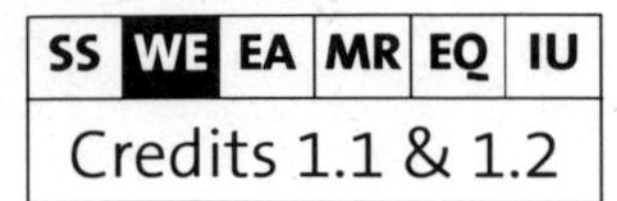
SS WE EA MR EQ IU
Credits 1.1 & 1.2

SS	**WE**	EA	MR	EQ	IU
Credit 2					

1 Point

Innovative Wastewater Technologies

Intent

Reduce generation of wastewater and potable water demand, while increasing the local aquifer recharge.

Requirements

Option A

- ❑ Reduce use of potable water for building sewage conveyance by 50%, based on water use baseline calculated for WE Prerequisite 1.

Option B

- ❑ Treat 100% of wastewater on site to tertiary standards.

Submittals – Initial Certification

Option A

- ❑ Provide a narrative description of measures implemented to reduce potable water sewage conveyance. Include calculations demonstrating that potable water sewage conveyance volumes are reduced by 50% over baseline conditions.
- ❑ Provide quarterly and annual water meter data over the performance period showing that 50% reduction is being achieved on an average annual basis.

Option B

- ❑ Provide a narrative description and schematic drawings detailing equipment locations and that 100% of building wastewater is directed to an on-site wastewater treatment system that provides treatment to tertiary levels. Include a letter from the local health department documenting compliance with local code.
- ❑ Provide quarterly water meter readings over the performance period documenting that 100% of building wastewater volume is directed to on-site wastewater treatment system that provides treatment to tertiary levels.

Note: If the building does not have separate metering for each water use (fixture use, process use, irrigation and other uses), the water use reduction achievements can be demonstrated with calculations.

Submittals – Recertification

- ❑ If there has been no change to the wastewater conveyance system or organizational policy regarding wastewater, provide quarterly and annual water meter data over the performance period showing that the requirements of Option A or B continue to be met.

OR

- ❑ If there has been a change to the wastewater conveyance system or organizational policy regarding wastewater, provide the same information as is required under Option A or B for initial LEED-EB filings.

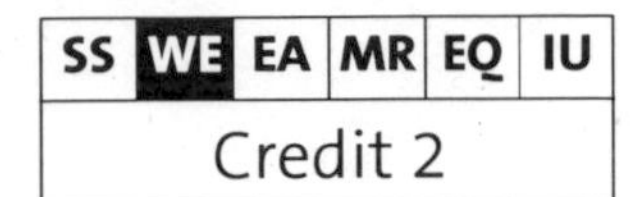

Summary of Referenced Standard

Energy Policy Act of 1992, Section 123 of Public Law 102–486

Publication 10CFR430.32 pages 266–273

U.S. Department of Energy (DOE)

www.doe.gov

(800) 363-3732

The Energy Policy Act of 1992 (EPAct) establishes minimum energy and water efficiency levels for classes of covered products. The EPAct standards relevant to LEED-EB set efficiency levels for plumbing fixture water usage performance. The types of plumbing fixtures that must be considered to establish a LEED-EB water use baseline are listed in Subpart C – Energy and Water Conservation Standards, and include: (o) Faucets, (p) Showerheads, (q) Water Closets, and (r) Urinals. **Table 1** below summarizes the standards for fixture water use.

To obtain a copy of EPAct, go to the U.S. Government Print Office (GPO) document retrieval web site (www.gpoaccess.gov/cfr/retrieve.html) or the following web link:

http://a257.g.akamaitech.net/7/257/2422/12feb20041500/edocket.access.gpo.gov/cfr_2004/janqtr/pdf/10cfr430.32.pdf

Green Building Concerns

Conventional wastewater systems require significant volumes of potable water to convey waste to municipal wastewater treatment facilities. However, graywater volumes from sinks, showers and other sources can substitute for potable water to flush toilets and urinals. Water can also be harvested from roof runoff volumes that would otherwise be absorbed into the ground or released to local water bodies. Low-flow fixtures, automatic controls and dry fixtures, such as composting toilet systems and non-water using urinals, can also reduce sewage volume generation.

Once wastewater enters treatment facilities, extensive treatment is required to remove contaminants before discharging to a water body. A more efficient method for handling wastewater is to treat it on site. On-site wastewater strategies reduce regional wastewater infrastructure costs and provide autonomy from public treatment works. A variety of on-site wastewater treatment options are available, including conventional biological treatment facilities similar to regional plants and "living machine" systems that mimic natural processes to treat wastewater.

Environmental Issues

On-site wastewater treatment systems transform perceived wastes into valuable resources that can be used on the building site. These include treated water volumes

Table 1: Energy Policy Act of 1992 Standards for Plumbing Fixture Water Usage

Fixture	Energy Policy Act of 1992 Standards for Plumbing Fixture Water Use
Water Closets [gpf]	1.60
Urinals [gpf]	1.00
Shower Heads [gpm]*	2.50
Faucets [gpm]**	2.20
Faucet Replacement Aerators**	2.20
Metering Faucets [gal/cycle]	0.25

** When measured at a flowing water pressure of 80 pounds per square inch (psi).*
*** When measured at a flowing water pressure of 60 pounds per square inch (psi).*

for potable and non-potable uses, and nutrients to improve soil conditions. Reducing wastewater treatment at a local facility minimizes public infrastructure, energy use and chemical use. In rural areas, on-site wastewater treatment systems avoid aquifer contamination problems prevalent in current septic system technology.

Economic Issues

Commercial and industrial facilities that generate large amounts of wastewater can realize considerable savings by recycling graywater and using it for sewage conveyance to replace potable water. A separate tank, filter and special emitters are often necessary for graywater systems, and additional energy costs may also be required.

Graywater recovery systems are most cost-effective in areas without a municipal water supply, where developed wells are unreliable, or where well water requires treatment. In some areas with a decentralized population, rainwater collection offers a low-cost alternative to a central piped water supply. Collecting and using rainwater or other site water for sewage conveyance will reduce site runoff and the need for runoff devices.

Wastewater treatment systems, graywater recovery systems, rainfall catchment systems and high-efficiency fixtures involve an initial capital investment, in addition to maintenance requirements. Savings on water and sewer bills offset these costs. A constructed wetland for wastewater treatment can also add value as a site enhancement. Wetlands are beneficial because they provide flood protection and stabilize soils on site.

Operating an on-site wastewater treatment system likely requires permitting from the local health board and local or state environmental agencies. Fees for permit acquisition and compliance should be considered when assessing the economic impact of installing an on-site system.

Strategies & Technologies

Option 1: Reduce Potable Water Used for Sewage Conveyance

Reduce potable water use for sewage conveyance by installing non-water using or high-efficiency fixtures or by utilizing rain or graywater systems. Low-flow and dual-flush water closets are available that use as little as 0.8 gpf.* **Table 2** below illustrates the variation in water efficiency between different types of fixtures.

Consider dry fixtures such as non-water using urinals and composting toilet systems. These non-water using technologies

Table 2: Sample Flush Fixture Types

Flush Fixture Type	Water Use [gpf]
Conventional Low-Flow Toilet (Water Closet)	1.6
High-Efficiency Toilet (Water Closet)	Below 1.3*
Dual-Flush Toilet	0.8 to 1.1/1.6**
Composting Toilet	0.0
Conventional Low-Flow Urinal	1.0
High-Efficiency Urinal	0.5 or below***
Non-Water Consuming Urinal	0.0***

**High-efficiency toilets (HETs) include dual-flush toilets, 1.0-gpf pressure-assist toilets and 1.28-gpf gravity-fed single-flush toilets.*
*** Dual flush toilets have an option of full flush (1.6 gal) or liquid-only flush (ranges between 0.8 gpf and 1.1 gpf, depend upon design). When calculating water use reductions from installation of these fixtures, use a composite (average) flush volume of 1.2 gal.*
****High-efficiency urinals are currently available at 0.5 gpf and 0.0 gpf. Urinals at 0.25 gpf will be available in 2005.*

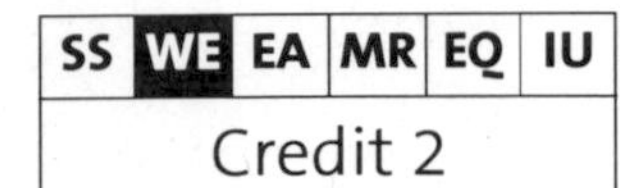

use zero water volume to cope with waste. Non-water using urinals use advanced hydraulic design and a buoyant fluid to maintain sanitary conditions, while composting toilet systems mix human waste with organic material to produce a nearly odorless end product that can be used as a soil amendment. The amount of water that can be saved by using these products is huge. For example, a building with 1,500 male occupants that replaces 100 urinals with non-water using substitutes will save 3,510,000 gallons of water annually, and $17,550 in water and sewer costs.[24] The payback period is extremely quick for a retrofit, usually between 1 and 3 years.

Non-potable water can also be used for flushing toilets and urinals, and for other uses that do not require potable water. Rainwater and graywater systems are other options. Rainwater collection systems harvest water otherwise absorbed into the ground or released to local water bodies, while graywater systems reuse the wastewater from sinks, showers and other sources for functions.

Option 2: On-site Wastewater Treatment

Consider an on-site wastewater treatment system such as a constructed wetland, a mechanical recirculating sand filter or an aerobic biological treatment reactor. Some systems imitate natural ecosystems to treat wastewater volumes biologically, while others use physical, chemical and biological technologies similar to municipal water treatment works. Both types of systems can turn blackwater into effluents that can be used for non-potable applications such as irrigation and toilet flushing.

The construction of artificial wetlands for wastewater treatment can be incorporated on multiple scales to accommodate projects ranging from single buildings to larger developments. As wastewater moves through the wetlands or bodies of water, plants and microbes naturally remove water contaminants. Creating an aquaculture system can turn wastewater contaminants into food for fish and plants. Check with local health departments about regulations governing the use of biological wastewater systems, as most areas require permits for them.

University campuses, military bases or similar campuses may have their own water treatment systems or use municipal treatment facilities. If an on-site wastewater treatment system treats 100 percent of the campus wastewater to tertiary standards, each building on the campus would qualify for this credit. (See the Definitions below for an explanation of tertiary treatment.)

The EPA has developed performance standards for wastewater treatment in the *Onsite Wastewater Treatment Systems Manual* (2002). The manual (EPA-625-R-00-008, available at http://cfpub.epa.gov/owm/septic/guidelines.cfm#7489) is a supplement to the agency's 1980 on-site treatment system design manual. The summary of the EPA treatment standards (TS) below highlight limits for various pollutants by treatment level, including tertiary treatment, as shown in **Table 3**. Local jurisdictions may have their own standards for tertiary treatment, so building sites with on-site wastewater treatment facilities should be careful to acquire any necessary permits and comply with local codes.

Synergies & Tradeoffs

Building location heavily influences the necessity for and availability of wastewater reuse and treatment strategies. In remote locations, an on-site wastewater treatment system is more likely to be cost-effective.

On-site wastewater treatment systems require ongoing inspection and maintenance to ensure they are operating safely and effectively. Suboptimal performance in on-site treatment facilities can result in human health issues as well as ground water and surface water pollution.

Check with local authorities, as most states require permits for graywater systems or on-site wastewater treatment. Failure to receive proper permitting can result in criminal and civil fines.

Calculations & Documentation

Calculations

Option 1: Reduce potable water for sewage conveyance by 50%

Create a water use baseline for sewage conveyance using the standards set in the Energy Policy Act of 1992. The baseline is set with the same process as in WE Prerequisite 1, except it should only include water closets, urinals and other fixtures used for sewage conveyance. See **Table 4** for an example of how to calculate the

Table 3: On-site Wastewater Treatment Performance Standards

Standard	BOD_5 [mg/L]	TSS [mg/L]	PO_4-P [mg/L]	NH_4-N [mg/L]	NO_3-N [mg/L]	Total N* [% removed]	Fecal coliform [CFU/L]
TS1– primary treatment							
TS1u – unfiltered	300	300	15	80	NA	NA	10,000,000
TS1f – filtered	200	15	80	80	NA	NA	10,000,000
TS2 – secondary treatment	30	30	15	10	NA	NA	50,000
TS3 – tertiary treatment	10	10	15	10	NA	NA	10,000
TS4 – nutrient reduction							
TS4n – nitrogen reduction	10	10	15	5	NA	50%	10,000
TS4p – phosphorus reduction	10	10	2	10	NA	25%	10,000
TS4np – N & P reduction	10	10	2	5	NA	50%	10,000
TS5 – bodily contact disinfection	10	10	15	10	NA	25%	200
TS6 – wastewater reuse	5	5	15	5	NA	50%	14
TS7 – near drinking water	5	5	1	5	10	75%	<1**

**Minimum percentage reduction of total nitrogen concentration in the raw, untreated wastewater.*
***Total coliform colony densities < 50 per 100 mL of effluent.*
Source: U.S. EPA Onsite Wastewater Treatment Systems Manual

Table 4: Example Water Use Baseline for Sewage Conveyance

Flush Fixture	Daily Uses	Flowrate [gpf]	Duration [flush]	Auto Controls	Occupants	Water Use [gal]
Conventional Water Closet (Male)	1	1.6	1	N/A	150	240
Conventional Water Closet (Female)	3	1.6	1	N/A	150	720
Conventional Urinal (Male)	2	1.0	1	N/A	150	300
Conventional Urinal (Female)	0	1.0	1	N/A	150	0
					Total Daily Volume [gal]	1,260
					Annual Work Days	260
					Total Annual Volume [gal]	**327,600**
					Multiply by 120%	**1.2**
					Water Use for Sewage Conveyance Baseline	**393,120**

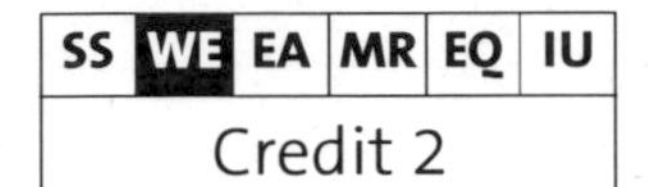

sewage conveyance baseline. Use the following assumptions:

- ❑ The ratio of males to females is 50:50 unless specifically documented otherwise.
- ❑ Female building occupants use water closets three times daily.
- ❑ Male occupants use water closets once and urinals twice daily.

Next, determine the actual potable water usage for sewage conveyance by using a similar table, but substituting the actual fixture water requirements. See **Table 5** for an example of actual water usage for the same building as the baseline calculations above. Use of low-flow water closets and non-water using urinals, combined with a graywater reuse system that supplies 36,000 gallons per year, saves this building 257,520 gallons of potable water per year, as compared to the baseline. This is a reduction of over 65 percent from the baseline calculations.

Documentation

All information needed to successfully document this credit can be found in the Submittals section of the LEED-EB Rating System and the LEED-EB Letter Templates.

Other Resources

Constructed Wetlands for Wastewater Treatment and Wildlife Habitat: 17 Case Studies

EPA Publication No. 832/B-93-005, 1993.

http://www.epa.gov/owow/wetlands/construc/

The case studies in this document provide brief descriptions of 17 wetland treatment systems that provide water quality benefits while also providing habitat. The projects described include systems involving constructed and natural wetlands, habitat creation and restoration, and the improvement of municipal effluent, urban stormwater and river water quality.

On-site Wastewater Treatment Systems Manual

www.epa.gov/owm/septic/pubs/septic_2002_osdm_all.pdf

This manual provides a focused and performance-based approach to on-site wastewater treatment and system management, including information on a variety of on-site sewage treatment options.

U.S. EPA Water-Saving Tips

www.epa.gov/OW/you/chap3.html

This EPA website provides guidance for commercial, industrial, and residential

Table 5: Example of Calculating Actual Water Usage for Sewage Conveyance

Flush Fixture	Daily Uses	Flowrate [gpf]	Duration [flush]	Auto Controls	Occupants	Water Use [gal]
Low-Flow Water Closet (Male)	1	1.1	1	N/A	150	165
Low-Flow Water Closet (Female)	3	1.1	1	N/A	150	495
Non-water using Urinal (Male)	2	0.0	1	N/A	150	0
Non-water using Urinal (Female)	0	0.0	1	N/A	150	0
					Total Daily Volume (gal)	660
					Annual Work Days	260
					Annual Volume (gal)	171,600
					Graywater Reuse Volume	(36,000)
					Total Annual Volume (gal)	**135,600**

water users on saving water and reducing sewage volumes.

Definitions

Aquatic systems are ecologically designed treatment systems that utilize a diverse community of biological organisms (e.g., bacteria, plants and fish) to treat wastewater to advanced levels.

Blackwater does not have a single definition that is accepted nationwide. Wastewater from toilets and urinals is always considered blackwater. Wastewater from kitchen sinks (perhaps differentiated by the use of a garbage disposal), showers, or bathtubs may be considered blackwater by state or local codes. Project teams should comply with blackwater definition as established by the authority having jurisdiction in their areas.

Composting toilet systems are dry plumbing fixtures that contain and treat human waste via microbiological processes.

Graywater is defined by the Uniform Plumbing Code (UPC) in its Appendix G, titled "Gray Water Systems for Single-Family Dwellings" as "untreated household waste water which has not come into contact with toilet waste. Grey water includes used water from bathtubs, showers, bathroom wash basins, and water from clothes-washer and laundry tubs. It shall not include waste water from kitchen sinks or dishwashers." The International Plumbing Code (IPC) defines graywater in its Appendix C, titled "Gray Water Recycling Systems" as "waste water discharged from lavatories, bathtubs, showers, clothes washers, and laundry sinks." Some states and local authorities allow kitchen sink wastewater to be included in graywater. Other differences with the UPC and IPC definitions can probably be found in state and local codes. Project teams should comply with graywater definitions as established by the authority having jurisdiction in their areas.

On-site wastewater treatment uses localized treatment systems to transport, store, treat and dispose of wastewater volumes generated on the project site.

Potable water is water that meets drinking water quality standards and is approved for human consumption by the state or local authorities having jurisdiction.

Tertiary treatment is the highest form of wastewater treatment that includes the removal of nutrients, organic and solid material, along with biological or chemical polishing (generally to effluent limits of 10 mg/L BOD_5 and 10 mg/L TSS).

A **non-water using urinal** is a urinal that uses no water, but instead replaces the water flush with a specially designed trap that contains a layer of buoyant liquid that floats above the urine layer, blocking sewer gas and urine odors from the room.

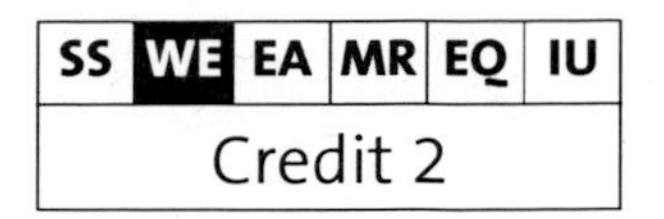

Case Study

King Street Center
Seattle, WA

LEED-EB Gold
Owner: King County

Photo courtesy of: Ned Ahrens

The King Street Center collects rainwater to flush its toilets throughout the year. The system is designed to collect rainwater from the building's roof to fill each of three 5,400-gallon tanks. The water fills and passes through all three tanks, then is filtered in small cylinders as it is pumped up to the toilets in the building in separate piping. If there is not enough rain to meet the building's flushing needs, domestic water is automatically added to the tanks.

The building uses approximately 2.2 million gallons of flushing water per year, with the reclamation system providing an estimated 1.4 million gallons, or over 60 percent of the flushing needs.

In addition to providing non-potable water for toilet flushing, much of the building's landscaping needs are met through diversion of water from the reclamation system.

SS | WE | EA | MR | EQ | IU

Credits 3.1 & 3.2

1–2 Points

Water Use Reduction

Intent

Maximize fixture potable water efficiency within buildings to reduce the burden on municipal water supply and wastewater systems.

Requirements

Have in place over the performance period strategies and systems that in aggregate produce a reduction of fixture potable water use from the calculated fixture water usage baseline established in WE Prerequisite 1. If the building does not have separate metering for each water use (fixture use, process use, irrigation and other uses), the water use reduction achievements can be demonstrated for WE 3.1 with calculations. At least one meter for the overall building water use is required and metering for cooling towers and other process water use encouraged but not required. To earn WE 3.2, measured fixture water use demonstrating required level of efficiency must be provided.

- ❑ WE 3.1: 10% reduction in fixture water use from the baseline. (1 point)
- ❑ WE 3.2: 20% reduction in fixture water use from the baseline. (1 point)

Submittals – Initial Certification

- ❑ Demonstrate the amount of annual fixture potable water use. Do this by providing fixture water meter data for the performance period OR by providing calculations, fixture cut sheets, and photographs (this second method is valid only for Credit 3.1).
- ❑ Provide annual water meter data for total water use in the building.

Submittals – Recertification

- ❑ Demonstrate the amount of annual fixture potable water use. Do this by providing fixture water meter data for the performance period OR by providing calculations, fixture cut sheets, and photographs (this second method is valid only for Credit 3.1).
- ❑ Provide annual water meter data for total water use in the building.

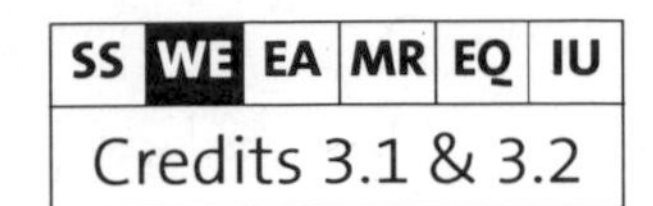

Summary of Referenced Standard

Energy Policy Act of 1992, Section 123 of Public Law 102–486

Publication 10CFR430.32 pages 266–273

U.S. Department of Energy (DOE)

www.doe.gov

(800) 363-3732

The Energy Policy Act of 1992 (EPAct) establishes minimum energy and water efficiency levels for classes of covered products. The EPAct standards relevant to LEED-EB set efficiency levels for plumbing fixture water usage performance. The types of plumbing fixtures that must be considered to establish a LEED-EB water use baseline are listed in Subpart C – Energy and Water Conservation Standards, and include: (o) Faucets, (p) Showerheads, (q) Water Closets, and (r) Urinals. **Table 1** below summarizes the standards for fixture water use.

To obtain a copy of EPAct, go to the U.S. Government Print Office (GPO) document retrieval web site (www.gpoaccess.gov/cfr/retrieve.html) or the following web link:

http://a257.g.akamaitech.net/7/257/2422/12feb20041500/edocket.access.gpo.gov/cfr_2004/janqtr/pdf/10cfr430.32.pdf

Green Building Concerns

See WE Prerequisite 1: Green Building Concerns.

Environmental Issues

See WE Prerequisite 1: Environmental Issues.

Economic Issues

See WE Prerequisite 1: Economic Issues.

Strategies & Technologies

WE Credits 3.1 and 3.2 focus on water use reduction beyond the requirements of WE Prerequisite 1. These credits do not require fixture replacement as many other options exist to reduce water use. To reduce fixture water use, develop a water use inventory, and then identify significant potable water demands and methods to minimize or eliminate these demands. Many strategies can save water in existing buildings. Select appropriate options for the building budget, upgrade schedule or planned renovations.

High-Efficiency Plumbing Fixtures

Install water-conserving plumbing fixtures that exceed the fixture requirements stated in EPAct. Consider high-efficiency toilets (HETs) and urinals (HEUs), faucets, showers and other fixtures. A variety of high-efficiency plumbing fixtures are

Table 1: Energy Policy Act of 1992 Standards for Plumbing Fixture Water Usage

Fixture	Energy Policy Act of 1992 Standards for Plumbing Fixture Water Use
Water Closets [gpf]	1.60
Urinals [gpf]	1.00
Shower Heads [gpm]*	2.50
Faucets [gpm]**	2.20
Faucet Replacement Aerators**	2.20
Metering Faucets [gal/cycle]	0.25

** When measured at a flowing water pressure of 80 pounds per square inch (psi).*
*** When measured at a flowing water pressure of 60 pounds per square inch (psi).*

currently available. Most are installed and used the same way as conventional low-flow fixtures. **Tables 2 and 3** below show the ranges of efficiency in plumbing fixtures available.

Water closets use a significant amount of potable water. Many water closets are available that use considerably less than 1.6 gpf, including pressure-assisted water closets at 1.0 gpf and dual-flush water closets that provide for "short flushes" (liquid only) of between 0.8 and 1.1 gpf and "long flushes" (liquid and solids) at 1.6 gpf. Actual water consumption, which includes water used by extra flushes needed because of inadequate performance, can only be determined by sub metering.

Water-efficient showerheads are also available that require less than 2.5 gpm. Bathroom faucets and fixtures that are typically used only for wetting purposes can be effective with as little as 1.0 gpm. Some water-saving faucet aerators are available that do not change the feel of the water flow and can be installed for a fraction of the cost of new fixtures.

Self-Closing and Sensor-Operated Fixtures

Automatic water control systems can also potentially reduce fixture potable water use. Install self-closing or electronic faucets, particularly in high-use areas where people may carelessly leave faucets running. No authoritative data exist on the water savings that might accrue from sensor-operated valves on faucets, toilets and urinals. However, estimate an average savings of 10 percent on sensor-operated

Table 2: Sample Flush Fixture Types

Flush Fixture Type	Water Use [gpf]
Conventional Low-Flow Toilet (Water Closet)	1.6
High-Efficiency Toilet (Water Closet)	Below 1.3*
Dual-Flush Toilet	0.8 to 1.1/1.6**
Composting Toilet	0.0
Conventional Low-Flow Urinal	1.0
High-Efficiency Urinal	0.5 or below***
Non-Water Consuming Urinal	0.0***

**High-efficiency toilets (HETs) include dual-flush toilets, 1.0-gpf pressure-assist toilets, and 1.28-gpf gravity-fed single-flush toilets.*

*** Dual flush toilets have an option of full flush (1.6 gal) or liquid-only flush (ranges between 0.8 gpf and 1.1 gpf, depend upon design). When calculating water use reductions from installation of these fixtures, use a composite (average) flush volume of 1.2 gal.*

****High-efficiency urinals are currently available at 0.5 gpf and 0.0 gpf. Urinals at 0.25 gpf will be available in 2005.*

Table 3: Sample Flow Fixture Fitting Types

Flow Fixture Type	Water Use [gpm]
Conventional Low-Flow Lavatory Faucet	2.2
High-Efficiency Lavatory Faucet	1.8
Conventional Low-Flow Kitchen Sink Faucet	2.2
High-Efficiency Kitchen Sink Faucet	1.8
Conventional Low-Flow Showerhead	2.5
High-Efficiency Showerhead	2.0 and below
Low-Flow Janitor Sink Faucet	2.5
Low–Flow Hand Wash Fountain	0.5
Conventional Low Flow Self Closing Faucet	0.25 gals./cycle
High Efficiency Self Closing Faucet	0.2 gals./cycle and below

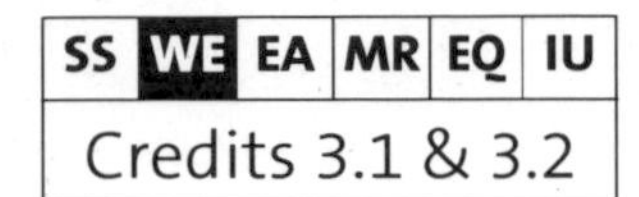

faucets. No savings can be attributed to sensor-operated flush valves.

Non-water using Technology

Consider dry fixtures such as non-water consuming urinals and composting toilet systems. Some non-water consuming urinals use a buoyant fluid to maintain sanitary conditions, while others use a mechanical seal or other means to provide the necessary trap seal. Composting toilet systems mix human waste with organic material to produce a nearly odorless end product that can be used as a soil amendment.

Potable water savings from non-water using technology can be significant. For example, a building with 1,500 male occupants that replaces 100 urinals with non-water consuming substitutes may save as much as 3.5 million gallons of water annually.[25] The ensuing water and savings costs can offset the initial investment, but maintenance costs for non-water consuming urinals may extend the payback period.

Non-potable Water Use

Many functions do not require high-quality water. Instead, water collection systems that process rain or graywater can provide suitable water for non-potable uses such as toilet flushing, janitorial tasks and irrigation. Note that use of non-potable water for flushing purposes may void some manufacturers' warranties if their product is designed for use with water that meets EPA potable water standards. It is recommended that product manufacturers be asked to extend warranties to explicitly include this type of usage if it is not covered. Although irrigation water use is not included in this credit, rainwater and graywater collection systems can be used to meet irrigation needs, as discussed in WE Credits 1.1-1.2.

Rainwater collection systems harvest water otherwise absorbed into the ground or released to local water bodies. Roof systems capture precipitation and transport it to a basement storage tank via gutters and downspouts. The water is filtered and treated to meet standards appropriate for future use, then stored in tanks until needed. If the water volume in the storage tank drops below the volume required for interior and/or exterior use, the system compensates by supplementing it with potable water. Storage tanks should be equipped with an overflow device to eliminate flooding.

Graywater systems also lessen dependence on potable water by reusing the wastewater from sinks, showers and other sources for functions. It is important to note that regulations for graywater reuse differ among jurisdictions. Check with your local health department and building department for regulations and codes governing the installation and use of graywater systems. For example, Texas and California have standards that encourage the use of graywater systems, while other states limit or prohibit graywater use in certain applications.

Communication with Building Occupants

Water-efficient fixtures must be used correctly to capitalize on their potential. Communicating with building occupants about water conservation goals, water saving features, and the overall function of building water systems will help maximize the benefit of water efficient fixtures. Consider posting signs that educates users on the proper way to operate these fixtures. This is especially important for technologies that do not function in the same manner as conventional models, such as low-flow fixtures, dual-flush toilets, composting toilet systems or fixtures that deliver non-potable water.

Planning Actions to Reduce Water Use

Estimating the water reductions associated with fixture upgrades will help de-

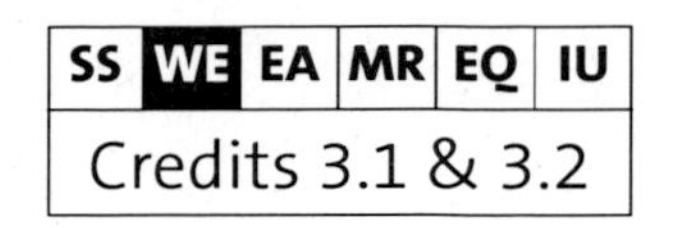

termine the extent of fixture replacement or other improvements necessary to meet LEED-EB fixture water use goals.

Examples of potential water use reduction actions include:

- ❑ Installing flow reduction aerators in faucets
- ❑ Installing automatic controls on lavatory faucets
- ❑ Using graywater volumes captured from showers, sinks and lavatories for use in water closets
- ❑ Replacing conventional urinals used in male restrooms with high-efficiency urinals (HEUs)
- ❑ Replacing fixtures on lavatories and kitchen sinks with fixtures that use 1.8 gpm or less
- ❑ Replacing showerheads with high-efficiency showerheads that use 1.8 gpm or less
- ❑ Installing high-efficiency toilets (HETs) that reduce per-flush water consumption by 20 percent or more.

Table 4 provides an example of water use reduction planning. The number of building occupants, workdays and the frequency-of-use data are identical for the baseline example and the planning case. The calculations indicate that these improvements would reduce annual water use to approximately 316,820 gallons. Comparison of the planning example to the baseline case (example in Prerequisite 1) indicates savings of about 399,220 gallons of potable water per year through the use of high-efficiency toilets and urinals, auto controls on lavatories and sinks, and reuse of graywater. This equates to savings of 56 percent over the baseline case.

Table 4: Water Use Reduction Planning Example

Flush Fixture	Daily Uses	Average Flowrate [gpf]	Duration [flush]	Auto Controls	Occupants	Water Use [gal/day]
High-efficiency Toilet (Male)	1	1.0	1	N/A	150	150
High-efficiency Toilet (Female)	3	1.0	1	N/A	150	450
Composting Toilet (Male)	0	0.0	1	N/A	150	0
Composting Toilet (Female)	0	0.0	1	N/A	150	0
High-efficiency Urinal (Male)	2	0.0	1	N/A	150	0
Fittings	**Daily Uses**	**Average Flowrate [gpm]**	**Duration [sec]**	**Auto Controls [% saved]**	**Occupants**	**Water Use [gal/day]**
High-efficiency Lavatory Faucet	3	1.8	15	10	300	365
High-efficiency Kitchen Sink Faucet	1	1.8	15	10	300	122
Shower	0.1	1.8	300		300	270
					Total Daily Volume (gal)	1,357
					Annual Work Days	260
					Annual Volume (gal)	352,820
					Graywater Reuse Volume	(36,000)
					Total Annual Volume (gal)	**316,820**

SS WE EA MR EQ IU

Credits 3.1 & 3.2

Synergies & Tradeoffs

Achieving reductions in fixture water use beyond that required in WE Prerequisite 1 requires greater use of advanced fixture technologies and practices. The strategies for achieving WE Credits 3.1 and 3.2 should be coordinated with the minimum practices required by WE Prerequisite 1.

Because of the relationship between water consumption and energy costs, increased levels of water savings should result in higher levels of energy conservation. However, increased water efficiency will require additional investment in advanced technologies.

Water use reduction strategies for existing buildings depend on the physical constraints of the building and site, and also on financial constraints that limit the pace of investments. Some technologies, such as graywater or rainwater collection, may not be economically feasible in an existing building unless extensive remodeling is taking place.

WE Credit 2: Innovative Wastewater Technologies also provides an opportunity for earning points and additional information on potable water reduction measures in buildings.

Calculations & Documentation

See WE Prerequisite 1: Calculations & Documentation

Other Resources

See WE Prerequisite 1: Other Resources

Case Study

Department of Ecology Headquarters

Olympia, Washington

LEED-EB Silver

Owner: State of Washington Department of Ecology

Photo courtesy of: State of Washington Department of Ecology

The State of Washington Department of Ecology Headquarters building is a 323,000 square foot office building constructed in 1993. The Department of Ecology is the main environmental regulatory agency for the State of Washington, and the incorporation of sustainable practices through the design, construction, and ongoing operation of the facility reflect that role. To meet water efficiency goals in the building, the LEED-EB project team performed a facility-wide fixture audit to assure full compliance with the Energy Policy Act of 1992 (EPAct). In addition to the use of water conserving low-flow water closets, urinals and shower heads used in the building, the agency has maintained an aggressive maintenance and repair program. Stuck flush valves, leaking fittings or dripping faucets are quickly repaired to prevent water loss. All fixtures are physically inspected regularly by facility staff and/or service providers. Water consuming kitchen appliances such as steam ovens, commercial dishwasher and prep sinks are also serviced regularly and deficiencies repaired. Water use in the Headquarters Building is roughly 28 percent less water than the LEED-EB baseline.

Endnotes

[1] Hutson, Susan S., et al. Estimated Use of Water in the Unites States in 2000. U.S. Geological Survey, Circular 1268, originally released March 2004, last revised February 2005. 4 May 2005 <http://water.usgs.gov/pubs/circ/2004/circ1268/htdocs/text-trends.html>.

[2] United States. Department of the Interior, U.S. Geological Survey. USGS Study Documents Water Level Changes in High Plains Aquifer. News Release: February 9, 2004. 23 February 2005 <http://www.usgs.gov/newsroom/article.asp?ID=121>.

[3] Solley, Wayne B., Robert R. Pierce, and Howard A. Perlman. Estimated Use of Water in the United States in 1995. U.S. Geological Survey Circular 1200, GPO, 1998. 23 February 2005 <http://water.usgs.gov/watuse/pdf1995/html/>.

[4] United Sates. Environmental Protection Agency, Office of Ground Water and Drinking Water. List of Drinking Water Contaminants & MCLS, February 2005. 23 February 2005 <http://www.epa.gov/safewater/mcl.html>.

[5] United States. Environmental Protection Agency, Office of Wastewater Management. Water Permitting 101, July 2002. 24 February 2005 <http://www.epa.gov/npdes/pubs/101pape.pdf>.

[6] Ibid.

[7] Hutson, Susan S., et al. Estimated Use of Water in the Unites States in 2000. U.S. Geological Survey, Circular 1268, originally release March 2004, last revised February 2005. 4 May 2005 <http://water.usgs.gov/pubs/circ/2004/circ1268/htdocs/text-trends.html>.

[8] Examples at: LEED Project List. U.S. Green Building Council. 23 February 2005 <https://www.usgbc.org/LEED/Project/project_list.asp>.

[9] Based on 650 building occupants each using an average of 20 gallons per day.

[10] The Benefits of Building Sustainably. 2000. City of Seattle. 23 February 2005 <http://www.cityofseattle.net/sustainablebuilding/benefits.htm>.

[11] United States. Department of Energy. Energy Information Administration. 1999 Commercial Buildings Energy Consumption Survey. 11 April 2005 <http://www.eia.doe.gov/emeu/cbecs/background.html>.

[12] United States. Environmental Protection Agency. Office of Wastewater Management. Water Use Efficiency Program: Low Flow Toilets April 2004. 21 February 2005 <http://www.epa.gov/owm/water-efficiency/toilets.htm>.

[13] United States. Environmental Protection Agency, National Pollutant Discharge Elimination System (NPDES). NPDES Permit Program Basics: Frequently Asked Questions December 2003. 11 April 2005 <http://cfpub.epa.gov/npdes/faqs.cfm?program_id=45>.

[14] United States. Environmental Protection Agency, Office of Water. Protecting the Nation's Water Through Effective NPDES Permits June 2001. EPA-833-R-01-001. 14 April 2005 <http://www.epa.gov/npdes/pubs/strategicplan.pdf>.

[15] United States. Environmental Protection Agency, Office of Wastewater Management,

NPDES Permitting Program. Stormwater Discharges from Construction Activities, Feb 2005. 18 Feb 2005 <http://cfpub.epa.gov/npdes/stormwater/const.cfm>.

[16] United States. Environmental Protection Agency, Office of Wastewater Management. National Pollutant Discharge Elimination System (NPDES) December 2003. 18 Feb 2005 <http://cfpub.epa.gov/npdes/index.cfm>.

[17] United States. Environmental Protection Agency, National Pollutant Discharge Elimination System (NPDES). NPDES Permit Program Basics: Frequently Asked Questions December 2003. 11 April 2005 <http://cfpub.epa.gov/npdes/faqs.cfm?program_id=45>.

[18] Ibid.

[19] Ibid.

[20] Ibid.

[21] United States. Environmental Protection Agency, Office of Water. Water-Efficient Landscaping. EPA Publication 832-F-02-002, September 2002. 21 January 2005 < http://www.epa.gov/owm/water-efficiency/final_final.pdf>.

[22] Connellan, Goeff. Efficient Irrigation: A Reference Manual for Turf and Landscape. University of Melbourne. 2002. 21 January 2005 <http://www.sewl.com.au/sewl/upload/document/WaterConManual.pdf>.

[23] Bilderback, T.E., and M.A. Powell. Efficient Irrigation. North Carolina Cooperative Extension Service, Publication Number AG-508-6, March 1996. 21 January 2005 <http://www.bae.ncsu.edu/programs/extension/publicat/wqwm/ag508_6.html>.

[24] Allen, Jim. “Going Green Pays Off.” Buildings Magazine, July 2004. 4 May 2005 <http://www.buildings.com/Articles/detail.asp?ArticleID=1970>.

[25] Ibid.

SS	WE	EA	MR	EQ	IU

Prerequisite 1

Required

Existing Building Commissioning

Intent

Verify that fundamental building systems and assemblies are performing as intended to meet current needs and sustainability requirements.

Requirements

Verify and ensure that fundamental building elements and systems are installed, calibrated and operating as intended so they can deliver functional and efficient performance. Carry out a comprehensive existing building commissioning including the following procedures:

1. Develop a comprehensive building operation plan that meets the requirements of current building usage, and addresses the heating system, cooling system, humidity control system, lighting system, safety systems and the building automation controls.
2. Prepare a commissioning plan for carrying out the testing of all building systems to verify that they are working according to the specifications of the building operation plan.
3. Implement the commissioning plan documenting all the results.
4. Repair or upgrade all systems components that are found to be not working according to the specifications of the building operation plan.
5. Re-test all building components that required repairs or upgrades to verify that they are working according to the specifications of the building operation plan.

OR

Submit a 1- to 5-Year Plan for continuous improvement of these aspects of commissioning requirements 1-5 until all aspects are completed. During the implementation of the continuous improvement plan, demonstrate continuous improvement on a yearly basis until all aspects are completed. All low-cost and no-cost measures must be implemented in the first two years of the implementation program.

Submittals – Initial Certification

- ❑ A narrative summary of the current building operation plan that highlights major building systems and assemblies.
- ❑ Documentation that all five actions in the Requirements have been completed.

OR

- ❑ If one or more aspects of the five actions in the Requirements have not been completed, submit a 5-Year Plan that includes a schedule of annual actions that will be implemented in order to complete all five actions in the Requirements within five years.

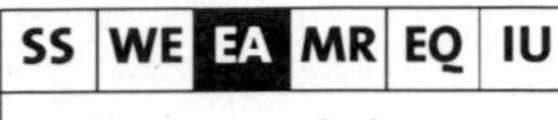

Submittals – Recertification

Provide an update of previous filings:

- ❑ A narrative summary of the current building operation plan that highlights major building systems and assemblies.

AND EITHER

- ❑ Documentation that all five actions in the requirements have been completed.

OR

- ❑ If one or more aspects of the five actions in the requirements were not completed in the original submittal, submit a progress report showing that the 5-Year Plan remains on schedule for meeting all of the requirements.

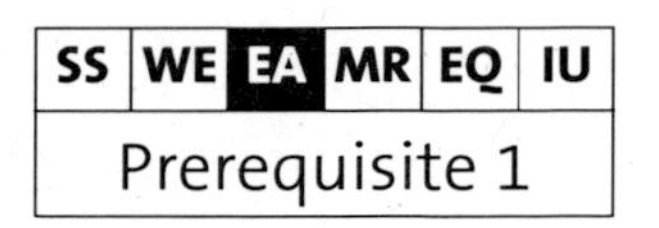

Summary of Referenced Standard

There is no standard referenced for this credit.

Green Building Concerns

Existing building commissioning is a systematic process for checking the performance of all building systems and repairing them as necessary to ensure that they perform in accordance with the building's operational needs. Commissioning activities involve performance testing and upgrades to meet building performance plan requirements. Building systems that are not performing as intended waste resources such as energy and water and increase the building's impact on the environment.

Environmental Issues

Commissioning optimizes energy efficiency and water efficiency, thereby minimizing environmental impacts associated with energy and water production and consumption. Energy and water conservation reduces the need for natural resource extraction and reduces emissions to the environment.

Economic Issues

Properly executed commissioning can result in substantial cost savings. These savings stem from a number of sources, including reduced maintenance/repair expenditures, reduced resource consumption through improved efficiency, and increased occupant productivity due to high indoor environmental quality.

Continually ensuring that systems are properly functioning prevents maintenance costs that accumulate due to negligence of repairs and upkeep. Preventing or addressing equipment problems early reduces the frequency of contractor call-back. Commissioning may also provide owners the opportunity to receive public benefit funds or utility rebates.

Increasing system performance through commissioning reduces operational resource consumption. Commissioning can increase energy efficiency by 5 to 10 percent. For example, the Oregon Office of Energy studied direct energy savings for two buildings after commissioning. In an 110,000-square-foot office building, commissioning helped realize energy savings of $12,276 per year (equivalent to $0.11 per square foot). In a 22,000-square-foot office building, energy savings equal to $7,630 per year ($0.35 per square foot) were achieved.[6]

Decreased occupant productivity is an indirect operational cost associated with subpar building performance. The Oregon study also estimated indirect costs associated with lost productivity due to occupant complaints about the indoor environment. The study estimated that if 20 percent of building occupants expended 30 minutes per month complaining about lighting or temperature conditions, the employer would lose $0.10 per square foot in annual productivity. For a 100,000-square-foot building, this equates to $10,000 per year.[7]. This loss does not factor in actual productivity reductions resulting from suboptimal working conditions, only complaint time. Other potential costs of poor building performance cited by the Oregon Office of Energy include employee illness, loss of tenants, liability related to indoor air quality and premature equipment replacement.

Strategies & Technologies

The existing building commissioning process starts with the preparation of a building operation plan that specifies the current operational needs of the building and how to meet them, followed by testing and repairing the building systems and equipment as necessary to ensure that they meet the plan. Since existing building commissioning may take some time to complete, the LEED-EB project team can either provide documentation that commissioning has been completed or provide a 5-year plan for completing the process.

Overall Strategy

The LEED-EB commissioning guidelines may be broadly applied to a diverse set of buildings, systems and equipment. It can also accommodate varying measurement technologies in existing buildings. Building managers should customize a building operation plan suitable to the building's current operational requirements and needs.

When developing a building operation plan, identify performance criteria essential for effective, efficient building operation, along with test and measurement procedures that can be conducted in a practical, cost-effective manner. The suggested approach is to identify high-level criteria for the whole building and primary systems for which test and measurement procedures are readily available. Methods that involve continuous monitoring as outlined in other sections of LEED-EB may also help meet this requirement.

For buildings that do not yet have continuous monitoring capabilities, some form of field test is required for building systems. While building owners can determine the most suitable methods for their needs, the suggested approach is to conduct performance testing for integrated systems. This concept assumes that an integrated system that does not pass a performance test must have one or more subsystems, equipment and/or components not in compliance with the building operation plan. If this is the case, specific testing and improvement for subsystems, equipment and/or components must be conducted to bring the overall system into compliance. These specific testing and improvement activities and the results of a commissioning retest must be documented and integrated into the building operation plan in subsequent applications for LEED-EB recertification.

For buildings with proactive building maintenance programs, the standards used in these existing programs may in aggregate provide much or all of what is needed to meet the LEED-EB requirement for a building operation plan.

Development of Building Operation Plan and Performance Testing

The following two sections provide examples of items to address in a building operation plan, although actual plans will vary depending on building features. For each area of building-level or system-level performance, define a Building Operation Plan and a Performance Testing Plan:

Building Operation Plan – For each area of the building or space-use type, document the intended hours of occupancy or operating schedules for the eight day-types (Monday through Sunday and holidays). Include seasonal variations if appropriate, a list of holidays, and a description of how partial and after-hour usage is accommodated.

Performance Testing – Complete Parts A and B below by the time of application or include a plan for completion within a maximum period of five years. The preference is to complete all these tasks by the time of submittal of the certification application. However, if this is not possible, it is acceptable to complete only some of the actions before submitting the application and include in the application a schedule for completing the remaining actions within five years.

Part A – Inspection – For automatic controls such as time clocks or direct digital controls, visually inspect and document settings for comparison with intended schedules. For manually controlled loads such as lighting operated by manual switches, provide documentation that sweeps are performed to ensure lights are off after occupied hours or provide other evidence that these loads are controlled in accordance with intended schedules.

Part B – Short Term or Continuous Measurements – Provide runtime reports and/or load profile data to demonstrate that controlled loads comply with intended operating schedules. These runtime reports can be developed using either temporary data loggers or building control systems that have this capability. Utilizing the continuous measurements method may also help earn other LEED-EB prerequisites and credits including the following:

- ❑ EA Credit 3.3: Building Systems Monitoring
- ❑ EA Credit 5.1–5.3: Performance Measurement and Verification.

I. Building-Level Performance

Space Environmental Conditions

Minimum IAQ performance, performance criteria, test and measurement procedures, and documentation requirements are specifically addressed in the following LEED-EB credits:

- ❑ IEQ Prerequisite 1: Outside Air Introduction and Exhaust Systems
- ❑ IEQ Credit 1: Outdoor Air Delivery Monitoring
- ❑ IEQ Credit 7.1: Thermal Comfort Compliance
- ❑ IEQ Credit 7.2: Thermal Comfort Permanent Monitoring System
- ❑ IEQ Credit 9: Contemporary IAQ Practice

To comply with EA Prerequisite 1, the building operation plan must identify intended setpoints of performance for each of three space environmental conditions listed below (space temperature, space pressurization, and building envelope). Setpoints should, at a minimum, reflect the minimum IAQ parameters mandated in IEQ Prerequisite 1. The performance criteria, test and measurement procedures, and documentation requirements of the LEED-EB IAQ performance credits listed above should be included in the building operation plan and performance tests if those credits are to be pursued in the LEED-EB application.

1. Space Temperature

   Building Operation Plan – For each area of the building or space-use type, document the intended space temperature setpoints for occupied and unoccupied heating and cooling. Describe how space temperatures are controlled (locally, remotely, and whether or not occupants have control), as well as any policies for control and enforcement of space temperatures.

   Performance Test – Complete both Parts A and B below at the time of application or include a plan for completion within a maximum period of five years.

   Part A – Inspection – Visually inspect and document a representative sample* of space temperature setpoints for comparison with intended setpoints. Submit any supporting documentation for policies on space temperature settings and how they are enforced.

   Part B – Short-Term or Continuous Measurements – Demonstrate compliance with intended setpoints in all seasons of operation by: 1) Installing loggers to monitor space temperature in representative areas of the building*; or 2) Using building automation system reports or trend log data. Utilizing the continuous measurements method may also help earn other LEED-EB prerequisites and credits including the following:

   - ❑ EA Credit 3.3: Building Systems Monitoring

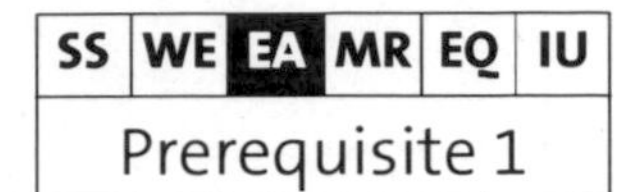

- ❑ EA Credit 5.1–5.3: Performance Measurement: Enhanced Metering
- ❑ IAQ Credit 7.1–7.2 Thermal Comfort

If setpoints or temperatures are not in compliance with the building operation plan, then submit a plan for continuous improvement. In subsequent years, submit documentation that improvement activities were conducted on the areas of the original sample, and submit the results of the acceptance retest. If tune-up commissioning or other system-related activities cannot achieve improvement, submit documentation describing the hurdles preventing improvement.

*Minimum sample size must be 10 percent or five space temperature control devices or locations, whichever is greater. Applicants are encouraged to exceed the minimum sample whenever possible. For sample sizes less than 10 percent, perform performance testing on a different sample each year.

Note: Thermal comfort, including humidity requirements, is specifically addressed in LEED-EB Indoor Environmental Quality Credit 7.

2. Space Pressurization

<u>Building Operation Plan</u> – For each area of the building or space-use type, document the intended space pressurization requirements.

<u>Performance Test</u> – Complete Option A or B at the time of application or include a plan for completion within a maximum of five years.

Option A – Instantaneous Measurements – Design and conduct a performance test, and submit documentation to demonstrate that space pressurization requirements have been met.

Option B – Short-Term or Continuous Measurements – Demonstrate compliance with intended space pressurization in all modes of operation by: 1) Installing loggers to monitor space pressure in strategic areas of the building; or 2) Using building automation system reports or trend log data. This method may also help earn other LEED-EB credits including:

- ❑ EA Credit 3.3: Building Systems Monitoring
- ❑ EA Credit 5.1–5.3: Performance Measurement: Enhanced Metering

For buildings in which space pressurization is critical for occupant safety, such as hospitals and laboratories, execute performance tests in accordance with applicable regulatory agency standards.

3. Building Envelope

<u>Building Operation Plan</u> – The building envelope must be caulked and sealed to minimize air infiltration.

<u>Performance Test</u> – Perform annual inspections of the following building envelope penetrations to ensure compliance with the operation plan:

- ❑ Basic envelope integrity (no holes, gaps or openings)
- ❑ Doors and door jams
- ❑ Windows and window frames
- ❑ Backdraft and mechanically operated dampers when fans are off

Provide documentation of corrections or a plan for correcting noncompliance. Each year, inspect 20 percent of the total conditioned space or 250,000 square feet, whichever is greater. For buildings 250,000 square feet or smaller, inspect the entire building.

Note: An Innovation Credit may be earned by conducting an infrared building scan once every five years and addressing any problems identified.

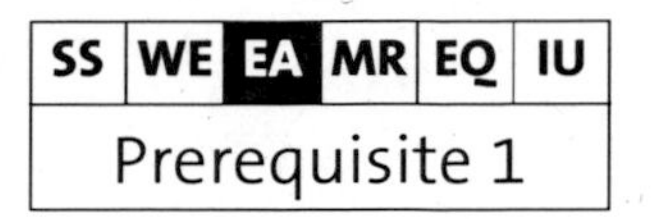

II. System-Level Performance

Primary HVAC Systems

1. Central Heating/Cooling Systems – Equipment Sequencing

   Building Operation Plan – Describe the intended sequence of operation for energizing, loading, unloading and de-energizing major, centralized equipment, such as boilers, chillers and cooling towers.

   Performance Test – Complete Option A or B at the time of application or include a plan for completion within a maximum of five years.

   Option A – Instantaneous Measurements – Design and conduct a performance test, and submit documentation to demonstrate that central heating and cooling systems are sequencing as intended.

   Option B – Short Term or Continuous Measurements – Demonstrate compliance with intended equipment sequencing by: 1) Installing appropriate data logging equipment; or 2) Using building automation system reports and/or trend log data. Utilizing the continuous measurements method may also help earn other LEED-EB prerequisites and credits including the following:

   - ❑ EA Credit 3.3: Building Systems Monitoring
   - ❑ EA Credit 5.1–5.3: Performance Measurement: Enhanced Metering

2. Central Heating/Cooling Systems – Supply Temperature Reset

   Building Operation Plan – For each applicable system (hot, chilled and condenser water), describe the intended sequence of operation for resetting supply water temperatures.

   Performance Test – Complete Option A or B at the time of application or include a plan for completion within five years.

   Option A – Instantaneous Measurements – Design and conduct a performance test, and submit documentation to demonstrate that supply water temperatures are being reset as intended.

   Option B – Short Term or Continuous Measurements – Demonstrate compliance with intended temperature reset by: 1) Installing appropriate logging equipment; or 2) Using building automation system reports and/or trend log data. Utilizing the continuous measurements method may also help earn other LEED-EB prerequisites and credits including the following:

   - ❑ EA Credit 3.3: Building Systems Monitoring
   - ❑ EA Credit 5.1–5.3: Performance Measurement: Enhanced Metering

3. Central Heating/Cooling Systems – Variable Volume Pumping Modulation

   Building Operation Plan – For each applicable variable volume pumping system, describe the sequence of operation and desired "turn-down" or performance criteria for modulation.

   Performance Test – Complete Option A or B at the time of application or include a plan for completion within five years.

   Option A – Instantaneous Measurements – Design and conduct performance tests, and submit documentation to demonstrate that variable volume pumping systems are modulating as intended.

   Option B – Short-Term or Continuous Measurements – Demonstrate compliance with intended variable volume modulation by 1) Installing appropriate logging equipment; or 2) Using building automation system reports and/or

trend log data. Utilizing the continuous measurements method may also help earn LEED-EB EA Credit 3.3: Building Systems Monitoring.

Air-Handling Units

1. Economizers

Building Operation Plan – Describe the intended sequence of operation for utilizing outdoor air to minimize mechanical cooling. Specify whether operation is based on enthalpy or dry bulb temperature.

Performance Test – Complete Option A or B at the time of application or include a plan for completion within five years.

Option A – Instantaneous Measurements – Conduct a field test, and submit documentation to demonstrate that air-handling unit economizers operate as intended. Note: It may be cost-effective to conduct this test at the same time as testing to comply with IAQ Prerequisite 1: Outside Air Introduction and Exhaust Systems.

Option B – Short Term or Continuous Measurements – Demonstrate compliance with intended economizer operation by: 1) Installing appropriate data logging equipment; or 2) Using building automation system reports and/or trend log data. Utilizing the continuous measurements method may also help earn other LEED-EB prerequisites and credits including the following:

- ❑ EA Credit 3.3: Building Systems Monitoring
- ❑ EA Credit 5.1–5.3: Performance Measurement: Enhanced Metering
- ❑ IEQ Credit 1: Outdoor Air Delivery Monitoring

2. Discharge Air Temperature Reset

Building Operation Plan – For each applicable air-handling unit (where terminal unit conditions are used to reset discharge air temperature) describe the intended sequence of operation.

Performance Test – Complete Option A or B at the time of application or include a plan for completion within five years.

Option A – Instantaneous Measurements – Design and conduct a performance test, and submit documentation to demonstrate that discharge air temperatures are being reset as intended.

Option B – Short-Term or Continuous Measurements – Demonstrate compliance with intended temperature reset by: 1) Installing appropriate logging equipment; or 2) Using building automation system reports and/or trend log data. Utilizing the continuous measurements method may also help earn other LEED-EB prerequisites and credits including the following:

- ❑ EA Credit 3.3: Building Systems Monitoring
- ❑ EA Credit 5.1–5.3: Performance Measurement: Enhanced Metering

3. Variable Air Volume Modulation

Building Operation Plan – For each air-handling unit with variable air volume capability, describe the sequence of operation and desired "turn-down" or performance criteria for modulation.

Performance Test – Complete Option A or B at the time of application or include a plan for completion within five years.

Option A – Instantaneous Measurements – Design and conduct a performance test, and submit documentation to demonstrate that variable air volume systems are modulating as intended.

Option B – Short-Term or Continuous Measurements – Demonstrate compliance with intended variable air volume modulation by: 1) Installing appropriate data logging equipment; or 2) Using building automation system reports and/or trend log data. Utilizing the continuous measurements method may also help earn other LEED-EB prerequisites and credits including the following:

- ❑ EA Credit 3.3: Building Systems Monitoring
- ❑ EA Credit 5.1–5.3: Performance Measurement: Enhanced Metering

Water Systems

One objective for this Existing Building Commissioning Prerequisite is to ensure that the water systems are operating in accordance with the current building operation plan. The LEED-EB Water Efficiency (WE) Section addresses plumbing fixture and irrigation system water usage and process equipment design efficiencies for dishwashers, cooling towers, evaporative cooling equipment, once-through process heating and cooling systems, humidification and make-up water systems. Operational efficiency (to ensure that these systems operate as intended) should be addressed as part of the system-level operation plan and associated performance tests outlined in this prerequisite. At a minimum, the building operation plan for water systems should include the performance criteria and validation outlined in WE Prerequisite 1: Minimum Water Efficiency and WE Prerequisite 2: Discharge Water Compliance.

Lighting Systems

Lighting systems, including all fixtures and their controls, play a vital role in both building energy use and IEQ. The objective for lighting systems in the Existing Building Commissioning Prerequisite is to ensure that they operate in accordance with the current building operation plan.

Control Systems

Building control systems play a vital role in both building energy use and IEQ.

Building Operation Plan – The control systems must operate according to the building operating schedule and provide equipment in the building with the appropriate signals to maintain the space environmental conditions in accordance with the building operation plan.

Performance Test – Demonstrate that the control systems are working in accordance with the current building operation plan. At a minimum, this demonstration needs to address building level performance, operating schedules, space environmental conditions, system level performance, primary HVAC systems, water systems and lighting systems.

Synergies & Tradeoffs

The commissioning process affects all dynamically operated components, equipment, systems and features. Site features on the project that require commissioning attention include alternative fueling stations and exterior lighting fixtures and systems. Water commissioning includes irrigation systems, plumbing fixtures and plumbing infrastructure. Energy commissioning covers HVAC systems, lighting, and energy generation equipment. Commissioning activities that affect IEQ include temperature and humidity controls, ventilation systems, monitoring equipment, occupant controls and daylighting systems.

Implementing an effective Existing Building Commissioning Program can help meet the requirements of other prerequisites and credits in the LEED-EB Rating System. These include:

- ❑ WE Prerequisite 1: Minimum Water Efficiency
- ❑ WE Prerequisite 2: Discharge Water Compliance

- ❑ EA Prerequisite 2: Minimum Energy Performance
- ❑ EA Credit 1: Optimize Energy Performance
- ❑ EA Credit 3.3: Building Systems Monitoring
- ❑ EA Credit 5.1–5.3: Performance Measurement
- ❑ IEQ Prerequisite 1: Outside Air Introduction and Exhaust Systems
- ❑ IEQ Credit 1: Outdoor Air Delivery Monitoring
- ❑ IEQ Credit 7.1–7.2: Thermal Comfort

Calculations & Documentation

Calculations

None.

Documentation

All information needed to successfully document this credit can be found in the Submittals and Requirements sections of the LEED-EB Rating System and the LEED-EB Letter Templates.

Other Resources

ASHRAE Guidelines

(800) 527-4723

www.ashrae.org

Several guidelines published by ASHRAE can be used as resources in developing and implementing an existing building commissioning plan. These include Guideline 0-2005 – The Commissioning Process and Guideline 1-1996 – The HVAC Commissioning Process. Both are available for purchase online (http://resourcecenter.ashrae.org/store/ashrae/).

California Commissioning Collaborative

(503) 595-4432

www.cacx.org

The California Commissioning Collaborative is a group of government, utility and building services professionals committed to developing and promoting viable building commissioning practices in California. Their online library (http://es57055.easystreet.com /library/) has over 300 resources, including articles, papers, guides and sample commissioning documents.

Energy Star® Building Manual

(888) STAR-YES

www.energystar.gov

This manual is a strategic guide for planning and implementing energy-saving building upgrades, including a chapter on recommissioning. It provides general methods and procedures for reviewing/adjusting system control settings, and testing/correcting calibration and operation of system components, such as sensors, actuators and controlled devices. The manual is available online at www.energystar.gov/index.cfm?c=business.bus_upgrade_manual.

A Practical Guide for Commissioning Existing Buildings

Report Number: ORNL/TM-1999/34 (May 1999)

http://eber.ed.ornl.gov/commercialproducts/retrocx.htm

This guide, prepared by Portland Energy Conservation, Inc. and Oak Ridge National Laboratory, provides information on rigorous functional performance and performance testing of many of the primary and secondary systems and components commonly found in existing buildings.

Retro-Commissioning Handbook for Facility Managers

www.energy.state.or.us/bus/comm/retrocx.pdf

Prepared for the Oregon Office of Energy by Portland Energy Conservation, Inc., this handbook provides building owners and manages with basic information about the retrocommissioning process.

Definitions

Existing Building Commissioning involves developing a building operation plan that identifies current building operating requirements and needs, conducting tests to proactively determine if the building and fundamental systems are operating in accordance with the building operation plan, and finally making any repairs needed so that the building and fundamental systems are operating according to the plan.

SS | WE | EA | MR | EQ | IU

Prerequisite 2

Required

Minimum Energy Performance

Intent

Establish the minimum level of energy efficiency for the building and systems.

Requirements

Demonstrate that the building has achieved an EPA ENERGY STAR rating of at least 60 utilizing the EPA's Portfolio Manager tool for building types addressed by ENERGY STAR,

OR

For building types not addressed by ENERGY STAR, demonstrate that the building has energy performance equivalent to an ENERGY STAR rating of at least 60, as calculated using the alternate method described in the LEED-EB Reference Guide.

Submittals – Initial Certification

- ❑ If the building type is addressed by ENERGY STAR, provide Portfolio Manager tool output, the Statement of Energy Performance, documenting that the building energy has achieved an EPA ENERGY STAR rating of at least 60.
- ❑ Provide a summary of the annual bills, including cost and usage amounts (kilowatt-hours, therms, gallons, etc.), for each type of energy used by the building.
- ❑ Provide copies of monthly building utility bills for the performance period (at least 3 months).

OR

- ❑ If the building is not a building type addressed by ENERGY STAR, provide calculations showing the building energy efficiency and performance meet the equivalent of an EPA ENERGY STAR rating of at least 60 using the alternate calculation method described in the LEED-EB Reference Guide.
- ❑ Provide a summary of the annual bills including cost and usage amounts (kilowatt-hours, therms, gallons, etc.) for each type of energy used by the building annually over the performance period.
- ❑ Provide copies of monthly building utility bills for the performance period (at least 3 months).

Submittals – Recertification

- ❑ If the building type is addressed by ENERGY STAR, provide an updated Statement of Energy Performance documenting that the building continues to maintain an EPA ENERGY STAR rating of at least 60.
- ❑ Provide a summary of the annual bills, including cost and usage amounts (kilowatt-hours, therms, gallons, etc.), for each type of energy used by the building annually over the performance period.
- ❑ Provide copies of monthly of building utility bills for the performance period (at least 12 months).

OR

- ❑ If the building is not a building type addressed by ENERGY STAR, provide calculations showing the building energy efficiency and performance continues to meet the equivalent of an EPA ENERGY STAR rating of at least 60 using the alternate calculation method described in the LEED-EB Reference Guide.
- ❑ Provide a summary of the annual bills, including cost and usage amounts (kilowatt-hours, therms, gallons, etc.), for each type of energy used by the building annually over the performance period.
- ❑ Provide copies of the most recent 12 months of building utility bills.

Summary of Referenced Standards

ENERGY STAR® Portfolio Manager

Tools for calculating the ENERGY STAR performance rating

U.S. Environmental Protection Agency

(888) 782-7937

www.energystar.gov

ENERGY STAR is a federal program helping businesses and individuals protect the environment through superior energy efficiency. Because a strategic approach to energy management can produce twice the savings—for the bottom line and the environment—as typical approaches, EPA's ENERGY STAR partnership offers a proven energy management strategy that helps in measuring current energy performance, setting goals, tracking savings, and rewarding improvements

Green Building Concerns

A variety of building mechanical systems and activities within buildings rely heavily on energy. Reducing energy use will decrease both operating costs and environmental degradation. As a result, well-planned energy efficiency upgrades can usually be designed and financed so the resulting energy cost savings pay for the investment over time.

Environmental Issues

Energy efficiency reduces the environmental burdens associated with energy production and use. Fossil fuels, the most common source of energy used in buildings, are a finite resource and the process of extracting and consuming energy from them causes many environmental impacts. These impacts include air pollution, solid waste generation and water pollution. Emissions of greenhouse gases and other pollutants that degrade air and water quality are of particular concern. In 2000, the U.S. industrial and commercial sectors accounted for nearly half of the nation's fossil fuel-related CO_2 emissions.[8] Furthermore, greenhouse gases and other emissions increase every year as overall energy consumption increases. Between 1990 and 2000, annual greenhouse gas emissions from U.S. energy use increased by nearly 14 percent.[9] As the far-reaching implications of global climate change are becoming more apparent and serious, reducing emissions through energy efficiency becomes more important.

Other sources of energy also carry environmental costs. Hydropower activities, for example, can alter aquatic ecosystems and have significant impacts on endangered species. Nuclear power plants also pose an environmental threat, as they are being decommissioned without sufficient storage sites for spent fuel materials. Given the environmental impacts inherent to most energy-production processes and limited energy supplies, efficiency measures are an important strategy for managing the impacts of energy consumption.

Economic Issues

Carefully designed energy efficiency upgrades in buildings can frequently pay for themselves from the resulting energy savings. Even small measures are significant. For instance, replacing an incandescent lamp with a fluorescent lamp uses up to 75 percent less energy and saves $30–$50 in energy costs over the lifetime of the lamp.[10] By bundling short payback actions like lighting upgrades with long payback options like chiller upgrades, efficiency actions can frequently be created that have payback periods that meet the financial performance requirements of the building owner.

ENERGY STAR offers businesses a suite of energy-related financial metrics to understand the effectiveness of current practices and find opportunities to improve

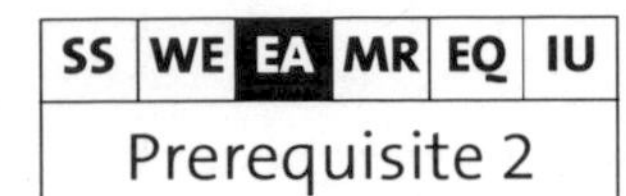

corporate energy management practices. The metrics allow senior decision-makers and financial analysts to gauge quickly and accurately a company's energy management performance within its specific industry. An online calculator to help determine the financial value of energy efficiency can be found at www.energystar.gov/index.cfm?c=assess value.bus financial value calculator. The metrics place organization-wide energy expenditures in a strategic financial context. They can be used to assess operating efficiency, business risk and growth potential.

Strategies & Technologies

Implement energy efficiency retrofits, effective building and equipment maintenance, and other energy-saving techniques to reduce energy use to the level required to meet this prerequisite. Use the resources below to determine current energy performance. Then identify opportunities for improvement by going to the ENERGY STAR web site (www.energystar.gov) and selecting "Reduce building and facility energy use in your organization" under the "Business Improvement" heading. Additional information on energy efficiency opportunities can be found under EA Credit 1: Optimize Energy Performance.

Assessing Building Performance with the ENERGY STAR Portfolio Manager

Use the ENERGY STAR Portfolio Manager on the ENERGY STAR web site (www.energystar.gov/index.cfm?c=evaluate performance.bus portfoliomanager) to assess the energy performance of your building:

- ❑ Enter the requested energy use and other building data
- ❑ Print out the data entered and the rating received. For covered building types, the impact of factors outside of your control (e.g., location, occupancy, and fuel type) are removed, providing a 1–100 ranking of a building's energy performance relative to the national building market.

For Building Types Not Covered by the ENERGY STAR Building Performance Rating System

See the Calculations section below. Contact the LEED-EB Hot Line (Email: leed-eb@usgbc.org, or 1-866-USGBC-EB) for the latest information on how to address EA Prerequisite 2 and EA Credit 1.

Synergies & Tradeoffs

Achievements beyond the minimum energy performance defined under this prerequisite may earn up to 10 points under EA Credit 1: Optimize Energy Performance. Further information about the synergies and tradeoffs of energy efficiency measures can be found under EA Credit 1.

Calculations & Documentation

Calculations

The Calculation methods presented below are used for this prerequisite as well as EA Credit 1: Optimize Energy Performance.

Buildings Covered by ENERGY STAR

For building types covered by the ENERGY STAR building energy performance rating system, gather the data required and input it into ENERGY STAR Benchmarking Tool calculator on the ENERGY STAR web site. Input data in the Portfolio Manager for all types of energy used in the building, including electricity, natural gas, fuel oil, diesel fuel, district steam or hot water, district chilled water, propane, liquid propane, and wood and others. Based on this information, assess the building's energy performance. Although not required by LEED-EB, building projects can then officially apply for the ENERGY STAR label by completing an Application Letter and having a professional engineer validate the Statement of Energy Performance.

The Professional Engineer's Guide to the ENERGY STAR ® Label for Buildings, at http://www.energystar.gov/ia/business/evaluate_performance/pm_pe_guide.pdf, explains how to use the Portfolio Manager. As stated in the guide, renewable energy generated on site should not be included in the Portfolio Manager for most projects. However, for LEED-EB purposes, projects applying for EA Credit 2: On-Site or Off-Site Renewable Energy must include renewable energy generated and consumed on site in the ENERGY STAR portfolio (enter this on-site renewable data by adding an "Other" meter type to the portfolio). This ensures that projects using renewable energy are fairly rewarded under LEED-EB, regardless of whether the renewable energy is generated on site or off site.

An ENERGY STAR rating of at least 60 is required to meet this prerequisite. The number of points awarded for EA Credit 1 is based on the building's ENERGY STAR rating as shown in the Requirements section of that credit.

Buildings Not Covered by ENERGY STAR

For building types not covered by the ENERGY STAR rating system, LEED-EB has developed a methodology for this prerequisite (and EA Credit 2) that can be used to evaluate improvements in building performance over time within a context of the performance of similar buildings. Because the ENERGY STAR rating system compares building performance with that of other buildings of similar type/climate, LEED-EB has integrated a number of strategies to most accurately model this approach for buildings that are not addressed by ENERGY STAR.

To achieve EA Prerequisite 2, the applicant must develop and document a **building energy performance baseline** from historical energy use data. The applicant must document a reduction in annual energy use of 10% or greater from the building energy performance baseline.

Points are awarded under EA Credit 2 corresponding with the reductions from the building energy performance baseline as described in **Table 1**.

Developing the Building Energy Performance Baseline

For building types not covered by the ENERGY STAR rating system, LEED-EB requires the development of a building energy performance baseline to determine current energy efficiency relative to past performance. Steps 1-3 below describe the process for establishing the building energy performance baseline.

Step 1: Determine Historical Average Energy Use

Determine the historical average energy use of the building by averaging 3 consecutive years of historical energy use data. The 3 years of data must fall within 6 years of the beginning of the application performance period. If major energy efficiency improvements have been made recently, the most advantageous approach is to use the energy use data from the most distant years within the 6-year interval.

Table 1: Point Scale for Energy Efficiency in Buildings Not Covered by ENERGY STAR

Reduction in Energy Use from the Baseline [%]	10	13	17	21	25	29	33	37	41	45	49
LEED-EB Points Earned	Meet EA Prereq. 2	1	2	3	4	5	6	7	8	9	10

Example: Historical Average Energy Use Calculation for a building applying for LEED-EB with a performance period beginning in 2005.

1999 Energy Use = 127,458 kBtu

2000 Energy Use = 127,478 kBtu

2001 Energy Use = 127,438 kBtu

Historical Average Energy Use = 127,458 kBtu

Step 2: Determine Percent Reduction in Energy Use Relative to Historical Average Energy Use

To use historical building energy use data to establish the building energy performance baseline, use **Equation 1** to compare current annual energy use to historical average energy use. The current and historical energy use data should include energy from all sources, such as electricity, natural gas, fuel oil, diesel fuel, district steam or hot water, district chilled water, propane, liquid propane and wood. Renewable energy generated and consumed on-site should only be included if the project is applying for EA Credit 2: On-Site and Off-Site Renewable Energy.

Example:

Current annual building energy use is 85,112 kBtu, and the three-year historical average energy use is 127,458 kBtu. The percent reduction in current energy use compared to the historical average energy use is 33 percent.

Step 3: Determine, and if necessary, Recalibrate Building Energy Performance Baseline

For building types not addressed by ENERGY STAR, LEED-EB determines the building energy performance baseline with the intent of establishing a proxy for the 'average energy performance of a similar building in a similar climate' represented by a score of 50 in the ENERGY STAR tool. Because historical data is insufficient to fully inform LEED-EB reviewers as to the performance of a building relative to similar buildings, the two options below are offered to applicants:

Note: This baseline is determined and set during the initial LEED-EB certification application and review process. Applications for LEED-EB recertification compare building energy performance with the building energy performance baseline set in the initial certification and review process.

Option A – Determine the Energy Performance Baseline Using Only Historical Data

If the Percent Reduction in Energy Use is *30 percent or less*, the historical average energy use is the building energy performance baseline. Points under EA Credit 2 are awarded based on this reduction corresponding to **Table 1**.

If the Percent Reduction in Energy Use is *more than 30 percent*, the baseline must be recalibrated so that current energy use equals a 30 percent reduction from the baseline. In this case the historic annual average is assumed to represent below-average energy performance as compared to similar buildings in a similar climate. Therefore, it is not equivalent to the ENERGY STAR methodology of comparing current energy performance to that of an average, similar building.

Using **only** the historical average data, a maximum of five points can be awarded (even if reductions correspond to higher point totals). Use **Equation 2** to set the baseline so that current energy use is equal to 30 percent of the baseline.

Example:

Because the Percent Reduction in Energy Use from the Equation 1 example above

Equation 1

Percent Reduction in Energy Use = ((Annual Baseline Energy Use - Current Annual Energy Use) / Baseline Energy Use) x 100

Equation 2

Building Energy Performance Baseline = Current Annual Energy Use / 0.7

Equation 3

Historical ratio = Sum of historical average energy use during performance period / Total historical average annual use

Equation 4

Annual energy use = Energy use during performance period (minimum of three consecutive months) / Historical ratio

is greater than 30 percent and data from other, similar buildings is not provided to substantiate the historical data as being representative of average for that building type, the baseline is not set at the historical average. Instead, the baseline is set at 123,890 kBtu, so that current energy use is equal to a 30 percent reduction in comparison to the baseline (85,112 / 0.7 = 121,589).

Option B – Determine the Energy Performance Baseline Using Historical Data and Data on the Average Performance of Comparable Buildings

In addition to the historical data for the building described in Option A, provide energy use data for other buildings with similar uses that convincingly establishes the "average energy performance of a similar building in a similar climate." Satisfactory provision of this information will allow for the integration of the data on similar buildings with the historic energy use data for the applicant building to determine the building energy performance baseline. Successful completion of this approach allows the applicant to earn up to ten points under EA Credit 2.

Performance Periods of Less than One Year for Buildings Not Covered by ENERGY STAR

Energy use data from the performance period is needed to demonstrate that the building's energy performance has been improved relative to the baseline. For first-time certification under LEED-EB, the minimum amount of performance period energy use data required is 3 consecutive months.

In order to compare current performance data to the baseline, compare the average annual energy use over the performance period with the energy use baseline. For performance periods of less than one year, extrapolate for the partial year data to annual energy use by using the method described below:

1. Calculate historical average energy use on a monthly basis as shown in **Table 2**.

2. Use **Equation 3** to determine the historical ratio of energy use during performance period months to annual energy use.

From the example in **Table 1**, the historical ratio for the months of June, July, and August is equal to 0.245456 ((9,743 + 10,552 + 10,990) / 127,458).

3. Use **Equation 4** to calculate annual energy use from performance period data and the historical ratio.

Expanding on the example above, **Table 3** provides performance period data from the months of June, July and August.

Based on energy use during the performance period of 27,683 kBtu and a historical ratio of 0.245456, annual energy use for this example is equal to 112,781.9 kBtu.

This calculation provides the effective annual energy consumption to use in

Table 2: Example of Historical Average Energy Use

	Energy Use from All Sources [kBtu]			
	2001	2002	2003	Historical Average
January	12,158	11,124	12,420	11,901
February	11,978	11,487	11,962	11,809
March	10,205	11,100	11,250	10,852
April	9,872	10,302	9,578	9,917
May	8,988	9,465	9,674	9,376
June	9,784	9,322	10,124	9,743
July	10,112	10,224	11,320	10,552
August	11,122	10,890	10,958	10,990
September	10,436	10,120	9,735	10,097
October	9,886	9,950	9,470	9,769
November	10,795	10,463	10,785	10,681
December	11,563	12,320	11,432	11,772
Totals	126,899	126,767	128,708	127,458

Table 3: Example of Performance Period Energy Use

	2004 Energy Use [kBtu]
June	8,643
July	9,720
August	9,320
Total	**27,683**

Based on energy use during the performance period of 27,683 kBtu and a historical ratio of 0.245456, annual energy use for this example is equal to 112,781.9 kBtu.

the performance evaluation to meet this prerequisite.

Recertification under LEED-EB for Buildings Not Covered by ENERGY STAR

The same baseline developed in the initial certification application and review process is used as the building energy performance baseline in the recertification applications.

Documentation

All information needed to successfully document this credit can be found in the Submittals section of the LEED-EB Rating System and the LEED-EB Letter Templates.

Other Resources

Advanced Buildings Technologies & Practices

www.advancedbuildings.org

This web resource supported by Natural Resources Canada presents energy-efficient technologies and strategies for commercial buildings, along with pertinent case studies.

American Council for an Energy Efficient Economy (ACEEE)

www.aceee.org

(202) 429-8873

ACEEE is a nonprofit organization dedicated to advancing energy efficiency through technical and policy assessments, advising policymakers and program managers, collaborating with businesses, public interest groups and other organizations, and providing education and outreach through conferences, workshops and publications.

American Society of Heating, Refrigeration and Air Conditioning Engineers (ASHRAE)

(800) 527-4723

www.ashrae.org

ASHRAE has developed a number of publications on energy use in existing buildings, including Standard 100-1995: Energy Conservation in Existing Buildings. This standard defines methods for energy surveys, provides guidance for operation and maintenance, and describes building and equipment modifications that result in energy conservation.

EPA Buildings Upgrade Manual

www.energystar.gov/index.cfm?c=business.bus_upgrade_manual&layout=print

This document is a guide for ENERGY STAR Buildings Partners to use in planning and implementing profitable energy-efficiency upgrades in their facilities and can be used as a comprehensive framework for an energy strategy.

IESNA Lighting Handbook (Ninth Edition), IESNA, 2000.

Mechanical and Electrical Equipment for Buildings, 9th Edition, by Benjamin Stein and John S. Reynolds, John Wiley and Sons, 2000

New Buildings Institute (NBI)

(509) 493-4468

www.newbuildings.org

The mission of NBI is to encourage the efficient use of energy in buildings and to mitigate the adverse environmental impacts resulting from energy use in buildings. The site includes information that may be helpful when planning building upgrades, such as the Advanced Lighting Guidelines that describe energy-efficient lighting strategies

U.S. Department of Energy (DOE) Office of Energy Efficiency and Renewable Energy

(202) 586-9220

www.eere.energy.gov

The EERE web site provides a portal to information about energy efficiency and renewable energy, including the Commercial Buildings Energy Consumption Tool for estimating end-use consumption in commercial buildings.

Definitions

The **Building Energy Performance Baseline** is the average building performance for the specific type of building. For building types covered by ENERGY STAR, this is a score of 50. For building types not covered by ENERGY STAR, the building energy performance baseline is established with historic building energy use data and/or energy use data from other, similar buildings.

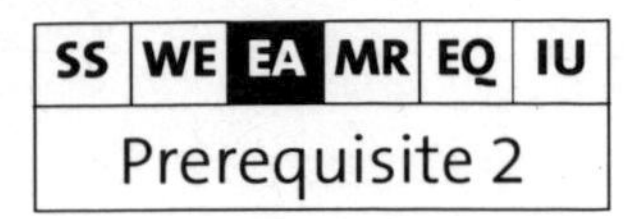

SS	WE	EA	MR	EQ	IU

Prerequisite 3

Required

Ozone Protection

Intent

Reduce ozone depletion.

Requirements

Zero use of CFC-based refrigerants in HVAC&R base building systems unless a third party (as defined in the LEED-EB Reference Guide) audit shows that system replacement or conversion is not economically feasible.

Definition of required economic analysis: The replacement of a chiller will be considered to be not economically feasible if the simple payback of the replacement is greater than 10 years. To determine the simple payback, divide the cost of implementing the replacement by the annual cost avoidance for energy that results from the replacement and any difference in maintenance costs. If CFC-based refrigerants are maintained in the building, reduce annual leakage to 5% or less using EPA Clean Air Act, Title VI, Rule 608 procedures governing refrigerant management and reporting and reduce the total leakage over the remaining life of the unit to less than 30% of its refrigerant charge.

Submittals – Initial Certification

- ❑ Provide documentation that base building HVAC&R systems do not use CFCs.

OR

- ❑ Provide results of third-party audit demonstrating that replacement is not economically feasible.
- ❑ Provide documentation showing compliance with EPA Clean Air Act, Title VI, Rule 608 governing refrigerant management and reporting.
- ❑ Provide documentation showing that the annual refrigerant leakage rate is below 5%, and the leakage over the remainder of unit life is being maintained below 30%.

Submittals – Recertification

Provide an update of previous filings:

- ❑ Provide documentation that base building HVAC&R systems do not use CFCs.

OR

- ❑ Provide results of a current (performed within the last five years) third-party audit demonstrating that replacement is not economically feasible.
- ❑ Provide documentation showing compliance with EPA Clean Air Act, Title VI, Rule 608 governing refrigerant management and reporting.
- ❑ Provide documentation showing that the annual refrigerant leakage rate is below 5% and the leakage over the remainder of unit life is being maintained below 30%.

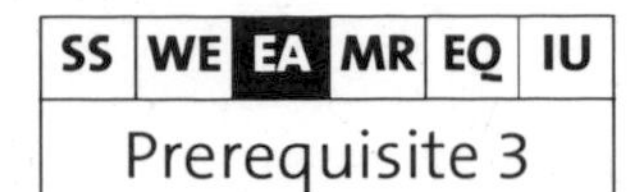

Summary of Referenced Standard

U.S. EPA Clean Air Act, Title VI, Section 608

Complying with the Section 608 Refrigerant Recycling Rule

U.S. Environmental Protection Agency

(800) 296-1996

www.epa.gov

Under Section 608 of the Clean Air Act, the EPA has established regulations on the use and recycling of ozone-depleting compounds. An overview of the pertinent regulations and information about compliance can be found at http://www.epa.gov/ozone/title6/608/608fact.html.

Green Building Concerns

Some refrigeration equipment in existing buildings use refrigerants containing chlorofluorocarbons (CFCs), which are halogenated substances that deplete the ozone layer in the Earth's atmosphere. The United States is one of the world's largest emitters of ozone-depleting substances. The world community has recognized the seriousness of ozone depletion, and 160 countries have signed the Montreal Protocol on Substances that Deplete the Ozone Layer. This treaty includes a timetable for the phase-out of production and use of ozone depleting substances, and, as a result, U.S. CFC production ceased in 1995.

As part of the U.S. commitment to implementing the Montreal Protocol, Congress included provisions in the Clean Air Act to protect the ozone layer. These provisions require EPA to develop and implement regulations for the responsible management of ozone-depleting substances in the United States. These regulations include programs for ending the production of ozone-depleting substances, identifying safe and effective alternatives to ozone-depleting substances, and requiring that manufacturers label products either containing or made with the most harmful Ozone Depletion Potentials (ODPs).

Environmental Issues

The use of CFCs in refrigeration equipment leads to their release into the stratospheric ozone layer, where they destroy ozone molecules through a catalytic process and deplete the Earth's natural shield for incoming ultraviolet radiation. CFCs in the stratosphere also absorb infrared radiation and function as potent greenhouse gases. Banning the use of CFCs in refrigerants slows the depletion of the ozone layer and reduces global warming effects.

Economic Issues

The standard practice in new buildings is to install equipment that does not use CFCs. However, existing buildings may already have chillers containing CFCs in place. The energy savings resulting from upgrading to more modern equipment may offset the cost of converting or replacing these existing systems. To earn this prerequisite, CFC equipment must be replaced if cost-effective. If it is demonstrated that it is not cost-effective to replace the CFC-containing chillers, they can remain in the building if refrigerant leakage is minimized.

For most older HVAC equipment (chillers) using CFC-based refrigerants, the efficiency increases resulting from advances in technology will often make replacement economically desirable. For example, replacing a 500-ton CFC chiller (0.85 kW/ton efficiency) with an efficient (0.56 kW/ton) non-CFC chiller can save $17,000/year, assuming a conservative $0.06/kWh.[11] However, if a third-party analysis shows that system replacement or conversion is not economically feasible, the HVAC&R base building systems using CFC-based refrigerants can continue

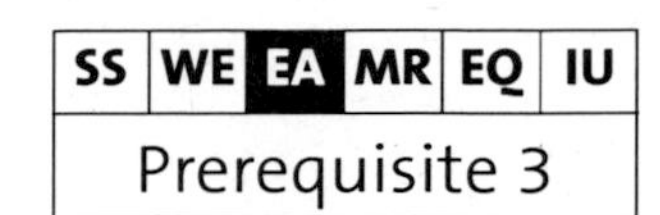

to be used in the building. A third party is someone not directly involved in the operation and maintenance of the affected HVAC&R base building systems.

Strategies & Technologies

Specify only non-CFC-based refrigerants in all new base building HVAC&R systems. Identify all existing CFC-based refrigerant uses and upgrade the identified equipment if economically feasible. If not, provide a third party analysis demonstrating that it is not feasible and implement a program to minimize leakage. The program to minimize leakage should specify loss minimization procedures and systems to meet annual loss minimization standards and reporting requirements. See the EPA's "Complying with the Section 608 Refrigerant Recycling Rule" for additional guidance.

For conversion or replacement systems, carefully consider the tradeoffs among the various CFC substitutes. Refrigerants have varying lifetimes, ozone depletion potentials (ODP) and global warming potentials (GWP). **Table 1** provides examples of lifetimes and ODP and GWP values for a variety of refrigerants used in HVAC equipment. It is beneficial to choose refrigerants with low lifetimes as well as low ODP and GWP values, since the longer a compound is present in the atmosphere, the more damage it can cause.

Upgrading HVAC equipment to meet this prerequisite can increase energy ef-

Table 1. Ozone-Depletion and Global-Warming Potentials of Refrigerants (100-yr values)

Refrigerant	ODP	GWP	Building Applications
Chlorofluorocarbons			
CFC-11	1.0	4,680	Centrifugal chillers
CFC-12	1.0	10,720	Refrigerators, chillers
CFC-114	0.94	9,800	Centrifugal chillers
CFC-500	0.605	7,900	Centrifugal chillers, humidifiers
CFC-502	0.221	4,600	low-temperature refrigeration
Hydrochlorofluorocarbons			
HCFC-22	0.04	1,780	Air conditioning, chillers
HCFC-123	0.02	76	CFC-11 replacement
Hydrofluorocarbons			
HFC-23	< 4x10-4	12,240	Ultra-low-temperature refrigeration
HFC-134a	< 1.5x10-5	1,320	CFC-12 or HCFC-22 replacement
HFC-245fa	~ 10-5	1,020	Insulation agent, centrifugal chillers
HFC-404A	~ 10-5	3,900	Low-temperature refrigeration
HFC-407C	~ 10-5	1,700	HCFC-22 replacement
HFC-410A	< 2x10-5	1,890	Air conditioning
HFC-507A	~ 10-5	3,900	Low-temperature refrigeration
Natural Refrigerants			
CO2	0	1	
NH3	0	0	
Propane	0	3	

Sources: Class I ozone-depleting substances, http://www.epa.gov/ozone/ods.html *U.S. EPA, 2002; Class II ozone-depleting substances,* http://www.epa.gov/ozone/ods2.html *U.S. EPA, 2002;. Global warming potentials of ODS substitutes, http://www.epa.gov/ozone/geninfo/gwps.html, U.S. EPA 2002; Inventory of U.S. Greenhouse Gas Emissions and Sinks, 291 pp., Washington, DC: EPA 430-R-04-003, 2004; "Scientific Assessment of Ozone Depletion: 2002," World Meteorological Organization Global Ozone Research and Monitoring Project, Nohende Ajavon et al., 2002, Report No. 47, http://www.unep.ch/ozone/Publications/index.asp.*

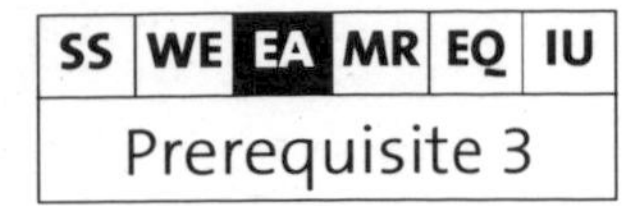

ficiency if equipment is chosen carefully. Unfortunately, there is no ideal alternative to CFCs. HCFC-123 and HFC-134a are the two most attractive substitutes at present. It is also important to check on phase-out periods for CFC substitutes being considered. Refrigerants phase out dates range from the near term to the long term. A schedule of phase-outs can be found at www.epa.gov/ozone/title6/phaseout/.

Synergies & Tradeoffs

This prerequisite is the first step in a two-step process to reduce a building's contribution to ozone depletion. The second step is discussed in EA Credit 4: Additional Ozone Protection.

Refrigeration equipment and refrigerant choices will impact the building's energy performance. Thus, it is important to balance energy efficiency with refrigeration choices. Depending on the age and other characteristics of the existing refrigeration equipment in the building, it may or may not be cost-effective to replace existing CFC-containing chillers with non-CFC equipment.

Calculations & Documentation

Calculations

The replacement of a chiller is considered economically infeasible if the simple payback of the replacement is greater than 10 years. To determine the simple payback, divide the cost of implementing the replacement by the annual cost avoidance for energy savings resulting from the replacement and any difference in maintenance costs. This must be determined by third-party analysis.

If CFC-based refrigerants are maintained in the building, reduce annual leakage to 5 percent or less using EPA Clean Air Act, Title VI, Section 608 procedures governing refrigerant management and reporting. Reduce the total leakage over the remaining life of the unit to less than 30 percent of its refrigerant charge.

For each HVAC&R system that uses CFC refrigerants, determine the percent refrigerant losses by using **Equation 1** below. If the performance period is not equal to one year, adjust the value determined in **Equation 1** to be the percent annual loss.

Documentation

- ❑ Documentation that base building HVAC&R systems do not use CFCs
  - Documentation should consist of a statement on organization letterhead signed by a responsible officer of the organization.

Other Resources

Benefits of CFC Phase-out

www.epa.gov/ozone/geninfo/benefits.html

This EPA document details the benefits of CFC phase-out, including brief case studies.

Building Owners Save Money, Save the Earth; Replace Your CFC Air Conditioning Chiller

www.epa.gov/ozone/title6/608/chiller1 07.pdf

This EPA brochure documents the environmental and financial reasons to replace CFC chillers with new, energy-efficient equipment.

Building Systems Analysis & Retrofit Manual, SMACNA, 1995.

Equation 1

Percent Refrigerant lost during the Performance Period = Refrigerant Lost During Performance Period [lbs.] / Total refrigerant contained in the Unit [lbs.]

This manual provides an overview of a number of topics relating to HVAC retrofits, including energy management retrofits and CFC/HCFC retrofits.

CFCs, HCFC and Halons: Professional and Practical Guidance on Substances that Deplete the Ozone Layer, CIBSE, 2000.

This booklet provides background information the environmental issues associated with CFCs, HCFCs, and halons design guidance, and strategies for refrigerant containment and leak detection.

Coping with the CFC Phase-out

www.facilitymanagement.com

This web site provides various articles on the issues of CFC phase-out from Facility Management magazine.

EPA's Significant New Alternatives Policy (SNAP)

www.epa.gov/ozone/snap/index.html

SNAP is an EPA program to identify alternatives to ozone-depleting substances. The program maintains up-to-date lists of environmentally friendly substitutes for refrigeration and air conditioning equipment, solvents, fire suppression systems, adhesives, coatings and other substances.

The Refrigerant Manual: Managing the Phase Out of CFCs, BOMA International, 1993.

This manual gives an overview of the phase out of CFCs, including information on retaining existing equipment, retrofitting existing equipment, or replacing equipment.

Stratospheric Ozone Protection: Moving to Alternative Refrigerants

http://es.epa.gov/program/epaorgs/oar/altrefrg.html

This EPA document includes 10 case histories on buildings that have been converted to accommodate non-CFC refrigerants.

Definitions

Chlorofluorocarbons (CFCs) are hydrocarbons that cause depletion of the stratospheric ozone layer and are used as refrigerants in buildings.

Halons are substances used in fire suppression systems and fire extinguishers in buildings and deplete the stratospheric ozone layer.

Hydrochlorofluorocarbons (HCFCs) are refrigerants that deplete the stratospheric ozone layer and are used in building equipment.

Refrigerants are the working fluids of refrigeration cycles that absorb heat from a reservoir at low temperatures and reject heat at higher temperatures

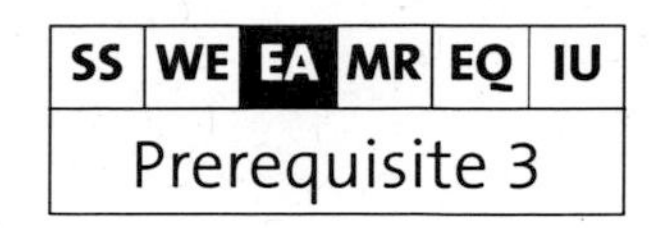

Case Study

National Geographic Society Headquarters

Washington, D.C.

Photo courtesy of: NGS Staff

LEED-EB Silver

Owner: National Geographic Society

The National Geographic Society (NGS) has systematically removed all CFCs refrigerants from major HVAC and refrigeration systems. CFCs have been replaced with more environment-friendly refrigerants in HVAC systems, food service refrigerators and freezers. The kitchen's centralized refrigeration system and specialized appliances, with the exception of drinking fountain water coolers, all use HFC refrigerants. All NGS chillers currently use HFC R-134a refrigerants, with the exception of two units, both of which are maintained in accordance with CAA Title VI, Rule 608. Maintenance records document an annual leak rate of 5% or less. Additionally, halons in fire suppression systems have been replaced with more environmentally-friendly agents.

SS	WE	EA	MR	EQ	IU
Credit 1					

1–10 points

Optimize Energy Performance

Intent

Achieve increasing levels of energy performance above the prerequisite standard to reduce environmental impacts associated with excessive energy use.

Requirements

Demonstrate the EPA ENERGY STAR energy performance rating that the building has achieved. Utilize ENERGY STAR'S Portfolio Manager tool for building types addressed by ENERGY STAR,

OR

For building types not addressed by ENERGY STAR, demonstrate the ENERGY STAR equivalent rating for the building energy use, calculated using the alternate method described in the LEED-EB Reference Guide.

ENERGY STAR Rating	LEED-EB Points
63	1
67	2
71	3
75	4
79	5
83	6
87	7
91	8
95	9
99	10

Submittals - Initial Certification

- ❑ Provide a summary of the annual bills, including cost and usage amounts (kilowatt-hours, therms, gallons, etc.), for each type of energy used by the building annually over the performance period.
- ❑ Provide copies of the most recent 12 months of building utility bills including both energy use and peak demand, if available.

AND EITHER

- ❑ If the building type is addressed by ENERGY STAR, provide Portfolio Manager tool output, the Statement of Energy Performance, documenting the building EPA ENERGY STAR rating over the performance period.
- ❑ If previously certified under LEED-NC, provide for the baseline (budget) building and design building projected energy consumption, projected peak demand and the energy points earned under LEED-NC.

OR

- ❑ If the building type is not addressed by ENERGY STAR, provide calculations showing the equivalent EPA ENERGY STAR rating for the building calculated using the alternate calculation method described in the LEED-EB Reference Guide.

Submittals - Recertification

Where documentation has been provided for EA Prerequisite 2, simply reference that material.

AND EITHER

- ❑ If the building type is addressed by ENERGY STAR, provide Portfolio Manager tool output, the Statement of Energy Performance, documenting the building EPA ENERGY STAR rating over the performance period.

OR

- ❑ If the building type is not addressed by ENERGY STAR, provide calculations showing equivalent EPA ENERGY STAR rating for the building calculated using the alternate calculation method described in the LEED-EB Reference Guide over the performance period.

Summary of Referenced Standard

Energy Star® Portfolio Manager

Tools for calculating the Energy Star performance rating

U.S. Environmental Protection Agency

(888) 782-7937

www.energystar.gov

Energy Star is a federal program helping businesses and individuals protect the environment through superior energy efficiency. Because a strategic approach to energy management can produce twice the savings—for the bottom line and the environment—as typical approaches, EPA's Energy Star partnership offers a proven energy management strategy that helps in measuring current energy performance, setting goals, tracking savings, and rewarding improvements

Green Building Concerns

Improving energy efficiency in buildings beyond minimum performance levels provides heightened benefits. Investing in high-efficiency equipment and other energy-saving practices provides a comfortable indoor environment, reduces operating costs and reduces the building's environmental impact without compromising building services or function. In existing buildings, well-planned energy efficiency upgrades can result in energy cost savings that exceed initial equipment costs.

Environmental Issues

Energy efficiency reduces air and water pollution, land degradation and the human health risks associated with energy production and use. Conventional forms of energy production have significant environmental impacts: burning fossil fuels creates air and water pollution, hydroelectric generation plants make waterways uninhabitable for indigenous fish and other aquatic species, and nuclear power generation poses safety concerns and problems with the disposal of spent fuel.

Economic Issues

Economic issues related to energy efficiency are discussed in Prerequisite 2: Minimum Energy Performance. By optimizing energy performance beyond the minimum requirements, operational costs can be further reduced. Because of the reliable energy cost savings in existing facilities, many organizations specialize in performing energy audits and offer energy performance contracts. These financing mechanisms attest to the cost-effectiveness of many energy efficiency improvements.

Strategies & Technologies

Improving your Energy Star score beyond that required in Prerequisite 2: Minimum Energy Performance could involve implementing major efficiency upgrades, employing additional energy-saving strategies beyond those currently in place or improving the effectiveness of current strategies. Options to reduce energy use include changes in occupant behavior, building operations improvements, upgrades to building equipment and systems, and improvements to the building site and shell.

Occupant Behavior

Building occupants can contribute to energy savings by turning on energy-consuming devices only when needed. For example, if building occupants set computers to "sleep" or "stand by" mode at the end of the day, they can save a significant amount of energy, particularly in office buildings with substantial quantities of computer equipment. Encouraging similar conservation practices for operating lighting systems, use of hot water, and

other energy-consuming activities can also help conservation efforts.

Building Operations

Commissioning, measurement and verification activities have a significant effect on energy use. Carefully monitor equipment to ensure that it is operating correctly to realize maximum energy savings. Set automated systems, such as HVAC and lighting equipment, to deliver conditions that reflect diurnal shifts in building occupancy. Window treatments can maximize passive solar gain and minimize heat loss during winter months, and minimize passive solar gain during summer months.

Equipment Upgrades

Consider energy efficiency when retrofitting or upgrading equipment. When purchasing new equipment in the building, from mechanical systems to small appliances or computer equipment, give preference to high-efficiency models. Make sure that the people responsible for purchasing energy-consuming equipment understand the energy efficiency goals so that they do not overlook opportunities to optimize energy efficiency. Coordinate water and energy efficiency goals, as water systems affect energy use. For example, low-flow plumbing fixtures can minimize the energy need for water pumps and hot water heating.

Site Improvements

Develop building site features to conserve energy. Landscaping can protect the building from wind, provide shade and not require automated irrigation systems that use energy. Site lighting can also have a significant effect on energy use, and should only be employed to the extent necessary to maintain safety conditions. Select site lighting that does not result in excessive lighting or direct light towards the night sky.

Building Shell Upgrades

Improvements to the building shell can lessen energy requirements needed to maintain space conditions within the building. Reflective roofing can reduce heat island effects and ambient temperature conditions, thus minimizing space cooling requirements. Upgrading windows can prevent heat transfer into and out of the building, thus providing opportunities to reduce the energy needed to heat and cool the building. Shell upgrades also provide an opportunity to incorporate daylighting features, which reduce the need for mechanical lighting systems.

Synergies & Tradeoffs

Energy consumption is closely linked to many building functions, which results in significant interaction between efficiency improvements and other green building issues. In many cases, sustainable improvements in another area will also improve energy efficiency, such as water efficiency measures. Conversely, tradeoffs between energy efficiency and other green building goals may be necessary. For example, in providing a high-quality indoor environment, balance provisions for energy efficiency with the preferred levels of thermal comfort and ventilation effectiveness.

LEED-EB prerequisites and credits related to energy efficiency include:

- ❑ SS Credit 1: Plan for Green Site and Building Exterior Management
- ❑ SS Credit 4: Reduced Site Disturbance
- ❑ SS Credit 6: Heat Island Reduction
- ❑ SS Credit 7: Light Pollution Reduction
- ❑ WE Prerequisite 1: Minimum Water Efficiency and Credit 3: Water Use Reduction
- ❑ WE Credit 1: Water Efficiency Landscaping

- ❑ EA Prerequisite 1: Existing Building Commissioning
- ❑ EA Prerequisite 2: Minimum Energy Performance
- ❑ EA Credit 2: On-Site and Off-Site Renewable Energy
- ❑ EA Credit 3: Building Operations and Maintenance
- ❑ EA Credit 5: Performance Measurement
- ❑ MR Prerequisite 2: Toxic Material Source Reduction – Reduced Mercury in Light Bulbs and MR Credit 6: Additional Toxic Material Source Reduction –Reduced Mercury in Light Bulbs
- ❑ IEQ Prerequisite 1: Outside Air Introduction and Exhaust systems
- ❑ IEQ Prerequisite 2: Environmental Tobacco Smoke (ETS) Control
- ❑ IEQ Credit 1: Outside Air Delivery Monitoring
- ❑ IEQ Credit 2: Increased Ventilation
- ❑ IEQ Credit 6: Controllability of Systems
- ❑ IEQ Credit 7: Thermal Comfort
- ❑ IEQ Credit 8: Daylighting and Views

In existing buildings, permanent building features may constrain opportunities to optimize energy efficiency. However, many efficiency upgrades in existing buildings are both feasible and cost effective with short payback periods. Project teams should consider which energy efficiency improvements are feasible, and then determine opportunities to incrementally implement them as funding and upgrade cycles allow.

Calculations & Documentation

Calculations

All calculations for this credit are described in EA Prerequisite 2: Minimum Energy Performance.

Documentation

All information needed to successfully document this credit can be found in the Submittals section of the LEED-EB Rating System and the LEED-EB Letter Templates.

Other Resources

Advanced Buildings Technologies & Practices

www.advancedbuildings.org

This web resource supported by Natural Resources Canada presents energy efficient technologies and strategies for commercial buildings, along with pertinent case studies.

American Council for an Energy Efficient Economy (ACEEE)

(202) 429-8873

www.aceee.org

ACEEE is a nonprofit organization dedicated to advancing energy efficiency through technical and policy assessments; advising policymakers and program managers; collaborating with businesses, public interest groups, and other organizations; and providing education and outreach through conferences, workshops, and publications.

American Society of Heating, Refrigeration and Air Conditioning Engineers (ASHRAE)

(800) 527-4723

www.ashrae.org

ASHRAE has developed a number of publications on energy use in existing buildings, including Standard 100-1995:

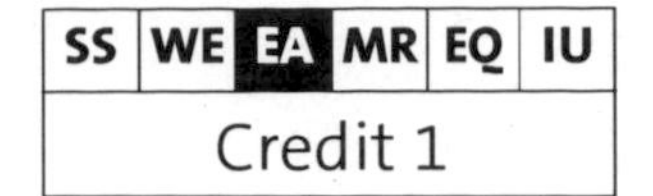

Energy Conservation in Existing Buildings. This standard defines methods for energy surveys, provides guidance for operation and maintenance, and describes building and equipment modifications that result in energy conservation.

EPA Buildings Upgrade Manual

www.energystar.gov/index.cfm?c=business.bus_upgrade_manual&layout=print

This document is a guide for ENERGY STAR Buildings Partners to use in planning and implementing profitable energy efficiency upgrades in their facilities, and can be used as a comprehensive framework for an energy strategy.

IESNA Lighting Handbook (Ninth Edition), IESNA, 2000.

This handbook for industry professionals includes comprehensive information about lighting concepts, techniques, application, procedures and systems.

Mechanical and Electrical Equipment for Buildings, 9th Edition, by Benjamin Stein and John S. Reynolds, John Wiley and Sons, 2000

This reference resource details information on the relationship between mechanical and electrical systems in buildings.

New Buildings Institute (NBI)

www.newbuildings.org

The mission of NBI is to encourage the efficient use of energy in buildings and to mitigate the adverse environmental impacts resulting from energy use. The site includes helpful information to plan building upgrades, such as the Advanced Lighting Guidelines that describe energy-efficient lighting strategies

U.S. Department of Energy (DOE) Office of Energy Efficiency and Renewable Energy (EERE)

(202) 586-9220

www.eere.energy.gov

The EERE web site provides a portal to information about energy efficiency and renewable energy, including the Commercial Buildings Energy Consumption Tool for estimating end-use consumption in commercial buildings.

Definitions

An **ENERGY STAR** rating is the rating a building earns using the ENERGY STAR Portfolio Manager to compare building energy performance to similar buildings in similar climates. A score of 50 represents average building performance.

Case Study

Karges-Faulconbridge Headquarters

St. Paul, Minnesota

LEED-EB Gold

Owner: Karges-Faulconbridge, Inc.

Photo courtesy of: Gallop Studios

Karges-Faulconbridge, Inc. (KFI) has a public goal of making their Headquarters building in St. Paul the most energy efficient of its kind in Minnesota. The design and upgrade of a variety of building mechanical and electrical systems to maximize energy efficiency have been implemented in pursuit of that goal. The building features a closed-loop ground source heat pump system, a constant volume energy recovery unit with passive desiccant wheel, an infrared heating system for the building core, multilevel switching, north facing vertical monitors with daylight harvesting sensors, and transient voltage suppression systems. These features and additional efficiency measures helped the KFI Headquarters achieve an Energy Star rating of 93.

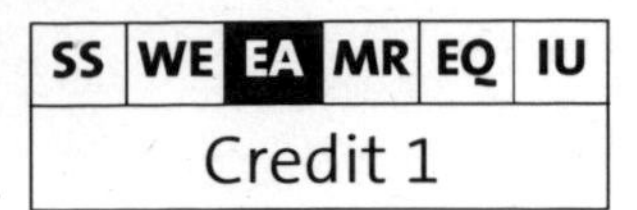

SS	WE	EA	MR	EQ	IU

Credits 2.1–2.4

1–4 points

On-Site and Off-Site Renewable Energy

Intent

Encourage and recognize increasing levels of on-site and off-site renewable energy in order to reduce environmental impacts associated with fossil fuel energy use.

Requirements

Over the performance period, meet some or all of the building's total energy use through the use of on-site or off-site renewable energy systems. Points are earned according to the following table. The percentages shown in the table are the percentage of building energy use over the performance period that is met by renewable energy.

Off-site renewable energy sources are as defined by the Center for Resource Solutions (CRS) Green-e products certification requirements or the equivalent. Green power may be procured from a Green-e certified power marketer, a Green-e accredited utility program, or through Green-e certified Tradable Renewable Certificates or the equivalent. At least 25% of any off-site green power or Green Certificates used to earn this credit needs to be from new sources (sources constructed after 1997). For on-site renewable energy that is claimed for LEED-EB credit, the associated environmental attributes must be retained or retired and cannot be sold.

Up to the four-point limit, any combination of individual actions will be awarded the sum of the points allocated to those individual actions. For example, one point would be awarded for implementing 3% of on-site renewable energy. Two additional points would be awarded for meeting 30% of the building's energy load with renewable power or certificates over the performance period.

LEED-EB Points	On-site Renewable Energy		Off-site Renewable Energy / Certificates
1	3 %	OR	15%
2	6 %	OR	30 %
3	9 %	OR	45%
4	12 %	OR	60%

Submittals – Initial Certification

- ❑ Provide system schematic diagrams and narrative highlighting on-site renewable energy systems installed in the building.
- ❑ Provide metered energy output of on-site renewable energy system over the performance period.
- ❑ Provide calculations documenting the percentage of the building's total energy requirements that was supplied by on-site renewable energy systems for the performance period.

OR

- ❑ Document the percentage of the building's total energy use that was met with renewable power or certificates over the performance period.

- ❑ Provide documentation demonstrating that the supplied renewable power or certificates over the performance period met the referenced Green-e requirements or the equivalent.
- ❑ Provide a letter stating a commitment to continue purchases of renewable power or certificates at the same or higher level over the next performance period.

Submittals – Recertification

Provide an update of previous filings:

- ❑ If there has been no change to the on-site renewable energy systems:
  - Provide metered energy output of on-site renewable energy system over the performance period.
  - Provide calculations documenting the percentage of the building's total energy requirements that was supplied by on-site renewable energy systems over the performance period.

OR

If there has been a change to the on-site renewable energy systems:

- ❑ Provide system schematic diagrams and narrative highlighting on-site renewable energy systems installed in the building.
- ❑ Provide metered energy output of on-site renewable energy system over the performance period.
- ❑ Provide calculations documenting the percentage of the building's total energy requirements that was supplied by on-site renewable energy systems for the performance period.

OR

- ❑ Document the percentage of the building's total energy use that was met with renewable power or certificates over the performance period.
- ❑ Provide documentation demonstrating that the supplied renewable power or certificates over the performance period met the referenced Green-e requirements or the equivalent.
- ❑ Provide a letter stating a commitment to continue purchases of renewable power or certificates at the same or higher level over the next performance period.

Summary of Referenced Standards

Green-e Renewable Electricity Certification Program

Green-e Standards for Renewable Energy

Center for Resource Solutions

(415) 561-2100

www.green-e.org

The Green-e Program is a voluntary certification and verification program for green electricity products. The program sets consumer protection and environmental standards for electricity products and verifies that Green-e certified products meet these standards.

Low Impact Hydropower Certification Program

Low Impact Hydropower Institute (LIHI)

(503) 227-1763

www.lowimpacthydro.org

LIHI's Low Impact Hydropower Certification Program certifies hydropower facilities that meet criteria regarding river flows, water quality, fish passage and protection, watershed protection, threatened and endangered species protection, cultural resource protection, recreation, and facilities recommended for removal. Facilities that meet the specifications of this certification program also qualify for certification through the Green-e program.

Green Building Concerns

Renewable energy sources include solar, wind, biomass and hydropower generation. Renewable energy is superior to conventional energy sources, such as coal, nuclear, oil, and natural gas, because power generation from renewable sources eliminates most of the negative environmental impacts of conventional sources. Although renewable, hydropower can have harmful environmental effects, including water quality degradation, fish injury and species endangerment. For this reason, this credit only covers low-impact hydropower.

In addition, renewable energy has a high coefficient of utilization (more electricity per unit of energy utilized) and does not require fuel transportation. Opportunities for renewable energy vary by location and climate, but there are many choices. On-site renewable energy technologies will reduce dependence on grid energy from fossil fuel and nuclear sources. Purchasing renewable energy from the grid or through the purchase of renewable energy certificates will also reduce harmful environmental impacts of electricity general from fossil fuels. Taking advantage of renewable energy, either on site or off site, is an excellent way for building owners to reduce the environmental impacts associated with a building's energy requirements.

Environmental Issues

The use of renewable energy reduces environmental impacts associated with the production and consumption of traditional fuels. These impacts include natural resource destruction, air pollution and water pollution. Renewable energy minimizes problems such as acid rain, smog and global climate change, and human health problems resulting from air contaminants. In addition, renewable resources avoid consumption of fossil fuels, production of nuclear waste, and operation of environmentally damaging hydropower dams.

The overall environmental benefit of renewable energy depends on the energy source and process by which energy is extracted from that source. For example, utilization of biomass can reduce the estimated 136 million tons of woody construction, demolition and land clearing waste annually sent to landfills.[12] Conversely, if these wastes are not processed properly, improper combustion could result in harmful air quality impacts. While green electricity is not environmentally benign, it drastically lessens the environmental impacts of power generation.

Economic Issues

Use of renewable energy sources can save energy costs in some areas. Utility and public benefit fund rebates may be available to reduce the initial cost of purchasing and installing renewable energy equipment. In some states, net metering can offset on-site renewable energy costs when excess electricity generated on site is sold back to the utility. For more information, contact local utilities, electric service providers or public benefit program managers.

The costs associated with purchasing renewable energy systems and green energy are becoming more comparable to traditional types of energy as technology improves and demand for renewable energy increases. In the future, renewable energy may even become less expensive than conventional energy as costs associated with human health and environmental degradation are factored into the price of electricity.

To some extent, renewable energy costs depend on the available sources. The cost of wind-generated electricity has decreased dramatically and is now available at costs very close to the cost of electricity generated by fossil fuels. The cost of electricity generated from photovoltaic cells has also decreased over time, although it is still higher than the cost of fossil fuel-generated electricity.

Strategies & Technologies

The two approaches under this credit can be applied separately or together to earn points. The first approach is to use on-site nonpolluting-source renewable technologies to contribute to the total energy requirements of the building and site. The second is to purchase renewable energy or renewable energy certificates (RECs) to meet some or all of the building's energy requirements.

On-Site Renewable Technologies

Employ on-site nonpolluting renewable technologies that contribute to the total energy requirements of the building and site. Technologies to consider include high-temperature solar, geothermal, wind, biomass (using only sustainably harvested fuel), and bio-gas. Some of these are described in further detail below. Note that passive solar, ground-source heat pumps and daylighting do not qualify for points under this credit - these strategies are recognized under EA Credit 1.

Photovoltaics (PVs) are composite materials that convert sunlight directly into electrical power that can be used to power any type of electronic device or load. In the past, these materials were assembled into PV panels that required a structure to orient them to the sun. In recent years, the efficiency of the cells has increased, the cost has dropped, and the panels are smaller in size. As a result, Building Integrated Photovoltaics (BIPVs) are now in production. BIPVs are incorporated into building elements such as the roof, cladding or window systems.

PVs generate direct current (DC) electricity, which generally must be converted to alternating current (AC) for mainstream building systems. The conversion process requires electronic devices between the PV module and electrically powered appliances. Both dispersed and central converter schemes are possible. The conversion process also affords net metering, where power is put back into the utility grid when the local demand is less than the capacity of the PV array.

As shown in **Table 2**, PV systems are rapidly becoming cost-effective. The

Table 2: Photovoltaic Economic Trends

Photovoltaic Data	1995	2000	2005	2020–2030
Module Efficiency [%]	7–17	8–18	10–20	15–25
System Cost [$/W]	7–15	5–12	4–8	1–1.5
System Lifetime [years]	10–20	>20	>25	>30
U.S. Cumulative Sales [MW]	175	500	1000-1500	>50,000

Source: Photovoltaics: Energy for the New Millennium, U.S. Department of Energy (January 2000).

general rule is that PVs are cost-effective for customers located farther than a quarter of a mile from the nearest utility line. When considering BIPVs, the costs should discount the marginal savings on the replaced elements of the building such as roofing or cladding.

Although PV sources make up only a fraction of U.S. power generation, the market has sustained growth upwards of 25 percent over the last decade. The number of U.S. companies producing PV panels has doubled since the late 1970s, providing new economic opportunities for manufacturing host communities. PV module production for terrestrial use has increased 500-fold in the past 20 years. Between 1994 and 2002, U.S. production of PV cells and modules more than tripled to over 110,000 kilowatts.[13] Solar energy contributed about 63 trillion Btu in 2003, making up roughly 1 percent of U.S. total energy supply.[14]

Solar Hot Water Heating is an effective way to gather and use solar energy in many areas. If you choose to use this resource, implement a program to document the amount of renewable energy delivered by the solar hot water heating system.

Geothermal Energy is not widely available, but where available is an effective renewable energy resource. If you area is blessed with underground hot water at a high enough temperature to contribute to meeting your building's energy needs, consider using this resource. If you choose to use this resource, implement a program to document the amount of renewable energy delivered by geothermal energy.

Biomass is plant material such as trees, grasses and crops. These materials are renewable and can be produced sustainably, providing a continuous feedstock source for fuel generation. To generate electricity, biomass fuel is converted to heat energy in a boiler or gasifier. The heat is converted to mechanical energy in a steam turbine, gas turbine or an internal combustion engine, and the mechanical device turns a generator that produces electricity. Current biomass technology produces heat in a direct-fired configuration. The next generation of equipment uses a co-firing configuration where biomass is substituted for a portion of coal in a standard power plant furnace. Biomass gasifiers that process biomass into bio-methane, a gas that can be used similar to natural gas, are also available to a limited extent.

The most economical and sustainable biomasses are residue materials from regional industrial processes. Example materials include organic by-products of food, fiber, and forest production such as sawdust, rice husks and bark. In urban areas, pallets and clean woody yard waste may be available. There also may be a steady supply of wood fiber from local waste collection of construction, demolition and land clearing (CDL) debris. The cost to generate electricity from biomass varies depending on the type of technology used, the size of the power plant, and the cost of the biomass fuel supply.

The U.S. Department of Energy (DOE) estimates that biomass power is now the largest source of renewable electricity in the United States, supplying 2.9 percent of energy consumed in the nation in 2003. The almost 60 billion kWh of electricity produced each year from biomass is more electricity than the entire state of Vermont uses annually.[15]

Wind energy systems convert moving air to electricity. Wind energy installations are becoming increasingly popular as corporate power users and utilities realize the benefits of clean, low-cost, reliable wind energy. Horizontal axis wind turbines, the conventional type of wind turbines, harness wind energy with a three-bladed rotor. Recent innovations include a larger rotor diameter using advanced airfoils and trailing-edge flaps for over-speed control. In the future, more advanced wind turbines incorporating the latest materials and mechanical technologies will enter the marketplace. Power generated from wind produces no air or water pollution, involves no toxic or hazardous substances, and poses minimal threats to public safety. Concerns over noise and potential bird strike should be addressed when siting wind turbines.

The cost of wind energy has dropped by 85 percent during the last 20 years. The American Wind Energy Association (AWEA) estimates that roughly 6,374 megawatts (MW) of wind power capacity were installed in the United States as of January 2004, generating over 16 billion kilowatt-hours (kWh) annually, providing enough electricity for about 1.6 million average American households' annual use.[16] Large wind farms are being constructed in many states for regional electricity requirements, while microturbines are being installed for specific applications. The market for small wind systems (< 100 kW) had an estimated growth of 35 percent in 1999.[17] These small wind systems power homes and small businesses such as farms and ranches. The electricity potential from wind generation is enormous; using present technology, North Dakota could provide 40 percent of the power consumed in the United States.[18]

Purchasing Renewable Energy Generated Off-Site

Purchase renewable energy or renewable energy tradable certificates to meet some or all of the building's energy requirements. Determine the energy needs of the building from historical energy use. Research power providers in the area and select a provider that guarantees that a fraction of its delivered electric power is derived from net nonpolluting renewable technologies. If the building is in a state with open market electric competition, investigate green power and power marketers licensed to provide power in that state. If not, explore what renewable energy offerings your utility provides. Renewable energy credits or renewable energy certificates (RECs), which provide the environmental benefits of renewable energy generated elsewhere, can also be purchased. These RECs are often cost competitive because they are bought and sold in the competitive marketplace. Renewable electricity that qualifies for this credit is Green-e Certified or its equivalent, and is produced by solar-electric, wind, geothermal, biomass, or certified low-impact hydropower.

Synergies & Tradeoffs

Some buildings sites are more compatible with renewable energy strategies than others. Equipment for generating renewable energy requires space that may limit other site uses. Renewable energy equipment will impact energy performance of the building and requires commissioning and measurement & verification attention. Some building PV systems can be integrated with daylighting strategies.

Calculations & Documentation

Calculations

To calculate the percent of the building's annual energy use provided by renewable sources, first determine total energy use from all sources. This should be the same value determined in EA Prerequisite 2: Minimum Energy Performance. Then determine the percent of total energy use provided by on-site or off-site renewable sources, as shown in **Equations 1–3** below. All energy should be reported in kBtu. To convert on-site or off-site renewable energy to kBtu, multiply the kWh of electricity by 3,413 Btu/kWh and divide by 1,000 to get a kBtu value.

Example:

From the example in Prerequisite 2, annual building energy use for the performance period was determined to be 99,112 kBtu and included no energy produced on site. Of this, 32,000 kBtu were purchases from an off-site renewable energy source. This is equal to 32 percent of total annual energy use, which earns 2 points under EA Credit 2.

To determine the number of points earned use the scale presented in the Requirements section of this credit. Up to four points can be earned, and any combination of actions will be awarded the sum of the points allocated to those individual actions.

Documentation

- ❑ Statement of commitment to continue purchasing renewable power or certificates
  - This letter should consist of a statement on organization letterhead, signed by a responsible officer of the organization.

Other Resources

American Bioenergy Association

www.biomass.org

The web site of the industry trade association dedicated to developing the entire breadth of the bioenergy industry from power to fuels to bio-based chemicals.

American Wind Energy Association (AWEA)

(202) 383-2500

www.awea.org

AWEA is a national trade association representing wind power plant developers, wind turbine manufacturers, utilities, consultants, insurers, financiers, researchers and others involved in the wind industry.

Equation 1

On-site Renewable Energy Use [kBtu] = PV [kBtu] + Wind [kBtu] + Solar hot water [kBtu] + Geothermal [kBtu] + Other on-site renewable energy [kBtu]*

** Note: Ground source heat pumps, daylighting, and passive solar energy may not be included here.*

Equation 2

Percent On-site Renewable Energy Use =
(On-site Renewable Energy Use [kBtu] / Total Building and Site Energy Use [kBtu]) x 100

Equation 3

Percent Off-site Renewable Energy Use =
[Off-site Renewable Energy Use [kBtu] / (Total Building and Site Energy Use [kBtu] – On-site Renewable Energy Use [kBtu])] x 100

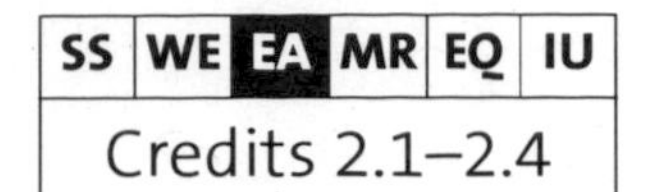

Database of State Incentives for Renewable Energy (DSIRE)

www.dsireusa.org

The North Carolina Solar Center developed this database to contain all available information on state financial and regulatory incentives (e.g., tax credits, grants and special utility rates) that are designed to promote the application of renewable energy technologies. DSIRE also offers additional features such as preparing and printing reports that detail the incentives on a state-by-state basis.

ENERGY Guide

www.energyguide.com

This web site provides information on different power types, including green power, as well as general information on energy efficiency and tools for selecting power providers based on various economic, environmental and other criteria.

Green Power Network

www.eere.energy.gov/greenpower

The Green Power Network provides news and information on green power markets and related activities and is maintained by the National Renewable Energy Laboratory for the U.S. Department of Energy.

National Center for Photovoltaics (NCPV)

www.nrel.gov/ncpv/

NCPV provides clearinghouse information on all aspects of PV systems.

National Renewable Energy Laboratory

www.nrel.gov

The National Renewable Energy Laboratory (NREL) is a leader in the U.S. Department of Energy's effort to secure an energy future for the nation that is environmentally and economically sustainable.

Office of Energy Efficiency and Renewable Energy (EERE)

www.eere.energy.gov

This web site includes information on all types of renewable energy technologies and energy efficiency.

U.S. EPA Green Power Partnership

www.epa.gov/greenpower/index.htm

EPA's Green Power Partnership provides assistance and recognition to organizations that demonstrate environmental leadership by choosing green power. It includes a buyer's guide with listings of providers of green power in each state.

Wind and Solar Power Systems, by Mukund Patel, CRC Press 1999.

This text offers information about the fundamental elements of wind and solar power generation, conversion and storage, and detailed information about the design, operation, and control methods of both stand-alone and grid-connected systems.

Wind Energy Comes of Age, by Paul Gipe, John Wiley & Sons 1995.

This book provides extensive information on the wind power industry, and is one of several books by the author covering general and technical information about wind power.

Definitions

Biomass is plant material such as trees, grasses and crops that can be converted to heat energy to produce electricity.

The **Environmental Attributes of Green Power** include emission reduction benefits that result from green power being used instead of conventional power sources.

Renewable energy certificates (RECs) are a representation of the environmental attributes of green power, and are sold separately from the electrons that make up the electricity. RECs allow the purchase of green power even when the electrons are not purchased.

Photovoltaic energy is electricity from photovoltaic cells that convert the energy in sunlight into electricity.

Renewable energy is energy from sources that are renewed on an ongoing basis. This includes energy from the sun, wind and small hydropower. Ways to capture energy from the sun include photovoltaic, thermal solar energy systems, and bioenergy. One issue with bioenergy is the amount of fossil fuel energy used to produce it.

Wind energy is electricity generated by wind machines.

Case Study

Len Foote Hike Inn

Dawsonville, Georgia

LEED-EB Gold

Owner: Georgia Department of Natural Resources

Photo courtesy of: Georgia DNR

The Len Foote Hike Inn is located at Amicalola Falls State Park in the North Georgia mountains. Operated by the Appalachian Education and Recreation Services and the Georgia Department of Natural Resources, the Hike Inn building is only accessible by foot using a five-mile trail. Upon arriving, each guest receives an educational tour featuring composting toilets, a rainwater collection system, worm bins that generate the compost from waste products, and the use of renewable/solar energy. The Len Foote Hike Inn building is equipped with photovoltaic panels producing at least 3,650 kilowatts DC of electrical power per year. The solar electric system was installed at a cost of $50,000.00 or $8.33 per sq ft and reduces annual operating costs.

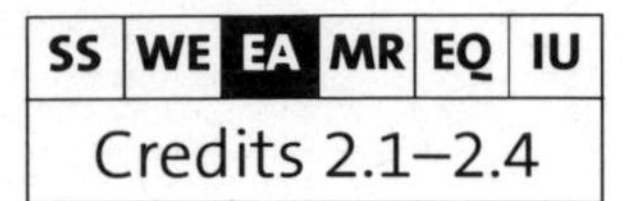
SS
WE
EA
MR
EQ
IU
Credits 2.1–2.4

SS	WE	EA	MR	EQ	IU

Credit 3.1

1 point

Building Operation & Maintenance

Staff Education

Intent

Support appropriate operations and maintenance of buildings and building systems so that they continue to deliver target building performance goals over the long term.

Requirements

Have in place over the performance period a building operations and maintenance staff education program that provides each staff person primarily working on building maintenance with at least 24 hours of education each year over the performance period. The education program should provide information on building and building systems operation, maintenance and achieving sustainable building performance. Training must be of high quality and relevant to building operations and maintenance.

Submittals – Initial Certification

- ❑ Provide documentation of the training received by building operations and maintenance staff for entire performance period.
- ❑ List the course titles and hours and annual total training hours for each staff person and the calculated annual average training hours for all by building operation and maintenance staff.

Submittals – Recertification

- ❑ Provide documentation of the training received by building operations and maintenance staff for entire performance period.
- ❑ List the course titles and hours and annual total training hours for each staff person and the calculated annual average training hours for all by building operations and maintenance staff.

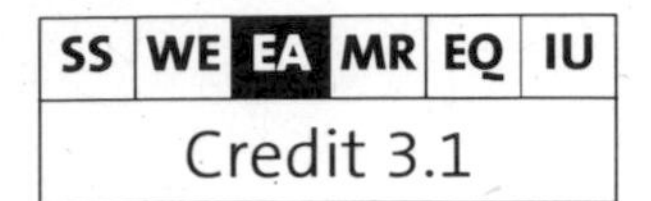

Summary of Referenced Standard

There is no standard referenced for this credit.

Green Building Concerns

This credit is not only relevant to EA, but also to all categories of green building. Establishing a minimum level of required training for building and site operation and maintenance staff ensures proper operation of a sustainable building. Site staff (e.g., building maintenance, building operation, landscaping, green cleaning) should be knowledgeable about green building operation and procedures in order to adhere to the building operation plan. All applicable staff should be familiar with building and site systems and policies, as well as general principles of green building and LEED. Proper education and training will improve indoor quality, site management, building operations, and materials use and disposal, and will provide the building and site with the knowledgeable and environmentally friendly caretakers it needs to be sustainable.

Environmental Issues

Optimizing building operation will reduce the building's environmental impacts. Educating staff about procurement and waste disposal policies, cleaning and maintenance procedures, and site maintenance methods will decrease unnecessary environmental effects due to negligence or ignorance. This is important in building systems operations, because proper commissioning of the building maximizes energy efficiency and minimizes the environmental impacts associated with energy production and consumption, such as natural resource extraction, air quality degradation and global climate change. In terms of green cleaning, some of the benefits of environmentally preferable cleaning products can be negated if the products are used or disposed of incorrectly.

Economic Issues

The costs associated with staff education need to be viewed relative to efficiency increases, extended equipment lifetimes and productivity increases resulting from superior operation of the building. Costs will include employee time to participate in educational events, as well as some development of materials and events, either by an outside consultant/vendor or a company employee.

Strategies & Technologies

Arrange on-site or off-site training for building and site operation and maintenance staff. The minimum 24 hours of training time per maintenance staff person can be delivered over the year in any combination of time increments. However, training sessions every few months over the course of the year help give green building operations a consistent and ongoing focus. Training should address building and building systems operation, maintenance and groundskeeping, and achievement of sustainable building and site requirements. Consider training and education on specific LEED-EB principles and credits to promote understanding of green building strategies. Educational sessions can be organized internally or by an outside source such as a consultant or a trade association. The Other Resources section of this credit lists organizations with training courses and/or materials.

Synergies & Tradeoffs

Regular training increases the capability of the operation and maintenance staff. However, training may take up time when the staff could be fulfilling other obligations and therefore must be scheduled to accommodate other responsibilities. Staff education can also indirectly assist

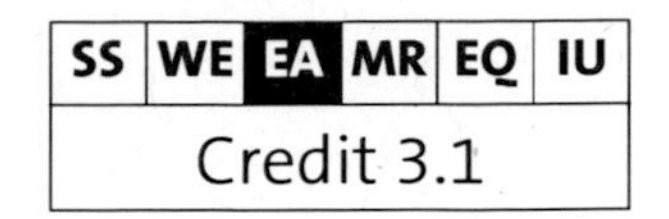

in meeting all LEED-EB prerequisites and credits.

Calculations & Documentation

Calculations

Compute and document the following statistics about training and education:

1. Total number of building and site operation and maintenance staff
2. Total number of training hours received by all building and site operation and maintenance staff
3. Average hours of training per applicable staff member
4. The highest and lowest number of training hours received by a single staff member.

Documentation

All information needed to successfully document this credit can be found in the Submittals section of the LEED-EB Rating System and the LEED-EB Letter Templates.

Other Resources

American Society of Heating, Refrigeration and Air Conditioning Engineers (ASHRAE)

www.ashrae.org

The ASHRAE Learning Institute (ALI) offers classes that utilize advanced information technologies, along with traditional instructor-based and self-directed studies.

Building Owners and Managers Association (BOMA)

www.boma.org/TrainingAndEducation/

BOMA provides training and education to facility managers and executives, corporate professionals, building owners and others.

International Facility Management Association (IFMA)

www.ifma.org

IFMA certifies facility managers, conducts research, provides educational programs and training, recognizes facility management degree and certificate programs and produces World Workplace, the largest facility management-related conference and exposition.

U.S. Green Building Council (USGBC) Workshops

www.usgbc.org

The USGBC offers training workshops for LEED and other green building topics.

Definitions

Operation and maintenance staff includes staff or contractors involved in operating, maintaining and cleaning the building and site.

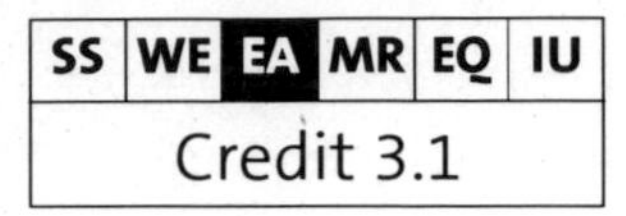
SS WE EA MR EQ IU
Credit 3.1

SS	WE	EA	MR	EQ	IU
Credit 3.2					

1 point

Building Operation & Maintenance

Building Systems Maintenance

Intent

Support appropriate operations and maintenance of buildings and building systems so that they continue to deliver target building performance goals over the long term.

Requirements

Have in place over the performance period a comprehensive Best Practices Equipment Preventative Maintenance Program that provides in-house resources or contractual services to deliver post-warranty maintenance.

Submittals – Initial Certification

- ❑ Document ongoing operation over the performance period of a Best Practices Equipment Preventative Maintenance Program including documentation of in-house resources or contractual services to deliver post-warranty maintenance.

Submittals – Recertification

- ❑ Document ongoing operation over the performance period of a Best Practices Equipment Preventative Maintenance Program including documentation of in-house resources or contractual services to deliver post-warranty maintenance.

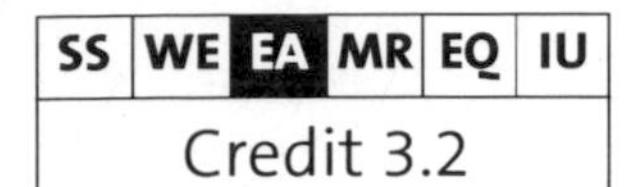

Summary of Referenced Standard

There is no standard referenced for this credit.

Green Building Concerns

If building systems are not well maintained, performance will diminish over time. Green buildings may have advanced systems, but insufficient maintenance will cause them to fail or function improperly, increasing operating costs and possibly offsetting the environmental benefits. Proper maintenance will ensure that potential environmental benefits are realized, increase the lives of the systems and postpone the expenses associated with complete system overhaul or replacement.

Environmental Issues

Scheduled maintenance increases energy efficiency and extends the lives of building systems, lowering replacement costs and the impact on material and energy resources. Energy efficiency depends greatly on the performance and efficiency of building systems; therefore, systems performing at optimal efficiency will have fewer environmental impacts than systems performing below par. Furthermore, building systems create large amounts of waste at the end of their useful lives, and the production of new systems can be costly in materials and energy, as well as economically. The best thing for both the environment and building owner is to keep all systems in proper working order through scheduled maintenance activities.

Economic Issues

Poor building equipment and system performance increase building energy use and operating costs. Periodic maintenance will reduce unscheduled downtime and ensure equipment is performing as intended. Scheduled maintenance also increases the life of the building systems, reducing or postponing costs associated with replacement. A study by Jones Lang LaSalle estimated that preventive maintenance programs have an average ROI of 545 percent due to increased efficiency and extended system lifetimes.[19]

Strategies & Technologies

Have in place over the performance period a comprehensive best-practices equipment preventative maintenance program. Schedule regular preventative maintenance for all of the equipment in the building, and document that maintenance activities are carried out according to the schedule. Include procedures to check for efficient operation of equipment in the preventive maintenance program, including evaluation of system controls. Internal staff or a contractor can carry out preventative maintenance.

Track scheduled maintenance activities on a spreadsheet. Include (1) name of the equipment, (2) scheduled date for preventive maintenance, (3) actual date the maintenance was completed, and (4) description of the preventive maintenance actions taken. More detailed records about maintenance and upgrade actions should also be kept.

Synergies & Tradeoffs

Preventative maintenance requires either staff time or money to hire an outside contractor. However, good preventative maintenance will result in paybacks from increased operating life of equipment, increased energy efficiency, and fewer unexpected equipment failures. Preventative maintenance can assist in meeting related credits, including EA Prerequisite 2: Minimum Energy Performance and EA Credit 1: Optimize Energy Performance.

Calculations & Documentation

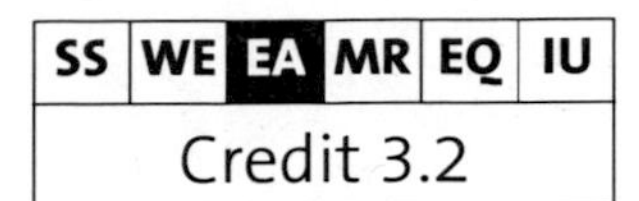

Calculations

None.

Documentation

All information needed to successfully document this credit can be found in the Submittals section of the LEED-EB Rating System and the LEED-EB Letter Templates.

Other Resources

Energy-Efficient Operation of Commercial Buildings, by Peter Herzog, McGraw-Hill 1997. This resource provides information about energy efficient building operation and management practices for commercial buildings.

Preventive Maintenance and Building Operation Efficiency

www.boma.org/ProductsAndResearch/PropertyManagement/PreventiveMaintenanceandBuildingOperationEfficiency.htm

This manual from the Building Owners and Managers Association (BOMA) gives insight into the newest developments in building operating efficiency and preventive maintenance.

Definitions

System lifetime is the length of time from installation to until a system needs to be replaced.

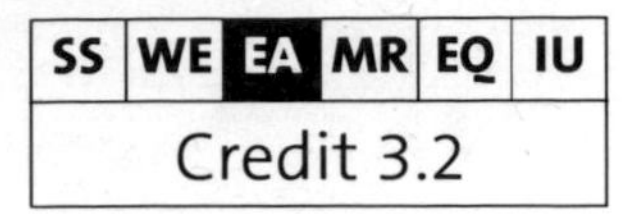
SS
WE
EA
MR
EQ
IU
Credit 3.2

SS | WE | EA | MR | EQ | IU

Credit 3.3

1 point

Building Operation & Maintenance

Building Systems Monitoring

Intent

Support appropriate operations and maintenance of buildings and building systems so that they continue to deliver target building performance goals over the long term.

Requirements

Have in place over the performance period a system for continuous tracking and optimization of systems that regulate indoor comfort and the conditions (temperature, humidity and CO_2) delivered in occupied spaces. The system must include:

- ❑ Continuous monitoring of system equipment performance and of the indoor environmental conditions delivered in the building.
- ❑ Alarms for performance or conditions that require repair.
- ❑ A system in place that delivers prompt repairs to problems identified.

Submittals – Initial Certification

For system descriptions provide:

- ❑ A narrative of the systems employed to continuously monitor equipment function and space conditions. The narrative must describe how these systems are used to identify and resolve equipment problems and to continuously deliver indoor comfort and the conditions delivered in occupied spaces.
- ❑ List of system equipment for which performance is monitored and the number of points monitored.
- ❑ List of the indoor environmental conditions parameters monitored and the number of points monitored for each.
- ❑ List of settings for alarms.
- ❑ Description of system in place for delivering prompt repairs to problems identified.

AND

For performance over the performance period provide:

- ❑ Documentation of alarms that occurred.
- ❑ Percentage of time that desired conditions are delivered in the building on a floor area weighted basis.

Submittals – Recertification

Provide an update of previous filings:

For system descriptions provide:

- ❑ Update of the description of the system in place if there have been any changes.

AND

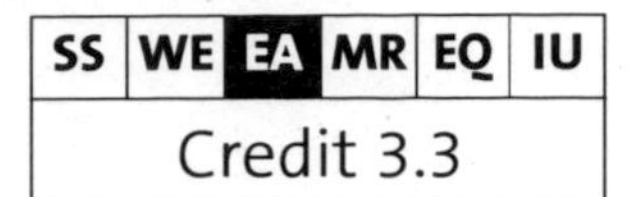

For performance over the performance period provide:

- ❑ Documentation of alarms that occurred.
- ❑ Percentage of time that desired conditions are delivered in the building on a floor area weighted basis.

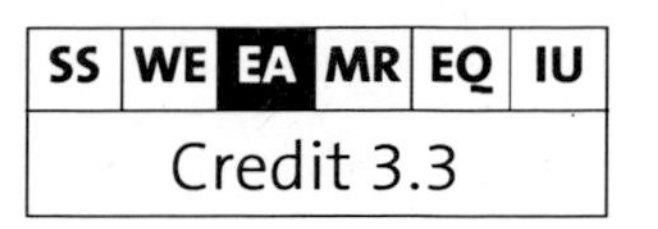

Summary of Referenced Standard

There is no standard referenced for this credit.

Green Building Concerns

Assuring the quality of the indoor environment for building occupants is important to make a building sustainable. Building controls systems have great capability for measuring, monitoring and providing alarms when desired temperature, humidity and carbon dioxide levels fall outside of the desired range. By using these capabilities and having a response program to fix problems as they are identified, the quality of the indoor environment delivered to the building occupants can be greatly improved.

In many buildings, occupant complaints are relied upon to identify deviations from desired ranges for temperature, humidity and carbon dioxide. By measuring, monitoring and responding to changes in temperature, humidity and carbon dioxide levels, facility staff can take a proactive approach to maintaining the desired indoor environmental conditions.

Environmental Issues

When buildings are monitored constantly, small fluctuations in indoor conditions can be sensed and addressed before they negatively affect building occupants. These systems also tend to provide increased energy efficiency, which reduces damage to the environment from energy use, such as air and water pollution, and damage from harvesting fossil fuels.

Economic Issues

Installing equipment to constantly measure the indoor environment incurs some costs. However, better control of the building's temperature, humidity and carbon dioxide levels should save energy and reduce the amount of productivity lost to occupant discomfort and complaints.

Monitoring equipment offers other advantages, as most automatic temperature control systems will allow automatic programming of temperature setpoints to save energy while the building is unoccupied. Programming the system to keep the temperature 10–15 degrees cooler for 8 hours each evening will result in a 5–15 percent savings on annual heating costs.[20] These systems can be set to increase the heat one half-hour before the office opens and to decrease it at night.

In addition to energy performance, decreased occupant productivity is an indirect operational cost associated with subpar building performance. An Oregon Office of Energy study estimated indirect costs associated with lost productivity due to occupant complaints about the indoor environment: if 20 percent of building occupants expended 30 minutes per month complaining about lighting or temperature conditions, the employer would lose $0.10 per square foot in annual productivity. For a 100,000-square-foot building, this equates to $10,000 per year.[21] Other potential costs of poor building performance cited by the Oregon Office of Energy include employee illness, loss of tenants, liability related to indoor air quality and premature equipment replacement.

Strategies & Technologies

This credit requires a system to be in place over the performance period for continuous tracking and optimization of mechanical systems that regulate indoor comfort and the conditions (temperature, humidity and CO_2) delivered in occupied spaces. The system must include (1) continuous monitoring of system equipment performance and of the indoor environmental conditions delivered in the building, (2) alarms for performance or conditions that require repair, and (3) a system in place that delivers prompt repairs to problems identified.

Synergies & Tradeoffs

Because monitoring building systems is helpful in maintaining proper indoor environmental conditions, the systems and strategies pursued for achieving this credit can also help earn IEQ Credits 7.1–7.2: Thermal Comfort and IEQ Credit 1: Outdoor Air Delivery Monitoring.

Calculations & Documentation

Calculations

None.

Documentation

All information needed to successfully document this credit can be found in the Submittals section of the LEED-EB Rating System and the LEED-EB Letter Templates.

Other Resources

American Society of Heating, Refrigerating and Air Conditioning Engineers (ASHRAE)

(800) 527-4723

www.ashrae.org

ASHRAE offers a number of resources related to operating mechanical building systems, including building automation systems.

Definitions

Monitoring points are locations where measurement sensors are installed.

Setpoints are normal ranges for building systems and indoor environmental quality outside which action is taken.

Case Study

Joe Serna Jr. CalEPA Building

Sacramento, California

LEED-EB Platinum
Manager: Thomas Properties Group

Photo courtesy of: John Swain Photo

Continuous commissioning of the CalEPA building environment is provided via automated building systems monitoring equipment. General building operating parameters are noted daily and regularly (air handlers, temperature, pressures, dampers and valve positions, fan status and etc.). Additionally, alarm and alert set points have been programmed into the automated system to indicate any conditions that may be out of range, resulting in critical alarm outputs to both of the engineering department operator workstations and main lobby security workstation. All comfort control zones, served by the variable air volume terminal units are checked for temperature and proper airflow on a floor-by-floor basis. Alarm and alert parameters are programmed for these units as well. Over time the building automation system has allowed engineering to tighten and fine turn the environmental controls.

SS	WE	EA	MR	EQ	IU
Credit 4					

1 point

Additional Ozone Protection

Intent

Reduce ozone depletion and support early compliance with the Montreal Protocol.

Requirements

Option A

- ❑ Do not operate base building HVAC, refrigeration or fire suppression systems that contain CFCs, HCFCs or Halons.

Option B

- ❑ Do not operate fire suppression systems that contain CFCs, HCFCs or halons,

  AND

  Reduce emissions of refrigerants from base building HVAC and refrigeration systems to less than 3% of charge per year over the performance period using EPA Clean Air Act, Title VI, Rule 608 procedures governing refrigerant management and reporting and reduce the leakage over the remainder of unit life to below 25%.

Submittals – Initial Certification

- ❑ Document that the base building HVAC, refrigeration and fire suppression systems do not contain CFCs, HCFCs or Halons.

Option B

- ❑ Document that fire suppression systems do not contain CFCs, HCFCs or halons.
- ❑ Document that emissions of refrigerants from base cooling equipment over the performance period are less than 3% of charge per year using EPA Clean Air Act, Title VI, Rule 608 procedures governing refrigerant management and reporting.
- ❑ Provide documentation showing that leakage over the remainder of unit life is being maintained below 25%.

Submittals – Recertification

Provide an update of previous filings:

- ❑ Document that the base building HVAC, refrigeration and fire suppression systems do not contain CFCs, HCFCs or Halons.

OR

- ❑ Document that fire suppression systems do not contain CFCs, HCFCs, or halons.
- ❑ Document that emissions of refrigerants from base cooling equipment over the performance period are less than 3% of charge per year using EPA Clean Air Act, Title VI, Rule 608 procedures governing refrigerant management and reporting.
- ❑ Provide documentation showing that leakage over the remainder of unit life is being maintained below 25%.

Summary of Referenced Standard

U.S. EPA Clean Air Act, Title VI, Section 608

Complying with the Section 608 Refrigerant Recycling Rule

U.S. Environmental Protection Agency

(800) 296-1996

www.epa.gov

Under Section 608 of the Clean Air Act, the EPA has established regulations regarding the use and recycling of ozone-depleting compounds. An overview of the pertinent regulations and information about compliance can be found at http://www.epa.gov/ozone/title6/608/608fact.html.

Green Building Concerns

EA Prerequisite 3 requires the phase-out of chlorofluorocarbons (CFCs) through substitution of hydrochlorofluorocarbons (HCFCs) and other low ozone-depleting refrigerants in building systems. While HCFCs are more environmentally friendly than CFCs, with ozone depletion potentials (ODPs) one-tenth or less than those of CFCs, the ODP of HCFCs is still significant. As a result, HCFCs will be phased out in the United States by 2030. HCFCs with the highest ODPs began to be phased out first, starting in 2003. This credit encourages additional ozone protection through the reduction of HCFCs and halons.

Halons are used in fire suppression systems and fire extinguishers. Halon production has been banned in the United States since 1994 due to high ODP values. Halons have particularly high ODPs because they contain bromine, which is many times more effective at destroying ozone than chlorine. Halons commonly used in buildings have ODPs ranging from 3 to 10, many times greater than ODPs for CFCs and HCFCs.

While HCFCs and halons are both addressed under this credit, their effects on the environment are significantly different. The environmental impacts of halons are typically an order of magnitude greater than HCFCs. See Table 1 for comparisons.

Environmental Issues

CFC and HCFC refrigerants both have negative impacts on the stratospheric ozone layer of the Earth's atmosphere. Similar to CFCs, elimination of HCFCs and halons in building systems reduces ozone depletion. Release of ozone-depleting substances to the stratospheric ozone layer destroys ozone molecules through a catalytic process, depleting the Earth's natural shield for incoming ultraviolet radiation. These refrigerants and their alternatives (usually HFCs) also impact climate change by virtue of their global warming potential through a very different process.

Economic Issues

Most new HVAC systems and refrigerants without CFCs and fire suppression systems without halons are cost-competitive. As an interim step, many owners are converting to HCFCs while eliminating the use of CFCs. However, HCFCs face a full ban in 2030. Therefore, it may be cost-effective to fully migrate to HFC-based equipment now, rather that relying on HCFCs as an interim step.

Strategies & Technologies

Identify all existing systems that use HCFCs and halons, and upgrade the identified equipment if possible. Specify that all upgrades utilize non-ozone-depleting equipment. Building systems to consider include HVAC, refrigeration, insulation and fire suppression systems. Common substitutes for HCFCs in HVAC and refrigeration systems are hydrofluorocarbons

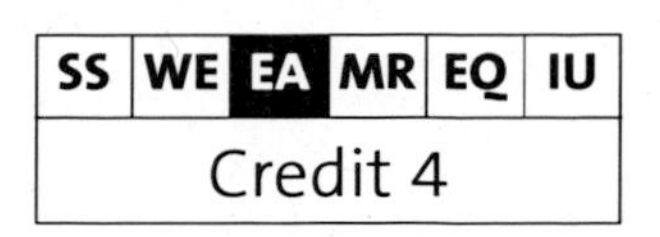

(HFCs). While HFCs have substantially lower ODPs, these substances have higher global warming potentials (GWPs). Thus, it is important to study different potential substitutes and to choose the most appropriate substitute with the lowest environmental impacts. See **Table 1** for a list of common refrigerants and their associated environmental data.

Consider the tradeoffs among refrigerants across a range of potential impacts, including worker safety, impacts on the ozone layer, energy efficiency and climate change. EPA's Significant New Alternatives Policy (SNAP) Program, which has a mandate to identify alternatives to ozone-depleting substances and to publish lists of acceptable and unacceptable substitutes, addresses these tradeoffs.

If you cannot replace all equipment containing ozone-depleting substances, implement a program to minimize refrigerant leakage and meet the credit requirements. The program should specify loss minimization procedures and systems to meet annual loss minimization standards and reporting requirements. See the U.S. EPA information "Complying with the Section 608 Refrigerant Recycling Rule" for additional guidance.

Table 1: Ozone-Depletion and Global-Warming Potentials of Refrigerants (100-yr values)

Refrigerant	ODP	GWP	Building Applications
Chlorofluorocarbons			
CFC-11	1.0	4,680	Centrifugal chillers
CFC-12	1.0	10,720	Refrigerators, chillers
CFC-114	0.94	9,800	Centrifugal chillers
CFC-500	0.605	7,900	Centrifugal chillers, humidifiers
CFC-502	0.221	4,600	Low-temperature refrigeration
Hydrochlorofluorocarbons			
HCFC-22	0.04	1,780	Air conditioning, chillers
HCFC-123	0.02	76	CFC-11 replacement
Hydrofluorocarbons			
HFC-23	< 4x10-4	12,240	Ultra-low-temperature refrigeration
HFC-134a	< 1.5x10-5	1,320	CFC-12 or HCFC-22 replacement
HFC-245fa	~ 10-5	1,020	Insulation agent, centrifugal chillers
HFC-404A	~ 10-5	3,900	Low-temperature refrigeration
HFC-407C	~ 10-5	1,700	HCFC-22 replacement
HFC-410A	< 2x10-5	1,890	Air conditioning
HFC-507A	~ 10-5	3,900	Low-temperature refrigeration
Natural Refrigerants			
CO_2	0	1	
NH_3	0	0	
Propane	0	3	
Halons			
Halon 1211	3	1300	
Halon 1301	10	1600	
Halon 2402	6		

Sources: Class I ozone-depleting substances, http://www.epa.gov/ozone/ods.html, *U.S. EPA, 2002; Class II ozone-depleting substances,* http://www.epa.gov/ozone/ods2.html, *U.S. EPA, 2002; Global warming potentials of ODS substitutes, http://www.epa.gov/ozone/geninfo/gwps.html, U.S. EPA, 2002; Inventory of U.S. Greenhouse Gas Emissions and Sinks, 291 pp., Washington, DC: EPA 430-R-04-003, 2004; "Scientific Assessment of Ozone Depletion: 2002," World Meteorological Organization Global Ozone Research and Monitoring Project, Nohende Ajavon et al., 2002, Report No. 47, http://www.unep.ch/ozone/Publications/index.asp.*

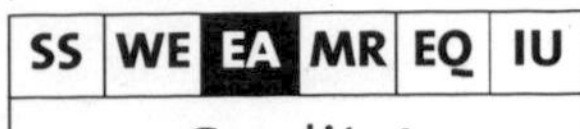

Credit 4

Synergies & Tradeoffs

This credit is closely tied with EA Prerequisite 3 and also has impacts on energy performance in the building. Economic and energy requirements should be considered when replacing existing building systems with non-ozone-depleting alternatives.

It is also important to check on phase-out periods for CFC substitutes being considered. Refrigerants phase out dates range from the near term to the long term. A schedule of phase-outs can be found at www.epa.gov/ozone/title6/phaseout/.

Calculations & Documentation

Calculations

If the building contains no base building HVAC, refrigeration or fire suppression systems containing CFCs, HCFCs or halons, no calculations are necessary. Document the absence of these chemicals in building systems in the LEED-EB application.

For each HVAC&R system that uses CFC or HCFC refrigerants, determine the percent refrigerant losses by using Equation 1 below. If the performance period is not equal to one year, adjust the value determined in Equation 1 to be the percent annual loss.

Documentation

All information needed to successfully document this credit can be found in the Submittals section of the LEED-EB Rating System and the LEED-EB Letter Templates.

Other Resources

DOE Phase-Out of Ozone Depleting Substances Information

www.epa.gov/ozone/title6/phaseout/index.html

EPA regulations issued under sections 601-607 of the Clean Air Act ended the production of several ozone-depleting substances (ODSs) and provided for the trading of production and consumption allowances. This web site provides fact sheets, regulations and guidance documents relating to phase-out of ODSs.

EPA Ozone Depleting Substances

www.epa.gov/ozone/ods.html

This site provides a listing of atmospheric lifetimes, ozone depletion potentials (ODPs) and global warming potentials (GWPs) for various substances and CFC substitutes under the SNAP program (see below).

EPA's Significant New Alternatives Policy (SNAP)

www.epa.gov/ozone/snap/index.html

SNAP is an EPA program to identify alternatives to ozone-depleting substances. The program maintains up-to-date lists of environmentally friendly substitutes for refrigeration and air conditioning equipment, solvents, fire suppression systems, adhesives, coatings and other substances.

Strategies for Managing Ozone-Depleting Refrigerants: Confronting the Future by Katharine B. Miller et al., Battelle Press, 1995.

This resource provides a comprehensive strategy for the phase out of ozone-depleting refrigerants.

Equation 1

Percent Refrigerant lost during the Performance Period = Refrigerant Lost During Performance Period [lbs.] / Total refrigerant contained in the Unit [lbs.]

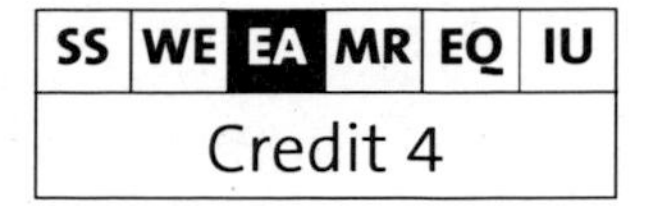

The HVAC/R Professional's Field Guide to Alternative Refrigerants by Richard Jazwin, Bookmasters, 1995.

This reference discusses the procedures and issues associated with retrofitting a system with alternative refrigerants.

Definitions

Halons are substances used in fire suppression systems and fire extinguishers in buildings; these substances deplete the stratospheric ozone layer.

Hydrochlorofluorocarbons (HCFCs) are refrigerants used in building equipment; these substances deplete the stratospheric ozone layer.

Hydrofluorocarbons (HFCs) are refrigerants that do not deplete the stratospheric ozone layer. However, some HFCs have high global warming potential, and thus are not environmentally benign.

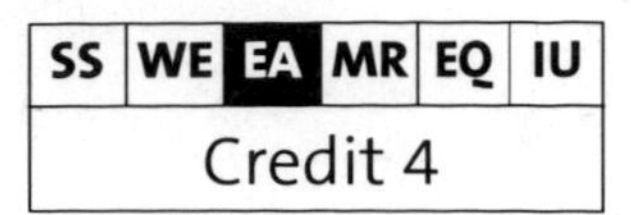

SS	WE	EA	MR	EQ	IU

Credits 5.1–5.3

1–3 points

Performance Measurement

Enhanced Metering

Intent

Demonstrate the ongoing accountability and optimization of building energy and water consumption performance over time and add incentives for additional energy reduction.

Requirements

Have in place over the performance period continuous metering for the following items: (Up to 3 points can be earned — one point is earned for each four actions implemented/maintained)

- ❑ Lighting systems and controls.
- ❑ Separate building electric meters that allow aggregation of all process electric loads (Process electric loads are defined in the LEED-EB Reference Guide).
- ❑ Separate building natural gas meters that allow aggregation of all process natural gas loads (Process natural gas loads are defined in the LEED-EB Reference Guide).
- ❑ Separate meters that allow aggregation of all indoor occupants' related water use for required fixtures.
- ❑ Separate meters that allow aggregation of all indoor process water use (Process water uses are defined in the LEED-EB Reference Guide).
- ❑ Separate meters that allow aggregation of all outdoor irrigation water use.
- ❑ Chilled water system efficiency at variable loads (kW/ton) or cooling loads (for non-chilled water systems).
- ❑ Cooling load.
- ❑ Air and water economizer and heat recovery cycle operation.
- ❑ Boiler efficiencies.
- ❑ Building specific process energy systems and equipment efficiency.
- ❑ Constant and variable motor loads.
- ❑ Variable frequency drive (VFD) operation.
- ❑ Air distribution, static pressure and ventilation air volumes.

For each item metered, prepare, implement and maintain a program for using the data gathered to improve building performance over time.

Submittals – Initial Certification

- ❑ For each item metered, provide a description of the performance improvement program implemented using the data gathered to improve system/building performance over time.
- ❑ Provide quarterly reports on the metered data gathered and, for each item metered, a report card of its performance.

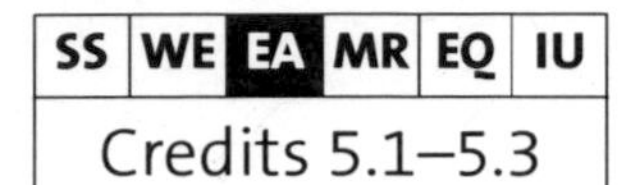

❑ Provide one day of actual output of all data recorded.

Submittals – Recertification

❑ If there have been any changes to the program implemented for using the data gathered for each item metered to improve building performance over time, provide an updated description of the program.

❑ Provide quarterly reports on the metered data gathered and, for each item metered, the resulting achievements in improving building performance.

❑ Provide one day of actual output of all data recorded.

SS	WE	EA	MR	EQ	IU
Credits 5.1–5.3					

Summary of Referenced Standard

There is no standard referenced for this credit.

Green Building Concerns

Because the lifetime of most buildings is 50 years or more, the benefits of optimal building operation can be substantial, especially in terms of energy and water performance. Even minor energy and water savings are significant in the aggregate. These long-term benefits can go unrealized due to maintenance personnel changes, aging of building equipment, and changing utility rate structures. Therefore, it is important to institute measurement, tracking and performance maintenance/improvement programs to maintain building system and equipment performance over the lifetime of the building.

Environmental Issues

Measurement of a building's ongoing energy and water consumption allows for improvement of building system and equipment performance over the life of the building. As a result, the environmental impacts associated with energy and water use can be minimized, reducing air pollution, water pollution and natural resource depletion.

Economic Issues

Proper metering and record-keeping will alert building staff to possible deficiencies or other problems with the systems so that they can be addressed and remedied while improving operating efficiencies. This saves money over time, because energy and water efficiency depend on the functionality of building systems. Metering can also be used as a baseline over which to improve. Maintaining and improving building system and equipment performance will reduce the building's energy use and overall operating costs.

Strategies & Technologies

Institute continuous metering for the identified categories of system and equipment performance over the performance period. Employ automation systems to perform measurement and tracking functions where applicable. Prepare, implement and maintain a performance improvement program to track each type of measurement for each item metered, and to track the actions taken to improve performance. The program should include (1) a list of each type of measurement taken for systems listed in the requirements, (2) a description of how these measurements are being tracked, and (3) a description of how this tracking is used to maintain and improve system performance over time.

Synergies & Tradeoffs

Measurement of a building's ongoing energy, water consumption and other performance indicators allows for ongoing improvement of building system and equipment performance over the lifetime of the building. Earning this credit involves actions that make it easier to earn several other credits, including EA Credit 3.3: Building Systems Monitoring and the credits for energy and water efficiency.

Calculations & Documentation

Calculations

None.

Documentation

All information needed to successfully document this credit can be found in the Submittals section of the LEED-EB Rating System and the LEED-EB Letter Templates.

Other Resources

International Performance Measurement and Verification Protocol (IPMVP)

www.ipmvp.org

IPMVP is a nonprofit organization that develops products and services to aid in measurement and verification of energy and water efficiency projects, quantifying emissions reductions due to these projects and conducting financial risk management.

Definitions

Submetering is metering added by the building owner and managers to track the amount of water and energy use and where it is occurring in the facility.

Utility metering involves the use of meters provided by utilities to measure consumption.

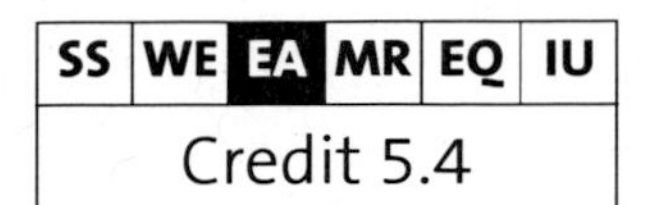

1 point

Performance Measurement

Emission Reduction Reporting

Intent

Document emission reduction benefits of building efficiency actions, retire a portion of the reductions and reduce emissions in the supply chain.

Requirements

Identify building performance parameters that reduce energy use and emissions.

- ❑ Track and record emission reductions delivered by energy efficiency, renewable energy and other building emission reduction actions.
- ❑ Report emission reductions using a third-party voluntary certification program.
- ❑ Retire at least 10% of the reported emission reductions through a third-party voluntary certification program. (To meet this requirement, the third-party voluntary emission reduction certification and retirement programs must be programs of credible organizations. Third-party programs shall notify any applicable local or regional emission reduction registries of the reported emission reductions.)
- ❑ Ask the suppliers of goods and services for the building to do the same by implementing actions of tracking, reporting, retiring emission reductions and asking their suppliers to do the same.

Submittals – Initial Certification

- ❑ Provide reporting of all building performance parameters that reduce energy use and calculate the total savings for each type of energy reduction.
- ❑ Provide reporting of renewable energy use and other emission reduction actions.
- ❑ Calculate and provide a report of the resulting reductions for the significant types of environmental emissions resulting from the energy-efficiency operations and other emission reduction actions using the emission reduction calculation protocol of a third-party voluntary certification program. Emission reductions to be documented include carbon dioxide (CO_2), sulfur dioxide (SO_2), nitrogen oxides (NO_x), mercury (Hg), small particulates (PM2.5), large particulates (PM10) and volatile organic compounds (VOCs).
- ❑ Provide documentation of the retirement of at least 10% of the reported emission reductions through a third-party voluntary certification program.
- ❑ Provide documentation that the suppliers for the building have been asked to:
  - Report energy savings, energy-efficiency actions, renewable energy use and other emission reduction actions.
  - Report all types of resulting emissions reductions.
  - Retire at least 10% of these reductions through a third-party voluntary certification program.
  - Ask their suppliers of goods and services to do the same.

- ❑ Provide documentation that a third-party voluntary certification program has notified any applicable local or regional emission reduction registries of the reported emission reductions.

Submittals – Recertification

Provide an update of previous filings:

- ❑ Track and record on an annual basis over the performance period the energy use and emission reductions delivered by energy efficiency, renewable energy and other building emission reduction actions.
- ❑ Report emission reductions on an annual basis over the performance period using a third-party voluntary certification program.
- ❑ Retire at least 10% of the reported emission reductions through a third-party voluntary certification program.
- ❑ Ask new suppliers of goods and services for the building since the previous LEED-EB filings to do the same by implementing requirements 1, 2 and 3 above.

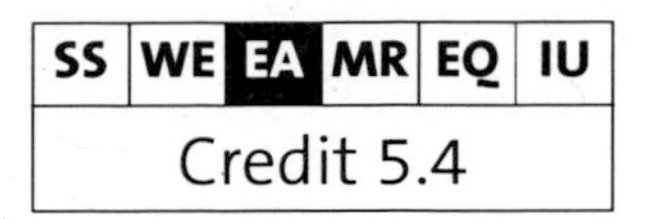

Summary of Referenced Standards

There is no standard referenced for this credit.

Green Building Concerns

Power plants and facilities with large amounts of on-site emissions have a financial incentive to reduce emissions through environmental regulatory programs. In contrast, building owners who use electricity from the grid produce no on-site emissions of this sort; the emissions produced by generation of their required electricity are released at the plant. As a result, although efficiency actions and renewable energy use by building owners reduce overall emissions, the emissions reduction benefits of these efforts are rarely rewarded financially. This is poor public policy as building energy efficiency actions are frequently the lowest cost way to reduce emissions.

Quantifying and publicizing the emission reductions delivered by energy efficiency and other actions help building owners recognize and be recognized for the full environmental benefits of their actions. Also, permanently retiring some of the quantified emission reductions assures ongoing environmental benefits. Building owners can also promote emissions reductions by asking suppliers to take the same actions. As much as 60 percent of the emissions associated with end-consumer actions are generated by the energy used in the production and delivery of goods and services.[22] This savings can therefore have a strong positive environmental impact.

Environmental Issues

Energy use causes a wide range of air emissions that degrade the environment and cause human health problems. Emissions caused by energy use include carbon dioxide (CO_2), sulfur dioxide (SO_2), nitrogen oxides (NOx), mercury (Hg), small particulates ($PM_{2.5}$), large particulates (PM_{10}) and volatile organic compounds (VOCs). Reducing energy use decreases all these emissions. This is true of both efficiency actions that reduce on-site combustion of fuel and reductions in electricity use that reduce emissions from generation plants burning fossil fuels elsewhere. Energy efficiency is the most complete way to reduce air emissions because it eliminates the environmental impacts of fuel extraction and the infrastructure needed to deliver the fuel to the user. Energy efficiency also reduces the environmental effects associated with the burning and use of the fuel.[23] **Table 1** below lists health and environmental impacts of the various emissions generated by energy use.

Traditional environmental regulation has been hampered by dealing with emissions one pollutant type at a time instead of in an integrated fashion. Just as integrated solutions are the key to sustainable building and operations, the key to reducing emissions efficiently is by dealing with multiple pollutants in an integrated way. Building owners can help promote integrated multi-pollutant approaches to pollution reduction by quantifying the environmental benefits of their energy efficiency and other emission reduction actions and by supporting programs that give recognition and rewards for these emission reductions.

Economic Issues

This credit creates additional benefits for the building's energy efficiency actions. For business or nongovernmental organization building owners, third-party certification of positive environmental actions creates the potential for increased sales resulting from preferential purchasing of goods and services by residential and commercial consumers.

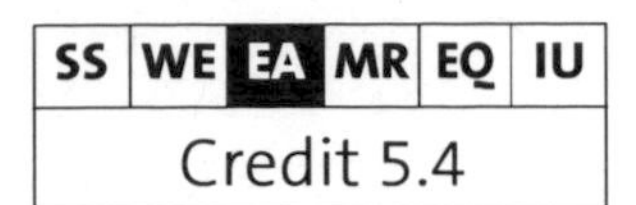

Table 1: Sources and Effects of Common Pollutants

Pollutant	Anthropogenic Sources	Human Health Effects	Environmental Effects
Ozone (O3)	Secondary pollutant formed by chemical reaction of VOCs and NOx in the presence of sunlight.	Breathing problems, reduced lung function, asthma, irritated eyes, stuffy nose, reduced resistance to colds and infections, premature aging of lung tissue.	Damages crops, forests, and other vegetation; damages rubber, fabric, and other materials; smog reduces visibility.
Nitrogen Oxides (NOx)	Burning of gasoline, natural gas, coal, oil. (Cars are a major source of NOx.)	Lung damage, respiratory illnesses, ozone (smog) effects.	Ozone (smog) effects; precursor of acid rain, which damages trees, lakes, and soil; aerosols can reduce visibility. Acid rain also causes buildings, statues, and monuments to deteriorate.
Carbon Monoxide (CO)	Burning of gasoline, natural gas, coal, oil.	Reduced ability of blood to bring oxygen to body cells and tissues.	
Volatile Organic Compounds (VOCs)	Fuel combustion, solvents, paint. (Cars are a major source of VOCs.)	Ozone (smog) effects, cancer, and other serious health problems.	Ozone (smog) effects, vegetation damage.
Particulate Matter (PM10 & PM2.5)	Emitted as particles or formed through chemical reactions; burning of wood, diesel, and other fuels; industrial processes; agriculture (plowing, field burning); unpaved roads.	Eye, nose and throat irritation; lung damage; bronchitis; cancer; early death.	Source of haze, which reduces visibility. Ashes, smoke, soot, and dust can dirty and discolor structures and property, including clothes and furniture.
Sulfur Dioxide (SO2)	Burning of coal and oil, especially high-sulfur coal; industrial processes (paper manufacturing, metal smelting).	Respiratory illness, breathing problems, may cause permanent damage to lungs.	Precursor of acid rain, which can damage trees, lakes, and soil; aerosols can reduce visibility. Acid rain also causes buildings, statues, and monuments to deteriorate.
Lead	Combustion of fossil fuels and leaded gasoline; paint; smelters (metal refineries); battery manufacturing.	Brain and nervous system damage (esp. children), digestive and other problems. Some lead-containing chemicals cause cancer in animals.	Harms wildlife and livestock.
Mercury	Fossil fuel combustion, waste disposal, industrial processes (incineration, smelting, chlor-alkali plants), mining.	Liver, kidney, and brain damage; neurological and developmental damage.	Accumulates in food chain. Harm to wildlife (e.g. fish, loons, and eagles)
Carbon Dioxide (CO2)	Fossil fuel combustion.		Contributes to global climate change

Source: Leonardo Academy (Table 1.4, pg. 7): Consumer Guide to Clean Energy Choices, 1999.

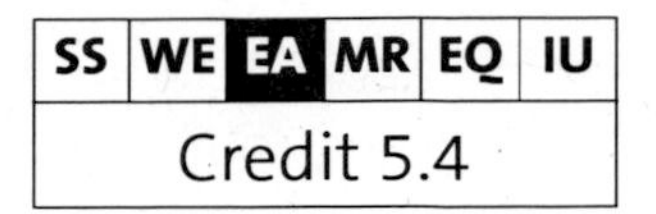

Strategies & Technologies

Address all significant types of pollutants reduced through energy efficiency. This is important because negative health effects and other environmental impacts result from many pollutants including CO_2, SO_2, NOx, Hg, $PM_{2.5}$, PM_{10} and VOCs as illustrated in **Table 1** above. Energy efficiency, renewable energy and other building emission reduction actions make important contributions towards improving health and environmental conditions at a low cost. To earn this credit, follow the two steps below:

1. Track whole building energy use, energy use reductions, renewable energy usage and other actions that reduce emissions.
2. Establish a baseline
3. Use a third-party emissions reduction reporting program or programs that help building owners (1) calculate and report all the different types of emission reductions delivered by their energy efficiency, renewable energy and other emission reduction actions, (2) retire at least 10 percent of these emission reductions
4. Ask the suppliers of goods and services to the building to take these same actions.

Synergies & Tradeoffs

This credit creates additional benefits supplementing the energy efficiency actions, renewable energy and other actions that reduce emissions implemented and maintained to earn other credits, such as the 10 points available for energy efficiency under EA Credit 1 and the 4 points for renewable energy available under EA Credit 2.

Calculations & Documentation

Calculations

Emission reductions for multiple pollutant types are based on annual energy use savings, plus on-site and off-site renewable energy purchases and any other well-documented emission reduction actions. Annual energy use savings are determined by comparing the performance period energy use to an established energy use baseline.

Setting the Baseline and Calculating the Energy Savings for Emission Reduction Calculations

The baseline is set using the same baseline used for LEED-EB EA Prerequisite 2 and Credit 1:

Option A: If the building is a type covered by ENERGY STAR, the energy use baseline is the energy the building would use if it had an ENERGY STAR score of 50.

Take the ENERGY STAR calculation you did for LEED-EB EA Prerequisite 2 and Credit 1 and incrementally increase the energy use inputs used in the ENERGY STAR calculation until the ENERGY STAR score is reduced to 50. Increase the energy use numbers proportionately for each type of energy used in the building if multiple energy types are used.

The base energy use reduction is the difference between the actual building energy use initially input and the adjusted energy use input to produce an ENERGY STAR score of 50. Account for energy savings by fuel type. Account for any on-site and off-site renewable energy used that meets the requirements of LEED-EB EA Credit 2 in addition to the base energy use reduction number in order to calculate total emission reductions. (See Table 2 below.)

Option B: If the building is a type not covered by ENERGY STAR, the energy use baseline is the same as that established

SS | WE | EA | MR | EQ | IU

Credit 5.4

for LEED-EB EA Prerequisite 2 and Credit 1.

The difference between the actual building energy use and the baseline is the base energy use reduction. Account for any on-site and off-site renewable energy used that meets the requirements of LEED-EB EA Credit 2 in addition to the base energy use reduction number in order to calculate total emission reductions. (See **Table 2** below.)

Emissions Calculations:

1. Energy savings for each type of energy are multiplied by the applicable emission rate for each pollutant type for the state where the building is located to obtain the annual emission reductions from energy savings.
2. On-site renewable energy for each type of energy is multiplied by the applicable emission rate for each pollutant type for the state where the building is located to obtain the annual emission reductions from energy savings.
3. Off-site renewable energy for each type of energy is multiplied by the applicable emission rate for each pollutant type for the state where the off-site renewable generation is located to obtain the annual emission reductions from energy savings.
4. Total annual emission reduction amounts for each pollutant type are the sum of annual emission reductions from energy savings, on-site renewable energy used, the off-site renewable energy used, and any other well documented emission reduction actions. **Table 2** shows an example for calculating the energy savings for CO_2 emission reduction calculations. Add emission factors columns for SO_2, NOx, $PM_{2.5}$, PM_{10}, VOCs and Hg to the table to calculate annual emission reductions for each pollutant type.

An online emissions reduction calculator, a guide to calculating these emission reductions using current emission reduction factors, and electricity and common fossil fuel emission rates for the required list of pollutant reductions to report (CO_2, SO_2, NOx, $PM_{2.5}$, PM_{10}, VOCs and Hg), for each state, can be found at www.cleanerandgreener.org/emission_reductions.htm. These emission rates for each state are based on U.S. EPA E-GRID data.

Documentation

All information needed to successfully document this credit can be found in the Submittals section of the LEED-EB Rating System and the LEED-EB Letter Templates.

Table 2: Calculating the Energy Savings for CO_2 Emission Reduction Calculations

	Baseline Annual Energy Use	Actual Annual Energy Use	Annual Energy Savings	Annual Renewable Energy Use	Unit of Measure Factor	CO2 Emission [lbs. per Unit of	CO2 Annual Measure] Emissions Reduction [lbs.]
Energy Use							
Electricity	2,000,000	1,700,000	300,000	N/A	kWh	1.771	531,300
On-site Nat. Gas	50,000	45,000	5,000	N/A	Therms	11.708	58,540
On-site Diesel Use	10,000	5,000	5,000	N/A	Gallons	25.000	125,000
Renewable Source							
On-site Renew.	N/A	N/A	N/A	10,000	kWh	1.771	17,710
Off-site Renew.	N/A	N/A	N/A	50,000	kWh	1.997	99,850
						Total CO_2 Emission Reduction [lbs.]	832,400

Other Resources

Cleaner and Greener℠ Certification Program

(608) 280-0255

www.cleanerandgreener.org

The Cleaner and Greener℠ Certification Program provides an online emissions reduction calculator, a guide to calculating all the major emission reductions from energy efficiency and renewable energy actions, and regularly updated emission reduction factors. These emission rates for each state are based on U.S. EPA E-GRID data. The Cleaner and Greener℠ program also helps building owners and organizations report emission reductions and retire emission reductions as well as recognizing them for positive emission reduction actions. The Leonardo Academy, an environmental nonprofit, runs the program.

International Performance Measurement and Verification Protocol (IPMVP)

www.ipmvp.org/

IPMVP is a nonprofit organization that develops products and services to aid in measurement and verification of energy and water efficiency projects.

Definitions

Emissions offsets are emissions reductions from one set of actions that are used to offset emission caused by another set of actions.

Renewable energy certificates (RECs) are a representation of the environmental attributes of green power, and are sold separately from the electrons that make up the electricity. RECs allow the purchase of green power even when the electrons are not purchased.

Case Study

Denver Place

Denver, Colorado

LEED-EB Gold

Owner: Amerimar Reality Management Co.

Photo courtesy of: Denver Place

Denver Place, an office complex and retail space in downtown Denver, achieved Level 4 certification under the Cleaner and Greener Emissions Reduction Certification Program of the Leonardo Academy. Denver Place completed a variety of energy saving actions, including lighting and technology upgrades as well as equipment use parameter adjustments, resulting in annual emissions reductions of over 20,000 lbs of SO_2, 26,000 lbs of mercury, and 9 million pounds of CO_2. Ten percent of these and other reductions in emissions were donated to the Cleaner and Greener program for retirement from 1996 through the end of 2004. Denver Place also encouraged their major suppliers to support a cleaner environment by taking steps to reduce their energy use and resulting emissions.

SS	WE	EA	MR	EQ	IU
Credit 6					

1 point

Documenting Sustainable Building Cost Impacts

Intent

Document sustainable building cost impacts.

Requirements

Document overall building operating costs for the previous five years (or length of building occupancy, if shorter), and track changes in overall building operating costs over the performance period. Document building operating cost and financial impacts of all of the aspects of LEED-EB implementation on an ongoing basis.

Submittals – Initial Certification

- ❑ Provide documentation of all building operating costs for the previous five years (or length of building occupancy, if shorter).
- ❑ Track changes in overall building operating costs over the performance period relative to sustainable performance improvement initiatives implemented and maintained for the building and the site.
- ❑ Document building operating cost and the financial impacts in building operation covering all aspects of LEED-EB implementation on an ongoing basis.

Submittals – Recertification

Provide an update of previous filings:

- ❑ Provide documentation of all building operating costs for the previous five years (or length of building occupancy, if shorter).
- ❑ Track changes in overall building operating costs over the performance period relative to sustainable performance improvement initiatives implemented and maintained for the building and the site.
- ❑ Document building operating cost and the financial impacts in building operation covering all aspects of LEED-EB implementation on an ongoing basis.

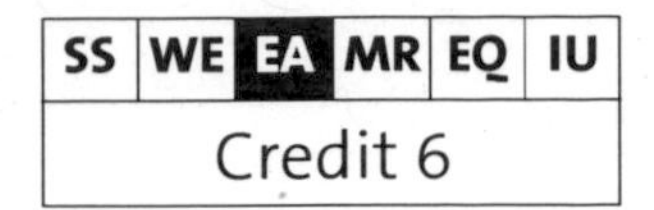

Summary of Referenced Standard

There is no standard referenced for this credit.

Green Building Concerns

A major factor in the implementation of sustainable building operation and upgrades involves understanding the costs and benefits. Gathering economic performance data for LEED-EB buildings will build a strong economic case for implementing LEED-EB, demonstrating both the financial and environmental benefits of sustainable buildings over time.

Environmental Issues

The magnitude of environmental impact reductions for a LEED-EB building is directly related to the number and type of sustainable building operations and upgrades implemented and maintained. Documenting the costs and benefits of implementing sustainable building operation and upgrades through LEED-EB is a key step in its broad adoption by building owners. Well-documented cost information will promote increased participation and higher levels of sustainable building achievements, therefore decreasing the overall environmental impacts of buildings.

Economic Issues

Many actions included in LEED-EB are low-cost or no-cost actions. For the LEED-EB pilot projects analyzed to date, overall implementation of LEED-EB has had an extremely short payback period. Green cleaning and green site management are excellent examples of low-cost or no-cost actions taken by pilot participants. Based on the preliminary information gathered to date, it is expected that reductions in building operating costs will provide sufficient benefits for broad LEED-EB adoption by building owners.

Many current expense streams for existing buildings can be reduced by the actions required for sustainable building operations and upgrades. Key opportunities include energy costs, water and sewer costs, and waste disposal costs. Tracking the financial aspects of sustainable buildings will help building owners identify opportunities for savings. In the long term, the quantification of productivity benefits associated with sustainable building operation and upgrades will add even more strength to the economic case for sustainable building operation and upgrades through LEED-EB.

Strategies & Technologies

Track building operating costs and benefits to identify impacts related to sustainable performance improvements of building and operations. For each prerequisite and credit earned, determine the costs and benefits of implementation over the performance period.

A good strategy is to start documenting costs and benefits early in the process and do so continually as new sustainable practices are implemented. This is easier than trying to reconstruct past costs and benefits from old invoices, utility bill and other paperwork.

Synergies & Tradeoffs

This credit encompasses all credits in the LEED-EB rating system and should be addressed according to which credits are pursued by the project team.

Calculations & Documentation

Calculations

A spreadsheet, similar to the tables below, is available from the USGBC to track building operating costs and benefits associated with implementation of building updates, programs and other LEED-EB improvements.

Gather and track two types of cost data to earn this credit:

Annual Operating Costs

(1) Track operating costs each year.

- Include the entire performance period.
- Include data for 5 years prior to initial LEED-EB Registration to the extent this is available.
- Break down the operating costs by account.

(2) Include comparison by account and total with comparables for the building type and location. Sources for operating cost information on comparable buildings include BOMA's Experience Exchange Report (EER), IFMA and APPA.

Costs and Benefits from Date of LEED-EB Registration to LEED-EB Certification

Benefits of sustainable building operation and upgrades include economic and other benefits of sustainability implementation in the building and on the site.

Costs of sustainable building operation and upgrades include the costs of all actions taken to implement sustainability in the building and on the site from the time that the decision to implement LEED-EB was made.

(1) Track costs and benefits for each prerequisite and credit.

- Include any incremental costs and incremental benefits due to striving to achieve desired LEED-EB points and rating.
- Do not include base cost of end-of-life replacements of equipment or systems.
- Calculate the simple payback by dividing the costs for each measure by the associated annual savings.

(2) Track costs of LEED-EB Application and certification process.

- Cost of consultants
- Fees
- Hours of internal staff time

Table 1: Operating Cost Tracking

Operating Cost Account Categories	Total Building Costs [$ / Account]	Building Costs [$ / ft²]	Comparable Building Costs [$ / ft2]	Comparison [$ / ft2]	Comparison [%]

Table 2: Implementation Costs and Benefits per Credit

Credit	Description of Actions	Costs of Implementation	Annual Savings/Costs	Simple Payback
Totals				

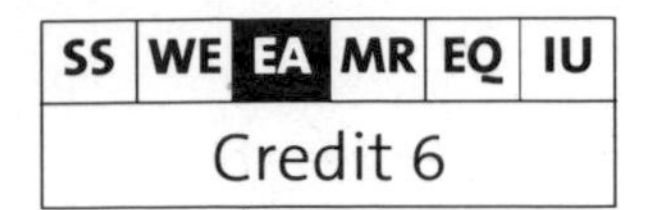

Examples on the Tracking of Costs and Benefits from Date of LEED-EB Registration to LEED-EB Certification:

Example 1

The building installed a high-efficiency chiller one month after registering for LEED-EB certification because the chiller reached its end of life. The cost of implementation would be the cost difference between replacing the existing chiller with a standard efficiency chiller versus the cost of the high-efficiency chiller. Cost benefits would include the annual energy cost savings of the high-efficiency chiller versus the standard efficiency chiller.

Example 2

The building sets up a recycling program to meet the requirements of MR Prerequisite 1.2 and gain credit for MR Credits 5.1–5.3. Implementation would include the cost of any recycling bins purchased for the program. Additional costs would include recycling educational materials developed and printed for occupants. Cost benefits would include decreased waste disposal cost and possible revenue from selling recycled material. Costs and benefits would be divided between MR Prerequisite 1.2 and MR Credits 5.1–5.3.

Example 3

The building installed occupancy sensors for lighting and water faucets. The cost of implementation would include the entire cost of the equipment since no equipment replacements are involved. Cost benefits would include energy cost savings from reduced lighting use and water cost and energy cost savings from reduced water consumption and reduced water heating and pumping.

Energy savings must be allocated between credits and cannot be double-counted. For example, water savings may include associated energy cost savings resulting from less pumping and hot water heating. These energy cost savings should not also be included in the energy performance credits.

The simple payback is calculated by dividing the costs for each measure by the associated annual savings.

Documentation

All information needed to successfully document this credit can be found in the Submittals section of the LEED-EB Rating System and the LEED-EB Letter Templates.

Endnotes

[1] United States. Department of Energy, Energy Information Administration. Annual Energy Review 2005. 12 February 2005 <http://www.eia.doe.gov/emeu/aer/>.

[2] United States. Department of Energy, Energy Information Administration. Commercial Buildings Energy Consumption Survey: Table C10 1999. 12 February 2005 <http://www.eia.doe.gov/emeu/cbecs/pdf/set9.pdf>.

[3] United States. Department of Energy, Energy Information Administration. United States Country Analysis Brief. January 2005. 12 February 2005 <http://www.eia.doe.gov/emeu/cabs/usa.pdf>.

[4] United States. Environmental Protection Agency. Clean Energy Web Site: Air Emissions February 2005. 13 February 2005 <http://www.epa.gov/cleanenergy/emissions.htm>.

[5] United States. Environmental Protection Agency, Office of Air Quality Planning & Standards. SO_2 – How Sulfur Dioxide Affects the Way We Live & Breathe. Research Triangle Park, NC, November 2000. 13 February 2005 <http://www.epa.gov/air/urbanair/so2/index.html>.

[6]State of Oregon. Oregon Department of Energy Building Commissioning Savings June 2004. 14 February 2005. <http://www.energy.state.or.us/bus/comm/commsave.htm>.

[7] Ibid.

[8] United States. Environmental Protection Agency, Office of Atmospheric Programs. Inventory of U.S. Greenhouse Gas Emissions and Sinks: 1990-2000. Publication Number EPA 430-R-02-003, April 2002. 15 Feb 2005 <www.epa.gov/globalwarming/publications/emissions>.

[9] Ibid.

[10] United States. Environmental Protection Agency, Climate Protection Partnerships Division. ENERGY STAR® Home Improvement Tips. 15 February 2005 <http://www.energystar.gov/index.cfm?c=home_improvement.hi_tips>.

[11] United States. Department of Energy, Office of Energy Efficiency and Renewable Energy. Energy Efficient Products. March 2004. 15 February 2005. <http://www.eere.energy.gov/femp/technologies/eep_wc_chillers.cfm>.

[12] United Sates. Environmental Protection Agency, Office of Solid Waste. C&D Debris March 2002. 14 February 2005 <http://www.epa.gov/epaoswer/non-hw/debris/>.

[13] United States. Department of Energy. Solar Thermal and Photovoltaic Collector Manufacturing Activities 2003. Energy Information Administration. 2004.

[14] United States. Department of Energy, Energy Information Administration. Renewable Energy Trends 2003 August 2004. 24 February 2005. <http://www.eia.doe.gov/cneaf/solar.renewables/page/trends/table1.html>.

[15] United States. Department of Energy, Energy Information Administration. Renewable

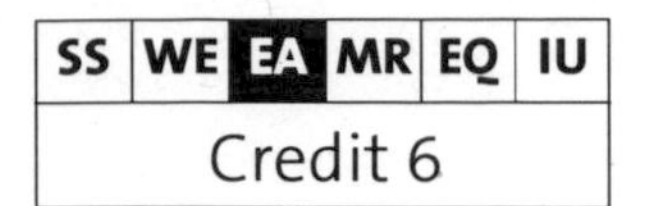

Energy Trends 2003. July 2004. 25 February 2005. <http://www.eia.doe.gov/cneaf/solar.renewables/page/trends/trends.pdf>.

[16] Wind Energy: An Untapped Resource. January 2004. American Wind Energy Association. 25 February 2005. <http://www.awea.org/pubs/factsheets/WindEnergyAnUntappedResource01-13-04.pdf>.

[17] Small Wind System. February 2005. American Wind Energy Association. 25 February 2005. <http://www.awea.org/smallwind.html>.

[18] Wind Power Today. August 2004. American Wind Energy Association. 25 February 2005. <http://www.awea.org/pubs/factsheets/WindPowerTodayFinal.pdf>.

[19] Lin Koo, Wei and Tracy Van Hoy, P.E. Determining the Economic Value of Preventive Maintenance. Jones Lang LaSalle, 2005. 25 February 2005 <http://www.joneslanglasalle.com/research/documents/PreventMaint.pdf>

[20] United States. Department of Energy. Automatic and Programmable Thermostats. DOE/GO-10097-375. March 1997. 25 March 2005 <http://www.eere.energy.gov/consumerinfo/factsheets/thermo.html>.

[21] State of Oregon. Oregon Department of Energy. Building Commissioning Savings June 2004. 14 February 2005 <http://www.energy.state.or.us/bus/comm/commsave.htm>.

[22] How We Cause Pollution. Leonardo Academy's Cleaner and Greener Program. 14 January 2005. <http://www.cleanerandgreener.org/schools/health.htm>.

[23] Consumer Guide to Green Energy Choices Report March 1999. Leonardo Academy. 25 March 2005 <www.cleanerandgreener.org/download/GreenEnergy.pdf>.

Materials and Resources

Buildings create a large amount of waste through their operation and use. Meeting the Materials & Resources (MR) credits can reduce the quantity of that waste while improving the building environment through responsible procurement choices. The credits in this section focus on: (1) choosing the materials brought into the building with reductions in environmental impacts in mind, and (2) managing the materials that leave the building as waste to minimize landfilling or incineration of these materials.

Materials selection plays a significant role in sustainable building operation because of the environmental and health consequences associated with the entire life cycle of materials, including extraction, processing, transportation, use, and disposal. These activities pollute water and air, destroy native habitats and deplete natural resources. Environmentally responsible procurement policies can significantly reduce these impacts. When purchasing materials and supplies, consider the relative environmental, social and health benefits of the available choices. For example, materials containing recycled content expand markets for recycled materials, slow the consumption of raw materials and reduce the amount of waste disposed of in landfills. Use of local materials supports local economies while reducing transportation impacts. Cleaning and other chemical products with fewer health and environmental impacts lead to a healthier workforce and a cleaner environment.

Waste generation also plays a large role in the environmental impact of a building due to the negative environmental aspects of waste disposal through landfilling or incineration. The EPA's three key strategies for waste reduction are (1) source reduction, (2) reuse and (3) recycling.[1] Source reduction is at the top of the EPA's hierarchy of waste reduction techniques because it reduces all impacts of the material life cycle including the supply chain, use, recycling and waste disposal. Reuse ranks second because reused materials do not become waste or produce the environmental impacts associated with recycling processes. Recycling ranks third—it does not deliver all the benefits of source reduction or reuse, but it does divert waste from landfills and incinerators and reduce the need for virgin materials.

A sustainable building operation plan requires policies that describe responsible procurement practices and effective waste management strategies. The MR prerequisites and credits set the foundation for effectively developing, implementing and documenting these policies. Practical waste management programs, in conjunction with purchasing policies that reduce waste and specify less harmful materials and supplies, can effectively reduce the overall impact a building has on the environment.

Overview of LEED® Prerequisites and Credits

MR Prerequisite 1.1
Source Reduction & Waste Management – Waste Stream Audit

MR Prerequisite 1.2
Source Reduction & Waste Management – Storage & Collection

MR Prerequisite 2
Toxic Material Source Reduction – Reduced Mercury in Light Bulbs

MR Credit 1.1
Construction, Demolition & Renovation Waste Management – Recycle 50%

MR Credit 1.2
Construction, Demolition & Renovation Waste Management – Recycle 75%

MR Credit 2.1
Optimize Use of Alternative Materials – 10% of Total Purchases

MR Credit 2.2
Optimize Use of Alternative Materials – 20% of Total Purchases

MR Credit 2.3
Optimize Use of Alternative Materials – 30% of Total Purchases

MR Credit 2.4
Optimize Use of Alternative Materials – 40% of Total Purchases

MR Credit 2.5
Optimize Use of Alternative Materials – 50% of Total Purchases

MR Credit 3.1
Optimize Use of IAQ Compliant Products – 45% of Annual Purchases

MR Credit 3.2
Optimize Use of IAQ Compliant Products – 90% of Annual Purchases

Overview of LEED® Prerequisites and Credits (continued)

MR Credit 4.1
Sustainable Cleaning Products & Materials – 30% of Annual Purchases

MR Credit 4.2
Sustainable Cleaning Products & Materials – 60% of Annual Purchases

MR Credit 4.3
Sustainable Cleaning Products & Materials – 90% of Annual Purchases

MR Credit 5.1
Occupant Recycling – Recycle 30% of the Total Waste Stream

MR Credit 5.2
Occupant Recycling – Recycle 40% of the Total Waste Stream

MR Credit 5.3
Occupant Recycling – Recycle 50% of the Total Waste Stream

MR Credit 6
Additional Toxic Material Source Reduction – Reduced Mercury in Light Bulbs

SS	WE	EA	**MR**	EQ	IU

Prerequisite 1.1

Required

Source Reduction and Waste Management

Waste Management Policy and Waste Stream Audit

Intent

Establish minimum source reduction and recycling program elements and quantify current waste stream production volume.

Requirements

Conduct a waste stream audit of the ongoing waste stream (not specific upgrade project waste) to establish a current building waste baseline that identifies the types of waste making up the waste stream and amounts of each type of waste in the waste stream. At a minimum, the audit should determine the amounts for paper, glass, plastics, cardboard and metals in the waste stream. Identify opportunities for source reduction and diversion. Operate over the performance period a waste reduction policy to reduce waste stream through source reduction purchasing strategies, collection station equipment, recycling and occupant education.

Submittals – Initial Certification

- ❑ Provide a copy of the waste stream audit to establish building waste baseline.
- ❑ Provide a copy of the waste reduction policy implemented to reduce waste stream through source reduction purchasing strategies, collection station equipment, recycling and occupant awareness notices.

Submittals – Recertification

Provide an update of previous filings:

- ❑ If there has been no change to the waste reduction policy implemented to reduce waste stream, provide a signed letter documenting its continued existence and implementation.

OR

- ❑ If the waste reduction policy implemented to reduce waste stream has changed, provide a copy of the policy highlighting any changes.
- ❑ Provide a signed letter documenting the revised plan's implementation.

Summary of Referenced Standard

There is no standard referenced for this prerequisite.

Green Building Concerns

Reducing the amount of waste disposed in landfills or incinerators is an important component of sustainable building operation. A waste stream audit, the first step in waste stream management, requires building operators to establish a system for tracking waste generation in the building. Auditing provides the information needed to identify opportunities to reduce waste. Reducing the waste stream can require allocating building space to separate and store waste materials, collaborating with procurement officials within the organization on source reduction, and communicating with building occupants about waste stream management practices and policies.

Environmental Issues

Buildings generate significant quantities of waste. Source reduction, reuse, recycling and other waste diversion strategies reduce both the volume of waste going to landfills or incineration and the use of new materials in manufacturing. Assessing the waste stream of a building helps identify opportunities for source reduction, reuse and recycling to divert waste from disposal through incineration or landfilling. These strategies reduce the environmental burden associated with waste disposal.

Economic Issues

Buying unnecessary materials and bringing them into buildings increases the amount of waste generated in the facility. This increase in waste generation raises the cost of building operation and maintenance in two ways: (1) unnecessary materials (such as packaging) add to the cost of products purchased, and (2) fees for landfilling or incineration increase as the amount of waste increases. Therefore, source reduction is the most economical way to reduce waste.

When source reduction is not possible, reuse and recycling can also save money. All three of these strategies can reduce building operating costs associated with unnecessary materials and waste. Highly effective waste stream management programs can even result in profit for the organization by reducing expenditures for waste disposal and generating revenue from recycling or resale proceeds.

Strategies & Technologies

An important first step in waste reduction is to understand the waste production patterns in the building and on site. Once waste sources have been identified and quantified, it is much easier to develop strategies for reduction. When developing a policy to reduce a building's waste stream, begin by conducting a waste stream audit to collect and analyze information about the amounts and types of waste generated by the facility.

Use the findings of the audit to evaluate how each type of waste in the waste stream can be reduced through source reduction, reuse, recycling or other waste diversion strategies. Then set goals for minimizing waste and disposal costs, maximizing revenues from recycling and maximizing savings from source reduction.

The final step is to develop, implement and maintain a waste reduction policy for the building that employs source reduction and diversion to reduce the amount of waste delivered to incinerators and landfills. Waste reduction policies should include source reduction purchasing strategies, reuse, recycling (including collection equipment and agreements) and occupant education to ensure the goals are met.

SS | WE | EA | **MR** | EQ | IU

Prerequisite 1.1

Synergies & Tradeoffs

Source reduction reduces purchasing costs and waste disposal fees. Selling waste stream material provides revenue that offsets waste disposal fees. Donating or giving away waste components provides public relations opportunities and benefits other organizations in the community. The audit conducted in this prerequisite will help set the stage for earning MR Prerequisite 1.2: Storage and Collection of Recyclables, as well as MR Credits 5.1–5.3: Occupant Recycling.

Calculations & Documentation

Calculations

A waste stream audit provides data on total waste amounts generated, reused, recycled and disposed of by landfilling or incineration. It also provides data on the component materials found in unsegregated waste. The waste audit should be used to evaluate and improve existing reuse and recycling programs, identify additional recycling opportunities and identify opportunities to reduce waste with source reduction programs.

MR Prerequisite 1.1 requires a waste audit that, at a minimum, assesses the amount of waste generated by type for paper, glass, plastic, cardboard, and metal. Aside from these mandatory waste categories, it is useful for the audit to identify all significant components of currently unsegregated waste. Waste amounts can be generated from either mass or volume measurements. However, LEED-EB requires reporting the final filed audit information by weight, because the mass of these materials is the best determinant of potential costs or revenues from increased recycling. It is recommended that all waste hauling contracts require weighing hauled waste in order to monitor the waste stream.

For a selected sample period, identify the total amount of solid waste produced and the amount of each component material, using weight or volume metrics. Waste that is already sorted on a regular basis may include office paper, glass, cardboard, metal cans or other specific types of waste. Waste that is not sorted on a regular basis should be sorted during the audit to determine its components.

Waste Audit Forms

The following tables simplify a waste audit. **Table 1** provides a form for gathering the information needed to calculate the total amount of waste created in the

Table 1: Waste Disposed of as Unsegregated Waste

Column A **List Each Waste Container**	Column B **Container Type (dumpster or compactor)**	Column C **Container Size [cu. yds.]**	Column D **Container Capacity [tons]**	Column E **Type of Waste**	Column F **Frequency of Collection (per month)**	Column G **Estimated % Filled**	Column H **Total Weight [tons/ Month]**	Column I **Total Weight [tons/year]**
Totals								

Notes: The goal of this table is to fill in Column I. If possible, enter information into this column directly from measurements from waste haulers. If these figures are not available, use the other columns in the table to compute the total weight of unsegregated waste.

Table 2: Waste Volume to Weight Conversions

Material	Volume	Weight [lbs]	Weight [tons]
Office paper	1 cubic yard	400	0.2
Corrugated, loose	1 cubic yard	285	0.1425
Corrugated, baled	1 cubic yard	507	0.2535
Glass, unbroken	1 cubic yard	660	0.33
Glass, broken	1 cubic yard	1125	0.05625
Glass, crushed, mech.	1 cubic yard	2060	1.03
Glass, uncrushed	55-gal dr.	300	0.15
Aluminum cans, whole	1 cubic yard	74	0.037
Aluminum cans, flat	1 cubic yard	250	0.125
Ferrous cans, whole	1 cubic yard	150	0.075
Ferrous cans, flat	1 cubic yard	850	0.425
PETE, soda bottles	1 cubic yard	30	0.015
HDPE, milk bottles	1 cubic yard	25	0.0125
PETE & HDPE mixed	1 cubic yard	30	0.015
PS	1 cubic yard	10	0.005
Leaves, uncompacted	1 cubic yard	400	0.2
Leaves, compacted	1 cubic yard	1000	0.5
Leaves, vacuumed	1 cubic yard	700	0.35
Grass, uncompacted	1 cubic yard	740	0.37
Wood chips	1 cubic yard	500	0.25
Wood waste (pallets)	1 cubic yard	286	0.143
Motor oil	1 gal	7	0.0035
Tires, cars	1	20	0.01
Tires, trucks	1	90	0.045
Auto batteries	1	33	0.0165
Concrete, brick & block	1 cy	4000	2
Asphalt (milled, ripped , crushed)	1 sq. yd.	115	0.0575
Food waste, solid & liquid fats	55-gal dr.	413	0.2063

Notes: Additional conversion factors:
(1) Compactor size in cubic yards / the compaction ratio (4) = compacted yards
(2) Compacted yards / 3.3 = Tonnage

building. **Table 2** provides factors to convert volume to weight, and **Table 3** provides a form for gathering the information needed to calculate the amount of currently recycled waste materials. **Table 4** provides a form for gathering information on the amounts of component materials in currently unsegregated waste, and **Table 5** provides a method to summarize overall waste composition and disposition. These forms are adapted from materials from the Passaic County, New Jersey, Office of Natural Resource Programs, "Simple as 1-2-3 Commercial Waste Audit."

Documentation

❑ Waste stream audit to establish building waste baseline

- A waste-stream audit is a one-time analysis of the volume and constituent parts of a building's solid waste.
- A waste-stream audit should be conducted over a single, representative period (determined by the participant) that represents a full and reasonable collection period for all wastes.

Table 3: Materials Currently Recycled

Column A **Material**	Column B **Quantity Recycled [tons/yr]**	Column C **Recycling Market Name and Address**
Newspaper		
Glass		
Aluminum		
Tin/bi-metal		
High grade paper		
Mixed paper		
Corrugated cardboard		
Plastics		
Scrap metals		
Construction/demolition		
Tires		
Used motor oil		
Auto batteries		
Leaves		
Grass		
Food waste		
Other		
Other		
Total [Tons/yr.]		

Notes: Column B: Fill in from recycling billing or payment records

SS WE EA MR EQ IU

Prerequisite 1.1

- The audit should be performed at the time of waste disposal, so that it integrates the total disposal volumes on a per-week, per-month or per-year basis.
- Participants should take care to perform the audit during a time period that accurately represents regular waste-generation conditions (i.e., not during a holiday or period likely to have additional or unusual waste of some type).
- The waste audit should include at a minimum the items described in the Rating System Requirements section as well as any other significant categories of diverted waste.

❑ Procurement/Management Policy

- Provide the procurement/management policy in hard copy or digital form on participant letterhead with the signature of the company officer responsible for its implementation, or a copy of the policy as it appears within the official organizational waste management plan adopted by the participant.
- Include samples or copies of any employee education materials or information that informs building occupants about the waste management program.

Other Resources

Municipal Solid Waste in the United States: 2001 Facts and Figures

www.epa.gov/epaoswer/non-hw/muncpl/msw99.htm

This report from the U.S. EPA describes the national waste stream based on data collected from 1960 through 2001, and demonstrates trends in municipal solid waste generation and waste management strategies.

U.S. EPA Waste Wise Program

www.epa.gov/wastewise/about/index.htm

Table 4: Materials Currently in Unsegregated Waste

Column A **Material**	Column B **Quantity for Period of Audit [pounds]**	Column C **Percent of Total Unsegregated Waste for Period of Audit**	Column D **Estimated Quantity of Each Material in Unsegregated Waste Per Year [tons/yr]**
Newspaper			
Glass			
Aluminum			
Tin/bi-metal			
High grade paper			
Mixed paper			
Corrugated			
Plastics			
Scrap metals			
Construction/Demolition			
Tires			
Used motor oil			
Auto batteries			
Leaves			
Grass			
Food waste			
Other:			
Other:			
Other:			
Totals	Pounds	100 %	Tons per year

Notes: Column B: Fill in from audit
Column C: (Column B / Total for Column B) x 100 (See **Equation 1***)*
Column D: Column C x Total Unsegregated Waste (See **Equation 2***)*

Equation 1

Percent of Total Unsegregated Waste = ((Quantity of Specified Material) / (Total Unsegregated Waste)) x 100

Equation 2

Quantity per Year = (Percent of Total Unsegregated Waste) x (Total Unsegregated Waste)

Equation 3

Percent of Total Waste = (Total Quantity of the Material / Total Quantity of All Materials) x 100

Equation 4

Recycling Rate [%] = (Quantity Recycled / Total Quantity of Material in Waste Stream) x 100

Waste Wise is a free, voluntary EPA program that helps U.S. organizations eliminate costly municipal solid waste disposal.

Waste at Work

(212) 788-7900

www.informinc.org/wasteatwork.php

This online document from Inform, Inc. and the Council on the Environment of New York City offers strategies and case studies for reducing workplace waste generation.

Definitions

An **Incinerator** is a furnace or container for burning waste materials.

Landfills are waste disposal sites for the deposit of solid waste from human activities.

Recycling is the collection, reprocessing, marketing and use of materials that were diverted or recovered from the solid waste stream. Recycling provides two categories of environmental benefits: (1) diversion of waste from landfilling or incineration and (2) reduces the need for virgin materials for the manufacture of new products.

Table 5: Overall Waste Consumption

Column A **Material**	Column B **Quantity Recycled [tons/yr]**	Column C **Estimated Quantity in Unsegregated Waste [tons/yr]**	Column D **Total Quantity [tons/yr]**	Column E **Percent Total Annual Waste [%]**	Column F **Current Recycling Rate [%]**
Newspaper					
Glass					
Aluminum					
Tin/bi-metal					
High grade paper					
Mixed paper					
Corrugated Cardboard					
Plastics					
Scrap metals					
Construction/ Demolition					
Tires					
Used motor oil					
Auto batteries					
Leaves					
Grass					
Food waste					
Other:					
Other:					
Other:					
Other:					
Other:					
Totals					

Notes: Column B: Fill in from Table 3, Column C
Column C: Fill in from Table 4, Column D
Column D: Column B + Column C
Column E: see **Equation 3**
Column F: see **Equation 4**

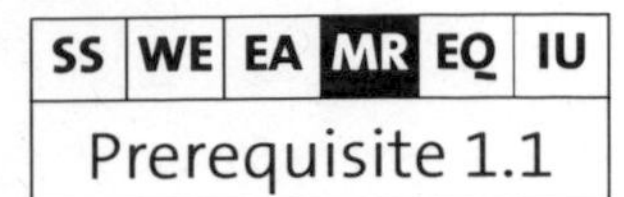

Source Reduction is reducing waste by reducing the amount of unnecessary material brought into a building. Purchasing products with less packaging is an example of source reduction.

Waste Disposal is the process of eliminating waste by means of burial in a landfill, combustion in an incinerator, dumping at sea, or eliminating waste in some other way that is not recycling or reuse.

Waste Diversion includes waste management activities that divert waste from disposal though incineration or landfilling. Typical waste diversion methods are reuse and recycling.

Waste Reduction includes source reduction and diversion of waste by means of reuse or recycling.

A **Waste Reduction Policy** includes: (1) A statement describing the organization's commitment to minimize waste disposal by using source reduction, reuse and recycling, (2) assignment of responsibility within the organization for implementation of waste reduction program, (3) a list of the general actions that will be implemented in the waste reduction program to reduce waste, and (4) a description of the tracking and review component in the waste reduction program to monitor waste reduction success and improve waste reduction performance over time.

Required

Source Reduction and Waste Management

Storage & Collection of Recyclables

Intent

Facilitate the reduction of waste generated by building occupants that is hauled to and disposed of in landfills or through incineration.

Requirements

Provide an easily accessible area that serves the entire building and is dedicated to the separation, collection and storage of materials for recycling. The recycling area needs to include (at a minimum) space for paper, glass, plastics, cardboard and metals. Recycling area capacity needs to be designed to accommodate at a minimum the potential recycling volumes identified in the waste stream audit for paper, corrugated cardboard, glass, plastics and metals.

If it can be documented for an existing building that there are no public or private recycling services available within the region where the building is located (within 50 miles of the building) for one or more of the identified materials, the building will be granted an exception to the requirement in this prerequisite for the identified material.

Submittals – Initial Certification

- ❑ Provide floor plans showing the area(s) dedicated to recycled material separation, collection and storage.

Submittals – Recertification

Provide an update of previous filings:

- ❑ If there has been no change to the building-wide recycling collection support systems, provide a signed letter documenting their continued existence and operation.

OR

- ❑ If the building-wide recycling collection support systems have changed, provide floor plans highlighting any changes to the collection, storage and separation locations for recycling.

Summary of Referenced Standard

There is no standard referenced for this prerequisite.

Green Building Concerns

Over the past few decades, recycling has increased in the United States. In 1960, only 6.4 percent of U.S. waste was recycled. By 2001, the amount had quadrupled to 29.7 percent.[2] Curbside recycling is now standard in many communities, and recycling facilities are available in almost all areas. In addition, many office workers recycle paper, airlines recycle aluminum cans and manufacturing facilities recycle scrap materials such as steel, plastic and wood.

Recycling is widely viewed as an integral aspect of environmentally responsible building management. Providing for the storage and collection of recyclables requires the allocation of building space. Finding this space in existing buildings to provide easily accessible recycling area may require some creativity. The designation of recycling areas should reflect which available space would most conveniently facilitate the deposit of materials by building occupants, as well as the collection and separation of materials by facility management staff.

Table 1: Sample Solid Waste Stream Characterization

Recyclable Material	Percentage (by volume)
High-grade paper	39.6%
Low-grade paper	20.2%
Glass	11.8%
Miscellaneous paper	7.4%
Newsprint	7.0%
Food waste	2.9%
Cardboard	2.8%
Plastic	2.6%
Metal	1.8%
Other	3.9%

Table 1 illustrates the potential for recycling, using a large federal office building as an example. Before recycling, the average weight of waste per employee was 2.9 pounds per day. Most of the listed materials could have been recycled instead of disposed of in landfills, drastically reducing the total building waste.

Environmental Issues

Waste going to landfills and incinerators directly and indirectly contributes to pollution and the depletion of natural resources. Landfills and incinerators both have direct negative impacts associated with their siting and construction, and waste disposal at these facilities has the potential to contaminate soil, air and groundwater. Disposing of waste, rather than reusing or recycling it, accelerates the harvesting rate of new materials, a process that strains natural resource stocks and causes environmental effects associated with transportation and energy use. Recycling has the potential to reduce these environmental burdens and extend the life of existing landfills.

Providing convenient recycling opportunities for building occupants can facilitate the diversion of a significant portion of the solid waste stream from disposal. Recycling also reduces the need to extract and process virgin natural resources. For example, recycling one ton of paper avoids the cutting of 17 trees and saves three cubic yards of landfill space. Recycling aluminum requires only 5 percent of the energy required to produce virgin aluminum from raw bauxite.

Economic Issues

Providing recycling storage and collection requires minimal initial cost to building owners and operators, and offers the potential to save money through reduced disposal fees. However, recycling storage and collection requires space that could be used for other activities. To minimize space requirements, equipment such as can crushers and cardboard balers can be installed if large volumes of recyclables are anticipated.

Recycling of some waste stream components may not fully offset the associated costs. Where recycling is economically competitive, it contributes to environmental protection and creates markets for otherwise discarded resources. Over time, markets are likely to place higher value on waste stream materials, leading to increased market demand and higher payments for these resources.

Strategies & Technologies

Strategies for waste reduction should place a preference on source reduction, followed by reuse and recycling, respectively. Establishing a waste management program consists of the steps listed below. In communities where recycling program are not currently in effect, project teams should develop facility plans for future recycling opportunities, stay abreast of new recycling opportunities, and prepare to communicate evolving recycling practices within the building to occupants.

Designate Collection Facilities

The most effective method to promote recycling is to make it convenient. Provide recycling collection areas throughout the building, as well as a central point to gather and store the recycled materials. Dispersed collection areas should be easily accessible throughout the building. Make sure that the central collection and storage area is adequately sized and conveniently located in the basement or on the ground level, with easy access to recyclable collection points throughout the building and access for allowing vehicles to move the gathered recyclables offsite. Collection and storage bins should accommodate a 75 percent diversion rate and provide easy access to custodial staff and collection workers. Consider bin designs that allow for easy cleaning to avoid health and air quality issues. Implement waste diversion tracking and reporting processes to ensure that collection and storage facilities are adequate for the volume of recyclables generated. There is no specific size requirement for compliance with MR Prerequisite 1.2, but **Table 2** can be used as a guideline to size the recycling area based on building square footage. It is based on the City of Seattle's ordinance on minimum areas for recycling and storage of recyclables in commercial and residential buildings.

In addition to designating space for the required material types (paper, glass, plastics, cardboard and metals), consider broadening the space allocation to provide dedicated spaces around the building for the collection of newspaper, organic waste (food and soiled paper) and other types of dry waste.

Identify Haulers

Identify local public and private recycling resources that provide services within a 50-mile radius of the building. Based on this information, develop a strategy for recycling as much of the building's waste stream as is feasible. Work with the

Table 2: Recycling Area Guidelines

Commercial Building Area [SF]	Minimum Recycling Area [SF]
0 to 5,000	82
5,001 to 15,000	125
15,001 to 50,000	175
50,001 to 100,000	225
100,001 to 200,000	275
200,001 or more	500

service providers selected to consider how cardboard balers, aluminum can crushers, recycling chutes and other waste management techniques can further enhance the recycling program.

Educate Occupants

Educate occupants and maintenance personnel about recycling procedures. Provide information about the types of materials recycled, the location of recycling collection area and other information about recycling procedures. Disseminate this information through employee handbooks, newsletters, signage and other communication modes. Let building occupants know about the environmental and financial benefits of recycling to increase their participation.

Additional Actions

Explore implementing source reduction programs to reduce the amount of waste. Encourage reduction and reuse of materials before they are recycled. For instance, building occupants can use reusable bottles, bags and other containers. Consider modifying purchasing practices to limit the amount of material brought into in the building that ultimately becomes waste. For example, seek out materials suppliers that minimize the packaging of their products.

Synergies & Tradeoffs

Dense urban areas typically have recycling infrastructure in place, but additional space for collection and storage within the building may be necessary and costly.

It is important to address possible adverse indoor environmental quality impacts due to recycling. Isolate activities that create odors, noise and air contaminants or perform them during non-occupant hours. These factors should be taken into account when developing a recycling plan.

Recycling of some materials may cost more than the resulting reduction in waste disposal fees. Although not economically ideal, recycling these materials is a valuable contribution to improving the environment because it helps develop markets for these waste streams.

Calculations & Documentation

Calculations

Use a table similar to **Table 3** to track recycling facilities available in the building.

Documentation

- ❑ Floor plan showing the area(s) dedicated to recycled material collection and storage
  - Floor plans should illustrate and highlight the areas where recyclable materials are collected.
  - Floor plans should identify floor or area-level collection stations, rather than containers serving individual offices or cubicles.

Table 3: Building Recycling Space

Recycling Space Location	Space Area [SF]
Total Area of Recycling Spaces in the Building [SF]	

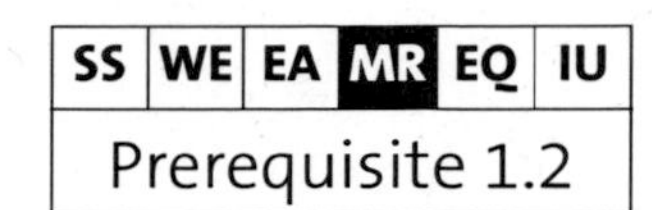

- If possible, the plan should note the type of materials collected at each station.
- In addition, it is suggested that participants include a narrative briefly describing:
  - The collection stations
  - How many people are served by each station
  - How often they are checked/emptied
  - Any unique challenges or circumstances affecting collection of recyclables
  - Photographs of example collection stations and signage that directs employees to recycling collection stations or identifies stations for use.

Other Resources

Business Resource Efficiency and Waste Reduction

www.ciwmb.ca.gov/bizwaste

This program from the California Integrated Waste Management Board assists in office recycling and waste reduction efforts.

City of Seattle Bills and Ordinances

www.clerk.ci.seattle.wa.us/~public/CBOR1.htm

This site provides electronic copies of ordinances from the City of Seattle, including the ordinance that requires minimum areas for recycling and storage of recyclables. These ordinances can be useful for municipalities or organizations drafting recycling policies.

Composting and Recycling Municipal Solid Waste by Luis Diaz, et. al., CRC Press, 1993.

This guide identifies and evaluates options for composing and recycling municipal solid waste.

Earth 911

1-877-EARTH911

www.earth911.org

This group provides information and education programs on recycling as well as links to regional recyclers.

McGraw-Hill Recycling Handbook by Herb Lund, McGraw-Hill, 2000.

The Recycling Handbook serves as a reference for individuals developing and operating recycling programs. It provides an overview of recycling laws, strategic goals for recycling programs, and information about the recycling process for each type of recyclable material.

National Recycling Coalition

www.nrc-recycle.org/

The National Recycling Coalition is a nonprofit organization dedicated to the advancement of recycling. The web site provides a range of information related to recycling.

Recycling at Work

(202) 293-7330

www.usmayors.org/USCM/recycle

This program from the U.S. Conference of Mayors provides information on workplace recycling efforts.

U.S. EPA Waste Wise Program

www.epa.gov/wastewise/about/index.htm

Waste Wise is a free, voluntary EPA program that helps U.S. organizations eliminate costly municipal solid waste disposal.

Definitions

An **Incinerator** is a furnace or container for burning waste materials.

Landfills are waste disposal sites for the deposit of solid waste from human activities.

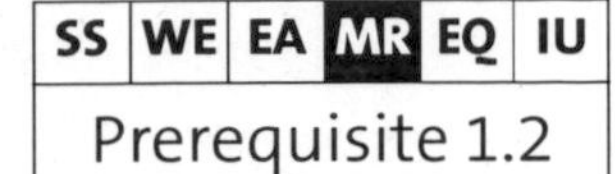

Recycling is the collection, reprocessing, marketing and use of materials that were diverted or recovered from the solid waste stream. Recycling provides two categories of environmental benefits: (1) diverts waste from landfilling or incineration and (2) reduces the need for virgin materials for the manufacture of new products.

Source Reduction is reducing waste by reducing the amount of unnecessary material brought into a building. Purchasing products with less packaging is a good example of source reduction.

Waste Disposal is the process of eliminating waste by means of burial in a landfill, combustion in an incinerator, dumping at sea or eliminating waste in some other way that is not recycling or reuse.

Waste Diversion includes waste management activities that divert waste from disposal though incineration or landfilling. Principal waste diversion methods are reuse and recycling waste.

Waste Reduction includes source reduction and diversion of waste by means of reuse or recycling.

A **Waste Reduction Policy** includes: (1) A statement describing the organization's commitment to minimize waste disposal by using source reduction, reuse and recycling, (2) assignment of responsibility within the organization for implementation of waste reduction program, (3) a list of the general actions that will be implemented in the waste reduction program to reduce waste and (4) a description of the tracking and review component in the waste reduction program to monitor waste reduction success and improve waste reduction performance over time.

Case Study – MR Prerequisite 1

Goizeuta Business School - Emory University

Atlanta, Georgia

LEED-EB Gold

Owner: Emory University

Photo courtesy of: Emory University

Emory University's Goizueta Business School recycles 33 percent of its 63 ton annual solid waste stream. The Goizueta School recycling program ensures that all building occupants, including both regular employees and students attending class, have opportunities to recycle. Recyclables collected from the building are delivered to the campus-wide Recycling Center, where they are processed with automated separation technology that separates cardboard, paper, glass, plastic and metals. In the future, Emory hopes to increase their recycling rate through promotional programs that convey the benefits of recycling to building users.

Emory is also exploring source reduction opportunities in their purchasing decisions. For example, a switch from folded paper towels to roll paper in lavatories is expected to result in less waste generation.

SS | WE | EA | MR | EQ | IU

Prerequisite 2

Required

Toxic Material Source Reduction

Reduced Mercury in Light Bulbs

Intent

Establish and maintain a toxic material source reduction program to reduce the amount of mercury brought into buildings through purchases of light bulbs.

Requirements

- ❑ Maintain mercury content of all mercury-containing light bulbs below 100 picograms per lumen hour, on weighted average, for all mercury-containing light bulbs acquired for the existing building and associated grounds.
- ❑ The weighted average mercury content of these mercury-containing light bulbs is calculated by: 1) adding up the total weight of mercury in all the mercury-containing light bulbs acquired during the performance period (picograms of Hg); and then, 2) dividing total mercury content (picograms of Hg) by the sum of the lumen hour output of all the light bulbs (lumen hours: calculated by multiplying the rated hours (life) of each light bulb by the mean light output in lumens).
  - Rated hours of life are defined as stated by the manufacturer based on consistent testing (three hours on/20 minutes off for linear fluorescents and compact fluorescents; 11 hours on for HID light bulbs) and are based on the design or mean light output of the light bulbs (in lumens, fluorescent light bulbs measured with a ballast having a ballast factor of 1.0 and measured using instant-start ballasts except for T-5s, which are measured using program start ballasts).
  - The mean light output in lumens is the light output at 40% of light bulb life.
  - These calculations need to show for all acquired mercury containing light bulbs:
    - The total mercury content in the light bulbs.
    - The total lumen hours of light output for all the light bulbs.
    - The number of light bulbs of each type.
    - The overall weighted average mercury content in picograms/lumen hour.
  - If the mercury content documentation shows a range of mercury contents in milligrams, use the highest value in the range in these calculations.

Submittals – Initial Certification

- ❑ Provide a copy of the organizational policy specifying that all future purchases of mercury-containing light bulbs will be made in such a way that the average mercury content of the light bulbs is less than the specified level in picograms/lumen hour.
- ❑ Provide records of all acquisitions during the performance period of mercury-containing light bulbs for use in the building and grounds.
- ❑ Include manufacturer Material Safety Data Sheets (MSDSs) for each type of light

bulb purchased showing mercury content of the light bulbs in milligrams.

- ❑ Provide calculations demonstrating that the weighted average mercury content of acquired light bulbs is less than the specified level in picograms per lumen hour. If an MSDS shows ranges of mercury contents in milligrams, use the highest value given in these calculations.

Submittals – Recertification

Provide an update of previous filings:

- ❑ Provide records of all acquisitions during the performance period of mercury-containing light bulbs for use in the building and grounds.
- ❑ Include manufacturer MSDS for each type of light bulb purchased showing mercury content of the light bulbs in milligrams.
- ❑ Provide calculations demonstrating that the weighted average mercury content of acquired light bulbs is less than the specified level in picograms per lumen hour.

AND EITHER

- ❑ If there has been no change to the purchasing policy specifying that the weighted average mercury content of these light bulbs is less than the specified level in picograms/lumen hour, provide a signed letter documenting its continued existence and implementation.

OR

- ❑ If the mercury-containing light bulb purchasing policy has changed, provide a copy of the revised plan highlighting any changes to the specified level picograms of mercury/lumen hour policy.

Summary of Referenced Standards

Light Bulb Life Measurement Standards:

IESNA LM-40-01 (01-Dec-2001) Standard for Life of Tubular Fluorescence

Note: Conduct life test using 3 hours on 20 minute off cycling and instant start ballast with a ballast factor of 1.

IESNA LM-47-01 (01-Dec-2001) Standard for Life of HID Lamps

IESNA LM-60-01 (01-Dec-2001) Standard for Life of Single-Ended Compact Fluorescent Lamps

Light Bulb Lumen Measurement Standards:

Lumens are measured in sphere following prescribed IES methods.

LM 9-Linear fluorescent

LM 66 Compact fluorescent

LM 51-HID lamps

Light Bulb Mercury Content Measurement Standards:

Option 1: Obtain manufacturer's certification as to mercury content (in milligrams) for each type of light bulb acquired. (If mercury content is provided as a range, use the high end of the range in these calculations.)

Option 2: Test each type of light bulb acquired using U.S. EPA Total Mercury by Cold Vapor Absorption Method 7471A.

Green Building Concerns

Mercury causes serious ecological and human health problems when released to the environment through human activities. Although coal-fired electricity plants are the largest source of mercury air emissions in the United States, mercury is also present in a number of products, including building supplies such as fluorescent light bulbs, some types of batteries, thermostats, thermometers and switches. Once these products leave buildings, they often become part of the solid waste stream and contribute to air, land and water contamination.

In addition to a threat to the environment, the disposal and handling of mercury-containing products presents health hazards for building occupants and maintenance personnel. Improper handling of these products can cause breakage, which releases elemental mercury vapor into the air. This situation is particularly dangerous in warm or poorly ventilated indoor spaces, as the vapor can be inhaled and absorbed through the lungs, impairing human health. Depending on exposure levels, health effects may include headaches, changes in nerve response, loss of cognitive function, kidney problems, respiratory failure or death.

Standard fluorescent light bulbs are used to light 90 percent of lit commercial floor space in the United States.[3] Other mercury-containing light bulbs used in buildings include compact fluorescent and high intensity discharge (HID) light bulbs. The mercury in these light bulbs allows for high-energy efficiency and long bulb life compared to other lighting options. Although currently there is no known method for completely eliminating mercury in fluorescent lights while maintaining energy efficiency, manufacturers have continuously reduced the amount of mercury in light bulbs. The total mercury contained in new fluorescent light bulbs was 17 tons in 1994, 13 tons in 1999, and 9 tons in 2001.[4] Light bulb consumers can further this trend by purchasing lower mercury content bulbs.

Three factors affect mercury brought into buildings through mercury-containing light bulbs, all of which require close attention: mercury content, length of life and lumen output. All three factors are captured by the picogram per lumen hour metric used in this prerequisite.

Since light bulbs are available with high-efficiency and low picogram per lumen hours, building owners and managers can directly reduce the mercury entering their buildings while indirectly reducing mercury emissions from coal-fired power pants through energy efficiency.

Environmental Issues

Although mercury naturally occurs in the environment, human activities have altered its global distribution. Coal-fired power plant emissions are the leading anthropogenic contributor to mercury in the environment,[5] as mercury previously contained underground in coal deposits is emitted into the atmosphere. Combustion of other fossil fuels also contributes to mercury pollution, along with disposal of mercury-containing products through incineration or landfilling.[6]

After being emitted into the air, mercury enters bodies of water through rain, deposition and runoff. Once in the water, microbial processes transform it to methylmercury, a bioaccumulating toxin.[7] Bioaccumulants are substances that increase in concentration in the living organisms exposed to them because they are very slowly metabolized or excreted.

Methylmercury in water bodies accumulates in fish, shellfish and eventually their predators. In humans, high levels of methylmercury exposure can damage the brain and organ systems, and act as an immunosuppressant. In infants and children, methylmercury exposure can cause neurological and developmental problems. Birds and mammals that prey on fish can be exposed to methylmercury levels that cause death, reproductive difficulties and suppressed growth and development.[8]

Economic Issues

Purchasing light bulbs with low mercury content, long life and/or high light output is the primary way to achieve the targeted mercury reduction in lamps. Each of these variables can help drive down the mercury content per lumen hour. For example, T-8 and T-5 fluorescent lamps offer low mercury content, long life and high light output.

The cost of these light bulbs is generally no higher than comparable ones with higher mercury content. Light bulbs with a longer life and higher output generally cost more than standard light bulbs. However, they reduce maintenance costs and improve lumens, lowering the quantity of light bulbs needed. Therefore, the combined purchasing and operating costs for the light bulbs in a building should be roughly constant or lower after fulfilling this prerequisite.

In some buildings, low mercury-content bulbs may not be available for a large enough portion of existing fixtures to meet the weighted average light bulb mercury content standard. In this case, some fixtures may need to be changed to accommodate low mercury content light bulbs. This one-time cost would need to be implemented for enough fixtures to achieve the average mercury content target. Fixture retrofits to accommodate low mercury fluorescent light bulbs may also result in energy savings that offset the cost of fixture replacements.

Strategies & Technologies

Although not required by MR Prerequisite 2, maintenance personnel should be trained to appropriately handle mercury-containing products to avoid breakage or implosion. Recycle all mercury-containing light bulbs through an appropriate facility at the end of their life. Helpful information about light bulb recycling procedures and service providers can be found on the North American Electrical Manufacturers Association's LampRecycle.org web site (www.nema.org/lamprecycle).

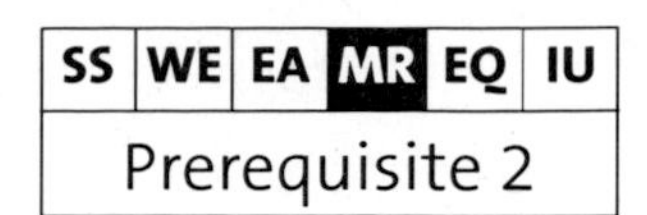

Establish and follow a light bulb purchasing program that keeps the weighted average mercury content below the specified level of picograms per lumen hour for mercury-containing light bulbs purchased during the performance period. To achieve the targeted level of weighted average mercury content, purchase light bulbs that have one or more of the following characteristics:

- ❑ Low mercury content
- ❑ Long life
- ❑ High lumen output

Non-mercury containing light bulbs, such as LEDs, may also be included in the picogram per lumen hour calculations for this prerequisite, but only if they have energy efficiency levels that are equal to or greater than the efficiency of comparable to mercury-containing light bulbs.

Develop and Implement a Plan for Achieving Targeted Picogram per Lumen Hour Levels

The following steps outline how to establish a light bulb purchasing program that meets the prerequisite requirements.

1. Project your mercury-containing light bulb replacement requirements for the performance period. It is a good idea to consider group light bulb replacement to maximize the energy efficiency of lighting and reduce unit costs.
2. Identify light bulb replacement options that fit the existing fixtures and meet mercury content, light bulb life and energy efficiency objectives.
   - Prepare a list of each type of light bulb used in the building and the number of each type.
   - Give this list to all available lighting suppliers representing all available manufacturers and ask them to assist you in identifying light bulbs for each application in your building and the bulbs' mercury content in milligrams, mean light output and life span.
   - For risk management purposes, ask suppliers to provide MSDSs for each type of light bulb or another formal company document stating the mercury content of each bulb type in milligrams.
   - Request that the suppliers include in their responses light bulbs manufactured by parent companies or affiliates in Europe of the manufacturers they represent that meet European standards for reduced mercury content in light bulbs.
3. For all projected acquisitions of mercury-containing light bulbs, create a spreadsheet (described in the Calculations & Documentation section below) and evaluate projected average mercury content of all mercury-containing light bulbs purchased over the performance period.
4. If the weighted average of the projected mercury content in light bulbs purchased over the performance period is too high, repeat step 2 using different combinations of bulbs and/or suppliers.
5. If the weighted average mercury content of light bulbs is still too high, identify opportunities to replace existing fixtures with those that accommodate lower mercury content light bulbs, and install lower mercury content light bulbs.
6. Repeat steps 4 and 5 until the weighted average mercury content of all mercury-containing light bulbs expected to be acquired over the performance period is far enough below the 100 picograms per lumen hour target to meet the prerequisite.
7. Track mercury content averages on a regular basis to make corrections as needed to meet performance period targets.

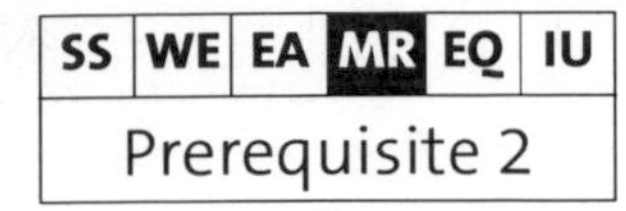

The European Union (EU) currently has a voluntary standard for mercury in florescent light bulbs requiring that regular-life tubular fluorescent light bulbs contain less that 5 milligrams of mercury. In 2006, the EU will require that regular-life tubular florescent light bulbs contain less than 5 milligrams of mercury. Since all manufacturers that sell fluorescent light bulbs in the EU must meet the 5-milligram mercury content requirement for regular life tubular fluorescent light bulbs, a wide variety of light bulbs with reduced mercury are becoming available. All major light bulb manufacturers currently produce regular-life tubular fluorescent light bulbs that contain less than 5 milligrams of mercury. Tubular fluorescent light bulbs with less than 5 milligrams of mercury and a typical life and light output will meet the 100 picograms per lumen hour requirement of this prerequisite.

Synergies & Tradeoffs

This prerequisite encourages the use of high efficiency, long life light bulbs with lower mercury content. Doing this helps meet this prerequisite, contributes to earning MR Credit 6 and helps earn points under EA Credit 1 for energy efficiency. Maintaining existing fluorescent fixtures and replacing other fixtures to accommodate fluorescent light bulbs will improve building energy efficiency. The best economic and environmental approach to lighting decisions is to optimize energy efficiency and light bulb life while minimizing mercury content.

MR Credit 6: Additional Toxic Material Reduction can be earned by lowering the mercury per lumen hour weighted average for mercury containing light bulbs to under 80 picograms per lumen hour. Consider the feasibility of earning this credit while developing a strategy for meeting MR Prerequisite 2.

This prerequisite addresses mercury pollution through source reduction. Other actions that further prevent mercury pollution include:

- ❑ Recycling mercury-containing light bulbs (MR Credit 5: Occupant Recycling)
- ❑ High energy efficiency, which indirectly reduces the amount of mercury released by coal-fired power plants (EA Prerequisite 2: Minimum Energy Performance and EA Credit 1: Optimize Energy Performance)

Calculations & Documentation

Calculations

Table 1 contains an example calculation of the weighted average mercury content of light bulbs for a building. A detailed calculation spreadsheet can be downloaded from the USGBC web site. The completed spreadsheet should contain both the plan for achieving reduced mercury content in the future and the mercury content of all mercury-containing light bulbs purchased during the performance period.

The same calculations apply to both MR Prerequisite 2 and MR Credit 6:

- ❑ If the weighted average mercury content of all the mercury-containing light bulbs is below 100 picograms per lumen hour, MR Prerequisite 2 is earned.
- ❑ If the weighted average mercury content of all the mercury-containing light bulbs is below 80 picograms per lumen hour, MR Credit 6 is earned and MR Prerequisite 2 is earned.

Documentation

- ❑ Organizational policy for light bulb purchases
  - Provide the light bulb purchasing policy in hard copy or digital form on participant letterhead with the signature of the company officer

responsible for its implementation, or as it appears within the official organizational purchasing plan adopted by the participant.

- A sample policy can be viewed on the following page.

- ❑ Records of all acquisitions during the performance period of mercury-containing light bulbs
  - Provide acquisition records even if the 100 picogram/lumen hour limitation is not met, if calculated based upon those purchases.
- ❑ Manufacturer Material Safety Data Sheets (MSDSs)
  - Provide manufacturer documentation that designates the mercury content (in milligrams) for each type/model of light bulb. This information should be documented in MSDSs, official company literature or a signed letter from the manufacturer.
- ❑ Calculations demonstrating the weighted average mercury content
  - If the mercury content information provided by the manufacturer is presented as a range of numbers, calculations for LEED-EB must use the highest mercury content of the range to ensure compliance.

Other Resources

ENERGY STAR® Business Improvement: Purchasing and Procurement

www.energystar.gov/index.cfm?c=bulk_purchasing.bus_purchasing

The ENERGY STAR web site provides resources designed to assist procurement officials in making smart purchasing decisions.

Inform Fact Sheet: Mercury-Containing Lamps

www.informinc.org/fact_P3mercury_lamps.php

This site provides information on mercury in fluorescent light bulbs, purchasing programs for low mercury-content bulbs, and related topics.

Table 1: Example Mercury Calculation for a Light Bulb Purchasing Plan

Column A Type of Light Bulb	Column B Quantity	Column C Hg Content per bulb [mg]	Column D Design Light Output per Bulb [lumens]	Column E Life per bulb [hours]	Column F Total Hg Content by Bulb Type [grams]	Column G Total Lumen Hours by Bulb Type [hours]
T-8 Four Foot	1000	3.5	2800	24000	3.5	67,200,000,000
Compact Fluorescent	30	1.4	1545	10000	0.042	463,500,000
HID	40	6.8	6800	12500	0.272	3,400,000,000
Totals					3.814	71,063,500,000
Mercury Content [Picograms / Lumen Hour]						53.7

Notes: Column A: From records or survey of building and building site
Column B: From records or survey of building
Column C: From light bulb manufacturer MSDS or signed letter from manufacturer
Column D: From manufacturer's product literature
Column E: From manufacturer's product literature
Column F: Mercury content of bulb type (column C) x quantity of bulbs (column B)
Column G: For each type of bulb: Mean Lumens (column D) x Life of bulb (column E) x quantity of bulbs (column B)
Total Mercury Content: Sum of the total mercury content for all types of bulbs
Total Lumen Hours: Sum of the lumen hours for all types of bulbs
Mercury Content [picograms/lumen Hour] = (Total Mercury Content / Total Lumen Hours) x 10^{12}

Sample Organization Policy Addressing Mercury in Lighting

Name of Organization: ______________________________

Organization Policy on Reduction of Mercury Content of Light Bulbs Purchased

Objective

This organization is committed to reducing the mercury content of the mercury containing light bulbs acquired for use in our building and on our site to less than [80 or 100] picograms per lumen hour, on average.

Implementation

Each year, the organization's maintenance department will prepare a plan for light bulb purchases for the next year. This purchasing plan will be used to set the maximum mercury content, life and lumen output for each type of bulb to be purchased such that the weighted average mercury content will be 10 percent less than the target. If necessary, some of the lighting fixtures will be changed to accommodate lower mercury light bulbs in order to reach this goal. The Purchasing Department will use these mercury content maximums for purchases of each type of light bulb.

Tracking

The purchasing department will maintain records of all purchases of mercury-containing light bulbs for use in the building and on the site and carry out calculations of the average monthly and weighted average annual mercury content of these light bulbs. If the monthly mercury content and cumulative annual mercury content is not at least 10 percent below the mercury/lumen hour target, the mercury content, life and lumen output of the light bulbs purchased for the remainder of the year will be reduced. This reduction in light bulb purchasing will maintain the weighted-annual mercury content per lumen hour at least 10 percent below the target of [80 or 100] picograms mercury/lumen hour.

Reporting

If at any time during the year corrective action is required to stay on track for achieving the mercury content reduction target, inform the Organization's Director of Facility Management that corrective action was required and the specific corrective action taken. Within 60 days of the end of the reporting year, report the mercury content of the mercury-containing light bulbs purchased during the last year, compare the actual reduction to the goal, and report any planned changes.

Signature of Head of Organization: ______________________________

Name of Head of Organization: ______________________________

Title: ______________________________

Name of Organization: ______________________________

Date: ______________________________

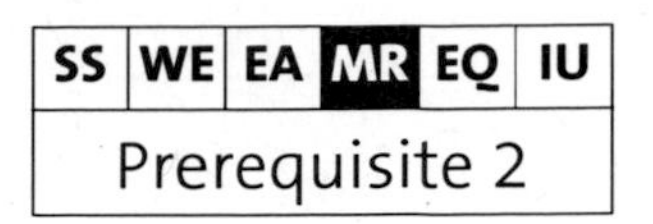

LampRecycle.org

www.nema.org/lamprecycle/

LampeRecycle.org is an online resource from the National Electric Manufacturers Association, and provides information on recycling spent mercury-containing light bulbs, including links to regulations and recycling service providers.

U.S. EPA Mercury Web Site

www.epa.gov/mercury/

This comprehensive site offers information about mercury emissions, the use of mercury in manufactured products, human and environmental health effects, and laws and regulations.

Definitions

Bioaccumulants are substances that increase in concentration in the living organisms exposed to them because they are very slowly metabolized or excreted.

Elemental mercury is pure mercury rather that a mercury containing compound, the vapor of which is commonly used in fluorescent and other light bulb types.

Light bulbs are devices that produce illumination, and include glass bulbs or tubes that emit light produce by electricity (as an incandescent bulb or fluorescent bulb).

Design light output is the light output of light bulbs at 40 percent of their useful life.

Light bulb life is the useful operating life of light bulbs.

A **lumen** is a unit of luminous flux equal to the light emitted in a unit solid angle by a uniform point source of one candle intensity.

Methylmercury is the term used to describe any of various toxic compounds of mercury containing the complex CH_3Hg- that often occur as pollutants and that bioaccumulate in living organisms, especially in higher levels of a food chain.

A **Picogram** is one trillionth of a gram.

Picograms per lumen hour is a measure of the amount of mercury in a light bulb per unit of light delivered over its useful life.

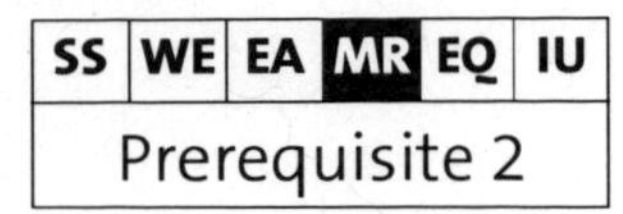

SS	WE	EA	MR	EQ	IU

Credits 1.1 & 1.2

1–2 Points

Construction, Demolition and Renovation

Intent

Divert construction, demolition and land-clearing debris from landfill and incineration disposal. Redirect recyclable recovered resources back to the manufacturing process. Redirect reusable materials to appropriate sites.

Requirements

Develop and implement a Waste Management Policy covering any future building retrofit, renovation or modification on the site. Quantify diversions of construction, demolition and land-clearing debris from landfill and incineration disposal by weight or volume.

- ❑ MR Credit 1.1: Divert at least 50% of construction, demolition and land-clearing waste from landfill and incineration disposal. (1 point)
- ❑ MR Credit 1.2: Divert at least 75% of construction, demolition and land-clearing waste from landfill and incineration disposal. (1 additional point)

Submittals – Initial Certification

- ❑ Provide a copy of the Waste Management Policy that specifies inclusion of waste management specifications for any future building retrofit, renovation or modification that may occur on the site.
- ❑ Provide documentation that the Waste Management Policy has been followed:
  - For any building retrofit, renovation or modification that has occurred in the building over the performance period, provide calculations on end-of-project waste management rates, salvage rates and landfill rates demonstrating that at least 50% for 1 point or 75% for 2 points (by weight or volume) of construction wastes were recycled, salvaged or otherwise diverted from landfill and incineration.

OR

  - Provide a written statement that no building retrofits, renovations or modifications were carried out in the building or on the site during the performance period.

Submittals – Recertification

Provide an update of previous filings:

OPTION 1

- ❑ If there has been no change to the Waste Management Policy that specifies inclusion of waste management specifications for any building retrofit, renovation or modification, provide a signed letter documenting its continued existence and implementation.
- ❑ Provide documentation that the Waste Management Policy has been followed:
  - For any building retrofit, renovation or modification that has occurred in the building over the performance period, provide calculations on end-of-project waste management rates, salvage rates, and landfill rates demonstrating that at least 50%

for 1 point or 75% for 2 points (by weight or volume) of construction wastes were recycled, salvaged or otherwise diverted from landfill and incineration.

OR

- Provide a written statement that no building retrofits, renovations or modifications were carried out in the building or on the site during the performance period.

OPTION 2

- ❑ If there has been a change to the Waste Management Policy that specifies inclusion of waste management specifications for any future building retrofit, renovation or modification, provide a copy of the revised plan highlighting any changes.
- ❑ Provide documentation that the revised Waste Management Policy has been followed:
  - For any building retrofit, renovation or modification that has occurred in the building over the performance period, provide calculations on end-of-project waste management rates, salvage rates, and landfill rates demonstrating that at least 50% for 1 point or 75% for 2 points (by weight or volume) of construction wastes were recycled, salvaged or otherwise diverted from landfill and incineration.

OR

- Provide a written statement that no building retrofits, renovations or modifications were carried out in the building or on the site during the performance period.

Summary of Referenced Standard

There is no standard referenced for this credit.

Green Building Concerns

Construction and demolition activities generate enormous quantities of solid waste. The U.S. EPA estimated that 136 million tons of construction and demolition debris (versus 209.7 million tons of municipal solid waste) were generated in 1996, 57 percent of it from non-residential construction, renovation and demolition.[9][10] This equates to 2.8 pounds per capita per day, nationwide.

Commercial construction generates between 2.0 and 2.5 pounds of solid waste per square foot, most of which can potentially be recycled. Diverting these materials preserves space in landfills and lessens the rate of natural resource consumption. Recycling opportunities are expanding rapidly in many communities, including recycling of metal, vegetation, concrete and asphalt. Materials such as paper, corrugated cardboard, plastics and clean wood can also be recycled in most communities. Other materials, such as gypsum wallboard, can be recycled only in regions with the necessary reprocessing plants. The recyclability of a demolished material often depends on the amount of contamination attached to it. Demolished wood, for instance, is often not reusable or recyclable unless it is deconstructed and de-nailed.

The composition of construction and demolition debris varies highly and depends on the building type, geographic location, and type of activity and structure. Because some types of construction and demolition debris are easier to recycle than others, knowing the composition of the debris waste stream is important to locate recycling services and develop pre-recycling collection and sorting practices. **Table 1** summarizes results of a 1998 study of waste composition for construction and demolition projects in Wisconsin. Note the differences in waste composition by project type.

Environmental Issues

Recycling of construction, demolition and land clearing (CDL) debris reduces demand for virgin resources, and can potentially reduce the environmental and health burdens associated with resource extraction, processing and transportation. Debris recycling also reduces dependence on landfills and incinerators. Landfills can contaminate groundwater and encroach upon valuable green space. Incinerators can pollute the air and contaminate groundwater. Effective construction waste management can extend the lifetime of existing

Table 1: Waste Stream Characterizations for Construction and Demolition Activities

Material	Percentage (by Weight) for Construction Projects	Percentage (by Weight) for Demolition Projects
Wood	39	28
Drywall	20	10
Cardboard	11	1
Scrap metal	10	6
Concrete/brick	6	14
Plastic	5	8
Shingles/roof materials	4	26
Carpet/textiles	1	4
Other	4	3

Adapted from Camp, Dresser, & McKee, "Quantity & Composition Study of Construction & Demolition Debris in Wisconsin," February 1998.

landfills, reducing the need for expansion or development of new landfill sites.

Economic Issues

In past years, many regions of the United States had readily available landfill capacity with low disposal fees, so recycling construction waste frequently cost more than it saved. Recycling infrastructure to process construction waste and marketplaces to resell it were not widely available. In recent years, however, increased materials and disposal costs, coupled with more stringent waste disposal regulations and decreasing landfill capacity, have changed the waste management equation. As landfill and incinerator fees escalate, recycling construction waste has become more economically attractive. As a rule of thumb, when disposal tipping fees exceed $50 per ton, recycling of construction waste is likely to save money.

Waste management plans require time and money to draft and implement, but can result in substantial savings throughout the construction process. Projects that recycle construction and demolition waste benefit from lower disposal tipping fees and associated hauling charges, which are often higher than associated costs for recycling collection and processing. Reuse of materials reduces the volume of new materials that need to be purchased.

Recyclable materials have different market values depending on reprocessing costs and the availability of virgin materials on the market. In general, metals have higher market values, while materials such as scrap wood and gypsum wallboard have lower market values. The market values of many recyclable materials, such as cardboard and plastics, fluctuate from month to month.

Project sites in urban areas may have little or no space available for waste separation activities, leading to additional expense to implement these strategies.

Strategies & Technologies

Develop and adopt a waste management policy for any construction occurring on the site. The policy should address reuse and/or recycling of corrugated cardboard, metals, concrete brick, asphalt, land clearing debris (if applicable), beverage containers, clean dimensional wood, plastic, glass, gypsum board and carpet. Also, evaluate the feasibility of recycling rigid insulation, engineered wood products and other materials. Using wood as a fuel is one option to divert wood waste from landfills or incineration. Land clearing debris is included in this credit, but excavated soil is not. This credit also includes materials that are removed and then reused, such as materials from partitions that are removed and used in the construction of new partitions. However, materials in a wall that is left in place are not included in this credit.

Identify deconstruction and salvage opportunities, licensed haulers and processors of recyclables, and potential markets for salvaged materials. Removal costs can be avoided by allowing private salvage companies access to the site. For combined demolition and construction projects, seek options for reusing materials from the demolished building in the new construction project. The policy should include estimated costs of recycling, salvaging and reusing materials, and should also address source reduction of materials used.

For waste volumes generated, identify and institute reuse, salvage and recycling whenever economics and logistics allow. Source reduction on the job site should be an integral part of the policy. Minimize factors that contribute to waste such as over-packaging, improper storage, ordering errors, ordering excess, poor planning, breakage, mishandling and contamination of construction materials.

On the construction site, designate an area to recycle construction and demolition waste. Train workers on the recycling protocols, and label recycling containers effectively, including labeling in the native language(s) of construction crew workers. Institute monthly reporting and feedback on the waste management policy to assess progress and address any problems. Post this information for all construction personnel to read.

Include the specifications of the construction and demolition waste management policy in contract language for general contractors and subcontractors. Seek contractors with experience in construction waste management, as their familiarity with reuse and recovery techniques will maximize the effectiveness of the waste reduction efforts. Provide stipulations in contract language for accountability and incentives to meet waste reduction goals.

Synergies & Tradeoffs

Construction activities in urban areas may have little or no space available for waste separation activities. Choose recycling collection areas wisely to avoid contaminating stormwater runoff and to protect stockpiled materials from the elements.

Calculations & Documentation

Calculations

The following calculation methodology supports the credit submittals listed in the Rating System. Use a spreadsheet (as provided in the LEED-EB Letter Templates) to track the weight of construction, demolition and land clearing (CDL) wastes that are landfilled and recycled. Note that excavation materials such as soil and clay are not considered CDL materials, and should not be included in the calculations. To calculate the recycling percentage, use **Equation 1**.

Tables 2 – 4 demonstrate waste calculations for an example project. The project recycled concrete, steel, wood, cardboard, gypsum wallboard, brick and land clearing debris. An estimated 243 tons of waste were recycled, while 43.7 tons were sent to the landfill. This results in a recycling rate

Equation 1

Recycling Rate [%] = (Recycled Waste [weight] / Recycled Waste + Waste to Landfill [weight]) x 100

Table 2: Example of Diverted Materials by Weight

Material Diverted	Means of Diversion		Weight [tons]
	Process	Placement of materials	
Concrete	Recycling	Delivered to Acme Concrete Recycling, Inc.	138.0
Land Clearing Debris	Recycling	Delivered to Municipal Compost Facility	56.2
Wood	Reuse	Donated to local nonprofit constructing affordable housing units, Housing Works, Inc.	19.6
Gypsum Wallboard (half sheets and larger in good condition)	Reuse	Donated to local nonprofit constructing affordable housing units, Housing Works, Inc.	3.5
Gypsum Wallboard (scraps that cannot be reused)	Recycling	Delivered to Acme Gypsum Recycling, Inc.	6.0
Brick	Reuse	Reused on site	9.4
Cardboard	Recycling	Delivered to Municipal Recycling Center	7.2
Steel	Recycling	Steel scrap sold to Smith's Scrap Metal Depot	3.1
Total			**243**

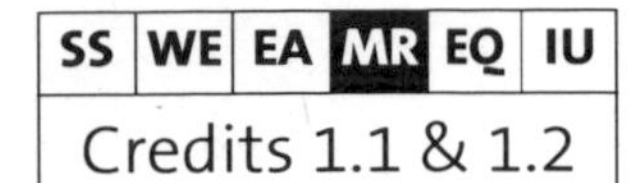

of 85 percent, qualifying for two points under this credit.

Typically, waste containers are sized by volume and weighed at the materials recovery facility or landfill. To assist in calculations, **Table 5** provides estimates to convert waste materials from volume to weight.

Documentation

❑ Waste Management Policy

- Submit the policy addressing construction, demolition and renovation waste management as it appears within the official organizational Waste Management Policy adopted by the participant, or as an individual document in hard copy or digital form on participant letterhead with the signature of the company officer responsible for its implementation.
- The policy should specify the percentage of construction waste that the participant is committed to diverting, the materials to be diverted and the method of diversion.

Sample Company Policy on Construction Waste Management

For any construction inside the project building or on the site (including retrofits, renovations or modifications), the construction plans and the contracting documents will include a requirement that all construction waste including demolition waste and land clearing waste (if applicable) be qualified by type of material by weight. Additionally, at least 75 percent (by weight) will be recycled and/or salvaged.

Table 3: Example of Materials Sent to Landfill by Weight

Waste to Landfill	Weight [tons]
Miscellaneous Waste	11.0
Miscellaneous Waste	9.0
Miscellaneous Waste	10.7
Miscellaneous Waste	13.0
Total	**43.7**

Table 4: Waste Diversion Rate

Waste	Weight [tons]
Total Waste Sent to Landfill (from Table 3)	43.7
Total Waste Diverted from Landfill (from Table 2)	243.0
Total Waste	286.7
Rate of Waste Diversion from Landfill	**85%**

Table 5: Solid Waste Conversion Factors

Material	Density [lbs/CY]
Rubble	1,400
Steel	1,000
Gypsum Wallboard	500
Mixed Waste	350
Wood	300
Cardboard	100

- ❑ Documentation of policy compliance
  - Provide calculations showing diversion rate for any building retrofit, renovation or modification during the performance period.
  - If no building retrofits, renovation or modifications were made during the performance period, provide a statement to that effect in hard copy or digital form on participant letterhead with the signature of the company officer responsible for waste management.

Other Resources

Building Savings

www.ilsr.org/recycling/buildingdebris.pdf

Building Savings is an online publication from the U.S. EPA offers strategies for construction waste and demolition debris.

Construction and Demolition Waste Recycling Information

(916) 341-6499

www.ciwmb.ca.gov/ConDemo

This program from the California Integrated Waste Management Board includes case studies, fact sheets and links.

Construction Waste Management Handbook

(202) 328-8160

www.smartgrowth.org/library/const-wastemgmt_hndbk.html

Part of the Smart Growth Network web site, this handbook provides information on residential construction waste management issues.

Contractors' Guide to Preventing Waste and Recycling

(206) 389-7304

www.metrokc.gov/dnrp/swd/construction-recycling/documents/ConGuide.pdf

The Contractors' Guide is an online guidebook on waste prevention in construction from the Business and Industry Resource Venture.

Construction Recycling and Waste Management

www.metrokc.gov/procure/green/waste-mgt.htm

This web site provides information from City of Seattle and Portland Metro construction waste management projects.

U.S. EPA Construction and Demolition Debris Web Site

www.epa.gov/epaoswer/non-hw/debris/index.htm

The Construction and Demolition Debris web site from the U.S. EPA provides construction and demolition debris statistics, and information and resources for managing and reducing waste.

Waste Spec: Model Specifications for Construction Waste Reduction, Reuse and Recycling

http://www.tjcog.dst.nc.us/cdwaste.htm

This resource from the Triangle J Council of Governments is a manual that provides model specifications and background information addressing waste reduction, reuse, and recycling before and during construction and demolition.

Definitions

Construction, demolition and land clearing (CDL) debris includes waste and recyclables generated from construction, land clearing (e.g., vegetation, but not soil), renovation, and demolition or deconstructing of pre-existing structures.

Hazardous waste is waste material made up of hazardous components that present a risk to human or environmental health.

Reuse is a strategy to return materials to active use in the same or a related capacity.

Recycling is the collection, reprocessing, marketing and use of materials that were diverted or recovered from the solid waste stream. Recycling provides two categories of environmental benefits: (1) diverts waste from land filling or incineration, and (2) reduces the need for virgin materials for the manufacture of new products.

Soil waste is unneeded or unusable soil from construction, demolition or renovation projects.

Tipping fees are fees charged by a landfill or incinerator for disposal of waste volumes (typically charged by the ton).

Source reduction reduces waste by reducing the amount of unnecessary material brought into a building. Purchasing products with less packaging is a good example of source reduction.

Waste disposal is the process of eliminating waste by means of burial in a landfill, combustion in an incinerator, dumping at sea, or eliminating waste in some other way that is not recycling or reuse.

Waste diversion is the practice of waste management activities that divert waste from disposal though incineration or landfilling. Principal waste diversion methods are reuse and recycling.

Waste reduction is the process of reducing waste through practices that result in less waste that needs to be disposed of through landfilling or incineration. Two components of waste reduction are source reduction and diversion.

A **Waste Reduction Policy** is a policy that includes: (1) a statement describing the organization's commitment to minimize waste disposal by using source reduction, reuse and recycling, (2) assignment of responsibility within the organization for implementation of waste reduction program, (3) a list of the general actions that will be implemented in the waste reduction program to reduce waste, and (4) a description of the tracking and review component in the waste reduction program to monitor waste reduction successes and improve waste reduction performance over time.

Wood waste is unneeded or unusable wood from construction, demolition or renovation projects.

Case Study – MR Credit 1

Karges-Faulconbridge Headquarters

St. Paul, MN

LEED-EB Gold

Owner: Karges-Faulconbridge, Inc.

Photo courtesy of: Gallop Studios

In 2002, Karges Faulconbridge, Inc. (KCI) purchased a vacant building, formerly a grocery store, for their new headquarters. During an aggressive building renovation project, KCI practiced careful waste management practices. Over 88 percent of the construction waste was diverted from landfills through reuse or recycling. Diverted materials included a variety of metals, exterior brick, wood, and an 89,700 sq. foot asphalt/concrete parking lot, which was almost entirely recycled by a local paving recycler.

SS	WE	EA	MR	EQ	IU
Credits 2.1–2.5					

1–5 Points

Optimize Use of Alternative Materials

Intent

Reduce the environmental impacts of the materials acquired for use in the operations, maintenance, and upgrades of building.

Requirements

Maintain a sustainable purchasing program covering at least office paper, office equipment, furniture, furnishings and building materials for use in the building and on the site. A template calculator will be provided for LEED-EB MR Credit 2.1–2.5. One point (up to a maximum of five) will be awarded for each 10% of total purchases over the performance period (on a dollar basis) that achieve at least one of the following sustainability criteria:

- ❑ Contains at least 70% salvaged material from off site or outside the organization.
- ❑ Contains at least 70% salvaged from on site through an internal organization materials & equipment reuse program.
- ❑ Contains at least 10% post-consumer or 20% post-industrial material.
- ❑ Contains at least 50% rapidly renewable materials.
- ❑ Is Forest Stewardship Council (FSC) certified wood.
- ❑ Contains at least 50% materials harvested and processed or extracted and processed within 500 miles of the project.

Note: In calculating the percentage of purchases over the performance period conforming to the requirements, each purchase can only receive credit against a single requirement (i.e., a purchase that contains both 10% post-consumer recycled content and is harvested within 500 miles of the project counts only once in this calculation).

Submittals – Initial Certification

- ❑ Provide a copy of the organizational policy that specifies use of sustainability criteria for purchases of covered materials for use in the building or on the site.
- ❑ Provide documentation of all covered materials purchased and total cost of these purchases over the performance period.
- ❑ Provide documentation of all covered materials purchased that meet one or more of the specified sustainability criteria and the cost of these purchases over the performance period.
- ❑ Provide a calculation of the fraction of covered materials purchased that meet one or more of the specified sustainability criteria (on a cost basis).

Submittals – Recertification

Provide an update of previous filings:

- ❑ If the organizational policy that specifies use of environmentally preferable purchasing standards for purchases of covered materials for use in the building or on the site has changed since the previous application for certification under LEED-EB, provide an updated copy of this organizational policy.

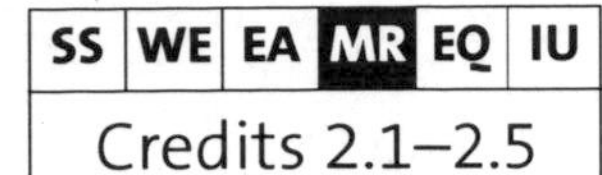

- ❑ Provide documentation of all covered materials purchased and total cost of these purchases over the performance period.
- ❑ Provide documentation of all covered materials purchased that meet one or more of the specified environmentally preferable purchasing standards and the cost of these purchases over the performance period.
- ❑ Provide a calculation of the fraction of covered materials purchased that meet one or more of the specified environmentally preferable purchasing standards (on a cost basis).

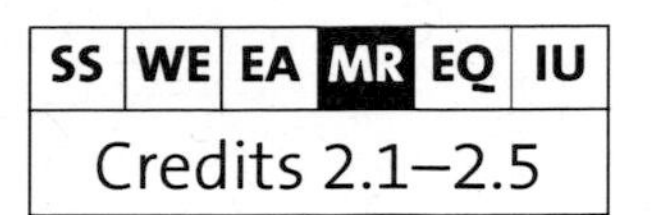

Summary of Referenced Standard

Forest Stewardship Council's Principles and Criteria

Forest Stewardship Council

www.fscus.org

(877) 372-5646

Forestry certification is available as a "seal of approval" for forest managers who adopt environmentally and socially responsible forest management practices, and for companies that manufacture and sell products made from certified wood. This seal enables consumers to identify and procure wood products from well-managed sources and use their purchasing power to influence and reward improved forest management activities around the world.

LEED accepts certification according to the comprehensive system established by the internationally recognized Forest Stewardship Council (FSC). FSC was created in 1993 to establish international forest management standards (known as the FSC Principles and Criteria) to ensure that forestry practices are environmentally responsible, socially beneficial and economically viable. These Principles and Criteria have been established to ensure the long-term health and productivity of forests for timber production, wildlife habitat, clean air and water supplies, climate stabilization, spiritual renewal and social benefit, such as lasting community employment derived from stable forestry operations. The global Principles and Criteria are translated into meaningful standards at a local level through the establishment of region-specific standards.

FSC also accredits and monitors certification organizations. These "certifiers" are independent, third-party auditors that are qualified to annually evaluate compliance with FSC standards on the ground and to award certifications. There are two types of certification:

- ❑ **Forest Management Certification** is awarded to responsible forest managers after their operations successfully complete audits of forestry practices and plans.
- ❑ **Chain of Custody Certification** is awarded after companies that process, manufacture and/or sell products made of certified wood successfully complete audits to ensure proper use of the FSC name and logo, segregation of certified and non-certified materials in manufacturing and distribution systems and observation of other relevant FSC rules (e.g., meeting minimum requirements for FSC fiber content in assembled and composite wood products).

Green Building Concerns

Building upgrades, maintenance and operations require the ongoing acquisition of materials. A wide variety of environmentally preferable materials are available. MR Credits 2.1–2.5 award points for five different categories of materials with reduced environmental impacts, each with its own set of considerations.

Salvaged Materials

Salvage and reuse activities are performed to extend the life of materials and to reduce overall first costs of materials. Use of salvaged materials can add character to the building and can be used effectively as architectural details. Some areas of the United States, such as New England, the Pacific Northwest, and California, have well-developed markets for salvaged materials, while other regions are just beginning to develop these markets.

Recycled Content Materials

Recycled content products contain materials recovered from consumer or industrial waste streams. They benefit the environment due to reduced virgin material use, manufacturing-related environmental and health burdens and solid waste volumes. The number of building products containing recycled content feedstock grows every year as recycling efforts increase and the marketplace for recycled materials matures. Many commonly used products are available with recycled content, including steel, aluminum, concrete, masonry, acoustic tile, paint, carpet, ceramic tile and insulation. Most recycled content products' performance compares favorably with products containing virgin materials, and they can be incorporated into building upgrade projects and operational practices without additional time or effort.

Rapidly Renewable Resources

Rapidly renewable resources substantially replenish themselves faster than traditional materials following extraction, are sustainably managed and do not result in significant biodiversity loss, increased erosion or reduced air quality. For the purposes of this credit, LEED defines rapidly renewable materials as being planted and harvested in less than a 10-year cycle. **Table 1** lists a few examples of rapidly renewable building materials.

Certified Wood

Wood products are used extensively in building structures and furnishings, and paper products are used in building operations and as office supplies. Wood can be a truly sustainable resource because it is renewable, biodegradable, non-toxic, energy efficient and recyclable. Responsible forestry meets the long-term product needs of humans, while maintaining the function and biodiversity of forested landscapes. The primary goal is to restore, enhance and sustain a full range of forestry values while producing a perpetual yield of quality forest products.

Table 1: Rapidly Renewable Materials

Examples of Rapidly Renewable Materials
Bamboo Flooring
Cork Flooring
Linoleum Flooring
Kenaf Paper
Sunflower Seed Board
Wheatgrass Cabinetry
Wool Carpet and Upholstery

Local/Regional Materials

Purchasing regionally manufactured building materials supports the local/regional economy and reduces environmental impacts and transportation costs. However, the availability of regionally manufactured building materials depends on the project location. In some areas, the majority of products required for a project can be obtained locally. For the purposes of LEED, "local/regional" is defined as area within a 500-mile radius of the project site. In other areas, only a small portion of the building materials can be found within this radius. It is also important to consider the source of the raw materials used to manufacture building products. Raw materials for some building products are harvested or extracted far from the point of manufacture, creating air and water pollution due to transportation between the point of extraction and point of manufacture.

Environmental Issues

The environmental burden of the harvesting, manufacture, consumption and disposal of materials varies by material type. Environmentally preferred materials have the potential to mitigate this burden relative to conventional materials. Different categories of environmentally preferable products address different aspects of sustainability.

Salvaged Materials

The salvage and reuse of materials from the waste stream reduces the need for landfill space and the associated water and air contamination issues, and avoids the environmental impacts of harvesting and

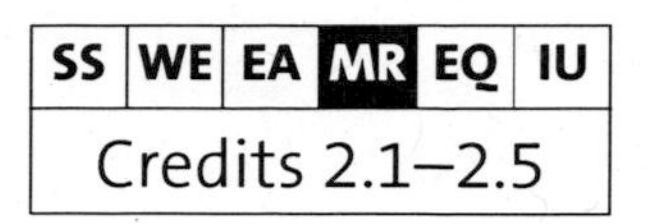

producing new product materials. These impacts are significant because buildings are estimated to use 40 percent of raw stone, gravel and sand, and 25 percent of virgin wood harvested globally.[11]

Recycled-Content Materials

Selecting materials with recycled content can reduce environmental impacts associated with extracting, harvesting and manufacturing virgin materials. It also can reduce the solid waste stream by diverting recyclable materials that would otherwise go to landfills or incinerators. Post-consumer and post-industrial recycled content differ in their origin. Recycled-content products are defined as post-consumer if the feedstock is collected from consumer waste, such as from curbside recycling of aluminum, glass and newspaper. Post-industrial recycled-content products contain waste from industrial processes. Although recycled-content materials are preferred to some products, recycling a material is not as environmentally beneficial as reusing it, since the transportation of materials to recycling facilities and the energy required to process these materials have a greater environmental impact. Therefore, reuse of building materials is preferred over recycling when possible.

Rapidly Renewable Resources

Rapidly renewable resources require significantly less land to produce the same amount of material as other resources. However, it is important to consider that a resource may only be renewable if its natural habitat is preserved. To avoid problems such as soil erosion and loss of biodiversity, it is important that rapidly renewable resource production includes sensitivity to the harvest area.

Certified Wood

The environmental impacts of conventional forest practices include soil erosion, stream sedimentation, habitat destruction, water pollution, air pollution and waste generation. The FSC referenced standard incorporates several criteria that contribute to the long-term viability of certified forests. These include the preservation of natural habitat areas and the reduction of damages related to soil erosion and water pollution.

Local/Regional Materials

The use of regional building materials reduces pollution and transportation costs associated with delivery of the materials to the job site. Trucks, trains, ships and other vehicles deplete finite reserves of fossil fuels and generate air pollution. Selecting building materials that are produced from regional materials reduces transportation impacts and supports the regional economy.

Economic Issues

Alternative materials can be less expensive, more expensive or equivalent in cost when compared to the purchasing price of conventional materials. Aside from first costs, issues such as product life span, durability, effectiveness, maintenance requirements and disposal costs can affect the economic desirability of alternative materials. These issues vary by product and alternative material type. Building location and function also affects the cost of using alternative materials.

Salvaged Materials

Some salvaged materials are more costly than new materials due to the high cost of labor to recover and refurbish them. However, salvaged materials are often of higher quality and more durable than new materials. Local demolition companies may be willing to sell materials recovered from existing buildings to avoid disposal tipping fees. In some areas, municipalities and waste management companies have established salvaged building material sales facilities at landfill sites or other locations. Be aware that sometimes the price of salvaged materials appears to be cost-effective, but there may be hidden costs for reprocessing, transportation or liabilities associated with contamination. However, certain salvaged materials may be impossible to duplicate (such as antique lumber and casework) and may well be worth the higher cost compared to new, but inferior, materials.

Recycled Content Materials

Some recycled content products cost more than equivalent virgin products due to the costs of research and design, innovative manufacturing equipment, new plants to produce the products, and the costs of the recycling process itself. However, many items from recycled material are comparably priced to those without recycled content. As demand for recycled products grows, the cost of recycled products is becoming more competitive with standard products. Many major product manufacturers have alternative recycled products available with negligible premiums.

Rapidly Renewable Resources

Because rapidly renewable resources replenish themselves more quickly than other resources, they require less land to produce the same quantity of material. This equates to lower land costs and a faster payback on investment for manufacturers. Despite these savings, many rapidly renewable materials are new to the marketplace and are subsequently more expensive than their conventional counterparts. As demand for rapidly renewable materials and products increases, their costs will likely become equivalent or lower than standard products.

Certified Wood

In the last 30 years, world trade in forest products has increased dramatically. By 1997, trade in primary forest products reached nearly $273 billion (U.S. dollars). North American and European countries account for the majority of international trade.[12] As more developing countries embrace world forest product markets and their growing economies encourage domestic consumption, the protection of endangered forests will become an even more critical issue. Currently, the cost of FSC-certified wood products is equal to or higher than conventional wood products. The limited availability of FSC products in certain regions further raises the price, as associated storage and distribution costs contribute to expenses. However, the price of FSC-certified wood products is expected to be more competitive with conventional wood products in future years as the world's forest resources are further depleted and the forest industry embraces more widespread adoption of sustainable forestry principles.

Local/Regional Materials

Regional building materials are generally more cost-effective for projects due to reduced transportation costs. Also, the support of regional manufacturers and labor forces retains capital within the region and creates a more stable tax base and healthier regional and local economies.

Strategies & Technologies

Specify the use of materials, supplies or equipment purchases that comply with one or more of the sustainability criteria established in this credit. When considering the use of alternative materials, ensure that they are appropriately durable and effective for their intended use. Strategies for assessing and exploiting opportunities for using sustainable products are presented below.

Salvaged Materials

Commonly salvaged or refurbished building materials and products include structural elements such as beams and posts, wood flooring, wood paneling, doors and frames, cabinetry and furniture, brick and other masonry products, and decorative items such as mantels, ironwork, and antique light fixtures. Salvaged material can also include office furniture, dividers and equipment. Research all salvaged and refurbished materials for durability, performance, code compliance and environmental considerations. Avoid items that generally should not be salvaged and reused, such as toilets (older models consume more water) and windows (older products are less energy efficient). The value of salvaged materials to calculate this credit is either the market value if purchased, or the estimated market value if the materials were not purchased (e.g., on-site salvage, donated materials, etc.).

When considering salvaged structural materials such as heavy timbers, it is imperative to check for structural integrity, code compliance and engineered rating. Verify compliance with the Uniform Building Code (UBC) for structural requirements. It may also be necessary to investigate salvaged materials for possible contamination by lead paint, asbestos, pesticides, rot, and toxic wood preservatives such as creosote, pentochlorophenol and arsenic.

For renovation or construction projects, develop a reuse strategy early in the schematic design phase to incorporate salvaged and refurbished building materials and set salvaged materials goals. Identify local sources for salvaged or refurbished building materials and products. It may be helpful to create and maintain a current list of the salvage material suppliers to use on other projects.

Recycled Content Materials

Consider how to incorporate recycled content materials into building operations and renovation/construction projects. Establish recycled content materials goals for ongoing operations and individual projects, and then determine whether recycled alternatives exist. For ongoing operations, incorporate the specified alternative materials into routine purchasing activities. For individual renovation/construction projects, incorporate specific recycling content materials goals into the project specifications and contracts.

Recycled content building materials are composed of components that have recycled content and are processed off-site. Examples include flooring, paint, cement and roofing materials. Materials including crushed brick, asphalt and concrete that are reused on site after on-site processing such as crushing are not considered recycled content materials because they do not support the recycled content marketplace. Instead, these materials should be assessed to determine if they meet the definition of salvaged material for this credit or can be counted towards MR Credit 1: Construction Waste Management.

Many building and office supplies are available with recycled content, including textiles, sanitary and office paper products, furniture and plastic products.

Ensure that recycled content materials perform equally well or better than virgin materials in terms of strength, maintenance and longevity. Maintain a list of manufacturers and suppliers of recycled content materials. Support regionally produced recycled content products to reduce the added costs of transportation.

Rapidly Renewable Resources

Research rapidly renewable materials for flooring, cabinetry, wood products and other project applications. Specify these materials in procurement documents and create a current list of rapidly renewable products for future reference. For the purposes of this credit, rapidly renewable products must be harvested within 10 years.

Certified Wood

Develop goals for certified wood use in the building and incorporate them into the organization's purchasing program and specifications. For example, specify that 50 percent (based on dollar value) of all wood-based materials coming into the building will be FSC-certified.

Local/Regional Materials

Specify and install regionally extracted, harvested and manufactured materials for facility operations or renovation/upgrade projects. Contact the state and local waste management boards for information about regional materials, and research them for durability, performance and other environmental considerations. Create and maintain a current listing of local manufacturers for future reference.

For construction projects on the building site, consider the incorporation of regionally sourced and manufactured building materials early in the schematic design stage. Specify appropriate regionally sourced and manufactured building materials in the construction documents.

For the purposes of this credit, regional materials are those harvested and processed, or extracted and processed, within 500 miles of the building. Purchases meeting this requirement must consist of at least 50 percent local/regional materials.

Synergies & Tradeoffs

Salvaged Materials

The availability of salvaged materials depends on the location of the project. Building projects in urban areas often have many opportunities to use salvaged materials, while rural projects probably do not have the same resources. To use on-site salvaged materials, coordinate plans with waste management practices, particularly as those related to MR Credit 1.1–1.2 – Construction, Demolition and Renovation Waste Management.

Recycled Content Materials

Research all recycled content materials for environmental considerations. For example, if the recycled content product is not as durable as its conventional counterpart, the environmental benefits may be compromised by the need for more frequent replacement. Also, check recycled content materials for problematic air emissions, especially with synthetic products such as plastic, rubber and polyester. Evaluate recycled content products in terms of their potential impacts on indoor air quality (IAQ). In some cases, chemical binders used in recycled content products or processes contain off-gassing ingredients that negatively affect IAQ. These off-gassing building products could harm the health of construction workers and of building occupants over the lifetime of the building.

Rapidly Renewable Resources

Many products made from rapidly renewable resources are relatively new, so their long-term performance characteristics may be unknown. For example, the performance and stability of bamboo flooring has improved in recent years through the use of laminated layers of the material. Therefore, it is important to evaluate a product's performance history before installing it.

It is also important to assess the IAQ impacts of all specified materials, as some rapidly renewable materials may off-gas contaminants and negatively impact IAQ. For example, while some products like bamboo may be rapidly renewable and meet the criteria for this credit, the binding agents may contain high levels of VOCs, which can be problematic for air quality and associated LEED-EB credits.

Certified Wood

Some certified wood products might not be locally available or could be difficult to locate. Some certified products also contain adhesives and chemicals that have off-gassing characteristics that may impact IAQ; therefore research these products to ensure low/no VOC content prior to specifying.

Local/Regional Materials

The location of the project site has a large effect on the availability of locally sourced materials. Remote sites often require the transport of construction materials from far away. In areas that do not have local manufacturing facilities, instead consider materials that are salvaged, contain recycled content, are rapidly renewable and/or (for wood products) are FSC-certified. When choosing local and regional materials, address VOC content as this can affect IAQ.

Calculations & Documentation

Calculations

LEED-EB Letter Templates are available to document purchases and conduct calculations. The final percentage of purchases that meet one or more of the standards should be rounded up to the nearest whole number. Below is a set of sample calculations to demonstrate an acceptable way to document and calculate purchases covered under this credit.

Sample Alternative Materials Calculations

Tables 2 through 7 document material purchases that comply with credit requirements. A separate table for each category of alternative materials was developed.

Table 8 provides information on the purchase of materials that do not meet any of the alternative materials standards. The purchases reported in Table 8 include those that do not meet the sustainability requirements but fall under the material types defined under the sustainable purchasing program (office paper, office equipment, furniture, furnishings, and building materials for use in the building and on the site).

Table 9 summarizes the value of alternative materials, total purchases and percentage of the total purchases that meet at least one of the standards defined by this credit.

Table 2: Purchases containing at least 70% salvaged material from offsite

Date of Purchase	Item	Cost or Value [$]
3/5/2005	6 metal shelves	$90.00
3/5/2005	2 office chairs	$20.00
Total Cost or Value		**$110.00**

Table 3: Purchases containing at least 70% salvaged material from on site

Date of Purchase	Item	Cost or Value [$]
5/30/2004	Wood wall molding	$150.00
Total Cost or Value		**$150.00**

Table 4: Purchases containing at least 10% post-consumer or 20% post-industrial material

Date of Purchase	Item	Cost or Value [$]
2/19/2005	30% post-consumer content recycled office paper, 100 reams	$420.00
Total Cost or Value		**$420.00**

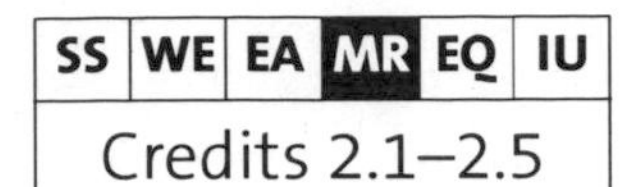

Table 5: Purchases containing at least 50% rapidly renewable materials

Date of Purchase	Item	Cost or Value
10/30/2004	150 yd^2 wool carpeting for conference room carpet replacement	$4,500
Total Cost or Value		**$4,500.00**

Table 6: Purchases that are FSC certified wood

Date of Purchase	Item	Cost or Value
9/18/2004	Conference table	$6,500.00
Total Cost or Value		**$6,500.00**

Table 7: Purchases containing at least 50% local/regional materials

Date of Purchase	Item	Cost or Value
7/25/2004	Wooden book shelves produced from locally harvested wood by local company	$400.00
Total Cost or Value	**$400.00**	

Table 8: Purchases that meet NONE of the alternative materials requirements

Date of Purchase	Item	Cost or Value
1/9/2005	Small envelopes, 10 boxes	$25.00
1/9/2005	Large envelopes, 5 boxes	$30.00
1/9/2005	Copy paper, 500 reams	$1,150.00
10/30/2004	Carpet, 675ft2, new carpet for 3 offices	$5,000.00
11/05/2004	3 office desks	$3,000.00
11/05/2004	3 desk chairs	$900.00
11/05/2004	2 upholstered chairs	$950.00
10/01/2004	60 4 X 8 drywall sheets	$600.00
9/18/2004	8 conference table chairs	$2,000.00
7/30/2004	10 plastic waste bins	$100.00
6/15/2004	4 storage shelving units	$800.00
Total Cost or Value		**$14,555.00**

Documentation

❑ Organizational policy for purchase of alternative materials

- Provide a copy of the organizational policy that specifies use of sustainability criteria for purchases in hard copy or digital form on participant letterhead with the signature of the company officer responsible for waste management.

❑ Documentation of purchases

- Document the type and cost of all materials purchased during the performance period that are covered under the organization's sustainable purchasing program, which at a minimum must include office paper, office equipment, furniture, furnishings and building materials.
- For purchases that meet one or more of the sustainability criteria outlined in this credit, include

Table 9: Summary of Purchases

Alternative Materials Standards	Cost/Value
Contains at least 70% salvaged material from offsite or outside the organization	$110.00
Contains at least 70% salvaged from on site through an internal organization materials & equipment reuse program	$150.00
Contains at least 10% post-consumer or 20% post-industrial material	$420.00
Contains at least 50% rapidly renewable materials	$4,500.00
Contains FSC-certified wood	$6,500.00
Contains at least 50% materials harvested and processed or extracted and processed within 500 miles of the project	$400.00
Total Value of Purchases that Meet One of these Standards	**$12,080.00**
Total Value of Purchases Not Meeting these Standards	**$14,555.00**
Total Cost or Value of all Applicable Purchases	**$26,635.00**
Percent of Total Purchases that Meet One of these Standards	**46%**

Alternative materials made up 46 percent of relevant purchases during the performance period, which earns 4 points under MR Credit 2.1–2.5.

a narrative description from the building owner's representative or manufacturer's documentation of the materials that describes how they meet credit requirements.

- ❑ Calculations
  - Demonstrate the fraction of materials purchased that meet one or more of the sustainability criteria on a cost basis.
  - Use the LEED-EB Letter Templates to perform calculations.

Other Resources

Bamboo Flooring

www.buildinggreen.com/products/bamboo.html

This article in Environmental Building News focuses on bamboo flooring, including a listing of bamboo flooring suppliers.

California Materials Exchange

www.ciwmb.ca.gov/CalMAX

The Materials Exchange program of the California Integrated Waste Management Board allows users to exchange waste items online.

EPA Comprehensive Procurement Guidelines (CPG)

www.epa.gov/cpg/

This program is part of the U.S. EPA's effort to promote the use of materials recovered from solid waste. The web site offers information about the guidelines, include Comprehensive Guideline for Procurement of Products Containing Recovered Materials; Recovered Materials Advisory Notice III; Final Rule (www.epa.gov/epaoswer/non-hw/procure/pdf/cpg-fr.pdf).

Forest Stewardship Council (FSC)

www.fsc.org/fsc

Information and resources on certified wood products can be found on the FSC's web site.

Recycled Content Product Directory

www.ciwmb.ca.gov/rcp

This online directory offers a searchable database for recycled content products. The directory was developed by the California Integrated Waste Management Board.

The Recycler's Exchange

www.recycle.net/exchange

The Recycler's Exchange is a free marketplace for buying and selling recyclables and salvaged materials.

Salvaged Building Materials Exchange

www.greenguide.com/exchange/search.html

This online resource offers another searchable database of salvaged building materials.

Definitions

Chain-of-Custody is a tracking procedure for documenting the status of a product from the point of harvest or extraction to the ultimate consumer end use.

Post-consumer waste recycling is the recycling of materials collected from consumer waste following consumer use of the products containing these materials.

Post-industrial waste recycling is the recycling of materials collected from industrial processes. This includes the collection and recycling of waste from industrial processes within the same manufacturing plant or from another manufacturing plant.

Rapidly renewable materials are materials that are planted and harvested in less than 10-year cycle.

Recycling is the collection, reprocessing, marketing and use of materials that were diverted or recovered from the solid waste stream. Recycling provides two categories of environmental benefits: (1) diverts waste from landfilling or incineration, and (2) reduces the need for virgin materials for the manufacture of new products.

Salvaged materials (Offsite) are building materials recovered from an offsite source that are reused in the existing building seeking LEED-EB certification.

Salvaged materials (On-site) are building materials recovered from and then reused at the same building site.

Source reduction reduces waste by reducing the amount of unnecessary material brought into a building. Purchasing products with less packaging is a good example of source reduction.

Sustainable forestry is the practice of managing forest resources in a manner that meets the long-term forest product needs of humans while maintaining the biodiversity of forested landscapes.

A **Sustainable Purchasing Program** includes the development, adoption and implementation of an organizational policy that outlines the types of materials that will be targeted to meet the sustainability criteria of this credit. Per the credit requirements, this program at a minimum must include office paper, office equipment, furniture, furnishings and building materials for use in the building and on the site.

A **Uniform Building Code** is a model building code published by the International Council of Building Officials (ICBO) that provides complete regulations covering all major aspects of building design and construction relating to fire and life safety and structural safety.

Waste disposal is the process of eliminating waste by means of burial in a landfill, combustion in an incinerator, dumping at sea, or eliminating waste in some other way that is not recycling or reuse.

Waste diversion is the practice of waste management activities that divert waste from disposal though incineration or landfilling. Principal waste diversion methods are reuse and recycling.

Waste reduction is the process of reducing waste through practices that result in less waste that needs to be disposed of through landfilling or incineration. Two components of waste reduction are source reduction and diversion.

Case Study

Denver Place

Denver, Colorado

LEED-EB Gold

Owner: Amerimar Reality Management Co.

Photo courtesy of: Denver Place

Amerimar's Denver Place is a downtown high rise office and retail complex. Amerimar has achieved outstanding resource reuse rates at Denver Place by using high-quality materials that are easy to disassemble and reuse during tenant changes. Specifying reusable doors, hardware, ceiling tiles and electrical, mechanical, and plumbing equipment wherever feasible has lead to a resource reuse rate of 42 percent over the LEED-EB performance period. In addition, Amerimar makes use of other alternative materials in Denver Place such as FSC-certified wood benches and wood doors.

SS	WE	EA	MR	EQ	IU

Credits 3.1 & 3.2

2 Points

Optimize Use of IAQ Compliant Products

Intent

Reduce the indoor air quality (IAQ) impacts of the materials acquired for use in the operation, maintenance and upgrades of buildings.

Requirements

Optimize use of air quality compliant materials inside the building to reduce the emissions from materials used in the building. Points are awarded for the existence of product purchasing policies for the building and site addressing the requirements of this credit and documentation of purchasing during the performance period in conformance with those policies, as described below. Subsequent re-certification is tied to both polices and purchasing performance, as described below. At a minimum, these policies must include the following product groups: paint and coatings, adhesives, sealants, carpet, composite panels, and agrifiber products. The building materials covered include any building materials covered by a.-e. below that are used for improvements, including upgrades, retrofits, renovations or modifications, inside the building.

One point shall be awarded, up to a maximum of 2 points, for each 45% of annual purchases calculated on a cost basis that conform with one of the following sustainability criteria:

a. Adhesives and sealants with a VOC content less than the current VOC content limits of South Coast Air Quality Management District (SCAQMD) Rule #1168, or sealants used as fillers that meet or exceed the requirements of the Bay Area Air Quality Management District Regulation 8, Rule 51.

OR

b. Paints and coatings with VOC emissions that do not exceed the VOC and chemical component limits of Green Seal's Standard GS-11 requirements.

OR

c. Carpet that meets the requirements of the CRI Green Label Plus Carpet Testing Program.

OR

d. Carpet cushion that meets the requirements of the CRI Green Label Testing Program.

OR

e. Composite panels and agrifiber products that contain no add urea-formaldehyde resins.

Submittals – Initial Certification

- ❑ Provide a copy of the organizational policy that specifies the use of these sustainability criteria for purchases of covered materials for use in the building.
- ❑ Provide documentation of all covered materials purchased and the total cost of these purchases over the performance period.
- ❑ Provide documentation of all covered materials purchased that meet one or more

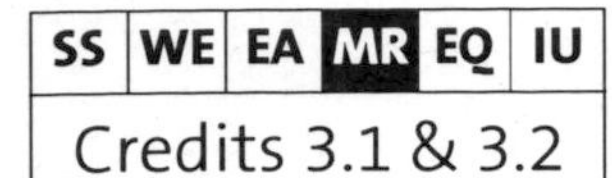

of the specified sustainability criteria and the cost of these purchases over the performance period.

- ❑ Provide a calculation of the percentage of covered materials purchased that meet one or more of the specified sustainability criteria (on a cost basis).

Submittals – Recertification

Provide an update of previous filings:

- ❑ If the organizational policy that specifies use of these sustainability criteria for purchases of covered materials for use in the building or on the site has changed since the previous application for certification under LEED-EB, provide an updated copy of this organizational policy.
- ❑ Provide documentation of all covered materials purchased and the total cost of these purchases over the performance period.
- ❑ Provide documentation of all covered materials purchases that meet one or more of the specified sustainability criteria and the cost of these purchases over the performance period.
- ❑ Provide a calculation of the percentage of covered materials purchased that meet one or more of the specified sustainability criteria (on a cost basis).

Summary of Referenced Standards

South Coast Rule 1168: Adhesive and Sealant Applications (Oct. 2003)

South Coast Air Quality Management District

www.aqmd.gov

(800) 288-7664

The South Coast Air Quality Management District is a public agency in Southern California with the mission to maintain healthful air quality. The organization established source-specific standards to reduce air quality impacts from Volatile Organic Compounds (VOCs). For LEED-EB purposes, this rule applies to the use of adhesives, adhesive bonding primers, adhesive primers, sealants, sealant primers or any other primers in buildings. **Tables 1–3** summarize the VOC limits required by Rule #1168 for selected applications. The October 2003 version of Rule 1168 can be located online at: www.arb.ca.gov/DRDB/SC/CURHTML/R1168.PDF.

Regulation 8: Organic Compounds, Rule 51: Adhesive and Sealant Products (July 2002)

Bay Area Air Quality Management District (BAAQMD)

www.baaqmd.gov

(415) 749-5000

This California regulatory agency develops and enforces air pollution regulations in its seven-county jurisdiction. **Table 4** summarizes Regulation 8, Rule 51 limits

Table 1: South Coast Rule #1168 VOC Limits – Architectural Adhesives

Application	VOC Limit [g/L]	Application	VOC Limit [g/L]
Indoor carpet adhesives	50	Carpet pad adhesives	50
Outdoor carpet adhesives	150	Wood flooring adhesives	100
Rubber floor adhesives	60	Subfloor adhesives	50
Ceramic tile adhesives	65	VCT and asphalt tile	50
Drywall and panel adhesives	50	Cove base adhesives	50
Multipurpose construction	70	Structural glazing	100

Table 2: South Coast Rule #1168 VOC Limits – Specialty Applications

Application	VOC Limit [g/L]	Application	VOC Limit [g/L]
PVC welding	285	CPVC welding	270
ABS welding	400	Plastic cement welding	250
Adhesive primer for plastic	250	Contact adhesive	80
Special purpose contact adhesive	250	Structural wood member adhesive	140
Sheet applied rubber lining	850	Top and trim adhesive	250

Table 3: South Coast Rule #1168 VOC Limits – Substrate-Specific Applications*

Application	VOC Limit [g/L]	Application	VOC Limit [g/L]
Metal to metal	30	Plastic foams	50
Porous material (except wood)	50	Wood	30
Fiberglass	80		80

**If an adhesive is used to bond dissimilar substrates together, the adhesive with the highest VOC content is allowed.*

Table 4: BAAQMD Regulation 8, Rule 51 Sealant and Sealant Primer VOC Limits

Sealant	VOC Limit [g/L]	Sealant Primer	VOC Limit [g/L]
Architectural	250	Architectural – nonporous	250
Other	420	Architectural – porous	775
		Other	750

on VOCs for sealants and sealant primers. An electronic copy of this standard can be found online at:

www.baaqmd.gov/dst/regulations/rg0851.pdf.

Green Seal GS-11 Environmental Requirements for Paints (May 1993)

Green Seal

www.greenseal.org

(202) 871-6400

Green Seal is a nonprofit organization that promotes the manufacture and sale of environmentally responsible consumer products. The Green Seal standard was developed for paints and anticorrosive paints, and addresses white paints without colorants. VOC limits are summarized in **Table 5**, and restricted chemical components are available on the Green Seal web site. An electronic version of the referenced standard can be found at:

www.greenseal.org/standards/paints.htm.

Table 5: Green Seal GS-11 VOC Limits

Coating	VOC Limit [g/L]
Interior non-flat	150
Interior flat	50

Green Label Plus Testing Program (2004) & the Green Label Testing Program (1992)

The Carpet and Rug Institute (CRI)

www.carpet-rug.com

(800) 882-8846

The Carpet and Rug Institute is a trade organization that established the Green Label Plus Testing Program to identify low-emitting carpet for consumers. The Green Label Testing program also addresses carpet cushion materials. The established limits on VOCs for carpets and cushions are summarized in **Table 6**. Online information about the Green Label and Green Label Plus Testing Programs can be found at:

www.carpet-rug.com/drill_down_2.cfm?page=8&sub=4&requesttimeout=350.

Green Building Concerns

Volatile Organic Compounds (VOCs) are chemical compounds that contribute to air pollution inside and outside buildings. Even non-reactive VOCs can have both acute and chronic impacts to building occupants, including eye, nose and throat irritation, headaches, loss of coordination and nausea, as well as damage to the liver, kidneys and the central nervous system.

Table 6: CRI Green Label Plus & Green Label Emission Limits for Carpet/Carpet Cushion

CRI Green Label Plus Limits for Compounds in Carpet	Limit [mg/m2]hr	CRI Green Label Limits for Compounds in Carpet Cushion	Limit [mg/m2]hr
Total VOC	0.50	Total VOC	1.00
4-PC	0.05	BHT	0.30
Formaldehyde	0.05	Formaldehyde	0.05
Styrene	0.40	4-PC	0.05

Selecting low-emitting materials for a building can prevent air-quality degradation indoors and provide a better indoor environment for occupants. Selecting low-emitting materials also reduces exposure of staff and contractors working with these materials. This credit targets building materials used indoors that commonly have high-VOC content, including adhesives, paints and coatings, carpet systems and composite wood and agrifiber products.

Environmental Issues

Many building products contain compounds that have a negative impact on indoor air quality and the earth's atmosphere. The most prominent of these compounds, volatile organic compounds (VOCs), contribute to smog generation and air pollution outdoors, and can harm the health of building occupants indoors.

When exposed to sunlight, reactive VOCs combine with nitrogen to form ground-level ozone, which can have a detrimental effect on human health, agricultural crops, forests and ecosystems. Ozone can damage lung tissue, reduce lung function and sensitize the lungs to other irritants. Ozone also can damage leaves and prevent food storage in plants.[13]

Economic Issues

Continued exposure to materials with high VOC content can ultimately cause illness and decrease occupant productivity. Health problems associated with VOC emissions include flu-like symptoms and more serious health problems. VOC emissions in the workplace may result in lost workdays or decreased productivity.

People living and working in a healthy indoor environment are, on average, more productive and have less illness-related absenteeism. This leads to higher productivity and may lower expenses for building owners and insurance companies. As a result, the construction market is driving product manufacturers to offer low-VOC alternatives to conventional building products. Costs for these low-VOC products are often competitive with conventional materials.

However, some low-VOC materials cost more than conventional materials, particularly when first introduced to the marketplace. Some low-VOC products may also be difficult to obtain. However, costs are equalizing and products are becoming easier to find as demand for low-VOC products increases.

Strategies & Technologies

Research and specify products containing VOC levels that fall within the limits in the referenced standards. Consider the durability, performance and environmental characteristics of the products. Material Safety Data Sheets (MSDSs) may not include information on VOC content, so it may be necessary to request emissions test data from product manufacturers and to compare this test data with similar products. VOC emissions data should exclude additives such as water, solvents and pigments.

Typical VOC-containing materials used in a building and on a building site include, but are not limited to, the following: paints, coatings, sealants and composite panels. Ensure that VOC limits are clearly stated in the organization's procurement policy where adhesives, sealants, coatings, carpets and composite woods are addressed, and that this policy is strictly followed. Consider monitoring VOC emissions during application and reviewing emission levels over the lifetime of the building via air quality testing.

Synergies & Tradeoffs

Existing buildings may already incorporate off-gassing materials. Therefore, it is important to prevent further contamina-

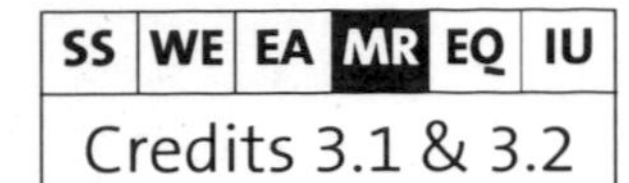

tion of IAQ from the introduction of additional VOC-containing materials and products. Material selection is especially important to create interior spaces with lower VOC levels. Choosing cleaning, construction and maintenance products with low VOC levels should not require extra expense, and will improve indoor air quality for the lifetime of the building.

Calculations & Documentation

Calculations

The products and materials included in the calculations include those purchased during the performance period that are field-applied inside the building for improvements, upgrades, retrofits, renovations, or modifications and fall under the following product groups used inside the building:

- ❑ Paints and coatings
- ❑ Adhesives
- ❑ Sealants
- ❑ Carpet
- ❑ Composite panels
- ❑ Agrifiber products
- ❑ Building materials

The following calculation methodology is used to support the credit submittals listed on the first page of this credit:

Use a table similar to **Table 7** to document purchases of products and materials that are compliant with credit requirements. In the table, record the date of purchase, the item purchased, the LEED-EB MR Credit 3.1–3.2 sustainability criteria met by the purchase, and the cost or value of the item. Use a table similar to **Table 8** to document purchases of products and materials that fall under the product groups defined by the credit but do not meet any of the credit requirements. Use a table similar to **Table 9** to summarize purchases and calculate the percentage of the total purchases that meet at least one of the credit standards.

Equation 1

Qualifying Percentage =
(Cost of Products Meeting Specifications) / Cost of All Applicable Products) x 100

Table 7: Purchases of Credit Compliant Products During the Performance Period

Date of Purchase	Item	Sustainability Criteria Met	Cost/Value [$]
Total cost or value of purchases that meet credit requirements			

Table 8: Purchases of Non-Credit Compliant Products During the Performance Period

Date of Purchase	Item	Cost/Value [$]
Total cost or value of purchases that do not meet credit requirements		

Table 9: Summary of Purchases

	Cost/Value [$]
(A) Total purchases that meet standards (from Table 7)	
(B) Total purchases not meeting standards (from Table 8)	
(C) Total purchases (Line A + Line B)	
Percent Qualifying Purchases ((Line A / Line C) x 100)	

The LEED-EB Letter Templates should be used to generate tables and calculations similar to the ones presented above.

Documentation

- ❑ Organizational policy for purchases of IAQ compliant products
  - Submit a copy of the sustainable purchasing policy addressing the purchasing of IAQ-compliant products as it appears within the official organizational purchasing policy in use by the participant, or as an individual document on participant letterhead with the signature of the company officer responsible for its implementation.
- ❑ Documentation of purchases
  - Document the type and cost of all materials purchased during the performance period that are used inside the building and are covered under the IAQ compliant product purchasing policy, which at a minimum must include paint and coatings, adhesives, sealants, carpet, composite panels, agrifiber products and building materials.
  - For purchases that meet one of the sustainability criteria outlined in this credit, provide manufacturer's documentation describing the nature of the product, and highlight product features that conform to the applicable referenced standards.
  - Provide sample invoices documenting purchase date, volume, dollar amount, etc.
- ❑ Calculations of percent qualifying purchases
  - Use the LEED-EB Letter Templates to make calculations

Other Resources

ASTM D5116-97: Standard Guide for Small-Scale Environmental Chamber Determinations of Organic Emissions from Indoor Materials / Products. ASTM, 1997.

Best Sustainable Indoor Air Quality Practices in Commercial Buildings

www.buildinggreen.com/elists/halpaper.html

This web site provides a primer on IAQ basics from Environmental Building News.

"Paint the Room Green" in Environmental Building News, Volume 8, Number 2, 1999.

This article describes the environmental issues associated with interior paints, including indoor environmental quality issues, resource use and pollution prevention. A list of alternative paint, zero-VOC conventional paint, and recycled paint manufacturers is provided.

Zero VOC Paint Manufacturers

www.aqmd.gov/business/brochures/zerovoc.html

This resource includes a listing of paint manufacturers that offer products with no VOC content, provided by the South Coast Air Quality Management District.

Definitions

Agrifiber products are products made from agricultural fiber. To qualify for this credit agrifiber products must contain no added urea-formaldehyde resins

Aromatic compounds, as defined by the referenced Green Seal Standard (GS-11), are "hydrocarbon compounds containing one or more 6-carbon benzene rings in the molecular structure."

Chemical Component Restrictions are a set of restrictions set by the referenced Green Seal Standard (GS-11). The standard requires that the manufacturer demonstrate that the chemical compounds included on the Chemical Component Restrictions list are not used as ingredients in the manufacture of the product.

Composite panels are panels made from several materials. Plywood and OSB (oriented strand board) are two examples of composite panels. To qualify for this credit composite panels must contain no added urea-formaldehyde resins.

Paints and Coatings, as defined by the referenced Green Seal Standard (GS-11), are "liquid, liquefiable or mastic composition that is converted to a solid protective, decorative, or functional adherent film after application as a thin layer. These coatings are intended for on-site application to interior or exterior surfaces of residential, commercial, institutional or industrial buildings." The Green Seal Standard (GS-11) does not include stains, clear finishes, or paints sold in aerosol cans within this category.

Volatile Organic Compounds (VOCs) are organic compounds that are volatile at typical room temperatures. The specific organic compounds addressed by the referenced Green Seal Standard (GS-11) are identified in U. S. Environmental Protection Agency (EPA) Reference Test Method 24 (Determination of Volatile Matter Content, Water Content, Density Volume Solids, and Weight Solids of Surface Coatings), Code of Federal Regulations Title 40, Part 60, Appendix A.

SS	WE	EA	MR	EQ	IU

Credits 4.1–4.3

1–3 Points

Sustainable Cleaning Products and Materials

Intent

Reduce the environmental impacts of cleaning products, disposable janitorial paper products and trash bags.

Requirements

Implement sustainable purchasing for cleaning materials and products, disposable janitorial paper products and trash bags. Cleaning product and material purchases include building purchases for use by in house staff or used by outsourced service providers. Calculate the percentage of the total sustainable material and product purchases that meet at least one of the specified sustainability criteria. The percentage of the total sustainable cleaning product and material purchases determine the number of points earned up to a total of 3 points. One point will be awarded for each 30% of the total annual purchases of these products (on a cost basis) that meet one of the following sustainability criteria:

- ❑ Cleaning products that meet the Green Seal GS-37 standard if applicable, OR if GS-37 is not applicable (e.g., for products such as carpet cleaners, floor finishes or strippers), use products that comply with the California Code of Regulations maximum allowable VOC levels.
- ❑ Disposable janitorial paper products and trash bags that meet the minimum requirements of U.S. EPA's Comprehensive Procurement Guidelines.

Submittals – Initial Certification

- ❑ Provide a copy of the organizational policy that specifies use of these sustainability criteria for purchases of covered materials for use in the building or on the site.
- ❑ Provide documentation of all covered materials purchased and the total cost of these purchases over the performance period.
- ❑ Provide documentation of all covered materials purchased that meet one or more of the specified sustainability criteria and the cost of these purchases over the performance period.
- ❑ Provide a calculation of the percentage of covered materials purchased that meet one or more of the specified sustainability criteria (on a cost basis).

Submittals – Recertification

Provide an update of previous filings:

- ❑ If the organizational policy that specifies use of these sustainability criteria for purchases of covered materials for use in the building or on the site has changed since the previous application for certification under LEED-EB, provide an updated copy of this organizational policy.
- ❑ Provide documentation of all covered materials purchased and the total cost of these purchases over the performance period.
- ❑ Provide documentation of all covered materials purchased that meet one or more of the specified sustainability criteria and the cost of these purchases over the performance period.

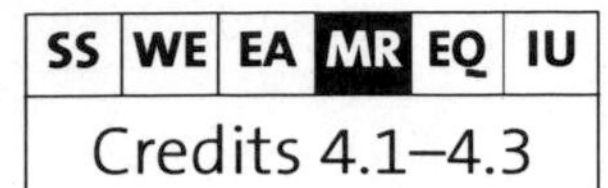

❑ Provide a calculation of the percentage of covered materials purchased that meet one or more of the specified sustainability criteria (on a cost basis).

Summary of Referenced Standard

Green Seal Standard GS-37 Industrial and Institutional Cleaners: General-purpose, Bathroom and Glass Cleaners (October 2000)

Green Seal

www.greenseal.com

(202) 872-6400

After rigorous testing, Green Seal GS-37 certifies cleaning products that meet requirements related to performance, health and environmental concerns, and labeling. Health and environmental requirements consider the product's IAQ properties, its potential as a water pollutant, and the presence of toxic compounds, carcinogens, reproductive toxins, and eye and skin irritants. The Green Seal web site has a full description of requirements. An electronic copy of GS-37 is at: www.greenseal.org/standards/industrialcleaners.htm.

Regulation for Reducing VOC Emissions From Consumer Products (September 2001)

Title 17, California Code of Regulations, Division 3, Chapter 1, Subchapter 8.5, Article 2

California Air Resource Board (CARB)

www.arb.ca.gov

(800) 242-4450

The California Air Resource Board (CARB), a Division of Cal EPA, developed this regulation to reduce VOC emissions from consumer products. This standard addresses the VOC content of various types of products and should be used for products not considered in the Green Seal GS-37 Standard (e.g., carpet cleaners, floor finishers or strippers). Full text of the standard is available on the web site: www.arb.ca.gov/consprod/regs/regs.htm.

EPA Comprehensive Procurement Guidelines (April 2004)

U.S. EPA

www.epa.gov/cpg

The Comprehensive Procurement Guideline (CPG) program is part of the U.S. EPA's continuing effort to promote the use of materials recovered from solid waste. It specifies recycled-content recommendations for a variety of products. For the purpose of this LEED-EB credit, CPG guidelines should be followed for toilet tissue, paper hand towels, facial tissues, industrial wipes and plastic trashcan liners. **Table 1** lists guidelines for commercial tissue products and recommended recycled content for plastic trash bags.

Green Building Concerns

Buildings require many materials during routine maintenance and ongoing operations. There are options for purchasing

Table 1: EPA Recommended Content Levels for Commercial/Industrial Paper Products

Item	Post-consumer Content [%]	Recovered Content [%]
Bathroom tissue	20-60	20-100
Paper towels	40-60	40-100
Paper napkins	30-60	30-100
Facial tissue	10-15	10-100
General purpose industrial wipers	40	40-100
Plastic trash bags	10-100	10-100

Note: The content levels should be read as "X% recovered content fiber, including Y% post-consumer content fiber" and not as "X% recovered content fiber plus Y% post-consumer content fiber."

products that are less toxic and that use materials more wisely than conventional methods.

Green Cleaning Products

Green cleaning products protect environmental health and indoor environmental quality. Unlike conventional cleaning products, they contain no carcinogens or chemicals that can cause reproductive health problems or irritate the eyes or skin, and contain reduced concentrations of volatile organic compounds (VOC) that diminish indoor air quality. Green cleaning products minimize the introduction of pollutants into buildings without compromising product performance or maintenance budget.

Recycled Content Janitorial Paper Products

Paper products that contain recycled content are beneficial because they reduce raw material extraction and minimize the introduction of pollutants such as chlorine into the environment. Recycled content and chlorine-free paper perform as well as conventional products, and usually cost no more.

Recycled Content Plastic Trashcan Liners

Most plastic trashcan liners are made from petroleum, a non-renewable resource. Using trashcan liners containing recycled material or omitting liners completely helps reduce the demand for this non-renewable material.

Environmental Issues

Sustainable cleaning products and materials are less toxic to the environment and use resources more wisely than conventional products. The environmental and human health benefits of sustainable products vary by product type.

Green Cleaning Products

Sustainable cleaning products not only improve indoor environmental quality, but also reduce negative environmental impacts on air, water and ecosystems. Cleaning commercial buildings consumes 6 billion pounds of chemicals annually, most of which are derived from non-renewable resources and pose significant threats to human and environmental health.[14] Green Seal-certified cleaning products are thoroughly tested for toxicity to aquatic life, biodegradability, contribution to eutrophication, air quality degradation and other factors related to human and environmental health. Regulations published by the California Air Resources Board (CARB) address the reduction of VOC emissions from many cleaning products not covered by Green Seal. VOC emissions affect both indoor and outdoor air quality.

Recycled Content Janitorial Paper Products

Recycled-content paper products reduce the environmental impact of ongoing building operations. Commercial and institutional buildings in the United States consume approximately 4.5 billion pounds of janitorial paper products[15] (e.g., toilet tissue and paper towels) per year, most of which is manufactured from virgin tree pulp. Recycled-content paper products also reduce environmental impacts associated with the extraction of raw materials (i.e., petroleum and trees) and reduce the demand for these resources. Additionally, diverting materials from landfills reduces land, water and air pollution associated with waste disposal.

Although not required by the EPA's procurement guidelines or by the LEED-EB requirements for this credit, an additional environmental measure to consider is purchasing paper products that are produced without the use of chlorine, a chemical that many paper manufacturers use during bleaching. Bleaching introduces chlorine into the environment, creating organochlorine toxins such as dioxin that bioaccumulate and can cause health problems including cancer, diabetes and birth defects. Because chlorine is not required to manufacture paper, many alternatives are currently available that do not use chlorine. Many of these chlorine-free products also contain recycled content.

Recycled Content Plastic Trashcan Liners

In 2001, 4 billion pounds of industrial liners, consumer trash bags and institutional trash bags were consumed in the United States. Consumption of plastic trash liners is expected to grow at a rate of 3.3 percent annually.[16] Plastic liners that contain recycled content can reduce the environmental impacts associated with plastic products. In addition to conserving raw materials and decreasing the amount of waste disposed of in landfills or through incineration, plastic recycling can minimize other environmental burdens associated with plastic production, such as energy consumption.[17]

Using trash liners with recycled material also helps establish and maintain a market for plastic recycling. Although not included in the requirements of this credit, another option is liners made from bio-based and/or renewable materials. Such liners provide a viable alternative to plastic trash bags and are becoming available from an increasing number of suppliers.

Economic Issues

Many green cleaning and recycled content products are priced similarly to their conventional counterparts. Locating suppliers of appropriate products can be a challenge, but a number of emerging directories allow efficient ordering and a mechanism for price comparison. The increasing demand for green products should continue to alleviate availability and pricing concerns. Although some green products may have a higher purchase price than conventional alternatives, these costs typically can be recouped and exceeded by savings over their life cycle.

Green Cleaning Products

Green cleaning products are becoming more prevalent on the market, and many companies that sell conventional products now also carry green products. The cost of green products is usually the same or nominally higher than other products, and should not be a huge factor when making the transition. An increase in cost from switching to a slightly more expensive green cleaning product may be alleviated by reduced costs to transport, store, handle and discard the products, since they require fewer permits, less staff training and reduced liability in the event of an accident.

Recycled Content Janitorial Paper Products

Janitorial paper products made from recycled materials do not usually cost more than conventional paper products, and can actually be less expensive than products made from raw materials. Unbleached paper processed without chlorine can also reduce expenses, as it usually costs less than bleached paper. These products are available in standard sizes and can easily replace conventional products in existing dispensers. However, in some cases, specialized dispensers may need to be installed. In these cases, you have an opportunity update to products that have the optimal combination of cost, recycled content, environmental benefits and user friendliness.

Recycled Content Plastic Trashcan Liners

Plastic trashcan liners are available in many recycled content options and should not involve any additional expense. Recycled alternatives to petroleum-based products can actually cost less, and this margin of savings could increase with increasing oil prices. Completely eliminating trashcan liners represents another option that could save significant amounts of money over time. Occasionally, updating receptacles is necessary, but this initial expenditure can be quickly returned, especially in large facilities.

Strategies & Technologies

When purchasing cleaning materials and supplies, specify products that meet one or more of the sustainability criteria listed in the credit requirements. Be sure to receive written confirmation from cleaning and janitorial product manufacturers that their products fulfill these specified standards.

Green Cleaning Products

Specify the procurement of products that meet the requirements of the Green Seal standard, as applicable, and the California Air Resource Board (CARB) Standards if the Green Seal standard is not applicable. See IEQ Credit 10 for additional information on green cleaning.

Recycled Content Janitorial Paper Products

Specify the procurement of janitorial paper products that meet the recycled content requirements of the EPA Comprehensive Procurement Guidelines. Purchasing such products is relatively straightforward, as numerous suppliers sell them.

Although not required by this credit, additional strategies can reduce the use of paper products and improve facility maintenance. These strategies include installing product dispensers that limit the amount of paper dispensed, hold multiple rolls, or hold coreless rolls that reduce packaging waste. Additionally, from a human health perspective, "hands-free" dispensers can reduce exposure to pathogenic organisms.

Energy-efficient electric hand dryers also can completely eliminate the need for paper towels in restrooms. The relative environmental benefits of the use of paper towels versus electric hand dryers in a specific building can be determined through comprehensive life cycle assessments of the options. One recent study indicates that the embodied energy of standard hand dryer use is about one-half that of paper towels, excluding energy consumed for disposal of paper towels, as measured in kilojoules per use. The study also looked at cost implications and found hand dryer use equated to less than 10 percent the cost per use when compared to paper towels.[18]

Recycled Content Plastic Trashcan Liners

Specify the procurement of plastic trashcan liners that meet the recycled content requirements of the EPA Comprehensive Procurement Guidelines. Purchase locally manufactured recycled content liners if possible to support the local recycling market and reduce transportation costs.

Consider using trashcan liners made from bio-based or renewable materials, or completely eliminate the use of trashcan liners to further reduce plastic consumption in the building.

Synergies & Tradeoffs

Procurement of green cleaning products should be coordinated with LEED-EB IEQ Credit 10.3: Green Cleaning – Low Environmental Impact Cleaning Policy. Also, purchasing green products that can be recycled at the end of their useful life, or come in recyclable containers or packaging, can help earn LEED-EB Occupant Recycling credits.

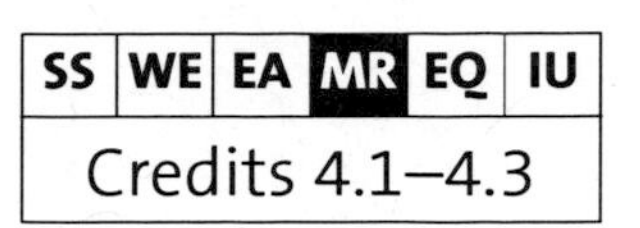

Calculations & Documentation

Calculations

The following calculation methodology supports the credit submittals as listed on the first page of this credit. The products and materials covered by this credit include those that are used as part of the janitorial practices within the building.

An example is provided below. Use a table similar to **Table 2** (found in the LEED-EB Letter Templates) to document purchases of products and materials that comply with credit requirements. For each purchase, note the date of purchase, the item purchased, and the credit requirement met by that purchase. **Table 3** provides a form for documenting purchases of cleaning products, janitorial paper and trashcan liners that do not meet the credit requirements. **Table 4** summarizes all purchases of relevant products and materials, and calculates the percentage of the total purchases that meet at least one of the credit requirements (**Equation 1**).

In this example, of the total purchases of relevant products, 40 percent meet the credit requirements, earning 1 point.

Table 2: Purchases of Credit Compliant Products During the Performance Period

Date of Purchase	Item	Meets Standard	Cost/Value
10/31/2004	Single-fold natural paper hand towels, 40% post-consumer recycled content, 8 cases	EPA Comprehensive Procurement Guidelines	$320.00
10/31/2004	Degreaser, 4 gallons	Green Seal GS-37	$60.00
Total cost or value of purchases that meet credit requirements			**$380.00**

Table 3: Purchases of Non Credit Compliant Products During the Performance Period

Date of Purchase	Item	Cost/Value
6/19/2004	Floor maintainer, 2 jugs	$80.00
7/15/2004	Industrial 60 gallon trash liners, 6 cases	$82.80
10/31/2004	Jumbo roll toilet tissue, 8 cases	$416.00
Total cost or value of purchases that do not meet credit requirements		**$578.80**

Table 4: Summary of Purchases

	Cost/Value
(A) Total purchases that meet credit requirements (from Table 2)	$380.00
(B) Total purchases not meeting credit requirements (from Table 3)	$578.80
(C) Total purchases (Line A + Line B)	$958.80
Percent Qualifying Purchases (Line A / Line C x 100)	**39.6%**

In this example, of the total purchases of relevant products, 40 percent meet the credit requirements, earning 1 point.

Equation 1

Qualifying Percentage = (Cost of compliant products / Cost of All Relevant Products) x 100

Documentation

- ❑ Organizational policy for sustainable cleaning products and materials
  - Provide a copy of the sustainable cleaning products and materials policy addressing the purchases of compliant cleaning products and materials as it appears within the official organization purchasing policy in use by the participant, or as an individual document on participant letterhead with the signature of the company officer responsible for its implementation.
- ❑ Documentation of purchases
  - Document the type and cost of all materials purchased during the performance period that are used inside the building and are covered under the sustainable cleaning products and materials purchasing policy.
  - For purchases that meet one of the sustainability criteria outlined in this credit, provide manufacturer's documentation describing the nature of the product, and highlight product features that conform to applicable referenced standards.
  - Provide sample invoices documenting purchase date, volume, dollar amount, etc.
- ❑ Calculations of percent qualifying purchases
  - Use the LEED-EB Letter Templates to perform calculations

Other Resources

Business and Sustainable Development: A Global Guide – Green Procurement

www.bsdglobal.com/tools/bt_green_pro.asp

This online resource, modeled on a toolkit developed by the Manitoba Green Procurement Network, offers resources and strategies for setting up green procurement programs within organizations.

California Integrated Waste Management Board Recycled-Content Product Directory

www.ciwmb.ca.gov/rcp/

This online directory lists thousands of recycled products and provides information on the companies that reprocess, manufacture and/or distribute recycled products, searchable by product name, product type and company name.

Comprehensive Procurement Guidelines Supplier Database

www.ergweb2.com/cpg/user/cpg_search.cfm

The EPA's database of product suppliers, including paper and trash bag manufacturers

GreenSpec® Menu

www.greenspec.com

This product information service from Building Green includes descriptions, manufacturer information and links to additional resources for environmentally preferable building products.

Definitions

Post-consumer recycled content is the percentage of material in a product that is recycled from consumer waste.

Post-industrial recycled content is the percentage of material in a product that is recycled from manufacturing waste.

Post-consumer waste recycling is the recycling of materials collected from consumer waste following consumer use of the products containing these materials.

Post-industrial waste recycling is the recycling of materials collected from industrial processes. This includes the collection and recycling of waste from industrial processes within the same manufacturing plant or from another manufacturing plant.

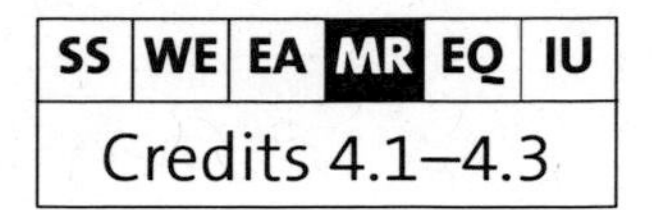

A **Sustainable Purchasing Policy** is the preferential purchasing of products that meet sustainability standards. Per this LEED-EB credit, the sustainable purchasing policy for cleaning products and materials should include all cleaning products, paper products and trashcan liners included in the U.S. EPA's Comprehensive Procurement Guidelines.

SS	WE	EA	MR	EQ	IU

Credits 5.1–5.3

1–3 Points

Occupant Recycling

Intent

Facilitate the reduction of waste and toxins generated by building occupants and building operations that are hauled to and disposed of in landfills or incineration.

Requirements

Have in place over the performance period a building occupant waste reduction and recycling program that addresses the separation, collection and storage of materials for recycling, including (at a minimum) paper, glass, plastics, cardboard/OCC, metals, batteries and fluorescent light bulbs and diversion from landfill disposal or incineration. Each time reusable architectural panels are moved and reinstalled, they can be counted as part of the total waste stream and included in the recycled component of the waste stream.

Collect and recycle at least 95% of the batteries used, and collect and recycle at least 95% of the fluorescent light bulbs used.

AND

- ❑ Divert/Recycle 30% of total waste stream (by weight or volume) (1 point)
- ❑ Divert/Recycle 40% of total waste stream (by weight or volume) (2 points)
- ❑ Divert/Recycle 50% of total waste stream (by weight or volume) (3 points)

Submittals – Initial Certification

- ❑ Provide a copy of the building occupant waste reduction and recycling policy.
- ❑ Provide quarterly summary reports on the total waste produced by the building along with hauler documentation and calculations of the amount of each type of waste that has been recycled over the performance period.

Submittals – Recertification

Provide an update of previous filings:

- ❑ If there has been no change to the building occupant waste reduction and recycling policy, provide a signed letter documenting its continued existence and implementation.
- ❑ Provide quarterly summary reports on the total waste produced by the building, along with hauler documentation and calculations of the amount of each type waste that has been recycled over the performance period.

OR

- ❑ If there has been a change to the building occupant waste reduction and recycling policy, provide a copy of the revised plan highlighting any changes.
- ❑ Provide quarterly summary reports on the total waste produced by the building, along with hauler documentation and calculations of the amount of each type of waste that has been recycled over the performance period.

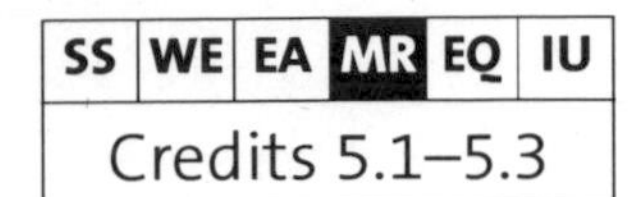

Summary of Referenced Standard

There is no standard referenced for this credit.

Green Building Concerns

One of the most important aspects of green building operation is waste reduction. Three principal strategies reduce the amount of waste going to a landfill or incinerator: source reduction, resource reuse, and recycling. A successful waste reduction program integrates all three strategies.

Source reduction is the most effective form of waste reduction, because items that never enter the site cannot become waste. Source reduction consists of evaluating the products, materials and packaging brought into the building and identifying opportunities to reduce the amount of waste by switching products, reducing the number of items or changing the associated packaging.

Reuse is the second essential approach to waste reduction by maximizing utilization or reuse of materials already in the building. Making unused or replaced office supplies and equipment available to other departments or organizations is an example of resource reuse. Resource reuse can save money by preventing unnecessary purchases and by reducing waste.

The third component of waste reduction is recycling. Recycling metal, glass, plastic and paper allows those materials to be manufactured into new products. Facility managers can encourage recycling within the building by providing appropriate facilities (such as collection bins and sorting stations) and managing the collection and processing of recyclable materials.

Environmental Issues

The environmental issues associated with waste reduction and recycling are similar to those discussed in MR Prerequisite 1.2. Landfills are a limited resource and, along with incineration, a major cause of soil, air and groundwater contamination.

Recycling provides materials for new products that would otherwise be harvested and manufactured from virgin materials. It prevents the extraction of raw natural resources and preserves limited landfill space. Recycling batteries and fluorescent light bulbs is especially important to prevent toxic materials from polluting air or ground water.

Economic Issues

The economic issues associated with this credit are similar to those discussed in MR Prerequisite 1.2. A successful recycling program requires time and energy to implement. Larger facilities may require an initial investment for equipment such as crushers and cardboard balers. Effective recycling programs require long-term monitoring and maintenance by facilities staff.

However, strong recycling programs can bring money into the organization. Through a combination of reduced waste disposal fees and payments received from recycling companies, recycling programs may generate revenues that exceed the costs. In addition, companies that achieve outstanding recycling rates are often noted in the press and viewed as good corporate neighbors.

Strategies & Technologies

MR Prerequisite 1.2 requires the establishment of a recycling program. This section addresses methods to improve existing programs to achieve MR Credit 5.1–5.3. First, use the building waste audit conducted for MR Prerequisite 1.1 to identify additional source reduction, reuse and recycling opportunities. For each material targeted for landfill or incinerator disposal, explore and evaluate what source reduction, reuse and recycling actions could reduce disposal volumes.

Optimizing a recycling program requires cooperation from maintenance staff and building occupants, so education should be a primary effort. Provide information on recycling procedures, including a list of recyclable materials and collection locations. Keep occupants informed about the success of the program, set goals for constant improvement and offer incentives. In addition, educate occupants on the environmental benefits of recycling to encourage participation.

The simplest and most effective way to encourage recycling is to make it easy. Placing recycling containers next to all trash receptacles means that occupants do not have to walk out of their way to recycle, which can significantly improve the success of a recycling program.

Another excellent way to reduce waste is to encourage building occupants to practice reuse. For example, provide reusable coffee mugs or bottles for employees instead of disposable cups, and collect lightly used paper to reuse for jotting notes or taking messages.

Synergies & Tradeoffs

Source reduction reduces purchasing costs and waste disposal fees, and selling waste stream materials provides revenue that offsets waste disposal fees. Donating or giving away waste components also reduces waste disposal fees while benefiting other organizations in the community.

Dense urban areas typically have recycling infrastructure in place, but additional space for collection and storage may be necessary and costly.

It is also important to address possible adverse indoor environmental quality impacts due to recycling activities. Activities that create odors, noise and air contaminants should be isolated or performed during non-occupant hours. These factors should be taken into account when developing a recycling plan.

Recycling of some components of the waste stream may cost more than the resulting reduction in disposal fees. Although not economically ideal, recycling these materials is a valuable contribution to improving the environment because it helps develop markets for them.

This credit is closely related to MR Prerequisite 1.1 and 1.2. Also, material purchasing programs, such as those described in MR Credits 2–5, can be developed to ensure that, to the extent possible, materials brought into the building are constructed of or packaged in materials that can be recycled through the building's recycling program.

Calculations & Documentation

Calculations

Waste diversion includes source reduction, reuse and recycling. The amount for each method of diversion must be quantified accurately and supported with documentation. The LEED-EB Letter Templates and the tables below show how to report waste diversion quantities and conduct calculations.

The waste audit tables in the Calculations section of MR Prerequisite 1 might be helpful for these calculations (also presented below as **Table 1**). **Tables 2–5** will help organize information about the recycling program in the building, and **Table 6** summarizes all values and calculations.

Documentation

- ❑ Organizational recycling policy
  - Submit a copy of the policy addressing occupant recycling as it appears within the official organizational waste management policy in use by the participant, or as an individual document on participant letterhead with the signature of the company officer responsible for its implementation.

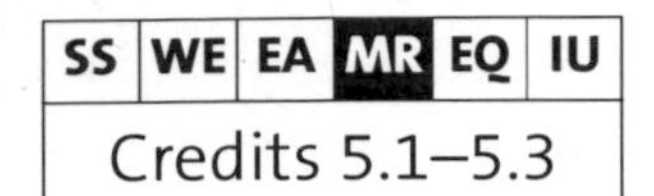

- The recycling policy should include a commitment to achieving the specific percentage of waste diverted/recycled.

Other Resources

Business Resource Efficiency and Waste Reduction

(916) 341-6000

www.ciwmb.ca.gov/bizwaste

This program from the California Integrated Waste Management Board promotes office recycling and waste reduction efforts.

Composting and Recycling Municipal Solid Waste by Luis Diaz, et. al., CRC Press, 1993.

This guide identifies and evaluates options for composing and recycling municipal solid waste.

McGraw-Hill Recycling Handbook by Herb Lund, McGraw-Hill, 2000.

The Recycling Handbook serves as a reference for individuals developing and operating recycling programs. It provides an overview of recycling laws, strategic goals for recycling programs, and information about the recycling process for each type of recyclable material.

National Recycling Coalition

(202) 347-0450

www.nrc-recycle.org/

The National Recycling Coalition is a nonprofit organization dedicated to the advancement of recycling. The web site provides a range of information related to recycling.

Recycling at Work

(202) 293-7330

www.usmayors.org/USCM/recycle

This program of the U.S. Conference of Mayors provides information on workplace recycling efforts.

U.S. EPA Waste Wise Program

www.epa.gov/wastewise/about/index.htm

Waste Wise is a free, voluntary EPA program that helps U.S. organizations eliminate costly municipal solid waste disposal.

Equation 1

Percent Diverted = (Source Reduction + Waste Recycled + Waste reused) / (Waste Disposal + Source Reduction + Waste Reused + Waste Recycled)

Table 1: Waste Not Diverted (Sent to Landfill, Incinerator or Other Disposal)

Column A	Column B	Column C	Column D	Column E	Column F	Column G	Column H	Column I
List Each Waste Container	**Container Type (dumpster or compactor)**	**Container Size [cu. yds.]**	**Container Capacity [tons]**	**Type of Waste**	**Frequency of collection [per month]**	**Estimated % Filled**	**Total Weight [tons/ Month]**	**Total Weight [tons/ year]**
Totals								

Notes: The goal of this table is to fill in Column I. If possible, enter information into this column directly from measurements from waste haulers. If these figures are not available, use the other columns in the table to compute the total weight of unsegregated waste.

SS	WE	EA	MR	EQ	IU
Credits 5.1–5.3					

Table 2: Source Reduction

Column A **Material**	Column B **Quantity Waste Material Avoided through Source Reduction [tons/yr]**	Column C **Description of Source Actions to Reduce Waste**
Newspaper		
Glass		
Aluminum		
Tin/bi-metal		
High grade paper		
Mixed paper		
Corrugated Cardboard		
Plastics		
Scrap metals		
Construction/Demolition		
Tires		
Used motor oil		
Auto batteries		
Leaves		
Grass		
Food waste		
Other		
Other		
Total [Tons/yr.]		

Table 3: Waste Material Reuse

Column A **Material**	Column B **Quantity of Each Material Reused [tons/yr]**	Column C **Description of Material Reuse Actions to Reduce Waste**
Newspaper		
Glass		
Aluminum		
Tin/bi-metal		
High grade paper		
Mixed paper		
Corrugated cardboard		
Plastics		
Scrap metals		
Construction/demolition		
Tires		
Used motor oil		
Auto batteries		
Leaves		
Grass		
Food waste		
Other		
Other		
Total [Tons/yr]		

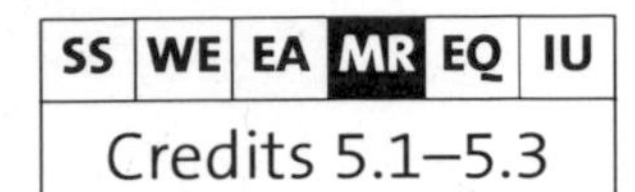

Table 4: Recycled Materials

Column A **Material**	Column B **Quantity Recycled [tons/yr]**	Column C **Recycling Market Name and Address**
Newspaper		
Glass		
Aluminum		
Tin/bi-metal		
High grade paper		
Mixed paper		
Corrugated cardboard		
Plastics		
Scrap metals		
Construction/demolition		
Tires		
Used motor oil		
Leaves		
Grass		
Food waste		
Other		
Other		
Total [Tons/yr]		

Note: Fill in Column B from recycling billing or payment records

Table 5: Battery and Fluorescent Lamp Recycling Rate

Column A **Material**	Column B **Quantity Recycled [tons/yr]**	Column C **Quantity Disposed [tons/yr]**	Column D **Percent Recycled**
Batteries			
Fluorescent Lamps			

Note: Column D is equal to (Column B / (Column B + Column C)) x 100

Definitions

An **incinerator** is a furnace or container for burning waste materials.

Landfills are waste disposal sites for the deposit of solid waste from human activities.

Recycling is the collection, reprocessing, marketing and use of materials that were diverted or recovered from the solid waste stream. Recycling provides two categories of environmental benefits: (1) diverts waste from land filling or incineration and (2) reduces the need for virgin materials for the manufacture of new products.

Source reduction is reducing waste by reducing the amount of unnecessary material brought into a building. Purchasing products with less packaging is a good example of source reduction.

Waste disposal is the process of eliminating waste by means of burial in a landfill, combustion in an incinerator, dumping at sea or eliminating waste in some other way that is not recycling or reuse

Waste diversion includes waste management activities that divert waste from disposal though incineration or landfilling. Typical waste diversion methods are reuse and recycling waste.

Waste reduction includes source reduction and diversion of waste by means of reuse or recycling.

A **Waste Reduction Policy** includes: (1) A statement describing the organization's commitment to minimize waste disposal by using source reduction, reuse and recycling, (2) assignment of responsibility within the organization for implementation of waste reduction program, (3) a list of the general actions that will be implemented in the waste reduction program to reduce waste and (4) a description of the tracking and review component in the waste reduction program to monitor waste reduction success and improve waste reduction performance over time.

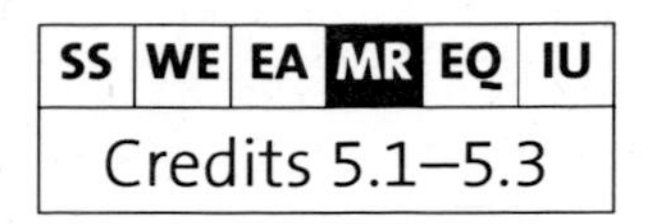

Table 6: Summary Table for Waste Diversion

	Column 2	Column 3
LN	**Category**	**Amount [Tons]**
1	Amount of Waste Avoided through source reduction	
2	Amount of Waste Avoided through reuse	
3	Amount of Waste Avoided through recycling	
4	**Total Amount of Waste Diversion**	
5	Total Amount of Waste sent to landfill/incinerator	
6	Sum of All Waste (Diverted & Landfilled/Incinerated)	
7	Waste Diversion Percentage	
8	Recycling rate for Mercury Containing Light Bulbs [%]	
9	Recycling rate for Mercury Containing Light Bulbs [%]	

Notes: Line 1: From Table 2 *Line 2: From Table 3*
Line 3: From Table 4 *Line 4: Sum of Lines 1, 2 and 3*
Line 5: From Table 1 *Line 6: Sum of Lines 4 and 5*
Line 7: (Line 4 / by Line 6) x 100 *Line 8: From Table 5, Column D*
Line 9: From Table 5, Column D

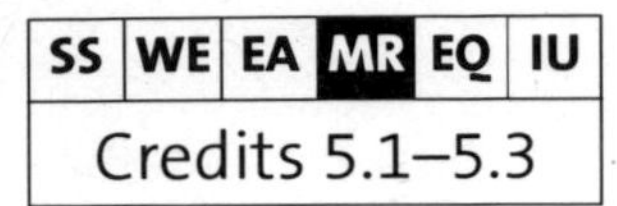
SS WE EA MR EQ IU
Credits 5.1–5.3

SS	WE	EA	MR	EQ	IU
Credit 6					

1 Point

Additional Toxic Material Reduction

Reduced Mercury in Light Bulbs

Intent

Establish and maintain a toxic material source reduction program to reduce the amount of mercury brought into buildings through purchases of light bulbs.

Requirements

- ❑ Maintain mercury content of all mercury-containing light bulbs below 80 picograms per lumen hour of light output (picogram/lumen hour), on weighted average, for all mercury-containing light bulbs acquired for the existing building and associated grounds. (The weighted average mercury content of these light bulbs is calculated as described in MR Prerequisite 2).

Submittals – Initial Certification

- ❑ Provide a copy of the organizational policy specifying that all future purchases of mercury-containing light bulbs will be made in such a way that the average mercury content of the light bulbs is less than the specified level in picograms per lumen hour.
- ❑ Provide records of all acquisitions during the performance period of mercury-containing light bulbs for use in the building and grounds.
- ❑ Include manufacturer MSDSs for each type of light bulb purchased showing mercury content of the light bulbs in milligrams.
- ❑ Provide calculations demonstrating that the weighted average mercury is less than the specified level in picograms per lumen hour for these light bulbs. If an MSDS shows ranges of mercury contents in milligrams, use the highest value given in these calculations.

Submittals – Recertification

Provide an update of previous filings:

- ❑ Provide records of all acquisitions during the performance period of mercury-containing light bulbs for use in the building and grounds.
- ❑ Include manufacturer MSDS for each type of light bulb purchased showing mercury content of the light bulbs in milligrams.
- ❑ Provide calculations demonstrating that the weighted average mercury content of all mercury-containing light bulbs acquired is less than the specified level in picograms per lumen hour for these light bulbs.

AND EITHER

- ❑ If there has been no change to the purchasing policy specifying that the weighted average mercury content of all mercury-containing light bulbs acquired is less than the specified level in picograms per lumen hour, provide a signed letter documenting its continued existence and implementation.

OR

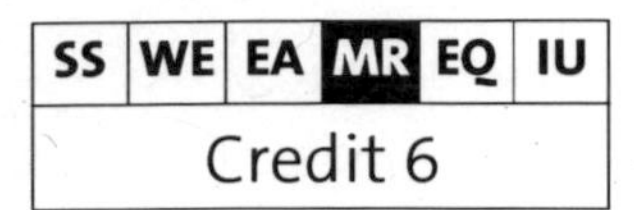

- ❑ If the mercury-containing light bulb purchasing policy has changed, provide a copy of the revised plan highlighting any changes to the specified level picograms of mercury per lumen hour policy.

Summary of Referenced Standard

Light Bulb Life Measurement Standards:

IESNA LM-40-01 (01-Dec-2001) Standard for Life of Tubular Fluorescence

Note: Conduct life test using 3 hours on 20 minute off cycling and instant start ballast with a ballast factor of 1.

IESNA LM-47-01 (01-Dec-2001) Standard for Life of HID Lamps

IESNA LM-60-01 (01-Dec-2001) Standard for Life of Single-Ended Compact Fluorescent Lamps

Light Bulb Lumen Measurement Standards:

Lumens are measured in sphere following prescribed IES methods.

LM 9-Linear fluorescent

LM 66 Compact fluorescent

LM 51-HID lamps

Light Bulb Mercury Content Measurement Standards:

Option 1: Obtain manufacturer's certification as to mercury content of each type of light bulb acquired. (If mercury content is provided as a range use the high end of the range in these calculations.)

Option 2: Test each type of light bulb acquired using U.S. EPA Total Mercury by Cold Vapor Absorption Method 7471A

Green Building Concerns

See MR-Prerequisite 2.0

Environmental Issues

See MR-Prerequisite 2.0

Economic Issues

See MR-Prerequisite 2.0

Strategies & Technologies

Establish and follow a light bulb purchasing program that keeps the weighted average mercury content below 80 picograms per lumen hour for mercury-containing light bulbs purchased during the performance period. Purchasing light bulbs with longer life has the added benefit of reducing maintenance costs. Calculating the picograms of mercury per lumen hour captures all three factors that affect the total amount of mercury brought into light bulbs over time: mercury content, light bulb life and light output. Consider all three measures in developing the light bulb purchasing plan for your building.

Synergies & Tradeoffs

See MR-Prerequisite 2.0

Calculations & Documentation

Calculations

Table 1 contains an example calculation of the weighted average mercury content of light bulbs on a building and its site. A detailed calculation spreadsheet can be downloaded from the USGBC web site. The spreadsheet should contain both the plan for achicving reduced mercury content and the mercury content of all light bulbs purchased during the performance period.

The same calculations apply to both MR Prerequisite 2 and MR Credit 6:

- ❑ If the weighted average mercury content of all the light bulbs is below 100 picograms per lumen hour, MR Prerequisite 2 is earned.
- ❑ If the weighted average mercury content of all the light bulbs is below 80 picograms per lumen hour, MR Credit 6 is earned and MR Prerequisite 2 is earned.

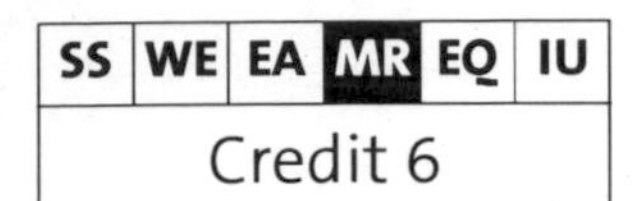

Documentation

- ❑ Organizational policy regarding light bulb purchases
  - This is a "going-forward" requirement for LEED-EB, meaning that the organizational policy should be designed to promote incremental changes as bulb replacement needs arise.
  - Provide the light-bulb purchasing policy in hard copy or digital form on participant letterhead with the signature of the company officer responsible for its implementation, or as it appears within the official organizational purchasing plan adopted by the participant.
  - A sample policy can be viewed below.
- ❑ Calculations establishing weighted average mercury content goals for the purchasing plan
  - If manufacturer provides mercury content as a range, calculations for LEED-EB must use the highest mercury content of the range to ensure compliance.
- ❑ Records of all acquisitions during the performance period of mercury-containing light bulbs
  - Provide acquisition records even if the 100 picogram/lumen hour limitation is not met if calculated based upon those purchases.
- ❑ Manufacturer Material Safety Data Sheets (MSDSs)
  - Provide manufacturer documentation to show the mercury content (in milligrams) for each type/model of light bulb, either in MSDSs or a signed letter from the manufacturer.
- ❑ Calculations demonstrating that pictogram per lumen hour requirements are met
  - If the manufacturer provides mercury content as a range, calculations for LEED-EB must use the highest mercury content of the range to ensure compliance.

Other Resources

See MR-Prerequisite 2.0

Table 1: Mercury Calculation Example for a Light Bulb Purchasing Plan for a Building

Column A	Column B	Column C	Column D	Column E	Column F	Column G
Type of Light Bulb	**Quantity**	**Hg Content per Bulb [mg]**	**Design Light Output per Bulb [Lumens]**	**Life per bulb [Hours]**	**Total Hg Content by Bulb Type [grams]**	**Total Lumen Hours by Bulb Type [Hours]**
T-8 Four Foot	1,000	3.5	2,800	24,000	3.5	67,200,000,000
Compact Fluorescent	30	1.4	1,545	10,000	0.042	463,500,000
HID	40	6.8	6,800	12,500	0.272	3,400,000,000
Totals					3.814	71,063,500,000
Mercury Content [Picograms/Lumen Hour]						53.7

Notes: Column A: From records or survey of building and building site
Column B: From records or survey of building
Column C: From light bulb manufacturer MDSDS signed letter from manufacturer
Column D: From manufacturer's product literature
Column E: From manufacturer's product literature
Column F: Mercury content of bulb type X quantity of bulbs
Column G: Mean Lumens X Life of bulb X number of bulbs
Total Mercury Content: sum of the total mercury content for all types of bulbs
Total Lumen Hours: sum of the lumen hours for all types of bulbs
Mercury Content [picograms/lumen Hour] = (Total Mercury Content / Total Lumen Hours) x 10^{12}

Definitions

See MR-Prerequisite 2.0

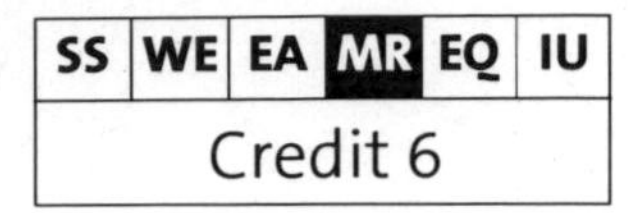
SS WE EA MR EQ IU
Credit 6

Endnotes

[1] United States. Environmental Protection Agency, Office of Solid Waste. Municipal Solid Waste: Basic Facts May 2005. 26 May 2005 <http://www.epa.gov/epaoswer/non-hw/muncpl/facts.htm>.

[2] United States. Environmental Protection Agency, Office of Solid Waste. Municipal Solid Waste: Basic Facts April 2004. 25 March 2005 < http://www.epa.gov/epaoswer/non-hw/muncpl/facts.htm>.

[3] United States. Department of Energy. 1999 Commercial Buildings Energy Consumption Survey, originally released August 2002, last revised July 2004. 15 March 2005 <http://www.eia.doe.gov/emeu/cbecs/detailed_tables_1999.html>.

[4] National Electrical Manufactures Association. Fluorescent Lamps and the Environment January 2001. Document 01BR.15 March 2005 <http://www.nema.org/stds/lamps-env.cfm>.

[5] United States. Environmental Protection Agency, Office of Air Quality Planning & Standards and Office of Research and Development. Mercury Study Report to Congress – Volume 1: Executive Summary. Publication EPA-452/R-97-003, December 1997.

[6] Ibid.

[7] United States. Environmental Protection Agency, Office of Air Quality Planning & Standards and Office of Research and Development. Mercury Study Report to Congress – Volume II1: Fate and Transport of Mercury in the Environment. Publication EPA-452/R-97-005, December 1997.

[8] United States. Environmental Protection Agency, Office of Air Quality Planning & Standards and Office of Research and Development. Mercury Study Report to Congress – Volume VI1: Characterization of Human and Wildlife Risks from Mercury Exposure in the United States. Publication EPA-452/R-97-009, December 1997.

[9] United States. Environmental Protection Agency, Office of Solid Waste. Construction & Demolition Debris: Basic Information February 2005. 15 March 2005. <http://www.epa.gov/epaoswer/non-hw/debris-new/basic.htm>.

[10] Roodman, David M. and Nicholas Lenssen. Worldwatch Paper #124: A Building Revolution: How Ecology and Health Concerns Are Transforming Construction. Washington, DC: Worldwatch Institute: 1995.

[11] Wood Products Trade 2003. World Forest Institute. 25 March 2005 <http://www.worldforestry.org/wfi/trade-1.htm>.

[12] United States. Environmental Protection Agency. Health and Environmental Impacts of Ground Level Ozone December 2004. 15 March 2005 <http://www.epa.gov/air/urbanair/ozone/hlth.html>.

[13] Ashkin, Stephen. "We Are Making a Difference: A cleaning industry expert reviews the ongoing changes in industry practices." EPP Buyer Update Volume 10 (January 2005). Massachusetts Operational Services Division, Environmental Preferable Products Procurement Program. 30 March 2005 <http://www.mass.gov/epp/EPPUPDATES/volume_10_january_2005.pdf>.

[14] Ibid.

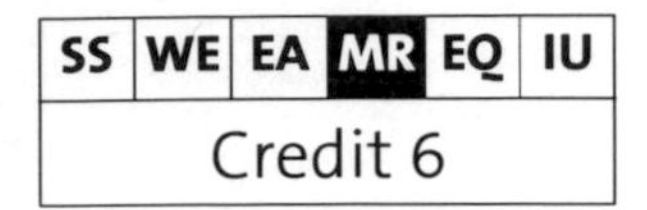

[15] Thedinger, Bart. "Trash Bags & Liners Grow at Rate of GDP." PlasticsTechnology: Your Business Outlook (March 2003). 30 March 2005 <http://www.plasticstechnology.com/articles/200303bib2.html>.

[16] Ross, Stuart and David Evans. "The environmental effect of reusing and recycling a plastic-based packaging system." Journal of Cleaner Production 11(2003): 561-571.

[17] "Energy Use Comparison of Paper Towels and Electric Hand Dryers". Environmental Building News 11.1 (January 2002). 31 March 2005 <http://www.buildinggreen.com/auth/article.cfm?filename=110106a.xml>.

Indoor Environmental Quality

Americans spend an average of 90 percent of their time indoors and as a result, the quality of the indoor environment has a significant influence on well-being, productivity and quality of life.[1] Following the EPA's designation of indoor air pollution as a top environmental risk to public health in reports released in 1987[2] and in 1990,[3] more attention has focused on integrated efforts to assess and manage indoor pollutants. Recent increases in building related illness (BRI) and sick building syndrome (SBS) have further heightened awareness of indoor air quality among building owners and occupants. An increasing number of legal cases have emphasized the need for strategies to maintain optimal IEQ.[4] Such strategies can potentially reduce liability for building owners, increase the resale value of the building and increase the health and productivity of building occupants.

In addition to health and liability concerns, productivity gains are also driving IEQ improvements. When calculating the 30-year cost of constructing, operating, maintaining and staffing a commercial building, 92 percent of the cost goes for employees' salaries.[5] With so much invested in people, it makes sense to keep them as healthy and productive as possible by improving and maintaining the quality of the indoor environment. The potential annual savings and productivity gains from improved IEQ in the United States are estimated as $6 to $14 billion from reduced respiratory disease, $1 to $4 billion from reduced allergies and asthma, $10 to $30 billion from reduced SBS symptoms, and $20 to $160 billion from direct improvements in worker performance that are unrelated to health.[6]

Effective IEQ strategies address issues related to indoor air quality (IAQ), such as ventilation effectiveness, moisture management and control of contaminants, in an integrated manner. Prevention of air quality problems is generally much less expensive than productivity losses or mitigation after problems occur. A study published by ASHRAE estimated the annual ROI for energy costs associated with increased ventilation as 600 percent. Other inexpensive and sensible ways to improve IAQ include enacting policies for construction activities to avoid contamination of materials or exposing building occupants to construction dust or harmful vapors. Specifying materials that release less and fewer harmful contaminants is even more beneficial.

To provide optimal environmental quality for building occupants, automatic sensors and individual controls can be integrated with the building systems to adjust temperature, humidity and the percentage of outside air introduced to occupied spaces. Sensors can also measure building CO_2 levels. High CO_2 levels indicate low outdoor airflow, which will lead to IAQ problems such as high VOC levels. Other IEQ issues addressed by the LEED-EB Rating System include daylighting and lighting quality, thermal comfort, acoustics, occupant control of building systems, and access to views. All of these issues have the potential to enhance the indoor environment and optimize interior spaces for building occupants.

Overview of LEED® Prerequisites and Credits

Overview of LEED® Prerequisites and Credits (continued)

EQ Credit 7.2
Thermal Comfort – Permanent Monitoring System

EQ Credit 8.1
Daylight & Views – Daylight for 50% of Spaces

EQ Credit 8.2
Daylight & Views – Daylight for 75% of Spaces

EQ Credit 8.3
Daylight & Views – Views for 45% of Spaces

EQ Credit 8.4
Daylight & Views – Views for 90% of Spaces

EQ Credit 9
Contemporary IAQ Practice

EQ Credit 10.1
Green Cleaning – Entryway Systems

EQ Credit 10.2
Green Cleaning – Isolation of Janitorial Closets

EQ Credit 10.3
Green Cleaning – Low Environmental Impact Cleaning Policy

EQ Credits 10.4-10.5
Green Cleaning – Low Environmental Impact Pest Management Policy

EQ Credit 10.6
Green Cleaning – Low Environmental Impact Cleaning Equipment Policy

SS	WE	EA	MR	EQ	IU
Prerequisite 1					

Required

Outside Air Introduction and Exhaust Systems

Intent

Establish minimum indoor air quality (IAQ) performance to enhance indoor air quality in buildings, thus contributing to the health and well-being of the occupants.

Requirements

- ❑ Modify or maintain existing building outside-air (OA) ventilation distribution system to supply at least the outdoor air ventilation rate required by ASHRAE 62.1-2004. If this is not feasible due to the physical constraints of the existing ventilation system, modify or maintain the system to supply at least 10 cubic feet per minute (CFM) per person.
- ❑ Implement and maintain an HVAC System Maintenance Program to ensure the proper operations and maintenance of HVAC components as they relate to IAQ.
- ❑ Test and maintain the operation of all building exhaust systems, including bathroom, shower, kitchen and parking exhaust system.

Submittals – Initial Certification

- ❑ Provide a letter and backup tabular information from a mechanical engineer or HVAC system specialist demonstrating that the existing building outside-air (OA) ventilation distribution system supplies at least the outdoor air ventilation rate required by ASHRAE 62.1-2004. If this is not feasible due to the physical constraints of the existing ventilation system, modify or maintain the system to supply at least 10 CFM/person.
- ❑ Provide a letter and backup tabular information from a mechanical engineer or HVAC system specialist demonstrating that the exhaust air HVAC systems serving the building are operating as designed.
- ❑ Provide the results of quarterly inspections of the building OA/exhaust air system to verify that the system is operating as intended over the performance period.

Submittals – Recertification

- ❑ Provide the results of quarterly inspections of the building OA/exhaust air system to verify that the system is operating as intended over the performance period.

AND EITHER

- ❑ If there has been no change to the HVAC system, provide a letter from the facility manager or an HVAC system specialist documenting its continued performance.

OR

- ❑ If there has been a change to the HVAC system, provide the documentation required for initial submittals under LEED-EB.

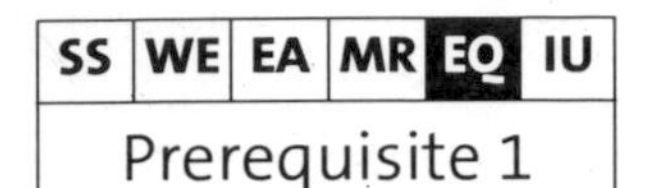

Summary of Referenced Standard

ASHRAE Standard 62.1-2004: Ventilation for Acceptable Indoor Air Quality

AHRAE

www.ashrae.org

(800) 527-4723

This standard addresses indoor air quality issues and prescribes minimum ventilation rates to reduce the potential for adverse health effects. The standard specifies the design of mechanical or natural ventilation systems to prevent uptake of contaminants, minimize the opportunity for growth and dissemination of microorganisms and, if necessary, filter particulates. The standard also specifies proper makeup air inlet and exhaust air outlet locations relative to potential sources of contamination.

A Ventilation Rate Procedure and an Indoor Air Quality Procedure offer alternative approaches to achieve compliance with the standard. The Ventilation Rate Procedure has recently been revised. The updated version redefines an occupied zone as a breathing zone and prescribes ventilation rates in both per-person and per-unit area values. The Indoor Air Quality Procedure requires establishment of both quantitative and subjective criteria for acceptable air quality and ventilation and/or air-cleaning as appropriate to achieve the established levels.

Green Building Concerns

Optimal IAQ performance in buildings results in improved occupant well-being and productivity. Key components for maintaining superior IAQ include using high-quality outdoor air and ensuring adequate ventilation rates.

Environmental Issues

Higher ventilation rates than those prescribed by ASHRAE Standard 62.1-2004 are sometimes necessary to improve IAQ and provide a healthy indoor environment. This can result in higher energy use to operate the building HVAC system. However, the additional need for energy can be mitigated by use of heat recovery ventilation and/or economizer strategies.

Economic Issues

Increased mechanical ventilation rates may result in greater annual heating and cooling energy costs (see www.epa.gov/iaq/largebldgs/eiaq_page.htm for the Energy Cost and IAQ Performance of Ventilation Systems and Controls Study). However, poor indoor air quality can cause occupant illnesses, resulting in increased expenses and liability costs for building owners, operators and insurance companies. Personnel costs are a significant percentage of operating costs, much greater than energy or maintenance costs. Thus, actions that affect employee attendance and productivity are significant.

Good IEQ reduces potential liability for architects, builders, owners, building operators and occupants and increases the value and marketability of the building.

Strategies & Technologies

Ensure that outside air capacity for the ventilation system can meet the requirements of ASHRAE 62.1-2004 in all modes of operation. Assess changes in occupant loads for renovation or retrofit projects and, where possible, plan for these future requirements. Remember to consider the maximum potential occupancy load when calculating outside air needs in all spaces. Avoid over-design and under-design of the ventilation system and anticipate future retrofits.

Identify, as designed, the outside air (OA) component of total air flow [cubic feet per minute (CFM)] for each fan system in the building. Conduct a visual inspection of OA air vent/dampers and remove any OA vent/louver obstructions that restrict full capacity to enter the distribution system. (Note: The standards for initial and ongoing maintenance can be found in EA Prerequisite 1 and Credit 3.) Conduct tests to measure and record airflow values (in terms of CFM) and document the outdoor and exhaust airflow. Compare measured flow to designed flow for each unit. Test the operation of each exhaust fan and verify that exhaust airflow is unobstructed.

Identify site activities that may have a negative impact on air quality such as construction activities, materials installed in the building, or chemical-handling activities that occur in the building. For renovation and rehabilitation projects, if using the Indoor Air Quality Procedure from ASHRAE 62.1-2004, establish concentration targets and perceived air quality percent satisfied.

Locate fresh air intakes away from possible sources of contamination (at least 25 feet is recommended and 40 plus feet is preferable). Possible sources of contamination include loading areas, building exhaust fans, cooling towers, street traffic, idling cars, standing water, parking garages, sanitary vents, dumpsters and outside smoking areas. Where possible sources of contamination are identified, move or remove the source of contaminants or move the intake.

Implement an operations and maintenance plan to maintain an uncontaminated HVAC system. Include regular maintenance of air filtration systems and consider systems upgrades. Follow U.S. EPA's detailed guidance for indoor air quality in commercial or institutional buildings.

Mold is an important IAQ issue. Actions to prevent mold include responding to water infiltration and drying affected building materials within 48 hours to discourage mold growth. Other mold prevention actions include decontamination best practices and air filtration. A good reference on this topic is the U.S. EPA's "Mold Remediation in Schools and Commercial Buildings," www.epa.gov/mold/mold_remediation.html.

Another potential IAQ issue is particulate accumulation on supply grills and adjacent ceiling and wall areas. These areas should be cleaned regularly by vacuuming and other measures.

Synergies & Tradeoffs

Additional efforts may be required in existing buildings to optimize the integration of the HVAC system with the layout of the structure and surrounding area. Site location and surrounding landscape design often influence the outdoor air volumes that can be circulated through the building. Dense neighborhoods, adjacent transportation facilities and existing site contamination can adversely affect the quality of outside air available for ventilation purposes.

Increased ventilation rates can solve some IAQ problems by diluting contaminant levels, but more intake flow increases energy use. Building commissioning and measurement & verification processes are tools that can improve indoor air quality levels while minimizing energy efficiency losses.

Coordinate ventilation activities with materials and practices that prevent contamination of air quality. During construction projects, protect building materials from moisture and specify building materials that do not release harmful or irritating chemicals such as volatile organic compounds (VOCs). VOC off-gassing from materials such as paints and solvents can contaminate the HVAC system. Occupant activities such as chemical handling and smoking can also contaminate the air in a space. Often, it may be more effective to reduce IAQ problems at the source, such as specifying low-VOC materials, than to use energy to ventilate the building and to condition a greater volume of air.

LEED-EB credits and prerequisites related to these issues include:

- ❑ EA Prerequisite 1: Existing Building Commissioning
- ❑ EA Credit 5: Performance Measurement
- ❑ MR Credit 3: Optimize Use of IAQ Compliant Products
- ❑ MR Credit 4: Sustainable Cleaning Products and Materials
- ❑ IEQ Prerequisite 2: Environmental Tobacco Smoke (ETS) Control
- ❑ IEQ Credit 1: Outside Air Delivery Monitoring
- ❑ IEQ Credit 2: Increased Ventilation
- ❑ IEQ Credit 3: Construction IAQ Management Plan
- ❑ IEQ Credit 5: Indoor Chemical and Pollutant Source Control
- ❑ IEQ Credit 10: Green Cleaning

Calculations & Documentation

Calculations

The ASHRAE Ventilation Rate Procedure has recently been revised. The updated version redefines an occupied zone as a breathing zone and describes ventilation rates in both per-person and per-unit area values. ASHRAE has introduced a spreadsheet called 62n-VRP.xls, which can be used to calculate the ventilation rate as outlined by the referenced standard.

Documentation

- ❑ Documentation that (OA) ventilation distribution system supplies the outdoor air ventilation rate required:
  - Engineer/System specialist may be an internal or third-party resource. The letter must be signed and appear on official letterhead, and should include information on the credentials of the signatory.
  - Documentation should reflect identification of key OA ventilation parameters for the building type and uses, as specified for compliance with ASHRAE 62.1-2004, and achievement of those parameters by the building under analysis. Alternately, documentation should also reference and reflect adherence to the 10CFM/person minimum.
- ❑ Documentation that the exhaust air HVAC systems are operating as designed:
  - Engineer/System specialist may be an internal or third-party resource. The letter must be signed and appear on official letterhead, and should include information on the credentials of the signatory. This letter may be integrated with the letter above into a single document.
  - Documentation should reflect identification of performance indicators for comparison of expected design OA ventilation performance, actual operating performance, and ongoing achievement of those indicators.
- ❑ Quarterly inspections of the building OA/exhaust air system:
  - The inspection results provided should include consecutive inspections that provide data covering all seasons.
  - If the performance period is less than one year, provide the number of inspections available, but at least one inspection must be completed.

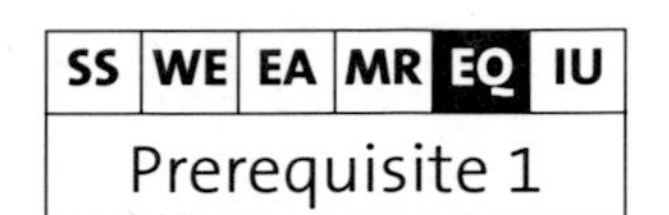

Other Resources

Air Contaminants and Industrial Hygiene Ventilation: A Handbook of Practical Calculations, Problems, and Solutions by Roger Wabeke, CRC Press & Lewis Publishers, 1998.

This reference text contains technical information for addressing industrial hygiene issues.

Building Air Quality: A Guide for Building Owners and Managers

http://www.epa.gov/iaq/largebldgs/baq-toc.html

This guide from the U.S. EPA provides practical suggestions on preventing, identifying and resolving IAQ problems in public and commercial buildings.

Environmental Design Links - Indoor Air Quality

www.outreach.missouri.edu/edninfo/air-quality.htm

This resource from the Department of Environmental Design, College of Human Environmental Sciences, University of Missouri – Columbia Outreach and Extension provides a directory of links related to IAQ building systems issues.

Handbook of Indoor Air Quality Management by Donald Moffat, Prentice Hall, 1997.

This comprehensive resource provides guidance for developing and implementing an IAQ management plan.

Improving Indoor Air Quality Through Design, Operation and Maintenance by Marvin Meckler, Prentice Hall, 1996.

This text provides information on the engineering, maintenance and operating procedures that can affect indoor air quality.

Indoor Air Quality (IAQ)

(800) 438-4318

www.epa.gov/iaq

This U.S. EPA site includes a wide variety of tools, publications and links to address IAQ concerns in schools and large buildings. The downloadable *IAQ Building Education and Assessment Model (I-BEAM)* (www.epa.gov/iaq/largebldgs/ibeam_page.htm) software program provides comprehensive IAQ management guidance and calculates the cost, revenue and productivity impacts of planned IAQ activities. Publications on the site include the *Energy Cost and IAQ Performance of Ventilation Systems and Controls Modeling Study*, the *Building Assessment, Survey and Evaluation Study* and the *Building Air Quality Action Plan.*

Indoor Air Quality Association (IAQA)

(301) 231- 8388

www.iaqa.org

The IAQA is a nonprofit organization dedicated to promoting the exchange of indoor environmental information through education and research.

Indoor Pollution: A Reference Handbook (Contemporary World Issues) by E. Willard Miller, et. al., Abc-Clio, 1998.

The sources, characteristics and human health effects of indoor pollutants are detailed in this text, along with an overview of the standards, controls, laws and regulations relevant to indoor air quality.

Mold Remediation in Schools and Commercial Buildings

http://www.epa.gov/mold/mold_remediation.html

This resource from the U.S. EPA (Publication No. EPA 402-K-01-001) presents guidelines for the remediation of mold and moisture problems in schools and commercial buildings. It is designed for use by building managers, custodians and other maintenance personnel.

Definitions

Building Related Illness is brought on by exposure to building air where symptoms

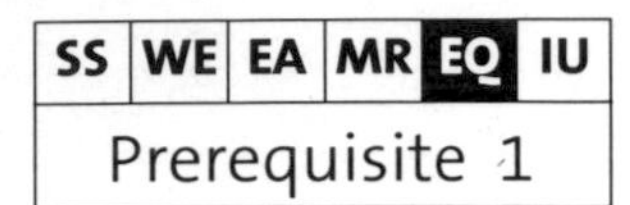

of diagnosable illness are identified and can be directly attributed to environmental agents in the air in the building.

Indoor Air Quality (IAQ) is the nature of air that affects the health and well-being of building occupants.

Sick Building Syndrome is a term used to describe situations where building occupants experience acute discomfort and negative health effects as a result of time spent in the building without any specific cause that can be identified, and the symptoms disappear soon after the occupants leave the building.

Ventilation is the process of supplying and removing air to and from interior spaces by natural or mechanical means.

SS	WE	EA	MR	EQ	IU
Prerequisite 2					

Required

Environmental Tobacco Smoke (ETS) Control

Intent

Prevent or minimize exposure of building occupants, indoor surfaces and systems to Environmental Tobacco Smoke (ETS).

Requirements

Option A. Prohibit smoking in the building.

- ❑ Prohibit smoking in the building.
- ❑ Locate any exterior designated smoking areas at least 25 feet away from building entries, outdoor air intakes and operable windows.

Option B. Establish negative pressure in the rooms with smoking.

- ❑ Prohibit smoking in the building except in designated smoking areas.
- ❑ Locate any exterior designated smoking areas at least 25 feet away from building entries, outdoor air intakes and operable windows.
- ❑ Provide one or more designated smoking rooms designed to effectively contain, capture and remove ETS from the building. At a minimum, the smoking room must be directly exhausted to the outdoors, away from air intakes and building entry paths, with no re-circulation of ETS-containing air to the non-smoking area of the building and enclosed with impermeable deck-to-deck partitions and operated at a negative pressure compared with the surrounding spaces of at least an average of 5 Pa (0.02 inches water gauge) and with a minimum of 1 Pa (0.004 inches water gauge) when the door(s) to the smoking room are closed.
- ❑ Verify performance of the smoking room differential air pressures by conducting 15 minutes of measurement, with a minimum of one measurement every 10 seconds, of the differential pressure in the smoking room with respect to each adjacent area and in each adjacent vertical chase with the doors to the smoking room closed. The testing will be conducted with each space configured for worst case conditions of transport of air from the smoking rooms to adjacent spaces.

Option C. Reduce air leakage between rooms with smoking and non-smoking areas in residential buildings.

Note that Option C is for residential buildings only.

- ❑ Prohibit smoking in all common areas of the building.
- ❑ Locate any exterior designated smoking areas at least 25 feet away from building entries, outdoor air intakes and operable windows opening to common areas.
- ❑ Minimize uncontrolled pathways for ETS transfer between individual residential units by sealing penetrations in walls, ceilings and floors in the residential units, and by sealing vertical chases adjacent to the units. In addition, all doors in the residential units leading to common hallways shall be weather-stripped to minimize air leakage into the hallway. Acceptable sealing of residential units shall be demonstrated by a blower door test conducted in accordance with ASTM-779-03, Standard Test Method for Determining Air Leakage Rate By Fan Pressurization, AND use of the

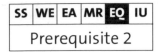

progressive sampling methodology defined in Chapter 7 (Home Energy Rating Systems (HERS) Required Verification And Diagnostic Testing) of the California Residential Alternative Calculation Method Approval Manual. Residential units must demonstrate less than 1.25 square inches leakage area per 100 square feet of enclosure area (i.e. sum of all wall, ceiling and floor areas).

Submittals – Initial Certification

- ❑ Provide a declaration signed by the building owner or responsible party, declaring that the building will be operated under a policy prohibiting smoking along with a statement describing the location of exterior smoking areas.

OR

- ❑ Provide a declaration signed by the facility manager or responsible party demonstrating that the criteria described in the credit requirements have been met and performance has been verified using the method described in the credit requirements.

Submittals – Recertification

- ❑ Provide a declaration, signed by the building owner or responsible party, declaring that the building will be operated under a policy prohibiting smoking along with a statement describing the location of exterior smoking areas.

OR

- ❑ Provide a declaration signed by the facility manager or responsible party demonstrating that the design criteria described in the credit requirements have been met and performance has been verified using the method described in the credit requirements.

Summary of Referenced Standards

Standard Test Method for Determining Air Leakage Rate by Fan Pressurization

ASTM Standard E 779-03

www.astm.org

(610) 832-9585

This test method covers a standardized technique for measuring air-leakage rates through a building envelope under controlled pressurization and de-pressurization, and is intended to produce a measure of air tightness of a building envelope.

California Residential Alternative Calculation Method Approval Manual

Topic Cited: Chapter 7 – Home Energy Rating Systems (HERS) Required Verification and Diagnostic Testing

California Energy Commission

www.energy.ca.gov/title24/residential acm

(916) 654-5106

This document establishes requirements for certifying the energy efficiency of residential buildings in accordance with the California Home Energy Rating System Program (California Code of Regulations, Title 20, Chapter 4, Article 8, Sections 1670-1675). Chapter 7 specifies procedures for sequentially designating sample residential units for verification.

Green Building Concerns

The relationship between smoking and various health risks, including lung disease, cancer, and heart disease, has been well documented. A strong link between Environmental Tobacco Smoke (ETS), or "secondhand smoke," and health risks has also been demonstrated. The most effective way to protect building occupants from the health problems associated with secondhand tobacco smoke is to prohibit smoking in all indoor areas. If this is not practical, designated indoor smoking areas should be isolated from nonsmoking areas and have separate ventilation systems to avoid the introduction of tobacco smoke contaminants into nonsmoking areas of the building.

Environmental Issues

Protecting indoor environments from contaminants such as ETS is essential for maintaining a healthy space for building occupants. ETS is a mixture of the smoke given off by the ignited end of tobacco products and the smoke exhaled by smokers. ETS contains thousands of chemicals, more than 50 of which are carcinogenic.[7] Exposure to ETS is linked to an increased risk of lung cancer and coronary heart disease in nonsmoking adults,[8] and is associated with increased risk for sudden infant death syndrome, asthma, bronchitis and pneumonia in children.[9]

Exposure to ETS is widespread, as an estimated 60 percent of people in the United States have biological evidence of exposure to ETS.[10] Building owners can prevent the damaging effects of ETS by eliminating or strictly controlling smoking in buildings.

Economic Issues

Providing separate smoking areas may incur costs to separate building spaces and alter mechanical ventilation systems, plus increased operating costs associated with the greater ventilation required for smoking areas.

Smoking within a building reduces indoor air quality and instigates occupant reactions ranging from irritation to illness to decreased productivity. These problems increase expenses and liability for building owners, operators and insurance companies.

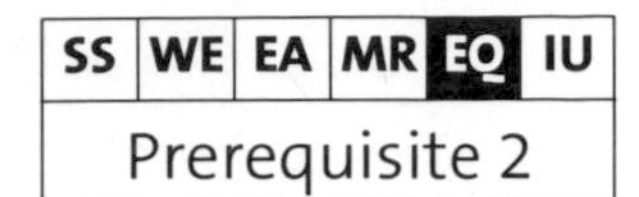

A nonsmoking policy avoids these problems and eliminates the need for a separate ventilation system for isolated smoking areas, thus incurring no costs. Prohibition of indoor smoking can also increase the useful life of interior fixtures and furnishings, resulting in reduced need for interior maintenance and cleaning.

Strategies & Technologies

Prohibition of smoking within the building is the simplest strategy to earn this prerequisite. Provide designated smoking areas outside the building in locations where ETS cannot enter the building or ventilation system, and away from concentrations of building occupants or pedestrian traffic.

For buildings where it is not feasible to prohibit smoking, design designated smoking areas in a manner that isolates and controls ETS from entering other areas of the building. A separate ventilation system must be installed and tested to ensure that the smoking areas are isolated from nonsmoking portions of the building, and a negative pressure must be maintained in these areas when compared with surrounding spaces. Verify the effectiveness of ETS control measures in the designated areas by following the testing procedures outlined in the credit requirements.

For residential buildings, a third option is to provide very tight construction to minimize ETS transfer among dwelling units and into common areas. Seal the penetrations in walls, ceilings and floors in each residential unit, and seal vertical chases adjacent to units. Equip all doors leading from units to common areas with weather stripping to minimize air leakage into hallways. Additionally, prohibit smoking in building common areas and locate any exterior designated smoking areas away from building entries, outdoor air intakes and operable windows.

Post information about smoking policies covering areas in and around the building.

Synergies & Tradeoffs

The use of separate ventilation systems to physically separate smoking areas from the rest of the building requires additional energy and requires commissioning and measurement & verification attention. On the other hand, smoking activities, both indoor and outdoor, affect the IAQ performance of the building. Smoke can enter the building areas through operable windows and intake vents or, for indoor smokers, through the ventilation system. It may be advantageous to address smoking-related contaminants in the building in conjunction with other sources of air pollutants.

Calculations & Documentation

Calculations

None.

Documentation

- ❑ Provide a declaration that the building will be operated under a policy prohibiting smoking.
  - Declaration should be a signed document appearing on company letterhead.

Other Resources

The Chemistry of Environmental Tobacco Smoke: Composition and Measurement, Second Edition by R.A. Jenkins, B.A. Tomkins and others, CRC Press & Lewis Publishers, 2000.

Fact Sheet: Respiratory Health Effects of Passive Smoking

www.epa.gov/smokefree/pubs/etsfs.html

This publication from the U.S. EPA is an assessment of the respiratory risks associated with secondhand smoke.

Setting the Record Straight: Secondhand Smoke is A Preventable Health Risk

www.epa.gov/iaq/ets/pubs/strsfs.html

An EPA document with a discussion of laboratory research on ETS and federal legislation aimed at curbing ETS problems.

The Smoke-Free Guide: How to Eliminate Tobacco Smoke from Your Environment by Arlene Galloway, Gordon Soules Book Publishers, 1988.

Definitions

Environmental Tobacco Smoke (ETS) or **Secondhand Smoke** consists of airborne particles emitted from the burning end of cigarettes, pipes, and cigars, and exhaled by smokers. These particles contain roughly 4,000 different compounds, up to 50 of which are known carcinogens.

Case Study

JohnsonDiversey Headquarters
Sturtevant, Wisconsin

LEED-EB Gold
Owner: JohnsonDiversey, Inc.

Photo courtesy of: JohnsonDiversey

JohnsonDiversey's facility includes one 12' x 12' designated smoking room for employees and guests. The smoking room has exhaust ventilation dedicated to serving only the smoking room and labs. The system is supplied with 100% outside air, and there is no recirculation. To ensure proper ventilation rates within the smoking area, JohnsonDiversey identified consultants who could reliably test the level of air change in the room. They found there is a minimum of 1600 cubic feet per minute of exhaust from the smoking room, resulting in 48 air changes per hour.

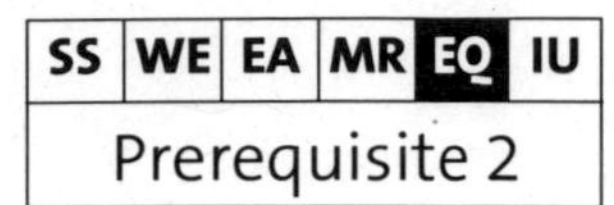

SS | WE | EA | MR | EQ | IU

Prerequisite 3

1 point

Asbestos Removal or Encapsulation

Intent

Reduce the potential exposure of building occupants to asbestos and prevent associated harmful effects of asbestos in existing buildings.

Requirements

- ❑ Have in place an asbestos management program.
- ❑ Identify the applicable regulatory requirements.
- ❑ Have survey records that identify where asbestos is located in the building and on the site so that the asbestos present can be addressed appropriately in the ongoing asbestos management program. If the existing survey records do not cover all areas of the building , conduct a survey to identify where asbestos-containing materials are present in the remaining areas of the building..

Submittals – Initial Certification

- ❑ Provide a letter from the facility manager, an accredited asbestos program manager or asbestos inspector stating that asbestos-containing materials are not present in the building, on the building exterior or on the site.

OR

- ❑ Provide a description of the current asbestos management program that identifies the applicable regulatory requirements and explains how the program is addressing asbestos remaining in the building on an ongoing basis.
- ❑ Review the past asbestos work done on the building and on the building site and use this data to prepare the history-based component of the asbestos survey for the building and the site by collecting the available information on: (1) where asbestos has been removed, (2) where asbestos remains and (3) how the remaining asbestos is being addressed.
- ❑ Update the asbestos survey for the building and the site with current information by: (1) sampling additional likely locations in the building and on the site for asbestos and (2) testing samples to see if asbestos is present.
- ❑ If the survey identifies any new locations with asbestos, add these to the description of how the asbestos management program is addressing asbestos remaining in the building on an ongoing basis.

Submittals – Recertification

Provide a description of the asbestos work done since the previous application for certification and provide any updates needed to the information submitted for the previous application for certification.

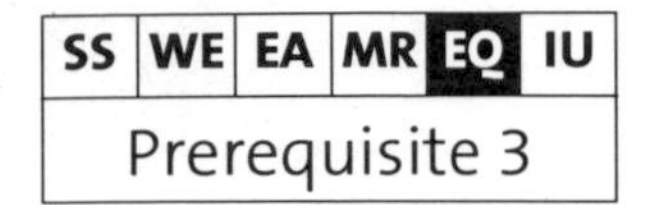

Summary of Referenced Standards

There is no standard referenced for this prerequisite.

Green Building Concerns

Asbestos in buildings has the potential to cause severe health effects. Individuals exposed to airborne asbestos can be at greater risk for developing two principal types of cancer: cancer of the lung and mesothelioma, a cancer of the thin membrane that surrounds the lung and other internal organs. These diseases do not develop immediately following exposure to asbestos, but appear only after a number of years. Asbestos-containing materials are often difficult to identify in older buildings, and may have degraded over time to a point of friability. Friability may result in a greater potential for the release of fibers into the air. Disturbance of asbestos-containing materials by maintenance workers can also result in the release of asbestos fibers, with subsequent exposure of the workers as well as other persons in the building and surrounding area.

Environmental Issues

The nature of asbestos and historical use patterns make asbestos important for building owners and operators to address as an indoor environmental pollutant. Asbestos represents a significant health hazard for workers who come in contact with it (See EPA Integrated Risk Information System www.epa.gov/iris/subst/index.html for more information). Additionally, building occupants may be exposed to airborne asbestos fibers due to the deterioration or damage of asbestos-containing building materials. Families are also at risk if workers bring home asbestos particles on clothing, hair, skin and equipment. The hazardous nature of this material requires regulated and careful disposal of asbestos-containing materials.

The following information is based on the U.S. EPA document "Asbestos: What Is It?" (www.epa.gov/asbestos/asbe.pdf):

Asbestos is a number of naturally occurring fibrous silicate minerals that have been mined for their useful properties such as thermal insulation, chemical and thermal stability, and high tensile strength. Asbestos deposits can be found throughout the world and are still mined in Australia, Canada, South Africa, and the former Soviet Union. The three most common types of asbestos are a) chrysotile, b) amosite, and c) crocidolite. Asbestos can only be identified under a microscope. Asbestos differs from other minerals in its crystal development. The crystal formation of asbestos is in the form of long thin fibers. Chrysotile makes up approximately 90 to 95 percent of all asbestos contained in buildings in the United States.

Asbestos is made up of microscopic bundles of fibers that may become airborne when distributed. These fibers are carried by the air and may become inhaled into the lungs, where they may cause significant health problems. Researchers still have not determined a "safe level" of exposure but we know the greater and the longer the exposure, the greater the risk of contracting an asbestos related disease. Some of these health problems include:

a) **Asbestosis** - a lung disease first found in naval shipyard workers. As asbestos fibers are inhaled they may become trapped in the lung tissue. The body tries to dissolve the fibers by producing an acid. This acid, due to the chemical resistance of the fiber, does little to damage the fiber, but may scar the surrounding tissue. Eventually, this scarring may become so severe that the lungs cannot function. The latency period (meaning the time it takes for the disease to become developed) is often 25 to 40 years.

b) **Mesothelioma** - a cancer of the pleura (the outer lining of the lung and chest cavity) and/or the peritoneum (the lining of the abdominal wall). This form of cancer is peculiar because the only known cause is from asbestos exposure. The latency period for mesothelioma is often 15 to 30 years.

c) **Lung Cancer** - caused by asbestos. The effects of lung cancer are often greatly increased by cigarette smoking (by about 50 percent).

Cancer of the gastrointestinal tract can also be caused by asbestos. The latency period for this cancer is often 15 to 30 years. Despite the common misconception, asbestos does not cause headaches, sore muscles or other immediate symptoms. As mentioned above, the effects often go unnoticed for 15 to 40 years.

Asbestos is not always an immediate hazard. In fact, if asbestos can be maintained in good condition so that it does not get into the air, the U.S. EPA recommends that it be left alone and periodic surveillance performed to monitor its condition. It is only when asbestos containing materials (ACMs) are disturbed or the materials become damaged that it becomes a hazard. When the materials become damaged, the fibers separate and may then become airborne. In the asbestos industry, the term '**friable**' is used to describe asbestos that can be reduced to dust by hand pressure. '**Non-friable**' means asbestos that is too hard to be reduced to dust by hand. Non-friable materials, such as transite siding and floor tiles are not regulated provided they do not become friable. Machine grinding, sanding and dry-buffing are ways of causing non-friable materials to become friable.

Economic Issues

Identification and removal of asbestos-containing materials can be an expensive and extensive process. For asbestos-containing materials that are intact, management of the asbestos in place may be a preferable alternative to removal. Building owners should be aware of liability issues surrounding the presence of asbestos, the identification, removal and encapsulation of it, and the effect on the sale/transfer of a property that contains asbestos.

Strategies & Technologies

Prepare a description of the current asbestos management program that identifies the applicable regulatory requirements and explains how the program addresses asbestos remaining in the building on an ongoing basis.

Review asbestos work done in the building and on the building site. Use this information to prepare the history-based component of the asbestos survey, collecting the available information describing: (1) where asbestos has been removed, (2) where asbestos remains, and (3) how the remaining asbestos is being addressed.

Update this survey with current information by having an appropriately accredited professional conduct any necessary follow-up surveys. The surveys may include: (1) sampling additional likely locations in the building and on the site for asbestos, and (2) testing samples to see if asbestos is present. If the surveys identify any new locations with asbestos, add these to the asbestos management program that addresses ongoing management of asbestos remaining in the building.

Synergies & Tradeoffs

A careful and thorough assessment of asbestos-containing materials in the building provides valuable information on health hazards as well as future liability. Removal of asbestos-containing material represents an opportunity to eliminate liability. For asbestos-containing materials that are intact, management in place may be a preferable alternative to removal.

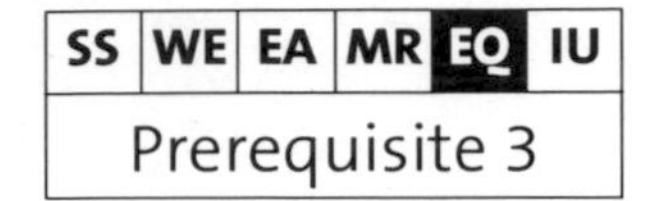

Calculations & Documentation

Calculations

None.

Documentation

- ❑ Letter from an accredited asbestos inspector stating that asbestos is not present:
  - Signatory should be an accredited inspector (Certified Industrial Hygienist or similar accreditation representing expertise in asbestos inspection/identification). Signatory may be a third party or internal company employee. The letter should appear on official letterhead.
  - If asbestos is present in the building, on the building exterior, or on the site, follow submittal requirements pertaining to the asbestos management program and asbestos survey.

Other Resources

ABIH®

(517) 321-2638

www.abih.org

The American Board of Industrial Hygiene (ABIH) is a nonprofit organization dedicated to improving the practices and educational standards of the profession of industrial hygiene. ABIH administers certification programs for industry professionals, including the Certified Industrial Hygienist (CIH®), Certified Associate Industrial Hygienist (CAIH®), and Industrial Hygienist-in-Training (IHIT®) programs. The ABIH web site includes a searchable database of certified professionals.

Asbestos and Vermiculite

(202) 566-0500

www.epa.gov/asbestos/

This U.S. EPA web site provides general information, links, summaries of laws and other asbestos-related resources.

Asbestos: Laws and Regulations

(202) 566-0500

www.epa.gov/asbestos/asbreg.html

This U.S. EPA resource provides an overview of and links to laws governing the use and handling of asbestos.

EPA-Approved State Accreditation Programs

http://www.epa.gov/asbestos/epaaprv.pdf

This resource provides information for those seeking certified professionals for asbestos assessment and management.

OSHA Safety and Health Topics: Asbestos

www.osha.gov/SLTC/asbestos/index.html

The asbestos section of the OSHA web site provides extensive links and resources on asbestos. Asbestos information specific to construction industry can be found at www.osha.gov/SLTC/constructionasbestos/index.html.

Source of Indoor Air Pollution – Asbestos

www.epa.gov/iaq/asbestos.html

This U.S. EPA web site provides information about asbestos as an indoor air pollutant.

Definitions

Friable is the term used in the asbestos industry to describe asbestos that can be reduced to dust by hand pressure.

Non-friable is the term used in the asbestos industry to describe asbestos too hard to be reduced to dust by hand.

Common Acronyms
ACM Asbestos Containing Materials
AHERA Asbestos Hazard Emergency Response Act
ASHARA Asbestos School Hazard Abatement Reauthorization Act
CAA Clean Air Act
CFR Code of Federal Regulations
FR Federal Register
NESHAPs National Emission Standards for Hazardous Air Pollutants
NDAAC National Directory of AHERA Accredited Courses
PLM Polarized Light Microscopy
TEM Transmission Electron Microscopy
TSCA Toxic Substance Control Act

Case Study

National Geographic Society Headquarters

Washington, D.C.

LEED-EB Silver

Owner: National Geographic Society

Photo courtesy of: NGS Staff

The National Geographic Society (NGS) Headquarters complex is comprised of four interconnected buildings ranging in age from 20 to 100 years. Asbestos-containing materials used in the original construction of the NGS Headquarters buildings have been systematically identified, and removed or encapsulated in accordance with OSHA and EPA regulations. The NGS engineering staff maintains detailed records of asbestos-containing materials testing, encapsulation, abatement and related work organized on a room-by-room basis. Each time an upgrade project is undertaken in the building, any known asbestos-containing materials related to the project are appropriately addressed. For example, pipe insulation in a boiler room was removed in accordance with OSHA and EPA regulations as part of a recent boiler plant upgrade.

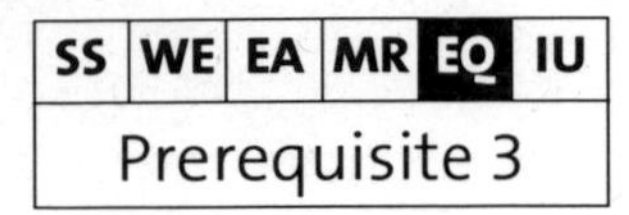

SS | WE | EA | MR | EQ | IU

Prerequisite 4

Required

Polychlorinated Biphenyl (PCB) Removal

Intent

Reduce the potential exposure of building occupants to PCBs and PCB combustion byproducts in case of fire in the building.

Requirements

- ❑ Have in place a PCB management program.
- ❑ Identify the applicable regulatory requirements.
- ❑ Have a current survey that identifies where PCBs are located in the building and on the site so that the PCBs present can be addressed appropriately in the ongoing PCB management program.

Submittals – Initial Certification

- ❑ Provide a letter from the facility manager or a qualified PCB management professional stating that PCB-containing materials are not present in the building or on the site.

OR

- ❑ Provide a description of the current PCB management program that identifies the applicable regulatory requirements and explains how the program is addressing PCBs remaining in the building on an ongoing basis.
- ❑ Review the past PCB work done on the building and on the building site and use this data to prepare the history-based component of the PCB survey for the building and the site collecting the available information on: (1) where PCBs have been removed, (2) where PCBs remain and (3) how the remaining PCBs are being addressed.
- ❑ Update the PCB survey for the building and the site with current information by: (1) sampling additional likely locations in building and on the site for PCBs and (2) testing samples to see if PCBs are present.
- ❑ If the survey identifies any new locations with PCBs, add these to the description of how the PCB management program is addressing PCBs remaining in the building on an ongoing basis.

Submittals – Recertification

- ❑ Provide a description of the PCB work done since the previous application for certification and provide any updates needed to the information submitted for the previous application for certification.

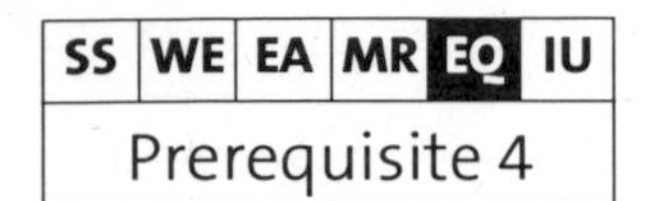

Summary of Referenced Standard

There is no standard referenced for this prerequisite.

Green Building Concerns

Due to their non-flammability, chemical stability, high boiling point and electrical insulating properties, PCBs have been used in hundreds of industrial and commercial applications. These include electrical, heat transfer, and hydraulic equipment; as plasticizers in paints, plastics and rubber products; in pigments, dyes and carbonless copy paper and many other applications.[11]

PCB-containing equipment in buildings poses a potential environmental risk from leakage due to deterioration or damage of the equipment. Such leakage also poses a risk to any workers or building occupants who have contact with the material. In case of fire, PCB-containing equipment poses a risk of exposure to hazardous combustion by-products.

Environmental Issues

PCBs have been demonstrated to cause a variety of adverse health effects and have been shown to cause cancer in animals. PCBs have also been shown to cause a number of serious non-cancer health effects in animals, including effects on the immune, reproductive, nervous and endocrine systems. Studies in humans provide supportive evidence for potential carcinogenic and non-carcinogenic effects of PCBs. The different health effects of PCBs may be interrelated, as alterations in one system may have significant implications for the other systems of the body.[12]

Economic Issues

Ensuring that existing regulatory requirements on PCB management are being followed reduces exposure to liability for building owners. The cost of contamination remediation following a spill or fire involving PCBs can be significant, due to both the closing of the building and removal of contaminants.

Alternative products free of PCBs are available. Alternative products cost the same as PCB products, or may carry a small additional cost. This small premium is expected to decline over time.

Strategies & Technologies

Survey the building to identify any remaining PCBs. Document that any PCBs identified in the building or on the site have been removed and disposed of appropriately or are being managed properly under the PCB management program. Review the current PCB management program, and prepare a description of it that identifies the applicable regulatory requirements and explains how the program will address PCBs remaining in the building and onsite on an ongoing basis.

Review PCB work done in the building and on the building site, and use this data to prepare the history-based component of the PCB survey by collecting the available information on: (1) where PCBs have been removed, (2) where PCBs remain and (3) how the remaining PCBs are being addressed.

PCBs have been included in commercial products sold under many names. Some of these names are listed below:

> Adkarel; Capacitor 21; EEC-18; Phenoclor; ALC; Chlorexto ; Eucarel; Pydraul; Apirolio; Chlorinol; Inclor; Pyralene; Arochlor B; Chlorphen; Kennechlor; Pyranol; Aroclor; Clophen; Magvar; Pyroclor; Asbestol; Diaclor; MCS 1489; Saf-T-Kuhl; ASK; DK; Nepolin; Santotherm; Askarel; Dykanol; No-Flamol; Santovac 1 and 2

Update the PCB survey with current information by: (1) sampling additional likely locations in building and on the site for PCBs, and (2) testing samples to see if PCBs are present. If the survey identifies any new locations with PCBs, add these to the description of how the PCB management program is addressing PCBs remaining in the building and onsite on an ongoing basis.

Synergies & Tradeoffs

For some existing buildings, it may be difficult to completely eliminate PCBs. In these instances, have an effective PCB management program. PCB content should be considered during the purchase and disposal of materials.

Fluorescent lighting systems in older buildings, though they encourage energy efficiency, may include PCBs in ballasts manufactured before July 1979. Evaluate older lighting systems that contain PCBs for facility contamination and liability potential, as well as the energy conservation potential that a lighting retrofit would provide. Ballasts containing PCBs should not be landfilled due to their status as hazardous waste as defined by EPA Regulation 40 CFR 761. Ballasts manufactured without PCBs are labeled "No PCBs."

Calculations & Documentation

Calculations

None.

Documentation

- ❑ Letter stating that PCB-containing materials are not present in the building or on the site.
  - The letter should appear on company letterhead and be signed by the facility manager or a qualified PCB management professional
  - If PCBs are present in the building, follow submittal requirements pertaining to a PCB management program and survey.

Other Resources

EPA Laws & Regulations: PCBs Manufacturing, Processing, Distribution in Commerce and Use Prohibitions (2003 40 CFR 761)

http://www.epa.gov/opptintr/pcb/2003pt761.pdf

This document established prohibitions and requirements for the manufacture, processing, distribution in commerce, use, disposal, storage and marking of PCBs and PCB items.

EPA PCB Home Page

www.epa.gov/opptintr/pcb/

This resource from the U.S. EPA provides general information about PCBs, information about health effects, laws and regulations, and more.

EPA PCB Identifier

www.epa.gov/toxteam/pcbid/

This reference document from the U.S. EPA provides the relevant names and numbers needed to correctly specify PCB species.

Definitions

Polychlorinated Biphenyls (PCBs) are mixtures of synthetic organic chemicals with the same basic chemical structure and similar physical properties ranging from oily liquids to waxy solids. More than 1.5 billion pounds of PCBs were manufactured in the United States prior to cessation of production in 1977. Concern over the toxicity and persistence in the environment of PCBs led Congress in 1976 to enact §6(e) of the Toxic Substances Control Act (TSCA) that included among other things, prohibitions on the manufacture, processing, and distribution in commerce of PCBs. TSCA legislated true "cradle to grave" (i.e., from manu-

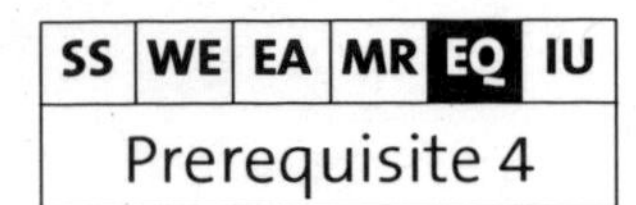

facture to disposal) management of PCBs in the United States. (This definition is from the U.S. EPA PCB web site, www.epa.gov/opptintr/pcb/).

SS | WE | EA | MR | EQ | IU

Credit 1

1 point

Outdoor Air Delivery Monitoring

Intent

Provide capacity for ventilation system monitoring to help sustain long-term occupant comfort and well- being.

Requirements

Install permanent monitoring systems that provide feedback on ventilation system performance to ensure that ventilation systems maintain minimum ventilation rates.

Option A

For mechanical ventilation systems that predominantly serve densely occupied spaces (spaces with a design occupant density greater than or equal to 25 people per 1,000 square feet (40 square feet per person)), do the following:

- ❑ Provide a CO_2 sensor or sampling location for each densely occupied space, and compare with outdoor ambient CO_2 concentrations.
- ❑ Test and calibrate CO_2 sensors to have an accuracy of no less than 75 ppm or 5% of the reading; whichever is greater. Sensors must be tested and calibrated at least once every five years or per manufacturers' recommendation.
- ❑ Monitor CO_2 sensors by a system capable of and configured to trend CO_2 concentrations on no more than 30 minute intervals.
- ❑ Configure system capability to generate an alarm visible to a system operator and, if desired, to building occupants if the CO_2 concentration in any zone rises more than 15% above that corresponding to the minimum outdoor air rate required by ASHRAE Standard 62 (see IEQ Prerequisite 1).
- ❑ CO_2 sensors may be used for demand-controlled ventilation provided the control strategy complies with ASHRAE Standard 62 (see IEQ Prerequisite 1), including maintaining the area-based component of the design ventilation rate.

Option B

For all other mechanical ventilation systems:

- ❑ An outdoor airflow measurement device must be provided that is capable of measuring (and, if necessary, controlling) the minimum outdoor airflow rate at all expected system operating conditions within 15% of the design minimum outdoor air rate.
- ❑ The outdoor airflow measurement device shall be monitored by a control system capable of and configured to trend outdoor airflow on no more that 15-minute intervals for a period of no less than six months.
- ❑ The control system shall be capable and configured to generate an alarm visible to the system operator if the minimum outdoor air rate falls more than 15% below the design minimum rate.

Option C

For natural ventilation systems, provide the following:

- ❑ CO_2 sensors located in the breathing zone of every densely populated room.
- ❑ CO_2 sensors located in the breathing zone of every natural ventilation zone.
- ❑ CO_2 sensor(s) located outdoors.
- ❑ CO_2 sensors shall provide an audible or visual alarm to the occupants in the space and building management if CO_2 conditions are greater than 530 parts per million above outdoor CO_2 levels or 1,000 parts per million absolute. The alarm signal should indicate that ventilation adjustments (i.e. opening windows) are required in the affected space.
- ❑ Operable windows areas must meet the requirements of ASHRAE 62.1-2004, section 5.1.

Submittals – Initial Certification

- ❑ Provide documentation that the requirements for this credit have been met.

Submittals – Recertification

- ❑ If building systems and building operating practices have not changed since the previous LEED-EB certification filing, provide a statement to this effect.

OR

- ❑ If building systems or building operating practices have changed since the previous LEED-EB certification filing, provide documentation that the requirements for this credit have been met.

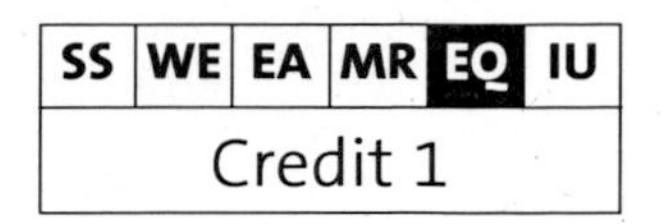

Summary of Referenced Standard

ASHRAE Standard 62.1-2004: Ventilation for Acceptable Indoor Air Quality

ASHRAE

www.ashrae.org

(800) 527-4723

This standard addresses indoor air quality issues and prescribes minimum ventilation rates to reduce the potential for adverse health effects. The standard specifies the design of mechanical or natural ventilation systems to prevent uptake of contaminants, minimize the opportunity for growth and dissemination of microorganisms, and if necessary, filter particulates. The standard also specifies proper makeup air inlet and exhaust air outlet locations relative to potential sources of contamination.

A Ventilation Rate Procedure and an Indoor Air Quality Procedure offer alternative approaches to achieve compliance with the standard. The Ventilation Rate Procedure has recently been revised. The updated version redefines an occupied zone as a breathing zone and prescribes ventilation rates in both per-person and per-unit area values. The Indoor Air Quality Procedure requires establishment of both quantitative and subjective criteria for acceptable air quality and ventilation and/or air-cleaning as appropriate to achieve the established levels.

Green Building Concerns

Buildings are supplied with outdoor air to flush airborne contaminants and to replenish fresh air on a regular basis. Measuring carbon dioxide (CO_2) concentrations to determine and maintain adequate outdoor air ventilation rates in buildings is one recommended method for achieving better indoor air quality. High CO_2 levels are generally an indication of low ventilation rates, and, by implication, poor dilution of occupant-related contaminants. Maintaining low CO_2 concentrations relative to those found outdoors is a strategy to optimize indoor air quality.

Environmental Issues

Measuring CO_2 concentrations in buildings may indicate that ventilation rates should be adjusted. Increasing ventilation rates may require additional energy inputs, which in turn causes additional air and water pollution. Conversely, CO_2 monitoring can reduce unnecessary over-ventilation, thereby saving energy.

CO_2 concentrations are an indicator of ventilation effectiveness, with elevated levels suggesting inadequate ventilation and possible build-up of indoor air pollutants. While relatively high concentrations of CO_2 alone are not known to cause serious health problems, they can lead to drowsiness and lethargy in building occupants. The implications of these indoor environmental pollutants include decreased occupant health, comfort and productivity.

Economic Issues

A permanent air monitoring system enables building owners, maintenance personnel and occupants to detect air quality problems quickly so that corrective actions can be implemented. Potential impacts of air quality problems range from reduced work productivity to temporary or permanent health issues of building occupants.

CO_2 monitoring systems incur equipment and installation costs. For each sampling point, initial costs typically range from $1,250 to $2,000.[13] Additional costs include annual calibration and maintenance expenditures.

Other savings can offset the initial cost of a monitoring system. Often, the lifetime of the HVAC system is extended and more efficient HVAC operation is achieved as a result of effective air quality monitoring. CO_2 monitoring can better control the amount of makeup air provided to ensure it accurately reflects building occupancy, thereby potentially reducing building energy use. Reduced absenteeism and increased occupant productivity resulting from improved indoor air quality can increase profitability.

Strategies & Technologies

Based on the ventilation systems serving the building (mechanical systems serving densely occupied spaces, other mechanical ventilation systems, or natural ventilation systems), develop an outdoor air delivery monitoring system that meets the credit requirements. Install/maintain permanent monitoring systems that provide feedback on ventilation system performance to ensure that those ventilation systems maintain minimum ventilation rates over time.

Install/maintain an independent system or make CO_2 monitoring a function of the building automation system. Such a system can control ventilation rates based on monitored CO_2 concentrations. Current systems include shared-sensor vacuum-draw systems and distributed sensors. Distributed sensors are either hard-wired or plugged into power circuitry and use carrier wave communication.

Situate monitoring locations in areas of the building with high occupant densities and at the ends of the longest runs of the distribution ductwork. Specify that system operation manuals require calibration of all of the sensors per manufacturer recommendations or at least once every five years. Include sensor and system operational testing and initial setpoint adjustment in the commissioning plan and report that was developed for EA Prerequisite 1: Existing Building Commissioning.

Monitoring of ventilation performance in occupied spaces is preferable to monitoring at the air handler because it accounts for the role of the distribution system in the quality of delivered air. Similarly, monitoring the amount of outdoor air received by the air handler fails to provide an assessment of the actual distribution of outside air to building occupants.

Synergies & Tradeoffs

CO_2 monitoring requires installation of additional equipment, additional commissioning, and measurement & verification attention. Constraints of systems in existing buildings may limit the optimization of ventilation rates due to inflexible HVAC equipment or inadequate outside air intakes. Use of CO_2 monitoring in control systems may allow constrained ventilation systems to get more makeup air to where it is needed most in the building.

Controlling system performance based on the results from monitoring of CO_2 levels has significant impacts on all indoor environmental quality issues, including overall IAQ performance, ventilation rates, chemical and pollutant control, thermal comfort and energy efficiency. Proper ventilation rates are integral to a successful air quality program and CO_2 monitoring can be used to deliver appropriate ventilation rates.

Calculations & Documentation

Calculations

Densely Occupied Spaces are those that have an occupant density greater than or equal to 25 people per 1,000 square feet of space. To calculate occupant density:

Occupant Density [people / 1,000 SF] = Number of People × 1,000 / Area of occupied space [SF]

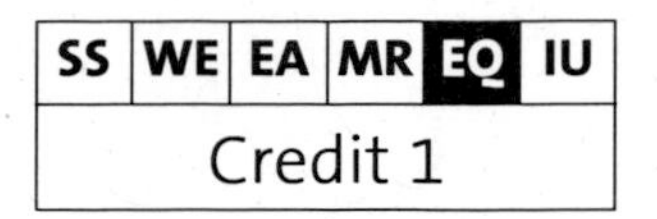

Documentation

- ❑ Provide documentation that the requirements for this credit have been met.
  - Documentation should include building floor plans noting locations of densely occupied spaces, CO_2 sensors, and outdoor airflow measurement devices.
  - Documentation of sensor and/or measurement device performance characteristics should consist of manufacturer specifications or similar literature.

Other Resources

ASHRAE

(800) 527-4723

www.ashrae.org

The ASHRAE web site provides information about the organization, industry updates and ASHRAE standards. ASHRAE standards relevant to this credit include **ASHRAE Standard 55-2004**: Thermal Comfort Conditions for Human Occupancy, and **ASHRAE Standard 62-2004**: Ventilation for Acceptable Indoor Air Quality.

Building Air Quality: A Guide for Building Owners and Facility Managers

www.epa.gov/iaq/largebldgs/baq_page.htm

A U.S. EPA publication on IEQ sources in buildings and methods to prevent and resolve IEQ problems.

Efficient Building Design Series, Volume 2: Heating, Ventilating, and Air Conditioning by J. Trost and Frederick Trost, Prentice Hall, 1998.

This book concisely details basic HVAC concepts, equipment choices, and efficiency opportunities.

IAQ Building Education and Assessment Model (I-BEAM)

www.epa.gov/iaq/largebldgs/ibeam_page.htm

This resource from the U.S. EPA IAQ contains comprehensive IAQ guidelines including checklists, forms and specific measures for improving IAQ.

Standard Guide for Using Indoor Carbon Dioxide Concentration to Evaluation Indoor Air Quality and Ventilation, ASTM Standard D 6245-98, 2002.

www.astm.org

This standard from ASTM describes how measured values of indoor CO_2 concentrations can be used to evaluate indoor air quality and building ventilation.

Definitions

Carbon Dioxide (CO_2) Monitoring is an indicator of ventilation effectiveness inside buildings. CO_2 concentrations greater than 530 ppm above outdoor CO_2 conditions are generally considered an indicator of inadequate ventilation. Absolute concentrations of CO_2 greater than 800 to 1000 ppm are generally considered an indicator of poor breathing air quality.

Return Air is air removed from conditioned spaces that is either re-circulated in the building or exhausted to the outside.

Supply Air is air delivered to conditioned spaces for use in ventilating, heating, cooling, humidifying and dehumidifying those spaces.

System Operator is a facility management staff person who is responsible for the operation of the building and for receiving and responding to HVAC system out of range performance alarms.

Case Study

Janssen Pharmaceutica Headquarters

Titusville, New Jersey

LEED-EB Silver

Owner: Janssen Pharmaceutica Inc.

Janssen Pharmaceutica installed a total of 20 CO_2 sensors in return ducts of the air handling units as part of its LEED-EB certification program. In addition, a CO_2 sensor was mounted to detect CO_2 levels of outside air. The sensors were integrated with the building automation system, and programmed to signal building operators when CO_2 levels inside rise more than 530 ppm when compared to outdoor levels. When this occurs, system operators can adjust outdoor air dampers to reduce CO_2 concentration to appropriate levels. Although the outside air introduction system itself was designed to provide adequate fresh air for building occupants, measuring CO_2 concentration levels helps guarantee adequate ventilation rates. The system also allows facility operators to identify any areas with air quality issues and to measure the effectiveness of corrective actions. Although the CO_2 sensors may at times increase loads on the HVAC system, Janssen believes that increases in employee productivity and reduction in employee sick time will offset any additional costs to operate the HVAC systems.

SS	WE	EA	MR	EQ	IU
Credit 2					

1 point

Increased Ventilation

Intent

Provide additional outdoor air ventilation to improve indoor air quality for improved occupant comfort, well- being and productivity.

Requirements

Option A

For Mechanically Ventilated Spaces:

- ❑ Increase outdoor air ventilation rates to all occupied spaces by at least 30% above the minimum required by ASHRAE 62.1-2004.

Option B

For Naturally Ventilated Spaces:

- ❑ Design natural ventilation systems for occupied spaces to meet the recommendations set forth in the "Good Practice Guide 237: Natural ventilation in non-domestic buildings" (1998). Determine that natural ventilation is an effective strategy for the project by following the flow diagram process shown in Figure 2.8 of the CIBSE Applications Manual 10: 2005, "Natural ventilation in non-domestic buildings."

AND EITHER

- ❑ Use diagrams and calculations to show that the design of the natural ventilation systems meets the recommendations set forth in the CIBSE Applications Manual 10: 2005, "Natural ventilation in non-domestic buildings."

OR

- ❑ Use a macroscopic, multi-zone, analytic model to predict that room-by-room airflows will effectively naturally ventilate at least 90% of occupied spaces.

Submittals – Initial Certification

Option A

For mechanical ventilation systems:

- ❑ Provide measurements demonstrating that actual ventilation rates exceed the minimum rates required by ASHRAE 62.1-2004 by at least 30%.

Option B

For natural ventilation systems:

- ❑ Provide documentation that natural ventilation is an effective strategy for the project and follows the design recommendations established by CIBSE.

AND EITHER

- ❑ Provide diagrams and calculations based on CIBSE Applications Manual 10.

OR

- ❑ Provide diagrams and calculations based on results provided by a multi-zone analytical model.

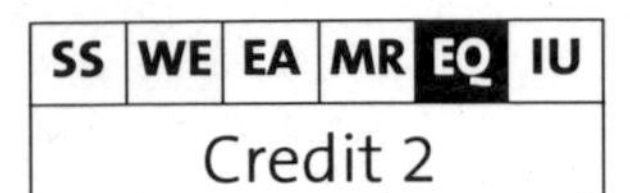

Submittals – Recertification

- ❑ If there has been no change since the previous filing, provide a statement to this effect.

OR

- ❑ If these have been changes since the previous filing, provide the same information as is required for initial filings.

Summary of Referenced Standard

ASHRAE Standard 62.1-2004: Ventilation for Acceptable Indoor Air Quality

ASHRAE

(800) 527-4723

www.ashrae.org

This standard addresses indoor air quality issues and prescribes minimum ventilation rates to reduce the potential for adverse health effects. The standard specifies the design of mechanical or natural ventilation systems to prevent uptake of contaminants, minimize the opportunity for growth and dissemination of microorganisms, and if necessary, filter particulates. The standard also specifies proper makeup air inlet and exhaust air outlet locations relative to potential sources of contamination.

A Ventilation Rate Procedure and an Indoor Air Quality Procedure offer alternative approaches to achieve compliance with the standard. The Ventilation Rate Procedure has recently been revised. The updated version redefines an occupied zone as a breathing zone and prescribes ventilation rates in both per-person and per-unit area values. The Indoor Air Quality Procedure requires establishment of both quantitative and subjective criteria for acceptable air quality and ventilation and/or air-cleaning as appropriate to achieve the established levels.

CIBSE Applications Manual 10: Natural Ventilation in Non-Domestic Buildings (2005)

Chartered Institution of Building Services Engineers (CIBSE)

+44 (0)20 8675 5211

www.cibse.org

CIBSE Applications Manual 10 provides guidance for implementing natural ventilation in non-residential buildings. It provides detailed information on how to implement a decision to adopt natural ventilation as the sole servicing strategy for a building or as an element in a mixed-mode design.

Good Practice Guide 237: Natural Ventilation in Non-Domestic Buildings [1998]

UK DETR Energy Efficiency Best Practice Programme

This document uses case studies to illustrate the benefits of and strategies for incorporating natural ventilation in commercial buildings. To obtain a copy of GPG 237, search for "GPG 237" on the Carbon Trust – Energy web site (www.thecarbontrust.co.uk/energy), or go to http://www.thecarbontrust.co.uk/energy/pages/publication_view.asp?PubID=4603#.

Green Building Concerns

Providing ventilation above the minimum rates required by ASHRAE Standard 62.1-2004 improves the air quality of a building's occupied spaces. Under-ventilation of buildings has negative impacts on occupant well-being and productivity. On the other hand, over-ventilation consumes significant amounts of energy.

Environmental Issues

Increased ventilation in buildings may require additional energy use and this may in turn create air and water pollution. However, improved IAQ benefits building occupants by providing a healthy indoor environment. Improving existing ventilation system design to take maximum advantage of regional climate characteristics can help reduce energy costs and increase ventilation options.

Economic Issues

Adequate ventilation may result in higher worker productivity, potentially leading to increased profitability for a company. However, increased ventilation requires increased costs for greater energy use to increase HVAC operation. HVAC systems should be operated in a manner that provides adequate ventilation effectiveness while avoiding over-ventilation of building spaces.

Improving existing ventilation system design to take maximum advantage of regional climate characteristics can help reduce energy costs and increase ventilation options. In regions with significant heating and/or cooling loads, using exhaust air to heat or cool the incoming air can significantly reduce energy usage and operating costs.

Natural ventilation strategies are typically less expensive to construct and operate than mechanical ventilation strategies, though they may be difficult to implement in large buildings and in existing buildings not originally designed for natural ventilation.

Strategies & Technologies

There are two approaches to ventilating buildings: mechanical ventilation and natural ventilation. Mechanical ventilation strategies use fan energy to ventilate occupied spaces. Mechanical systems provide the most reliability and control. Natural ventilation strategies take advantage of physical properties of the building design and site such as stack effects, operable windows, and site wind patterns to ventilate occupied spaces. Natural ventilation strategies provide a connection to the outdoors and have relatively low operation and maintenance costs.

In existing buildings, ventilation strategies may be limited because overall airflow, building location and building orientation are already determined. Regional climate characteristics of the building location may dictate whether mechanical or natural ventilation strategies can be used. In some locations it may not be possible to employ natural ventilation solutions due to poor outdoor air quality, prevailing air flows, undesirable outdoor temperatures or security concerns.

Improving existing ventilation system design to take maximum advantage of regional climate characteristics can help cut down on energy costs and increase ventilation options. Implement natural ventilation strategies in the building wherever possible to decrease operating costs. Some existing buildings may have been originally designed for natural ventilation, making it quite feasible to restore the use of natural ventilation.

Project teams should evaluate the strengths and weaknesses of the two approaches, including building location, regional climate patterns, and building occupant preferences in the final decisions for ventilation system alterations. Additionally, a combination of mechanical and natural ventilation strategies might be appropriate in some buildings. Buildings with a "mixed-mode" approach to ventilation should comply with the referenced standards applicable to the ventilation strategies in use. CIBSE Application Manual 13: Mixed Mode Ventilation includes additional information for successfully implementing mixed-mode ventilation strategies.

Option A

If the existing building has a mechanical ventilation system, measure and compare the ventilation rates in the spaces to ASHRAE Standard 62.1-2004. If the ventilation rates are less than 30 percent above the minimum rates in ASHRAE Standard 62.1-2004, the outside air dampers should be adjusted to allow the desired increased ventilation rates.

Option B

If the existing building is naturally ventilated, show that the system complies

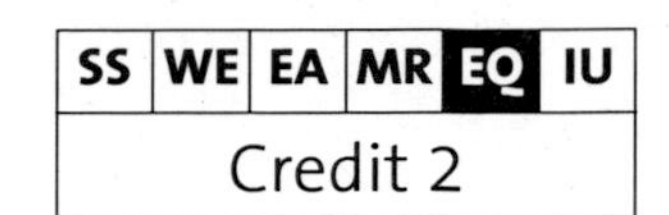

with the recommendations set forth in the CIBSE Application Manual 10 – Natural Ventilation in Non-Domestic Buildings.

Synergies & Tradeoffs

Ventilation strategies influence the overall energy performance of the building and require commissioning and measurement & verification. Increased ventilation, particularly when delivered by mechanical systems, can increase energy consumption. The use of heat transfer equipment, like heat recover wheels, can precondition intake air. This minimizes the extent to which increased ventilation requires additional energy to heat or cool intake air.

Natural ventilation strategies can improve overall building energy performance, though opportunities for employing these strategies may be limited by existing building features, site design and local climatic conditions.

Installing a permanent ventilation performance monitoring system, as required in IEQ Credit 1: Outdoor Air Delivery Monitoring, can facilitate the achievement and maintenance of increased ventilation.

Calculations & Documentation

Calculations

The ASHRAE Ventilation Rate Procedure has recently been revised. The updated version redefines an occupied zone as a breathing zone and describes ventilation rates in both per-person and per-unit area values. ASHARE has introduced a spreadsheet called 62n-VRP.xls, which can be used to calculate the ventilation rate as outlined by the referenced standard.

Documentation

Option A

For mechanical ventilation systems:

❑ Provide measurements demonstrating that actual ventilation rates exceed the minimum rates required by ASHRAE 62.1-2004 by at least 30 percent.

- Documentation should reflect identification of ventilation rates for the building type and uses as specified for compliance with ASHRAE 62.1-2004, and evidence that those parameters have been surpassed in the building by at least 30 percent.

Other Resources

ASHRAE Handbook: Fundamentals, ASHRAE, 2001.

This resource details basic principles and data regarding HVAC&R design.

ASHRAE Handbook: HVAC Systems and Equipment, ASHRAE, 2004.

This handbook aids system designers and operators in selecting and using equipment.

Heating, Ventilating, and Air Conditioning: Analysis and Design, 5th Edition, by Faye McQuiston, Jerald Parker, and Jeffrey Spitler, John Wiley & Sons, 2000.

This text is a comprehensive guide to HVAC systems, and includes information about load calculation, indoor air quality procedures, and environmentally acceptable refrigerants.

Mixed Mode Ventilation, Application Manual 13, CIBSE, 2000.

This CIBSE publication provides the information needed to make strategic decisions about mixed-mode ventilation systems, including potential barriers and solutions for successful use of mixed-mode systems.

Definitions

The **Breathing Zone** is the region in an occupied space from 3 inches above the

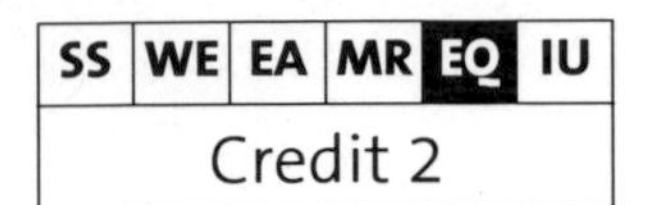

floor to 72 inches above the floor and greater than 2 feet from walls or fixed air conditioning equipment.

Conditioned Space is the portion of the building that is heated or cooled, or both, for the comfort of building occupants.

Natural Ventilation is the process of supplying and removing air by natural means in building spaces by using openings such as windows and doors, wind towers, non-powered ventilators, and infiltration processes.

Ventilation is the process of supplying and removing air by natural or mechanical means in building spaces.

SS	WE	EA	MR	EQ	IU
Credit 3					

1 point

Construction IAQ Management Plan

Intent

Prevent indoor air quality problems resulting from any construction/renovation projects in order to help sustain the comfort and well-being of construction workers and building occupants.

Requirements

Develop and implement an Indoor Air Quality (IAQ) Management Plan for the construction and occupancy phases of the building as follows:

- ❑ During construction, meet or exceed the recommended Design Approaches of the Sheet Metal and Air Conditioning National Contractors Association (SMACNA) IAQ Guideline for Occupied Buildings Under Construction, 1995, Chapter 3.
- ❑ Protect stored on-site or installed absorptive materials from moisture damage.
- ❑ If air handlers must be used during construction, filtration media with a Minimum Efficiency Reporting Value (MERV) of 8 must be used at each return air grill, as determined by ASHRAE 52.2-1999.
- ❑ Replace all filtration media immediately prior to occupancy.
- ❑ Remove contaminants that may be remaining at the end of the construction period.
  - Conduct a minimum two-week building flush-out with new filtration media with 100% outside air after construction ends and prior to occupancy of the affected space. After the flush-out, replace the filtration media with new media, except for filters solely processing outside air.

  OR

  - After construction ends conduct a baseline indoor air quality testing procedure for the affected space in the building that demonstrates that the concentration levels for the chemical air contaminants are below specified levels. For each sampling point where the maximum concentration limits are exceeded conduct a partial building flush-out, for a minimum of two weeks, then retest the specific parameter(s) that were exceeded to indicate the requirements are achieved. Repeat procedure until all requirements have been met.

Chemical Contaminate	Maximum Concentration
Formaldehyde	0.05 parts per million
Particulates (PM10)	20 micrograms per cubic meter above outside air conditions
Total Volatile Organic Compounds (TVOC)	500 micrograms per cubic meter
4-Phenylcyclohexene (4-PCH)	3 micrograms per cubic meter
Carbon Monoxide (CO)	9 parts per million

The air sample testing shall be conducted as follows:

- ❑ Air samples collected for every 25,000 square feet, or for each contiguous floor area, whichever is greater.

- Measurements conducted with the building ventilation system starting at normal daily start time and operated at the minimum outside air flow rate for the occupied mode throughout duration of the air testing.
- Building shall be fully finished and unoccupied. Furniture can be included in the testing if desired but it is not required.
- Test with time weight values of four hours with data logging.
- When re-testing non-complying building areas, take samples from the same locations as in first test.
- Copies of the IAQ testing results should describe the contaminant sampling and analytical methods, the locations and duration of contaminant samples, the field sampling log sheets and laboratory analytical data, and the methods and results utilized to determine that the ventilation system was started at the normal daily start time and operated at the minimum outside air flow rate for the occupied mode through the duration of the air testing.

Submittals – Initial Certification

- Provide a copy of the Construction IAQ Management Plan that specifies inclusion of Construction IAQ Management specification provisions for any construction projects that may occur in the building.
- Application of management plan to any construction projects carried out in the building in the performance period.
  - If there have not been any construction projects during the performance period, provide a statement to this effect.
  - If there have been any construction projects carried out in the building during the performance period provide:
  - A list of the construction projects implemented during the performance period and for each one provide:
    - A copy of the construction IAQ Management Plan highlighting the six requirements of SMACNA IAQ Guideline for Occupied Buildings under Construction, 1995, Chapter 3.
    - Photographs of construction IAQ management measures such as protection of ducts and on-site stored or installed absorptive materials.
    - Technical information on filtration media used during construction and installed immediately prior to occupancy with MERV values highlighted.
    - Documentation of post construction flush-out or measurement of contaminant concentrations.

Submittals – Recertification

Provide an update of previous filings:

- Construction IAQ Management Plan that specifies inclusion of Construction IAQ Management specification provisions for the any construction projects that may occur in the building.
  - If there has been no change to the plan, provide a statement to this effect.

- If there has been a change, provide the updated plan.

- ❑ Application of IAQ Management Plan to any construction projects carried out in the building during the performance period.
  - If there were no construction projects during the performance period, provide a statement to this effect.
  - If there were construction projects during the performance period, list these projects and document that the IAQ Management Plan was followed for each project.

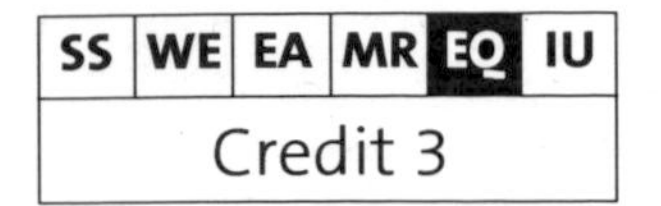

Summary of Referenced Standard

SMACNA IAQ Guidelines for Occupied Buildings Under Construction (1995)

Topic cited: Chapter 3 – Control Measures

SMACNA

(703) 803-2980

www.smacna.org

The Sheet Metal and Air Conditioning Contractors' National Association (SMACNA) is an international association of union contractors that developed these guidelines for maintaining healthy indoor air quality during demolition, renovation or construction activities. The full document covers the source of air pollutants, control measures, how to manage the IAQ process, quality control and documentation, communication with occupants, sample projects, tables, references, resources and checklists.

ASHRAE 52.2-1999: Method of Testing General Ventilation Air-Cleaning Devices for Removal Efficiency by Particle Size (ANSI approved)

Topic cited: Standards for filtration media - Minimum Efficiency Reporting Value (MERV)

ASHRAE

(800) 527-4723

www.ashrae.org

This standard from the American Society of Heating, Refrigerating and Air Conditioning Engineers (ASHRAE) establishes a test procedure for evaluating the performance of air-cleaning devices as a function of particle size. The standard addresses two air cleaner performance characteristics: the ability of the device to remove particles from the air stream and its resistance to airflow. The test procedure uses laboratory-generated potassium chloride particles dispersed into the air stream as the test aerosol. This standard delineates a method of loading the air cleaner with synthetic dust to simulate field conditions.

Green Building Concerns

Building renovation or upgrade processes invariably include activities that have the potential to contaminate the building during construction. Often, these activities result in residual building contamination that continues to impact indoor air quality over the lifetime of the building. HVAC systems are especially prone to contamination from particulate matter generated during construction activities. This particulate matter can include dust, volatile organic components (VOCs), microorganisms and other contaminants that remain in HVAC systems for years. Building occupants may experience reduced productivity and adverse well-being effects as a result. Contaminants in the indoor air can also negatively affect furnishings and equipment in the building.

Fortunately, management strategies can be instituted during construction to minimize the potential for building contamination and to remediate or clean up any contamination that has occurred. Protection of HVAC systems during construction, flush-out of the building following construction and source control are some of the effective methods to reduce construction impacts on IAQ and occupant health.

Environmental Issues

Effective ventilation for construction IAQ management in buildings may require additional energy use, which contributes to air and water pollution. However, contaminant reduction improves the indoor environment and benefits building occupants, resulting in lower absenteeism and greater productivity.

Economic Issues

Additional time, labor and other resources may be required during and after construction to protect and clean ventilation systems. However, these actions can extend the lifetime of the ventilation system and improve its efficiency, resulting in reduced energy use.

The additional effort during a construction project can prevent air quality and other contamination problems that could impair occupant health and productivity over the life of the building.

Sequencing the installation of materials may require additional time and could potentially delay the date when occupants return to the space. Early coordination between the construction contractors and subcontractors can minimize or eliminate delays.

Strategies & Technologies

This credit involves planning for and implementing practices that minimize the negative effects of construction projects on IAQ. Develop a Construction IAQ Management Plan that meets the credit requirements, and implement it whenever construction projects occur on the building site.

It is imperative that, prior to the start of construction projects, the components of the Construction IAQ Management Plan are communicated to the general contractor, and the general contractor agrees to abide by all its elements. In some cases, the contractor might tailor general concepts within the plan to the specific situation. Construction-related IAQ procedures should be included in pre-construction and construction progress meeting agendas. All participants in the construction process must be aware of the IAQ procedures and understand the importance of the goals of the IAQ Management Plan. Identify an owner's representative as the IAQ Manager to identify IAQ problems, initiate mitigation as necessary, and ensure that all preventive measures included in the plan are properly executed.

The Construction IAQ Management Plan should address protection of the ventilation system components during construction and cleanup of contaminated components after construction is complete. Consider incorporating the following strategies in the plan:

- ❑ Specify containment control strategies, including protecting the HVAC system, controlling pollutant sources, interrupting pathways for contamination, enforcing proper housekeeping and coordinating schedules to minimize disruption.
- ❑ Specify the construction sequencing to install absorptive materials after the prescribed dry or cure time of wet finishes to minimize adverse impacts on IAQ. Materials directly exposed to moisture through precipitation, plumbing leaks, or condensation from the HVAC system are susceptible to microbial contamination.
- ❑ Use protective covers and sequencing of installation to protect absorptive materials including insulation, carpeting, ceiling tiles and gypsum products.
- ❑ Appoint an IAQ Manager with owner's authority to inspect IEQ problems and require mitigation as necessary.
- ❑ Sequence the application of building materials so that materials that may be significant sources of contaminants (e.g., composite wood products and wet products such as adhesives, paints and coatings, and glazing) significantly dissipate their emissions prior to the introduction of products with the capacity to absorb or trap contaminants (e.g., carpet and padding, fabric wall covering, acoustic tiles, and upholstered furniture). Where protection

cannot be provided by sequence of installations, protect adsorbing surfaces with vapor barriers and provide air exchange through temporary or permanent ventilation systems.

- ❑ Perform a flush-out when new materials are installed, such as new carpet.
- ❑ Use a recognized measurement protocol for IAQ testing such as the U.S. EPA "Compendium of Methods for the Determination of Air Pollutants in Indoor Air."
- ❑ Clean ducts and related equipment as part of the renovation process. Sequencing this task carefully with the overall construction process can mitigate contamination of the remainder of the ducts.

Meeting or exceeding the recommendations in SMACNA's IAQ Guidelines for Occupied Buildings Under Construction is necessary to earn this credit. The guidelines include control measures in the following areas: HVAC protection, source control, pathway interruption, housekeeping and scheduling.

HVAC Protection – Shut down the return side of the HVAC system (which is, by definition, ductwork under negative pressure) whenever possible during heavy construction or demolition. The system should be isolated from the surrounding environment whenever possible. If the ventilation system must be operated during construction, fit it with temporary filters that can be replaced with clean media just prior to substantial completion of the project. The standard recommends that filter efficiency be upgraded where major loading is expected to occur on operating HVAC systems.

The return side of the HVAC system should be dampered off in the heaviest work areas and return system openings; diffusers and window units on the supply system should be sealed with plastic for further protection. Duct cleaning should also be considered to ensure that the dust generated is effectively removed or cleaned. Timing of duct cleaning should be sequenced carefully with the overall IAQ plan.

Source Control – Control building contamination at its source by different strategies such as product substitution (using products with low-emitting materials), modifying equipment operation, changing work practices and implementing temporary local exhaust. Specify nontoxic materials when selecting items such as paints, carpet and finishes. (Nontoxic materials selection is covered under Materials & Resources Credit 5.) The project team should identify materials that have no low-toxic alternatives so that the contractor can institute appropriate control measures.

Pathway Interruption – During construction, isolate areas of work to prevent contamination of clean or occupied spaces. Depending on the climate, ventilate using 100 percent outside air to exhaust contaminated air directly to the outside during installation of VOC-emitting materials. Pressure differentials between construction areas and clean areas can be utilized to prevent contaminated air from entering clean areas. Such strategies often require the erection of temporary barriers between work areas and non-work areas. Consider expanding the use of temporary entryway matting systems to minimize the tracking of dust and other contaminants from the construction area into occupied space. (Selection criteria of entryway matting systems can be found in IEQ Credit 10.1.)

Housekeeping – To prevent occupied spaces from excessive construction dust, spills or volatile organic compounds (VOCs), expand standard housekeeping procedures to deal with construction-related problems. Use high-efficiency vacuum cleaners and micro-fiber dusting cloths and mops to capture and remove fine particles. (The selection of vacuum cleaners is covered in IEQ Credit 10.6.) Consider cleaning occupied space more frequently during construction to minimize exposures to occupants and delicate office equipment and building systems. Keep furniture, equipment and floors clean, and remove spills or excess applications with products that do not emit odors. It is also important to keep the areas dry and address water accumulation as soon as possible. Also pay particular attention to worksite sanitation to ensure that workers are properly disposing of food items and other wastes that could attract pests to avoid a source of future problems after construction is complete.

Scheduling – Specify construction sequencing to reduce absorption of VOCs by materials that act as sinks or contaminant sources. Complete applications of wet and odorous materials such as paints, sealants and coatings before installing "sink" or absorbent materials such as ceiling tiles, carpets, insulation, gypsum products and fabric-covered furnishings. Materials directly exposed to moisture through precipitation, plumbing leaks, or condensation from the HVAC system are susceptible to microbial contamination. Treat materials exposed to moisture properly so that microbial contamination does not become a problem.

Synergies & Tradeoffs

Proper construction waste management procedures can minimize the possibility of building contamination. It is also beneficial to choose building materials that have a low potential for contaminating the building, such as low VOC paints, adhesives and sealants (MR Credit 3: Optimize Use of IAQ Compliant Products).

Calculations & Documentation

Calculations

None.

Documentation

- ❑ Copy of the Construction IAQ Management Plan
  - Submit the official Construction IAQ Management Plan adopted by your organization and highlight the sections that address the credit requirements.
- ❑ Application of the management plan to construction projects during the performance period
  - If no construction projects have occurred during the performance period, documentation should include a statement to that effect that appears on organization letterhead and is signed by an officer of the organization.

Other Resources

EPA Fact Sheet: Ventilation and Air Quality in Offices

www.epa.gov/iaq/pubs/ventilat.html

This U.S. EPA publication addresses IEQ issues for office buildings.

Definitions

A **Construction IAQ Management Plan** is a document specific to a building project that outlines measures to minimize contamination in the building during construction, and procedures to flush the building of contaminants prior to occupancy.

HVAC Systems include heating, ventilating and air conditioning systems used to provide thermal comfort and ventilation for building interiors.

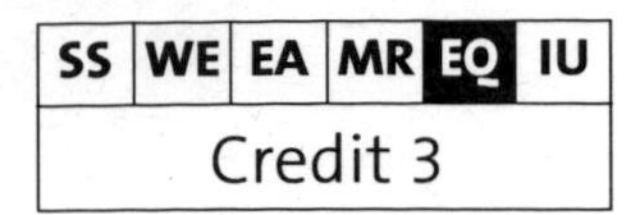

SS	WE	EA	MR	EQ	IU

Credit 4.1

1 point

Documenting Productivity Impacts

Absenteeism and Health Care Cost Impacts

Intent

Document absenteeism, health care cost and productivity impacts of sustainable building performance improvements.

Requirements

Document the history of absenteeism and health care costs for building occupants for the previous five years (or length of building occupancy with a minimum of 12 months) and track changes in absenteeism and health care costs (claim costs must be provided and any reductions in premium costs should be provided if available) for building occupants over the performance period relative to sustainable building performance improvements.

Submittals – Initial Certification

- ❑ Provide documentation of the history of absenteeism and health care costs for building occupants for the previous five years (or length of building occupancy with a minimum of 12 months).
- ❑ Track changes in absenteeism and health care costs (claim costs must be provided and any reductions in premium costs should be provided if available) for building occupants over the performance period relative to sustainable building performance improvements.

Submittals – Recertification

- ❑ Provide documentation of the history of absenteeism and health care costs for building occupants for the previous five years (or length of building occupancy with a minimum of 12 months).
- ❑ Track changes in absenteeism and health care costs (claim costs must be provided and any reductions in premium costs should be provided if available) for building occupants over the performance period relative to sustainable building performance improvements.

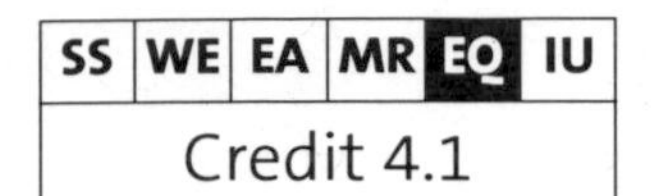

Summary of Referenced Standard

There is no standard referenced for this credit.

Green Building Concerns

Better occupant health is a major benefit of improved indoor environmental quality in buildings. Improved building design, operation and maintenance can minimize the negative effects of buildings on human health, including reduced instances of communicable respiratory illnesses, allergies, asthma symptoms, and other symptoms. IEQ improvement measures reduce the presence of allergens, minimize the introduction of toxic chemicals into the building, and improve air filtration and ventilation, all of which contribute to occupant well-being. Additionally, daylighting and views can promote mental health and diminish the effects of Seasonal Affective Disorder (SAD).

Sick Building Syndrome (SBS) is a term used to describe a host of building-related health symptoms, including eye, nose and skin irritation, headache, fatigue and difficulty breathing that appear to be linked to time spent in a building, but no specific illness or cause can be identified. Building Related Illness (BRI) is the term used when symptoms of diagnosable illness are identified and can be attributed directly to building contaminants. Symptoms of BRI include cough, chest tightness, fever, chills and aches. Building factors that influence SBS and BRI include ventilation systems, chemical and microbial pollution, and indoor temperature and humidity.

Documenting the health benefits associated with green building design and operation are an important element of expanding the green building movement.

Environmental Issues

Many factors that influence indoor environmental quality also carry environmental benefits. Documenting absenteeism and health care cost impacts associated with IEQ will help promote green building practices, which will benefit occupant health and the environment.

Economic Issues

The economic costs of adverse health effects in buildings are substantial. Poor indoor environmental quality can result in:

- ❑ Direct medical costs for people whose health is affected by poor indoor air quality and receive treatment;
- ❑ Lost productivity from absence due to illness;
- ❑ Decreased efficiency on the job;.
- ❑ Materials and equipment damages due to exposure to indoor air pollutants.

High-quality indoor environments reduce these costs, and also may enhance an organization's ability to recruit and retain employees. Potential savings within the United States from improved IEQ are estimated to range from $40 billion to $200 billion annually (in 1996 dollars).[14]

Communicable respiratory illnesses (common cold, influenza, pneumonia, bronchitis, etc.) contribute to health care expenditures and the cost of work absences. Additionally, respiratory illnesses decrease productivity due to impaired work performance. In 2000, one study determined the total annual cost of respiratory infections in the United States to be approximately $70 billion.[15]

SBS is associated with reduced worker productivity due to decreased accuracy and efficiency in task performance. Productivity drops an estimated 2 to 3 percent due to SBS. Based on a 2 percent decline in productivity, the annual costs

SS	WE	EA	MR	EQ	IU
Credit 4.1					

associated with SBS nationwide were estimated at $60 billion in 2000.[16]

BRI includes toxic illness (e.g., carbon monoxide poisoning), infectious disease (e.g., Legionnaires' disease), and allergic diseases (e.g., asthma and hay fever). Depending on the type of BRI, economic costs might include prolonged absences from work or chronic health issues, leading to decreased efficiency and productivity. An estimated 20 million Americans have asthma, with the annual direct (treatment) and indirect (productivity loss) costs of asthma totaling $16.1 billion in 2004.[17] This cost is expected to increase in future years, along with increased numbers of allergy and asthma sufferers.

Documenting the productivity impacts of green building operations helps promote practices that minimize IEQ-associated health and productivity costs.

Strategies & Technologies

Track absenteeism and health care costs for building occupants to identify any positive impacts related to sustainable performance improvements to building IEQ and operations. This may require working with the organization's human resource department and health insurance provider. Efforts to track health insurance premium costs should note other changes important in determining premiums, such as the number of individuals covered and national increases in health care costs.

Synergies & Tradeoffs

Tracking health care expenditures and absenteeism can guide future building improvements. For example, analysis of health care claims might indicate that many building occupants suffer from allergies or asthma, making additional IAQ improvements a priority for future building improvement projects.

Calculations & Documentation

Calculations

Use tables similar to the ones below as a guide to track changes in absenteeism (**Table 1**) and health care costs (**Table 2**) relative to green building improvements.

Documentation

All information needed to successfully document this credit can be found in the Submittals section of the LEED-EB Rating System and the LEED-EB Letter Templates.

Other Resources

Health and Productivity Gains from Better Indoor Environments and Their Relationship with Building Energy Efficiency, William J. Fisk, 2000

www.usgbc.org/Docs/Resources/Fisk(LBNL)HealthandProductivityEE2000.pdf

Table 1: Absenteeism Data

Year	Total number of sick days (absent for health care reasons) for all building occupants	Total number of building occupants	Average number of sick days taken per occupant per year	LEED-EB Score for Year	Other

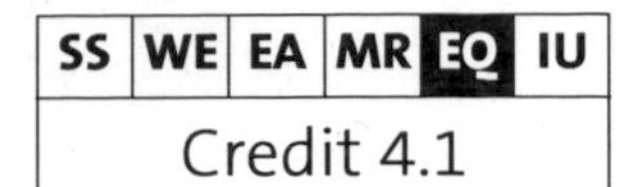

This publication summarizes numerous studies that relate indoor environments to productivity and provides estimates of the nationwide implications for health and productivity.

EPA Indoor Air Facts No. 4 (revised): Sick Building Syndrome (SBS)

www.epa.gov/iaq/pubs/sbs.html

This fact sheet provides information about the indicators of SBS and BRI, and the causes and solutions to SBS.

Definitions

Building Related Illness (BRI) is a term to describe diagnosable illnesses that can be directly attributed to airborne building contaminants.

Seasonal Affective Disorder (SAD) is a form of depression thought to be triggered by a decrease in exposure to sunlight.

Sick Building Syndrome is a term used to describe situations where building occupants experience acute discomfort and negative health effects as a result of time spent in the building without any specific cause that can be identified, and the symptoms disappear soon after the occupants leave the building.

Table 2: Health Care Cost Data

Year	Health insurance premiums + co-pays (all building occupants)	Total number of building occupants	Per occupant cost health insurance premiums + co-pays	Health insurance claims and co-pays [all building occupants]	Per occupant cost health insurance claims and co-pays	LEED-EB Score for Year	Other
	$		$	$	$		
	$		$	$	$		
	$		$	$	$		
	$		$	$	$		
	$		$	$	$		

SS	WE	EA	MR	EQ	IU
Credit 4.2					

1 point

Documenting Productivity Impacts

Other Productivity Impacts

Intent

Documentation of the other productivity impacts (beyond those identified in IEQ Credit 4.1) of sustainable building performance improvements.

Requirements

Document the other productivity impacts (beyond those identified in IEQ Credit 4.1) of sustainable building performance improvements for building occupants. Address and track changes in the impact on the amount of work done and errors made or other productivity impacts for building occupants over the performance period relative to sustainable building performance improvements. This documentation needs to be provided for the previous five years (or length of building occupancy with a minimum of 12 months).

Submittals – Initial Certification

- ❑ Provide documentation of the other productivity impacts for building occupants (beyond those identified in IEQ Credit 4.1) of sustainable building performance improvements. The documentation needs to address the impact on the amount of work done and errors made by building occupants relative to sustainable building performance improvements. This documentation also needs to be provided for the previous five years (or length of building occupancy with a minimum of 12 months).

Submittals – Recertification

- ❑ Provide updated documentation over the performance period of the other productivity impacts for building occupants (beyond those identified in IEQ Credit 4.1) of sustainable building performance improvements. The documentation needs to address the impact on the amount of work done and errors made by building occupants relative to sustainable building performance improvements. This documentation also needs to be provided for the previous five years (or length of building occupancy with a minimum of 12 months).

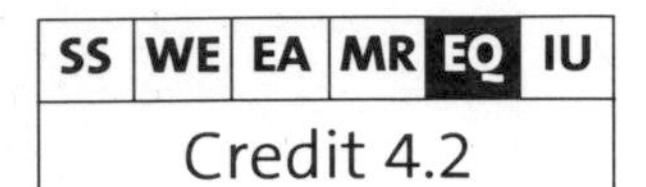

Summary of Referenced Standard

There is no standard referenced for this credit.

Green Building Concerns

Beyond minimizing the productivity losses due to illness and absenteeism, high indoor environmental quality can improve work performance and productivity. Productivity benefits associated with green buildings have been documented in office spaces, classrooms and retail stores. Building design and operating practices—including comfortable temperature and humidity levels, adequate ventilation, access to daylighting and views, and indoor spaces devoid of pollutants—can contribute to heightened levels of worker productivity. In office settings, building features can influence workers to perform 1 to 20 percent better or worse than average.[18]

Environmental Issues

Many factors that influence IEQ also carry environmental benefits. Documenting productivity impacts beyond absenteeism and health care costs associated with IEQ will help further promote green building practices, which will benefit occupant health and the environment.

Economic Issues

Worker salaries are often the largest expense an organization faces. Documentation of productivity impacts allows building owners to understanding ways to improve building operations in a manner that enhances worker performance. Because salaries are a large portion of an organization's overall budget, productivity increases of only a few percentage points represent significant savings, maximizing the value of an organization's investment in its building and employees.

Strategies & Technologies

IEQ Credit 4.1 involves reformatting absenteeism and health care cost data that most organizations already collect into appropriate formats to address the impact of sustainable buildings. IEQ Credit 4.2 is aimed at encouraging the participation of building owners and managers in the development and implementation of serious scientific studies of the impact of sustainable buildings on the productivity of building occupants.

Ongoing LEED-EB recertification provides data on the level of sustainability being delivered in the building. The challenge of this credit for building owners, managers and their scientific collaborators is to devise scientifically meaningful measures of building occupant performance impacts in buildings.

Such productivity studies involve setting up a system to track productivity impacts (such as changes in the amount of work done, errors made by building occupants, or sales volume) over the performance period for one or more buildings and comparing the productivity performance with the LEED-EB ratings levels achieved for the building or buildings in the studies. Tracking the employee turnover rate is one relatively simple method for determining the productivity impacts of green buildings.

Synergies & Tradeoffs

Tracking employee productivity and its relationship to building features and practices can guide future building improvements. For example, analysis of access to daylighting on employee performance might indicate that the expansion of daylit areas is a priority for future building improvement projects.

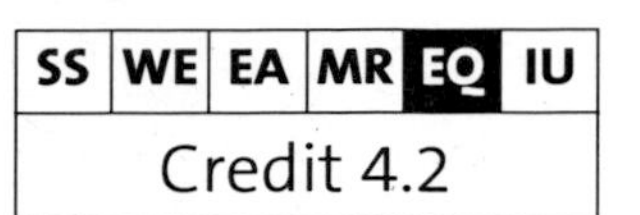

Calculations & Documentation

Calculations

Use spreadsheets similar to **Tables 1–3** below as guides to gather information on the productivity benefits of LEED-EB certified buildings. Carefully design productivity studies so that effects of LEED-EB are isolated from other factors affecting productivity.

Documentation

All information needed to successfully document this credit can be found in the Submittals section of the LEED-EB Rating System and the LEED-EB Letter Templates.

Table 1: Example 1 - Comparing Retail Store Sales within a Company

LEED-EB Certified Building (Store 1)		Conventional Building (Store 2)	
Month	**Monthly Sales**	**Month**	**Monthly Sales**
January		January	
February		February	
March		March	
April		April	
May		May	
June		June	
July		July	
August		August	
September		September	
October		October	
November		November	
December		December	
Total		Total	
[Store 1 Annual Sales] Minus [Store 2 Annual Sales]			
Difference Divided by Store 1 Annual Sales			

Table 2: Comparing Employee Productivity within a Company

LEED-EB Certified Building (Building 1)		Conventional Building (Building 2)	
Month	**Monthly Production**	**Month**	**Monthly Production**
January		January	
February		February	
March		March	
April		April	
May		May	
June		June	
July		July	
August		August	
September		September	
October		October	
November		November	
December		December	
Total		Total	
[Building 1 Annual Production] Minus [Building 2 Annual Production]			
Difference Divided by Building 1 Annual Production			

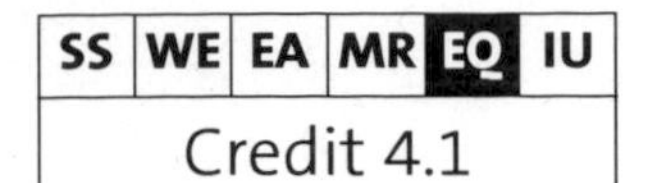

Table 3: Example 3 – Tracking Employee Turnover Rates

Year	Total Number of Voluntary Departures of Employees	Total Number of Employees	Turnover Rate	LEED-EB Score for Year

Other Resources

Analysis of the Performance of Students in Daylit Schools

www.innovativedesign.net/paper_a.htm#student

Study by Nicklas and Bailey, Innovative Design, Raleigh, NC, considering the influence of daylighting on student performance on standardized testing. This is a good resource for conducting productivity studies.

California Energy Commission Public Interest Energy Research (PIER) Program

www.energy.ca.gov/pier/index.html

The PIER Program supports energy research, development and demonstration projects, including those related to windows, daylighting and productivity. Copies of relevant studies are available on the Integrate Energy Systems: Productivity & Building Science portion of the web site (http://www.energy.ca.gov/pier/final_project_reports/500-03-082.html), including:

- ❑ Windows and Offices: A Study of Office Worker Performance and the Indoor Environment
- ❑ Windows and Classrooms: A Study of Student Performance and the Indoor Environment
- ❑ Daylight and Retail Sales

Daylighting in Schools: An Investigation into the Relationship Between Daylighting and Human Performance

www.pge.com/003_save_energy/003c_edu_train/pec/daylight/di_pubs/SchoolDetailed820App.PDF

This study considers the effect of daylighting on human performance through analyses of the correlation between student performance data and the amount of daylight in the classroom environment.

Indoor Health & Productivity (IHP) Project

www.dc.lbl.gov/IHP/

A project of the National Science and Technology Council, IHP is an effort to advance the understanding of the relationships between the physical attributes of workplaces and the health and productivity of occupants.

Definitions

Productivity is the quantity and quality of employee output per unit time.

SS | WE | EA | MR | EQ | IU

Credit 5.1

1 point

Indoor Chemical and Pollutant Source Control

Non-Cleaning System – Reduce Particulates in Air Distribution

Intent

Reduce exposure of building occupants and maintenance personnel to potentially hazardous particle contaminants, which adversely impact air quality, health, building finishes, building systems and the environment.

Requirements

Have filters with particle removal effectiveness MERV 13 or greater in place over the performance period for all outside air intakes and for the returns for the re-circulation of inside air. Establish and follow a regular schedule for maintenance and replacement of these filters.

Submittals – Initial Certification

- ❑ Document that the building has had filters in place over the performance period with particle removal effectiveness MERV 13 or greater for all outside air intakes and for the returns for the re-circulation of inside air.
- ❑ Document that a regular schedule for maintenance and replacement of these filters has been established and followed over the performance period.

Submittals – Recertification

- ❑ Document that the building has had filters in place over the performance period with particle removal effectiveness MERV 13 or greater for all outside air intakes and for the returns for the re-circulation of inside air.
- ❑ Document that a regular schedule for maintenance and replacement of these filters has been established and followed over the performance period.

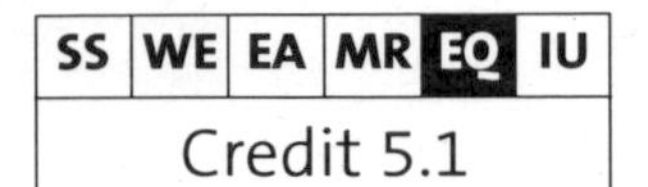

Summary of Referenced Standard

ASHRAE 52.2-1999: Method of Testing General Ventilation Air-Cleaning Devices for Removal Efficiency by Particle Size (ANSI approved)

Topic cited: Standards for filtration media - Minimum Efficiency Reporting Value (MERV)

ASHRAE

(800) 527-4723

www.ashrae.org

This standard from the American Society of Heating, Refrigerating and Air Conditioning Engineers (ASHRAE) establishes a test procedure for evaluating the performance of air-cleaning devices as a function of particle size. The standard addresses two air cleaner performance characteristics: the ability of the device to remove particles from the air stream and its resistance to airflow. The test procedure uses laboratory-generated potassium chloride particles dispersed into the air stream as the test aerosol. This standard delineates a method of loading the air cleaner with synthetic dust to simulate field conditions.

Green Building Concerns

Particulate matter in the air degrades the indoor environment. A wide variety of particles occur in indoor environments, including lint, dirt, carpet fibers, dust particles, dust mites, mold, bacteria, pollen and animal dander. These airborne particulates can exacerbate respiratory problems like allergies, asthma, emphysema and chronic lung disease. Air filtration reduces the exposure of building occupants to these airborne contaminants.

Environmental Issues

The primary goal of reducing particulates in air distribution is to improve the indoor environment. Indoor air pollutants can have a significantly negative influence on human health since people spend a large amount of time indoors.

Economic Issues

The use of higher efficiency filters may increase the operating costs of the ventilation system, due to the greater cost of replacement filters and increased energy use due to the higher pressure drop posed by the filters. On the other hand, reduced soiling of building materials would result in cost savings from reduced cleaning and maintenance costs. Additionally, enhanced occupant comfort and well-being may result in greater productivity and indirect economic benefits.

Strategies & Technologies

Install and maintain filters with a particle removal effectiveness of MERV 13 or greater for all outside air intakes and for the returns for the re-circulation of inside air. Based on information provided by the filter manufacturer, establish and follow a regular schedule for maintenance and replacement of these filters.

Synergies & Tradeoffs

Better air filtration provides cleaner air for building occupants. It also requires more expensive filters, more frequent filter replacement, and more energy used to circulate the air in the building.

Because many indoor particulates originate outside of the building, developing landscaping and grounds maintenance plans that minimize pollen distribution, allergens, dust and other air pollutants can help improve indoor air quality (SS Credit 1: Plan for Green Site and Building Exterior Management).

Calculations & Documentation

Calculations

None.

Documentation

- ❑ Document that the building has filters with ratings of MERV 13 or greater.
  - Provide manufacturers specifications or literature indicating the particle removal effectiveness of the filters.
- ❑ Document the establishment and implementation of regular maintenance schedules.
  - A schedule for the maintenance and replacement of filters might include the information featured in **Table 1** below:

Definitions

HEPA Filters or High Efficiency Particulate Air (HEPA) filters have a filtration efficiency of at least 99.97 percent for 0.3 microns particles.

MERV 13 is a filter efficiency rating category based on a test method established by the American Society of Heating, Refrigerating, and Air Conditioning Engineers (ASHRAE 52.2-1999, Method of Testing General Ventilation Air Cleaning Devices for Removal Efficiency by Particle Size). MERV is an acronym for "minimum efficiency reporting value." The MERV efficiency categories range from 1 to 16 (very low to very high efficiency).

Other Resources

Department of Energy High Efficiency Particulate Air (HEPA) Filters Web Site

www.eh.doe.gov/hepa

This site provides information about filtration and ventilation issues with special reference to the use and testing of HEPA filters.

EPA Indoor Air Quality Division

www.epa.gov/iaq/

This web site provides comprehensive information about IAQ.

Table 1: Filter Replacement Log

Date	Location in System	Type of Filter Installed	MERV Rating	Scheduled Frequency of Replacement per Year	Notes

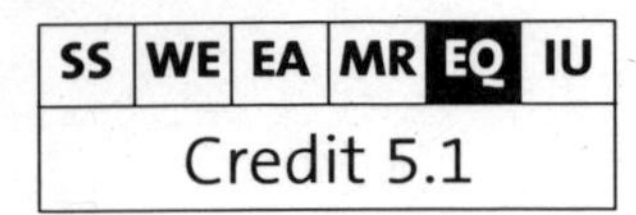
SS
WE
EA
MR
EQ
IU
Credit 5.1

SS	WE	EA	MR	EQ	IU

Credit 5.2

1 point

Indoor Chemical and Pollutant Source Control

Isolation of High-Volume Copying/Print Rooms/Fax Stations

Intent

Reduce exposure of building occupants and maintenance personnel to potentially hazardous chemical, biological and particle contaminants, which adversely impact air quality, health, building finishes, building systems and the environment.

Requirements

Have in place over the performance period structural deck-to-deck partitions with separate outside exhausting, no air re-circulation and negative pressure to contain and isolate high volume copying/print rooms/fax stations. High volume means any copy machine, print or fax station with a monthly copy usage of more than 40,000 pages. This credit can also be earned by putting all copiers, printers, and fax machines exceeding a lower monthly capacity or usage threshold (selected by the building owner) in isolated separately ventilated rooms.

Submittals – Initial Certification

- ❑ Provide a building plan showing all locations of high-volume copying/print rooms/fax stations and photographs or drawings of structural deck-to-deck partitions.
- ❑ Provide documentation of separate outside exhausting, no air re-circulation and negative pressure relative to surrounding occupied areas and isolation of high-volume copying/print rooms/fax stations.

Submittals – Recertification

- ❑ If the building systems pertaining to high-volume copying/print rooms/fax stations have not been changed, provide a letter documenting their continued existence and use.

OR

- ❑ If the systems pertaining to high-volume copying/print rooms/fax stations have been changed, provide a building plan showing all locations of high-volume copying/print rooms/fax stations and photographs or drawings of structural deck-to-deck partitions.
- ❑ Provide documentation of separate outside exhausting, no air re-circulation and negative pressure relative to surrounding occupied areas and isolation of high volume copying/print rooms/fax stations.

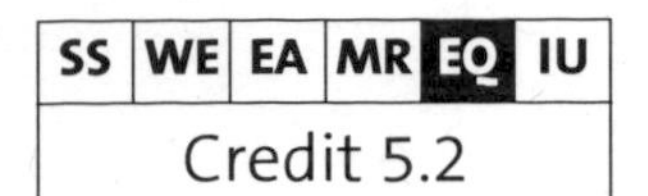

Summary of Referenced Standard

There is no standard referenced for this credit.

Green Building Concerns

High-volume copiers, printers, fax machines and similar equipment produce volatile organic chemicals (VOCs), ozone, dust and other particles that can affect both occupant well-being and productivity, as well as damage sensitive equipment, fabrics and other surfaces.

In existing buildings, isolating copiers/print rooms/fax stations may require a renovation project to designate space and install separate outside exhaust.

Environmental Issues

Additional materials and energy may be required to provide isolated areas, which can increase natural resource consumption as well as air and water pollution. However, preventing air contaminants from entering the occupied spaces of the building preserves indoor environmental quality and protects occupant health. Air contaminants from printing/copying can cause irritation of the eyes, skin, and respiratory tract; coughing; nausea; headaches and other symptoms.

Economic Issues

Additional separation and separate exhausts for copying/print rooms/fax stations can be costly, and probably will not be cost-effective unless other renovation or building updates are taking place. However, this separation eliminates the potential of contaminants from the print processes from entering the occupied spaces, and the resulting human health benefits should prove economically sound over the lifetime of the building.

Strategies & Technologies

Contain and isolate air from high-volume copying/print rooms/fax stations via structural deck-to-deck partitions with separate outside exhausting, negative pressure, and no air re-circulation. Develop a plan to minimize unnecessary use of convenience printers and copiers by moving larger copying and printing jobs to high-volume printers and copiers in isolated spaces meeting the requirements of this credit.

Locate high-volume equipment (e.g., copiers, printers, and fax machines) away from regularly occupied areas and physically isolate this equipment. Provide dedicated localized exhaust systems and locate discharge points away from HVAC system air intakes.

Calculate the monthly and annual output of all the printers, copiers and fax machines in the building and evaluate the benefits of creating an isolated and separately ventilated room for high-volume copying, printing, and fax printing.

Consider outsourcing high-volume copying, printing and fax printing to a service provider operating in an isolated and separately ventilated space. Having an outsourcing contract for high-volume copying, printing and fax printing (more than 40,000 pages on average) is an alternative way to earn this credit.

This credit can also be earned by putting all copiers exceeding a lower capacity or usage threshold (selected by the building owner) in isolated separately ventilated rooms.

Synergies & Tradeoffs

Isolating high-volume copying/print rooms/fax stations reduces noise in the general spaces of the building and prevents emissions from these processes getting into the rest of the building. On the other hand, care must be given in layout to minimize inefficiencies that occur with increased ducting to the high-volume station.

Emissions from copying/print rooms/fax stations can be further prevented by using equipment with low ozone emission specifications and/or an activated carbon filter, properly maintaining equipment, regularly replacing filters and using containerized toner systems.

Calculations & Documentation

Calculations

None.

Documentation

All information needed to successfully document this credit can be found in the Submittals section of the LEED-EB Rating System and the LEED-EB Letter Templates.

Other Resources

Energy Star Office Equipment

www.energystar.gov/index.cfm?c=ofc_equip.pr_office_equipment

This Energy Star web site has a guide to efficient and environmentally friendly copiers, printers, fax machines and other equipment.

Office Equipment: Design, Indoor Air Emissions, and Pollution Prevention Opportunities by R. Hetes, M. Moore, and C. Northeim, U.S. EPA Project Summary, EPA/600/SR-95/045, Research Triangle Park, North Carolina, 1995.

This report summarizes available information on office equipment design, indoor air emissions from office equipment, and pollution prevention approaches.

Definitions

Convenience Copier describes low-volume copying machines distributed around the building for the convenience of the building occupants.

High-Volume Copiers are used to copy many pages on a continuous basis.

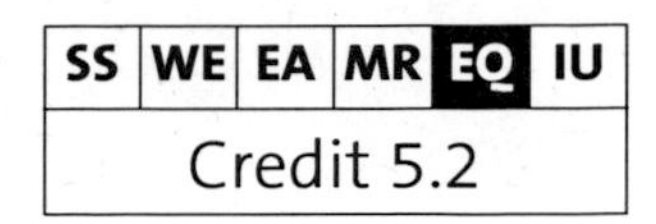

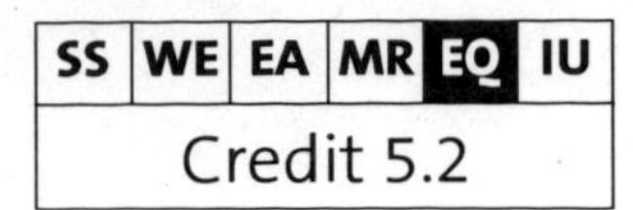
SS WE EA MR EQ IU
Credit 5.2

SS	WE	EA	MR	EQ	IU

Credit 6.1

1 point

Controllability of Systems

Lighting

Intent

Provide a high level of temperature, ventilation and lighting control by individual occupants or specific groups in multi-occupant spaces (e.g., classrooms or conference areas) to promote the productivity, comfort and well-being of building occupants.

Requirements

Provide lighting controls, for at least 50% of building occupants, enabling adjustments to suit individual task needs and preferences, or those of a group sharing a multi-occupant space or workgroup area.

Submittals – Initial Certification

- ❑ Provide documentation signed by the responsible party, demonstrating and declaring that the required lighting controls are provided.
- ❑ Provide drawings showing location of lighting controls.

Submittals – Recertification

- ❑ If there has been no change to the occupant lighting control strategy or related occupant use of the building since the previous LEED-EB filing, provide a statement that the system continues to deliver required occupant control.

OR

- ❑ If there has been a change to this information since the previous LEED-EB filing, provide an updated documentation, signed by the responsible party, demonstrating the changes made and declaring that the required lighting controls are provided.

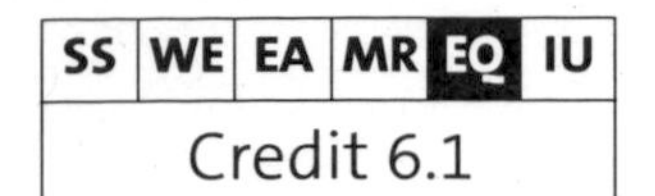

Summary of Referenced Standard

There is no standard referenced for this credit.

Green Building Concerns

Many existing buildings were designed to have overhead lighting systems with no occupant controls. Such an environment can result in occupant discomfort due to undesirable light levels. Providing individual lighting controls can improve the comfort and productivity of building occupants and save energy. Individual controls allow occupants to set light levels appropriate to the current task, time of day in spaces with daylighting, personal preferences and individual variation in visual acuity.

Environmental Issues

In 1999, lighting was estimated to account for 23 percent, or 716 trillion Btu, of electricity consumption in U.S. commercial buildings.[19] Individual control of lighting systems saves energy by eliminating unnecessary lighting. According to UC Berkeley's Center for the Built Environment, building occupants use 40 percent less lighting energy when given convenient individual control of lights.[20] This results in reduced natural resource consumption and air quality impacts from energy production and consumption activities.

Economic Issues

Adding lighting controls and task lighting fixtures incurs equipment first costs. However, energy savings and increased occupant comfort and productivity can offset these costs. Lighting controls can also extend the calendar life of lamps, thereby creating a longer interval between lamp replacements and savings on maintenance labor costs.

Strategies & Technologies

Implement system and occupant control of lighting by employing ambient and task lighting. Use ambient and task lighting that provide basic space lighting with occupant controls to suit the needs of specific tasks or individual preferences. Provide individual or integrated controls systems that control lighting in individual rooms and/or work areas.

Simple switching controls are adequate for meeting credit requirements. However, providing more sophisticated occupant controls, such as dimming capabilities, may result in increased energy savings and enhanced occupant comfort.

Installation of individual lighting controls in core locations of a floor plan is a relatively straightforward project. Further control can then be provided at the individual level with task lighting. For example, furniture systems can include built-in task lighting. Under the LEED-NC Rating System, task lighting must be hardwired to meet the credit requirements, and cannot include lamps that are plugged into outlets. However, since providing hardwired task lighting in existing buildings might require substantial renovations, while outlet-powered task lighting provides an simple and effective way to add occupant controls in existing buildings, LEED-EB does not mandate hardwired task lighting. For finer control, larger ambient lighting zones can be sub-switched to provide smaller lighting zones.

Educate occupants on individual control of their office space environment. A monitoring system can be implemented to maintain proper system operation. Signage may help in reminding occupants of their responsibilities (e.g., turning off task lights as they leave for the day).

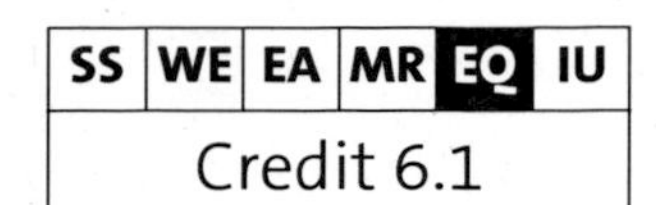

Synergies & Tradeoffs

Individual control of lighting systems may not be feasible for all building types. If the building type or use prohibits individual controls for at least 50 percent of the building occupants, this credit cannot be achieved. Alteration of the lighting scheme may change the energy performance of the building and require commissioning and measurement & verification attention (EA Prerequisite 1: Existing Building Commissioning and EA Prerequisite 2 and Credit 1: Energy Performance).

Calculations & Documentation

Calculations

Calculate the percent of occupants with access to lighting controls for both Individual Workspaces and Multi-occupant Group Spaces based on the methodologies presented below. The criteria for both types of spaces must be met to earn this credit.

Calculations for Individual Occupant Workspaces

Include all workspaces that regularly accommodate a single occupant in these calculations. This includes workstations in both private offices and individual multi-occupant spaces, such as individual workstations within an open office floor layout. Do not include areas that are not regularly occupied, such as hallways and lobbies, in these calculations

To meet the credit requirements, 50 percent of occupants in individual workspaces must have access to lighting controls. For LEED-EB, individual lighting controls can be lighting devices that are either permanently installed (hardwired) or portable (not hardwired). Follow the steps below to determine if this requirement is met. An example is presented in **Table 1**.

Step 1: Identify the number of individual workspaces in the building.

Step 2: Determine how many of the individual workspaces contain lighting controls that enable adjustments to suit individual task needs and preferences.

Step 3: Use **Equation 1** below to determine the percentage of individual occupant workspaces meeting this requirement.

Equation 1:

Percent of Individual Occupant Workspaces with Lighting Controls [%] =
(Number of Individual Occupant Workspace with Lighting Controls / Total Number of Individual Occupant Workspaces) x 100

Table 1: Sample Calculations for Individual Occupant Workspace Controls

Floor	Private Offices		Individual Workstations in Multi-Occupant Spaces		Other Individual Workstations		Total Number of Workspaces	Number with Lighting Controls
	Total Number	Number with Controls	Total Number	Number with Controls	Total Number	Number with Controls		
1	4	4	10	0	2	0	16	4
2	6	6	16	8	2	2	24	16
3	6	6	14	6	4	2	24	14
Totals							**64**	**34**
Percent of Individual Occupant Workspaces with Lighting Controls								**53%**

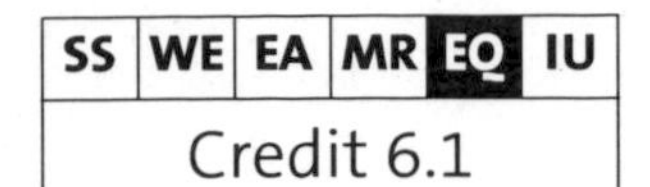

Calculations for Group Multi-Occupant Spaces

Group Multi-Occupant Spaces include spaces used as a place of congregation, such as conference rooms, classrooms and meeting halls. Note that open office plans that contain standard individual workstations are not considered group multi-occupant spaces.

Individuals using these spaces share the lighting controls. To meet the credit requirements, 50 percent of these spaces must meet the lighting control requirements. For group spaces with floor areas less than or equal to 10,000 square feet, there must be at least 3 lighting controls per 2,500 square feet of floor area. For group spaces with floor areas greater than 10,000 square feet, there must be at least 3 lighting controls per 10,000 square feet of floor area. Note that the number of controls needed should be rounded to the nearest whole number, unless that number is zero, in which case it should be round to one.

Because group multi-occupant spaces are populated irregularly and by groups of varying size and duration, area-based analysis of occupant controls is necessary. To determine the percentage of building occupants served by group multi-occupant space controls, use the steps below. An example is presented in **Table 2**.

Step 1: Identify each Group Multi-Occupant Space within the building, and determine its square footage.

Step 2: Determine if each space meets the requirements for the number of lighting controls specified above.

Step 3: Sum the floor areas of Group Multi-Occupant Spaces that meet or exceed the required number of lighting controls, and use **Equation 2** below to determine what percent it is of total Group Multi-Occupant Space floor area.

Documentation

- ❑ Documentation demonstrating and declaring that the required lighting controls are provided.

Equation 2

Percent of Group Multi-Occupant Spaces with Lighting Controls [%] =
(Floor Area of Group Multi-Occupant Spaces Meeting Lighting Control Requirements [SF] / Total Floor Area of Group Multi-Occupant Spaces [SF]) x 100

Table 2: Sample Calculations for Group Multi-Occupant Space Controls

Room	Area [SF]	Controls		Qualifying Space
		# Required	# Present	
Conference Hall A	12,000	3.6	4	Yes
Conference Hall B	15,500	4.7	4	No
Meeting Room A	1,000	1.2	1	Yes
Meeting Room B	1,400	1.7	2	Yes
Classroom A	2,600	3.1	2	No
Classroom B	2,500	3.0	3	Yes
Classroom C	4,000	4.8	5	Yes
Area of Qualifying Group Multi-Occupant Spaces [SF]				**20,900**
Total Area of Group Multi-Occupant Spaces [SF]				**39,000**
Percent Qualifying Group Multi-Occupant Spaces				**53.6 %**

- Documentation should be provided on organization letterhead, signed by an officer of the organization.
- Documentation should demonstrate that the requirements are met for BOTH individual occupant workspaces and group multi-occupant spaces.

❑ Provide drawings showing location of lighting controls.

- Drawings should consist of building plans illustrating sample workspaces and how lighting controls are located. Photographs may be provided to supplement drawings.

Other Resources

Controls and Automation for Facilities Managers: Applications Engineering by Viktor Boed, CRC Press, 1998.

This resource is directed at facility managers and includes information about control and automation systems for new and retrofit buildings.

Giving Occupants What They Want: Guidelines for Implement Personal Environmental Control in Your Building

www.cbe.berkeley.edu/research/pdf_files/FBau_WorldWk1999.pdf

This article by Fred Bauman from the Center for the Built Environment focuses on the benefits and technology available for implementing personal controls in buildings.

Increased Energy Savings by Individual Lighting Control

www.iaeel.org/IAEEL/Archive/Right_Light_Proceedings/Proceedings_body/BOK4/RL4embre.pdf

This study by Rob Embrechts and Chris Van Bellegem includes an analysis of the energy savings and occupant satisfaction levels associated with individual lighting controls.

Lighting Research Center (LCR)

www.lrc.rpi.edu

Part of the Rensselaer Polytechnic Institute, the LRC is a university-based research center devoted to lighting. Its web site provides references for lighting controls research, including the National Lighting Product Information Project (NLPIP).

Saving Energy with High-Tech Lighting Systems

http://www.edcmag.com/CDA/ArticleInformation/features/BNP_Features_Item/0,4120,77293,00.html

An article from Environmental Design and Construction magazine about lighting.

Definitions

Group Multi-Occupant Spaces include conference rooms, classrooms and other indoor spaces used as places of congregation for presentations, training sessions, etc. Individuals using these spaces share the lighting and temperature controls. Group multi-occupant spaces do not include open office plans that contain standard individual workstations.

Individual Occupant Workspaces are those in which individuals occupy standard workstations for the purpose of conducting individual tasks. These workstations can be located in private offices or multi-occupant spaces, such as open office areas.

Non-Occupied Spaces include all rooms used by maintenance personnel and not open for use by occupants, such as janitorial, storage and equipment rooms, and closets.

Non-Regularly Occupied Spaces include corridors, hallways, lobbies, break rooms, copy rooms, storage rooms, kitchens, restrooms, stairwells, etc.

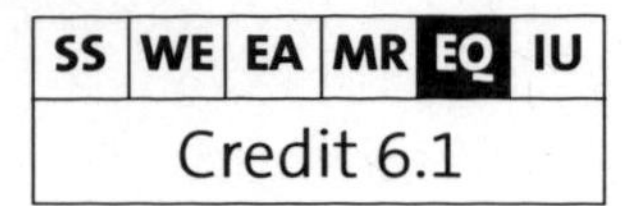
SS
WE
EA
MR
EQ
IU
Credit 6.1

SS	WE	EA	MR	EQ	IU
Credit 6.2					

1 point

Controllability of Systems

Temperature & Ventilation

Intent

Provide a high level of temperature and ventilation control by individual occupants or specific groups in multi-occupant spaces (e.g., classrooms or conference areas) to promote the productivity, comfort and well-being of building occupants.

Requirements

Provide individual temperature and ventilation controls for at least 50% of the building occupants, enabling adjustments to suit individual needs and preferences, or those of a group sharing a multi-occupant space or workgroup area. Operable windows may be used in lieu of individual controls for occupants in spaces near the windows (20 feet inside of and 10 feet to either side of the operable part of the window), and where the operable windows meet the requirements of ASHRAE 62.1-2004 paragraph 5.1.

Submittals – Initial Certification

Provide documentation, signed by the responsible party, demonstrating and declaring that the required ventilation and temperature controls are provided.

Submittals – Recertification

- ❑ If there has been no change to the temperature and ventilation control strategy or related occupant use of the building since the previous LEED-EB filing, provide a statement that the system continues to deliver required occupant control.

OR

- ❑ If there has been a change to this information since the previous LEED-EB filing, provide updated documentation, signed by the responsible party, demonstrating the changes made and declaring that the required temperature and ventilation controls are provided.

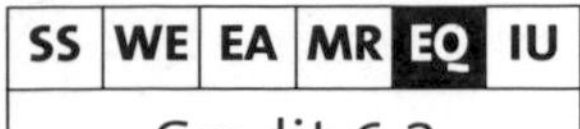

Summary of Referenced Standard

ASHRAE Standard 62.1-2004: Ventilation for Acceptable Indoor Air Quality

Topic Cited: Paragraph 5.1 – Natural Ventilation

ASHRAE

www.ashrae.org

(800) 527-4723

This standard addresses indoor air quality issues and prescribes minimum ventilation rates to reduce the potential for adverse health effects. The standard specifies the design of mechanical or natural ventilation systems to prevent uptake of contaminants, minimize the opportunity for growth and dissemination of microorganisms, and if necessary, to filter particulates. The standard also specifies proper makeup air inlet and exhaust air outlet locations relative to potential sources of contamination.

A Ventilation Rate Procedure and an Indoor Air Quality Procedure offer alternative approaches to achieve compliance with the standard. The Ventilation Rate Procedure has recently been revised. The updated version redefines an occupied zone as a breathing zone and prescribes ventilation rates in both per-person and per-unit area values. The Indoor Air Quality Procedure requires establishment of both quantitative and subjective criteria for acceptable air quality and ventilation and/or air-cleaning as appropriate to achieve the established levels.

Paragraph 5.1 of the standard addresses the use of natural ventilation systems in lieu of or in conjunction with mechanical ventilation systems and specifies the location, size, control and accessibility of the operable openings.

Green Building Concerns

Many existing buildings were designed as sealed environments with no occupant controls and no physical connection to the building grounds and neighboring areas. Such an environment can result in occupant discomfort due to undesirable temperature and ventilation, as well as a lack of connection to the outdoors. By providing individual controls such as thermostats, vents, operable windows (where available) and shading devices, building occupants can customize the indoor environment to their own preferences.

Allowing occupants to control their individual spaces may lead to higher worker productivity, while reducing the amount of time and effort maintenance personnel spend responding to thermal discomfort complaints.

Environmental Issues

Individual control of building systems may save energy by eliminating unwanted or unnecessary space conditioning. This results in reduced natural resource consumption and air quality impacts from energy production and consumption activities. Controllability of systems allows for an indoor environment that is well suited for occupant health and comfort.

Economic Issues

Providing localized or individual temperature and ventilation controls, or operable windows (if available and practical), may require materials and installation expenditures. Some existing buildings, however, may have originally been designed and constructed with operable windows. For other existing buildings, providing localized or individual temperature and ventilation controls, or operable windows, may require significant expenditures. In these buildings it may be possible to offset the costs through reduced costs of responding to occupant complaints and by energy

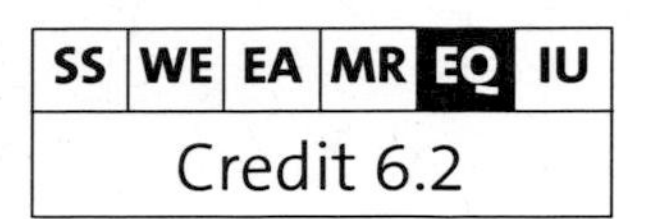

savings through lower conditioned temperatures, natural ventilation (if available and practical), and less solar gain through proper use of shading devices.

Conversely, misuse of personal controls such as setting thermostats too high or leaving windows open during non-working hours could increase energy costs. Therefore, building occupant education on the proper use of controls is an important part of localized or individual control of ventilation and temperature. Heightened occupant comfort may increase productivity and reduce the cost of responding to occupant complaints.

Strategies & Technologies

Evaluate how to provide localized and individual occupant temperature and ventilation controls in the existing building. Consider capabilities already present in the building (for example, it may have been built with operable windows), and what improvements can be added over the course of future building upgrades.

Consider the practicality of strategies like adding under-floor HVAC systems with individual diffusers, displacement ventilation systems with control devices, operable windows at perimeter spaces, ventilation walls and mullions.

As part of building upgrades over time, it may be possible to add under-floor air distribution systems. Under-floor air distribution systems are a very effective way to deliver individual control over both ventilation and temperature. They make it practical to provide individual floor vents that give individuals control over both ventilation and temperature. A number of new systems combine an under-floor air distribution systems with individual controls at the desktop. These Personal Environmental Control (PEC) systems transfer a large portion of the HVAC system control from the capital improvement budget to the furnishing budget. This can create challenges or opportunities, depending on the financial structure of the planned upgrade projects for the existing building.

If operable windows are already part of the building, or if the addition of operable windows is being considered, recognize the need to develop and implement strategies that coordinate the use of the windows with the HVAC system. In modern buildings, good engineering practices lead to a positive ventilation scheme for all regularly occupied spaces. In a traditional HVAC mixing system such as VAV, operable windows are difficult to accommodate. Either the windows need to be modest in size and low in quantity or a control interface with the HVAC system is needed to prevent counterproductive operation of the windows and the HVAC system.

A simple control interface might include a light indicating when the HVAC is operating and closed windows will provide the greatest comfort. An intermediate system might only allow economizer operations when windows are open. A more complex scheme might sense how many windows are open and the location of these windows, signal the building energy management system to close the windows with actuators, and then start up the HVAC system.

Educate occupants on individual control of their office space environment. A monitoring system can be implemented to maintain proper system operation, and signage can remind occupants of their responsibilities (e.g., turning down the thermostat at night and closing windows).

Synergies & Tradeoffs

Most existing buildings have relatively large temperature and ventilation zones with relatively few controls. To successfully integrate localized and individual controls into existing buildings, compare

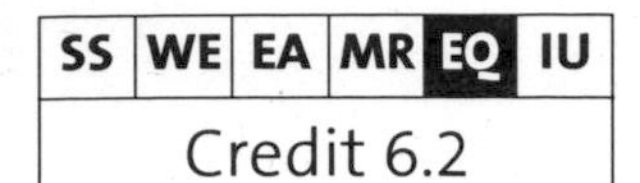

the economic benefits of user satisfaction and productivity with the costs.

Localized and individual controls for temperature and ventilation may not be feasible for all existing buildings. If the building cannot achieve localized or individual controls for at least 50 percent of the building occupants, the building cannot earn this credit.

Alteration of the ventilation and temperature control strategy for an existing building may change the energy performance of the building and require commissioning and measurement & verification attention. However, many existing buildings were initially designed when there was more dependence on natural ventilation, and the location and size of operable windows may well support cross-ventilation and controllability by building occupants. The degree of occupant controls will affect the performance of the ventilation systems.

Other LEED-EB prerequisites and credits related to temperature and ventilation controls include:

- ❑ EA Prerequisite 1: Existing Building Commissioning
- ❑ EA Prerequisite 2 and Credit 1: Energy Performance
- ❑ IEQ Prerequisite 1: Outside Air Introduction and Exhaust Systems
- ❑ IEQ Credit 1: Outside Air Delivery Monitoring
- ❑ IEQ Credit 2: Increased Ventilation
- ❑ IEQ Credit 7: Thermal Comfort
- ❑ IEQ Credit 8: Daylighting and Views

Calculations & Documentation

Calculations

Calculate the percent of occupants with access to temperature and ventilation controls for both Individual Workspaces and Multi-occupant Group Spaces based on the methodologies presented below. The criteria for both types of spaces must be met to earn this credit.

Calculations for Individual Occupant Workspaces

Include all workspaces that regularly accommodate a single occupant in these calculations. This includes workstations in both private offices and individual multi-occupant spaces, such as individual workstations within an open office floor layout. Areas that are not regularly occupied, such as hallways and lobbies, should not be included in these calculations

To meet the credit requirements, 50 percent of occupants in individual workspaces must have access to temperature and ventilation controls. Airflow and temperature controls must be devised that allow occupants to actively control the space's thermal condition. Control devises must be easily adjustable (i.e., less than six feet above the floor) and readily accessible (i.e., not locked in an enclosure) by the occupants. Operable windows may be used in lieu of individual controls for occupants in spaces near the windows, provided they meet the requirements of ASHRAE 62.1-2004 paragraph 5.1. Follow the steps below to determine if this requirement is met. An example is presented in **Table 1**.

Step 1: Identify the number of individual workspaces in the building.

Step 2: Determine how many of the individual workspaces contain at least one airflow and one temperature control that enable adjustments to suit individual task needs and preferences.

Step 3: Use **Equation 1** below to determine the percentage of individual occupant workspaces meeting this requirement.

SS | WE | EA | MR | **EQ** | IU

Credit 6.2

Calculations for Group Multi-Occupant Spaces

Group Multi-Occupant Spaces include spaces used as a place of congregation, such as conference rooms, classrooms and meeting halls. Note that open office plans that contain standard individual workstations are not considered group multi-occupant spaces.

Individuals using these spaces share the temperature and ventilation controls. To meet the credit requirements, 50 percent of these spaces must meet the control requirements. For group spaces with floor areas less than or equal to 10,000 square feet, there must be at least one airflow control and one temperature control per 2,500 square feet of floor area. For group spaces with floor areas greater than 10,000 square feet, there must be at least one airflow control and one temperature control per 10,000 square feet of floor area. Note that the number of controls needed should be rounded to the nearest whole number, unless that number is zero, in which case it should be rounded to one.

Because group multi-occupant spaces are populated irregularly and by groups of varying size and duration, area-based analysis of occupant controls is necessary. To determine the percentage of building occupants served by group multi-occupant space controls, use the steps below. An example is presented in **Table 2**.

Step 1: Identify each Group Multi-Occupant Space within the building, and determine its square footage.

Step 2: Determine if each space meets the requirements for the number of controls specified above.

Step 3: Sum the floor areas of Group Multi-Occupant Spaces that meet or exceed the required number of controls, and use **Equation 2** below to determine what percent it is of total Group Multi-Occupant Space floor area.

Documentation

- ❑ Documentation demonstrating and declaring that the required controls are provided.
  - Documentation should include a narrative description of the ventilation and temperature control

Equation 1

Percent of Individual Occupant Workspaces with Temperature and Ventilation Controls [%] = (Number of Individual Occupant Workspace with Controls / Total Number of Individual Occupant Workspaces) x 100

Table 1: Sample Calculations for Individual Occupant Workspace Controls

Floor	Private Offices		Individual Workstations in Multi-Occupant Spaces		Other Individual Workstations		Total Number of Workspaces	Number with Temperature & Ventilation Controls
	Total Number	Number with Controls	Total Number	Number with Controls	Total Number	Number with Controls		
1	4	4	10	0	2	0	16	4
2	6	6	16	8	2	2	24	16
3	6	6	14	6	4	2	24	14
Totals							**64**	**34**
Percent of Individual Occupant Workspaces with Lighting Controls								**53%**

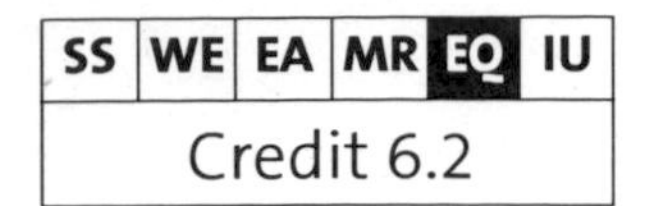

strategy and technical controls provided to individual occupants. This description should appear on organization letterhead and be signed by the officer of the organization responsible for this issue.

- Documentation should also include drawings showing locations of controls for spaces as appropriate.
- Documentation should demonstrate that the requirements are met for BOTH individual occupant workspaces and group multi-occupant spaces.

Other Resources

Controls and Automation for Facilities Managers: Applications Engineering by Viktor Boed, CRC Press, 1998.

A Field Study of Personal Environmental Module Performance in Bank of American's San Francisco Office Buildings

http://www.cbe.berkeley.edu/research/pdf_files/bauman1998_bofa.pdf

This study by Bauman et al. from the Center for Environmental Design Research at UC-Berkeley assesses the impact of installing Personal Environmental Modules on worker satisfaction.

Giving Occupants What They Want: Guidelines for Implement Personal Environmental Control in Your Building

www.cbe.berkeley.edu/research/pdf_files/FBau_WorldWk1999.pdf

This article by Fred Bauman from the Center for the Built Environment focuses on the benefits and technology available for implementing personal controls in buildings.

Definitions

Group Multi-Occupant Spaces include conference rooms, classrooms and other indoor spaces used as places of congregation for presentations, training sessions, etc. Individuals using these spaces share the lighting and temperature controls. Group multi-occupant spaces do not include open office plans that contain standard individual workstations.

Individual Occupant Workspaces are those in which individuals occupy

Equation 2

Percent of Group Multi-Occupant Spaces with Temperature and Ventilation Controls [%] =
(Floor Area of Group Multi-Occupant Spaces Meeting Control Requirements [SF] / Total Floor Area of Group Multi-Occupant Spaces [SF]) x 100

Table 2: Sample Calculations for Group Multi-Occupant Space Controls

Room	Area [SF]	Temp. Controls		Airflow Controls		Qualifying Space
		# Required	# Present	# Required	# Present	
Conference Hall A	12,000	1.2	1	1.2	1	Yes
Conference Hall B	15,500	1.6	1	1.6	2	No
Meeting Room A	1,000	0.4	1	0.4	1	Yes
Meeting Room B	1,400	0.6	1	0.6	1	Yes
Classroom A	2,600	1.0	1	1.0	1	Yes
Classroom B	2,500	1.0	1	1.0	1	Yes
Classroom C	4,000	1.6	1	1.6	1	No
Area of Qualifying Group Multi-Occupant Spaces [SF]						**19,500**
Total Area of Group Multi-Occupant Spaces [SF]						**39,000**
Percent Qualifying Group Multi-Occupant Spaces						**50 %**

standard workstations for the purpose of conducting individual tasks. These workstations can be located in private offices or multi-occupant spaces, such as open office areas.

Non-Occupied Spaces include all rooms used by maintenance personnel and not open for use by occupants. Included are janitorial, storage and equipment rooms, and closets.

Non-Regularly Occupied Spaces include corridors, hallways, lobbies, break rooms, copy rooms, storage rooms, kitchens, restrooms, stairwells, etc.

Personal Environmental Controls (PECs) are office furniture with heating, ventilation and lighting built into the furniture.

Variable Air Volume (VAV) is a type of HVAC system that varies the volume of conditioned air delivered to rooms.

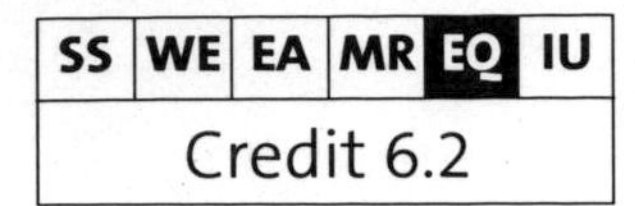
SS WE EA MR EQ IU
Credit 6.2

SS | WE | EA | MR | EQ | IU

Credit 7.1

1 point

Thermal Comfort

Compliance

Intent

Provide a comfortable thermal environment that supports the productivity and well-being of building occupants.

Requirements

Comply with ASHRAE Standard 55-2004, Thermal Comfort Conditions for Human Occupancy.

Submittals – Initial Certification

- ❑ Provide documentation that the project complies with ASHRAE Standard 55-2004.

Submittals – Recertification

Provide update of previous filings:

- ❑ Provide documentation that the project complies with ASHRAE Standard 55-2004.

AND EITHER

- ❑ If there have been no changes to comfort criteria, building systems or related occupant use of the building since the previous LEED-EB filing, provide a statement that the building continues to comply with the specified standard per the original submittal.

OR

- ❑ If there have been changes to comfort criteria, building or building systems, or occupant use of the building, update the documentation to reflect comfort criteria and compliance as the building is currently configured and used.

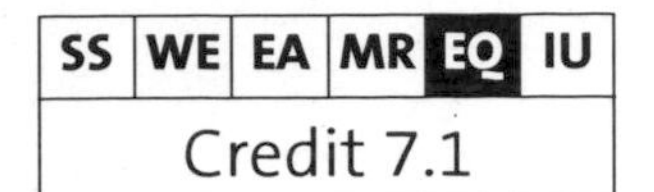

Summary of Referenced Standard

ASHRAE 55-2004: Thermal Environmental Conditions for Human Occupancy

ASHRAE

www.ashrae.org

(800) 527-4723

This standard specifies the combinations of indoor thermal environmental factors and personal factors that produce thermal environmental conditions acceptable to a certain percentage of the occupants within a defined space. The standard is intended for use in design, commissioning and testing of buildings and other occupied spaces and their HVAC systems and for the evaluation of thermal environments. The major elements of meeting the standard include determining the conditions that provide thermal comfort in a specific building, designing or upgrading HVAC systems so they have the capacity to deliver appropriate thermal conditions, and evaluating the thermal environment to ensure it meets thermal comfort criteria.

Green Building Concerns

Thermal comfort is an important component of occupant satisfaction with indoor environmental conditions. However, occupant surveys indicate that thermal satisfaction is often lower than satisfaction with other elements of the indoor environment.[21] Optimal temperature levels depend on occupant activity levels, air movement in the space, humidity levels and individual preferences. Dissatisfaction with the thermal environment may cause health problems and reduce productivity. A properly outfitted building can provide optimal temperature and humidity levels throughout the year. Furthermore, an HVAC system with controls to monitor temperature and humidity can avoid problems.

In addition to thermal comfort, spaces with low humidity promote static electricity that has detrimental effects on office equipment, human respiratory systems and certain furniture. Spaces with excessive humidity can promote the growth of mold and mildew on furnishings and interior surfaces, creating health hazards and increased maintenance requirements.

Environmental Issues

Maintaining optimal temperature and humidity levels may increase energy requirements for the building, resulting in air and water pollution impacts. In instances of unnecessarily elevated temperatures, maintaining optimal temperature can reduce energy requirements, thereby reducing the pollution impacts associated with energy consumption.

Thermal comfort is a major component of IEQ. Optimal building operation increases occupant productivity and reduces illnesses and absenteeism. Elevated temperatures are correlated with increased illness symptoms, headaches, and incidence of sick building syndrome (SBS).[22] Excessive humidity can also contribute to health issues in building occupants, and is associated with increase risk of respiratory symptoms and infection, fatigue, and headache.[23]

Economic Issues

The most frequent complaints from building occupants involve lack of thermal comfort, accounting for 75 percent of all indoor environmental complaints.[24] Estimates indicate that improving thermal comfort, and therefore avoiding complaints, could decrease labor costs by $2 billion annually.[25] Thermal discomfort can decrease occupant productivity and increase absenteeism, both of which reduce business profitability. Improving thermal environments in office buildings is estimated to result in a direct increase in productivity worth $12 to $125 billion annually.[26] Improving thermal comfort can also decrease the labor costs associated with building operators responding to complaints.

In instances where thermal discomfort is attributed to excessive heating or cooling, improving the thermal environment can result in decreased energy costs. For situations where additional heating or cooling is necessary to improve thermal comfort, energy costs may increase.

Undesirable humidity issues can also impact occupant productivity and may harm building fixtures and furnishings. Replacement costs for fixtures and furnishings contaminated with mold and mildew are often high. However, a humidification system that is needed for only a short period during the year may be cost-prohibitive, both in initial cost and in maintenance costs over the lifetime of the building.

Strategies & Technologies

Compliance with ASHRAE Standard 55-2004 involves determining acceptable thermal conditions for a specific building based on the expected satisfaction of a majority of the occupants, and then ensuring that actual thermal conditions fall within the acceptable ranges.

Determine Acceptable Thermal Conditions

The referenced standard provides a process by which building owners and facility managers can use environmental factors to calculate the acceptable thermal conditions for a specific building. (See ASHRAE 55-2004, Section 5: Conditions that Provide Thermal Comfort.) This is the first step in complying with the standard.

The environmental parameters that affect human thermal comfort are air temperature, radiation exchange, air velocity, humidity, clothing and activity. An assessment of building and system design, outdoor conditions, occupants' clothing and occupants' activity levels is incorporated into defining acceptable thermal conditions via ASHRAE 55-2004. Because of variations in clothing and activity level from one building the next, the ASHRAE standard does not mandate operating setpoints for buildings. Instead, it provides a method to define thermal conditions appropriate for specific buildings.

Use one of the two methodologies outlined in Section 5 to assess the relevant environmental parameters and determine acceptable thermal conditions for the building. For most buildings, Section 5.2: Method for Determining Acceptable Thermal Conditions in Occupied Spaces should be used. A second methodology (Section 5.3: Optional Method for Determining Acceptable Thermal Conditions in Naturally Conditioned Spaces) may be used for buildings that are "naturally conditioned" as defined in Section 5.3.

Document which methodology was used to determine acceptable thermal conditions, the logic of the assessments involved, and the resulting range of thermal conditions deemed acceptable for each thermal environmental variable.

System Design Compliance with Acceptable Thermal Conditions

Once acceptable thermal conditions for the building have been established, ensure that building mechanical systems, control systems and thermal envelopes have the capacity to deliver acceptable thermal conditions. ASHRAE 55-2004 does not provide specific guidance regarding mechanical and control systems or other building features. However, building systems must be in place that, at design conditions, are able to maintain conditions compliant with the thermal comfort conditions determine in Section 5.

Assess the ability of current building systems to provide acceptable thermal con-

SS	WE	EA	MR	EQ	IU
Credit 7.1					

ditions based on the ASHRAE 55-2004 requirements. If existing systems are inadequate, consider upgrading equipment, adding system controls or implementing other improvements to ensure building systems are capable of delivering the desire thermal conditions.

See Section 6: Compliance of ASHRAE 55-2004 for more information on mechanical system requirements.

Evaluate the Thermal Environment

Section 7 of ASHRAE 55-2004 provides means to validate that acceptable thermal conditions are maintained in the building. Evaluate the building's actual thermal environment as specified in the standard to achieve this credit as well as provide ongoing monitoring of thermal comfort in the building.

There are two viable methods for evaluating the thermal environment: Survey of Occupants and Analyze Environmental Variables. Both are described in paragraph 7.6 of the standard.

The standard's purpose is to ensure that an occupied space is comfortable for a substantial majority (at least 80 percent) of the occupants. Surveying the occupants for every operating mode, in every design condition, is one effective way to evaluate the environmental conditions of the space. Even though the Analyze Environmental Variables method is the more commonly used evaluation technique, the use of an occupant survey is also encouraged. Standard ASHRAE 55-2004 specifies the minimum data required from the occupants.

For projects validating thermal comfort conditions through the Analyze Environment Variables method, measurements should be made using the ASHRAE 55-20004 guidelines. Section 7 of the standard provides guidelines for measuring device criteria, measurement positions, measurement periods, and measuring conditions.

Synergies & Tradeoffs

Addition of temperature and humidity monitoring equipment can affect the energy performance of the building and requires commissioning and measurement & verification attention. Temperature and humidity monitoring and control can be challenging in existing buildings because the building systems are already in place.

Thermal and humidity measures can be integrated with CO_2 sensors, ventilation systems and occupant controls. Due to variation in individual preferences, individual controls may be the most effective way to deliver thermal comfort to building occupants.

Calculations & Documentation

Calculations

None.

Documentation

- ❑ Provide documentation that the project complies with ASHRAE Standard 55-2004.
  - Documentation should reflect identification of key thermal comfort conditions for the building type and uses as specified for compliance with ASHRAE 55-2004.
  - Document the validation method used to ensure compliance. Validation of compliance with thermal comfort criteria is described in Paragraph 7.6 of ASHRAE Standard 55-2004. This section of the standard outlines the means to validate compliance of the comfort criteria, and also provides guidelines for providing ongoing monitoring of thermal comfort performance of the building. The standard allows either of two validation methods: 1) Survey Oc-

cupants (Paragraph 7.6.2.1), or 2) Analyze Environment Variables (Paragraph 7.6.2.2). Compliance with the standard can be achieved with either validation method, though applying both methods would facilitate continuous improvement in facility performance and is encouraged.

Other Resources

ASHRAE

www.ashrae.org

The ASHRAE web site provides information about the organization, industry updates, standards, and guidelines for air quality in buildings.

Center for the Built Environment

www.cbe.berkeley.edu

From the University of California, Berkeley, this group's mission is to provide timely, unbiased information on promising new building technologies and design techniques. The Center offers a large amount of information on HVAC systems, IEQ, envelope systems and building information technology.

ISO Standard 7726-1998: Ergonomics of the thermal environment – Instruments for measuring physical quantities.

ISO, 1998

ISO Standard 7730-1994: Moderate thermal environments – Determination of the PMV and PPD indices and specification of the conditions for thermal comfort.

ISO, 1994

Definitions

Occupied Zone is the region normally occupied by people within a space. Per ASHRAE 55-2004, it is defined to generally consist of the space between the floor and 1.8 meters above the floor, and more than 1.0 meters from outside walls/windows or fixed heating, ventilating, or air conditioning equipment and 0.3 meters from internal walls.

Relative Humidity is the ratio of partial density of water vapor in the air to the saturation density of water vapor at the same temperature.

Thermal Comfort is a condition of mind experienced by building occupants expressing satisfaction with the thermal environment.

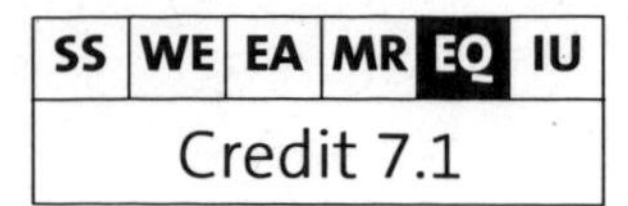

SS	WE	EA	MR	EQ	IU
Credit 7.2					

1 point

Thermal Comfort

Permanent Monitoring System

Intent

Provide a comfortable thermal environment that supports the productivity and well-being of building occupants.

Requirements

Provide a permanent monitoring system to ensure building performance to the desired comfort criteria as determined by IEQ Credit 7.1, Thermal Comfort: Compliance.

Submittals – Initial Certification

Provide documentation signed by the engineer or responsible party that identifies the comfort criteria, the strategy for ensuring performance to the comfort criteria, a description of the permanent monitoring system implemented and the process for corrective action to meet the requirement.

Submittals – Recertification

Provide an update of previous filings:

- ❑ Provide performance documentation to the comfort criteria as generated by the permanent monitoring system, indicating performance compliance and/or exceptions experienced with corrective actions taken for the period since the last LEED-EB certification.

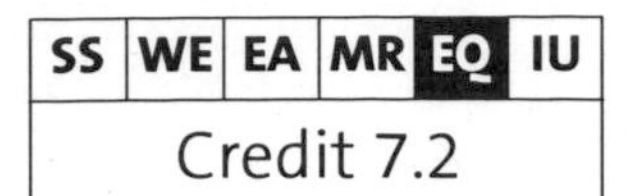

Summary of Referenced Standard

ASHRAE 55-2004: Thermal Environmental Conditions for Human Occupancy

ASHRAE

www.ashrae.org

(800) 527-4723

This standard specifies the combinations of indoor thermal environmental factors and personal factors that produce thermal environmental conditions acceptable to a certain percentage of the occupants within a defined space. The standard is intended for use in design, commissioning and testing of buildings and other occupied spaces and their HVAC systems and for the evaluation of thermal environments. The major elements of meeting the standard include determining the conditions that provide thermal comfort in a specific building, designing or upgrading HVAC systems so they have the capacity to deliver appropriate thermal conditions, and evaluating the thermal environment to ensure it meets thermal comfort criteria.

Green Building Concerns

See IEQ 7.1

Environmental Issues

See IEQ 7.1

Economic Issues

See IEQ 7.1

Strategies & Technologies

Implement systematic monitoring of the actual performance of the building to the comfort criteria defined by IEQ Credit 7.1 by analyzing environmental variables on a continuous basis. Monitoring might include measurement and trending of temperatures, relative humidity, CO_2 or air speed at locations selected according to their variability and impact on occupant comfort.

Install and maintain a temperature and humidity monitoring system for key areas of the building (i.e., at the perimeter and spaces provided with humidity control). This function can be satisfied by the building automation system. Analyze existing building HVAC systems and coil capacities relative to the ASHRAE requirements.

Synergies & Tradeoffs

See IEQ 7.1

Calculations & Documentation

See IEQ 7.1

Other Resources

See IEQ 7.1

Definitions

See IEQ 7.1

Case Study

Brengel Technology Center
Milwaukee, Wisconsin

LEED-EB Gold
Owner: Johnson Controls, Inc.

Photo courtesy of: Johnson Controls, Inc.

The Brengel Technology Center, a 130,000-square-foot office building in downtown Milwaukee, is equipped with temperature and humidity sensors in the discharge air plenums at all major air handling systems, as well as in select occupied spaces in the building. The occupied spaces monitored are representative of areas in the building that may experience temperature and/or humidity difficulties during certain occupancy patterns and/or periods of year. The temperature and humidity sensors are tied into the building automation system and monitored constantly. When temperatures exceed the allowable range (68–74 degrees F in the winter and 73–79 degrees F in the summer), the building automation system alerts building operators so they can address the conditions.

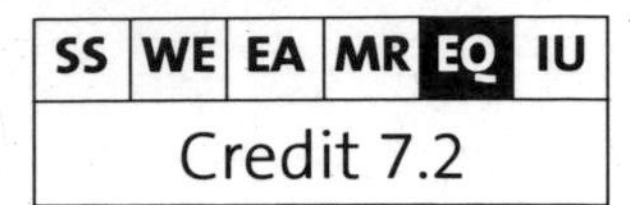

SS	WE	EA	MR	EQ	IU

Credits 8.1 & 8.2

2 points

Daylight and Views

Daylight

Intent

Provide a connection between indoor spaces and the outdoor environment through introduction of daylight and views into the occupied areas of the building.

Requirements

Achieve a minimum Daylight Factor of 2% (excluding all direct sunlight penetration) in space occupied for critical visual tasks, not including copy rooms, storage areas, mechanical, laundry and other low-occupancy support areas. Exceptions include those spaces where tasks would be hindered by the use of daylight or where accomplishing the specific tasks within a space would be enhanced by the direct penetration of sunlight. Provide glare control for all windows where direct penetration of sunlight would interfere with normal occupant activities.

Achievement of a 2% daylight factor in:

- ❑ IEQ Credit 8.1: 50% of all spaces occupied for critical visual tasks. (1 point)
- ❑ IEQ Credit 8.2: 75% of all spaces occupied for critical visual tasks. (1 point)

Submittals – Initial Certification

- ❑ Provide building floor plan copies and calculations indicating where the space plan has been implemented on the percentage of the total building area. Include area calculations defining the daylighting and daylight prediction calculations demonstrating a minimum Daylight Factor of 2% in these areas.
- ❑ Provide documentation of glare control features for all windows where direct penetration of sunlight would interfere with normal occupant activities.

Submittals – Recertification

Provide an update of previous filings:

- ❑ Provide documentation of glare control features for all windows where direct penetration of sunlight would interfere with normal occupant activities.

AND EITHER

- ❑ If there has been no change to the amount of daylighting since the previous LEED-EB filing, provide a statement that the required daylighting percentages are achieved.

OR

- ❑ If there has been a change to the amount of daylighting since the previous LEED-EB filing, provide building floor plan copies and calculations indicating where the space plan has been implemented on a percentage of the total building area. Include area calculations defining the daylighting and daylight prediction calculations demonstrating a minimum Daylight Factor of 2% in these areas.

Summary of Reference Standard

There is no standard referenced for this credit.

Green Building Concerns

Daylighting improves the indoor environment of buildings by exposing occupants to natural light. Studies (see "Other Resources" below) have demonstrated that productivity increases dramatically for building occupants working in daylit areas. In addition, daylighting decreases energy costs for buildings by providing natural solar lighting, and reduces space-cooling loads by minimizing waste heat generated by lights. A well-designed daylit building is estimated to reduce energy use by 50 to 80 percent.[27]

For existing buildings not originally constructed with daylighting, renovation projects may provide an opportunity for incorporating daylight into the building interior. Daylighting design involves a careful balance of heat gain and loss, glare control and variations in daylight availability. Shading devices, light shelves, courtyards, atriums and window glazing are all strategies employed in daylighting design. Important considerations include building orientation, window size and spacing, glass selection, reflectance of interior finishes, and locations of interior walls. Adding daylighting features to a building may impact maintenance activities such as regular glass-cleaning and a systems maintenance schedule.

Environmental Issues

Daylighting reduces the need for electric lighting and space cooling of building interiors, resulting in decreased energy use. This conserves natural resources and reduces air pollution impacts due to decreased energy production and consumption. Daylit spaces also provide an indoor environment that increases occupant productivity and reduces absenteeism and illness.

Adding daylighting features to existing building envelopes may require renovation projects, which have the potential to generate waste, cause IAQ contamination and contribute to other environmental issues.

Economic Issues

Specialized glazing can increase initial costs for a project and can lead to excessive heat gain if not designed properly. Adding daylighting features to existing buildings will incur renovation and materials expenses. Glazing provides less insulating effect compared to standard walls and requires additional maintenance. However, offices with sufficient natural daylight have proven to increase occupant comfort and performance (see "Other Resources" for example studies). In most cases, occupant salaries significantly outweigh first costs of incorporating daylighting measures into a building design.

Daylighting can significantly reduce artificial lighting requirements and energy costs in many commercial and industrial buildings, as well as schools, libraries and hospitals. In some facilities, daylighting has reduced energy use for interior lighting by 80 percent.[28] In addition to lighting energy savings, daylighting can decrease the energy load for mechanical cooling systems, boosting energy savings to as much as one-third of total energy costs.[29]

Strategies & Technologies

Implement renovation design strategies to provide access to daylight and views to the outdoors in a glare-free way using vision panels, low partitions, exterior sun shading, interior light shelves and/or window treatments.

Determine if daylighting and direct line of sight to the outdoors is feasible and appropriate for the building. Some buildings cannot utilize natural daylighting due to site constraints or specialized building uses that prohibit sunlight penetration.

It is not possible to re-orient existing buildings on the project site to maximize daylighting options, so creative use of existing features and any opportunities created by building renovations are likely strategies.

Courtyards, atriums, clerestory windows, skylights, interior light shelves, exterior fins, louvers and adjustable blinds, used alone or in combination, are effective strategies to achieve deep daylight penetration. The desired amount of daylight will differ depending on the tasks occurring in a daylit space. Daylit buildings often have several daylight zones with differing target light levels. In addition to light levels, daylighting strategies should address interior color schemes, direct beam penetration, and integration with the electric lighting system.

Glare control is perhaps the most common failure in daylighting strategies. Large window areas provide generous amounts of daylight to the task area, and if not controlled properly, this daylight can produce unwanted glare. Measures to control glare include light shelves, louvers, blinds, fins and shades.

Daylighting design often uses computer modeling applications to simulate conditions. Daylighting applications produce continuous daylight contours to simulate the daylighting conditions of interior spaces and to account for combined effects of multiple windows within a daylit space.

Photo-responsive controls for electric lighting can be incorporated into daylighting strategies to maintain consistent light levels and to minimize occupant perception of the transition from natural light to artificial light. These controls result in energy savings by reducing electric lighting in high daylight conditions while preserving foot-candle levels on the task surface.

Synergies & Tradeoffs

The existing building orientation has a significant effect on the success of daylighting strategies. Vertical site elements such as neighboring buildings and trees may reduce the potential for daylighting. Due to these factors, existing buildings may have limited daylighting potential due to their orientation, number and size of building openings, and floor plate size. Older existing buildings often feature larger window openings. This may provide good opportunities for creative strategies for daylighting. Light sensors and automatic controls will affect the energy performance of the building and will require commissioning and measurement & verification attention.

The inclusion of daylight in buildings may influence lighting and HVAC needs. Consider how daylighting features can work in concert with natural ventilation, passive solar heating and cooling, artificial lighting control systems, and landscaping features.

Calculations & Documentation

Calculations

The daylighting calculation methodology below can be applied to approximate the daylight factor for each regularly occupied room in the building. The Daylight Factor (DF) is the ratio of exterior illumination to interior illumination expressed as a percentage. The variables used to determine the daylight factor include the floor area, window area, window geometry, visible transmittance (T_{vis}) and window height. This calculation method aims to

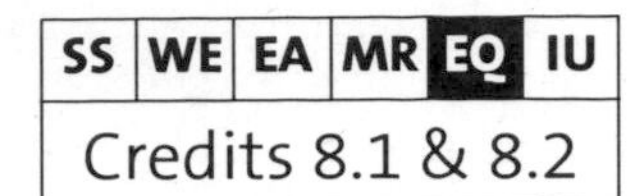

provide a minimum 2 percent DF at the back of a space.

Areas to include in the daylighting calculations include all regularly occupied spaces such as office spaces, meeting areas, and cafeterias. Areas that should not be considered include support areas for copying, storage, mechanical equipment, laundry and restrooms.

The daylighting calculation methodology includes the following steps:

1. Create a spreadsheet and identify all regularly occupied rooms. Determine the floor area of each applicable room using construction documents.
2. For each room identified, note the window types and estimate the window areas. **Table 1** lists the range of acceptable window types.
3. Glare control is required for each window where direct penetration of sunlight would interfere with normal occupant activities. **Table 1** provides best practice glare control measures for different window types. Create a second spreadsheet that identifies the type of glare control applied to each window type. Provide rationale for any window not protected (e.g., window facing north in northern latitudes).
4. For each window type, insert the appropriate geometry factor, minimum T_{vis}, and height factor as listed in **Table 1**.
   - ❑ The geometry factor indicates the effectiveness of a particular aperture to distribute daylight relative to window location.
   - ❑ The minimum T_{vis} is the recommended level of transmittance for selected glazing.
   - ❑ The height factor accounts for where light is introduced to the space.
     - Window areas above 7'6" are considered to be daylight glazing. Glazing at this height is the most effective at distributing daylight deep into the interior space.
     - Window areas from 2'6" to 7'6" are considered to be vision glazing. These window areas are primarily used for viewing and lighting interior spaces close to the building perimeter.
     - Window areas below 2'6" do not generally contribute significantly to daylighting of interior spaces and are excluded

Table 1: Daylight Design Criteria

Window Type	Geometry Factor	Minimum Tvis	Height Factor	Best Practice Glare Control
Sidelight Daylight Glazing	0.1	0.7	1.4	Adjustable blinds Interior light shelves Fixed translucent exterior Shading devices
Sidelighting Vision Glazing	0.1	0.4	0.8	Adjustable blinds Exterior shading devices
Toplighting Vertical Monitor	0.2	0.4	1.0	Fixed interior Adjustable exterior blinds
Toplighting Sawtooth Monitor	0.33	0.4	1.0	Fixed interior Exterior louvers
Toplighting Horizontal Skylights	0.5	0.4	1.0	Interior fins Exterior fins Louvers

from the calculations. (Note: If the building design includes exterior light shelves of open perimeter floor space, designed to reflect daylighting into the interior spaces, window areas below 2'6" may play a role in daylighting for interior spaces. If this is true for the building, make the case for how this works and include it in the calculations.)

5. Calculate the Daylight Factor for each window type using **Equation 1**. For rooms with more than one window type, sum all window types to obtain a total Daylight Factor for the room.

6. If the total daylight factor for a room is 2 percent or greater, then the square footage of the room is applicable to the credit.

7. Sum the square footage of all applicable rooms and divide by the total square footage of all regularly occupied spaces. If this percentage is greater than 50 percent, then the building qualifies for the first point of this credit (IEQ Credit 8.1). If this percentage is greater than 75 percent, then the building qualifies for the second point of this credit (IEQ Credit 8.2).

Table 2 provides an example of daylighting calculations for an office building. All of the offices are considered to be regularly occupied spaces while support areas such as hallways, foyers, storage areas, mechanical rooms and restrooms are not considered to be regularly occupied.

Equation 1

Daylight factor = (Window area [SF] / Floor area [SF]) x Window Geometry x (Tvis / Minimum Tvis) x Window Height Factor

Table 2: Sample Daylighting Calculations

Office/ Room	Floor Area [SF]	Glazing Area [SF]	Window Type	Geometry Factor	Tvis		Window Height Factor	Daylight Factor		Daylit Area	Sun Control
					Actual	Min		Each [%]	Room [%]	[SF]	
A	820	120	vision	0.1	0.9	0.4	0.8	2.6	3.3	820	Ext shading device
		40	daylight	0.1	0.7	0.7	1.4	0.7			Interior blinds
B	410	75	vision	0.1	0.9	0.4	0.8	1.6	2.5	410	Ext shading device
		25	daylight	0.1	0.7	0.7	1.4	0.9			Interior blinds
C	120	36	vision	0.1	0.4	0.4	0.8	2.4	2.4	120	Ext shading device
D	95	25	vision	0.1	0.4	0.4	0.8	2.1	2.1	95	Ext shading device
E	410	75	vision	0.1	0.9	0.4	0.8	3.3	4.1	410	Ext shading device
		25	daylight	0.1	0.7	0.7	1.4	0.9			Interior blinds
F	410	75	vision	0.1	0.9	0.4	0.8	3.3	4.1	410	Ext shading device
		25	daylight	0.1	0.7	0.7	1.4	0.9			Interior blinds
G	120	36	vision	0.1	0.4	0.4	1.4	4.2	4.2	120	Ext shading device
H	120	36	vision	0.1	0.4	0.4	1.4	4.2	4.2	120	Ext shading device
I	95	32	vision	0.1	0.4	0.4	1.4	4.7	4.7	95	Ext shading device
J	95	32	vision	0.1	0.4	0.4	1.4	4.7	4.7	95	Ext shading device
K	410	36	sawtooth	0.3	0.4	0.7	1.0	1.5	1.5	0	Interior blinds
L	410	36	sawtooth	0.3	0.4	0.7	1.0	1.5	1.5	0	Interior blinds
M	120	24	sawtooth	0.3	0.4	0.7	1.0	3.4	3.4	120	Interior blinds
N	95	24	sawtooth	0.3	0.4	0.7	1.0	3.4	3.4	95	Interior blinds
Totals	**3,730**									**2,910**	
		Percentage of Rooms Meeting 2% daylight Factor Requirement								**78%**	

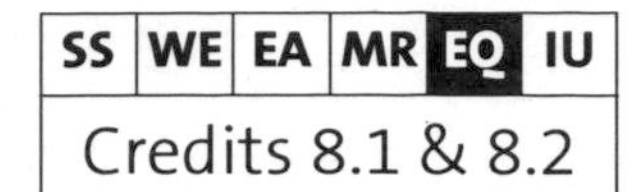

For each regularly occupied room, the floor area, window area, window geometry, transmittance and window height are noted. The daylighting factor is calculated using the provided equation (Equation 1). Rooms with a total daylighting factor of 2.0 percent or greater qualify as being daylit. Where a room has more than one window type (such as Office A), the daylight factors for each type (daylight and vision windows) are computed and then summed to obtain a total Daylight Factor for the room. Note that some rooms in the example have a Daylight Factor of less than 2 percent and do not qualify as daylit rooms.

Once daylighting factors have been calculated for all regularly occupied space, the sum of regularly occupied space and the sum of daylit area is determined. The total daylit percentage is then calculated by dividing the total daylit area by the total regularly occupied area.

Glare control devices are listed in **Table 2** for the daylit rooms. The example qualifies for the first point of this credit because it exceeds the minimum square footage of daylit rooms and includes glare control on all windows in daylit rooms.

Documentation

- ❑ Provide documentation of glare control features.
  - Documentation of glare control features should include photographs of the glare control features in place, as well as manufacturer literature where appropriate.

Other Resources

Analysis of the Performance of Students in Daylit Schools

www.innovativedesign.net/paper_a.htm#student

This study by Nicklas and Bailey, Innovative Design, Raleigh, NC, considers the influence of daylighting on student performance on standardized testing, and can serve as a resource for conducting productivity studies.

California Energy Commission Public Interest Energy Research (PIER) Program

www.energy.ca.gov/pier/index.html

The PIER Program supports energy research, development and demonstration projects, including those related to windows, daylighting and productivity. Copies of relevant studies are available on the Integrate Energy Systems: Productivity & Building Science portion of the web site (http://www.energy.ca.gov/pier/final_project_reports/500-03-082.html), including:

- ❑ *Windows and Offices: A Study of Office Worker Performance and the Indoor Environment*
- ❑ *Windows and Classrooms: A Study of Student Performance and the Indoor Environment*
- ❑ *Daylight and Retail Sales*

Daylighting Performance and Design, by Gregg D. Ander, John Wiley and Sons, 2003.

This book contains information on daylighting strategies, materials and methods of construction.

Tips for Daylighting with Windows

http://windows.lbl.gov/daylighting/designguide/designguide.html

This comprehensive daylighting guide is from Lawrence Berkeley National Laboratory.

Windows and Daylighting Homepage

http://windows.lbl.gov

This resource from the Lawrence Berkeley National Laboratory provides product research, software tools and other daylighting-related information.

The Whole Building Design Guide

http://www.wbdg.org/

The Daylighting and Lighting Control section provides a wealth of resources including definitions, fundamentals, materials and tools.

Definitions

Daylight Factor (DF) is the ratio of exterior illumination to interior illumination and is expressed as a percentage. The variables used to determine the daylight factor include the floor area, window area, window geometry, visible transmittance (T_{vis}) and window height.

Daylight Glazing is vertical window area that is located 7'6" above the floor of the room. Glazing at this height is the most effective at distributing daylight deep into the interior space.

Daylighting is the controlled admission of natural light into a space through glazing with the intent of reducing or eliminating electric lighting. By utilizing solar light, daylighting creates a stimulating and productive environment for building occupants.

Glare is defined as any excessively bright source of light within the visual field that creates discomfort or loss in visibility.

Space Occupied for Critical Visual Tasks are rooms used for tasks like reading and computer monitor use.

Visible Transmittance (T_{vis}) is the ratio of total transmitted light to total incident light. In other words, it is the amount of light passing through a glazing surface divided by the amount of light striking the glazing surface. A higher T_{vis} value indicates that a greater amount of incident light is passing through the glazing.

Vision Glazing is glazing that provides views of outdoor landscapes to building occupants for vertical windows between 2'6" and 7'6" above the floor. Windows below 2'6" and windows above 7'6" (including daylight glazing, skylights, and roof monitors) do not count as vision glazing for this credit.

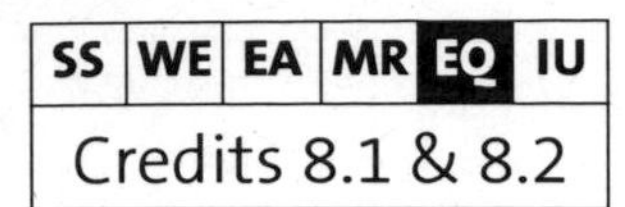

SS | WE | EA | MR | EQ | IU

Credits 8.3 & 8.4

1 point

Daylight and Views

Views

Intent

Provide a connection between indoor spaces and the outdoor environment through introduction of daylight and views into the occupied areas of the building.

Requirements

Develop and adopt a space churn renovation plan and policy that specifies the goal of achieving direct line of sight to vision glazing for building occupants from 90% of all regularly occupied spaces (not including copy rooms, storage areas, mechanical, laundry and other low-occupancy support areas).

AND

- ❑ IEQ Credit 8.3: Achieve direct line of sight to vision glazing for building occupants from 45% of regularly occupied spaces. (1 point)
- ❑ IEQ Credit 8.4: Achieve direct line of sight to vision glazing for building occupants from 90% of regularly occupied spaces. (1 point)

Regularly occupied spaces are considered as having access to views if they provide direct line of sight to vision glazing, where horizontal view angles to the vision glazing are not less than 10 degrees (must include partition base and glazing frame if appropriate). Vision glazing is vertical windows between 2'6" and 7'6" above the floor. Views to vision glazing may be direct or through interior windows.

Submittals – Initial Certification

- ❑ Provide a copy of the building space churn renovation plan and policy that specifies the goal of achieving direct line of sight to vision glazing from 90% of all regularly occupied spaces, (not including copy rooms, storage areas, mechanical, laundry and other low-occupancy support areas).
- ❑ Provide building floor plan copies and calculations indicating where the space plan has been implemented:
  - For 45% of all regularly occupied spaces.
  - For an additional 45% (90% total) of all regularly occupied spaces.

Submittals – Recertification

Provide an update of previous filings:

- ❑ If there has been no change to the occupant views achievements since the previous LEED-EB filing, provide a statement that the building continues to meet the credit requirements.

OR

- ❑ If there has been a change to the occupant views achievements since the previous LEED-EB filing, provide a copy of the building space churn renovation plan and policy that specifies the goal of achieving direct line of sight to vision glazing from

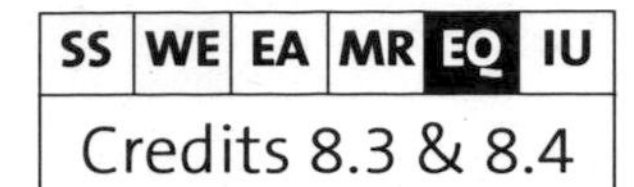

90% of all regularly occupied spaces, (not including copy rooms, storage areas, mechanical, laundry and other low-occupancy support areas).

- ❑ Provide building floor plan copies and calculations indicating where the space plan has been implemented:
  - For 45% of all regularly occupied spaces.
  - For an additional 45% (90% total) of all regularly occupied spaces.

Summary of Referenced Standard

There is no standard referenced for this credit.

Green Building Concerns

Building occupants with access to outside views have an increased sense of well-being, leading to higher productivity and increased job satisfaction. Important considerations for providing views include building orientation, window size and spacing, glass selection and locations of interior walls.

For existing buildings not initially constructed with views, renovation projects may provide an opportunity to add views, though the limitation of the existing structure may constrain options. Following the addition of windows to the building envelope, building maintenance schedules should be altered to accommodate regular glass-cleaning and other maintenance.

Environmental Issues

The use of windows to provide access to views can result in daylighting that reduces the need for electric lighting of building interiors, resulting in decreased energy use. If operable windows are provided, natural ventilation options can also reduce energy consumption. This conserves natural resources and reduces air pollution impacts due to decreased energy production and consumption.

On the other hand, renovation projects for adding windows to the building envelope have the potential to generate waste and require material inputs that may deplete natural resources.

Views can also provide a connection between building occupants and the outdoors, creating a more appealing indoor environment. Job satisfaction and work attitudes among office workers are significantly related to the presence of windows in the workplace.[30]

Economic Issues

Adding views to an existing building may necessitate rearranging building floor plans, divider walls and furniture. To minimize the costs associated with adding views, plans should be developed to make incremental steps toward increasing occupant views during future renovation projects.

Spaces with daylighting and views increase occupant productivity, reduce absenteeism and illness, and can help recruit and retain employees. In most cases, occupant salaries significantly outweigh first costs of incorporating views into a building design.

Strategies & Technologies

Develop and implement a space renovation plan and policy that specifies the goal of achieving direct line of sight to vision glazing from 90 percent of all regularly occupied spaces. Utilize opportunities created by churn to gradually implement this plan over time.

Determine if direct line of sight to the outdoors is feasible and appropriate for the building. Some buildings cannot provide adequate views due to site constraints or specialized building uses that prohibit sunlight penetration.

Consider how to rearrange interior walls and furnishings to maximize access to views from occupant workspaces.

Assess the feasibility of adding windows to the building envelope during renovation projects. Size, spacing, glazing and other factors can affect the quality of the view provided by windows, and should be considering during renovation design planning.

Implement renovation design strategies to provide access to views to the outdoors in a glare-free way using vision panels, low partitions, exterior sun shading, interior light shelves and/or window treatments. Glare control is perhaps the most common failure in window systems. Glare is defined as any excessively bright source of light within the visual field that creates discomfort or loss in visibility. Large window areas provide generous amounts of daylight to the task area, and if not controlled properly, this daylight can produce unwanted glare.

Implement green building principles during window renovation projects, such as selecting energy-efficient windows that are manufactured with environmentally friendly materials. Care should also be taken to minimize and properly manage waste generated during window renovations and preserving IAQ during renovation projects.

Synergies &Tradeoffs

Providing building occupants with access to views to the outside of the building is consistent with increasing the amount of daylighting in the building.

Operable windows may also contribute to the achievement of goals for increasing ventilation and providing occupant controls.

High efficiency windows can improve building energy efficiency and reduce HVAC loads, while poorly designed window systems can promote undesirable solar heat gain or building heat loss to the outdoors.

The integration of views into renovation plans should take into consideration points of visual interest viewable from the building, and should be mindful of landscaping and other site maintenance activities. Landscaping and grounds maintenance activities can preserve and promote these desirable views from window lines of sight.

Calculate the percent of occupants with access to views for both Individual Occupant Workspaces and Multi-occupant Group Spaces based on the methodologies presented below. The criteria for both types of spaces must be met to earn this credit.

Views are required for at least 45 percent of all regularly occupied spaces for IEQ Credit 8.3 and for at least 90 percent of all regularly occupied spaces for IEQ Credit 8.4. Use the following steps to perform view calculations:

Calculations for Individual Occupant Workspaces

Include all workspaces that regularly accommodate a single occupant in these calculations. This includes workstations in both private offices and individual multi-occupant spaces, such as individual workstations within an open office floor layout. Do not include areas that are not regularly occupied, such as hallways and lobbies, in these calculations

1. Using the Views spreadsheet in **Table 1** below, note the view vision glazing in each room containing individual occupant workspaces. Vision glazing is vertical windows between 2'6" and 7'6" above the floor. Windows below 2'6" and windows above 7'6" (including daylight glazing, skylights and roof monitors) do not count as vision glazing for this credit. For best results, use a copy of the floor plan and track the total number of regularly occupied workspaces and the number of workspaces within each room that have a direct line of sight. Construct line of sight lines at each window to identify non-view workspaces in each room. Remember to take into account the wall thickness when determining oblique angles of sight through windows because wall thickness affects the angle of sight. Visually inspect each room and compare workspaces with direct views against those without.

Table 1: Sample Views Calculations for Individual Occupant Workspaces

Office/Room	Description	Number of Workspaces with Access to Views	Total Number of Workspaces
A	Multi-occupant room w/ workspaces divided by partitions	6	11
B	Reception area	3	3
C	Private office	1	1
D	Private office	1	1
E	Multi-occupant room w/ workspaces divided by partitions	6	12
F	Interior multi-occupant room	0	6
G	Multi-occupant room w/ workspaces divided by partitions	5	10
H	Interior shared office	0	3
I	Private office	1	1
J	Private office	0	1
Totals		**23**	**49**
Percent of Workspaces with Access to Views			**47%**

Views to vision glazing may be direct or through interior windows.

2. Calculate the percent of regularly occupied workspaces with access to views by summing the number of individual occupant workspaces with access to views and dividing by the total number of individual occupant workspaces within the building.

Table 1 below provides an example of view calculations for an office. For each room containing individual occupant workspaces, the total number of workspaces and the portion of them with access to views is noted.

Calculations for Group Multi-Occupant Spaces

Group Multi-Occupant Spaces include spaces used as a place of congregation, such as conference rooms, classrooms and meeting halls. Note that open office plans that contain standard individual workstations are not considered group multi-occupant spaces.

Because group multi-occupant spaces are populated irregularly and by groups of varying size and duration, area-based analysis of views is necessary. To determine the percentage of building occupants served by views in group multi-occupant spaces, use the steps below. An example is presented in **Table 2.**

1. Identify each Group Multi-Occupant Space within the building, and determine its square footage.
2. For each space, note if views are provided by vision glazing (vertical windows between 2'6" and 7'6" above the floor). The entire space is considered to have adequate views if direct line of sight to vision glazing is present for 90 percent or more of the floor space.
3. Calculated the percent of Total Group Multi-Occupant Space floor area with access to views by summing the floor areas of the Group Multi-Occupant Spaces that meet or exceed the view criteria outlined in Step 2 above, and dividing by the total floor area of all Group Multi-Occupant Spaces.

Because 47 percent of Individual Occupant Workspaces have access to views

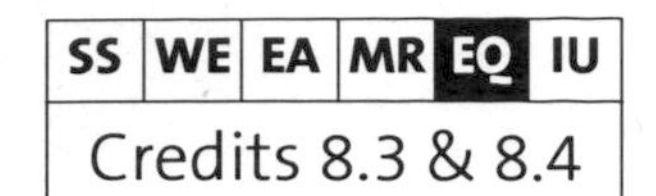

Table 2: Sample Views Calculations for Group Multi-Occupant Spaces

Room	Area [SF]	Area of Room with Access to Views [SF]	Qualifying Space	
			Yes/No	Area [SF]
Conference Hall A	12,000	0	No	0
Meeting Room A	1,000	950	Yes	1,000
Meeting Room B	1,400	1,300	Yes	1,400
Classroom A	2,600	2,500	Yes	2,600
Classroom B	2,500	2,350	Yes	2,500
Classroom C	4,000	3,700	Yes	4,000
Classroom D	750	200	No	0
Area of Qualifying Group Multi-Occupant Spaces [SF]				**12,250**
Total Area of Group Multi-Occupant Spaces [SF]				**24,250**
Percent Qualifying Group Multi-Occupant Spaces				**50.5 %**

and 46.4 percent of Group Multi-Occupant Spaces include access to views, this example qualifies for IEQ Credit 8.3, but *not* IEQ Credit 8.4.

Documentation

- ❑ Provide a copy of the building space churn renovation plan and policy.
  - Building space churn renovation plan and policy should appear on official organization letterhead.
- ❑ Provide building floor plan copies and calculations.
  - Floor plans should clearly identify areas where the space plan has been implemented.

Other Resources

Efficient Windows Collaborative

www.efficientwindows.org

This site, jointly developed by the University of Minnesota, Alliance to Save Energy, and Lawrence Berkeley National Laboratory, provides information about the benefits of energy-efficient windows, descriptions of how they work, and recommendations for their selection and use.

Tips for Daylighting with Windows

http://windows.lbl.gov/daylighting/designguide/designguide.html

This comprehensive daylighting guide is from the Lawrence Berkeley National Laboratory.

Whole Building Design Guide: Windows and Glazing

www.wbdg.org/design/windows.php

This section of the Whole Building Design Guide web site provides information about window systems technologies and the benefits windows provide for indoor environmental quality.

Windows and Daylighting Homepage

http://windows.lbl.gov

This site from the Lawrence Berkeley National Laboratory provides information about window and daylighting technology.

Definitions

Group Multi-Occupant Spaces include conference rooms, classrooms and other indoor spaces used as places of congregation for presentations, training sessions, etc. Individuals using these spaces share the lighting and temperature controls. Group multi-occupant spaces do not include open office plans that contain standard individual workstations.

Individual Occupant Workspaces are those in which individuals occupy standard workstations for the purpose

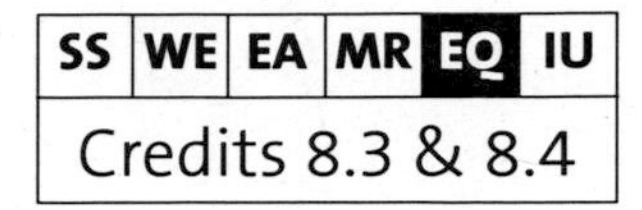

of conducting individual tasks. These workstations can be located in private offices or multi-occupant spaces, such as open office areas.

Non-Occupied Spaces include all rooms used by maintenance personnel and not open for use by occupants. Included are janitorial, storage and equipment rooms, and closets.

Non-Regularly Occupied Spaces include corridors, hallways, lobbies, break rooms, copy rooms, storage rooms, kitchens, restrooms, stairwells, etc.

Regularly Occupied Spaces are areas where workers are seated or standing as they work inside a building.

Vision Glazing is glazing that provides views of outdoor landscapes to building occupants for vertical windows between 2'6" and 7'6" above the floor. Windows below 2'6" and windows above 7'6" (including daylight glazing, skylights, and roof monitors) do not count as vision glazing for this credit.

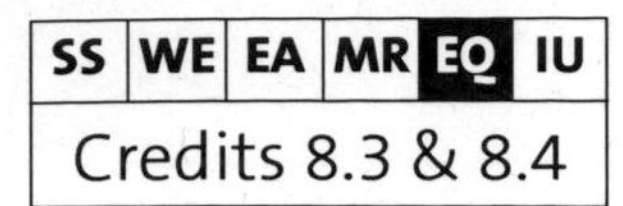
SS WE EA MR EQ IU
Credits 8.3 & 8.4

SS	WE	EA	MR	EQ	IU
Credit 9					

1 point

Contemporary IAQ Practice

Intent

Enhance IAQ performance by optimizing practices to prevent the development of indoor air quality problems in buildings correcting indoor air quality problems when they occur and, maintaining the well- being of the occupants.

Requirements

Develop and implement on an ongoing basis an IAQ management program for buildings based on the EPA document "Building Air Quality: A Guide for Building Owners and Facility Managers," EPA Reference Number 402-F-91-102, December 1991, which is available on the EPA Web site, www.epa.gov/iaq/largebldgs/graphics/iaq.pdf.

Submittals – Initial Certification

- ❑ Provide a copy of the IAQ management program for the building based on the EPA document "Building Air Quality: A Guide for Building Owners and Facility Managers."
- ❑ Provide documentation of the ongoing implementation over the performance period of the IAQ management program for the building.

Submittals – Recertification

Provide an update of previous filings:

- ❑ If there has been no change to the IAQ management program for the building since the previous LEED-EB filing, provide a statement that there has been no change.

OR

- ❑ If there has been a change to the IAQ management program for the building since the previous LEED-EB filing, provide updated information. Provide an updated copy of the IAQ management program for the building based on the EPA document "Building Air Quality: A Guide for Building Owners and Facility Managers."
- ❑ Provide documentation of the ongoing implementation over the performance period of the IAQ management program for the building.

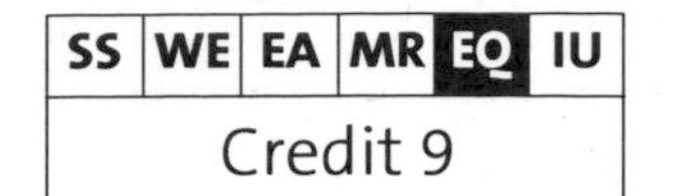

Summary of Referenced Standard

Building Air Quality: A Guide for Building Owners and Facility Managers

Reference Number 402-F-91-102, December 1991

U.S. EPA

www.epa.gov

(202) 272-0167

This document is a guide for the prevention and resolution of IAQ problems in buildings. It recommends actions that can be carried out by facility staff and contractors. It is available online in PDF format at http://www.epa.gov/iaq/largebldgs/graphics/iaq.pdf.

Green Building Concerns

Indoor air quality (IAQ) is of central importance to the comfort, health and productivity of building occupants. IAQ problems can negatively influence building occupants in a number of ways, including contributing to instances of sick building syndrome (SBS) and building related illness (BRI), and reducing productivity duc to absenteeism and occupant discomfort.

Preventing IAQ problems and quickly addressing them as they arise requires an understanding of the complex factors that influence air quality and effective communication between building owners, managers, and occupants. Contaminant sources, HAVC systems, pollutant pathways and building occupants each play a role in IAQ. Contemporary IAQ practices involve considering these elements in a comprehensive manner that facilitates a healthy and comfortable indoor environment.

Environmental Issues

Quality indoor air improves occupant health and comfort, leading to higher workplace productivity. Ventilation flush-outs and other IAQ strategies may require additional energy use, which is associated with air and water pollution. However, contaminant reduction in the indoor environment is beneficial to building occupants, resulting in greater comfort, lower absenteeism and greater productivity.

Economic Issues

Superior indoor air quality is likely to increase worker productivity, translating to greater profitability for companies. Additional time and labor may be required to protect and clean ventilation systems. However, these actions can extend the lifetime of the ventilation system and improve its efficiency, resulting in reduced energy use. High IAQ can also slow the deterioration of other building equipment and furnishings, which saves money by extending their replacement cycles. Typically, preventive measures are less expensive than remediation of IAQ problems once they develop, and can avoid liability problems. Buildings with superior IAQ can also realize economic benefits related to their competitive advantage in leasing and real estate markets.

Strategies & Technologies

Over the performance period, operate a program to enhance IAQ performance by optimizing practices to prevent the development of IAQ problems in buildings, thereby maintaining occupants' well-being. Survey the building and evaluate systems to identify potential problems. Implement a program to prevent these problems from occurring and to maintain a high level of IAQ on an ongoing basis. Include in the program a plan for preventing moisture accumulation and mold in the building. For additional information see the U.S. EPA IAQ web page: www.epa.gov/iaq/largebldgs/baqtoc.html.

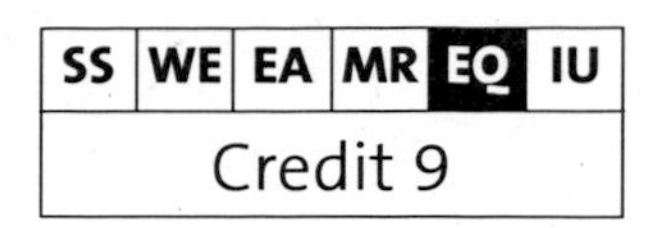

Include proactive measures in the building IAQ maintenance program that:

- ❑ Eliminate common causes of IAQ problems in buildings;
- ❑ Incorporate references to targets in plans and specifications for HVAC system retrofits;
- ❑ Ensure ventilation system outdoor air capacity can meet standards in all modes of operation;
- ❑ Locate building outdoor air intakes away from loading areas, building exhaust fans, cooling towers, and other sources of contamination. If this is not possible due to physical limitations of the building, include documentation demonstrating acceptable ambient air quality at the intakes;
- ❑ Include a narrative explaining measures taken to mitigate potential negative impacts on IAQ.
- ❑ Include a plan for preventing moisture accumulation and mold in the building. Include operational testing in the building commissioning report where possible. Design cooling coil drain pans to ensure complete draining.

Synergies & Tradeoffs

A comprehensive IAQ management plan can complement and coordinate with commissioning and upgrade schedules for HVAC equipment, green cleaning practices, purchasing plans for low-VOC content materials and resources, and grounds maintenance. Other LEED-EB prerequisites and credits related to IAQ include:

- ❑ SS Credit 1: Plan for Green Site and Building Exterior Management
- ❑ EA Prerequisite 1: Existing Building Commissioning
- ❑ EA Prerequisite 2 and Credit 1: Energy Performance
- ❑ MR Credit 3: Optimize use of IAQ Compliant Products
- ❑ MR Credit 4: Sustainable Cleaning Products and Materials
- ❑ IEQ Prerequisite 1: Outside Air Introduction and Exhaust Systems
- ❑ IEQ Prerequisite 2: Environmental Tobacco Smoke Control
- ❑ IEQ Credit 1: Outdoor Air Delivery Monitoring
- ❑ IEQ Credit 2: Increased Ventilation
- ❑ IEQ Credit 3: Construction IAQ Management Plan
- ❑ IEQ Credit 5: Indoor Chemical and Pollutant Source Control
- ❑ IEQ Credit 6: Controllability of Systems
- ❑ IEQ Credit 10: Green Cleaning

Calculations & Documentation

Calculations

None.

Documentation

- ❑ Provide a copy of the IAQ management program.
  - ■ The building IAQ Management Program should be an official document reflecting the organization's commitment to the program parameters described.
- ❑ Provide documentation of the ongoing implementation of the IAQ management program over the performance period.
  - ■ Documentation of implementation might include (but is not limited to) quarterly reports or other records describing IAQ management practices and performance monitoring.

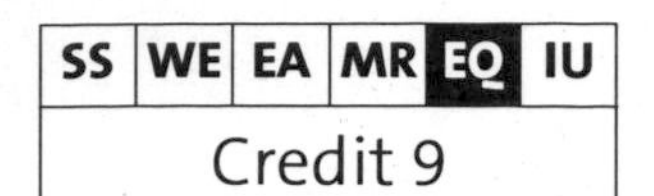

Other Resources

American Indoor Air Quality Council

www.indoor-air-quality.org

This nonprofit association promotes awareness, education, and certification in the field of indoor air quality.

EPA Indoor Air Quality Web Site

www.epa.gov/iaq

This site from the U.S. EPA contains information about indoor pollutants, the ensuing health effects in building occupants, and design and operation strategies for improving IAQ.

Definitions

Building Related Illness (BRI) is a term to describe diagnosable illnesses that can be directly attributed to airborne building contaminants

Sick Building Syndrome (SBS) is a term used to describe situations where building occupants experience acute discomfort and negative health effects as a result of time spent in the building without any specific cause that can be identified and the symptoms disappear soon after the occupants leave the building.

SS	WE	EA	MR	EQ	IU
Credit 10.1					

1 point

Green Cleaning

Entryway Systems

Intent

Reduce exposure of building occupants and maintenance personnel to potentially hazardous chemical, biological and particle contaminants, which adversely impact air quality, health, building finishes, building systems, and the environment.

Requirements

Utilize over the performance period entryway systems (grills, grates, mats etc.) to reduce the amount of dirt, dust, pollen and other particles entering the building at all entryways, and develop the associated cleaning strategies to maintain those entryway systems, as well as the exterior walkways.

Submittals – Initial Certification

- ❑ Provide a building plan and photos showing all high-volume entryways and installed entryway systems (grills, grates, mats, etc.) and the written procedures for cleaning and maintaining these entryway systems.
- ❑ Provide quarterly reports over the performance period documenting that these entryway systems have been effectively used, cleaned and maintained on a regular basis.

Submittals – Recertification

Provide an update of previous filings:

- ❑ If the building entryway systems have not been changed, provide a letter documenting that the procedures for cleaning and maintaining these entryway systems have not been changed.
- ❑ Provide quarterly reports over the performance period documenting that these entryway systems have been effectively used, cleaned and maintained on a regular basis.

OR

- ❑ If the building entryway systems have been changed or the procedures for cleaning and maintaining these entryway systems have been changed, provide a building plan showing all high-volume entryways and photos of installed entryway systems (grills, grates, mats, etc.) and the procedures for cleaning and maintaining these entryway systems have not been changed. Highlight the changes that have been made.
- ❑ Provide quarterly reports over the performance period documenting that these entryway systems have been effectively used, cleaned and maintained on a regular basis.

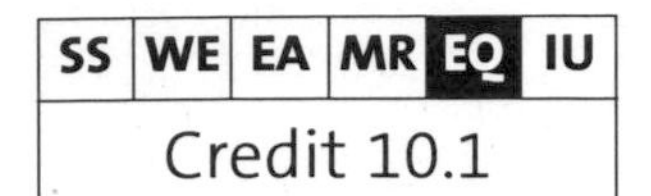

Summary of Reference Standard

There is no standard referenced for this credit.

Green Building Concerns

Occupants and visitors entering the building bring in contaminants on their shoes that can infiltrate the ventilation system, affect delicate equipment and controls, act as an abrasive that can damage flooring materials, and be directly inhaled by occupants. The installation and maintenance of entry systems can reduce the contaminant load resulting from people entering the building especially in residential applications.

Environmental Issues

Additional materials and energy may be required to provide entryway systems. This can increase natural resource consumption and air and water pollution. However, the appropriate use and maintenance of entryway systems can increase the life of flooring materials (e.g., carpets, stone, and resilient tile) throughout the entire building, and reduce the chemicals, energy and overall maintenance needs of those flooring materials. Entryway systems also contribute to healthy and productive IEQ.

Economic Issues

Anecdotal evidence from the commercial cleaning industry suggests that as much as 80 percent of all dust and dirt in a building is tracked in on the shoes of those entering the building.[31] Thus, reducing contaminants, especially soils containing grit and sand, can save costs by reducing spending to maintain flooring materials to an acceptable appearance level, and by increasing the longevity of the flooring materials themselves. Furthermore, appropriate entryway systems that are well maintained can also reduce the liability and costs associated with people slipping and falling on wet floors during inclement weather. Cleaner indoor air that results from prevention of contaminants improves worker productivity, which translates into increased profitability for the company.

Strategies & Technologies

Equip all exterior entrances with entryway systems (grills, grates, mats, etc.) to catch and hold dirt particles and to prevent contamination of the building interior. In existing buildings without grills and grates already in place, mats provide an opportunity to earn this credit without substantial alteration of existing entryways. During renovation projects, consider the installation of permanent systems such as grill and grates.

Considerations for Mat Selection

Matting systems can be designed for use both outside and immediately inside entryways. Matting systems should be appropriate to the climate—for example, durable course mats with large open loops used outside the entryway are appropriate for capturing sand, mud or snow—and should have a Class 1 fire retardant rating. High quality mats with a softer, finer texture are appropriate for use indoors to capture smaller, finer particles such as dust and salt from ice-melting compounds, and to remove moisture (dry shoes) before entering the building. In general, the size of the mats needs to be large enough for each foot to hit the mat two times when walking (approximately 12 feet in length) but should be sized based on the climate and weather conditions.

High void volume within fibers provides space for removed dirt to be trapped below the matting face surface and allows water to spread to a larger mat area for improved drying. This inhibits dirt retracing and mold/mildew growth. High void volume mats are easier to clean more thoroughly when vacuumed or shaken out. Fiber height provides maximum scrapping surface at the shoe and mat interface. Fiber height also improves vacuuming suction efficiency.

Solid backing captures the dirt and moisture in the mat. This prevents soiling under the center of a mat and reduces re-dirtying of the floor surface under the mat when being returned after cleaning. A non-porous backing inhibits mold and mildew growth within the backing. The use of mold- and mildew-resistant materials in the mat construction can also prevent mold and mildew growth within the materials. Other performance features to seek in a mat are:

- ❑ Fire Retardant ratings that exceed DOC-FF-1-70, such as NFPA (National Fire Protection Association) -253 Class I and II, which can reduce insurance costs.
- ❑ Electrostatic Propensity levels of less then 2.5 KV, which means that contact should not produce electrical discharges when contacting other people or objects.

Mats constructed with recycled content and rubber backing are preferable. Consult a local mat supplier for proper specification and recommendations on the maintenance program.

Development of a Plan for Management Practices for Entryway Systems

Develop, document and record maintenance practices that keep entryway grates or mats clean and effective in their purpose. The cleaning plan should specifically include strategies for both the exterior and interiors of entryways, maintenance of matting systems, and for cleaning, drying or temporary replacement of mats when they become wet from inclement weather. Keep a log of cleaning records that notes and tracks performance. Reduce maintenance and replacement needs for entryway mats by keeping exterior walkways clean to control the source of contamination and by utilizing high quality mats. Increasing the frequency of cleaning activities such as vacuuming, extracting, or pressure-washing mats, as compared to the routine cleaning and maintenance of carpets and other flooring materials in other parts of the building, can also reduce replacement needs.

Synergies & Tradeoffs

Developing landscaping and building exterior maintenance plans that control the volume of contaminants near entryways aid IEQ goals and reduce maintenance and replacement needs for entryway mats. Coordination efforts might include:

- ❑ Selecting landscaping vegetation for entryway areas that comply with integrated pest management (IPM) strategies and do not yield berries, flowers or leaves that can be tracked into the building;
- ❑ Establishing a schedule for sweeping and pressure-washing exterior walkways;
- ❑ Ensuring that drainage patterns on impervious exterior surfaces do not deliver debris to building entrances.

Entryway systems significantly reduce the amount of dirt tracked into buildings by occupants. This may alter the staff time and cleaning materials necessary for janitorial tasks.

Calculations & Documentation

Calculations

None.

Documentation

- ❑ Building plan showing all high-volume entryways, photos of installed entry-

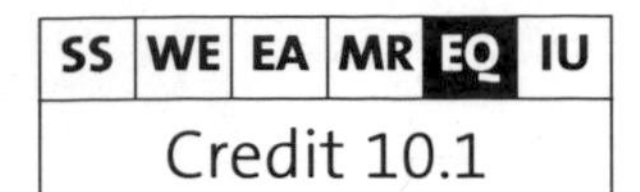

way systems, and the procedures for cleaning/maintaining them.

- Building plans should identify location and type of each high-volume entryway system. Maintenance procedures should appear as part of the building maintenance program or as regular work orders.

Other Resources

Protecting the Built Environment: Cleaning for Health by Michael A. Berry, Tricomm Twenty First Press, 1994

Definitions

Integrated Pest Management (IPM) is the coordinated use of pest and environmental information and pest control methods to prevent unacceptable levels of pest damage by the most economical means, and with the least possible hazard to people, property and the environment.

Walk-Off Mats are mats placed inside or outside building entrances to remove dirt from the feet of people and off equipment entering the building.

SS	WE	EA	MR	EQ	IU
Credit 10.2					

1 point

Green Cleaning

Isolation of Janitorial Closets

Intent

Reduce exposure of building occupants and maintenance personnel to potentially hazardous chemical, biological and particle contaminants, which adversely impact air quality, health, building finishes, building systems, and the environment.

Requirements

Have in place over the performance period structural deck-to-deck partitions with separate outside exhausting, no air re-circulation and negative pressure in all janitorial closets. Provide hot and cold water and drains plumbed for appropriate disposal of liquid waste in areas where janitorial equipment and chemicals are stored and/or water and cleaning chemical concentrate mixing occurs.

Submittals – Initial Certification

- ❑ Provide a building plan showing all areas where janitorial closets are located where cleaning chemical storage, janitorial equipment storage and/or water and cleaning chemical concentrate mixing occurs.
- ❑ For janitorial closets, provide photos or drawings of structural deck-to-deck partitions, and documentation of separate outside exhausting, no air re-circulation, negative pressure relative to surrounding occupied areas and drains plumbed for appropriate disposal of liquid waste.
- ❑ Provide a copy of the cleaning chemical storage guidelines and policy adopted by your organization.
- ❑ Provide a written description of how the janitorial closets were used for cleaning chemical storage over the performance period.

Submittals – Recertification

Provide an update of previous filings:

- ❑ If the building systems pertaining to cleaning chemical mixing and storage have not been changed, provide a letter documenting their continued existence and use.
- ❑ Provide a written description of how the janitorial closets were used over the performance period.

OR

- ❑ If the systems pertaining to cleaning chemical mixing and storage have been changed, provide a building plan showing all areas where janitorial closets are located where chemical storage, janitorial equipment storage, and/or water and chemical concentrate mixing occurs.
- ❑ For cleaning chemical mixing and storage areas, provide photos or drawings of structural deck-to-deck partitions, and documentation of separate outside exhausting, no air re-circulation, negative pressure relative to surrounding occupied areas and drains plumbed for appropriate disposal of liquid waste.

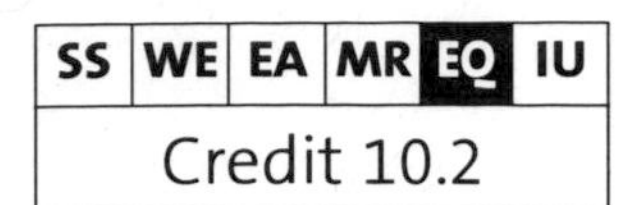

- ❑ Provide a copy of the cleaning chemical storage guidelines and policy adopted by your organization.
- ❑ Provide a written description of how the janitorial closets were used for cleaning chemical storage over the performance period.

Summary of Referenced Standard

There is no standard referenced for this credit.

Green Building Concerns

Some common building activities have a negative impact on IAQ. The storage and mixing of cleaning chemicals, as well as janitorial equipment such as mops, buckets, vacuum cleaners, floor machines and other materials, can contribute significantly to airborne contaminants including particles, VOCs and biological contaminants (e.g. mold spores) affecting the well-being and productivity of building occupants. By reducing the impacts of these activities, superior indoor air quality can be maintained.

Environmental Issues

With the appropriate isolation of chemical storage and mixing facilities, building occupants are protected from inadvertent exposure to hazardous materials. Janitorial equipment is an often overlooked source of volatile emissions and should also be stored in isolation to reduce occupant exposures.

Economic Issues

Additional sinks, drains, electrical outlets to charge battery-powered equipment and separate exhausts for janitorial areas represent an initial added cost. However, adequate services and room for cleaning materials can result in a quicker ability to respond to spills. This extends the life of fabrics, floor coverings and other materials, and reduces the potential for people slipping and falling. Proper services (hot and cold water, along with a sink for disposing of mop bucket water and other wastes) will result in the ability to use automated chemical dispensing equipment. This can reduce the cost of cleaning chemicals by accurately measuring concentrated products and thereby reducing overuse and waste.

When appropriate ventilation is used, the potential of contaminants from the storage and mixing of chemicals is eliminated, and other contaminant sources (e.g., from wet mops) are prevented from entering the building. When coupled with good human health initiatives, these efforts should prove economically sound over the lifetime of the building.

Strategies & Technologies

Physically isolate activities associated with janitorial chemical storage and use. Have structural deck-to-deck partitions with separate outside exhausting, no air re-circulation and negative pressure in place in all janitorial closets over the performance period. Isolation measures include adequate and secure storage areas for cleaning equipment and products.

Provide hot and cold water and drains plumbed for appropriate disposal of liquid waste in areas where staff mix water and cleaning chemical concentrate and store janitorial equipment. If dilution equipment is installed, institute appropriate measures to prevent back-flow of chemicals into the potable water supply.

Implement policies, procedures and mixing systems that minimize exposure of cleaning staff to concentrated cleaning chemicals. To ensure that these features remain effective over time, building owners should institute operations and maintenance training programs for chemical usage and storage.

Chemicals in buildings are not limited to cleaning and housekeeping. Facility managers must develop guidelines and policies on the storage of all chemicals in their buildings, and review performance against them on at least an annual basis.

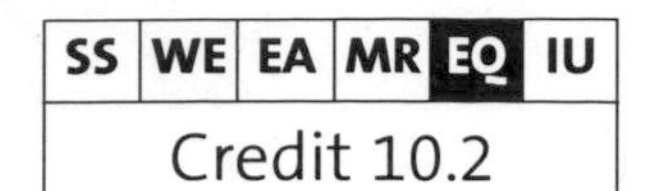

Synergies & Tradeoffs

Construction of isolated janitorial closets with sinks, drains and ventilation systems will result in increased construction and energy costs. However, operation cost savings may be achieved if such facilities result in more efficient use of cleaning supplies and equipment. Additional cost benefits may be achieved as a result of lower costs for responding to occupant complaints. Cost benefits also include reduced liability and potential health problems due to exposures to air contaminants from janitorial chemicals, supplies and equipment. Importantly, the productivity and well-being of building occupants will be enhanced by the resulting improvement in building air quality.

Storage and use facilities for janitorial chemicals can be more effective when implemented in conjunction with employee training programs. Consider developing a staff education program that promotes proper use of isolated janitorial closets for the protection of janitorial workers and building occupants (see EA Credit 3.1: Building Operations and Maintenance – Staff Education).

Calculations & Documentation

Calculations

None.

Documentation

All information needed to successfully document this credit can be found in the Submittals section of the LEED-EB Rating System and the LEED-EB Letter Templates.

Other Resources

International Sanitary Supply Association (ISSA)

1-800-225-4772

www.issa.com

ISSA is an association of companies that manufacture, market and distribute cleaning and maintenance products, equipment and services. Its web site provides information about the cleaning industry, cleaning technologies and more.

Definitions

Janitorial Closets are rooms where janitorial equipment and supplies are stored.

SS	WE	EA	MR	**EQ**	IU

Credit 10.3

1 point

Green Cleaning

Low Environmental Impact Cleaning Policy

Intent

Reduce exposure of building occupants and maintenance personnel to potentially hazardous chemical, biological and particle contaminants, which adversely impact air quality, health, building finishes, building systems, and the environment.

Requirements

Have in place over the performance period a low-impact environmental cleaning policy addressing:

- ❑ Sustainable cleaning systems.
- ❑ Use of sustainable cleaning products.
- ❑ Use of chemical concentrates and appropriate dilution systems.
- ❑ Proper training of maintenance personnel in the hazards, use, maintenance and disposal of cleaning chemicals, dispensing equipment and packaging.
- ❑ Use of hand soaps that do not contain antimicrobial agents (other than as a preservative system), except where required by health codes and other regulations (i.e., food service and health care requirements).
- ❑ Use of cleaning equipment that reduces impacts on IAQ.

Submittals – Initial Certification

- ❑ Provide a copy of the low environmental impact cleaning policy adopted by your organization.
- ❑ Provide documentation that this policy has been followed over the performance period.
  - Provide documentation/specifications on the chemical and cleaner dispensing and dilution equipment used.
  - Provide documentation identifying the date and activities associated with floor maintenance.
  - Provide documentation of cleaning worker training.

Submittals – Recertification

Provide an update of previous filings:

- ❑ If the low environmental impact cleaning policy has not been changed, provide a letter documenting its continued existence and implementation.
  - Provide documentation that this policy has been followed over the performance period.
  - Provide documentation identifying the date and activities relative to floor care maintenance.
  - Provide documentation of cleaning worker training.

- Provide documentation on the chemical and cleaner dispensing and dilution equipment used.
- Provide documentation identifying the date and activities associated with floor maintenance.

OR

- ❑ If the low environmental impact cleaning policy has been changed, provide a copy of the low environmental impact cleaning policy adopted by your organization highlighting all changes.
  - Provide documentation that this policy has been followed over the performance period.
  - Provide documentation of cleaning worker training.
  - Provide documentation identifying the date and activities associated with floor maintenance.
  - Provide documentation on the chemical and cleaner dispensing and dilution equipment used.

Summary of Referenced Standard

There is no standard referenced for this credit.

Green Building Concerns

The appropriate selection and use of cleaning products is critically important to building occupant hygiene and safety. Chemical technologies play an important role in sanitation of bathrooms, food preparation areas and common use areas, reducing the risk of disease transmission. Chemical applications can also reduce the risk of occupant injury from slips and falls—one of the most common workplace injury causes.

However, cleaning products and activities can also harm environmental and human health. The U.S. EPA has determined that cleaning products can contribute to indoor air quality (IAQ) problems as the chemicals evaporate and volatile organic compounds (VOCs) are circulated throughout the building via the ventilation system. In addition to potential IAQ problems, cleaning products can leave residues that can burn the eyes and skin of occupants who inadvertently touch improperly prepared surfaces, can be absorbed through the skin to affect health, can be ingested to cause poisoning, and can be inadvertently mixed to create harmful gases and cause fires. These risks are borne by both building occupants and cleaning workers. Furthermore, the inappropriate maintenance and cleaning of floors can contribute to slipping or falling accidents that are among the highest causes for litigation within buildings.

It is critical to recognize that the solution to these problems is not to clean less, as cleaning is essential to protecting occupant well-being and safety. Rather, the solution is the appropriate selection and use of cleaning and maintenance products along with appropriate staffing levels, procedures and janitorial management designed to create the healthiest and most productive indoor environment possible based on the unique needs of the building itself and its occupants.

Environmental Issues

The commercial cleaning industry uses approximately 6 billion pounds of chemicals to clean and maintain commercial and institutional buildings in the United States.[32] In addition to affecting IAQ, cleaning products are released to the outdoor environment through evaporation of volatile compounds or disposal of residual cleaning compounds down drains. Many cleaning product ingredients can be toxic to human health and cause long-term environmental problems. Cleaning agents that contain volatile organic compounds (VOCs) diminish air quality by contributing to smog, while those containing phosphates and nitrates contribute to nutrient-loading in water bodies, to the detriment of water quality and aquatic ecology.[33] Additionally, cleaning product residues in inadequately treated wastewater can be toxic to aquatic species, and can deliver endocrine disrupters to wildlife exposed to polluted waters. Endocrine disrupters cause adverse reproductive effects.[34]

Reducing the quantity and the toxicity of the products used in cleaning can reduce the negative impacts on the environment. Furthermore, many products are formulated from ingredients derived from non-renewable resources.

Economic Issues

The use of low impact cleaning systems that are environmentally benign, as well as those that reduce impact to human health, can result in significant economic savings. Additionally, because the cost of cleaning is 80 to 90 percent labor, efficient material use, labor scheduling and work processes can result in the best outcomes at the most economical cost.[35] Custodial workers are among the most injured job categories, and many of their injuries result from exposure to hazardous cleaning chemicals (e.g., highly acidic bathroom cleaners and highly alkaline floor stripping compounds). By using low impact products, worker's compensation can be reduced, as can owner liability. Furthermore, the rate of turnover among custodial workers can be reduced, as a portion of turnover is directly attributed to workers who choose to leave the profession to reduce their exposures to hazardous chemicals.

In addition, the use of low impact cleaning products can enhance occupant productivity. Many traditional products emit VOCs and other compounds that can affect occupant health. By replacing these products with those that do not adversely affect occupant health, improved worker productivity translates into increased profitability.

The implementation of a low impact environmental cleaning program can be cost neutral compared to the use of a well-designed and managed traditional cleaning program due to the increased availability and competition among product manufacturers, as well as the advancements in the performance of the products themselves. However, in buildings where the current cleaning program is haphazard and the frequency of cleaning is below that which is necessary to protect human health and maintain a high performance indoor environment (i.e., cleaning programs designed to maintain the appearance of public areas with cleaning of occupants' space limited to little more than emptying trash cans and keeping restrooms stocked with supplies), an increase in cleaning frequency and supply usage may be necessary, resulting in an increased cost of cleaning. However, these costs are often more than offset by increases in occupant productivity and performance and the decrease of turnover and absenteeism.

Strategies & Technologies

Appropriate selection and use of cleaning chemicals is important to worker and occupant hygiene and safety (refer to MR Credit 4: Sustainable Cleaning Products and Materials for information regarding the selection of cleaning chemicals and janitorial paper products). Technologies that reduce negative effects on both health and the environment should be considered by facility managers in the selection of cleaning products and systems.

Policy Development

There are multiple strategies that may be considered to achieve sustainable cleaning and hard flooring coating systems. Facility managers must first assess the areas and substrates to be maintained, facility usage patterns, and overall goals of the cleaning program. Suppliers of cleaning products and services can then be engaged to develop a comprehensive approach to the maintenance of the facility and specification of products and labor components to be used. These specifications should be incorporated in the Low Environmental Impact Cleaning Policy and used to educate in-house cleaning staff. The policy should also inform planning and preparing of RFPs to identify and contract with outside service and/or product providers.

Development of cleaning strategies should employ a comprehensive approach focusing on efficient use of chemicals and supplies; meet the hygiene and appearance goals of the cleaning program; and protect building occupants, systems and finishes from contaminants that adversely affect their performance. More frequent and intensive cleaning should be directed towards building entryways, bathrooms, and food preparation and consumption areas, while fewer resources can be devoted to less frequently used areas. It may be more effective to clean more often than to use stronger chemicals. The development of cleaning specifications that include frequency of operations should be undertaken with the assistance of the in-house facility manager or a cleaning service provider.

To ensure that these features remain effective over time, it is critical that building owners institute operations and maintenance training and documentation programs for chemical usage and floor maintenance procedures. This requirement should be included in the low impact cleaning policy. Assistance in developing and administering the programs should be sought from the cleaning product and/or service providers.

To achieve leadership in environmental responsibility within cleaning systems, facility managers must consider the life cycle of their building materials and maintenance methods, and incorporate concepts of total cost of performance, safety in use and application, and overall environmental impact. "Sustainable cleaning" encompasses more than the concept of minimizing exposure of personnel to potentially hazardous chemicals. All stages of sustainable cleaning can be measured for environmental performance, including product and equipment manufacturing processes, installation, operation, long-term maintenance and eventual disposal.

Use of cleaning chemicals may be reduced by using more efficient (e.g., micro-fiber cleaning cloths instead of paper towels) or labor-intensive cleaning strategies, increasing the "life" of a floor finish, and using concentrated products with appropriate dilution controls.

Policy Components

Consider including the following environmental and safety elements in the low-impact environmental cleaning policy:

- ❑ Facility safety, health and environmental practices should comply with applicable local regulatory requirements.
- ❑ The Facility manager should develop and communicate proper disposal methods for all cleaning wastes, including floor care stripping wastes.
- ❑ Janitorial service personnel should be properly trained in the use, maintenance and disposal of cleaning chemicals, dispensing equipment and packaging. Training records certifying each person's specific training dates should be documented.
- ❑ Cleaning products procured for use in the building should meet the requirements of MR Credit 4: Sustainable Cleaning Products and Materials
- ❑ When selecting floor coating products, preference should go to those that are free of zinc.
- ❑ A log should be kept that details all housekeeping chemicals used or stored on the premises (stored products include those that are no longer used, but still in the building). Attachments to the log should include manufacturer's Material Safety Data Sheets (MSDSs) and Technical Bulletins. MSDSs from suppliers should provide full disclosure (see definition) of ingredients. Additionally, suppliers must provide training materials on the hazards and proper use of housekeeping chemicals for workers. If ingredient disclosure is not reported on MSDSs, then disclosure can be provided by suppliers through other means that are easily accessible to health and safety personnel.
- ❑ When available, chemical concentrates dispensed from portion-controlled, closed dilution systems should be used as alternatives to open dilution systems or non-concentrated products.
- ❑ Selection of flooring used in the facility, whether a new installation or replacement, should reflect all potential

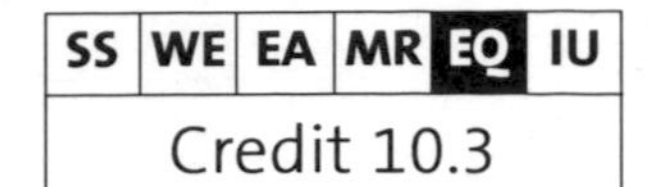

environmental impacts over the full life of the floor system, including raw material extraction and use, installation practices, maintenance requirements, overall useful life, hygiene, appearance and safety attributes, and eventual disposal. A scoring system should be used to develop and evaluate alternatives, including consideration of the total cost of ownership. The selection of flooring materials and their maintenance should consider the full life cycle impacts in order to ensure they will offer the most sustainable floor care system.

- Resilient tile and hard flooring coating systems, including floor finishes and restoration products, should be slip-resistant (as defined by ASTM Std D-2047). Additionally, these floor coating systems should be highly durable in order to maintain an acceptable level of protection and appearance for a minimum of one year before stripping/removal and re-coating is necessary.
- A written floor maintenance plan and log should be kept that details the number of coats of floor finish applied as the base and top coats, along with relevant maintenance/restoration practices and the dates of these activities. The duration between stripping and re-coat cycles should be documented.

Chemical Concentrates

Use of chemical concentrates may have several environmental benefits:

- Significantly lower transportation costs between manufacturer and end-user;
- Significantly lower use of packaging materials;
- Lower chemical use to obtain same performance;
- Potentially lower exposure of maintenance personnel to hazardous chemicals.

Portion-controlled dilution devices can reduce chemical consumption by 30 to 65 percent compared to non-portion controlled dilution methods resulting in significant reductions in environmental impacts. However, if improperly used, chemical concentrates may present higher hazards upon exposure. Proper containment, storage and dispensing are critical to avoid employee exposures. Exposure to hazardous chemicals can be minimized by using closed dispensing systems. Concentrates sold for manual dilution in buckets or bottles can increase the risk of employee exposure. Installation of proper hot and cold water supplies and drain systems in janitor closets will facilitate the utilization of chemical dispensing equipment for the proper dilution of concentrated cleaning chemicals.

Using portion control dilution equipment or pre-measured pouches will assure that the appropriate amount of concentrated products are used, and will minimize overall usage of chemical as well as reduce packaging wastes. To avoid risks posed by potential exposure to chemical concentrates, specify and use only closed dispensing systems. If utilizing mechanical or automated dilution equipment, it is important that they meet the appropriate local plumbing codes and are maintained properly to ensure that accurate dilution rates not only at the time of installation, but also on an ongoing basis.

Increasing Floor Life

To increase the "life" of the floor finish, which in turn reduces the frequency of stripping and re-coating, several strategies can be employed. First, it is necessary to analyze the substrate and the expected traffic pattern of the floor under consideration. This must then be matched to a floor finish product and maintenance system that will produce the required appearance while minimizing the maintenance and prolonging the useful life prior to stripping. It may be necessary to

SS	WE	EA	MR	EQ	IU
Credit 10.3					

establish an initial base of floor finish thick enough to maintained (buffed, burnished, scrubbed, etc.) for a minimum of one year. Depending on the durability of the floor finish and the percentage of solids, it may require an initial base of 6 to 12 coats.

Once the base coat is applied, develop a strategy of finish protection. Address grit and fine particles, which act as abrasives to damage the floor coating, by utilizing high-quality entryway matting systems, frequently dust mopping or vacuuming hard floors, and damp mopping. It should be noted that vacuuming of hard floors is an acceptable strategy for removing grit and other abrasive materials. Additionally, a thorough interim floor maintenance program should be implemented, which may include auto scrubbing, deep scrubbing and top coating the floor.

Green Cleaning Products

Reduced environmental impact is assured by specifying cleaning fluids used for general or all-purpose cleaning, glass and bathroom, and carpet extraction cleaners that meet the criteria of MR Credit 4: Sustainable Cleaning Products and Materials.

Additional Strategies

Additional strategies should include efforts to reduce the total amount of materials consumed. This is especially true for janitorial paper products. Some of the specific strategies include:

- Product dispensers that limit the amount of paper being dispensed;
- Product dispensers that can hold two rolls, which eliminates waste as custodians may feel the need to replace partial rolls so that they do not run out prior to restocking;
- Core-less rolls of paper products, which reduce packaging waste;
- From a human health perspective, "hands-free" dispensers that eliminate levers and cranks that users share when getting paper can reduce potential exposure to pathogenic organisms.

Synergies & Tradeoffs

Having a Green Cleaning policy in place provides coordination of all of the components of green cleaning implemented in the building and facilitates adoption of green cleaning on an institutional level. Other IEQ Green Cleaning credits and MR Credit 4: Sustainable Cleaning Products and Materials should be considered during policy development.

Policy development and implementation may initially require additional staff time and attention. Cooperation between procurement officials, janitorial staff, facility managers and building occupants will promote the successful implementation of a green cleaning policy.

Calculations & Documentation

Calculations

None.

Documentation

All information needed to successfully document this credit can be found in the Submittals section of the LEED-EB Rating System and the LEED-EB Letter Templates.

Other Resources

CA Air Resource Board/CA Code of Regulations: Standards for Consumer Products

Title 17 Section 94509 - (Topic cited: Standards for low VOC cleaning products.)

http://www.arb.ca.gov/regs/title17/94509.pdf

This set of California regulations establishes standards for reducing VOC emissions from consumer products.

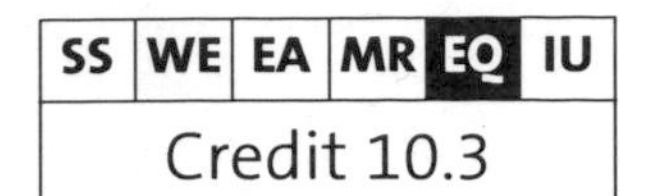

Collaborative for High Performance Schools

www.chps.net

This organization provides information on providing healthy and sustainable school environments, including a variety of information dealing with IAQ, maintenance, and operations issues.

EPA Environmentally Preferable Purchasing

www.epa.gov/oppt/epp/documents/docback.htm

This web site has specific background and policy information on a host of issues relative to environmentally preferable purchasing.

EPA Environmentally Preferable Purchasing Case Studies

http://www.epa.gov/oppt/epp/documents/doccase.htm

Providing information about organization approaches to the incorporation of environmental considerations into their purchasing decisions, this web site offers pertinent background documents, such as Executive Orders and Memorandums of Agreement, specifically beneficial to federal users.

Green Seal Standard GS-37

www.greenseal.org

Green Seal is an independent, nonprofit organization that strives to achieve a healthier and cleaner environment by identifying and promoting products and services that cause less toxic pollution and waste, conserve resources and habitats, and minimize global warming and ozone depletion. GS-37 provides standards for low VOC cleaning products.

Pennsylvania Green Building Operations and Maintenance Manual

www.dgs.state.pa.us/dgs/lib/dgs/green bldg/greenbuildingbook.pdf

The Commonwealth of Pennsylvania's Department of General Services has published a comprehensive Green Building Maintenance Manual. This Manual includes chapters on cleaning procedures, green landscaping, HVAC & lighting maintenance, and more.

Definitions

Concentrate is a product that must be diluted by at least eight parts by volume water (1:8 dilution ratio) prior to its intended use. (Green Seal GS-37)

Full Disclosure for products that are not formulated with listed suspect carcinogens is defined as (i) disclosure of all ingredients (both hazardous and non-hazardous) that make up 1 percent or more of the undiluted product and (ii) use of concentration ranges for each of the disclosed ingredients. "Full Disclosure" for products that are formulated with listed suspect carcinogens is defined as (i) disclosure of listed suspect carcinogens that make up 0.1 percent or more of the undiluted product, (ii) disclosure of all remaining ingredients (both hazardous and non-hazardous) that make up 1.0 percent or more of the undiluted product, and (iii) use of concentration ranges for each of the disclosed ingredients. Suspect carcinogens are those that are listed on authoritative lists available for MSDS preparation: IARC, NTP, and California Proposition 65 lists. Concentration range definitions are available from OSHA or Canada WHMIS Standards.

Case Study

Brengel Technology Center
Milwaukee, Wisconsin

LEED-EB Gold
Owner: Johnson Controls, Inc.

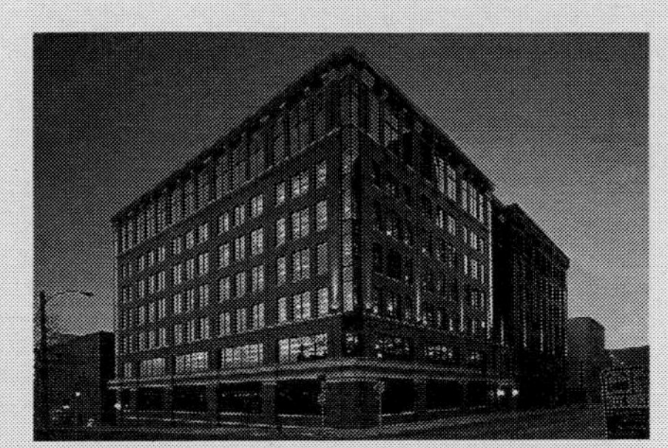

Photo courtesy of: Johnson Control, Inc.

The Brengel Technology Center, a 130,000-square-foot office building in downtown Milwaukee, has adopted a comprehensive low environmental impact cleaning policy for building maintenance and upkeep. The Green Housekeeping Plan integrates a number of critical elements for the safe and sustainable cleaning of the building, including the use of sustainable cleaning products and cleaning systems. Entryway systems, floor care and carpet maintenance are conducted with green performance measurement in mind and specific equipment options designated based on environmental criteria. Chemical concentrates are emphasized when chemical cleaning product use is deemed necessary to minimize the transportation and packaging costs associated with the product life-cycle, and all storage and mixing is restricted to designated, properly isolated and ventilated chemical storage areas.

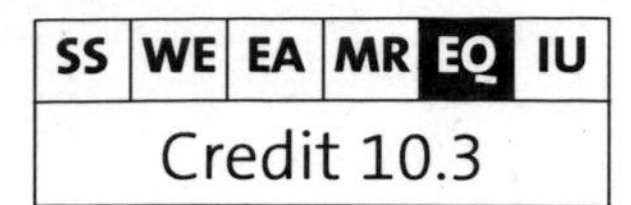

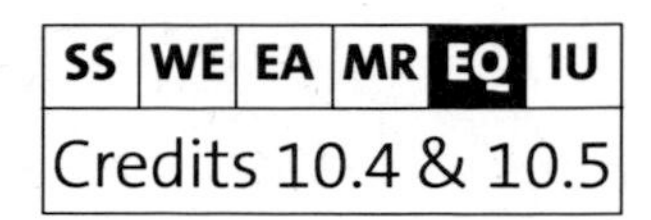

2 points

Green Cleaning

Low Environmental Impact Pest Management Policy

Intent

Reduce exposure of building occupants and maintenance personnel to potentially hazardous chemical, biological and particle contaminants, which adversely impact air quality, health, building finishes, building systems, and the environment.

Requirements

Develop, implement and maintain a low environmental impact integrated indoor pest management policy. Any cleaning products included in the integrated pest management policy must meet the requirements identified in MR Credit 4.1–4.3.

Submittals – Initial Certification

❑ Provide a copy of the low environmental impact pest management policy adopted by the organization:

- The plan shall promote safer alternatives to chemical pesticides while preventing economic and health damage caused by pests. The plan shall implement the use of IPM techniques to reduce the need for reliance on chemical pesticides. When pesticides may be necessary, the plan shall ensure that clear and accurate notification concerning the use of pesticides be made available so that measures may be taken to prevent and address pest problems effectively without endangering occupants, janitorial workers or visitors.
- The plan should address:
  - Integrated methods.
  - Site or pest inspections.
  - Pest population monitoring.
  - An evaluation of the need for pest control.
  - One or more pest control methods, including sanitation, structural repairs, mechanical and living biological controls, other non-chemical methods and, if nontoxic options are unreasonable and have been exhausted, a least toxic pesticide.
- The plan shall include a communication strategy to provide notification of the IPM system. This shall include information and notice to tenants or directly to occupants in an owner-occupied building. The notice shall include a description of the integrated pest management system and a list of all pesticides, including any least toxic pesticide that may be used in the building as part of the integrated pest management system; the name, address, and telephone number of the contact person of the building; and a statement that the contact person maintains the product label and material safety data sheet (MSDS) of each pesticide used by the building, that the label or MSDS is available for review upon request, and that the contact person is available for information and comment.

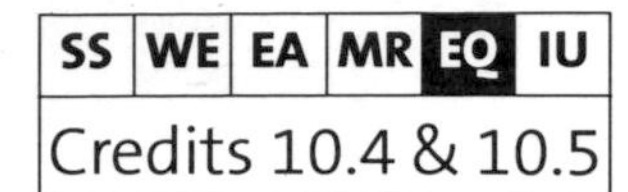

- The communications strategy shall address "Universal Notification," which requires notification not less than 72 hours before a pesticide, other than a least toxic pesticide, is applied in a building or on surrounding grounds that the building maintains.
- The plan shall address under what circumstances an emergency application of pesticides in a building or on surrounding grounds being maintained by the building can be conducted without complying with the earlier provisions. In addition, address notification strategies to ensure that occupants and janitorial workers are notified 24 hours in advance of the pesticide application.

❑ Provide documentation that the Low Environmental Impact Pest Management Policy has been followed during the performance period.

Submittals – Recertification

Provide an update of previous filings:

❑ Provide documentation that the Low Environmental Impact Pest Management Policy has been followed during the performance period.

AND EITHER

❑ If there has been no change to this policy since the previous LEED-EB filing, provide a statement that there has been no change.

OR

❑ If there has been a change to this policy since the previous LEED-EB filing, provide an updated policy.

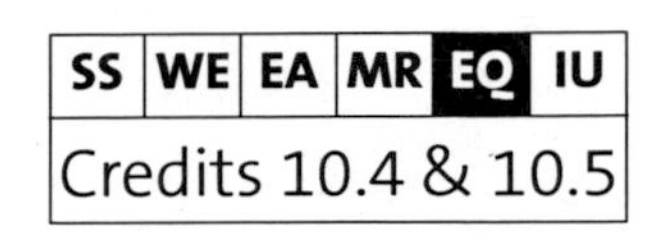

Summary of Referenced Standard

There is no standard referenced for this credit.

Green Building Concerns

Pests can be very harmful to the building itself while serving as disease vectors affecting occupant well-being and productivity. However, the use of many traditional pesticide products can also harm occupants, especially in buildings occupied with infants, small children and the elderly. An integrated pest management (IPM) strategy can prevent pests and the need for pesticides by creating an environment that is not conducive to insects, rodents and other pests. Developing strategies to prevent pests from entering the building, while maintaining an indoor environment free from pest food and water sources, can minimize the need for toxic pesticides. When pesticides must be used, minimizing the amounts used, selecting the least-toxic materials, and maximizing application techniques can reduce the potential for adverse effects on building occupants and the environment.

According to the U.S. EPA, the benefits of an IPM strategy include:[36]

- ❑ Cost-effective methods of pest control
- ❑ Greater flexibility through using a variety of pest management options
- ❑ More control in decision making and problem solving so that decisions are proactive rather than reactive
- ❑ Risk-reduction benefits that result from using fewer and lower-risk pesticides
- ❑ Improved targeting of pesticide applications so that chemicals are used only when necessary to avoid negative impacts on people and the environment
- ❑ Less chance of occupant illnesses, poisonings and liability lawsuits, due to better pest management with less chemical risk

Environmental Issues

Each year, 1 billion pounds of conventional pesticides (includes active ingredient only) are applied in the United States. These pesticides come in over 20,000 different products, and contain 620 different active ingredients.[37] Releasing these chemicals into the environment poses serious risks to human and environmental health. Pesticides can collect in lakes and rivers, harming ecosystems and contaminating drinking water. These chemicals can also persist for some time, causing cancer, birth defects, respiratory problems and more serious conditions in humans, especially children, and other fauna. Careful selection and reduced use of pest control products can significantly reduce or eliminate the environmental effects if pesticides are used.

Economic Issues

One of the benefits of IPM is that it is less expensive than most other pest management programs. Because the methods involve proactive approaches such as pest prevention rather than relying solely on reactive measures, IPM will reduce the costs of pest control products, and reduce the amount of time that maintenance staff must devote to pest control.

Strategies & Technologies

Evaluate current strategies for pest management in the building, and determine the measures necessary to construct an IPM program with low environmental impact. The IPM plan should be in accordance with the requirements of this credit and product specifications for VOC levels in MR Credit 4.1–4.3.

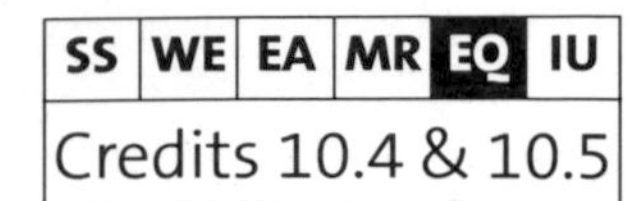

Pest prevention should begin outside the building. Design landscaping features to eliminate safe heavens for pests and rodents. It is a good idea to keep shrubs and other plant cover at least eighteen inches from the building, and to fill this space with small stones or a similar substrate.

Install barriers to prevent pests from entering the building. This includes sealing cracks, crevices and holes in external walls, as well as inspecting the seals around doors and windows. Site inspection and monitoring will prevent infestations and minimize the potential need for more toxic pesticides. Traps for both insects and rodents can be carefully and strategically placed throughout the building and monitored for early signs of a pest problem.

When a pest problem is identified, baits and traps should typically be the first line of defense. When necessary, the least toxic pesticide should be used, and the product should be specific to the species being eliminated. At least 72 hours before applying any pesticide, notify building occupants so that those who are sensitive to pesticides, pregnant, or have a preexisting health condition may plan accordingly.

In order to ensure occupants are not accidentally welcoming harmful pests into the building, eliminate or control all food and water sources. Food service areas and break rooms should be thoroughly cleaned and food and waste kept in airtight containers. Fix dripping faucets or leaking pipes. Rinse beverage containers before collection so as not to attract sugar-loving pests, and clean all spills as soon as possible. Also, eliminate clutter to simplify cleaning and minimize hiding places for pests.

Synergies & Tradeoffs

Elimination of habitat for pests and rodents through landscape modification might also result in reduction of habitat for desirable native wildlife. Minimization of cover near the building should be coordinated with landscaping plans and site maintenance practices.

Calculations & Documentation

Calculations

None.

Documentation

All information needed to successfully document this credit can be found in the Submittals section of the LEED-EB Rating System and the LEED-EB Letter Templates.

Other Resources

Beyond Pesticides

www.beyondpesticides.org

Started in 1981 as the National Coalition Against the Misuse of Pesticides, this nonprofit membership organization was formed to serve as a national network committed to pesticide safety and the adoption of alternative pest management strategies that reduce or eliminate a dependency on toxic chemicals.

EPA – Pesticides Web Site

www.epa.gov/pesticides

This site from the EPA provides information on integrated pest management (IPM), and the environmental effects of pesticides.

Integrated Pest Management Institute to North America, Inc.

www.ipminstitute.org

This organization provides news, standards, and information about integrated pest management (IPM) practices.

Definitions

Integrated Pest Management (IPM) is the coordinated use of pest and envi-

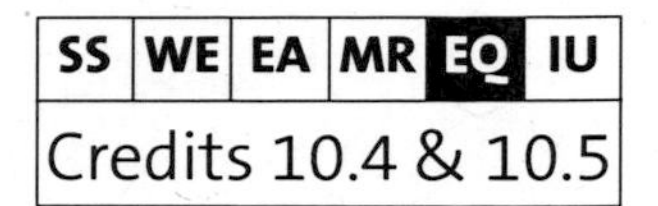

ronmental information and pest control methods to prevent unacceptable levels of pest damage by the most economical means, and with the least possible hazard to people, property and the environment.

Least toxic pesticides include boric acid and disodium octoborate tetrahydrate; silica gels; diatomaceous earth; nonvolatile insect and rodent baits in tamper-resistant containers or for crack and crevice treatment only; microbe-based insecticides; pesticides made with essential oils (not including synthetic pyrethroids) without toxic synergists; and materials for which the inert ingredients are nontoxic and disclosed. A least toxic pesticide does not include a pesticide that: is determined by the U.S. Environmental Protection Agency as a probable, likely, or known carcinogen or endocrine disruptor; is a mutagen, reproductive toxin, developmental neurotoxin, or immune system toxin; is classified by the U.S. Environmental Protection Agency as a toxicity I or II pesticide; is in the organophosphate or carbamate chemical family; or contains inert ingredients categorized as "List 1: Inerts of Toxicological Concern." Least toxic pesticides do not include any application of pesticides using a broadcast spray, dust, tenting, fogging or baseboard spray application.

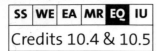

SS	WE	EA	MR	EQ	IU
Credit 10.6					

1 point

Green Cleaning

Low Environmental Impact Cleaning Equipment Policy

Intent

Reduce exposure of building occupants and maintenance personnel to potentially hazardous chemical, biological and particle contaminants, which adversely impact air quality, health, building finishes, building systems and the environment.

Requirements

Implement a policy for the use of janitorial equipment that maximizes effective reduction of building contaminants with minimum environmental impact.

Cleaning equipment policy needs to specify that:

- ❑ Vacuum cleaners meet the requirements of the Carpet & Rug Institute "Green Label" Testing Program- Vacuum Cleaner Criteria and are capable of capturing 96% of particulates 0.3 microns in size and operate with a sound level less than 70dBA.
- ❑ Hot water extraction equipment for deep cleaning carpets is capable of removing sufficient moisture such that carpets can dry in less than 24 hours.
- ❑ Powered maintenance equipment including floor buffers, burnishers and automatic scrubbers is equipped with vacuums, guards and/or other devices for capturing fine particulates, and shall operate with a sound level less than 70dBA.
- ❑ Propane-powered floor equipment has high-efficiency, low-emissions engines.
- ❑ Automated scrubbing machines are equipped with variable-speed feed pumps to optimize the use of cleaning fluids.
- ❑ Battery-powered equipment is equipped with environmentally preferable gel batteries.
- ❑ Where appropriate, active micro fiber technology is used to reduce cleaning chemical consumption and prolong life of disposable scrubbing pads.
- ❑ Powered equipment is ergonomically designed to minimize vibration, noise and user fatigue.
- ❑ Equipment has rubber bumpers to reduce potential damage to building surfaces.
- ❑ A log will be kept for all powered housekeeping equipment to document the date of equipment purchase and all repair and maintenance activities and include vendor cut sheets for each type of equipment in use in the logbook.

Submittals – Initial Certification

- ❑ Provide a copy of the low environmental impact janitorial equipment policy adopted by your organization.
- ❑ Provide a record of the janitorial equipment used in the building and a log of the maintenance of each piece of equipment over the performance period. Include vendor specifications for each type of equipment in use.

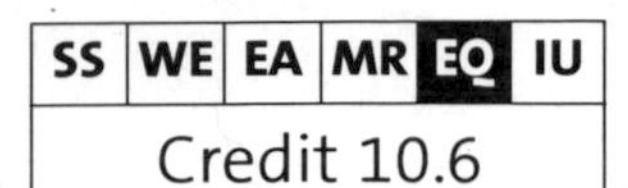

Submittals – Recertification

Provide an update of previous filings:

- ❑ If there has been no change to the low environmental impact janitorial equipment policy since the previous LEED-EB filing, provide a statement verifying its continued existence and operation.
- ❑ Provide a record of the janitorial equipment used in the building and a log of the maintenance of each piece of equipment over the performance period. Include vendor specifications for each type of equipment in use.

OR

- ❑ If there has been a change in the low environmental impact janitorial equipment policy, provide a copy of the plan highlighting any changes.
- ❑ Provide a record of the janitorial equipment used in the building and a log of the maintenance of each piece of equipment over the performance period. Include vendor specifications for each type of equipment in use.

Summary of Referenced Standard

"Green Label" Testing Program - Vacuum Cleaner Criteria

The Carpet and Rug Institute (CRI)

www.carpet-rug.org

(800) 882-8846

This program certifies vacuum cleaners that show superior performance at removing soil, capturing dust and fine particles, and improving the appearance of carpets without causing damage. More information about the CRI "Green Label" vacuum cleaner certification program can be found online (www.carpet-rug.org/drill_down_2.cfm?page=8&sub=9).

Green Building Concerns

Many vacuums cannot capture the very fine particles that cause respiratory problems and damage building systems and delicate electronic equipment. In addition, the use of some floor machines (e.g., burnishers and buffers) can create large amounts of dust, reducing the quality of the indoor environment. These machines can be equipped with active dust control systems including vacuums, guards and skirts to alleviate dust problems. High-efficiency carpet cleaners are also available that use less water and allow carpets to dry more quickly, minimizing the potential for mold growth and associated problems. Utilizing these devices will have a positive impact on IAQ, occupant health and productivity.[38]

Environmental Issues

This credit was designed to minimize waste production, energy use and harmful impacts to IEQ (i.e., noise pollution and indoor air degradation). Careful purchasing and use of janitorial equipment extends the lives of carpets and floors, thereby preventing all the environmental effects of their replacement, including the effects of energy use, resource extraction, transportation and waste production. The required equipment will also keep microscopic particulates out of the air, reducing stress on building systems, electronic equipment and building occupants. Janitorial equipment using electric or propane motors should be energy-efficient to reduce energy use and produce low emission levels to promote healthy IAQ.

Economic Issues

Highly effective janitorial equipment often has greater up-front costs than lower performing equipment. However, quality equipment results in reduced hours for maintenance personnel and fewer equipment repairs. These benefits, along with IEQ impacts that protect occupant health and improve productivity, will save money compared to average cleaning equipment. In addition, the majority of injuries to janitorial workers are muscular-skeletal injuries (such as back injuries), resulting in part from the use of equipment designed with poor ergonomics. Equipment that offers improved ergonomics (e.g., backpack vacuums) can reduce back injuries, workman's compensation claims, and worker turnover.

Strategies & Technologies

Develop, implement and maintain a policy for the use of janitorial equipment that maximizes effective reduction of building contaminants with minimum environmental impacts and injury risks to equipment users. Evaluate the janitorial equipment in use, and make a plan to upgrade to janitorial equipment when replacements are necessary or financially feasible. All equipment should meet the specifications in the Requirements section of this credit.

Keep a log of all powered housekeeping equipment that identifies the date of

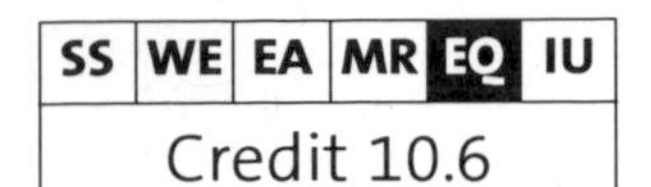

purchase and all repair and maintenance activities. Include vendor cut sheets for each type of equipment for records and LEED-EB submission.

An alternative to a CRI-certified vacuum cleaner is a centralized vacuum system that exhausts outdoors. This system must have the capability of capturing 96 percent of particulates 0.3 microns in size and operate within the required decibel levels. The exhaust point for the central vacuum must be directed away from building air intakes and any occupied areas.

Synergies & Tradeoffs

Implementation of the required cleaning equipment policy may result in higher initial costs for equipment and supplies. Once implemented, however, the program will achieve reduced costs in addition to the positive environmental impacts. Also, any cleaning products used in janitorial equipment should comply with the policies discussed in IEQ Credit 10.3 and MR Credits 4.1–4.3.

Calculations & Documentation

Calculations

None.

Documentation

- ❑ Copy of the low environmental impact janitorial equipment policy:
  - All items listed in the Requirements should be addressed in the organizational janitorial equipment policy even if they do not apply to current building operational programs.

Other Resources

Collaborative for High Performance Schools

www.chps.net

This organization provides information on providing healthy and sustainable school environments, including a variety of information dealing with IAQ issues.

EPA Environmentally Preferable Purchasing

www.epa.gov/oppt/epp/documents/docback.htm

This web site has specific background information on a host of issues relative to environmentally preferable purchasing.

EPA Environmentally Preferable Purchasing Case Studies

www.epa.gov/oppt/epp/documents/doccase.htm

Providing information about organization approaches to the incorporation of environmental considerations into their purchasing decisions, this web site offers pertinent background documents, such as Executive Orders and Memorandums of Agreement, specifically beneficial to federal users.

Pennsylvania Green Building Operations and Maintenance Manual

www.dgs.state.pa.us/dgs/lib/dgs/green bldg/greenbuildingbook.pdf

The Commonwealth of Pennsylvania's Department of General Services has published a comprehensive Green Building Maintenance Manual with chapters that address green cleaning.

Definitions

Green Cleaning is the use of cleaning products and practices that have reduced environmental impacts in comparison with conventional products and practices.

Endnotes

[1] United States. Environmental Protection Agency. Health Buildings, Healthy People: A Vision for the 21st Century October 2001. 18 February 2005 <http://www.epa.gov/iaq/hbhp/hbhptoc.html>.

[2] United States. Environmental Protection Agency. Unfinished Business: A Comparative Assessment of Environmental Problems. Washington, DC, 1987.

[3] United States. Environmental Protection Agency. Reducing Risk: Setting Priorities and Strategies for Environmental Protection. SAB-EC-90-0021. Washington, DC, 1990.

[4] United States. Environmental Protection Agency. Indoor Air in Large Buildings October 2002. 17 February 2005 <http://www.epa.gov/iaq/largebldgs/i-beam_html/ch8-budg.htm>.

[5] City of San Francisco. San Francisco's Green Building Report 1999-2002. 16 February 2005 <http://temp.sfgov.org/sfenvironment/aboutus/innovative/greenbldg/gb_report.pdf>.

[6] Fisk, W.J. "Health and Productivity Gains From Better Indoor Environments and Their Relationship with Building Energy Efficiency." Annual Rev. Energy Environ. 25:537-66. 2000.

[7] United States. Department of Health and Human Services. National Institutes of Health, National Cancer Institute. Health Effects of Exposure to Environmental Tobacco Smoke. Smoking and Tobacco Control Monograph 10, 1999. NIH Pub. No. 99-4645. 24 May 2005 <http://cancercontrol.cancer.gov/tcrb/monographs/10/m10_complete.pdf>

[8] Ibid.

[9] United States. Department of Health and Human Services, Public Health Service, Office of the Surgeon General. Women and Smoking: A Report of the Surgeon General. Rockville, MD: 2001. 24 May 2005 <http://www.cdc.gov/tobacco/sgr/sgr_forwomen/index.htm>.

[10] United States. Department of Health and Human Service, Center for Disease Control, National Center for Environmental Health. Second National Report on Human Exposure to Environmental Chemicals: Tobacco Smoke. NCEH Pub. No. 03-0022, Atlanta, GA: 2003. 24 May 2005 <http://www.cdc.gov/exposurereport/>.

[11] United States. Environmental Protection Agency. Polychlorinated Biphenyls (PCBs) December 2004. 11 February 2005 <http://www.epa.gov/opptintr/pcb/>.

[12] United States. Environmental Protection Agency. Health Effects of PCBs September 2004. 11 February 2005 <http://www.epa.gov/opptintr/pcb/effects.html>.

[13] Kentucky State University, Department of Architectural Engineering & Construction Science. GreenBuild Tech Bulletin: Carbon Dioxide Monitoring July 2004. 11

February 2005 <http://www.edcmag.com/FILES/HTML/PDF/2005_01-GBTB-CO2_Monitoring.pdf>.

[14] Fisk, William J. "Health and Productivity Gains from Better Indoor Environments and Their Relationship with Building Energy Efficiency." Annual Revue Energy Environment 25, 537-566. 2000. 27 May 2005 <http://www.usgbc.org/Docs/Resources/Fisk(LBNL)HealthandProductivityEE2000.pdf>.

[15] Ibid.

[16] Ibid.

[17] United States. Department of Health and Human Services, Public Heath Service, National Institutes of Health, National Heart, Lung, and Blood Institute. Morbidity & Mortality: 2004 Chart Book on Cardiovascular, Lung, and Blood Diseases, 2004. 11 February 2005 <http://www.nhlbi.nih.gov/resources/docs/04_chtbk.pdf>.

[18] California Energy Commission. Windows and Offices: A Study of Office Worker Performance and the Indoor Environment, P500-03-082-A-9, 2003. Prepared by Heschong Mahone Group, Inc. Managed by New Buildings Institute. 15 March 2005 <http://www.newbuildings.org/pier/downloadsFinal.htm>.

[19] United States. Energy Information Administration, Department of Energy, Commercial Buildings. Preliminary End-Use Consumption Estimates – 1999 Commercial Buildings Energy Consumption Survey, October 2003. 11 February 2005 <http://www.eia.doe.gov/emeu/cbecs/enduse_consumption/intro.html>.

[20] University of California – Berkeley. College of Environmental Design, Center for the Built Environment. Development of a Prototype Wireless Lighting Control System 2002. 11 February 2005 <http://www.cbe.berkeley.edu/research/wireless_lighting.htm>. Efficiency data is from a pilot installation of the lighting control prototype. CBE is expanding research in this area.

[21] Leaman, A., and B. Bordass. "Assessing Building Performance in Use 4: The Probe Occupant Surveys and Their Implications." Building Research and Information 29.2 (2001): 129-143.

[22] Wyon, David P. "Indoor Environmental Effects on Productivity." In Teichman, K.Y., ed. Proceedings of IAQ 96-Paths to Better Building Environments. ASHRAE, Atlanta, 5-15, 1996.

[23] Bornehag, C., et al. "Dampness in Buildings and Health." Indoor Air 11.2 (2001): 72-86.

[24] Federspiel, Clifford C. "Statistical Analysis of Unsolicited Thermal Sensation Complaints in Commercial Buildings." ASHRAE Transactions 104.1 (1998): 912-923.

[25] Martin, Rodney, A., Clifford C. Federspiel, and David M. Auslander. "Responding to Thermal Sensation Complaints in Buildings." ASHRAE Transactions 112.1 (2002): 407-412.

[26] Wyon, David P. "Enhancing Productivity While Reducing Energy Use in Buildings." Proceedings of the E-Vision 2000 Conference, October 11-13, 2000, Washington, D.C. Available online from RAND Corporation, Arlington, VA. 15 February 2005 <http://www.rand.org/publications/CF/CF170.1.1/CF170.1.wyon.pdf>. Figure cited is a summary of estimates developed by Wyon (Healthy building and their impact on productivity, 1993; The economic benefits of a healthy indoor environment, 1994; Indoor environmental effects on productivity, 1996) and Fisk and Rosenfeld (Estimates of improved productivity and health from better indoor environments, 1997).

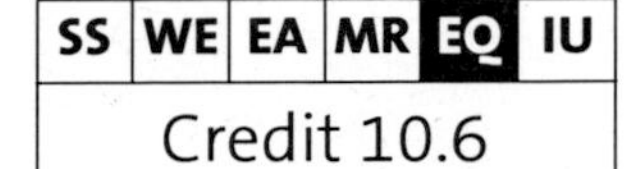

[27]Loren E. Abraham, "Chapter 9: Daylighting," Sustainable Building Technical Manual: Green Building Design, Construction, and Operations (Public Technology Inc. and U.S. Green Building Council, 1996).

[28] United States. Department of Energy, Office of Energy Efficiency and Renewable Energy, Federal Energy Management Program. FEMP Focus – March/April 2002: Federal Energy Managers See Daylight To Energy Savings February 2004. 4 March 2005 <http://www.eere.energy.gov/femp/newsevents/fempfocus_article.cfm/news_id=7148>.

[29] Ibid.

[30] Finnegan, M.C., and L.A. Solomon. "Work attitudes in windowed vs. windowless environments." Journal of Social Psychology 115 (1981): 291-291.

[31] Information supplied by Stephen Ashkin, President, The Ashkin Group, LLC. Figure also published in: Ashkin, Stephen. "Implementing Green Cleaning: Steps Toward a Healthier Facility." Destination Green 1.1 (2005). 11 March 2005 <http://www.imakenews.com/theashkingroup/e_article000353594.cfm?x=b11,b312Nd0N,w>.

[32] Information supplied by Stephen Ashkin, President, The Ashkin Group, LLC. www.ashkingroup.com.

[33] United States. Environmental Protection Agency, Office of Pollution Prevention & Toxics. Environmentally Preferable Purchasing: Green Your Purchase of Cleaning Products October 2004. 4 March 2005 <http://www.epa.gov/oppt/epp/documents/clean/cleaning.htm>.

[34] Ibid.

[35] Information supplied by Stephen Ashkin, President, The Ashkin Group, LLC. www.ashkingroup.com.

[36] United States. Environmental Protection Agency. Guide to IPM May 2003. 16 February 2005 <http://www.epa.gov/seahome/child/pesticide/iguide_m.htm>.

[37] United States. Environmental Protection Agency, National Health and Environmental Effects Research Laboratory. Health and Environmental Health Research January 2005. 16 February 2005 <http://www.epa.gov/NHEERL/research/human_health.html>.

[38] Ashkin, Stephen. "Stewardship, Cleaning and IAQ." Today's Facility Manager June 2004.

Innovation in Upgrades, Operations and Maintenance

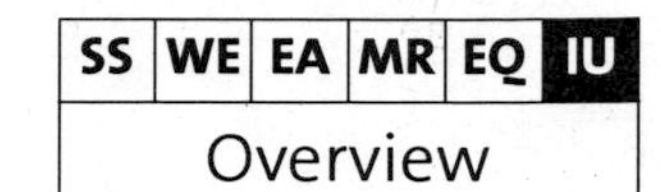

Strategies for operating buildings more sustainably are constantly evolving and improving. New technologies are continually introduced to the marketplace and up-to-date scientific research influences building operation, design and function. The purpose of this LEED-EB category is to recognize projects for innovative building features/practices and sustainable building knowledge which generate increased environmental benefits beyond those addressed or specified by LEED-EB. Additionally, expertise in sustainable building principles is essential to the upgrades, operations, and maintenance processes. Innovation in Upgrades, Operations and Maintenance (IU) credits reward these elements of sustainability.

IU credits are of particular value to the growth and development of the LEED-EB rating system. Successful IU credits represent valuable input from the building operations industry as to developments in the field, as well as the metrics used to assess performance on key environmental issues. The USGBC reviews IU credits as a means of ensuring that LEED-EB continues to keep pace with the direction and standards of the industry.

Overview of LEED® Credits

IU Credit 1
Innovation in Upgrades, Operations and Maintenance

IU Credit 2
LEED® Accredited Professional

There are 5 points available in the Innovation in Upgrades, Operations and Maintenance category.

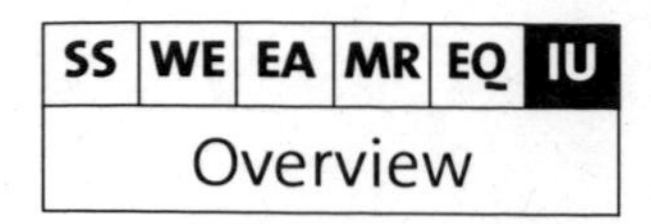

SS	WE	EA	MR	EQ	IU

Credit 1

1–4 points

Innovation in Upgrades, Operations and Maintenance

Intent

To provide building operation and upgrade teams with the opportunity to be awarded points for additional environmental benefits achieved beyond those already addressed by LEED-EB Rating System

Requirements

Credit 1.1 (1 point)	Provide documentation of each proposed innovation credit, including a description of the achievement, the additional environmental benefits delivered and the performance metrics used to document the additional environmental benefits delivered over the performance period.
Credit 1.2 (1 point)	Same as Credit 1.1
Credit 1.3 (1 point)	Same as Credit 1.1
Credit 1.4 (1 point)	Same as Credit 1.1

Submittals – Initial Certification

❑ Provide documentation of each proposed innovation credit, including a description of the achievement, the additional environmental benefits delivered , and the performance metrics used to document the additional environmental benefits delivered over the performance period.

Submittals – Recertification

❑ Provide documentation of each proposed innovation credit, including a description of the achievement, the additional environmental benefits delivered, and the performance metrics used to document the additional environmental benefits delivered over the performance period.

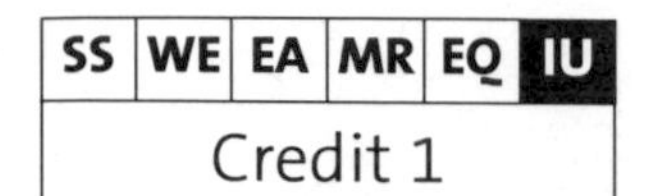

Summary of Referenced Standard

There is no standard referenced for this credit.

Green Building Concerns

The LEED-EB Green Building Rating System was developed to address current sustainability issues and opportunities related to existing buildings. As the building management and upgrade industry is constantly evolving and introducing new strategies for sustainable operations, many new opportunities to generate additional environmental benefits will continue to emerge. IU credits are intended to provide recognition and credit within the LEED-EB rating system for those efforts that either deliver a greatly increased environmental benefit in one of the existing LEED-EB prerequisite or credit areas, or deliver meaningful environmental benefits in an area that is not currently addressed by LEED-EB. Areas that are not currently addressed by LEED-EB may include unique local environmental concerns or opportunities, as well as broader environmental issues not addressed in the rating system.

Environmental Issues

With all sustainable design strategies and measures, it is important to consider the environmental impacts and to assure that other building aspects are not adversely impacted. Project teams should be prepared to demonstrate the environmental benefit of the innovative strategies used within the building, and are encouraged to investigate opportunities that provide an environmental benefit of particular significance in the area.

Economic Issues

Innovative strategies and measures have a range of first costs and operating costs that depend on the degree of complexity, materials incorporated and novelty of the technology. Initial costs can range from free to prohibitively expensive. To understand the implications of innovative strategies and technologies, a life cycle analysis should be considered as a way to determine if the strategy or technology is cost effective over the lifetime of the building. Many early innovators decide the value of being a pioneer and driving change outweighs the higher cost of innovative measures.

Strategies & Technologies

Credits in this section may be earned by documenting increased benefits to the environment in one of two ways. A building strategy or measure which results in building performance that greatly exceeds that required by an existing LEED-EB credit may be eligible for an IU credit. In addition, IU credits can be earned by other projects, efforts, or sustainability strategies that produce environmental benefits beyond those addressed by any LEED-EB prerequisite or credit.

Project teams are encouraged to investigate opportunities for innovative actions that will be particularly meaningful to the surrounding community in terms of their environmental benefit. For example, buildings located in an area with water shortages might take measures to significantly exceed the water efficiency requirements of LEED-EB.

Suggested Topics for Innovation Credits

Only those strategies and measures that have significant environmental benefits are applicable to this credit, and the standard for earning IU credits is high. For example, an environmental educational program consisting of simple signage in a building would not by itself be considered a significant benefit. Conversely, a visitor's center and interactive display, coupled with a web site and video would be an appropriate level of effort for earning an innovation credit.

The following list contains sample actions that might meet the criteria for earning IU credits. Project teams are encouraged to explore the full range of innovative opportunities within their buildings.

- ❑ Provide an education program for the building occupants on the environmental and human health benefits of green building practices, and how occupants can help improve the buildings green performance achievements. Evaluate results and refine the occupant education program to increase its impact. The program should consist of elements that significantly engage building occupants and visitors in understanding green building issues.
- ❑ Increase public awareness of green buildings, sustainable building operations, and your LEED-EB project by providing a public outreach program that builds on Energy & Atmosphere Credit 6. Produce a detailed case study of the project, give presentations about the project to interested local and regional groups, and provide tours of the building to guests and interested parties.
- ❑ Evaluate any product or material, being used or being considered for use in the building, on the basis of an ISO 14040 life-cycle assessment.
- ❑ Develop ride sharing programs that include providing a database on ride sharing opportunities and a guaranteed get-home policy for participants that get stranded due to unexpected conditions.
- ❑ Provide incentives for using public and alternative transportation that lead to significant participation by building occupants.

Calculations & Documentation

Calculations

For IU credits that substantially exceed the performance required by existing LEED-EB credits, calculations based on the same methodology outlined for the exceeded credit should be included.

Documentation

Documentation submitted in support of IU credits should be detailed, and include a description of the measure, its environmental benefits, and the achievements delivered over the performance period. A separate set of detailed submittals is required for each point awarded.

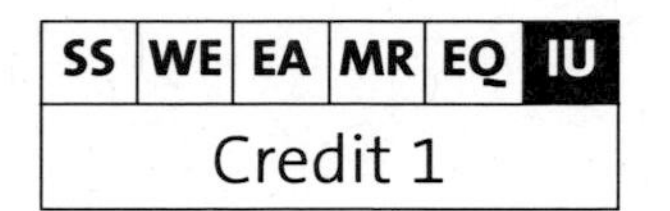

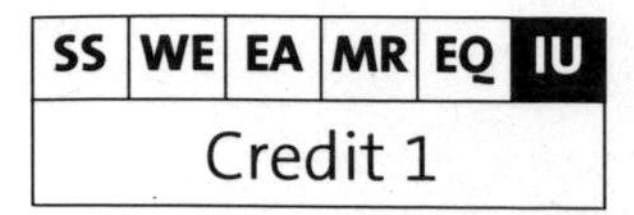
SS WE EA MR EQ IU
Credit 1

SS | WE | EA | MR | EQ | IU

Credit 2

1 point

LEED Accredited Professional

Intent

To support and encourage the operation, upgrade and project team integration required for LEED-EB implementation in buildings and to streamline the application and certification process.

Requirements

At least one principal participant of the project team is a LEED Accredited Professional.

Submittals – Initial Certification

- ❑ Provide documentation stating the LEED Accredited Professional's name, title, company and contact information.

Submittals – Recertification

- ❑ Provide documentation stating the LEED Accredited Professional's name, title, company and contact information.

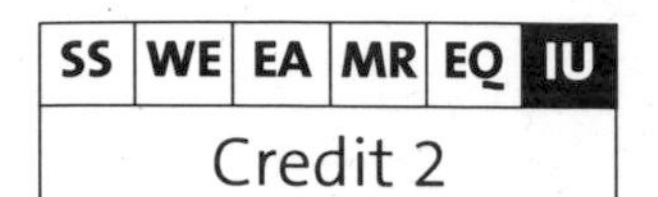

Summary of Referenced Standard

LEED Accredited Professional

U.S. Green Building Council

www.usgbc.org/DisplayPage.aspx?CMSPageID=69&

(202)828-7422

Individuals are accredited as LEED Accredited Professionals (LEED APs) after successfully completing the LEED Professional Accreditation exam. The purpose of the certification exam is to ensure that the successful candidate has the knowledge and skill necessary to participate in the LEED application and certification process, and to test understanding of green building practices and principles, and familiarity with LEED requirements, resources, and processes.

Green Building Concerns

LEED APs have the expertise required to integrate sustainability into building operating and upgrade practices. The Accredited Professional understands the importance of considering interactions between the prerequisites and credits and their respective criteria. Facility managers, engineers, consultants, building owners, architects and others that have a strong interest in sustainable buildings are all appropriate candidates for accreditation. The Accredited Professional should be the champion for the project's LEED-EB application and this person should be an integral member of the project team.

Strategies & Technologies

The participation of a LEED Accredited Professional in the LEED-EB application process is considered a valuable and important step. Although not required by LEED-EB, the presence of a LEED AP ensures that the project team is well-informed on the key elements of the rating system and understands the importance of considering interactions between the prerequisites and credits and their respective criteria.

Currently, the LEED Professional Accreditation exam is based on LEED-NC Version 2.1. In the future, the LEED AP exam will include an additional section for individuals specializing in LEED-EB. Including an individual who has been certified under any current or future LEED AP exam on the project team meets the credit requirements. Strategies for including a LEED AP on the project team include:

- ❑ Engaging an individual within your organization who is already a LEED AP
- ❑ Having someone in your organization prepare for and complete the LEED AP accreditation process. Attending a LEED Workshop and reviewing the LEED Rating Systems are effective ways to prepare for the exam.
- ❑ Hire a LEED AP to support your project. Consider selecting a LEED AP experienced with LEED-EB or who has also taken the LEED-EB specialization portion of the LEED Accreditation exam (once available).

For more information on workshops and the Accreditation Exam testing locations, fees, and topics covered, visit the USGBC web site (www.usgbc.org).

Glossary of Terms

Advanced Technology Vehicles (ATVs) **SS C3.3**

A type of alternative vehicles that use advanced technologies for powertrains, emissions controls, and other vehicle features that allow for improved environmental performance. Electric hybrid vehicles and fuel cell vehicles are examples of ATVs.

Agrifiber Products **MR C3**

Products made from agricultural fiber.

Albedo **SS C 6.1**

See solar reflectance.

Alternative Fuel Vehicles (AFVs) **SS C3.3**

A type of alternative vehicles that use low-polluting fuels such as electricity, propane or compressed natural gas, liquid natural gas, methanol and ethanol.

Aquatic Systems **WE C2**

Ecologically designed treatment systems that utilize a diverse community of biological organisms (e.g., bacteria, plants and fish) to treat wastewater to advanced levels.

Aromatic Compounds **MR C3**

Defined by the Green Seal Standard (GS-11) as "hydrocarbon compounds containing one or more 6-carbon benzene rings in the molecular structure."

Bicycle Racks **SS C3.2**

Include outdoor bicycle racks, bicycle lockers or indoor bicycle storage rooms.

Bioaccumulants **MR P2**

Substances that increase in concentration in the living organisms exposed to them because they are very slowly metabolized or excreted

Biomass **EA C2**

Plant material such as trees, grasses and crops that can be converted to heat energy to produce electricity.

Blackwater **WE P1, WE C1, WE C2**

No single definition is accepted nationwide. Wastewater from toilets and urinals is always considered blackwater. Wastewater from kitchen sinks (perhaps differentiated by the use of a garbage disposal), showers, or bathtubs may be considered blackwater by state or local codes. Project teams should comply with blackwater definition as established by the authority having jurisdiction in their areas.

Breathing Zone **IEQ C2**

The region in an occupied space from 3 inches above the floor to 72 inches above the floor and greater than 2 feet from walls or fixed air conditioning equipment.

Building Density — SS C2

The floor area of the building divided by the total area of the property (square feet per acre).

Building Energy Performance Baseline — EA P2

The average building performance for the specific type of building. For building types covered by ENERGY STAR, this is a score of 50. For building types not covered by ENERGY STAR, the building energy performance baseline is established with historic building energy use data and/or energy use data from other, similar buildings.

Building Footprint — SS C4

The area of the site that is occupied by the building structure, not including parking lots, landscapes and other non-building facilities.

Building Related Illness — IEQ P1, IEQ C4.1, IEQ C9

Diagnosable illnesses that can be directly attributed to airborne building contaminants.

Carbon Dioxide (CO_2) Monitoring — IEQ C1

An indicator of ventilation effectiveness inside buildings. CO_2 concentrations greater than 530 ppm above outdoor CO_2 conditions are generally considered an indicator of inadequate ventilation. Absolute concentrations of CO_2 greater than 800 to 1000 ppm are generally considered an indicator of poor breathing air quality.

Carpool — SS C3.4

An arrangement in which two or more people share a vehicle together for transportation.

Chain-of-Custody — MR C2

A tracking procedure for documenting the status of a product from the point of harvest or extraction to the ultimate consumer end use.

Chemical Component Restrictions — MR C3

A set of restrictions set by the Green Seal Standard (GS-11) requiring that the manufacturer demonstrate that the chemical compounds included on the Chemical Component Restrictions list are not used as ingredients in the manufacture of the product.

Chlorofluorocarbons (CFCs) — EA P3

Hydrocarbons that cause depletion of the stratospheric ozone layer and are used as refrigerants in buildings.

Composite Panels — MR C3

Panels made from several materials. Plywood and OSB (oriented strand board) are two examples of composite panels.

Composting Toilet Systems — WE P1, WE C2

Dry plumbing fixtures that contain and treat human waste via microbiological processes.

Concentrate IEQ C10.3

A product that must be diluted by at least eight parts by volume water (1:8 dilution ratio) prior to its intended use. (Green Seal GS-37)

Conditioned Space IEQ C2

The portion of the building that is heated and/or cooled for the comfort of building occupants.

Constructed Wetlands SS C5

Wastewater treatment systems designed to simulate natural wetland functions for water purification by removing contaminants from wastewaters.

Construction, Demolition and Land Clearing (CDL) Debris MR C1

Includes waste and recyclables generated from construction, land clearing (e.g., vegetation, but not soil), renovation, and demolition or deconstructing of pre-existing structures.

Construction IAQ Management Plan IEQ C3

A document specific to a building project that outlines measures to minimize contamination in the building during construction, and procedures to flush the building of contaminants prior to occupancy.

Convenience Copier IEQ C5.2

Low-volume copying machines distributed around the building for the convenience of the building occupants.

Conventional Irrigation WE C1

The most common irrigation system used in the region where the building is located. A common conventional irrigation system uses pressure to deliver water and distributes it through sprinkler heads above the ground.

Curfew Hours SS C7

Locally determined times when greater lighting restrictions are imposed.

Daylight Factor (DF) IEQ C8

The ratio of exterior illumination to interior illumination and is expressed as a percentage. The variables used to determine the daylight factor include the floor area, window area, window geometry, visible transmittance (T_{vis}) and window height.

Daylight Glazing IEQ C8

Vertical window area that is located 7'6" above the floor of the room. Glazing at this height is the most effective at distributing daylight deep into the interior space.

Daylighting IEQ C8

The controlled admission of natural light into a space through glazing with the intent of reducing or eliminating electric lighting. By utilizing solar light, daylighting creates a stimulating and productive environment for building occupants.

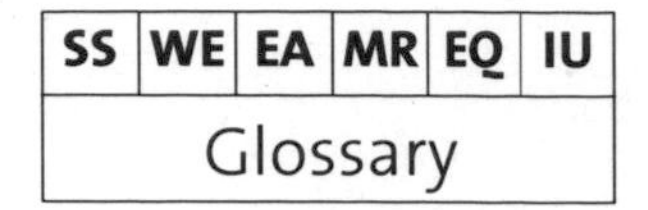

Design Light Output — **MR P2**

The light output of light bulbs at 40 percent of their useful life.

Detention Ponds — **SS C5**

Ponds that capture stormwater runoff and allow pollutants to drop out before release to a stormwater or water body. A variety of detention pond designs are available, with some utilizing only gravity while others use mechanical equipment such as pipes and pumps to facilitate transport. Some ponds are dry except during storm events and other ponds permanently store water volumes.

Drip Irrigation — **WE C1**

A high-efficiency irrigation method in which water is delivered at low pressure through buried mains and sub-mains. From the sub-mains, water is distributed to the soil from a network of perforated tubes or emitters. Drip irrigation is a type of micro-irrigation.

Ecological Restoration — **SS C4**

The process of assisting in the recovery and management of ecological integrity, which includes a critical range of variability in biodiversity, ecological processes and structures, regional and historical context, and sustainable cultural practices.

Ecologically Appropriate Site Features — **SS C4**

Natural site elements that maintain or restore the ecological integrity of the site, and may include native/adapted vegetation, water bodies, exposed rock, un-vegetated ground, or other features that are part of the historic natural landscape within the region and provide habitat value.

Elemental Mercury — **MR P2**

Pure mercury rather that a mercury containing compound, the vapor of which is commonly used in fluorescent and other light bulb types.

Emissions Offsets — **EA C5.4**

Emissions reductions from one set of actions that are used to offset emission caused by another set of actions.

Emissivity — **SS C6.1**

The ratio of the radiation emitted by a surface to the radiation emitted by a blackbody at the same temperature.

ENERGY STAR Rating — **EA C1**

The rating a building earns using the ENERGY STAR® Portfolio Manager to compare building energy performance to similar buildings in similar climates. A score of 50 represents average building performance

Environmental Attributes of Green Power — **EA C2**

Emission reduction benefits that result from green power being used instead of conventional power sources.

Environmental Tobacco Smoke (ETS) or Second Hand Smoke **IEQ P2**

Airborne particles emitted from the burning end of cigarettes, pipes, and cigars, and exhaled by smokers. These particles contain roughly 4,000 different compounds, up to 50 of which are known carcinogens.

Erosion **SS P1**

A combination of processes by which materials of the earth's surface are loosened, dissolved, or worn away, and transported from one place to another by natural agents.

Eutrophication **SS P1**

The process by which lakes and ponds age. Water, through natural or human sources, becomes rich in nutrients and promotes the proliferation of plant life (especially algae) that reduces the dissolved oxygen content of the water and often causes the extinction of other organisms within the water body.

Existing Building Commissioning **EA P1**

Developing a building operation plan that identifies current building operating requirements and needs, conducting tests to proactively determine if the building and fundamental systems are operating in accordance with the building operation plan, and making any repairs needed so that the building and fundamental systems are operating according to the plan.

Filtration Basins **SS C5**

Basins that remove sediment and pollutants from stormwater runoff using a filter media such as sand or gravel. A sediment trap is usually included to remove sediment from stormwater before filtering to avoid clogging.

Fixture sensors **WE P1**

Motion sensors that automatically turn on/off lavatories, sinks, water closets and urinals.

Footcandle (fc) **SS C7**

A unit of light intensity and is equal to the quantity of light falling on a one-square foot area from a one candela light source at a distance of one foot.

Friable **IEQ P3**

The term used in the asbestos industry to describe asbestos that can be reduced to dust by hand pressure.

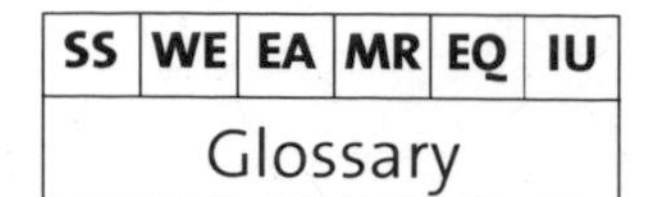

Full Disclosure — IEQ C10.3

For products that are not formulated with listed suspect carcinogens, full disclosure is defined as (i) disclosure of all ingredients (both hazardous and non-hazardous) that make up 1 percent or more of the undiluted product and (ii) use of concentration ranges for each of the disclosed ingredients. "Full Disclosure" for products that are formulated with listed suspect carcinogens is defined as (i) disclosure of listed suspect carcinogens that make up 0.1 percent or more of the undiluted product, (ii) disclosure of all remaining ingredients (both hazardous and non-hazardous) that make up 1.0 percent or more of the undiluted product, and (iii) use of concentration ranges for each of the disclosed ingredients. Suspect carcinogens are those that are listed on authoritative lists available for MSDS preparation: IARC, NTP, and California Proposition 65 lists. Concentration range definitions are available from OSHA or Canada WHMIS Standards.

Full-Time Equivalent Building Occupants — SS C3.2

The total number of hours all building occupants spend in the building during the peak 8-hour occupancy period divided by 8 hours. For buildings used for multiple shifts each day, the shift with the greatest number of FTE building occupants sets the overall FTE building occupants for the building.

Glare — IEQ C8

Any excessively bright source of light within the visual field that creates discomfort or loss in visibility.

Grassed Swales — SS C5

Trenches or ditches covered with vegetation to encourage subsurface infiltration, similar to infiltration basins and trenches. They utilize vegetation to filter sediment and pollutants from stormwater.

Graywater — WE P1, WE C1, WE C2

Defined by the Uniform Plumbing Code (UPC) in its Appendix G, titled "Gray Water Systems for Single-Family Dwellings" as "untreated household waste water which has not come into contact with toilet waste. Grey water includes used water from bathtubs, showers, bathroom wash basins, and water from clothes-washer and laundry tubs. It shall not include waste water from kitchen sinks or dishwashers." The International Plumbing Code (IPC) defines graywater in its Appendix C, titled "Gray Water Recycling Systems" as "waste water discharged from lavatories, bathtubs, showers, clothes washers, and laundry sinks." Some states and local authorities allow kitchen sink wastewater to be included in graywater. Other differences with the UPC and IPC definitions can probably be found in state and local codes.

Green Cleaning — IEQ C10.6

The use of cleaning products and practices that have reduced environmental impacts in comparison with conventional products and practices.

Greenfield — SS C2, SS C4

Undeveloped land or land that has not been impacted by human activity.

Group Multi-Occupant Spaces — **IEQ C6, IEQ C8.3 & 8.4**

Conference rooms, classrooms and other indoor spaces used as places of congregation for presentations, training sessions, etc. Individuals using these spaces share the lighting and temperature controls. Group multi-occupant spaces do not include open office plans that contain standard individual workstations.

Halons — **EA P3, EA C4**

Substances that are used in fire suppression systems and fire extinguishers in buildings and deplete the stratospheric ozone layer.

Hazardous Waste — **MR C1**

Waste material made up of hazardous components that present a risk to human or environmental health.

Heat Island Effect — **SS C6.1**

Urban air and surface temperatures that are higher than nearby rural areas. Principle contributing factors include additions of dark, non-reflective surfaces, elimination of trees and vegetation, waste heat from vehicles, factories, and air conditioners and reduced airflow from tall buildings and narrow streets.

HEPA Filters — **IEQ C5.1**

High Efficiency Particulate Air (HEPA) filters have a filtration efficiency of at least 99.97 percent for 0.3 microns particles

High Occupancy Vehicles — **SS C3.4**

Vehicles with more that one occupant.

High-Volume Copiers — **IEQ C5.2**

Machines used to copy many pages on a continuous basis.

HVAC Systems — **IEQ C3**

Heating, ventilating and air conditioning systems used to provide thermal comfort and ventilation for building interiors.

Hybrid Vehicles — **SS C3.3**

Vehicles that use a gasoline engine to drive an electric generator and use the electric generator and/or storage batteries to power electric motors that drive the vehicle's wheels.

Hydrochlorofluorocarbons (HCFCs) — **EA P3, EA C4**

Refrigerants that deplete the stratospheric ozone layer and are used in building equipment.

Hydrofluorocarbons (HFCs) — **EA C4**

Refrigerants that do not deplete the stratospheric ozone layer. However, some HFCs have high global warming potential, and thus are not environmentally benign.

Impervious Surfaces **SS C5**

Surfaces that promote runoff of precipitation volumes instead of infiltration into the subsurface. The imperviousness or degree of runoff potential can be estimated for different surface materials.

Imperviousness **SS C6.1**

Resistance to penetration by a liquid, calculated as the percentage of area covered by a paving system that does not allow moisture to soak into the earth below the paving system.

Incinerator **MR P1, MR C5**

A furnace or container for burning waste materials.

Individual Occupant Workspaces **IEQ C6, IEQ C8.3 & 8.4**

Workspaces in which individuals occupy standard workstations for the purpose of conducting individual tasks. These workstations can be located in private offices or multi-occupant spaces, such as open office areas.

Indoor Air Quality (IAQ) **IEQ P1**

The nature of air that affects the health and well-being of building occupants.

Infiltration Basins & Trenches **SS C5**

Land forms used to encourage subsurface infiltration of runoff volumes through temporary surface storage. Basins are ponds that can store large volumes of stormwater. They need to drain within 72 hours to maintain aerobic conditions and to be available for the next storm event. Trenches are similar to infiltration basins except that they are shallower and function as a subsurface reservoir for stormwater volumes. Pretreatment to remove sediment and oil may be necessary to avoid clogging of infiltration devices. Infiltration trenches are more common in areas where infiltration basins are not possible.

Infrared Emittance **SS C6.1**

A parameter between 0 and 1 that indicates the ability of a material to shed infrared radiation. The wavelength of this radiant energy is roughly 5 to 40 micrometers. Most building materials (including glass) are opaque in this part of the spectrum, and have an emittance of roughly 0.9. Materials such as clean, bare metals are the most important exceptions to the 0.9 rule. Thus clean, untarnished galvanized steel has low emittance, and aluminum roof coatings have intermediate emittance levels.

Integrated Pest Management (IPM) **SS C1, IEQ C10**

The coordinated use of pest and environmental information and pest control methods to prevent unacceptable levels of pest damage by the most economical means, and with the least possible hazard to people, property and the environment.

Janitorial Closets **IEQ C10.2**

Rooms where janitorial equipment and supplies are stored.

Landfills **MR P1, MR C5**

Waste disposal sites for the deposit of solid waste from human activities.

Landscape Architecture SS C4

The analysis, planning, design, management and stewardship of the natural and built environments.

Landscape area WE C1

Equal to the total site area less the building footprint, paved surfaces, water bodies, patios, etc.

Least Toxic Pesticides IEQ 10.4-5

These include boric acid and disodium octoborate tetrahydrate; silica gels; diatomaceous earth; nonvolatile insect and rodent baits in tamper-resistant containers or for crack and crevice treatment only; microbe-based insecticides; pesticides made with essential oils (not including synthetic pyrethroids) without toxic synergists; and materials for which the inert ingredients are nontoxic and disclosed. A least toxic pesticide does not include a pesticide that: is determined by the U.S. Environmental Protection Agency as a probable, likely, or known carcinogen or endocrine disruptor; is a mutagen, reproductive toxin, developmental neurotoxin, or immune system toxin; is classified by the U.S. Environmental Protection Agency as a toxicity I or II pesticide; is in the organophosphate or carbamate chemical family; or contains inert ingredients categorized as "List 1: Inerts of Toxicological Concern." Least toxic pesticides do not include any application of pesticides using a broadcast spray, dust, tenting, fogging or baseboard spray application.

Light Bulb Life MR P2

The useful operating life of light bulbs.

Light Bulbs

Devices that produce illumination, and include glass bulbs or tubes that emit light produce by electricity (as an incandescent bulb or fluorescent bulb).

Light Pollution SS C7

Waste light from building sites that produces glare, compromises astronomical research, and adversely affects the environment. Waste light does not increase nighttime safety, utility, or security and needlessly consumes energy and natural resources.

Local Zoning Requirements SS C4

Local government regulations imposed to promote orderly development of private lands and to prevent land use conflicts.

Lumen MR P2

A unit of luminous flux equal to the light emitted in a unit solid angle by a uniform point source of one candle intensity.

Mass Transit SS C3.1

Transportation facilities designed to transport large groups of persons in a single vehicle such as buses or trains

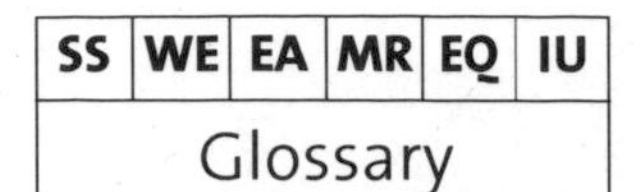

MERV 13 — IEQ C5.1

A filter efficiency rating category based on a test method established by the American Society of Heating, Refrigerating, and Air Conditioning Engineers (ASHRAE 52.2-1999, Method of Testing General Ventilation Air Cleaning Devices for Removal Efficiency by Particle Size). MERV is an acronym for "minimum efficiency reporting value." The MERV efficiency categories range from 1 to 16 (very low to very high efficiency).

Methylmercury — MR P2

The term used to describe any of various toxic compounds of mercury containing the complex CH_3Hg- that often occur as pollutants and that bioaccumulate in living organisms, especially in higher levels of a food chain.

Micro-Irrigation — WE C1

Involves irrigation systems with small sprinklers and microjets or drippers designed to apply small volumes of water. The sprinklers and microjets are installed within a few centimeters of the ground, while drippers are laid on or below grade.

Mitigated Stormwater — SS C5

The volume of precipitation falling on the site that does not become runoff. Runoff is defined as stormwater leaving the site via means of uncontrolled surface streams, rivers, drains, or sewers. Factors affecting stormwater mitigation include site perviousness, stormwater management practices (structural and non-structural), and onsite capture and reuse of rainwater.

Monitoring Points — EA C3.3

Locations where measurement sensors are installed.

Native/Adapted Vegetation — SS C4

Plants indigenous to a locality or cultivars of native plants that are adapted to the local climate and are not considered invasive species or noxious weeds, and which require only limited irrigation following establishment, do not require active maintenance such as mowing, and provide habitat value and promote biodiversity through avoidance of monoculture plantings.

Natural Areas — SS C4

Areas covered with native or adapted vegetation or other ecologically appropriate features.

Natural Ventilation — IEQ C2

The process of supplying and removing air by natural means in building spaces by using openings such as windows and doors, wind towers, non-powered ventilators, and infiltration processes.

Non-Friable — IEQ P3

The term used in the asbestos industry to describe asbestos too hard to be reduced to dust by hand.

Non-Occupied Spaces IEQ C6, IEQ C8.3 & 8.4

All rooms used by maintenance personnel and not open for use by occupants, such as janitorial, storage and equipment rooms, and closets.

Non-Regularly Occupied Spaces IEQ C6, IEQ C8.3 & 8.4

Corridors, hallways, lobbies, break rooms, copy rooms, storage rooms, kitchens, restrooms, stairwells, etc.

Non-Roof Impervious Surfaces SS C6.1

All surfaces on the site with a perviousness of less than 50 percent, not including the roof of the building. Examples of typically impervious surfaces include parking lots, roads, sidewalks and plazas.

Non-Water Using Urinal WE P2, WE C2

A urinal that uses no water, but instead replaces the water flush with a specially designed trap that contains a layer of buoyant liquid that floats above the urine layer, blocking sewer gas and urine odors from the room.

Occupied Zone IEQ C7

The region normally occupied by people within a space. Per ASHRAE 55-2004, it is defined to generally consist of the space between the floor and 1.8 meters above the floor, and more than 1.0 meters from outside walls/windows or fixed heating, ventilating, or air conditioning equipment and 0.3 meters from internal walls.

On-Site Wastewater Treatment WE C2

Localized treatment systems to transport, store, treat and dispose of wastewater volumes generated on the project site.

Open Site Area SS C4

Total site area less the footprint of the building.

Operation and maintenance staff EA C3.1

Include staff or contractors involved in operating, maintaining and cleaning the building and site.

Paints and Coatings MR C3

Defined by the referenced Green Seal Standard (GS-11) as "liquid, liquefiable or mastic composition that is converted to a solid protective, decorative, or functional adherent film after application as a thin layer. These coatings are intended for on-site application to interior or exterior surfaces of residential, commercial, institutional or industrial buildings." The Green Seal Standard (GS-11) does not include stains, clear finishes, or paints sold in aerosol cans within this category.

Parking Subsidies SS C3.4

The costs of providing occupant parking that are not recovered in parking fees.

Permeable Surfaces **SS C5**

Surfaces used as a substitute for impermeable surfaces to allow runoff to infiltrate into the subsurface. These surfaces are typically maintained with a vacuuming regime to avoid potential clogging and failure problems. Porous pavement is one type of permeable surface.

Personal Environmental Controls (PECs) **IEQ C6.2**

Office furniture with heating, ventilation and lighting built into the furniture.

Perviousness **SS C6.1**

The percent of area covered by a paving system that is open and allows moisture to soak into the earth below the paving system.

Photovoltaic energy **EA C2**

Electricity from photovoltaic cells that convert the energy in sunlight into electricity.

Picogram **MR P2**

One trillionth of a gram.

Picograms per lumen hour **MR P2**

A measure of the amount of mercury in a light bulb per unit of light delivered over its useful life.

Point Source **WE P2**

A discrete conveyance of a pollutant, such as a pipe or man-made ditch. As stated in the NPDSES Permit Program Basics: Frequently Asked Questions, a point source is "any discernible, confined and discrete conveyance, such as a pipe, ditch, channel, tunnel, conduit, discrete fissure, or container."

Pollutants **WE P2**

Include "any type of industrial, municipal, and agricultural waste discharged into water." Those regulated in the NPDES program include conventional pollutants (such as BOD5, total suspended solids, pH, fecal coliform, and oil and grease), toxic pollutants (such as metals and manmade compounds), and non-conventional pollutants (such as ammonia, nitrogen, phosphorus). The definition of "pollutant" as it pertains to the Clean Water Act and NDPES permitting is subject to change based on ongoing litigation and increased understanding about the environmental affects of discharged substances. An agent of the NPDES should be consulted regarding the pollutant status of discharge from specific buildings.

Polychlorinated Biphenyls (PCBs) **IEQ P4**

Mixtures of synthetic organic chemicals with the same basic chemical structure and similar physical properties ranging from oily liquids to waxy solids. More than 1.5 billion pounds of PCBs were manufactured in the United States prior to cessation of production in 1977. Concern over the toxicity and persistence in the environment of PCBs led Congress in 1976 to enact §6(e) of the Toxic Substances Control Act (TSCA) that included among other things, prohibitions on the manufacture, processing, and distribution in commerce of PCBs. TSCA legislated true "cradle to grave" (i.e., from manufacture to disposal) management of PCBs in the United States. (This definition is from the U.S. EPA PCB web site, www.epa.gov/opptintr/pcb/).

Post-Consumer Recycled Content **MR C4**

The percentage of material in a product that is recycled from consumer waste.

Post-Consumer Waste Recycling **MR C2, MR C4**

The recycling of materials collected from consumer waste following consumer use of the products containing these materials.

Post-Industrial Recycled Content **MR C4**

The percentage of material in a product that is recycled from manufacturing waste.

Post-Industrial Waste Recycling **MR C2, MR C4**

The recycling of materials collected from industrial processes. This includes the collection and recycling of waste from industrial processes within the same manufacturing plant or from another manufacturing plant.

Potable Water **WE P1, WE C1, WE C2**

Water that is suitable for drinking and is supplied from wells or municipal water systems.

Preferred Parking **SS C3.3, SS C3.4**

Parking that is preferentially available to particular users, usually located closer to the building.

Process Water **WE P1**

Water used for industrial processes and building systems such as cooling towers, boilers and chillers.

Productivity **IEQ C4.2**

The quantity and quality of employee output per unit time.

Property Area **SS C2**

The total area within the legal property boundaries of a building and includes all areas of the site including constructed areas and non-constructed areas.

Public Transportation **SS C3.1**

Bus, rail, or other transportation service provided for the general public on a regular, continual basis that is publicly or privately owned.

Rapidly Renewable Materials **MR C2**

Materials that are planted and harvested in less than 10-year cycle.

Recycling **MR P1, MR C1, MR C2, MR C5**

The collection, reprocessing, marketing and use of materials that were diverted or recovered from the solid waste stream. Recycling provides two categories of environmental benefits: (1) diversion of waste from landfilling or incineration and (2) reduces the need for virgin materials for the manufacture of new products.

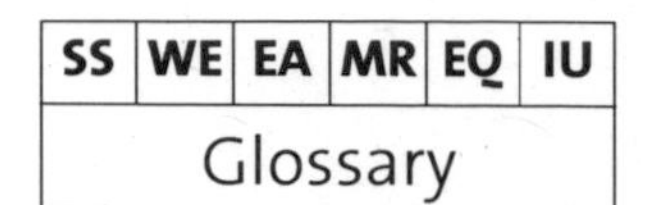

Refrigerants **EA P3**

The working fluids of refrigeration cycles that absorb heat from a reservoir at low temperatures and reject heat at higher temperatures

Regularly Occupied Spaces **IEQ C8.3-8.4**

Areas where workers are seated or standing as they work inside a building.

Relative Humidity **IEQ C7**

The ratio of partial density of water vapor in the air to the saturation density of water vapor at the same temperature.

Renewable Energy

Energy from sources that are renewed on an ongoing basis. This includes energy from the sun, wind and small hydropower. Ways to capture energy from the sun include photovoltaic, thermal solar energy systems, and bioenergy. One issue with bioenergy is the amount of fossil fuel energy used to produce it.

Renewable Energy Certificates (RECs) **EA C2, EA C5**

A representation of the environmental attributes of green power that are sold separately from the electrons that make up the electricity. RECs allow the purchase of green power even when the electrons are not purchased.

Return Air **IEQ C1**

Air removed from conditioned spaces that is either re-circulated in the building or exhausted to the outside.

Reuse **MR C1**

A strategy to return materials to active use in the same or a related capacity.

Salvaged Materials (Off-site) **MR C2**

Building materials recovered from an offsite source that are reused in the existing building seeking LEED-EB certification.

Salvaged Materials (On-site) **MR C2**

Building materials recovered from and then reused at the same building site.

Seasonal Affective Disorder (SAD) **IEQ C4.1**

A form of depression thought to be triggered by a decrease in exposure to sunlight.

Sedimentation **SS P1**

The addition of soil particles to water bodies by natural and human-related activities. Sedimentation often decreases water quality and can accelerate the aging process of lakes, rivers and streams.

Setpoints **EA C3.3**

Normal ranges for building systems and indoor environmental quality outside which action is taken.

Sick Building Syndrome (SBS) — IEQ P1, IEQ C4.1, IEQ C9

A term used to describe situations where building occupants experience acute discomfort and negative health effects as a result of time spent in the building without any specific cause that can be identified, and the symptoms disappear soon after the occupants leave the building.

Soil Waste — MR C1

Unneeded or unusable soil from construction, demolition or renovation projects.

Solar Reflectance — SS C6

A measure of the ability of a surface material to reflect sunlight – including the visible, infrared, and ultraviolet wavelengths – on a scale of 0 to 1. Solar reflectance is also called albedo. White paint (titanium dioxide) is defined to a have a solar reflectance of 1 while black paint has a solar reflectance of 0.

Source Reduction — MR P1, MR C1, MR C2, MR C5

Reducing waste by reducing the amount of unnecessary material brought into a building. Purchasing products with less packaging is an example of source reduction.

Space Occupied for Critical Visual Tasks — IEQ C8

Rooms used for tasks like reading and computer monitor use.

Square Footage of a Building — SS C2

The total floor area in square feet of all rooms including corridors, elevators, stairwells, and shaft spaces.

Stormwater Runoff — SS C5

Water volumes that are created during precipitation events and flow over surfaces into sewer systems or receiving waters. All precipitation waters that leave project site boundaries on the surface are considered to be stormwater runoff volumes.

Submetering — EA C5

Metering added by the building owner and managers to track the amount of water and energy use and where it is occurring in the facility.

Supply Air — IEQ C1

Air delivered to conditioned spaces for use in ventilating, heating, cooling, humidifying and dehumidifying those spaces.

Sustainable Forestry — MR C2

The practice of managing forest resources in a manner that meets the long-term forest product needs of humans while maintaining the biodiversity of forested landscapes.

Sustainable Purchasing Policy — MR C4

The preferential purchasing of products that meet sustainability standards. Per this MR Credit 4, the sustainable purchasing policy for cleaning products and materials should include all cleaning products, paper products and trashcan liners included in the U.S. EPA's Comprehensive Procurement Guidelines.

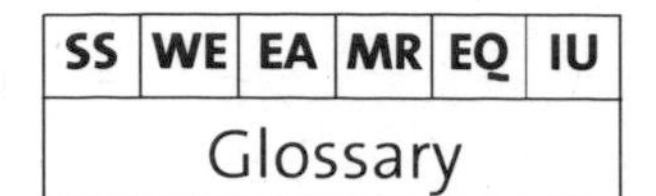

Sustainable Purchasing Program **MR C2**

Includes the development, adoption and implementation of an organizational policy that outlines the types of materials that will be targeted to meet the sustainability criteria of this credit. Per the credit requirements, this program at a minimum must include office paper, office equipment, furniture, furnishings and building materials for use in the building and on the site.

System Lifetime **EA C3.2**

The length of time from installation to until a system needs to be replaced.

System Operator **IEQ C1**

A facility management staff person who is responsible for the operation of the building and for receiving and responding to HVAC system out of range performance alarms.

Telecommuting **SS C3.4**

Work that is done through the use of telecommunications and computer technology from a location other than the usual or traditional place of business — for example, home, a satellite office or a telework center.

Tertiary Treatment **WE C2**

The highest form of wastewater treatment that includes the removal of nutrients, organic and solid material, along with biological or chemical polishing (generally to effluent limits of 10 mg/L BOD_5 and 10 mg/L TSS).

Thermal Comfort **IEQ C7**

A condition of mind experienced by building occupants expressing satisfaction with the thermal environment.

Thermal Emittance **SS C6.2**

The ratio of the radiant heat flux emitted by a sample to that emitted by a blackbody radiator at the same temperature.

Tipping Fees **MR C1**

Fees charged by a landfill or incinerator for disposal of waste volumes (typically charged by the ton).

Turbidity **SS P1**

The state of having sediment stirred up or suspended. Turbidity in lakes or estuaries affects water clarity, light penetration, and their suitability as habitat for aquatic plants and animals.

Underground Parking **SS C6.1**

A "tuck-under" or stacked parking structure that reduces the exposed parking surface area.

Uniform Building Code **MR C2**

A model building code published by the International Council of Building Officials (ICBO) that provides complete regulations covering all major aspects of building design and construction relating to fire and life safety and structural safety.

Utility Metering **EA C5**

Involves the use of meters provided by utilities to measure consumption.

Variable Air Volume (VAV) **IEQ C6.2**

A type of HVAC system that varies the volume of conditioned air delivered to rooms.

Vegetated Filter Strips **SS C5**

Strips of vegetation to filter sediment and pollutants from stormwater. Strips are appropriate for treating low-velocity surface sheet flows in areas where runoff is not concentrated. They are often used as pretreatment for other stormwater measures such as infiltration basins and trenches.

Ventilation **IEQ P1, IEQ C2**

The process of supplying and removing air to and from interior spaces by natural or mechanical means.

Visible Transmittance (T_{vis}) **IEQ C8**

The ratio of total transmitted light to total incident light. In other words, it is the amount of light passing through a glazing surface divided by the amount of light striking the glazing surface. A higher T_{vis} value indicates that a greater amount of incident light is passing through the glazing.

Vision Glazing **IEQ C8**

Glazing that provides views of outdoor landscapes to building occupants for vertical windows between 2'6" and 7'6" above the floor. Windows below 2'6" and windows above 7'6" (including daylight glazing, skylights, and roof monitors) do not count as vision glazing for this credit.

Volatile Organic Compounds (VOCs) **MR C3**

Organic compounds that are volatile at typical room temperatures. The specific organic compounds addressed by the referenced Green Seal Standard (GS-11) are identified in U. S. Environmental Protection Agency (EPA) Reference Test Method 24 (Determination of Volatile Matter Content, Water Content, Density Volume Solids, and Weight Solids of Surface Coatings), Code of Federal Regulations Title 40, Part 60, Appendix A.

Walk-Off Mats **IEQ C 10.1**

Mats placed inside or outside building entrances to remove dirt from the feet of people and off equipment entering the building.

Waste Disposal **MR P1, MR C1, MR C2, MR C5**

The process of eliminating waste by means of burial in a landfill, combustion in an incinerator, dumping at sea, or eliminating waste in some other way that is not recycling or reuse.

Waste Diversion **MR P1, MR C1, MR C2, MR C5**

Includes waste management activities that divert waste from disposal though incineration or landfilling. Typical waste diversion methods are reuse and recycling.

Waste Reduction MR P1, MR C1, MR C2, MR C5

Includes source reduction and diversion of waste by means of reuse or recycling.

Waste Reduction Policy MR P1, MR C1, MR C5

Includes (1) A statement describing the organization's commitment to minimize waste disposal by using source reduction, reuse and recycling, (2) assignment of responsibility within the organization for implementation of waste reduction program, (3) a list of the general actions that will be implemented in the waste reduction program to reduce waste, and (4) a description of the tracking and review component in the waste reduction program to monitor waste reduction success and improve waste reduction performance over time.

Weathered Radiative Properties SS C6.2

The solar reflectance and thermal emittance of a roofing product after three years of exposure to the weather.

Wind Energy EA C2

Electricity generated by wind machines.

Wood Waste MR C1

Unneeded or unusable wood from construction, demolition or renovation projects.